Jacobus de Voragine

The Golden Legend

Readings on the Saints

TRANSLATED BY

William Granger Ryan

VOLUME I

Princeton University Press

PRINCETON, N.J.

Copyright © 1993 by Princeton University Press
Published by Princeton University Press, 41 William Street,
Princeton, New Jersey 08540
In the United Kingdom: Princeton University Press,
Chichester, West Sussex

Library of Congress Cataloging-in-Publication Data

Jacobus de Voragine, ca. 1229-1298.
[Legenda aurea. English]
The golden legend: readings on the saints / Jacobus de Voragine;
translated by William Granger Ryan.
p. cm.
Includes bibliographical references and index.
ISBN 0-691-00865-5 (v.1, hardback)
ISBN 0-691-00153-7 (v.1, paperback)
ISBN 0-691-03178-9 (v.2, hardback)
ISBN 0-691-00154-5 (v.2, paperback)
1. Christian saints—Biography. I. Ryan, William Granger,
1905–. II. Title.
BX4654.J334 1993
282'.092'2—dc20
[B] 92-300068

This book has been composed in Adobe Bembo
Designed by Jan Lilly

Princeton University Press books are printed on acid-free paper
and meet the guidelines for permanence and durability of the Committee
on Production Guidelines for Book Longevity of the
Council on Library Resources

Printed in the United States of America

Fourth printing, and first paperback printing, 1995

6 8 10 9 7

TO

Dominique de Menil

CONTENTS

VOLUME I

ACKNOWLEDGMENTS
xi

INTRODUCTION
xiii

CONTENTS

CONTENTS

INDEX
389

VOLUME II

CONTENTS

ACKNOWLEDGMENTS

This translation of Jacobus de Voragine's *Legenda aurea* is based on the only modern Latin edition of the work, produced by Dr. Th. Graesse in 1845. The translator acknowledges his indebtedness not only to Graesse but to two translations, one in French, *La légende dorée de Jacques de Voragine*, by the Abbé J.-B. M. Roze, 3 vols. (Paris: Edouard Rouveyre, Editeur, 1902), and the other in German, *Iacobus de Voragine Legenda aurea*, by Richard Benz, 2 vols. (Jena: Eugen Diederichs, 1917–1921). I am grateful to my colleagues at Yale Divinity School, and particularly to Professor John W. Cook, Director of the Institute of Sacred Music, Worship, and the Arts, for their encouragement as the work progressed. My sister Margot Ryan gave valued assistance by proofreading the text, and Mark Looney, of the Institute staff, helped substantially in the final preparation of the manuscript. Above all I owe thanks to the Menil Foundation, and to Dominique de Menil in person, for support and encouragement in carrying this undertaking to conclusion.

INTRODUCTION

The *Golden Legend* is a thirteenth-century work, dated about 1260, whose author is commonly called and cataloged as Jacobus de Voragine. The author was
a native of the town of Varazze on the Genoese Riviera. His name was Jacopo
(Jacobus in Latin, James in English); in these pages he will be called Jacobus. He
was born about A.D. 1230, entered the Dominican Order (O.P., the Order of
Friars Preachers) in 1244, and, in the course of four decades, held high offices in
the Order as teacher and administrator. In 1292 he became archbishop of Genoa,
where he was esteemed as a peacemaker and a father to the poor. He died in
1298, was beatified (whence the title "Blessed") by Pope Pius VII in 1816, and
is venerated as a saint by the Dominican Order and the city and province of
Genoa.[1]

Jacobus left several volumes of sermons and a *Chronicle of Genoa* and other
minor writings, as well as the present work, which originally was called simply
Legenda Sanctorum (Readings on the saints).[2] The lasting popularity of the work
caused it to be called *Legenda Aurea*, the *Golden Legend*. (It also acquired a sub-
title, "The History of the Lombards," because in his penultimate chapter, "Saint
Pelagius, Pope," Jacobus followed a one-line acknowledgment of the pope's
career with an account, in some ten thousand words, of the "history of the
Lombards" from mid–sixth century to shortly before 1250.) The popularity of
the *Legend* was such that some one thousand manuscripts have survived, and,
with the advent of printing in the 1450s, editions both in the original Latin and
in every Western European language multiplied into the hundreds. It has been
said that in the late Middle Ages the only book more widely read was the Bible.

The version here offered is the first complete modern translation in English.
It is based on the Latin text published by Th. Graesse in 1845. The second
edition (the one used for this translation) was published in 1850,[3] and a third in
Dresden-Leipzig in 1890. The second and third editions are identical, and a
photo-offset reproduction came out at Osnabrück in 1969. Graesse says in his
brief preface (signed and dated *Scripsi Dresdae Kal. Novembr. MDCCCXLV*) that
his text is based on an edition (Lexic. Bibliogr. T.1, p. 872, sq. nr. 10672[b]),

---

[1] For information about Jacobus, see E. C. Richardson, *Materials for a Life of Jacoopo da Varagine*
(New York: The H. W. Wilson Company, 1935).

[2] The headline over the Prologue reads "*Incipit prologus super legenda sanctorum*": here *legenda* is
neuter plural and means "readings."

[3] Jacobi a Voragine, *Legenda aurea vulgo historia lombardica dicta*, recensuit Dr. Th. Graesse, editio
secunda (Leipzig, 1850).

preserved in the Royal Public Library in Dresden, giving no further information about the source edition itself. Graesse accepted 182 chapters or legends as Jacobus's work, and added 61 by authors other than Jacobus. These added chapters are not included in the present translation.

The *Golden Legend* is basically the work of a compiler. Abbé Roze[4] identifies some 130 sources quoted or referred to in the *Legend*, grouping them by centuries from the second to the thirteenth. The lists include the Latin and Greek Fathers (the latter known from Latin anthologies and encyclopedias like Isidore of Seville's *Etymologiae*) and most of the authors then regarded as reliable authorities. Some of Jacobus's sources were known to be apocryphal and not trustworthy, and Jacobus says so, but does not hesitate to repeat some of their statements and stories. He was concerned about differences regarding dates, places, and persons occurring in his sources, and tried repeatedly to reconcile them; but the accuracy of a number or a date or a fact was less important to him than its doctrinal or moral or mystical significance. His overall subject was the dealings of God with humankind—with *salvation history* as it revealed itself in God's agents and instruments, the saints. The "History of the Lombards" mentioned above, for instance, contains little of the history we would expect, but gives attention to developments in Church doctrine and liturgy, to heresies, to saints and miracles.

The *Legend* was translated, as has been mentioned, into every Western European language. The only surviving early translation in English was made and published by William Caxton, man of letters and printer-publisher, in 1483.[5] He mentions as his sources an earlier English translation, now unknown, a French version, and a Latin edition. Caxton omitted some of Jacobus's saints and added some sixty not in Jacobus, many of the latter being English or Irish. Caxton's is the only English translation undertaken, so far as I know, until 1941, when, with the assistance of the late Helmut Ripperger, I made a new "translation and adaptation,"[6] omitting material that at the time was considered expendable. The present translation is entirely new and includes every line of each of the 182 chapters offered by Graesse as authentic. I should note that while scholars have in recent years turned their attention to Jacobus's work,[7] much remains to be done on the *Legend*—for example, to establish a *textus receptus* by collating the manuscript material, to locate Jacobus's quotations from other authors, and to evaluate the use he made of his sources. The present work does not include any such research. It is not a study of the *Golden Legend*: it *is* the *Golden Legend*.

---

[4] J.-B. M. Roze, in the preface of his translation of the *Legend*, *La légende dorée*, 3 vols. (Paris: Ed. Rouveyre, 1902), 1:xiv–xvii.

[5] *The Golden Legend or Lives of the Saints as Englished by William Caxton*, 7 vols. (London: Dent & Sons, 1931).

[6] *The Golden Legend of Jacobus de Voragine* (New York: Longmans, Green & Co.), 1941.

[7] Two interesting and informative recent studies are by A. Boureau, *La légende dorée* (Paris: Editions du Cerf, 1984), and by S. L. Reames, *The Legenda aurea: A Reexamination of Its Paradoxical History*, (Madison: University of Wisconsin Press, 1985), 1.

But why a new and complete English translation? In a word, to provide a ready tool for study in the fields of myth and legend, of hagiography and folklore, of medieval history, literature, art, and religion. Let us quote Emile Mâle, historian of medieval art:

> The *Golden Legend* remains one of the most interesting books of its time for those who seek in medieval literature for the spirit of the age to which it belonged. Its fidelity in reproducing earlier stories, and its very absence of originality, make it of special value to us. . . . Nearly all the bas-reliefs and windows which deal with legends can be interpreted with its help, and in re-editing it Graesse rendered a valuable service to the history of art, if not also to the history of religion.[8]

The *Golden Legend* is, first and foremost, a religious work, but students of medieval history can see in it how "scientific" history, as distinguished from "sacred" or "salvation" history, was interpreted, misinterpreted, or simply ignored by Jacobus and the authors he consulted, notably Vincent of Beauvais in his *Mirror of History*. Students of the late medieval mystery plays and miracle plays will see that many of these plays may well have drawn upon the *Legend* for setting, characters, action, dialogue, and "business."[9] The book has long been used as an aid in the study of medieval statuary and stained glass.

A preliminary question: who are the saints about whom Jacobus compiled his readings? The answer is that they are, so to speak, the "official" saints, whom the Church, up to Jacobus's time, had declared to be worthy of public veneration, and particularly those whose feast days were celebrated in the Church's liturgy. There were already official readings about these saints in the existing martyrologies and legendaries. To these readings or "legends" Jacobus added new material gleaned from his sources, and assembled them within the framework of the Church's liturgical calendar. Then he distributed the readings on the saints according to the dates of their feast days within the several seasons of the liturgical year—Advent, Christmas, Lent, Easter, and the time after Pentecost.[10] As for the myriad other saints—the martyrs, the confessors and virgins, and all the good men and good women who by God's grace are with him in heaven—Jacobus devoted to them his chapter for the Feast of All Saints.

The chapter on All Saints is a typical example of Jacobus's way of developing his argument. One feature of his method meets the reader from the first sentence on: there were four "causes" (reasons, purposes) for the institution of the feast; each of the four will be studied under three, four, five subdivisions, and each subdivision under a number of sub-subdivisions. This structuring by numbers is typical, but the numbers are not the method, which essentially includes three

---

[8] Emile Mâle, *The Gothic Image*, trans. Dora Nussey (New York: Harper & Row, 1972), 273.

[9] As one among a number of examples, see the account of Christ's visit to hell in the chapter of the Lord's resurrection.

[10] No dates are attached to the saints' legends in the Graesse edition or in this translation. Some of the feasts included by Jacobus have been suppressed and the dates of others changed.

elements, namely, Scripture, authorities, and narrative. As a general rule Jacobus supports each point he is making with one or several texts from Scripture—texts of which frequently only the first few words are quoted.[11] To the scriptural proofs he usually adds one or more references to, or quotations from, his author-ities. But the authorities are interpreting and explaining the biblical texts. The whole foundation of Jacobus's argumentation in the *Golden Legend* is scriptural. He does not philosophize or theologize in the scholastic manner. Instead he accumulates texts and authorities, sometimes by the dozen: the greater the num-ber, the stronger the argument itself.

Narrative is the third essential element in the method. Jacobus interlards his argument with narrative, most frequently stories of miracles. That most of these narratives were at least partially fictional—or better, the product of generations of oral retelling—in no way diminished their effectiveness. They served an im-portant purpose: they humanized and dramatized the doctrinal point to be made. In them men and women were seen as *living* the doctrine. The saints the people heard about in church, and talked about and prayed to, are alive in the *Legend,* and they move and talk and act like the men and women Jacobus saw passing by his window on the road to heaven. A primary purpose of these narra-tives was to prove that the person concerned was truly a saint. Very little was known about the actual lives of most of the saints memorialized in the *Legend.* Martyrdom was an ipso facto proof of sainthood. For nonmartyrs, the practice of heroic virtue *and* the performance of miracles, all graphically narrated, showed that God was working through the individual, thus proving that he or she was indeed a saint. Miracles were *expected* of the saint, and the saint's miracle was the work of God.

The miracle stories, if they are to make any sense to modern readers, require a special effort, which consists in trying to see life and the world the way medie-val Christians did. For these people in general, God was not a philosophical abstraction but a living, ever-present, caring *actor,* the creator and giver of life. Their life was a pilgrimage through a world that was passing, to which they were not to become attached, since the reason for their being was to be united with God in heaven; meanwhile they grubbed a hard living from the reluctant earth. The world was a scene of warfare between good and evil, a world peopled with demons and angels. The demons, in order to deceive and mislead God's chil-dren, resorted to a marvelous bag of tricks but always wound up looking foolish. The angels protected God's people. The Church, the sacraments, the mysteries of Christ celebrated in the liturgy, formed a milieu for the Christian's progress from birth to death, from earthly life to eternal life. "If you be risen with Christ, seek the things that are above, not the things that are upon the earth" (Col. 3:1–2).

To people who saw the hand of God working in the world and in the mira-cles of the saints, the miracles, the "wonderworks"—cures, control of natural

---

[11] In this translation enough of the quoted text has been added to make its relevancy clear.

forces, foreknowledge—while astonishing, were unquestionably believable. To the modern reader the multiplication of these events in Jacobus's stories may seem excessive and boring. The multiplication itself, however, like the accumulation of authorities already referred to, was used to confirm the saint's sanctity and/or the truth to which he or she bore witness; and, to judge by the "popular" literature of the Middle Ages, the wonderful, of which the miraculous is a subcategory, was never boring. Of course some of the stories are ridiculous as well as occasionally vulgar. Some are so preposterous that Jacobus pointed out the likelihood that they were "apocryphal," but kept them in nonetheless. They are part of the stuff of medieval hagiography, and they tell us something about the habits and manners, as well as about the piety, of medieval Christians—even, perhaps, about their sense of humor.

A note may be made here about the "etymologies" that preface most of the legends of the saints. The humanist critics of the sixteenth and later centuries scoffed at them, and Graesse calls them "those most perverse etymologies, in which more than anywhere else our Jacobus limps."[12] In fact they are admirable examples of Jacobus's whole method. To him, a name is the symbol of the person who bears it, and in its letters and syllables can be found the indication of what the person's life, with its virtues and its triumphs, is to be. So he dissolves the compound of the name, so to speak, into its component elements; and he shows—frequently by recourse to Greek, of which he obviously knew little,[13] and at times to Hebrew, of which he knew less—what the name meant when by the providence of God it was conferred on the future saint.[14] As with numbers and facts and dates and places, therefore, so also with names: it is the hidden meaning and the spiritual message which things convey that must be sought.

Scholars do not agree on Jacobus's purpose in composing the *Golden Legend*, nor on the audience he had in mind. The work was written in Latin and therefore would seem to have had clerics as its primary audience. Jacobus was a Friar Preacher, and A. Boureau, in his *La légende dorée*,[15] makes a case for the likelihood that the book's first purpose was to serve as material for preachers and teachers of preaching, particularly in the houses of study of the Dominican Order. Boureau also notes that the trend in the thirteenth-century Church was to direct the faithful to the Book and to books, perhaps in order to bring about a more binding contact between laity and clergy. This would suppose, for one thing, that the ability to read was becoming more common, and, for another, that the multiplication of copies and translations of the *Legend* and books like it occurred in response to an existing demand. The chapters bearing directly on Jesus Christ—Advent (which includes the Last Judgment), Christmas, Circum-

---

[12] . . . *etymologias illas perversissimas, quibus maxime claudicat Jacobus noster.* . . . *Legenda aurea*, iv.

[13] Knowledge of the Greek language did not spread in Western Europe, even among the literati, until the fifteenth century.

[14] His "analysis" of the name varies when the name belongs to different persons and must conform to the personality of each one.

[15] Boureau, *La légende dorée*, 21–25.

cision, Epiphany, Annunciation, Passion, Resurrection, Ascension, Pentecost, and on Blessed Mary's Nativity and Assumption and her ubiquitous activity throughout the whole story—besides being heavy with doctrine and spiritual inspiration, are crowded with fascinating and instructive anecdotes. That the *Legend* became a book for private reading and devotion seems indisputable.

The probability that Jacobus intended the book to be primarily a manual for preachers would help to explain not only what it contained or did, but what it lacked or did not do. There is no systematic attempt in the *Legend* to expound or to outline a pattern of sainthood for the laity, nor even a pattern for a happy and holy *family* life, such as is prescribed by Saint Paul in Col. 3:17–25, or caroled in more down-to-earth terms in Psalm 127 (128). In the *Legend*, marriage is obviously a second-class way of life: Saint Jerome is quoted as saying that there is as much difference between wedlock and virginity as there is between not sinning and being a saint. Women are simply presumed to occupy the same status in the Church and in society as Saint Paul assigned to them. Of the approximately two hundred saints celebrated by name in the *Legend*, only forty-one were women and only five had been married. The ideal of the holy Christian life, as it emerges from the various legends, turns out to be a monastic and ascetical pattern, based on "contempt for the things of earth" and on the practice of humility, chastity, obedience to God and the Church, and patience with the trials of this life (not specified existentially), in view of the hope of heaven and the gaining of merit toward that end. The vast majority of Christians will be saved by obeying the laws of God and the Church, and, as we have seen, they will be honored on the Feast of All Saints.

There is none of what is now called "social doctrine" in the *Legend*. No attention was directed to what would have to have been radical solutions of problems of civil government and law and order, of slavery and serfdom, of labor and just compensation, of poverty and famine, of the equitable sharing of natural resources. Jacobus and his time saw these problems not as problems to be solved but as trials to be borne. Furthermore, there is no evidence in the *Legend* of what is now called ecumenism, that is, any outreach toward non-Christian religions and their followers, or toward "heretical" Christians. Difference begot hostility. Toward Muslim men and women and children, hostility then took the form of the Crusades. For Jewish men and women and children, hostility meant the ghetto. The Inquisition dealt with recalcitrant heretics.

Jacobus was a man of his time and wrote for his time. He was no radical and does not seem to have thought of his preachers as reformers of the earthly society in which they lived. The reforms he envisaged were in preparation for the Last Judgment.

W.G.R.

May 1992
Institute of Sacred Music, Worship and the Arts
Yale University

THE GOLDEN LEGEND

Prologue

Here begins the Prologue to *Readings on the Saints*, otherwise called the *History of the Lombards*, which was compiled by Brother Jacobus, Genoese, of the Order of Friars Preachers.

The whole time-span of this present life comprises four distinct periods: the time of deviation or turning from the right way, the time of renewal or of being called back, the time of reconciliation, and the time of pilgrimage. The time of deviation began with Adam, or rather with his turning away from God, and lasted until Moses. The Church represents this period from Septuagesima to Easter, and the Book of Genesis is read, since that book tells of the fall of our first parents. The time of renewal or of being called back began with Moses and ended with the birth of Christ, during which time mankind was renewed and called back to faith by the prophets. The Church observes it from the beginning of Advent until the Nativity of the Lord. Isaiah is read then, because he treats clearly of this recall. The time of reconciliation is that during which we were reconciled by Christ, and the Church marks it from Easter to Pentecost: the Book of the Apocalypse, or Revelation, in which the mystery of this reconciliation is fully treated, is read. The time of pilgrimage is that of our present life, for we are on pilgrimage and constantly engaged in warfare. The Church observes this time from the octave of Pentecost to the beginning of Advent, and the Books of Kings and of Maccabees are read because they record many wars, thus reminding us of our own spiritual struggles. Finally, the interval between the Lord's birthday and Septuagesima falls partly within the time of reconciliation, a time of rejoicing, namely, from Christmas to the octave of Epiphany, and [partly in the time of pilgrimage, namely, from the octave of Epiphany] to Septuagesima.[1] This fourfold division of historic time can be related to the seasons of the year, winter corresponding to the first period, spring to the second, summer to the third, autumn to the fourth, and the sense of this comparison is clear enough. Or it may be related to the phases of the day, the first time to night, the second to morning, the third to midday, the fourth to evening.

Although the time of turning from the right way came before renewal, the Church begins the cycle of her offices with the time of renewal rather than with that of deviation—in other words, with Advent rather than Septuagesima—and this for two reasons. She does not wish to start from error, for she puts reality

---

[1] The words in brackets, missing in Graesse, are supplied from Jacobus de Varagine, *Legenda aurea* (Ulm: Joh. Zainer, ca. 1476), in Yale's Beinecke Library, 1972/+117.

3

before the sequence of time, just as the Evangelists often do; and besides, the renewal of all things came with the coming of Christ, and therefore the season of Advent is designated the time of renewal and recall: "Behold, I make all things new" (Apoc. 21:5). So it is proper for the Church to renew the sequence of her offices with this season.

In order to keep the sequence of times as the Church has set it, we shall deal first with the feast days that fall within the time of renewal, which she observes from the beginning of Advent to the birth of Christ. Next we shall dwell on those that occur within the period that falls partly within the time of reconciliation and partly within that of pilgrimage—the period represented by the Church from Advent to Septuagesima. Thirdly, we shall see the feast days celebrated in the time of deviation, from Septuagesima to Easter, and fourthly those within the time of reconciliation, from Easter through the octave of Pentecost. Lastly, we shall treat of feasts occurring within the time of pilgrimage, from the octave of Pentecost to the beginning of Advent.

1: The Advent of the Lord

The Lord's advent is celebrated for four weeks to signify that his coming is fourfold: he came to us in the flesh, he comes into our hearts, he comes to us at death, and he will come to judge us. The fourth week is seldom completed, because the glory of the saints, which will be bestowed at the last coming, will never end. So it is, too, that the first responsory for the first Sunday of Advent, which includes the *Gloria Patri*, has four verses corresponding to the aforesaid four comings; let the attentive reader figure out which verse best fits each coming.

While the Lord's comings are four, the Church specially memorializes two of them, the one in the flesh and the one at the Last Judgment, as is clear from the office of the season. Therefore the Advent fast[1] is partly one of rejoicing, by reason of Christ's coming in the flesh, and partly one of anxiety at the thought of the Judgment. To bring this to our minds the Church sings some of her joyful chants because of the coming of mercy and rejoicing, and puts aside some others because the Judgment will be very strict and prompts anxiety.

---

[1] The penitential fast used to be of precept in Advent as well as in Lent.

With regard to the Lord's coming in the flesh three aspects are to be examined—its timeliness, its necessity, and its usefulness.

The timeliness is manifest first as regards man himself, who by the law of his nature lacked knowledge of God. Hence he fell into the worst errors of idolatry. Therefore he was compelled to cry out: "Enlighten my eyes."[2] Then came the Law with its commandments, and man became aware that he was powerless to obey. Previously he had cried: "There are those willing to fulfill the command, but not yet anyone to command." For thus far he was only instructed, not freed from sin nor helped by any grace to do good; so now he was compelled to cry out: "There is one to command but no one to fulfill the command." Therefore the coming of the Son of God was opportune and timely, since man was now convicted of ignorance and helplessness: if Christ had come earlier, man might have attributed salvation to his own merits and would not have been thankful for his cure.

Secondly, the Lord's advent was timely because he came in the fullness of time: "When the fullness of time was come, God sent his Son."[3] Augustine says: "There are many who ask why Christ did not come sooner. It was because by the will of him who made all things in time, the fullness of time had not arrived. When that fullness had come, the One came who freed us from time, and, freed from time, we are to come to that eternity in which there will be no time." Thirdly, the whole world was wounded and ailing, and since the disease was universal it was the moment for a universal medicine to be applied. Augustine: "The great physician came when throughout the world mankind lay like a great invalid."

Hence the Church, in the seven antiphons that are sung before the Lord's birthday, shows the multiplicity of our ills and for each of them begs a remedy of the physician. Before the Son of God came in the flesh, we were ignorant or blind, liable to eternal punishment, slaves of the devil, shackled with sinful habits, enveloped in darkness, exiles driven from our true country. Therefore we had need of a teacher, a redeemer, a liberator, an emancipator, an enlightener, and a savior. Because we were ignorant and needed to be taught by him, we call out in the first antiphon: "O Wisdom, you came forth from the mouth of the Most High, reaching from end to end and ordering all things mightily and sweetly. Come, and teach us the way of prudence!" Yet it would be of little profit if we were taught but not redeemed, so we ask to be redeemed by him when we cry to God in the second antiphon: "O Adonai and leader of the house of Israel, you appeared to Moses in the flames of the burning bush, and on Sinai gave him the Law. Come, stretch out your arm and redeem us." And what good would it do if we were instructed and redeemed, if after redemption we were still held captive? Therefore we pray to be set free, when we plead in the third antiphon: "O Root of Jesse, you are raised as a banner to the peoples. Before

[2] Ps. 13:4.   [3] Gal. 4:4.

you kings shall remain silent, with you all nations will plead for help. Come to set us free, do not delay!" Yet of what use would it be to captives if, being redeemed and given their freedom, their shackles were still not stricken from them so that they could be under their own control and go freely wherever they wished? So it would do us little good if he redeemed and freed us but left us in chains. Therefore in the fourth antiphon we pray to be delivered of all the bonds of sin: "O Key of David, you open and no one closes, you close and no one opens. Come, and from the prison house release man enchained and sitting in the shadow of death!" But because the eyes of those who have been in prison for a long time grow dim and they no longer see clearly, even after we are set free from prison, we still have to have our eyes opened to the light, so that we may see where we ought to go. Therefore in the fifth antiphon we pray: "O rising Dawn, splendor of light eternal and sun of justice! Come, and enlighten those who sit in darkness and the shadow of death." And if we were taught, redeemed, freed from all enemies, and enlightened, how would it benefit us unless we were to be saved? So in the next two antiphons we beg for the gift of salvation, saying: "O King of the Gentiles, for whom they long, O Headstone who make the two one! Come and save man, whom you formed out of the slime of the earth." And likewise, "O Emmanuel, our king and our lawgiver, awaited by the nations and their savior! Come and save us, O Lord our God!" So first we plead for the salvation of the pagans, saying, "O King of the Gentiles," and then pray for the salvation of the Jews, to whom God gave the Law.

THE USEFULNESS OF THE COMING OF THE LORD

As for the usefulness of Christ's coming, different saints define it differently. God himself testifies that he came and was sent to be useful in seven ways, as we see in the fourth chapter of Luke: "The Spirit of the Lord is upon me, etc."[4] There he states the reasons one after the other: to console the poor, to heal the sorrowful, to free the captives, to enlighten the ignorant, to remit sins, to redeem the whole human race, and to reward merit.

Augustine points to three ways in which Christ's coming is useful, saying: "In this evil age what is there in abundance except to be born, to labor, and to die? These are the wares in which here on earth we trade, and to trade in them our merchant came down. And because every merchant gives what he has and receives what he does not have, Christ gave and received in this market. He received what there is plenty of here, namely, birth, toil, and death, and what he gave us is to be reborn, to rise again, and to reign for all eternity. This tradesman from heaven came to us to receive shame and give honor, to undergo death and give life, to bring ignominy upon himself and give glory."

---

[4] Luke 4:18–19.

Gregory proposes four causes or kinds of usefulness for the Lord's advent: "All the proud of heart born of Adam's race look for the good things of life, shun adversity, flee humiliation, seek glory. The Lord incarnate came into their midst seeking adversity, spurning the world's goods, embracing opprobrium, fleeing glory. So the long-awaited Christ came and taught new things, wrought new wonders by his teaching, and, doing wonders, bore ills."

Bernard has it otherwise, saying: "Miserably we labor under a threefold sickness. We are easily misled, weak in action, and fragile in resistance. If we wish to distinguish between good and evil, we are deceived; if we attempt to do good, we lack strength; if we strive to resist evil, we are overcome. So the coming of the Savior is necessary. Dwelling in us he enlightens our blindness; remaining with us he helps our infirmity; standing for us he protects and defends our fragility." Thus Bernard.

Concerning the second advent, namely, the Last Judgment, we should consider both what will precede it and what will accompany it. Three things will precede it: fearful signs, the fallacious claims of the Antichrist, and a storm of fire. Luke's gospel sets down five signs to precede the Judgment: "There shall be signs in the sun and the moon and the stars, and upon the earth distress of nations by reason of the confusion of the roaring of the sea and the waves."[5] The book of Apocalypse describes the first three signs: "The sun became black as sackcloth, and the moon red as blood, and the stars from heaven fell upon the earth." Rev.[6] The sun is said to be darkened because its light was taken away so that it might seem to be mourning the father of a family, namely, man; or because a greater light, that of the radiance of Christ, had risen; or, to express it metaphorically, because, as Augustine says, the divine vengeance will be so severe that even the sun will not dare to look upon it. Or, according to a mystical interpretation, Christ the sun of justice will be darkened because no one will have the courage to confess him. "Heaven" here means the upper air, and "stars" means shooting stars or meteors, because by their substance they resemble stars, and in common speech stars are said to "fall from heaven" when meteors are seen. In this case Scripture adopts the common usage. The event will certainly create a powerful impression because of its fiery nature, and the Lord does this to terrify sinners. Or the stars are said to fall because they emit fiery tails, or because many men who appeared to be stars in the Church will fall headlong, or because the stars will withdraw their light and become invisible.

About the fourth sign, distress of nations, we read in Matthew 24: "There shall then be great tribulation, such as there has not been from the beginning of the world."[7] As for the fifth sign, the confusion of the roaring of the sea, some think this means that with a thundering noise the sea will cease to be what it was before, as Apocalypse says: "The sea is no more."[8] Others understand the roar-

---

[5] Luke 21:25. [6] Rev 6:12–13.
[7] Matt. 24:21. [8] Rev. 21:1.

ing as the great noise made as the sea rises forty cubits above the mountains and then crashes down. Gregory reads the text literally: "Then there was a new and unheard-of disturbance of the sea and the waves."

Jerome, in his *Annals of the Hebrews*, finds fifteen signs preceding the Judgment, but does not say whether they will be continuous or intermittent. On the first day the sea will rise forty cubits above the tops of the mountains, standing in place like a wall. Only on the second day will it come down and be almost invisible. On the third day the sea beasts will come out above the surface and will roar to the heavens, and God alone will understand their bellowing. On the fourth day the sea and the waters will burn up. On the fifth the trees and grasses will exude a bloody dew: also on this fifth day, as others assert, all the birds in the sky will gather together in the fields, each species in its place, not feeding or drinking but frightened by the imminent coming of the Judge. On the sixth day buildings will collapse. It is said that on this same sixth day fiery thunderbolts will pour out of the setting sun and run across the sky all the way to its rising. On the seventh the rocks will collide with each other and split into four parts, and each part, it is said, will crash against the other; and no man will hear the sound, only God. On the eighth will come a worldwide earthquake, which will, we are told, be so great that neither man nor beast will be able to stand, and all will fall prostrate on the ground. On the ninth the earth will be leveled and the mountains and hills reduced to dust. On the tenth, men will come out of the caves and go about as if demented, unable to speak to each other. The eleventh day will see the bones of the dead rise and stand above the tombs from the rising of the sun to its setting, so that the dead will be able to come out. On the twelfth the stars will fall: all the fixed and wandering stars will spread fiery trains, and then will again be generated from their substance. It is said that on that day, too, all the animals will come into the fields, growling and grunting, not feeding, not drinking. On the thirteenth the living will die in order to rise again with the dead. On the fourteenth heaven and earth will be burned up. On the fifteenth a new heaven and a new earth will come to be, and all the dead will rise again.

Also to precede the Last Judgment will be the false pretensions of the Antichrist. He will try to deceive all men in four ways, first by cunning argument or false exposition of the Scriptures. His aim will be to persuade people, and to prove from Scripture that he is the Messiah promised in the Law, and he will destroy the law of Christ and establish his own: "Appoint, O Lord, a lawgiver over them";[9] and the *Gloss*: "That is the Antichrist, giver of perverse law." The book of Daniel has: "They shall place [in the sanctuary] the abomination unto desolation";[10] and the *Gloss*: "The Antichrist will sit in the temple of God pretending to be God, in order to do away with the law of God."

He will also try to deceive by working miracles; 2 Thessalonians: "Whose coming is according to the working of Satan, in all words and signs and lying

[9] Ps. 9:21. [10] Dan. 11:31.

wonders";[11] Apocalypse: "He did great signs, so that he made also fire to come down from heaven unto the earth";[12] and the *Gloss*: "As the Holy Spirit was given to the apostles in the form of fire, the wicked spirit will also be given in the form of fire." A third means of deception will be his conferring of gifts. Daniel: "He shall give them power over many and shall divide the land gratis";[13] and the *Gloss*: "The Antichrist will give many gifts to those he deceives, and will distribute the land to his army, for those whom he could not conquer by terror he will overcome through avarice." His fourth method will be the infliction of torments; Daniel: "He shall lay all things waste and shall prosper and do more than can be believed."[14] And, speaking of the Antichrist, Gregory comments: "He kills the strong, conquering in the body those who had remained unconquered."

The last occurrence preceding the Judgment will be the storm of fire, which will go before the face of the Judge. God will send this fire, firstly for the renewal of the world: he will purge and renew all the elements. Like the waters of the Deluge, the fire will climb fifteen cubits higher than the mountains, as the *Scholastic History* says, "higher than the works of men could reach." Secondly, the fire will be for men's purification, because the place of purgatory will be for those who are then found still living. Thirdly, the fire will increase the torments of the damned and, fourthly, will provide greater illumination of the saints. According to Saint Basil, once the purgation of the world is accomplished, God will separate the heat of the fire from its light and will send all the heat to the region of the damned to torture them, and all the light to the region of the blessed for their greater enjoyment.

Several circumstances will be attendant upon the Last Judgment itself. Firstly, the Judge's procedure in judging. He will come down into the valley of Josaphat and judge the good and the wicked, setting the good on his right and the wicked on the left. It is to be believed that he will occupy an elevated place, so that all may see him. Nor should we think that the whole gathering would be crowded into that small valley; to think so, Jerome says, would be childish. They will be both in the valley and in the surrounding areas: countless thousands of people can stand in a small space, especially if they are pressed closely together. Moreover, if need be, the elect, due to the lightness of their bodies, could hover in the air, while the damned could be held aloft by the power of God.

Then the Judge will address himself to the wicked, upbraiding them for failing to do the works of mercy. At this all will lament for themselves, as John Chrysostom, commenting on Matthew, says: "The Jews will lament, seeing the One they thought of as a dead man now living and life-giving, and at the sight of his wounded body will be unable to deny their crime and will know themselves convicted. The Gentiles also will lament because, having allowed them-

---

[11] Rev. 2:9. [12] Rev. 13:13.
[13] Dan. 11:39. [14] Dan. 8:24.

selves to be deceived by the philosophers' reasonings, they thought that to worship a crucified God was irrational and stupid. Christian sinners will lament on account of their sins, because they loved the world more than God and Christ. Heretics will lament because they called the Crucified a mere man and now see him, whom the Jews made to suffer, as the Judge. And all the tribes of the earth will mourn, because there no longer is any power to resist him nor possibility of escaping from his presence nor room for repentance nor time to make satisfaction. All is distress, nothing is left to them but grief."

Secondly, among those to be judged, different ranks or groups will be set apart. According to Gregory there will be four divisions, two among the reprobate, two among the elect. There are some who will be judged and will perish, such as those to whom it is said: "I was hungry and you gave me no food, etc."[15] Others are condemned without being judged, such as those of whom it is said: "He who does not believe is already judged."[16] They will not hear any word from the Judge, since they were unwilling to receive his word in faith. Then there are those who are judged and who reign. As the perfected, they will judge others—not that they will pronounce sentence, this being the prerogative of the Judge himself, but they are said to judge insofar as they will assist the one judging. This assistance is granted them to honor the saints, since to sit with him who judges is a great honor, as the Lord promised: "When the Son of man shall sit on his glorious throne, you also will sit on twelve seats, judging the twelve tribes of Israel."[17] It also confirms the sentence, as at times those who assist the judge approve his sentence and put their signatures to it as a mark of approval: "To execute on them the judgment written, this is glory for all his faithful ones."[18] Again, by so assisting the Judge, the saints condemn the wicked by the fact that they lived their lives righteously.

A third accompaniment to the Judgment will be the insignia of the Lord's passion, namely, the cross, the nails, and the marks of his wounds. First, they will give evidence of his glorious victory; therefore they will appear resplendent in glory. Hence Chrysostom, commenting on Matthew, says: "The cross and the wounds will shine more brightly than the sun's rays." Consider also the great power of the cross. The sun will be darkened and the moon will not give her light, that you may learn how much more radiant the cross is than the moon, how much more splendid than the sun. Second, the insignia will put his mercy in evidence, showing how great is the mercy by which the good are saved. Third, they will show forth his justice, making clear how justly the wicked are condemned because they had no regard for the precious blood he shed for them. He will reproach them in such words as Chrysostom, in his commentary on Matthew, has him say: "For your sake I became man, was bound and mocked and scourged and crucified; and what service did you render me in return for the

---

[15] Matt. 25:42. [16] John 3:18.
[17] Matt. 19:28. [18] Ps. 149:9.

price of my blood? I held you higher than my glory, I, who being God came as a man; and you held me lower, viler than all your possessions. The most worthless things on earth you loved more dearly than my goodness and my faith." Thus Chrysostom.

Fourthly, have in mind the sternness of the one judging. "No fear can influence him, for he is omnipotent": so Chrysostom. Nor is there any power that can resist him, nor possibility of fleeing from him. "Bribes cannot corrupt him because he is so rich," says Bernard. And Augustine: "He will come on that day, when pure hearts will be of more avail than shrewd words, and a good conscience more than full purses; he is not fooled by words nor swayed by gifts." The day of judgment is awaited, and that most impartial judge will be present. He is no respecter of powerful persons, and no bishop or abbot or count will be able to corrupt his palace with gold or silver. Being all good, he is not moved by hatred, because hate cannot fall upon the good: "Thou hatest none of the things which thou hast made."[19] Love will not dissuade him, because he is most just, so he will not let even his brothers, i.e., false Christians, go free: "No brother can redeem."[20] He will not err, because he is all wise. Pope Leo says: "Tremendous is his insight, which penetrates the impervious, to which every secret is open, the obscure is lightened, the speechless respond, silence confesses, the mind speaks even without words. And therefore, since such and so great is his wisdom, against it no arguments of lawyers, no sophisms of philosophers, no eloquent speeches by orators, no subtleties from the sharp-witted, will have the slightest weight." And Jerome comments: "'How much better off the tongue-tied and mute will be than the fluent of speech, shepherds than philosophers, rustics than orators; how the mutterings of dullards will do better than the astute arguments of Cicero!"

Fifthly, there will be the dread accuser. Indeed, three accusers will stand up against the sinner. The first to accuse will be the devil. Augustine writes: "The devil will then be there, reciting the words of our profession and throwing up to us our actions, the places and times of our sins, and what good we should have done at those moments. And then this adversary will say: 'O most just Judge, give judgment that this sinner is mine because of his sin, since he did not choose to be yours by grace. He is yours by his nature, mine by his misery, yours due to your passion, mine by my persuasion; you he disobeyed, me he obeyed; from you he received the robe of immortality, from me the rags he now is clothed with; he threw off your robe and comes here with mine. O fairest of judges, judge that he is mine and must be damned with me.' Woe to such a one! How could he open his mouth, being found deserving to be counted with the devil!" Thus far Augustine.

The second accuser will be one's own sin. Each one's own sins will accuse him; "They shall come with fear at the thought of their sins, and their iniquities

---

[19] Wisd. 11:25.   [20] Ps. 48:8 (Douay).

shall stand against them to convict them."[21] Bernard writes: "Then all his deeds will speak together: 'You did us, we are your actions; we will always be with you and will go with you to judgment.'" Many and divers crimes will be his accusers.

The third accuser will be the whole world. Hear Gregory: "If you ask who will accuse you, I say, 'The whole world. When the Creator is offended the entire creation is offended.'" Chrysostom comments on Matthew: "There will be nothing we can say in response on that day when heaven and earth, the waters, the sun and the moon, night and day and the whole world will oppose us before God, testifying to our sins; and if all were silent, our very thoughts and especially our works will stand against us before God, forcefully accusing us."

Sixthly, there will be the infallible witness. The sinner will indeed have three witnesses against him. One will be above him, namely, God, who will be judge and witness: "I am judge and witness, says the Lord."[22] Another will be within him, namely, his conscience. Augustine: "Whoever you are who fear your future judge, straighten your conscience at present; for what will speak to your case is the testimony of your conscience." A third witness will be at his side, his own angel assigned to be his guardian; and the angel, knowing everything he has done, will bring testimony against him. "The heavens (i.e., the angels) will reveal his iniquity."[23]

Seventhly, there is the sinner's self-accusation concerning all this. So Gregory says: "Oh how narrow are the ways for the condemned! Above them an angry judge, below them the horrid abyss, on the right their accusing sins, on the left hordes of demons dragging them to torment, inside of them their burning conscience, outside, the world afire. So straitened, whither shall the sinner flee? To hide will be impossible, to show himself, intolerable."

Eighthly, the irrevocable sentence; for that sentence can never be revoked, nor can there be any appeal from it. In judicial cases no appeal is acceptable, for any of three reasons. The first is the supremacy of the judge: hence no appeal can be made from a king's sentence within his kingdom, because in his kingdom he has no one above him. Likewise there is no appeal against the emperor or the pope. The clear evidence of the crime is a second reason, because when the crime is known to all, there is no appeal. The third reason is that the case may not be deferred, because some harm might follow upon such deferral. So in the present case no appeal is possible. The judge is supreme: he has no one above him, he is beyond all by his eternity, his dignity, and his power. There might be some way to appeal from an emperor or a pope to God, but none from God to anyone else, there being no one higher. Furthermore, the crime is evident: all the crimes and misdeeds of the condemned will then be known and manifest. Jerome: "That day will come when our deeds will be visible as in a painted picture." Finally the case cannot be deferred. Nothing done there is subject to delay: everything will be accomplished in a moment, in the twinkling of an eye.

---

[21] Wisd. 4:20.   [22] Jer. 29:23.   [23] Job 20:27.

2. Saint Andrew, Apostle

Andrew is interpreted beautiful, or responding, or manly, from *ander*, which means male, a man; or Andrew, Andreas, is like *anthropos*, i.e., man, from *ana*, above, and *tropos*, a turning. So Andrew was one who turned upward toward heavenly things and was lifted up to his Creator. He was beautiful in his life, responding in wise doctrine, manly in suffering, and raised up in glory. The presbyters and deacons of Achaia wrote an account of his martyrdom, which they had witnessed with their own eyes.

Andrew and several other disciples were called by our Lord three times. The first time he called them to know him. That was the day when Andrew, standing with John his teacher and another disciple, heard John say: "Behold the lamb of God who takes away the sins of the world." Immediately he and the other disciple went and saw where Jesus lived, and they stayed with him all day; and later Andrew found his brother Simon and led him to Jesus. The next day they returned to fishing, their regular occupation. Later Jesus called them a second time, this time to his friendship. Coming with a great crowd to the shore of the lake of Genesareth, which is also called the sea of Galilee, he went into the boat that belonged to Simon and Andrew, and at his bidding they made a large haul of fish. Then Andrew called James and John, who were in another boat, and they followed the Lord, after which they again returned to their work. But soon Jesus called them again, this time to be his disciples. Walking one day beside the same lake, he signaled them to throw aside their nets, and said: "Follow me, I will make you fishers of men." And they followed him and did not go back to their usual work. Still a fourth time, moreover, the Lord called Andrew, on this occasion to be his apostle, as Mark reports in his third chapter: "He called those he had chosen for himself and they came to him, and he saw to it that they were twelve in number."

    After the Lord's ascension into heaven the apostles separated, and Andrew went to Scythia, while Matthew went to Murgundia, also called Ethiopia. But the Ethiopians, refusing to heed Matthew's preaching, put out his eyes, bound him with chains, and threw him into prison, intending to put him to death in a few days. Meanwhile the angel of the Lord appeared to Andrew and commanded him to go to Ethiopia to be with blessed Matthew. Andrew answered that he did not know the way there, whereupon the angel ordered him to go to the seacoast, and there to board the first ship he encountered. This Andrew promptly did, and the ship, aided by a favorable wind, swiftly carried him to the town where Matthew was. Then, the angel guiding him, he made his way into the evangelist's prison, which he found open. Seeing Matthew he wept much and prayed; and the Lord, in answer to his prayer, restored to Matthew the sight of his eyes, which the cruelty of the unbelievers had taken from him.

Matthew then departed and went to Antioch. Andrew stayed in Murgundia, where the inhabitants, furious at their prisoner's escape, seized the apostle and dragged him from place to place with his hands bound. His blood flowed freely, but he prayed to God unceasingly for his tormentors and in the end converted them. Then he set out for Achaia. This, at any rate, is what we are told; but I find the story very hard to believe, because Matthew's deliverance and cure by Andrew would imply—and this is very unlikely—that the great evangelist was unable to obtain for himself what Andrew secured for him so easily.

A young man of noble family had been converted by Saint Andrew and joined his company against the will of his parents, whereupon they set fire to the house where he lived with the apostle. When the flames were at their height, the young man sprinkled a vial of water on them and the fire died out. Then the parents said: "Our son has been turned into a sorcerer." They brought a ladder and tried to climb up and rescue their son; but God struck them blind, so that they could no longer see the rungs of the ladder. A man who was passing called up to them: "Why go to so much trouble? Do you not see that God is fighting for them? Stop now, or God's wrath may fall upon you!" Many, witnessing this, believed in the Lord. As for the youth's parents, they died after fifty days and were buried in a tomb.

A woman who had married a murderer was brought to bed but could not give birth. She said to her sister: "Go and pray to our mistress Diana for me." The sister prayed, but it was the devil, not Diana, who answered: "It is useless to invoke me, for I can do nothing for you. Go instead and find Andrew the apostle: he can help your sister." She went therefore and sought out Saint Andrew, and brought him to the bedside of her ailing sister. "You deserve your suffering," he said to her; "you married badly, conceived badly, and called upon the devil. But repent, believe in Christ, and you will be delivered." The woman made an act of faith and brought forth a stillborn child; and her pangs ceased.

An old man named Nicholas came to Andrew and told him: "Master, I am now seventy years old and have always been given to sins of lust. Yet I have read the gospel and have prayed to God to grant me the gift of continence, but I cannot resist concupiscence, and I fall back into my evil ways. Now it has happened that driven by lust and forgetting that I carried the gospel on my person, I went to a brothel; but the harlot, when she saw me, cried out: 'Get out, old man, get out! Don't touch me or try to come near me. I see marvelous things about you, and I know you are an angel of God!' Astonished by what she said, I remembered that I was carrying the gospel. Now, holy man of God, let your prayer obtain my salvation!" Hearing all this the saint began to weep and remained in prayer for hours; and then he refused to eat, saying: "I will eat nothing until I know that the Lord will take pity on this old man." After he had fasted for five days, a voice came to him: "Andrew, your prayer is granted. But just as you have mortified your body by fasting for him, so likewise he must fast in order to win salvation." The old man did so. For six months he fasted on bread and water, and then fell asleep in peace, full of good works. And again Andrew heard the voice, this time saying to him: "Your prayer has restored to me Nicholas whom I had lost."

A certain Christian youth told Saint Andrew in secret: "My mother, seeing my good figure, tried to make me do wrong with her; and when I absolutely refused, she went to the judge and accused me of that very crime. Pray for me and save me from an unjust death, because I will not defend myself. I would rather die than expose my mother to such shame." So the young man was summoned before the judge, and Andrew went with him. The mother insistently charged her son with wanting to violate her, and the son, despite being asked several times whether this was true, said not a word. Then Andrew spoke to the mother: "O cruelest of women, your own lust makes you willing to send your only son to death!" The woman said to the judge: "Sir, my son attached himself to this man after failing to have his way with me." This made the judge very angry, so he ordered the young man to be put in a sack smeared with pitch and tar and thrown into the river, and Andrew to be kept in jail until he, the judge, decided on a form of torture that would kill him. But Andrew prayed, whereupon a stupendous clap of thunder terrified them all, a huge earthquake threw them to the ground, and the woman, struck by lightning, shriveled up and crumbled to ashes. The others begged the apostle to pray that they might be spared. Andrew prayed for them, and the storm fell calm. At this the judge believed, as did his whole household.

When the apostle came to the city of Nicaea, the townspeople told him that seven devils had stationed themselves along the road outside the city gate and were killing anyone who passed that way. The saint, with all the people looking on, commanded the demons to come to him, and at once they came in the shape of dogs. The apostle ordered them to be off to some place where they could not harm anyone. The devils vanished, and those who had witnessed the miracle accepted the faith of Christ. But when Andrew arrived at the gate of another town, he came upon the body of a young man being carried out for burial. Asking what had happened to the youth, he was told that seven dogs had come and killed him in his bed. The apostle, in tears, cried out: "I know, Lord, that these were the seven demons I chased out of Nicaea!" Then he said to the father: "What will you give me if I restore your son to life?" "I have nothing dearer to me than my son," the father answered, "so I will give him to you." And when Andrew had prayed to the Lord, the young man rose and followed him.

Some men, to the number of forty, were on their way by sea to receive the word of faith from Andrew, when the devil raised a storm and all were drowned. But their bodies were cast up on the shore by the waves. The apostle quickly brought them back to life, and they all told what had befallen them. Whence it is that we read in a hymn from the saint's office:

Quaterdenos juvenes,
Submersos maris fluctibus,
Vitae reddidit usibus.[1]

Then blessed Andrew settled in Achaia, filled the whole region with churches, and led a great number of people to the Christian faith. Among others, he converted the wife of the proconsul Aegeus and baptized her. As soon as the proconsul heard of this, he came to the town of Patras and commanded the Christians to sacrifice to the idols. Then Andrew came to meet him and said: "You have earned the right to judge men on earth. Now what you ought to do is to recognize your judge who is in heaven, worship him, and turn completely away from false gods." Aegeus spoke: "So you are that Andrew who preaches the superstitious sect which the princes of Rome recently ordered us to exterminate." Andrew: "That is because the Roman rulers have not yet known that the Son of God has come on earth, and has taught that your idols are demons and their teaching an offense to God. So God, being offended, turns away from those who worship them and does not hear their prayers; and they, no longer heard by God, are made captive by the devil and deluded by him until their naked souls leave their bodies, carrying nothing with them but their sins." "Yes," Aegeus retorted, "and because your Jesus was teaching this nonsense, they nailed him to a cross." Andrew replied: "It was to give us salvation, and not to expiate any misdeeds of his own, that he freely accepted the agony of the cross." Then said Aegeus: "How can you say that he freely suffered death, when we know that he was handed over by one of his disciples, imprisoned by the Jews, and crucified by the soldiers?"

Andrew thereupon set out to prove, by five arguments, that the passion of Christ was voluntary. Christ had foreseen his passion and had foretold it to his disciples, saying: "Behold, we go up to Jerusalem, and the Son of man shall be betrayed."[2] When Peter tried to dissuade him, Jesus said: "Go behind me, Satan!"[3] He made it plain that he had the power both to suffer death and to rise again, saying: "I have the power to lay it (my life) down, and I have power to take it up again."[4] He knew in advance the man who would betray him, since he dipped bread and gave it to him, and still made no attempt to avoid him. Finally, he had chosen the place where he knew the traitor would come to betray him. Andrew also declared that he himself had been present at all these moments; and he added that the cross was a great mystery. "It is not a mystery

---

[1] Forty young men, / who had been drowned in the waves of the sea, / he restored to the uses of life.

[2] Matt. 20:18.

[3] Matt. 16:23.

[4] John 10:17–18.

at all," Aegeus replied, "but a punishment. However, if you refuse to obey my command, I will give you a taste of your mystery!" "If I were afraid of the pain of the cross," Andrew answered, "I would not be preaching the glory of the cross. But first let me teach you its mystery. Maybe you will believe in it, worship it, and be saved."

He then began to explain the mystery of redemption to the proconsul, proving, by five arguments, how necessary and appropriate this mystery is. Since the first man had brought death into the world by means of wood, a tree, it was appropriate that the Son of man should banish death by dying on a cross of wood. Since the sinner had been formed out of clean earth, it was fitting that the reconciler should be born of an immaculate virgin. Since Adam had stretched out his greedy hands toward the forbidden fruit, it was fitting that the second Adam should open his guiltless hands on the cross. Since Adam had tasted the sweetness of the apple, Jesus had to taste the bitterness of gall. And since he was giving his own immortality to man, it was by a fitting exchange that he took human mortality, because if God had not become man, man could not have become immortal. To all this Aegeus's reply was: "Go teach these inanities to your own people, but now obey me and offer sacrifice to the all-powerful gods!" And Andrew: "To almighty God I offer daily a Lamb without stain, who remains alive and whole after all the people have eaten him." Aegeus asked how this could be, and Andrew answered: "Become his disciple and I will tell you." Aegeus: "Well, then, I will torture an answer out of you"; and, enraged, he had him imprisoned.

The next morning, taking his place in the judgment seat, he again called upon Andrew to sacrifice to the idols, saying: "If you refuse to obey me, I shall have you hung upon the cross you boast about!" And he threatened him with other torments. The apostle responded: "Make them the worst you can think of! The more bravely I bear suffering in his name, the more acceptable I shall be to my king." Aegeus commanded twenty-one men to seize him, flog him, and bind him hand and foot to a cross, so as to make his agony last longer.

While the saint was being led to the cross, a great crowd gathered, shouting: "An innocent man is condemned to shed his blood without cause!" The apostle, however, begged them not to try to save him from martyrdom. Then, seeing the cross in the distance, he greeted it, saying: "Hail, O cross sanctified by the body of Christ and adorned with his limbs as with precious stones! Before the Lord was lifted up on you, you were greatly feared on earth, but now you draw down love from heaven and are accepted as a blessing. I come to you assured and rejoicing, so that you may joyfully accept me, the disciple of him who hung upon you, for I have always loved you and yearned to embrace you. O good cross, honored and beautified by the limbs of the Lord, long desired, constantly loved, ceaselessly sought, and now prepared for my wishful heart! Take me away from the world of men and return me to my Master, that he, having redeemed me by means of you, may receive me from you." Having said these words, he shed his garments and gave them to the executioners, who fixed him to the cross as they had been commanded. For two days Andrew hung there alive and preached to twenty thousand people. On the third day the crowd began to threaten the proconsul Aegeus with death, saying that a saintly, gentle man should not be made to suffer so; and Aegeus came to have the saint released. Seeing him, Andrew exclaimed: "Why have you come here, Aegeus? If to seek forgiveness, you will be forgiven; but if to take me down from the cross, know that I will not come down alive, for already I see my king awaiting me." When the soldiers tried to free him, they could not even touch him: their arms fell powerless at their sides. Meanwhile Andrew, knowing that the people wanted to rescue him, uttered this prayer from the cross, as Augustine quotes it in his book *On Penance*: "Lord, do not let me come down alive! It is time for you to entrust my body to the earth. You entrusted it to me, and I have borne it so long and watched over it and worked so hard, and now I wish to be discharged of this obedience and relieved of this most burdensome garment. I think of how I have labored to carry its weight, to control its unruliness, to support its weakness, to compel its slow responses. You know, O Lord, how often it has struggled to draw me away from the purity of contemplation and awaken me from the repose of that most sweet stillness, how many and how grave pains it has inflicted on me. O most kind Father, I have resisted the assaults of this body for so long, and with your help I have mastered it. Just and loving Rewarder, I beg of you not to leave it any longer in my care! I give back what you entrusted to me. Commend it to the earth so that I will not have to take care of it, and it will not curb and hamper me, thirsting as I am to come freely to you, the inexhaustible source of life and joy." Thus Augustine.

As Andrew finished his prayer, a dazzling light shone out of heaven and enveloped him for the space of a half hour, hiding him from sight; and as the light faded, he breathed his last. Maximilla, Aegeus's wife, took away the body of the holy apostle and gave it honorable burial. But Aegeus, before ever he got back to his house, was seized by a demon and died in the street, with the crowd looking on.

We are told also that a flourlike manna and sweet-smelling oil used to issue from Saint Andrew's tomb, and that by this sign the people of the region could predict the next year's crops. If the flow was meager, the crops would be poor; if abundant, the yield would be plentiful. This may have been true in the past, but now it is said that the saint's body was transferred to Constantinople.

A certain truly devout bishop venerated Saint Andrew above all other saints and began whatever he was about to do with the invocation, "To the honor of God and Saint Andrew." This aroused the devil's envy, and he turned all his cunning to the task of deceiving the bishop. So he took the form of a marvelously beautiful woman, who came to the bishop's palace and said that she wanted to confess to him. The bishop sent word that she should apply to his own confessor, to whom he gave the necessary faculties, but she refused on the ground that the bishop himself was the only one to whom she could reveal the secrets of her conscience. In the end he allowed her to be brought before him, and she said: "I pray you, my lord, have pity on me, young as I am as you can see, tenderly nurtured and of royal blood. I have come here, alone and in the garb of a pilgrim. My father, a mighty king, wanted to give me in marriage to a great prince, but I told him that I held the marriage bed in horror because I had vowed perpetual virginity to Christ, and could never consent to carnal commerce. With the choice of either yielding to his will or suffering dire punishment, I got away secretly, preferring to live in exile rather than break faith with my spouse. The fame of your sanctity had come to my ears, and I have sought refuge under the wings of your protection, hoping to find a place with you where I might enjoy the secret silence of holy contemplation, avoid the pitfalls of life, and escape from the disorders of the noisy world."

The bishop, admiring her noble origin and her physical beauty as well as her fervor and eloquence, answered her kindly: "Be reassured, my child, and have no fear. He for whose love you have given up everything, yourself, your kin, and all your possessions, will heap graces upon you in this life and the fullness of glory in the next. I, as his servant, offer you all that is mine. Please choose wherever you wish to dwell; and today I invite you to dine with me." "O my father," she replied, "do not ask this of me. It might stir up some suspicion that would damage your good name." "Not at all!" said the bishop. "There will be others present, we shall not be alone. There cannot be the slightest suspicion that there is anything amiss."

So the bishop, the woman, and the rest of the company went to the table, the woman seated facing the prelate and the others to either side. The bishop could not take his eyes from her face nor contain his admiration for her beauty; and, the eye being fixed, the inner man was wounded. The ancient enemy, aware of this, drove his dart deep into the bishop's heart, at the same time making the alluring face more and more beautiful. The bishop was on the verge of consenting to the thought of proposing a wicked act to the woman at the first opportunity, when suddenly a pilgrim came pounding on the door and loudly demanded admittance. As no one opened to the stranger and the noise from outside increased, the bishop asked the woman whether she would mind if the pilgrim was allowed to come in. She replied: "We shall propose a very difficult question to him. If he can give a satisfactory answer, let him in. If not, let him be driven away as an ignorant person, unworthy to be in the presence of a bishop!"

The plan appealed to all present, and they looked around to see who might be wise enough to propound the question. Then the bishop said to the woman: "No one of us, my lady, is so well able to do this as you are. You surpass us all in wisdom and eloquence, so you shall propose the question." So the woman said: "Ask him to name the most wonderful thing that God has made in a small form." The question was relayed to the stranger, who answered the messenger:

"It is the variety and excellence of the human face: for among so many human beings, from the beginning of the world to its end, no two could be discovered whose faces resembled each other in every respect, or ever will be; yet in each face, small as it may be, God places the seat of all the senses of the body." This solution pleased the company, and they said: "This is a true and excellent answer." Then the woman said: "Let us propose a second and harder problem, so that we may better gauge his knowledge: ask him at what point earth is higher than the heavens." The stranger replied: "It is in the empyrean heaven, for there the body of Christ resides; and the body of Christ is higher than any heaven, yet it was formed of our flesh, and our flesh was made of earth. Therefore at that point earth is higher than the heavens." Hearing this, the company applauded the stranger's wisdom, but the woman spoke again: "We shall give him one more question, this one far more difficult, more obscure, harder to solve than any other could be. This will let us plumb the depth of his knowledge. If he has the answer, he is indeed worthy to sit at the bishop's table. Ask him therefore how far it is from earth to heaven." The pilgrim's reply to the messenger was: "Go back to the one who sent you to me and put that question carefully to him. He knows the answer better than I do and can answer it better, because he traversed the distance when he fell from heaven into the abyss. I never fell from heaven and so never measured the distance. He is not a woman but the devil, who took on a woman's likeness." The messenger, frightened by what he had heard, hurried to report it to those inside. They sat stunned and bewildered by the message, but the ancient enemy vanished from their midst.

The bishop, coming to himself, bitterly reproached himself and with tears prayed for pardon for his fault. He sent the porter to bring the pilgrim into the house, but the stranger was nowhere to be found. Then he called the people together, explained to them everything that had happened, and asked them to fast and pray that God might deign to reveal the identity of the stranger who had saved him from so great a danger. That very night it was revealed to the bishop that it was Saint Andrew himself who, to save him, had come dressed as a pilgrim. Thereafter the bishop was more than ever devout in his veneration of the holy apostle.

The prefect of a certain city had taken possession of a field that belonged to a church dedicated to Saint Andrew. At the prayer of the bishop, the prefect was immediately stricken with fever as a punishment for his sin. He thereupon asked the bishop to pray for him, promising to return the field to the church if he recovered his health; but once he had been made well he took back the field. Then the bishop again resorted to prayer and extinguished all the lights in the church, saying: "There will be no more light until the Lord is avenged upon his enemy and the church recovers its loss." The prefect promptly fell ill again, this time with a higher fever, so once more he begged the bishop to pray for him, saying that he would give back the stolen field and another of equal size. The bishop's answer was: "I have already prayed, and God has answered my prayer."

The sick man then had himself carried to the bishop, whom he forced to go into the church to pray for him again; but hardly had the bishop entered the church when the prefect died, and the field was restored to the church.

3. Saint Nicholas

The name Nicholas comes from *nicos*, which means victory, and *laos*, people; so Nicholas may be interpreted as meaning victory over a people, i.e., either victory over vices, which are many and mean, or as victory in the full sense, because Nicholas, by his way of life and his doctrine, taught the peoples to conquer sin and vice. Or the name is formed from *nicos*, victory, and *laus*, praise—so, victorious praise—or from *nitor*, shining whiteness, and *laos*, people, as meaning the bright cleanness of the people. Nicholas had in him that which makes for shining cleanness, since, according to Ambrose, "the word of God makes clean, as do true confession, holy thoughts, and good works."

The life of Saint Nicholas was written by learned men of Argos, called Argolics, Argos being, according to Isidore, a town in Greece, so the Greeks are also called Argolics. Elsewhere we read that his legend was written in Greek by the patriarch Methodius and translated into Latin by John the Deacon, who added much to it.

Nicholas, a citizen of Patera, was born of rich and pious parents. His father was named Epiphanes, his mother, Johanna. When, in the flower of their youth, they had brought him into the world, they adopted the celibate life thenceforth. While the infant was being bathed on the first day of his life, he stood straight up in the bath. From then on he took the breast only once on Wednesdays and Fridays. As a youth he avoided the dissolute pleasures of his peers, preferring to spend time in churches; and whatever he could understand of the Holy Scriptures he committed to memory.

After the death of his parents he began to consider how he might make use of his great wealth, not in order to win men's praise but to give glory to God. At the time a certain fellow townsman of his, a man of noble origin but very poor, was thinking of prostituting his three virgin daughters in order to make a living out of this vile transaction. When the saint learned of this, abhorring the crime he wrapped a quantity of gold in a cloth and, under cover of darkness, threw it through a window of the other man's house and withdrew unseen. Rising in the morning, the man found the gold, gave thanks to God, and celebrated the wedding of his eldest daughter. Not long thereafter the servant of God did the same thing again. This time the man, finding the gold and bursting into loud praises, determined to be on the watch so as to find out who had come to the relief of his penury. Some little time later Nicholas threw a double sum of gold into the house. The noise awakened the man and he pursued the fleeing figure, calling out, "Stop! Stop! Don't hide from me!" and ran faster and faster until he saw that it was Nicholas. Falling to the ground he wanted to kiss his benefactor's feet, but the saint drew away and exacted a promise that the secret would be kept until after his death.

Some time later the bishop of Myra died, and all the bishops of the region gathered to choose a successor. Among them was one bishop of great authority, upon whose opinion the decision of the others would depend. This prelate exhorted the others to fast and pray; and that very night he heard a voice telling him to post himself at the doors of the church in the morning, and to consecrate as bishop the first man he saw coming in, whose name would be Nicholas. In the morning he made this known to his colleagues and went outside the church to wait. Meanwhile Nicholas, miraculously guided by God, went early to the church and was the first to enter. The bishop, coming up to him, asked his name; and he, filled with the simplicity of a dove, bowed his head and answered, "Nicholas, the servant of your holiness." Then all the bishops led him in and installed him on the episcopal throne. But he, amidst his honors, always preserved his former humility and gravity of manner. He passed the night in prayer, mortified his body, and shunned the society of women. He was humble in his attitude toward others, persuasive in speech, forceful in counsel, and strict when reprimands were called for. A chronicle also states that Nicholas took part in the Council of Nicaea.

One day some seamen, threatened by a violent storm at sea, shed tears and prayed as follows: "Nicholas, servant of God, if what we have heard about you is true, let us experience your help now." At once there appeared before them a figure resembling the saint, who said to them: "You called me, here I am!" And he began to assist them with the sails and ropes and other rigging of the ship, and the storm died down immediately. The sailors eventually came to the church where Nicholas was and recognized him instantly, although they had never seen him in the flesh. They thanked him then for their deliverance, but he told them to thank God, since their rescue was due not to his merits, but only to the divine mercy and their own faith.

There came a time when Saint Nicholas's province was beset by a famine so severe that no one had anything to eat. The man of God learned that several ships laden with grain were anchored in the harbor. He hastened there promptly and begged the ships' people to come to the aid of those who were starving, if only by allowing them a hundred measures of wheat from each ship. But they replied: "Father, we dare not, because our cargo was measured at Alexandria and we must deliver it whole and entire to the emperor's granaries." The saint answered: "Do what I tell you, and I promise you in God's power that the imperial customsmen will not find your cargo short." The men did so, and when they arrived at their destination, they turned over to the imperial granaries the same quantity of grain that had been measured out at Alexandria. They spread news of the miracle and glorified God in his saint. Meanwhile the grain they had relinquished was distributed by Nicholas to each according to his needs, and so miraculously that not only did it suffice to feed the whole region for two years but supplied enough for the sowing.

In the past this region had worshiped idols; and even in Saint Nicholas's time there were rustics who practiced pagan rites under a tree dedicated to the wicked goddess Diana. To put a stop to this idolatry the saint ordered the tree cut down. This infuriated the ancient enemy, who concocted an unnatural oil that had the property of burning on water or on stone. Then, assuming the form of a nun, he came alongside a ship carrying people on their way to visit the saint and called to them: "I wanted so much to come with you to the holy man of God, but I cannot. May I ask you to offer this oil at his church and to paint the walls with it in memory of me." And forthwith he vanished. Then they saw another craft nearing them with honest people aboard, including one person who bore a striking likeness to Saint Nicholas, and this one asked them: "What did that woman say to you and what did she bring to you?" The people gave a full account of what had taken place. "That was the shameless Diana herself," he replied, "and if you want proof of it, throw that oil out over the water." They did so, and a huge fire flared up on the sea and, contrary to nature, burned for hours. When the travelers finally came to the servant of God, they said: "Truly you are the one who appeared to us at sea and delivered us from the wiles of the devil."

About that time there was a tribe that had risen in rebellion against the Roman Empire, and the emperor sent three princes, Nepotian, Ursus, and Apilion, to put them down. The three were forced by adverse winds to put in at an Adriatic port, and Nicholas, anxious to have them restrain their men from robbing his people on market days—something that happened regularly—invited them to his house. Meanwhile, during the saint's absence, the Roman consul, corrupted by a bribe, had ordered three innocent soldiers to be beheaded. As soon as the holy man heard of this, he asked his guests to accompany him, and they hurried to the spot where the execution was to take place. There he found the condemned men already on their knees, their faces veiled, and the executioner brandishing his sword over their heads. Nicholas, afire with zeal, threw himself upon the headsman, snatched his sword from his hand, unbound the innocent men, and led them away safe and sound.

The saint then hastened to the consul's headquarters and forced the door, which was locked. The consul came hurriedly to greet him, but Nicholas spurned him and said: "You enemy of God, you perverter of the law, how dare you look us in the eye with so great a crime on your conscience?" And he heaped reproaches upon him, but the princes pleaded for him, and the saint, seeing the man repentant, forgave him kindly. Thereupon the imperial emissaries, having received the bishop's blessing, continued their journey and put down the rebels without bloodshed; and when they returned to the emperor, he gave them a splendid reception.

Some other courtiers, however, envying their good fortune, bribed the imperial prefect to go to the emperor and accuse the princes of lese majesty. The emperor was beside himself with anger at the charge, and ordered the accused to be thrown into jail immediately and to be put to death without trial that very night. When the three heard this from their jailer, they tore their garments and wept bitterly. Then one of them, Nepotian, recalled that the blessed Nicholas had lately, in their presence, saved three innocent men from death, and exhorted his companions to invoke the holy man's aid. The result of their prayer was that Saint Nicholas appeared that night to Emperor Constantine and said: "Why have you had these princes arrested unjustly and condemned them to death when they are innocent? Hurry, get up and order them to be set free at once! Otherwise I shall pray God to stir up a war in which you will go down to defeat and be fed to the beasts." "Who are you," the emperor asked, "to come into my palace at night and talk to me this way?" Nicholas answered: "I am Nicholas, bishop of the city of Myra." The saint also appeared that night to the prefect, whom he terrified by saying: "Mindless and senseless man, why did you agree to the killing of innocent men? Go at once and see that they are set free. If you don't, your body will be devoured by worms and your house swiftly destroyed." The prefect retorted: "Who are you, to face us with such threats?" "Know," the holy man replied, "that I am Nicholas, bishop of the city of Myra."

The emperor and the prefect rose from sleep, told each other their dreams, and lost no time summoning the three princes. "Are you sorcerers," the emperor demanded, "to delude us with such visions?" They replied that they were not sorcerers, and that they had done nothing to deserve the sentence of death. Then said the emperor: "Do you know a man named Nicholas?" At the mention of the name they raised their hands to heaven and prayed God to save them, by the merits of Saint Nicholas, from the peril in which they found themselves. And when the emperor had heard from them about the life and miracles of the saint, he said: "Go, and thank God, who has saved you at the prayer of this Nicholas. But also bring gifts to Nicholas in my name and ask him not to threaten us anymore, but to pray the Lord for me and my reign."

Some days later the princes went to visit the servant of God. They threw themselves at his feet saying: "Truly you are a servant of God, truly you love and worship Christ." Then they told him everything that had happened; and he, raising his hands to heaven, offered heartfelt praise to God and sent the princes home after instructing them thoroughly in the truths of the faith.

When the Lord wished to call Nicholas to himself, the saint prayed that he would send his angels. And when he saw them coming, he bowed his head and recited the Psalm *In te Domine speravi*; and coming to the words *In manus tuas Domine commendo spiritum meum*, which mean "Into your hands, O Lord, I commend my spirit," he breathed forth his soul to the sound of heavenly music. This was in the year 343. He was buried in a marble tomb, and a fountain of oil began to flow from his head and a fountain of water from his feet. Even today a holy oil issues from his members and brings health to many.

One day this oil stopped flowing. This happened when the successor of Saint Nicholas, a worthy man, was driven from his see by jealous rivals. As soon as the bishop was restored, however, the oil flowed again. Long afterward, the Turks razed the city of Myra. Forty-seven soldiers from the town of Bari happened to be passing through, and four monks opened the tomb of Saint Nicholas to them: they removed his bones, which were immersed in oil, and carried them to Bari, in the year of the Lord 1087.

A man had borrowed some money from a Jew, giving him his oath on the altar of Saint Nicholas that he would repay it as soon as possible. As he was slow in paying, the Jew demanded his money, but the man declared that he had repaid it. He was summoned before the judge, who ordered him to swear that he had paid his debt. However, the man had put the money in a hollow staff, and before giving his oath he asked the Jew to hold the staff for him. He then swore that he had returned the money and more besides, and took back his staff: the Jew handed it over all unaware of the ruse. On his way home the dishonest fellow fell asleep by the roadside, and a coach, coming along at high speed, ran over him and killed him, also breaking open the staff and spilling the money. Being informed of this, the Jew hurried to the spot and saw through the trick; but, though the bystanders urged him to pick up his money, he refused unless the dead man were restored to life by the merits of Saint Nicholas, in which case he himself would become a Christian and accept baptism. At once the dead man was revived, and the Jew was baptized in the name of Jesus Christ.

Another Jew, seeing the miraculous power of Saint Nicholas, ordered a statue of the saint and placed it in his house. Whenever he had to be away for a long time, he addressed the statue in these or similar words: "Nicholas, I leave you in charge of my goods, and if you do not watch over them as I demand, I shall avenge myself by beating you." Then, one time when he was absent, thieves broke in and carried off all they found, leaving only the statue. When the Jew came home and saw that he had been robbed, he said to the statue: "Sir Nicholas, did I not put you in my house to guard my goods? Why then did you not do so and keep the thieves away? Well, then, you will pay the penalty! I shall make up for my loss and cool my anger by smashing you to bits!" And he did indeed beat the statue. But then a wondrous thing happened! The saint appeared to the robbers as they were dividing their spoils and said to them: "See how I have been beaten on your account! My body is still black and blue! Quick! Go and give back what you have taken, or the anger of God will fall upon you, your crime will become common knowledge, and you will every one of you be hanged." "And who are you," the thieves answered, "to talk this way to us?" "I am Nicholas, the servant of Jesus Christ," he replied, "and the Jew whom you robbed has beaten me in revenge!" Terrified, they ran to the Jew's house, told him of their vision, learned from him what he had done to the statue, restored all his property, and returned to the path of righteousness. The Jew, for his part, embraced the faith of the Savior.

A certain man, for love of his son who was learning his letters at school, annually celebrated the feast of Saint Nicholas in solemn fashion. On one particular occasion the boy's father laid on a sumptuous feast, to which he invited many clerks. During the meal the devil, dressed as a pilgrim, knocked at the door and asked for alms. The father ordered his son to take alms to the pilgrim, and the youth, not finding him at the door, pursued him to a crossroad, where the demon waylaid and strangled him. Hearing this, the father moaned with grief, carried the body back to the house and laid it on a bed, and cried: "O dearest son, how could this have happened to you? And, Saint Nicholas, is this my reward for the honor I have paid you all this time?" And while he was saying these things, the lad opened his eyes as if he were just waking up, and rose from the bed.

A nobleman had asked Saint Nicholas to pray the Lord to grant him a son, and promised that he would go with his son to the saint's tomb and would offer him a gold cup. His prayer was answered and he ordered the cup to be made, but he was so pleased with it that he kept it for himself and ordered another of like value. Then he took ship with the boy, to travel to the saint's tomb. On the way the father told his son to fetch him some water in the first cup. The boy tried to fill the cup with water, but fell into the sea and disappeared. Though stricken with grief, the father pursued his journey in order to fulfill his vow. He came to the church of Saint Nicholas and placed the second cup on the altar, whereupon an unseen hand thrust him back with the cup and threw him to the ground. He picked himself up, returned to the altar, and again was thrown down. And then, to the astonishment of all, the boy arrived whole and unharmed, carrying the first cup in his hands. He told how, the minute he had fallen into the water, Saint Nicholas had plucked him out and had kept him hale and hearty. At this the father rejoiced and offered both cups to the blessed Nicholas.

A rich man had obtained a son through the intercession of Saint Nicholas and called him Adeodatus. He also built a chapel in his house in honor of the saint and there solemnly celebrated his feast every year. The place was close to the territory of the Agarenes, and it happened that Adeodatus was captured by the Agarenes and carried off to serve their king as a slave. The following year, while the father was devoutly celebrating the feast of Saint Nicholas, the boy, serving the king with a precious cup in his hands, thought of his capture, his parents' grief, and the joy that used to be theirs on the feast day, and began to sigh and weep. The king demanded the reason for his tears and said: "Your Nicholas can do as he likes, but you are going to stay right here." Suddenly a mighty wind blew up, demolished the king's palace, snatched up the boy and the cup, and carried him to the threshold of the chapel where the parents were celebrating, to the great joy of all. Other sources would have it, however, that the aforesaid youth was of Norman origin and was on his way to the Holy Land when he was captured by the sultan, who had him whipped on the feast of Saint Nicholas and threw him into prison. There the boy fell asleep and woke to find himself in the chapel his father had built.

4. Saint Lucy, Virgin

Lucy comes from *lux*, which means light. Light is beautiful to look upon; for, as Ambrose says, it is the nature of light that all grace is in its appearance. Light also radiates without being soiled; no matter how unclean may be the places where its beams penetrate, it is still clean. It goes in straight lines, without curvature, and traverses the greatest distances without losing its speed. Thus we are shown that the blessed virgin Lucy possessed the beauty of virginity without trace of corruption; that she radiated charity without any impure love; her progress toward God was straight and without deviation, and went far in God's works without neglect or delay. Or the name is interpreted "way of light."

Lucy, the daughter of a noble family of Syracusa, saw how the fame of Saint Agatha was spreading throughout Sicily. She went to the tomb of this saint with her mother Euthicia, who for four years had suffered from an incurable flow of blood. The two women arrived at the church during the mass, at the moment when the passage of the Gospel was being read that tells of the Lord's cure of a woman similarly afflicted. Then Lucy said to her mother: "If you believe what you have just heard, you should also believe that Agatha is always in the presence of him for whose name she suffered martyrdom; and if in this faith you touch the saint's tomb, you will instantly recover your health."

So, when all the people had left the church, the mother and her daughter stayed to pray at the tomb. Lucy then fell asleep, and had a vision of Agatha standing surrounded by angels and adorned with precious stones, and Agatha said to her: "My sister Lucy, virgin consecrated to God, why do you ask me for something that you yourself can do for your mother? Indeed, your faith has already cured her." Lucy, awakening, said to her mother: "Mother, you are healed! But in the name of her to whose prayers you owe your cure, I beg of you to release me from my espousals, and to give to the poor whatever you have been saving for my dowry." "Why not wait until you have closed my eyes," the mother answered, "and then do whatever you wish with our wealth?" But Lucy replied: "What you give away at death you cannot take with you. Give while you live and you will be rewarded."

When they returned home, they began day after day to give away their possessions to satisfy the needs of the poor. Lucy's betrothed, hearing about this, asked the girl's nurse what was going on. She put him off by answering that Lucy had found a better property which she wished to buy in his name, and for that reason was selling some of her possessions. Being a stupid fellow he saw a future gain for himself and began to help out in the selling. But when everything had been sold and the proceeds given to the poor, he turned Lucy over to the consul Paschasius, accusing her of being a Christian and acting contrary to the laws of the emperors.

Paschasius summoned her and commanded her to offer sacrifice to the idols. Lucy's answer was: "The sacrifice that is pleasing to God is to visit the poor and help them in their need. And since I have nothing left to offer, I offer myself to the Lord." Paschasius retorted: "Tell that story to fools like yourself, but I abide by the decrees of my masters, so don't tell it to me." Lucy: "You obey your masters' laws, and I shall obey the laws of my God. You fear your masters and I fear God. You are careful not to offend them, I take pains not to offend God. You want to please them, I wish to please Christ. Do then what you think will be of benefit to you, and I shall do what I think is good for me." Paschasius: "You have squandered your patrimony with seducers, and so you talk like a whore"; but Lucy replied, "As for my patrimony, I have put it in a safe place, and never have had anything to do with any seducers of the body or of the mind." Paschasius: "Who are these seducers of the body and the mind?" Lucy: "You and those like you are seducers of the mind, because you induce souls to turn away from their Creator. As for the seducers of the body, they are those who would have us put the pleasures of the flesh ahead of eternal joys."

This moved Paschasius to say: "The sting of the whip will silence your lip!" Lucy: "The words of God cannot be stilled!" Paschasius: "So you are God?" Lucy: "I am the handmaid of God, who said to his disciples, 'You shall be brought before governors and before kings for my sake, but when they shall deliver you up, take no thought how or what to say, for it is not you that speak but the Holy Spirit that speaks in you.'" Paschasius: "So the Holy Spirit is in you?" Lucy: "Those who live chaste lives are the temples of the Holy Spirit." "Then I shall have you taken to a brothel," said Paschasius, "your body will be defiled and you will lose the Holy Spirit." "The body is not defiled," Lucy responded, "unless the mind consents. If you have me ravished against my will, my chastity will be doubled and the crown will be mine. You will never be able to force my will. As for my body, here it is, ready for every torture. What are you waiting for? Son of the devil, begin! Carry out your cruel designs!"

Then Paschasius summoned procurers and said to them: "Invite a crowd to take their pleasure with this woman, and let them abuse her until she is dead." But when they tried to carry her off, the Holy Spirit fixed her in place so firmly that they could not move her. Paschasius called in a thousand men and had her hands and feet bound, but still they could not lift her. He sent for a thousand yoke of oxen: the Lord's holy virgin could not be moved. Magicians were brought in to try to move her by their incantations: they did no better. "What is this witchery," Paschasius exclaimed, "that makes a thousand men unable to budge a lone maiden!" "There is no witchery here," said Lucy, "but the power of Christ; and even if you add ten thousand more, you will find me still unmovable." Paschasius had heard somewhere that urine would chase away magic, so he had the maiden drenched with urine: no effect. Next the consul, at the end of his wits, had a roaring fire built around her and boiling oil poured over her. And Lucy said: "I have prayed for this prolongation of my martyrdom in order to free believers from the fear of suffering, and to give unbelievers time to insult me!"

At this point the consul's friends, seeing how distressed he was, plunged a dagger into the martyr's throat; but, far from losing the power of speech, she said: "I make known to you that peace has been restored to the Church! This very day Maximian has died, and Diocletian has been driven from the throne. And just as God has given my sister Agatha to the city of Catania as protectress, so I am given to the city of Syracusa as mediatrix."

While the virgin was still speaking, envoys from Rome arrived to seize Paschasius and take him in chains to Rome, because Caesar had heard that he had pillaged the whole province. Arriving in Rome he was tried by the Senate and punished by decapitation. As for the virgin Lucy, she did not stir from the spot where she had suffered, nor did she breathe her last before priests had brought her the Body of the Lord and all those present had responded Amen to the Lord. There also she was buried and a church was raised in her honor. Her martyrdom took place about the year of the Lord 310.

5. Saint Thomas, Apostle

The name Thomas means abyss; or it means twofold, the Greek word for which is *didimus*; or it comes from *thomos*, which means a dividing or separating. Thomas is called abyss because he was granted insight into the depths of God's being when Christ, in answer to his question, said: "I am the way and the truth and the life." He is called twofold because he came to know the Lord's resurrection in two ways—not only by sight, like the others, but by seeing and touching. He is called dividing or separating because he separated his heart from the love of the world; or because he set himself apart from the other disciples by not at first believing that Christ had risen. Or again, Thomas comes from *totus means*, a total wanderer, one who is wholly outside himself in the love and contemplation of God; for there were three wondrous things about him that showed his love of God. Prosper speaks of this in the book *On the Contemplative Life:* "What is loving God other than to have in one's heart a fervent desire to see God, to hate sin, and to despise the world?" Or Thomas comes from *theos*, God, and *meus*, my, and therefore means "my God," because he said "My Lord and my God" when he was sure that Christ had risen.

Thomas the apostle was at Caesarea when the Lord appeared to him, saying: "Gundofor, king of India, has sent his provost Abbanes to find a man skilled in architecture. Come along and I will send you with him." Thomas answered: "Lord, send me anywhere you wish except India." God replied: "Go in safety, because I will be your guardian; and when you have converted the Indians, you shall come to me with the palm of martyrdom." Thomas: "You are my Lord and I am your servant: your will be done."

The provost was walking in the marketplace, and the Lord asked him: "Young man, what are you looking for?" The man's answer was: "My master sent me to bring home men learned in the architectural arts, to build a palace in the Roman style." Then the Lord introduced Thomas to him, stating that he was expert in that art.

The two took ship and put in at a city where the king was celebrating his daughter's nuptials and had issued an order bidding everyone to attend; otherwise his majesty would be offended. So Abbanes and the apostle went to the wedding feast. A Hebrew girl with a flute in her hand was going around saying complimentary things to each of the guests. She saw the apostle and recognized him as a Hebrew because he ate nothing and kept his eyes directed heavenwards, so she sang to him in the Hebrew tongue: "One is the God of the Hebrews, who created all things and established the seas in their place." The apostle troubled her to repeat those very same words. The wine steward meanwhile, noticing that the apostle was not eating or drinking but sat with his eyes turned toward heaven, struck him a blow on the cheek. The apostle addressed him: "It is better for you to receive here and now a punishment of brief duration, and to be granted forgiveness in the life to come. Know that I shall not leave this table before the hand that struck me is brought here by dogs." The servant went out to draw water, a lion killed him and drank his blood, dogs tore his body to pieces, and a black one carried his right hand into the midst of the feast. This greatly disturbed the whole company. The girl told them what the apostle had said, and then, throwing aside her flute, prostrated herself at Thomas's feet.

Augustine, in his book *Against Faustus*, will have none of this act of vengeance and declares that the incident is apocryphal, for which reason it is regarded as suspect on more than one point. It may, however, be surmised that what the apostle said to the steward was not intended as seeking revenge but as teaching a lesson: if Augustine's words are weighed carefully, they do not seem to express outright disapproval. In the book quoted he says: "The Manicheans read apocryphal books that were written under apostles' names by unknown fablemongers. At the time these books were written, they might well have been received by holy Church as authoritative, if saintly and learned men then living were able to examine them and found elements of truth in them. In any case those people read there that when the apostle Thomas was present, as a pilgrim and totally unknown, at a nuptial banquet, a servant slapped him with his open hand, and the apostle invoked upon him a cruel and immediate punishment; for when the man went to fetch water for the guests, a lion attacked and killed him and a dog carried to the apostle's table the hand that had dealt him a light blow on the head. What could be more cruel than this? Yet this may not be true, because, if I am not mistaken, the book also says that the apostle prayed for the offender to receive pardon in the world to come. So the compensation of a greater benefice was effected, so that by the fear aroused it was made known to those who had not known him how dear to God the apostle was, and the other man was assured of eternal happiness after this life, which had to end sooner or later.

"Whether this story is true or false is of no interest to me now. Certainly the Manicheans, who accept these writings as serious and true although the Church canon rejects them, are at least compelled to admit that the virtue of patience, which the Lord taught when he said: 'If someone strikes you on the right cheek, turn the other to him also,' can exist in the heart though not expressed outwardly by word or gesture. So the apostle, who had received the blow, rather than offering the other cheek to the servingman or urging him to strike again, would have prayed the Lord to spare the wrongdoer in the afterlife but not to let the wrong go unpunished here below. Certainly his inward disposition was one of love while he sought the outward correction as an example. Moreover, whether this story be fact or fiction, why are the Manicheans unwilling to believe that this was the thought and intention in which God's servant Moses struck down makers of idols with the sword? And if we compare punishments, what difference does it make whether the penalty be to die by the sword or to be torn to pieces by wild beasts? After all, judges, enforcing the public laws, condemn those who commit major crimes either to the beasts or to the headsman." Thus far Augustine.

Back, then, to Thomas . . . At the king's request the apostle blessed the bridegroom and the bride, saying: "Lord, give these young people the blessing of your right hand and sow in their hearts the seed of life." Then he left them, and the bridegroom found in his hand a palm branch laden with dates. After eating the fruit the couple fell asleep and both dreamed the same dream. They saw a king adorned with precious gems, who embraced them and said: "The apostle has blessed you in order that you may share eternal life." They awoke and told each other their dream, and the apostle came in to them and told them: "My King has just appeared to you, and he brings me here though the doors are closed, that through my blessing upon you you may preserve the purity of your bodies—that purity which is the queen of virtues and the fruit of eternal salvation. Virginity is the sister of the angels, the possession of all goods, victory over the passions, the prize and reward of faith, the overthrow of the demons, and the assurance of eternal joys. Lust begets corruption, of corruption pollution is born, guilt rises from pollution, confusion follows upon guilt." When he had said these things, two angels appeared to them and said: "We are the angels sent to be your guardians, and, if you are faithful to the apostle's counsel, we offer all your prayers to God." Thereupon the apostle baptized them and diligently instructed them in the truths of faith. After a long time the bride, whose name was Pelagia and who had taken the holy veil of consecration, suffered martyrdom. Her husband, called Dionysius, was ordained bishop of that city.

The apostle and Abbanes pursued their journey and came to the court of the king of India. Thomas drew up the plans for a magnificent palace, and the king gave him a large store of treasure so that he might get on with the building of the palace. Then the king set out for another province; and the apostle distributed to the people all the money he had received from the king.

During the two years of the king's absence the apostle was zealous in preaching and converted great multitudes to the faith. But when the king returned and learned what Thomas had done, he threw him into a dungeon, and Abbanes with him, intending to have them flayed and burned alive. Thereupon the king's brother, whose name was Gad, died, and preparations were under way to give him a splendid funeral. But on the fourth day after his death he returned to life, and all who saw him were terrified and fled. Gad said to the king: "Brother, the man whom you wish to have flayed and burned alive is a friend of God, and all the angels are his servants. These angels brought me to paradise and showed me a marvelous palace built of gold and silver and precious stones; and while I was admiring its beauty, they told me: 'This is the palace that Thomas built for your brother.' I said to them: 'I would like to be the doorkeeper here!' They answered: 'Your brother has shown himself unworthy of it. If you yourself wish to have it for your dwelling, we will pray the Lord to raise you to life, and you can buy the palace from your brother and pay him all the treasure he thinks he has lost.'" Gad then ran to the prison, begged the apostle to forgive his brother, struck off his chains, and pressed him to accept a precious mantle. Thomas's answer was: "Do you not know that those who yearn for power in heavenly things have no desire for earthly possessions?"

The apostle now emerged from his prison. The king came to meet him, threw himself at his feet, and pleaded for pardon. "God has granted both of you much," Thomas said, "in order that he might show you his secrets. Believe in

Christ and be baptized, so that you may share in the everlasting kingdom." The king's brother said: "I have seen the palace you built for my brother and have bought it for myself!" The apostle responded: "That depends on your brother's decision." The king broke in: "The palace will be mine! Let the apostle build you another; or if that is not possible, we shall live there together!" Thomas told them: "In heaven there are countless palaces, prepared from the beginning of time, and they are won by prayer and the giving of alms. As for your riches, they can precede you there but they cannot follow you."

A month later, the apostle called together all the poor people of the region, and when they were all assembled, he summoned the sick, the lame, and the feeble to come forth from the crowd. Then he prayed over them, and those among them who had received the faith responded Amen. Then a great light came from heaven and flashed over the apostle and all the rest for half an hour, and they fell to the ground as if struck dead by lightning. The apostle rose and said: "Stand up! My Lord has come like lightning and has cured them all!" So everybody stood up whole and healthy, and glorified God and his apostle.

Then Thomas began to teach the people and explained to them the twelve degrees of virtue. The first degree is to believe in a God one in essence and trine in persons. The apostle showed them by means of tangible examples how three persons can be in one essence, and said: "Man's wisdom is one, yet it is composed of understanding, memory, and reason. Reason is the power by which you discover what you have not yet learned; memory enables you to retain what you have learned; understanding allows you to comprehend what is shown or taught to you. The vine, too, is made up of three elements, wood, leaves, and fruit, and yet they form one vine. One head comprises four senses—sight, taste, hearing, and smell—they being several and the head being one." The second degree of virtue consists in receiving baptism; the third in abstaining from fornication; the fourth in controlling greed; the fifth in shunning gluttony; the sixth in doing penance; the seventh in perseverance in good works; the eighth in generous care of strangers; the ninth in seeking the will of God and doing it willingly; the tenth in seeking out what God does not want us to do and not doing it; the eleventh in love of friends and enemies; the twelfth in watchful care to observe all of this. And when the apostle had finished his preaching, he baptized nine thousand men, not to mention the women and children.

Next Thomas went to Upper India and gained fame by his many miracles. He brought the light of faith to Syntice, who was a friend of Migdomia the wife of Carisius, a cousin of the king. Migdomia asked Syntice: "Do you think I might see the apostle?" Then, taking her friend's advice, she put off her rich garments and mingled with the poor women who were hearing the apostle's preaching. Thomas began to expound upon the misery of this life and said, among other things: "This is indeed a miserable life, subject to all sorts of misfortune, and so fleeting that when one thinks one has it well in hand, it slips away and is gone." Then he exhorted his hearers to receive the word of God gladly and offered four reasons, comparing the word to four kinds of things: to an eye-salve, because it enlightens the eyes of our intellect; to a potion, for it purifies and cleanses our will of all carnal love; to a plaster, because it heals the wounds of our sins; and to food, because it delights us with the love of the things of heaven. And just as these things can do no good to the ailing person unless he uses them well, so the word of God cannot benefit the ailing soul unless it is heard devoutly. Migdomia believed the apostle's preaching and thereafter shunned her husband's bed with horror. At this Carisius complained to the king and had Thomas thrown into prison. Migdomia visited him there and implored him to pardon her for being the cause of his plight; but he consoled her kindly and said that he was happy to bear all his suffering. Then Carisius asked the king to send the queen, his wife's sister, to his wife, hoping that she might bring Migdomia back to him. But the queen, carrying out her mission, was converted by the very one she sought to lead astray; and seeing the great miracles the apostle performed, she said: "Those who refuse to believe so many signs and works are damned by God!" Meanwhile Thomas spoke briefly to all present on three points: they should love the Church, honor the priests, and come together gladly to hear the word of God.

When the queen returned home, the king asked her: "What kept you away so long?" The queen's answer was: "I thought Migdomia was stupid, but on the contrary she is very wise. She led me to the apostle of God and let me learn the way of truth. The really stupid ones are those who will not believe in Christ!" And from then on she refused to lie with her husband. The king, dumbfounded, said to his brother-in-law: "I tried to get your wife back for you, and instead I have lost my own; she treats me worse than yours treats you!"

The king then ordered the apostle to be brought before him, hands bound, and commanded him to counsel the wives to return to their husbands. The apostle proceeded to prove to the king, by three examples—a king, a tower, a spring of water—that as long as the men persisted in their error, the women must not do as commanded. "You," he said, "being a king, want no dirty servants around you, but only clean servingmen and handmaids. How much more surely should you believe that God loves chaste, clean servants? Am I wrong in preaching that God loves in his servants what you love in yours? I have raised a high tower, and you tell me, the builder, to tear it down? I have dug a deep well and brought up a flowing spring, and you tell me to shut it off?"

This was too much for the king. He sent for iron plates fired to red heat and ordered the apostle to stand barefoot on them. Instantly, at a sign from God, a spring rose from the ground and cooled the iron. Then the king, following his brother-in-law's advice, had him thrown into a fiery furnace, but it was extinguished immediately, and the apostle emerged unharmed the next morning. Carisius said to the king: "Command him to sacrifice to the god of the sun. That will bring down on him the wrath of his god, who so far has been protecting him." So they tried to force Thomas to do this, but he said to the king: "You are greater than the things you make, yet you spurn the worship of the true God and worship a handmade idol instead. You think, as Carisius does, that my God will be angered with me after I worship your god; but it is against your god that he will be angered, and he will destroy him the moment I adore him. If my God does not destroy yours when I offer him worship, I will offer sacrifice: if the contrary, promise me that you will believe my God." To this the king retorted: "How dare you speak to me as equal to equal!"

Now the apostle, speaking in Hebrew, commanded the demon who was in the idol to demolish it as soon as he bent the knee before it. Then, falling to his knees, he said: "See, I adore, but not this idol; I worship, but not this metal; I adore, but not this graven image. I adore my Lord Jesus Christ, in whose name I command you, O demon lurking inside, to destroy the idol!" And at once the image melted as if it were made of wax. At this all the priests bellowed like cattle, and the high priest of the temple, raising his sword, drove it through the apostle, crying: "Thus shall I avenge the insult done to my god!" The king and Carisius fled, seeing that the people wished to avenge the apostle and burn the high priest alive. The Christians meanwhile carried away the saint's body and gave it honorable burial.

Long afterwards, around the year of our Lord 230, Emperor Alexander, at the request of the Syrians, transferred the apostle's body to the city of Edessa, which formerly was called Rages of the Medes. In that city no heretic, no Jew, no pagan can live, no tyrant can do harm, since Abgar, king of the city, had been found worthy of receiving a letter written by the hand of the Lord. If any people stirs up an insurrection against the city, a baptized child, standing above the city gate, reads the letter; and that very day, thanks to the Savior's writing and the merits of Thomas the apostle, the enemy either goes away or makes peace.

In his book *On the Life and Death of the Saints* Isidore says of Saint Thomas: "Thomas, a disciple of Christ who bore a resemblance to the Savior, not believing what he heard, believed when he saw the Lord. He preached the Gospel to the Parthians, the Medes, the Persians, the Hircanians, and the Bactrians. Setting foot on the shores of the Orient and penetrating into the interior, he preached to the peoples there until the day of his martyrdom. He died from the thrust of a lance." So Isidore. Chrysostom also says that Thomas made his way to the land of the Magi who had come to adore the Christ, and that he baptized them and they helped to propagate the Christian faith.

*About the feasts that occur within
the time that falls partly in the time of reconciliation and
partly in the time of pilgrimage*

We have spoken about the feasts that occur in the time of renewal, which began with Moses and the prophets and lasted until the advent of Christ in the flesh, and which the Church represents from the beginning of Advent to the Birth of Christ. We now take up the feast days that occur within the period that falls partly in the time of reconciliation and partly in the time of pilgrimage. This period the Church represents from the Birth of Christ to Septuagesima, as was noted in the Prologue.

6. The Birth of Our Lord Jesus Christ According to the Flesh

The birth of our Lord Jesus Christ in the flesh took place, according to some sources, 5,228 years after Adam, while others say 6,000 years, or, according to Eusebius of Caesarea in his chronicle, 5,199. Methodius seems to have arrived at the figure 6,000 by mystical rather than chronological calculation.

In any case Octavian was the Roman emperor at the time. His first given name was Octavian: he was called Caesar after Julius Caesar whose nephew he was, Augustus because he augmented the state, Emperor to pay honor to his dignity by distinguishing him from the earlier kings, he being the first to bear this title. When the Son of God became incarnate, the universe enjoyed such peace that the emperor of the Romans reigned alone and peacefully over the whole world. It was the Lord's will that since he was coming to give us peace in time and in eternity, temporal peace should lend luster to the time of his birth.

In those days Caesar Augustus, being master of the world, wished to know how many provinces, cities, fortresses, villages, and men there were in the world. He therefore decreed, as we read in the *Scholastic History*, that all the men in his empire should go to the city from which they drew their origin, and pay to the governor of the province a silver denarius as a profession of their submission to the Roman Empire, since the coin bore Caesar's name and image. This payment was called both profession and enrollment, but for different reasons. The word *profession* was used because each man, when he remitted the head tax (the aforementioned denarius) to the provincial governor, placed it on his own head and declared aloud and in public that he was a subject of the empire. *Enrollment* meant that those who paid the head tax were given a number which was recorded in the rolls.

This first enrollment was carried out by Cyrinus the governor of Syria. It was designated "first" (as we are told in the *Scholastic History* regarding Cyrinus) because Judea is said to be the umbilicus of our habitable earth, and therefore the census was initiated there and later carried on throughout the surrounding regions and by other governors. Or "first" here stands for "universal," the others being local; or perhaps the first enrollment was the head count made in the city by the governor, the second counted the cities in a region and was made by Caesar's legate, and the third accounted for the regions and was made in the presence of Caesar.

Joseph, being of the house and family of David, went up from Nazareth to Bethlehem to be enrolled. The time was approaching for Mary to be delivered, and Joseph took her with him. Not knowing how long he would be away, and unwilling to leave this treasure that God had entrusted to him in the care of strangers, he preferred to guard her with his own vigilant attention. As they drew near to Bethlehem (as Brother Bartholomew, drawing upon the *Book of the Infancy of the Savior*, testifies in his compilation), the Virgin saw part of the populace rejoicing and part lamenting. An angel explained this to her, saying: "Those who rejoice are the people of the Gentiles, who in the seed of Abraham will receive eternal blessing. Those who grieve are the Jewish people, rejected by God in accordance with their deserts."

So Joseph and Mary came to Bethlehem. They were poor and could find no lodging in the inns, which already were full of people who had come for the same purpose; so they had to take shelter in a public passage. This passage, according to the *Scholastic History*, was located between two houses. It provided some overhead covering and served as a meeting place for townspeople who came there to talk or eat together in their free time, or when the weather was bad. Perhaps Joseph set up a manger for his ox and his ass, or, as some think, peasants coming in to market were used to tying up their animals there and the crib was ready to hand. In that place, at midnight, the eve of Sunday, the blessed Virgin gave birth to her Son and laid him on hay in the manger. This hay, which the ox and the ass abstained from eating, was brought to Rome by Saint Helena, as we learn from the *Scholastic History*.

The birth of Christ was miraculous as regards the mother, the child born of her, and the mode of the birth.

As regards the mother, she was a virgin both before and after giving birth, and the fact that she remained a virgin is assured by five proofs. The first is from the prophet Isaiah, who in his seventh chapter says: "Behold, a virgin shall conceive and bear a son, and his name shall be called Emmanuel." The second is by way of figure: it was prefigured both by Aaron's rod, which blossomed without any human care, and by Ezechiel's gate, which always remained closed. The third is Joseph's guardianship: he watched over her and so was a witness to her virginity. There is a fourth proof, for Bartholomew (apparently borrowing from the *Book of the Infancy of the Savior*) has it that when the hour had come for Mary to be delivered, Joseph called two midwives, the one being called Zebel and the other Salome—not that he doubted that the Virgin would bring forth the Son of God, but that he was following the custom of the country. When Zebel, probing and realizing that Mary was a virgin, cried out that a virgin had given birth, Salome did not believe it and tried to find out for herself, but her hand instantly withered; then an angel appeared and told her to touch the child, and she was cured immediately. The fifth proof is a miraculous event. As Pope Innocent III testifies, during the twelve years when Rome enjoyed peace, the Romans built a Temple of Peace and placed a statue of Romulus in it. Apollo was asked how long the temple would stand, and the answer was that it would be until a virgin bore a child. Hearing this, the people said that the temple was eternal, for they thought it impossible that such a thing could happen; and an inscription, TEMPLUM PACIS AETERNUM, was carved over the doors. But in the very night when Mary bore Christ, the temple crumbled to the ground, and on its site the church of Santa Maria Nuova stands today.

The birth of the Lord was no less miraculous as regards the Child himself. As Bernard says, in one and the same person the eternal, the ancient, and the new wondrously came together: the eternal, namely, the Godhead, the ancient, namely, the flesh descended from Adam, and the new, since a new soul was created. Moreover, as the same author says, God wrought three mixtures or three works, so marvelously singular that such things had not been done before nor would be done ever again. For God and man, a mother and a virgin, faith and the human heart, were conjoined. The first is indeed a marvel, because God and the slime of the earth, majesty and infirmity, such great degrees of baseness and sublimity were joined; for nothing is more sublime than God and nothing more base than mud. The second conjunction is just as miraculous. From the beginning of the world it was unheard-of that there was a virgin who became a mother or a mother who remained a virgin. The third wonder is inferior to the other two but great nonetheless: the marvel is that the human heart could believe that God became man and the virgin who bore him was still a virgin. So far Bernard.

The mode of the birth also was miraculous. It was above nature, by the fact that a virgin conceived; above reason in that God was begotten; above the human condition, in that the birth was painless; and above what is customary, since the conception was by the Holy Spirit, for the Virgin begot her Son not from human seed but from a mystic breath. Indeed the Holy Spirit took the most pure and most chaste blood of the Virgin and out of it formed that body. So it is that God showed a fourth wondrous way of making man. Anselm says: "God can make man in four ways, namely, without a man or a woman (as he made Adam), from a man without a woman (as he made Eve), from a man and a woman (the usual way), and from a woman without a man (as was done miraculously today)."

The birth of the Lord was made known in a multiplicity of ways. To begin with, it was made manifest through every level or class of creatures. There are the creatures which have existence only, such as things that are simply material or corporeal, like stones; others have existence and life, like plants and trees; others have existence, life, and sensation, namely, the animals; still others, in addition to the above endowments, have reason, as human beings do; and finally some creatures have understanding, or knowledge, and these are the angels.

Through all these creatures the birth of Christ is today made known. Of those that are purely corporeal there are three kinds, the opaque, the transparent or pervious, and the lucid, or luminous. Opaque creatures manifested the Nativity, for example by the destruction of the temple in Rome, as above described, and also by the collapse of other statues that fell in a great many other places. For instance, we read in the *Scholastic History* that the prophet Jeremiah, going down to Egypt after the death of Godolias, indicated to the Egyptian kings that their idols would fall to pieces when a virgin bore a son. For that reason the priests of the idols made a statue of a virgin holding a male child in her lap, set it up in a secret place in the temple, and there worshiped it. When King Ptolemy asked them the meaning of this, they told him that it was a mystery handed down by the fathers, who had received it from a holy man, a prophet, and they believed that what was foretold would really happen.

Now regarding transparent or pervious corporeal beings: in the night of the Lord's birth the darkness of night was turned into the brightness of day. In Rome it also happened (as attested by Orosius and Pope Innocent III) that a fountain of water turned to oil and burst into the Tiber, spreading very widely all that day; and the Sibyl had foretold that when a fountain of oil sprang up, a Savior would be born.

Then there are the luminous corporeal creatures, such as the supercelestial: these too revealed the Nativity. For on that very day, according to what the ancients relate and Chrysostom affirms, the Magi were praying on a mountain-top and a star appeared above them. This star had the shape of a most beautiful boy over whose head a cross shone brilliantly. He spoke to the Magi and told them to make their way to Judea, where they would find a newborn child. That same day three suns appeared in the East and gradually melded into one solar body. This signified that knowledge of the one and triune God was about to be given to the world, or that he in whom soul, flesh, and divinity were united had now been born. In the *Scholastic History*, however, it is said that the three suns appeared not on the day of the Nativity but some time earlier: Eusebius in his chronicle puts it after the death of Julius Caesar. The emperor Octavian (as Pope Innocent says) had brought the whole world under Roman rule, and the Senate was so well pleased that they wished to worship him as a god. The prudent emperor, however, knowing full well that he was mortal, refused to usurp the title of immortality. The senators insisted that he summon the sibylline prophet-ess and find out, through her oracles, whether someone greater than he was to be born in the world. When, therefore, on the day of Christ's birth, the council was convoked to study this matter and the Sibyl, alone in a room with the emperor, consulted her oracles, at midday a golden circle appeared around the sun, and in the middle of the circle a most beautiful virgin holding a child in her lap. The Sibyl showed this to Caesar, and while the emperor marveled at the vision, he heard a voice saying to him: "This is the altar of Heaven." The Sibyl then told him: "This child is greater than you, and it is he that you must wor-ship." That same room was dedicated to the honor of Holy Mary and to this day is called Santa Maria Ara Coeli.

The emperor, understanding that the child he had seen was greater than he, offered incense to him and refused to be called God. With reference to this Orosius says: "In Octavian's day, about the third hour, in the limpid, pure, serene sky, a circle that looked like a rainbow surrounded the orb of the sun, as if to show that One was to come who alone had made the sun and the whole world and ruled it." So far Orosius. Eutropius gives a similar account of the event. And Timotheus the historian reports that he had learned from ancient Roman histories that in the thirty-fifth year of his reign Octavian went up the Capitoline hill and anxiously asked the gods who would succeed him as ruler of the empire. He then heard a voice telling him that an ethereal child, begotten in eternity of the living God, was presently to be born of a virgin undefiled, the God-man without stain. Having heard this, he erected an altar on which he inscribed the title: THIS IS THE ALTAR OF THE SON OF THE LIVING GOD.

Christ's birth was manifested also by creatures having existence and life, like plants and trees. Thus, on the night of the Christ's birth, the vineyards of Engedi, which produce balsam, bloomed and bore fruit from which balsam flowed.

Living and sentient creatures gave their own testimony. Setting out for Bethlehem with Mary, who was with child, Joseph took along an ox (perhaps to sell it for money to pay the head tax and buy food and the like) and an ass, no doubt for Mary to ride on. The ox and the ass, miraculously recognizing the Lord, went to their knees and worshiped him.

Humankind, the creatures possessed of reason and discernment, were represented by the shepherds. At the hour of the Nativity they were watching over their flock, as was customary twice a year on the longest and shortest nights. It was the custom among the Gentiles to observe these nocturnal vigils at each solstice, namely, the summer one around the feast of John the Baptist and the winter one close to Christmas, by way of veneration of the sun; and the Jews may have borrowed the practice from the neighboring peoples. So the angel of the Lord appeared to the shepherds, announced the birth of the Savior, and told them how they could find him, whereupon a host of angels sang: "Glory to God in the highest and peace to men of good will." The shepherds went and found everything just as the angel had told them.

We have noted that this manifestation came also through Caesar Augustus, who then decreed that no one should dare to call him God, as Orosius testified. In some chronicle we also read that as the day of the Lord's birth drew near, Octavian built public roads throughout his empire and remitted all the Romans' debts. And even the sodomites gave witness by being exterminated wherever they were in the world on that night, as Jerome says: "A light rose over them so bright that all who practiced this vice were wiped out; and Christ did this in order that no such uncleanness might be found in the nature he had assumed." For, as Augustine says, God, seeing that a vice contrary to nature was rife in human nature, hesitated to become incarnate.

Lastly, the creatures possessing existence, life, discernment, and understanding showed forth the birth of the Lord, when the angels announced it to the shepherds, as noted above.

We may also consider that the manifestation of Christ's birth was useful to us in several ways. Firstly, it served to confound the demons, for they could no longer overpower us as they had before. We read that Saint Hugh, abbot of Cluny, on the night of the Nativity had a vision of the Blessed Virgin holding her Son in her arms and saying: "The day is come when the oracles of the prophets are fulfilled. Where now is the Enemy who until now prevailed over men?" At the sound of her voice the devil came up through the floor to taunt the Virgin; but iniquity gave the lie to itself, because while he prowled around the monks' quarters, their devoutness drove him from the oratory, their pious readings from the refectory, their scant bedding from the dormitory, their patience from the chapter house. Furthermore we read in a book by Peter of Cluny that the night before the birth of the Lord the Blessed Virgin appeared to Saint Hugh, abbot of Cluny, holding her Son in her lap and playing with him, and the Child said: "You know, Mother, that the Church celebrates my birthday with great praise, feasting, and dancing. And where now is the power of the devil? What can he do now? What can he say?" Then the devil was seen to rise out of the ground, as it were, and say: "Even if I cannot enter the church where your praises are chanted, I shall get into the chapter house, the dormitory, the refectory!" But when he tried to do this, he found the chapter house door too narrow for his gross girth, the door of the dormitory too low for his height, and the door of the refectory fastened with bars and bolts, these being the charity of those who served there, their eagerness to hear the readings, and the sparseness of the food and drink consumed there. So, confounded, he vanished.

Secondly, Christ's birth is useful to us in obtaining pardon for sin. We read in a certain book of examples that a fallen woman, finally repenting of her sins, despaired of pardon. Thinking of the Last Judgment she considered herself worthy of hell; turning her mind to heaven she thought of herself as unclean; dwelling on the Lord's passion, she knew she had been ungrateful. But then she thought to herself that children are more ready to be kind, so she appealed to Christ in the name of his childhood, and a voice told her that she had won forgiveness.

Thirdly, the Nativity benefits us by curing our infirmities. Bernard says about this benefit: "The human race labored under a threefold malady, beginning, middle, and end. Man's birth was unclean, his life perverse, his death perilous. Christ came and brought a threefold remedy: his birth cleansed ours, his life put order in ours, his death destroyed ours." Thus far Bernard.

Lastly, the Lord's birth serves us by humbling our pride. So Augustine says that the humility of the Son of God, which he demonstrated in his incarnation, was for us "an example, a sacrament, and a medicine. A most fitting example it was for man's imitation, a high sacrament by which we were delivered from the bonds of sin, and a most powerful medicine, which heals the tumor of our pride." So far Augustine. For the pride of the first man was cured by the humility of Christ. Note how exactly the Savior's humility corresponds to the pride of the betrayer. The first man's pride was against God; it went as high as God and even above God. It was against God because it was contrary to the commandment by which he forbade eating from the tree of the knowledge of good and evil. It reached God's height because Adam aspired to divinity, believing what the devil had said: "You will be like gods." It was above God, as Anselm says, because it willed what God willed that man should not will. Thus Adam placed his own will above the will of God. But God's Son, according to John of Damascus, humbled himself for the sake of mankind, not against us: his humility reached man's level and above man. It was for men's sake because it was for their welfare and salvation; it reached men's level because the mode of birth was similar, and it was above them by the dissimilarity of the birth. In one way Christ's birth was like our own, namely, that he was born of a woman and came forth through the same portal, but in another way it was unlike ours, because he was conceived by the Holy Spirit and born of the Virgin Mary.

※

7. Saint Anastasia

The name Anastasia is derived from *ana*, meaning above, and *stasis*, meaning standing or stand; for the saint stood on high, raised above vice and sin to virtue.

Anastasia was born into a noble Roman family; her father, Praetaxtatus, was a pagan, but her mother Faustina was Christian. Anastasia was raised in the Christian faith by her mother and Saint Chrysogonus. Given in marriage against her will to a young man named Publius, she feigned an enfeebling sickness and kept herself apart from him. Then he found out that she was visiting the Christians in prison and ministering to their needs, dressed as a poor woman and accompanied by one of her handmaids. He therefore kept her in strict confinement, even denying her food, hoping to cause her death and to live in luxury on her great wealth. Anastasia, expecting to die, wrote piteous letters to Chrysogonus, who replied with consolatory messages. However, it was her husband who died, and she was set free.

She had three very beautiful servingmaids who were sisters, of whom one was named Agapete, the second Theonia, the third Irene. All three were Christians. A certain prefect was smitten with desire for them and, when they refused his advances, had them shut up in a room where the cooking utensils were stored.

There he went, intent upon having his way with them; but he was deprived of his senses and, thinking that he was dealing with the three virgins, caressed and kissed the stoves, kettles, pots, and other utensils. Having satisfied himself in this manner he went out blackened with soot and his clothes in tatters. His slaves, who were waiting for him outside and saw him in this condition, thought they were seeing a demon, beat him with sticks, and ran away, leaving him alone. He set out to complain to the emperor, and on the way some struck him with rods; others threw mud and dust at him, thinking he had gone mad. His eyes, however, were blinded and he could not see how he looked to others, nor could he understand why they were mocking him instead of paying him the honor to which he was accustomed. He thought, of course, that he was dressed in white clothes as everybody else was. Finally he was told of his sorry state and thought that the maidens had worked some magic upon him. He therefore commanded that they be brought before him and stripped, so that he might at least enjoy the sight of their nudity, but it turned out that their clothing clung so tightly to their bodies that no one could take it off. The prefect was surprised at this and fell into a sleep so deep that he snored and could not be awakened even by blows. Finally the virgins were crowned with martyrdom.

As for Anastasia, the emperor handed her over to another prefect, with permission to marry her if he could make her sacrifice to the gods. The prefect led her to the bridal chamber and tried to embrace her: instantly he was stricken blind. He went to the idols and asked if he might be cured. Their answer was: "Because you saddened the holy Anastasia, you have been turned over to us to be tortured forever with us in hell." And as he was being led to his house, he died in the arms of his servants.

Anastasia was then entrusted to still another prefect, with orders to hold her in the tightest security. This man knew that she was very rich and said to her secretly: "Anastasia, if you want to be a Christian, do as your Lord commanded when he said that anyone who did not renounce all his possessions could not be his disciple. Give me therefore all that is yours, then go wherever you wish and be a true Christian!" But she replied: "God commanded that I give up all that I have and give to the poor, not to the rich. But you are rich! Therefore if I gave you anything, I would go against God's command."

Then Anastasia was thrown into a dreadful prison to be starved to death, but Saint Theodora, who already had gained the crown of martyrdom, fed her for two months with food from heaven. Finally she was taken, with two hundred virgins, to the island of Palmaria, to which many Christians had been banished. Some days later the prefect summoned all of them to his presence, and had Anastasia bound to a stake and burned alive; the rest he put to death in various ways. Among them there was a man who had been despoiled of his wealth several times, and who repeated over and over: "At least you cannot take Christ away from me!" Apollonia had the body of Saint Anastasia buried in her garden, and there built a church in her honor. She suffered martyrdom in the reign of Diocletian, which began about the year of the Lord 287.

8. Saint Stephen

The name Stephen—Stephanus in Latin—comes from the Greek word for crown—*stephanos*: in Hebrew the name means norm or rule. Stephen was the crown of the martyrs in the sense that he was the first martyr under the New Testament, as Abel was under the Old. He was a norm, i.e., an example or rule, showing others how to suffer for Christ, as well as how to act and live according to the truth, or how to pray for one's enemies. Or Stephen (Stephanus) comes from *strenue fans*, speaking strenuously or with zeal, as the saint showed in his manner of speaking and his brilliant preaching of the word of God. Or Stephen may be understood as *strenue stans* or *fans anus*, laudably standing and instructing and ruling over old women, here meaning widows, because the apostles put him in charge of the widows, who were literally old women. So Stephen is a crown because he is first in martyrdom, a norm by his example in suffering and his way of life, a zealous speaker in his praiseworthy teaching of the widows.

Stephen was one of the seven deacons whom the apostles ordained for ministry. As the number of the disciples increased, the Christians of Gentile origin began to murmur against those converted from Judaism, because the widows among the former were being neglected in the daily ministry. The cause of these complaints may have been either that the widows were not allowed to do any service, or that they were given too much work to do in the daily round. Whatever the trouble was, the apostles had assigned some services to the widows, so that they could devote themselves entirely to preaching. Now, confronted with these complaints, they called all the disciples together and said to them: "It is not right that we should give up preaching the word of God to serve tables . . . (The *Gloss* adds: 'Because the food of the mind is better than feasts for the body.') . . . Therefore, brethren, pick out from among you seven men of good repute, full of the spirit and of wisdom, whom we may appoint to this duty . . . (The *Gloss*: '. . . to serve or to supervise the servers.') . . . But we will devote ourselves to prayer and to the preaching of the word." This plan pleased the assemblage and they elected seven men, of whom Stephen stood out foremost and as leader, and brought them to the apostles, who imposed hands on them.

Now Stephen, full of grace and fortitude, did great wonders and signs among the people. Then the Jews, being jealous of him and wanting to discredit him and find him guilty, joined issue with him in three ways—by argument, by suborning false witnesses, and by putting him to the torture. But he won the arguments, convicted the false witnesses, and triumphed over his torturers, and in each encounter aid was given him from heaven. In the first, the Holy Spirit aided him with divine wisdom. In the second it was his face, like the face of an angel, that terrified the false witnesses. In the third Christ himself appeared, ready to give aid and to strengthen the martyr. In each of the three conflicts, therefore, three aspects are to be noted—the battle joined, the aid given, and the triumph achieved. A brief review of the incidents will show all this clearly.

Thus, when Stephen's miracles and preaching aroused the envy of the Jews, they launched the first battle, trying to defeat him by argument. Some of them who rose belonged to the synagogue of the Libertines, so called either after the region they came from or because they were sons of people called *Liberti*, i.e., freedmen, men manumitted from slavery and given their freedom. So they were of servile stock and at first resisted the faith. There were also Cyrenians from the city of Cyrene, Alexandrians, and men from Cilicia and Asia. All of them disputed with Stephen. There we have the first battle. Then comes the triumph: they could not stand up against his wisdom. Lastly, there is the aid—the Spirit, who spoke in him.

Stephen's opponents saw that they could not overcome him by that approach and craftily turned to the second one, namely, the testimony of false witnesses. Into the council they brought two false witnesses who accused the saint of four blasphemies, namely, against God, against Moses, against the Law, and against the Tabernacle or Temple. There is the battle. All of those sitting in the council gazed upon Stephen and saw that his face was like the face of an angel. There is the aid. Then came the victory, when the false witnesses were refuted point by point. The high priest asked Stephen if their testimony was true, and the blessed one proved that he was innocent of the four charges brought against him, taking them in order. Blasphemy against God? The God, he said, who spoke to the fathers and the prophets was the God of glory, and he praised God's glory according to the three ways the term could be explained. God is the God of glory in the sense that he bestows glory: "Whosoever shall glorify me, him will I glorify."[1] He is the God of glory in the sense that he contains glory in himself: "With me are riches and glory."[2] He is the God to whom all creation owes glory: "To the King of the ages, immortal, invisible, the only God, be honor and glory forever."[3] So God glorifies, is glorified, and is worthy of glorification.

Stephen then took up the second accusation, blasphemy against Moses, by commending Moses on many grounds, but principally on three—the fervor of his zeal when he struck and killed an Egyptian; his working of miracles, which he performed in Egypt and in the desert; and his familiar friendship with God, since he spoke familiarly with God more than once. As for the charge of blasphemy against the Law, he commended the Law on three grounds: by reason of the Giver, God himself, of the administrator, mighty Moses, and of the purpose, because the Law gives life. Coming to the accusation of blasphemy against the Temple, he refuted it by commending the Temple on four grounds: that it was

---

[1] 3 Kings 2:30.   [2] Prov. 8:18.   [3] 1 Tim. 1:17.

ordered by God, that the way it was to be built was shown in a vision, that it was completed by Moses, and that it contained the Ark of the Covenant. The Temple, he added, succeeded the Tabernacle. By his reasoning, therefore, blessed Stephen proved himself clean of the crimes of which he was accused.

The Jews realized that the second attack was as futile as the first, so they resorted to the third, the inflicting of torture and pain, thus embarking on the third battle. Blessed Stephen saw what they were about and, wishing to observe the Lord's command regarding fraternal correction, tried to correct them and recall them from such malice by three means: first, by shaming them; second, by arousing their fear; third, by demonstrating his love for them. To shame them he reproached them for their hardness of heart and for putting saints to death. "You, stiff-necked and uncircumcised in heart and ears, you have always resisted the Holy Spirit. Like father, like son! Which of the prophets did your fathers not persecute? They even killed those who foretold the coming of the just One." Thus, as the *Gloss* says, he posited three degrees of wickedness—resisting the Holy Spirit, persecuting the prophets, some of whom, with increasing malice, they put to death. Shame on them! The forehead of a strumpet was theirs; they knew not how to blush and so be deterred from pursuing their evil designs. But, far from feeling shame, his hearers were cut to the heart and gnashed their teeth at him.

Next, therefore, he tried to correct them by fear, saying that he saw Jesus standing at God's right hand as though ready to help him and condemn his adversaries. Indeed Stephen, full of the Holy Spirit and looking up steadfastly to heaven, saw the glory of God and said: "Behold, I see the heavens opened and Jesus standing on the right hand of God!" But for all his efforts to correct them through shame and fear, they not only did not desist but were worse than before, and, crying out with a loud voice, they stopped their ears (so as not to hear blasphemy, the *Gloss* explains) and with one accord ran violently upon him, cast him outside the city, and stoned him. In doing this they judged that they were acting according to the Law, which made it mandatory to stone a blasphemer outside the camp. And the two false witnesses, who by law were to cast the first stone, took off their garments (lest these be made unclean by contact with the blasphemer, or in order to be more at ease while throwing the stones) and laid them at the feet of a young man whose name was Saul and who later was called Paul. He, by standing guard over their garments and giving them more freedom to stone the victim, shared the guilt of all of them in the stoning.

Stephen had failed to win them over through shame or fear: now he had recourse to his third weapon, love. Could he have shown greater love than by praying for himself and for them? He prayed for himself, that his passion might not be prolonged and their guilt thereby augmented, and for them, that they be not held guilty of this sin. We read that as they were stoning him, he called upon God and said: "Lord Jesus, receive my spirit." And, falling to his knees, he cried out with a loud voice, saying: "Lord, lay not this sin to their charge, because they know not what they do!" See here his wondrous love! He stood while praying for himself, but praying for those who stoned him he knelt, as though he desired that the prayer he offered for them be heard even more than the prayer he poured out for himself. He knelt for them rather than for himself, because, as the *Gloss* says at this place, their greater iniquity demanded a greater supplication to remedy it. In this the martyr also imitated Christ, who in his passion prayed for himself, saying: "Into thy hands I commend my spirit"; and for his executioners, saying: "Father, forgive them, for they know not what they do." And when Stephen had made his prayer, he fell asleep in the Lord. The *Gloss* notes: "How beautifully it is said that he fell asleep, and not that he died, because he offered a sacrifice of love and fell asleep in the hope of resurrection."

Stephen's martyrdom took place on the third day of August in the year of our Lord's ascension. Saint Gamaliel, and Nicodemus who stood up for the Christians in all the councils of the Jews, buried him in a plot of land that belonged to Gamaliel, and made great mourning over him.

A violent persecution now broke out against the Christians who were in Jerusalem: since Stephen, one of their leaders, had been killed, the rest were hotly pursued, to the point that all the Christians (except the apostles, who were braver than the others) scattered throughout the territory of the Jews. This accorded with the Lord's command to them: "If they persecute you in one town, flee to another."

The eminent doctor Augustine relates that the blessed Stephen shone because of the countless miracles attributed to him. He raised six dead persons to life, cured many who were suffering from various illnesses, and performed other miracles worth remembering. Augustine says, for instance, that flowers which had been laid on the saint's altar cured sick persons to whom they were later applied. Cloths laid on the altar likewise cured many. In the twenty-second book of *The City of God* he reports that a blind woman recovered her sight when flowers taken from the altar were applied to her eyes. In the same book he tells the story of one of the city's leading men, named Martial, who was an unbeliever and absolutely refused to be converted. This man fell gravely ill, and his son-in-law, a devout Christian, went to the church of Saint Stephen, took some flowers from the altar, and placed them secretly on the bed near his father-in-law's head. The sick man slept on them and, when he awoke at the break of dawn, called out that someone should go and bring the bishop to him. The bishop was not at home, but another priest came to Martial's bedside. Martial declared that he now believed, and asked to be baptized. Thereafter, as long as he lived, he repeated the words: "Christ, receive my spirit," not knowing that these were Saint Stephen's last words.

Augustine also tells of a lady named Petronia, who had suffered for a long time from a very serious illness and had tried many remedies without the slightest success. At one point she consulted a certain Jew, who gave her a ring with a stone in it and advised her to tie it with a string against her bare flesh, because the stone had power to cure her. She followed his advice, but it did her no good. Then she went to the church of the first martyr and prayed earnestly to Saint Stephen for help. Immediately the ring fell to the ground, although the string was unbroken and the ring and the stone undamaged; and at that instant the woman's health was completely restored.

Still another miracle from the same source. . . . At Caesarea of Cappadocia lived a noble lady who was bereft of her husband but was surrounded by a fine flock of children, including seven boys and three girls. One day they offended their mother and she laid a curse upon them. Divine punishment followed the mother's curse, and the children were stricken with a dreadful ailment. Their limbs were afflicted by a horrible trembling, and they were ashamed to be seen by the people around them; so they wandered far and wide, and wherever they went, they were stared at. Two of them, a brother and a sister named Paul and Palladia, reached Hippo and told their story to Saint Augustine, who was bishop of that city. It was then two weeks before Easter, and the brother and sister went every day to the church of Saint Stephen, beseeching the saint to obtain their health. On Easter day, when the church was filled with the faithful, Paul suddenly went through the gates of the sanctuary and prostrated himself in faith and reverence before the altar, praying; and while the assemblage waited for him to come out, suddenly he stood up cured, and the trembling of his body never returned. The lad was brought to Augustine, who showed him to the people and promised to write an account of this miracle and read it to them the next day. While he was still speaking and the sister, Palladia, was standing there shaking in every limb, she suddenly broke from the crowd, went through the gates to Saint Stephen's altar, seemed to fall asleep, and rose entirely cured. She in turn was shown to the assembly, and a great chorus of thanksgiving went up to God and Saint Stephen for the health of the two young people. We should add that Orosius, coming back to Augustine after a visit to Saint Jerome, had brought relics of Saint Stephen, and it was through these relics that the miracles just described, and many others, were effected.

It is worth noting that Saint Stephen's martyrdom occurred not on the day after the Lord's birth, but, as we have already said, on the morning of the third day of August, the day the finding of his body is celebrated. The reason for this exchange will be explained when we treat of the Finding. For the present suffice it to say that the Church had two motives in placing the three feasts which follow the Nativity as they now stand. The first was that Christ, the spouse and head, might have his companions close by him. When Christ, spouse of his spouse the Church, was born into this world, he took to himself three companions. Of these the Song of Solomon says: "My beloved is white and ruddy, chosen out of thousands." "White" refers to John the Evangelist, the beloved confessor; "ruddy" to Stephen the first martyr; "chosen out of thousands" to the virginal multitude of the Holy Innocents. The Church's second motive was to group together, in the order of their dignity, all the different classes of martyrs, associating them closely with the birth of Christ, which was the cause of their martyrdom. For there are three kinds of martyrdom: the first is willed and endured, the second willed but not endured, the third endured without being willed. Saint Stephen is an example of the first, Saint John of the second, the Holy Innocents of the third.

---

9. Saint John, Apostle and Evangelist

John (Johannes) is interpreted grace of God, or one in whom is God's grace, or one to whom a gift is given, or to whom a particular grace is given by God. By this we understand four privileges which God bestowed upon Saint John. The first is the special love of Christ for him. Christ loved John above the other apostles and gave him greater signs of love and familiar friendship. Hence he is called the grace of God, because to the Lord he was graced. Christ is also seen to have loved him more than Peter. But there is the love which is in the heart and the love which is manifested outwardly, and the latter is of two kinds—one which consists in showing familiar friendship, the other in the conferring of outward benefactions. As regards the love of the heart, Christ loved the two apostles equally; as to the showing of familiar friendship, he loved John more, and as to outward benefactions he showed Peter more love.

The gift referred to in the second meaning of the name is John's freedom from fleshly corruption, because he was chosen as a virgin and so is one who had in him the grace of virginal chastity: he had thought of marrying but instead was called by the Lord. Thirdly, the name means one to whom a gift is given, and in John's case this gift was the revelation of secrets. For to him it was given to know many profound secrets, such as the divinity of the Word and the end of the world. And the particular grace or favor implied in the fourth meaning was the entrusting to John of the mother of God. For this he was called the one to whom God has given a gift; indeed the greatest possible gift was given by the Lord to John when the mother of God was entrusted to his care.

The life of the apostle was written by Miletus, bishop of Laodicea, and was summarized by Isidore in his book *On the Birth, Life, and Death of the Holy Fathers.*

When, after Pentecost, the apostles separated, John, apostle and evangelist, be-loved of Christ and chosen as a virgin, went to Asia and there founded many churches. The emperor Domitian, hearing of his fame, summoned him to Rome and had him plunged into a caldron of boiling oil outside the gate called the Porta Latina; but the blessed John came out untouched, just as he had avoided corruption of the flesh. Seeing that this treatment had not deterred him from preaching, the emperor exiled him to the island of Patmos, where, living alone, he wrote the Apocalypse, the Book of Revelation. That same year the emperor was murdered because of his cruelty, and the Senate revoked all his decrees. Thus it came about that John, who had been deported unjustly, re-turned to Ephesus with honor, and the crowds ran out to meet him, crying: "Blessed is he who comes in the name of the Lord!"

As he entered the city, a woman named Drusiana, who had been a dear friend of his and had looked forward more than anyone to his return, was being carried out for burial. This woman's kinsmen, and the widows and orphans of Ephesus, said to Saint John: "Here we are about to bury Drusiana, who, following your directions, nourished all of us with the word of God. Yearning for your return she used to say: 'Ah, if only I could see the apostle of God once more before I die!' And now you have come back, and she was not able to see you." John thereupon ordered them to set down the bier and unbind the body, and said: "Drusiana, may my Lord Jesus Christ raise you to life! Arise, go to your house and prepare food for me!" Drusiana got up and went straight to her house as the apostle had commanded, and it seemed to her that she had awakened from sleep, not from death.

The day after the apostle arrived in Ephesus, a philosopher named Crato called the people together in the public square to show them how they should despise the world. He had ordered two young men, brothers and very rich, to sell their entire patrimony, to buy the most priceless gems with the proceeds, and to smash them to bits while everybody watched. The apostle, however, happened to be passing, and he called the philosopher and denounced this sort of contempt of the world, citing three reasons. For one thing it wins the praise of men but is condemned by divine judgment. For another, such contempt cures no vices and therefore is worthless, as any medicine that never cures a disease is said to be worthless. Thirdly, contempt of riches is meritorious only when they are given away to the poor, as the Lord said to the rich young man: "If you wish to be perfect, go and sell all you have and give to the poor."

Hearing this, Crato replied: "If your master is truly God, and if it is his will that these gems should benefit the poor, then you put them together again, thus winning glory for him as I have won the applause of men." Saint John gathered the fragments of the gems in his hand and prayed; and the stones were restored to their former shape. At this the philosopher and the two young men believed, and they sold the gems and gave the money to the poor.

Their example induced two other young highborn young men to sell every-thing they owned and give the proceeds to the poor, and they became the apostle's followers. But one day they saw their former slaves flaunting elegant and costly raiment while they themselves had but one cloak between them, and they began to have regrets. Saint John saw this in their gloomy expression, so he had some sticks and pebbles brought to him from the seashore, and turned them into gold and precious stones. Then he sent the youths to show their new pos-sessions to all the goldsmiths and jewelers, and they came back a week later to tell him that those experts had never seen gold so pure or gems so fine. The apostle said to them: "Go and buy back the lands you sold! Since you have lost the treasures of heaven, flourish, but only to wither; be rich for a time, but only to be beggars for eternity!" He then went on to speak against riches, enumerat-ing six reasons that should deter us from an inordinate desire for wealth. The first is in Scripture, and he told the story of the gluttonous rich man, whom God rejected, and the poor man Lazarus, whom God rewarded. The second comes from nature itself: man is born naked and without wealth, and he dies without wealth. The third is seen in creation: just as the sun, the moon, and the stars, the rains and the air, are common to all and their benefits shared by all, so among men everything should be held in common. The next reason is fortune itself. The rich man is the slave of his money; he does not possess it, it possesses him; and he is the slave of the devil, because the Gospel says that the lover of money is a slave of mammon. Fifth comes care and worry: the rich worry day and night about how to get more and how to keep what they have. Sixth and last, he showed that wealth involves the risk of loss. In the acquisition of riches there lies a twofold evil: it leads to swollen pride in the present life and to eternal damna-tion in the next; and for those doomed to damnation there is a double loss—of divine grace at present and of eternal glory in the future.

While Saint John was carrying on this discourse against riches, a young man who had been married only a month before was carried out for burial. His mother, his widow, and the rest of the mourners came and prostrated themselves at the apostle's feet, begging him to revive him in the name of God, as he had done for Drusiana. The apostle, after weeping and praying for a long time, raised the dead man to life and ordered him to tell the two disciples already mentioned how great a penalty they had incurred and how much glory they had lost. He did so, speaking at length about the glories of paradise and the pains of hell, which he had seen; and he said: "O wretched men, I saw your angels weeping and the demons gloating over you!" He further told them they had lost eternal palaces built of shining gems, filled with banquets, abounding in delights and lasting joys. He also spoke about the eight pains of hell, which are named in the following verse:

> Vermes et tenebrae flagellum frigus et ignis
> Daemonis adspectus scelerum confusio luctus,

i.e., worms, darkness, the lash, cold, fire, the sight of the devil, remorse for sins, grief.

The revived man and the other two then fell at the apostle's feet and implored him to obtain mercy for them. Saint John replied: "Do penance for thirty days, and during that time pray that the sticks and stones may revert to their former nature." After this was accomplished, he said to them: "Go and put those things back where you found them." They did so, and the sticks and stones became again what they had been before. Thereupon the young men received the grace of all the virtues that had been theirs.

When Saint John had preached throughout the region of Asia, the idol-worshipers stirred up a riot among the populace, and they dragged him to the temple of Diana and tried to force him to offer sacrifice to the goddess. Then the saint proposed this alternative: if by invoking Diana they overturned the church of Christ, he would offer sacrifice to the idols; but if by invoking Christ he destroyed Diana's temple, they would believe in Christ. To this proposal the greater number of the people gave their consent. When all had gone out of the building, the apostle prayed, the temple collapsed to the ground, and the statue of Diana was reduced to dust.

Thereupon the high priest Aristodemus incited a still greater commotion among the people, and two parties were at the point of coming to blows. The apostle asked the priest: "What do you want me to do to restore order?" He answered: "If you want me to believe in your God, I will give you poison to drink. If it does you no harm, it will be clear that your master is the true God." John replied: "Do as you say!" "But first," came the answer, "I want you to see it kill some others, to make you fear its power the more." So Aristodemus hied himself to the proconsul, obtained the release of two criminals condemned to decapitation, and, in the presence of the crowd, gave them the poison. They drank it and fell dead. Then the apostle took the cup, armed himself with the sign of the cross, drained the drink, and suffered no harm; and all present began to praise God.

Aristodemus, however, was not yet convinced and said: "If you can bring the two dead men back to life, I will not hesitate to believe." The apostle handed him his cloak. "Why do you give me your cloak?" the other asked. John's answer: "To make you think twice and give up your unbelief!" "No mantle of yours will ever make me believe!" the priest retorted. John said: "Go and spread this cloak over the corpses, and say, 'The apostle of Christ has sent me to you, that you may rise in the name of Christ.'" He did as he was bidden, and the dead men arose at once. Then the high priest and the proconsul believed, and the apostle baptized them and their families. At a later time they built a church in honor of Saint John.

Saint Clement relates, as we find in Book IV of the *Ecclesiastical History*, that the blessed John once converted a handsome but headstrong young man and commended him as a "deposit" to a certain bishop. Some time later, however, the young man left the bishop and became the leader of a band of robbers. Eventually the apostle came back to the bishop and asked him to return his deposit. The bishop, thinking that he was talking about money, was taken aback, but the apostle explained that he meant the young man whom he had so solicitously entrusted to his care. The bishop answered: "O my venerable father, that man is dead, spiritually at least; he lives on yonder mountain with a band of thieves and has become their chief." At that the saint tore his mantle, beat himself about the head with his fists, and cried: "A fine guardian you have been for the soul of a brother whom I left with you!"

Quickly he ordered a horse saddled, and rode fearlessly toward the mountain. The young man, seeing him coming, was overwhelmed with shame, mounted his horse, and rode off at top speed. The apostle, forgetting his age, put spurs to his mount and chased the fugitive, calling after him: "What, beloved son! Do you flee from your father, an old man, unarmed? My son, you have nothing to fear! I shall account for you to Christ, and be sure I will gladly die for you, as Christ died for all of us. Come back, my son, come back! The Lord himself has sent me after you!" Hearing this, the young man, filled with remorse, turned back and wept bitterly. The apostle knelt at his feet and, as though repentance had already cleansed it, began to kiss his hand. Then he fasted and prayed for the penitent, obtained God's pardon for him, and later ordained him a bishop.

We also learn from the *Ecclesiastical History* (and from the *Gloss* on the second canonical epistle of John) that once when John went to take a bath in Ephesus, he saw the heretic Cerinthus in the baths and immediately hurried out, saying: "Let us get out for fear the bathhouse might cave in on us, because Cerinthus, an enemy of the truth, is bathing here."

Someone gave a live partridge to the blessed John (as Cassian tells us in his *Conferences*), and he gently held and stroked the bird. Seeing this, a boy laughed and called to his companions: "Come and watch this old man playing with a little bird like a child!" The saint, knowing by the spirit what was going on, called him and asked what it was that the youngster held in his hand. The boy said that it was a bow, and John asked what he did with it. The answer was: "We shoot birds and animals!" Then the lad stretched his bow and held it taut in his hand, but when the apostle said nothing, he loosened it. John asked him why he loosened the bowstring, and he replied: "Because if you keep it stretched too long, it gets too weak to shoot the arrows." So John told him: "That's how it is with human fragility: we would have less strength for contemplation if we never relaxed and refused to give in now and then to our own weakness. So too the eagle, which flies higher than any other bird and looks straight into the sun, yet by its nature must come down again; and the human spirit, after it rests awhile from contemplation, is refreshed and returns more ardently to heavenly thoughts."

According to Jerome, Saint John stayed on in Ephesus into his extreme old age. He grew so feeble that he had to be supported by his disciples on his way to the church and was hardly able to speak. At every pause, however, he re-peated the same words: "My sons, love one another!" One day the brethren, wondering at this, asked him: "Master, why are you always saying the same thing?" The saint replied: "Because it is the commandment of the Lord, and if this alone is obeyed, it is enough."

Helinandus reports that when Saint John was about to write his gospel, he first called upon the faithful to fast and to pray that his writing might be worthy of the subject. We are told also that when he retired to the remote place where he was to write the divine book, he prayed that he might not be disturbed at his work by wind or rain; and even today the elements maintain the same reverence for the spot. Thus Helinandus.

Finally, according to Isidore, when the saint was in his ninety-ninth year, the sixty-seventh from the Lord's passion, Christ appeared to him with his disciples and said: "Come to me, my beloved, the time has come for you to feast at my table with your brothers." John rose and prepared to go, but the Lord said: "You will come to me on Sunday." Early Sunday morning the whole populace gath-ered in the church that had been built in his name. At the first cockcrow he preached to them, exhorting them to be steadfast in the faith and fervent in observing the commandments of God. Then he had a square grave dug near the altar and saw to it that the earth was carried outside the church. He went down into the grave and, raising his hands to God, said: "Lord Jesus Christ, you have invited me to your table, and behold I come! I thank you for welcoming me there and knowing that I have longed for you with all my heart." When he had said this prayer, a light shone around him, so bright that he was hidden from sight. When the light faded away, the grave was seen to be filled with manna, which continues to be generated to this day, so that the bottom of the grave looks as if it were covered with fine sand, as would happen at the bottom of a spring.

Saint Edmund, king of England, never refused anyone who asked a favor in the name of Saint John the Evangelist. Thus it happened one day when the royal chamberlain was absent that a pilgrim importuned the king in the saint's name for an alms. The king, having nothing else at hand, gave him the precious ring from his finger. Some time later an English soldier on overseas duty received the ring from the same pilgrim, to be restored to the king with the following mes-sage: "He for whose love you gave this ring sends it back to you." Hence it was obvious that Saint John had appeared to him in the guise of a pilgrim.

In his *Life and Death of the Saints* Isidore wrote: "John changed branches from the forest trees into gold and the pebbles of the beach into precious stones; he made broken jewels whole; at his command the widow came back to life; a youth was revived and the soul returned to his body; unharmed he drank a poisonous draft and restored life to those whom the poison had killed."

10. The Holy Innocents

The Holy Innocents are so called for three reasons—by reason of their life, of the death they suffered, and of the innocence they attained. They are called innocent because their life was in-nocent, i.e., not doing injury, since they never injured anyone: not God by disobedience, nor their neighobor by injustice, nor themselves by any sin. Therefore the Psalm says: "The innocent and the upright have adhered to me"; for they were innocent in their lives and upright in faith. They suffered innocently and unjustly; hence the Psalmist: "They have poured out [innocent] blood." And by their martyrdom they attained baptismal innocence, being cleansed of original sin. Of this innocence the Psalm says: "Keep innocence and behold justice"; i.e., keep the innocence of baptism and thereafter behold the justice of good works.

The Holy Innocents were put to death by Herod of Ascalon. Holy Scripture mentions three Herods, all three notorious for their cruelty. The first is called Herod of Ascalon. During his reign the Lord was born, and by him the Innocents were killed. The second is called Herod Antipas. He ordered the beheading of Saint John the Baptist. The third is Herod Agrippa, who put Saint James to death and imprisoned Saint Peter. All this is expressed in the following verse:

> Ascalonita necat pueros, Antipa Johannem,
> Agrippa Jacobum, claudens in carcere Petrum.

Let us look briefly at the story of the first Herod. Antipater the Idumaean, as we read in the *Ecclesiastical History*, married a niece of the king of the Arabs, and by her had a son whom he called Herod and who later was surnamed Herod of Ascalon. This Herod was appointed king of Judea by Caesar Augustus, and so the scepter was for the first time taken away from Judea. Herod had six sons—Antipater, Alexander, Aristobulus, Archelaus, Herod Antipas, and Philip. Alexander and Aristobulus were born of the same mother, a Jewess, and were sent to Rome to be educated in the liberal arts: after their return home Alexander became a grammarian and Aristobulus was known for the vehemence of his oratory. The two often quarreled with their father over the succession to the throne. Herod was offended by these disputes and took steps to make Antipater his heir, so the two brothers began to plot his death. For this reason he drove them out, and they went to Caesar to make complaint about the wrong done them by their father.

It was about this time that the Magi came to Jerusalem and diligently sought information about the birth of the new king. Herod was troubled when he heard of this, fearing that someone might have been born of the true royal line and might expel him as a usurper of the throne. He asked the Magi to bring him word of the child once they had found him, pretending that he too wished to worship the newborn king, although his intention was to kill him; but the Magi went back by another way into their country. Herod, when he saw that they did not return to him, thought that they had been deceived by the star and had been ashamed to face him, so he decided to give up his search for the child. However, when he heard what the shepherds had reported and what Simeon and Anna had prophesied, all his fears returned. He thought the Magi had played a low trick on him, and he determined to massacre all the male infants in Bethlehem so that the unknown child of whom he was afraid would be sure to perish.

But Joseph was warned by an angel and took the Child and his mother into Egypt, to the city of Hermopolis, where he stayed for seven years, until the death of Herod. And when the Lord came into Egypt, all the idols in the land were destroyed, as had been foretold by the prophet Isaiah. It is also said that just as when the exodus of the children of Israel from Egypt took place the firstborn lay dead in every house in Egypt, so now there was no temple in which the idol was not shattered. And Cassiodorus tells us in his *Tripartite History* that in Hermopolis in the Thebaid there is a tree called *persidis*, which cures any sickness if one of its fruits, or a leaf, or a piece of its bark is applied to the neck of the sick person. When blessed Mary fled into Egypt with her Son, this tree bent down to the ground and devoutly adored the Christ. Thus Cassiodorus.

While Herod was planning the murder of the children in Bethlehem, he was summoned by letter to appear before Caesar Augustus to answer the accusations of his two sons. His journey toward Rome took him to Tharsis, and it occurred to him that the Magi had taken passage in ships from that city. He therefore had all their ships destroyed by fire, fulfilling the prediction: "With a vehement wind thou shalt break in pieces the ships of Tharsis."

After the father and his sons had presented their arguments before Caesar, the emperor decreed that the sons should obey their father in all things, and that the king should pass on the kingdom to whomever he wished. Herod then returned from Rome emboldened by the confirmation of his authority, and forthwith ordered the killing of all the male children in Bethlehem who were two years old and under, figuring from the time he had learned from the Magi.

But the phrase "two years old and under" can be taken two ways. If "under" is read as referring to time elapsed, the sense would be "from infants two years old down to babies one day old." Herod had gathered from the Magi that the Lord was born the day the star appeared to them; and since a year had passed with his journey to and from Rome, he concluded that the Lord was a year old plus any remaining days. So, fearing that the child might be a changeling—in other words (since even the stars were at his service), he might have changed his age or his bodily appearance—the king vented his rage on children older than this one child and up to two years of age, or *under*, i.e., down to, the age of one day. This interpretation is more in keeping with common usage and is regarded as the truer one.

Yet the phrase is differently construed according to Chrysostom, and "under" indicates the order or sequence of numbers, so the sense is "from children the age of two and on down to three, four, etc." Chrysostom says that the star appeared to the Magi for a year previous to the Savior's birth, and that after Herod had heard the Magi, he was away for another year on his trip to Rome. He thought that Jesus was born when the Magi saw the star and would now be two years old, so he killed all the males two years old and *down to* the age of five but not *under* two. There seems to be some likelihood to this interpretation, because some of the Holy Innocents' bones have been preserved and are so large that they could not have come from two-year-olds. Yet it might be thought that at that time men grew far larger than they do now.

Herod was punished immediately. Macrobius tells us, and we also read in a chronicle, that an infant son of the king had been given to a woman in Bethlehem for nursing and was slain with the other children. Then what the prophet had foretold came to pass: "the sound of weeping and wailing"—namely, the voices of the bereaved mothers—"was heard in Rama," i.e., on high. And, as we read in the *Scholastic History*, God, the most just Judge, did not allow Herod's great wickedness to go without further punishment. By divine decree it happened that the one who had deprived many fathers of their sons should be even more miserably deprived of his own. Once more, then, Herod had reason to suspect his sons Alexander and Aristobulus. One of their accomplices confessed that Alexander had promised him many gifts if he succeeded in poisoning his father. Moreover, Herod's barber told of the rewards promised him if he slashed the king's throat while shaving him, and added that Alexander had warned him not to hope for much from an old man who had his hair dyed in order to look young.

All this made the father angry. He had the two put to death and designated Antipater as the future king, but later substituted Herod Antipas to reign instead of Antipater. Moreover, he had a paternal fondness for Agrippa and for Philip's wife Herodias, the children of Aristobulus, whom he had adopted. For this double reason Antipater conceived a hatred for his father so unbearable that he tried to poison him, but Herod, foreseeing this, put him in prison. When Caesar Augustus heard that he had done away with his sons, he said: "I would rather be Herod's swine than his son, because he spares his swine but kills his sons."

Finally, when Herod was seventy years old, he fell ill with a deadly disease, being tormented by high fever, an itch all over his body, incessant pain, inflammation of the feet, worms in the testicles, a horrible smell, and shortness and irregularity of breath. His physicians placed him in a bath of oil, but he was taken out almost dead. Then, hearing that the Jews were looking forward joyfully to the moment of his death, he had young men from the noblest families in all Judea taken into custody, imprisoned them, and said to his sister Salome: "Well I know that the Jews will rejoice at my death, but I foresee many of them grieving and many stately funerals if you carry out my wish: just kill all those young Jews I hold in prison. Then all Judea will mourn over me, against their will though it be."

It was Herod's custom to eat an apple, which he peeled himself, after every meal. One day, while peeling his apple, he was seized with a violent coughing spell and turned his knife against his breast, looking around to see that no one could prevent him from killing himself; but a nephew of his grasped his hand and stopped him. However, a great cry erupted in the palace, as though the king were indeed dead. Antipater, hearing the noise, was overjoyed and promised large rewards to his jailers if they would free him. This in turn came to Herod's ear, and, taking his son's exultation more grievously than his own imminent death, he sent some of his sergeants to put an end to him, and named Archelaus to succeed to the throne.

Five days later Herod died, most fortunate of men in many ways, yet most unhappy in domestic matters. His daughter Salome freed all those whom he had ordered her to execute. But Remy, in his commentary on Saint Matthew, says that Herod did stab himself to death with his paring knife, and that Salome put the prisoners to death as her brother had commanded.

※

---

11. Saint Thomas of Canterbury

Thomas means depth, or twofold, or cut down. He was profound in his humility, as is shown by his hair shirt and his washing the feet of the poor; twofold in his office, teaching the people by word and example; and cut down in his martyrdom.

Thomas of Canterbury, while he was at the court of the king of England, saw things happening that were contrary to religion. He therefore left the court and took service with the archbishop of Canterbury, who made him his archdeacon. At the archbishop's request, however, he accepted the office of chancellor to the king, so that he might use the prudence with which he was endowed to put a stop to the wrongs being done to the Church by evil men. The king conceived so strong an affection for him that when the archbishop died, he nominated Thomas to the see of Canterbury. Thomas, although he strenuously resisted the offer, finally obeyed and bent his shoulders to the burden. The new dignity immediately made him a different and perfect man. He began to mortify his flesh by fasting and wearing a hair shirt and haircloth drawers that came down to the knees. He was careful to hide his holiness: mindful of the proprieties, he made his outer dress and his furnishings conformable to what those around him wore. Every day he went on his knees and washed the feet of thirteen poor men, saw to their food, and gave each one four silver pennies.

But the king made every effort to bend Thomas to his will at the expense of the Church. He wanted the archbishop to confirm certain customs that were contrary to the Church's liberties, as his predecessors had done. Thomas absolutely refused, thus drawing upon himself the wrath of the king and the barons. There came a time, however, when with the rest of the bishops he was harassed by the king, even with threats of death; and, misled by the advice of the chief men of the state, he gave oral consent to the royal demands. But when he saw the danger to souls that would ensue from his action, he imposed ever more severe penances upon himself and suspended himself from the ministry of the altar until the pope should judge him worthy to be reinstated. Then the king demanded that he confirm in writing the verbal approval he had given. He refused manfully and, holding high his cross of office, walked out, while the impious shouted after him: "Lay hold of the thief! Hang the traitor!"

Now two of the foremost barons, who were loyal to Thomas, came to him shedding tears and told him under oath that many of the barons were conspiring to murder him. Therefore the man of God, fearing for the Church more than for himself, took flight, and was welcomed in Sens by Pope Alexander. The pontiff recommended him to the monastery at Pontigny, and he settled down in France. In the interim the king had sent to Rome, asking that legates come and put an end to their differences; but the request was repulsed, and this exacerbated his anger against the archbishop. Therefore he laid hands on everything that belonged to Thomas and his kinsmen and condemned the whole family to exile, without consideration of age, sex, rank, or condition. Meanwhile Thomas was praying daily for England and the king. Then it was revealed to him that he was to return to his church, and subsequently to leave this world with the palm of martyrdom and be with Christ in heaven. So, after seven years of exile, he was allowed to go back to England and was received with full honors.

Some days before the saint's martyrdom a young man, who had died and miraculously returned to life, said that he had been led to the highest circle of the saints and amidst the apostles had seen one empty throne. He had asked whose throne that was, and an angel had answered that it was reserved for a great priest from England.

There was a priest who celebrated the mass every day in honor of the Blessed Virgin Mary. He was accused of this and summoned before the archbishop, who suspended him from his office as being simpleminded and unlearned. At the time Saint Thomas had to mend his hair shirt, which he hid under his bed until he could find time to take care of it. Then Blessed Mary appeared to the priest and said: "Go to the archbishop and tell him that she for love of whom you said those masses has mended his hair shirt, which is under his bed, and has left there the red silk she used in the sewing. Tell him also that she sent you to him, and that he is to lift the suspension he imposed on you." Hearing this, Thomas was astounded to find his shirt mended, lifted the priest's suspension, and ordered him to keep the whole matter secret.

The archbishop continued to maintain the rights of the Church as in the past, and the king was unable to move him by pleas or by force. Therefore the king's armed soldiers went to the church and loudly asked where the archbishop was. Thomas went to meet them and said: "Here I am! what do you want?" They answered: "We have come to kill you! You cannot live any longer!" He said to them: "I am ready to die for God, to defend justice, and to protect the freedom of the Church. If therefore you are looking for me, I adjure you, in the name of almighty God and under pain of anathema, to do no harm to any of those around me. As for me, I commend myself and the cause of the Church to God, the Blessed Virgin Mary, Saint Denis, and all the saints." Having said these words, he bowed his venerable head to the swords of the wicked, and they split his skull and spilled his brains over the pavement of the church. Thus the martyr was consecrated to the Lord, in the year of the Lord 1174.

It is said that at the moment when the clergy were about to intone the *Requiem aeternam*, the mass of the dead, choirs of angels came and interrupted the singers, and began to chant the mass of the martyrs, *Laetabitur justus in Domino*, with the clergy joining in. This change was certainly the work of the right hand of the Most High—a chant of sorrow turning into a canticle of praise, and what had begun as prayers for the dead becoming hymns of praise for him who died as a martyr. Indeed he is shown to have been endowed with extraordinary sanctity and to be a glorious martyr of the Lord, since angels visited such honor upon him and ushered him into the choir of the martyrs. Saint Thomas suffered for the Church, in a church, a holy place, at a sacred moment, among his priests and religious, in order to bring out both the holiness of the one who suffered and the cruelty of his persecutors.

God deigned to work many other miracles through his saint. By Thomas's merits the blind saw, the deaf heard, the lame walked, the dead were brought back to life. Indeed the water in which cloths stained by his blood were washed brought healing to many.

An English lady, who was eager to attract men's attention and therefore to be more beautiful, wanted her eyes to change color, so she made a vow and walked barefoot to the tomb of Saint Thomas. There she knelt in prayer but, when she stood up, found that she was blind. Repentant, she began to pray to the saint that her eyes, even if their color was unchanged, be restored as they had been before—a favor that was granted her, but not before she had been at great pains to obtain it.

A trickster carried a pitcher of ordinary water instead of Saint Thomas's water to his master at table. The master said: "If you have never stolen anything from me, may Saint Thomas allow you to bring water in; but if you have been guilty of theft, may it evaporate at once!" The servant agreed, knowing that he had just filled the pitcher with water. Wonder of wonders! They tipped the pitcher and found it empty, and the servant was caught in a lie and, worse still, was exposed as a thief.

A bird that had learned to speak was being chased by a hawk, and cried out a phrase it had been taught: "Saint Thomas, help me!" The hawk fell dead and the bird escaped.

A man for whom Saint Thomas had had great affection fell gravely ill. He went to the saint's tomb, prayed for health, and was made whole. But when he got home cured of his illness, he began to think that perhaps the cure was not in the best interest of his soul. So back he went to the tomb and prayed that if health was not propitious for his spiritual good, he would rather be ill; and promptly he was ill again.

As for the saint's killers, the wrath of God dealt with them severely. Some of them gnawed their fingers to bits, others became slavering idiots; some were stricken with paralysis, still others went mad and perished miserably.

12. Saint Silvester

Silvester is derived from *sile*, which means light, and *terra*, earth, as though to say the light of the earth, i.e., the Church, which, like good earth, has fertility in good works, the blackness of humiliation, and the sweetness of devotion. Good earth is recognized by these three qualities, as Palladius says. Or the name comes from *silva*, forest, and *theos*, God, because Saint Silvester drew savage, untaught, insensitive men to the faith. Or, as the *Glossary* says, the name means verdant, devoted to plowing and planting, shaded, thickly wooded; and Silvester was verdant in his contemplation of heavenly things, a farmer in his cultivation of himself, shaded in his cool withdrawal from all fleshly desires, and wooded, being planted amidst the trees of heaven. Eusebius of Caesarea compiled his legend, and Saint Blaise, in a council of seventy bishops, recommended it as worthy of being read by Catholics.

Silvester's mother, whose name was Justa, was just in name and in reality. A priest called Cyrinus taught him his lessons. He was known for his generous hospitality. Timothy, a very devout Christian, was received into his household, although other people avoided the man for fear of persecution. Timothy steadfastly preached the faith of Christ for a year and three months, after which he gained the crown of martyrdom. The prefect, Tarquin by name, thought that Timothy had been a very wealthy man and demanded his riches of Silvester, threatening him with death; but later, when he was assured that the martyr had not possessed wealth, he ordered Silvester to offer sacrifice to the idols, or to undergo various kinds of torture on the following day. Silvester's reply was: "Fool, you will die tonight and will suffer perpetual torments, and, willing or not, will recognize the God we worship as true God!"

Silvester therefore was committed to jail and Tarquin was invited to dinner. While he was eating, a fish bone stuck in his throat, and he could neither swallow it nor spit it out. So it happened that Tarquin died in the middle of the night and was carried to the tomb amid mourning, while Silvester was set free from prison amid rejoicing, because he was held in deep affection not only by Christians but even by pagans: he was angelic in appearance, polished in speech, shapely in body, holy in his actions, wise in council, Catholic in his faith, patient in hope, and unstinting in charity.

Melchiades, the bishop of the city of Rome, died, and Silvester, despite his strenuous resistance, was elected supreme pontiff by the entire populace. He had the names of all orphans, widows, and poor people collected in a register, and saw to it that their needs were provided for. He decreed that Wednesdays, Fridays, and Saturdays were to be observed as fast days, and Thursday to be solemnized like Sunday. To the Greek Christians who said that Saturday should be solemnized rather than Thursday, Silvester responded that this was not right, both because what he ordered was in conformity with the apostolic tradition and because Saturday should commemorate the Lord's lying in the tomb. The Greeks replied: "Christ was buried for only one Saturday, and his burial is observed by fasting once every year." Silvester: "Just as every Sunday celebrates the glory of the Resurrection, so every Saturday honors the Lord's burial." So the Greeks gave in regarding Saturday but continued to argue forcefully about Thursday, saying that there was no reason for Christians to solemnize that day. Silvester, however, upheld the dignity of Thursday on three counts: on that day the Lord ascended into heaven and instituted the sacrament of his body and blood, and the Church confected the holy chrism. Finally all parties gave their assent to this reasoning.

Constantine continued to persecute the Christians, and Silvester left the city and settled in the mountains with his clerics. The emperor himself, in punishment for his tyrannical persecution, fell victim to the incurable disease of leprosy. In time, upon the advice of the priests of the idols, three thousand infants were brought together to be slaughtered so that the emperor could bathe in their fresh, warm blood; but when he came out to the place where the bath was to be prepared, the children's mothers crowded forward to meet him with their hair in disarray, crying and wailing pitifully. Constantine wept and halted his chariot, stood up, and said: "Hear me, counts and fellow knights and all you people here present! The honor of the Roman people is born of the font of piety.[1] Piety gave us the law by which anyone who kills a child in war shall incur the sentence of death. What cruelty it would be, therefore, if we did to our own children what we are forbidden to do to aliens! What do we gain by conquering barbarians if we allow cruelty to conquer us? To have vanquished foreign nations by superior power is proper to warlike peoples, but vice and sin are overcome by moral strength. In warfare we consider ourselves stronger than our enemies, but in this moral contest we overcome ourselves. Whoever is bested in this latter struggle wins victory by being conquered, whereas a victor is conquered after his victory if cruelty wins out over piety. Therefore let piety win in this conjuncture. Well it is for us to be victorious over all our adversaries if we win by piety alone. He indeed proves himself to be master of all, who shows himself to be the servant of piety. It is better for me, therefore, to die, the life of these innocents being spared, than by their destruction to recover my life—an uncertain recovery at best, whereas what is certain is that the life so recovered is a cruel one."

Constantine then ordered the children to be returned to their mothers and an abundance of gifts and plenty of wagons to be provided for them. So the mothers, who had come in tears, went home rejoicing.

The emperor returned to his palace. That night Saints Peter and Paul appeared to him and said: "Because you shrank from shedding innocent blood, the Lord Jesus Christ has sent us to tell you how to regain your health. Summon Silvester the bishop, who is in hiding on Mount Sirapte. He will show you a pool into which you will immerse yourself three times and so be fully cured of the disease of leprosy. In exchange you are to do something for Christ: demolish the temples of the idols, restore the Christian churches, and become a worshiper of Christ henceforth!" Constantine awoke and immediately sent soldiers after Silvester, who, seeing them coming, thought that he was called to receive the palm of martyrdom. He commended himself to God, encouraged the men who were with him, and went fearlessly to face the emperor. Constantine saluted him with the words: "We are happy that you came!" After Silvester greeted him in return, he gave a full account of the vision he had had in a dream. He asked who

---

[1] Piety: the traditional Roman virtue of *pietas* consisted of dutifulness toward gods, parents and family, and society. It included kindness and compassion.

the two gods were who had appeared to him, and Silvester answered that they were not gods but apostles of Christ. Then, at the emperor's request, the bishop sent for images of the apostles, and Constantine, examining them, exclaimed that they looked like the two who had appeared to him. Silvester therefore made him a catechumen, imposed a week-long fast upon him, and told him to open the jails. When the emperor went down into the water of baptism, a marvelous, brilliant light shone around him: he emerged from the pool clean of his leprosy and made it known that he had seen Christ.

The first day after his baptism, Constantine proclaimed as law that in the city of Rome Christ was to be worshiped as truly God; the second day, that anyone who blasphemed Christ would be punished; the third day, that anyone doing a Christian a wrong would be shorn of half his goods; on the fourth, that just as the Roman emperor was supreme in the world, so the bishop of Rome would be the head of all the world's bishops; on the fifth, that anyone taking refuge in a church was to be held immune from all injury; the sixth, no one could build a church within the walls of any city without the permission of the local bishop; on the seventh, that the tenth part of the royal income was allotted to the building of churches. On the eighth day the emperor went to the church of Saint Peter and tearfully accused himself of his faults. Afterwards he picked up a tool and turned over the first shovelful of earth at the foundation of the basilica that was to be built there, then carried out twelve baskets of earth on his shoulders and threw it outside the building site.

When Helena, mother of Constantine Augustus, who was in Bethany at the time, heard about her son's conversion, she wrote a letter praising him for renouncing the worship of false gods, but upbraiding him roundly because he was leaving behind the God of the Jews to worship a crucified man as God. The emperor wrote back that Helena should bring with her to Rome the foremost doctors of the Jews, whom he would confront with the Christian doctors so as to bring out the true faith by mutual discussion. Saint Helena therefore brought 161 of the most learned men of the Jews, among whom there were twelve who outshone the rest by their wisdom and eloquence. When Silvester and his clergy and the aforesaid Jews came together to debate in the emperor's presence, by common consent they established as judges two Gentiles named Crato and Zenophilus, men of great learning and high reputation, whose role was to act as arbiters between the disputants. Though they were pagans, they were nonetheless fair and faithful judges. They decided between them that when one speaker stood up and was speaking, no one could interrupt.

Now the first from among the twelve, Abiathar by name, began by saying: "Since these people say that there are three Gods, the Father, the Son, and the Holy Spirit, it is obvious that they go against the Law, which says, 'See ye that I alone am God and there is no other God besides me.'[2] And if they say that

---

[2] Isa. 45:5.

Christ is God because he wrought many signs, under our Law also there have been many who worked a great number of miracles yet never dared on that account to claim for themselves the name of divinity, as does the one whom these people adore." Silvester answered him as follows: "We worship one God, but we do not think of him as being so alone as not to have the joy of having a Son. Moreover, we can show you the trinity of Persons out of your own books. We say there is the Father, of whom the prophet says, 'He shall cry out to me, Thou art my Father, my God.'[3] We say there is the Son, of whom the same says, 'The Lord said to me, Thou art my Son, this day I have begotten thee.'[4] And of the Holy Spirit the same says, 'By the word of the Lord the heavens were established, and all the power of them by the Spirit of his mouth.'[5] Also, when God said, 'Let us make man to our own image and likeness,'[6] he clearly demonstrated both the plurality of Persons and the oneness of the divine nature. Although there are three Persons, God is one, and we can show this by a visible example." He took hold of the emperor's purple mantle and made three folds in the cloth, saying: "Here you see three folds." Then he unfolded the cloth and said: "You see that the three folds are one piece of fabric, as the three Persons are one God. . . . It has also been said that Christ should not be believed to be God on account of his miracles, since many other holy men performed miracles without claiming to be God as Christ willed to assert his divinity on the ground of his works. Certainly God never allowed those who rose up in pride against him to escape dire punishment, as is obvious in the examples of Dathan and Abiron and many others. How then could Christ have lied, saying that he was God if he was not, since no punishment befell him as a result of his claim, which was accompanied by many a display of divine powers?" Then the judges spoke: "Clearly Abiathar is outdone by Silvester, because reason itself teaches that if Christ were not God and yet said he was God, he never could have brought the dead to life."

So the first Jewish doctor stepped down and the second, whose name was Jonas, took his place. "Abraham," he said, "received from God the order to be circumcised and was justified thereby, and all the sons of Abraham were justified through circumcision. Therefore anyone who is not circumcised will not be justified." Silvester answered him: "We know that before being circumcised Abraham pleased God and was called God's friend. Therefore it was not circumcision that sanctified him but his faith and righteousness that made him pleasing to God. He did not receive circumcision to sanctify him but to mark him with a difference."

Jonas thus defeated, the third master, Godolias, came forward and said: "How can your Christ be God, since you state that he was born, tempted, betrayed, stripped naked, given gall to drink, was bound, and was buried, whereas all these things are impossible in God?" Silvester: "We prove from your own books that all these things were predicted of Christ. Of his birth Isaiah said, 'Behold a virgin shall conceive and bear a son.'[7] Zechariah said of his temptation, 'The Lord showed me Jesus the high priest standing before the angel of the Lord, and Satan stood on his right hand to be his adversary.'[8] The psalmist says of his betrayal, 'My bosom friend, in whom I trusted, who ate of my bread, has lifted his heel against me.'[9] He was stripped of his clothing, and the psalmist says, 'They parted my garments amongst them, and upon my vesture they cast lots.'[10] Of his bitter drink, the psalmist says, 'They gave me gall for my food, and in my thirst they gave me vinegar to drink.'[11] He was bound, and Ezra says, 'You have bound me not as a father who freed you from the land of Egypt, crying out before the judge's tribunal; you have humiliated me, hanging me upon the wood; you have betrayed me.' Of his burial Jeremiah says, 'In his burial the dead will live again.'" And when Godolias could make no response, judgment was given and he was dismissed.

It was now the turn of the fourth master, Annas, who said: "This Silvester affirms that the things that were said of others were predicted of his Christ. He still has to prove that these things really were foretold of his Christ." Silvester: "Give me someone other than Christ whom a virgin conceived, who was fed with gall, crowned with thorns, and crucified, who died and was buried, rose from the dead and ascended into heaven!" At this Constantine said: "If he can give us no one else, let him admit that he has lost the argument." When Annas could not name anyone, he stepped to one side and the fifth doctor, Doeth by name, came forward.

Doeth began: "If Christ was born of the seed of David and sanctified, as you say he was, then he should not have been baptized in order to be sanctified again." Silvester: "As Christ's circumcision put an end to circumcision, so in Christ's baptism our baptism was instituted for sanctification. Christ was not baptized to be sanctified but to sanctify." Doeth said nothing, and Constantine spoke: "Doeth would not remain silent if he had anything to say by way of refutation."

Then came the sixth doctor, Chusi, who said: "We would like to have this Silvester expound to us the reasons for this virginal birth." Silvester: "The earth from which Adam was formed was incorrupt and virginal, because it had neither opened itself to drink human blood nor been cursed with the curse of thorns; it had not had a dead man buried in it nor been given to the serpent to eat. Therefore it was fitting that the new Adam be born of the Virgin Mary, in order that as the serpent had conquered a man formed from the virgin earth, he might be conquered by one born of a virgin, and that he who had emerged as Adam's conqueror in paradise should become the Lord's tempter in the desert, so that having conquered Adam eating, he should be conquered by Christ fasting."

[7] Isa. 7:14.   [8] Zech. 3:1.   [9] Ps. 41:9.
[10] Ps. 22:18.   [11] Ps. 69:21.

Chusi was finished, and Benjamin, the seventh master, said: "How can your Christ, who could be tempted by the devil by being challenged to make bread out of stones when he was hungry, then by being lifted up to the pinnacle of the Temple, again by being bidden to adore the devil himself . . . how could he be the Son of God?" Silvester answered: "If the devil conquered because he was listened to by Adam eating, it is certain that he was overcome by Christ fasting and spurning him. We profess that Christ was tempted not in his divinity but as man. Moreover, he was tempted in three ways in order to ward off all temptations from us and to show us how to deal with them. It often happens in human experience that a victory by continence is followed by the temptation to worldly glory, and this temptation is accompanied by a craving for power and eminence. Therefore Christ overcame these temptations to give us a lesson in withstanding them."

Now the eighth master, Aroel, spoke. "It is certain that God is the summit of perfection and that he needs no one. Of what use, then, could it be to him to be born in Christ? Secondly, how do you call Christ the Word, for this too is certain, that before he had a son, God could not be called Father; therefore if afterwards he is called Christ's Father, he has become subject to change." Silvester replied: "The Son was begotten of the Father before all time, in order to create what did not yet exist, and he was born in time to remake those that had been lost. He could have remade them by his sole word, but he could not redeem them by his passion unless he became man, because he was not capable of suffering in his divinity. Nor was it an imperfection but a perfection, that in his divinity he could not suffer. Moreover, it is clear that the Son of God is called the Word, because the prophet says, 'My heart has uttered a good word.' God also was always Father because his Son always existed, for his Son is his Word and his Wisdom and his Power. The Son was always in the Father as his Word, according to the text, 'My heart has uttered a Word.'[12] He was always the Father's Wisdom: 'I came out of the mouth of the Most High, the firstborn before all creatures.'[13] He was always the Power: 'Before the hills I was brought forth, nor had the fountains of waters as yet sprung out.'[14] Since, therefore, the Father was never without his Word, his Wisdom, and his Power, how can you think that the name Father came to him in time?"

Aroel being dismissed, Jubal, the ninth doctor, said: "We know that God did not condemn nor curse marriage. Why therefore do you refuse to have the one you worship born of a marriage—unless it is your intention to denigrate marriage? Another question: how can one who is almighty be tempted, and how does one who is power suffer, or one who is life die? And lastly, you are forced to say that there are two sons, the one whom the Father begets, the other born of the virgin. And again, how can it be that the humanity which is assumed suffers without injury to the divinity which assumed the humanity?"

---

[12] Ps. 44:2.　　　[13] Sir. 24:5.　　　[14] Prov. 25:24.

To all this, Silvester responded: "It is not to condemn marriage that we say Christ was born of a virgin, and we have already stated the reasons for his virginal birth. Nor is marriage discredited by that assertion; on the contrary, it is honored, because this virgin who became Christ's mother was herself the child of a marriage. Christ was tempted in order to vanquish all the devil's temptations; he suffered in order to bring all suffering under subjection; he died to thwart the reign of death. In Christ there is the one and only Son of God: as Christ is truly God's invisible Son, the Son is the visible Christ. What is invisible in him is God, what is visible is man. We may show by an example that the man assumed can suffer while the godhead assuming does not suffer. Let us use the emperor's purple mantle as an example. It was wool, and blood was applied to this wool and gave it its purple color, but when the wool was held in the fingers and twisted into thread, what was twisted? The color that signifies the royal dignity, or the wool that was wool before it was dyed purple? So then, the wool stands for the man, the purple color for God. God was present in Christ's passion when Christ suffered on the cross, but was not subjected to suffering in any way."

The tenth master, Thara, said: "I am not pleased by this example, because the color is twisted with the wool!" All present disagreed, but Silvester said: "Very well, take another example! Imagine a tree filled with the splendor of sunlight. When the tree is cut down, it feels the sharp bite of the ax, but the sunlight suffers nothing from the blow! So, when the man suffered, the divinity underwent no suffering."

Sileon, the eleventh doctor, now spoke. "If the prophets foretold these things about your Christ," he said, "we would like to know the reasons for all this mockery and suffering and death!" Silvester: "Christ suffered hunger that he might feed us; he thirsted in order to quench our dryness with a life-giving draft; he was tempted to liberate us from temptation; he was taken captive to deliver us from capture by the demons; he was mocked to free us from the demons' mockery; he was bound in order to untie for us the knot of bondage and malediction; he was humiliated in order to exalt us; he was stripped of his garments to clothe with his pardon the nakedness of our primal privation; he accepted the crown of thorns in order to give back to us the lost flowers of paradise; he was hung upon the tree to condemn the evil desires that a tree had stirred; he was given gall and vinegar to drink in order to bring man into a land flowing with milk and honey and to open for us fountains running with honey; he took mortality upon himself to confer immortality upon us; he was buried to bless the tombs of the saints; he rose to restore life to the dead; he ascended into heaven to open heaven's gates; he is seated at God's right hand to hear and grant the prayers of the faithful."

When Silvester had finished speaking, applause rang out from the whole company, including the emperor and the Jews; but Zambri, the twelfth Jewish master, was highly indignant and said: "It's a wonder to me that you, all-wise judges, are beguiled by these ambiguous word games and allow that the omnipotence of God can be comprehended by human reason! But enough of words, let us get down to deeds! Great fools they are who worship a crucified man, for I know the name of the almighty God, a name the power of which the rocks cannot withstand and which no creature can bear to hear! And so that you may have proof that I am speaking the truth, let a wild bull be led here to me, and when I murmur that name in its ear the bull will die instantly!" Silvester asked him: "How is it that you have heard that name and did not die?" "You, enemy of the Jews that you are," Zambri retorted, "cannot know this mystery!"

A bull was brought in, so ferocious that a hundred men could hardly restrain it; and when Zambri whispered a name in its ear, the animal roared, rolled its eyes, and fell dead. At this all the Jews cheered and hurled insults at Silvester, who said: "He did not utter the name of God but the name of the foulest of demons! Our God not only lets the living die but also brings the dead to life. To kill and not restore life . . . lions, serpents, wild beasts can do that! If this doctor wants me to believe that the name he pronounced was not that of a demon, let him pronounce it again and bring what he killed back to life! For it is written of God, 'I will kill and I will make to live.' If he cannot do this, there is no doubt but that he named a demon who can kill a living being but cannot bring a dead one to life."

The judges then pressed Zambri to awaken the bull, but Zambri said: "Let Silvester awaken it in the name of Jesus the Galilean, and we will all believe in Jesus, for even if Silvester can sprout wings and fly, he cannot do this!" All the Jews then promised that they would believe if Silvester brought the bull to life. He therefore prayed and, bending down to the bull's ear, said: "Bull, get up and go back nicely to your herd!" The bull got to its feet and went away gently and quietly. Thereupon the queen, the Jews, the judges, and everybody else were converted to the faith.

Some days later, the priests of the false gods came to the emperor and said: "O holy emperor, since you adopted the Christian faith, the dragon we have in the pit has killed more than three hundred people a day with its breath!" Constantine consulted Silvester about this, and the bishop answered: "I, by the power of Christ, will make the beast desist from all such mischief!" The priests promised that if he did this, they would believe. Silvester prayed and the Holy Ghost appeared to him, saying: "You will be safe. Go down to the dragon with two priests, and when you reach the beast, speak to it as follows, 'Our Lord Jesus Christ, who was born of a virgin, crucified, and buried, who rose again and is seated at the right hand of the Father, is to come to judge the living and the dead. Therefore you, Satan, wait for him here in this pit until he comes.' Then you will tie up its mouth with a thread and seal it with a ring with a cross on it. Come back to me afterwards hale and unharmed, and you all will eat the bread I shall have prepared for you."

Silvester, with his two priests carrying lanterns, went down by forty steps into the pit, and he spoke to the dragon as instructed. Then, while the animal growled and hissed, he tied up its maw and sealed it. On their way up out of the pit they met two magicians, who had followed them to see whether they actually went all the way to the dragon: the two were almost dead, overcome by the brute's foul breath. The saint brought them out with him unharmed, and the two, with a countless multitude, were converted at once. Thus the Roman people were delivered from a twofold death, namely, from the worship of the devil and the dragon's venom.

At length the blessed Silvester, nearing death, admonished his clergy on three points: they should practice charity among themselves, should rule their churches with diligence, and should protect the flock from being bitten by wolves. After that he fell asleep happily in the Lord about the year of the Lord 320.

※

---

13. The Circumcision of the Lord

The day of the Lord's circumcision is noteworthy and solemn for four reasons: it is the octave of his birth, and it commemorates the imposition of a new and saving name, the shedding of his blood, and the seal of circumcision.

First, it is the octave of the birth of Christ. If the octaves of other saints are solemn days, how much more solemn should the octave day of the Saint of saints be! Yet it does not seem that the Lord's nativity should have an octave: his birth led to death, whereas the deaths of the saints have octaves for the reason that the saints are then born with the birth which leads to eternal life and thus to their eventual rising in glorious bodies. For the same reason the birthdays of the Blessed Virgin and Saint John the Baptist should not have octaves, nor should the Lord's resurrection, which has taken place already.

But note that, as Praepositivus says, there are supplementary octaves, for instance, the octave of the birth of Christ, in which we supplement what had been inadequately celebrated on the feast itself, namely, the office of the one who bore him; for that reason it was customary in former times to sing the mass *Vultum tuum*[1] in honor of the Blessed Virgin. There are also octaves of veneration, including Easter, Pentecost, certain of Mary's feasts, and that of Saint John the Baptist; octaves of devotion, which can be instituted for any saint; and

---

[1] *Vultum tuum*, first words of a mass for feasts and commemorations of the Blessed Virgin in the old Roman missal.

octaves of figuration instituted for saints as signifying the octave of resurrection.

Secondly, this day is solemnized because of the imposition of a new and saving name. On this day indeed a new name was conferred upon the Child, the name that came from the mouth of God the Father; and there is no other by which we can be saved. This is the name that, according to Bernard, is honey in the mouth, music in the ear, and a cry of joy in the heart. He also says that the name is like oil: it gives light, it nourishes when preached, it brings calm when meditated, and anoints when invoked.

We know from the gospels that the Lord had three names—Son of God, Christ, and Jesus. He is called Son of God because he is God from God; Christ, because he is man, assumed as to his human nature by a divine Person; Jesus, because he is God united to humanity. Regarding this triple name Bernard says: "O you who are in the dust, wake up and give praise! Lo, your Lord comes with salvation, he comes with anointing, he comes with glory; for Jesus does not come without salvation, nor Christ without anointing, nor the Son of God without glory, for he himself is salvation and ointment and glory."

Previous to the Lord's passion this triple name was not perfectly known. The first was known by conjecture, as, for instance, by the demons who said that he was God's Son. The second also was known to a particular few who recognized him as the Christ. As for the third, it was known as the name by which he was called, Jesus, but not as to its meaning, which is savior.

After the Resurrection, however, the full meaning of the three names was more clearly manifested; of the first by the certain knowledge that he is the Son of God, of the second by its diffusion throughout the world, of the third as to the reason for the name. Consider the first name, Son of God. That this name rightly belonged to Jesus is brought out by Hilary in his book *On the Trinity*: "That our Lord Jesus Christ is truly the only-begotten Son of God is made known in many ways—by the Father's testimony, by his own statements about himself, by the apostles' preaching, by the faith of religious people, by the demons' admission, by the Jews' denial, by the Gentiles' recognition of him in his passion." Hilary also says: "We know our Lord Jesus Christ in these ways—by his name, his birth, his nature, his power, and what he said of himself."

The second name, Christ, means anointed, for he was anointed with the oil of gladness above his fellows. That he is called the anointed one implies that he was prophet, pugilist, priest, and king, because these four types of persons were usually anointed with oil. He was a prophet in his knowledge of doctrine, a pugilist in his bouts with the devil, a priest in reconciling all with the Father, and a king in his distribution of rewards. We ourselves are named after this second name, Christ, from which comes the title Christian. Of this name Augustine says: "Christian is the name of justice, kindness, integrity, patience, chastity, modesty, humanity, innocence, and piety. And you, how can you claim that name and defend your right to it—you, in whom so few of that great number of virtues subsist? A Christian is one who is Christian not in name only but in action." So far Augustine.

The third name is Jesus. According to Bernard, this name suggests food, a fountain, a remedy, and a light. This food has a multiple effect; it enlivens, it fattens, it strengthens, and it invigorates. Bernard says: "This name Jesus is food. Are you not strengthened every time you recall it? What else builds up the spirit of the one pondering it as this name does? What so refreshes the tired heart, strengthens the virtues, fosters chaste loves?"

The holy name is also a fountain, and the same Bernard says: "Jesus is a sealed fountain of life, which flows out into the plains in four streams. So Jesus became for us wisdom, righteousness, sanctification, and redemption—wisdom in his preaching, righteousness in absolving us of sin, sanctification in behavior or in conversion, redemption in his passion." Thus Bernard. And elsewhere he says: "Three streams flowed from Jesus—the word of sorrow, in which is confession, the sprinkled blood, in which is affliction, and the water of cleansing, in which is repentance."

Thirdly, the name Jesus is a remedy, and Bernard says: "This name Jesus is a medicine. Nothing else so inhibits outbursts of anger, calms the tumor of pride, heals the wound of envy, restrains the welling up of unchaste desire, extinguishes the flame of lust, allays thirst, soothes the itch of greed and of every sort of vice." And fourthly, the name is a light, and he says: "Where in the whole world, think you, is there so bright and sudden a light of faith as shines from Jesus preaching or from Jesus preached? This is the light that Paul carried to the Gentiles like a lamp on a lampstand."

Furthermore this name has much sweetness, whence Bernard says: "What you write has no taste for me unless I read in it the name of Jesus. If you debate or make speeches, I find no savor unless I hear his name." Likewise Richard of Saint Victor: "Jesus is a sweet name, a name of delight, a name that comforts the sinner, a name of blessed hope. Therefore, Jesus, be to me Jesus!" It is also a name of great power, as Peter of Ravenna says: "You shall call his name Jesus, i.e., the name that gave sight to the blind, hearing to the deaf, walking to the lame, speech to the mute, life to the dead; and the power of this name drove all the might of the devil from the bodies of the possessed." It is a most excellent and sublime name; so says Bernard: "It is the name of our Savior, of my brother, of my flesh and my blood, the name hidden from the ages but revealed at the end of the ages, so wonderful, so ineffable, so inestimable a name, the more inestimable that it is more wonderful, the more welcome that it is freely given!"

The name of Jesus was imposed upon him by God the eternal, by the angel, and by his putative father, Joseph. Jesus is interpreted savior, and he is called savior for three reasons, namely, on account of his power to save, his disposition to save, and his act of saving. Insofar as the name bespeaks power to save, it was fitting that it be imposed by God the eternal; signifying the disposition to save, it was imposed by the angel as belonging to him from the moment of his conception; denoting the act of saving, it was imposed by Joseph in anticipation of the Lord's passion. Therefore the *Gloss* on the text "You shall call his name Jesus" says: "You shall impose the name that was imposed by the angel or by the eternal." And here the *Gloss* touches upon the threefold naming above set forth. When it is said: "You shall impose . . . ," the naming by Joseph is referred to; ". . . that was imposed by the angel or by the eternal" refers to the other two namings. Rightly therefore on this day, which is the head of the year by decree of Rome the head of the world and is designated by the head letter (A) of the alphabet, Christ, the head of the Church, was circumcised, a name was imposed upon him, and the octave day of his birth is honored.

The third reason for solemnizing this day is the shedding of Christ's blood, because today marks the first time he shed his blood for us, as he was to do five times in all. The first was the circumcision, and this was the beginning of our redemption. The second was when he prayed in the garden, and this showed his desire for our redemption. The third, the scourging, merited our redemption, because by his bruises we are healed. The fourth was his crucifixion, and this was the price of our redemption, since he made payment for what he had not taken away. The fifth was when the soldier opened his side with a spear, and this was the sacrament of our redemption, for blood and water issued forth: this prefigured our cleansing by the water of baptism, because that sacrament has its efficacy from the blood of Christ.

Fourthly, we pointed to the circumcision as a seal that Christ deigned to receive on this day. He had many reasons for wanting to be circumcised. The first was for his own sake, to show that he had assumed a real human body, because he knew that there would be those who would say his body was not real but a phantasm. Therefore, to refute their error, he chose to be circumcised and to shed blood, because no phantasm can bleed. The second was for our sake, to show us that we should be circumcised in the spirit. According to Bernard the circumcision we should undergo is twofold—external in the flesh, internal in the spirit. The external circumcision takes three forms, namely, in our manner of living, lest it be blameworthy, in our actions, lest they merit reproach, and in our speech, lest it evoke contempt. Internal circumcision likewise has three forms, namely, in our thoughts, which must be holy, in our affections, which must be pure, and in our intention, which must be right. So far Saint Bernard.

Moreover, Christ was circumcised for our sake in order to save us. As one member might have to be cauterized to preserve the health of the whole body, so Christ chose to be cauterized in one member in order to bring health to the whole mystical body: "In whom you are circumcised not with circumcision made by hand in despoiling of the body of the flesh, but in the circumcision of Christ."[2] To this the *Gloss* adds: "from vices, as with a very sharp rock, 'for the rock was Christ.'"[3] This recalls Exodus: "Immediately Sephora took a very sharp stone and circumcised the foreskin of her son."[4] The *Gloss* explains this in

[2] Col. 2:11.   [3] 1 Cor. 10:4.   [4] Exod. 4:25.

two ways. The first way goes as follows: "You are circumcised, I say, with a circumcision not made by hand, i.e., not by the work of man but by the work of God—by a spiritual circumcision. This circumcision consists in the stripping off of the body of flesh, in other words, in putting off the carnal man, meaning the man of fleshly vices and desires, in the sense in which the word flesh is used. Thus Saint Paul: 'Flesh and blood cannot possess the kingdom of God.'[5] You are, I say, circumcised with a circumcision not made by hand but with a spiritual circumcision." The second way: "You are circumcised, I say, in Christ, and this by a circumcision not made by hand, i.e., not by circumcision according to the Law, which is done by stripping away the flesh of the body, namely, the skin of the flesh that is removed by legal circumcision. You are not, I say, circumcised with that circumcision, but by Christ's circumcision, the spiritual one which amputates all the vices. Hence we read in Romans: 'He is not a real Jew who is one outwardly, nor is true circumcision something external and physical. He is a Jew who is one inwardly, and real circumcision is a matter of the heart, spiritual and not literal. His praise is not from men but from God.'[6] So you are circumcised with a circumcision not made by hand in the despoiling of the body of flesh, but with the circumcision of Christ."

The Lord's third reason for accepting circumcision had to do with the Jews, who thus would have no excuse. For if he were not circumcised, the Jews could have excused themselves, saying: "We do not accept you because you are not like our fathers." And his fourth reason had the demons in mind, to keep them from learning the mystery of his incarnation. Since circumcision was done as a counteragent to original sin, the devil thought that this man, who was circumcised, was also a sinner who needed the remedy of circumcision. For the same reason the Lord willed that his mother, though a perpetual virgin, should be married.

The fifth reason for Christ's circumcision was that all justice might be fulfilled. Just as he wished to be baptized so that all righteousness, i.e., perfect humility (which means subjecting oneself to an inferior) would be fulfilled, so also he chose to be circumcised in order to show us the same humility, in that he, the author and master of the Law, subjected himself to the Law. And a sixth reason was to demonstrate approval of the Law of Moses, which was good and holy and was to be fulfilled. He had come not to destroy the Law but to fulfill it: "For I say that Christ Jesus was minister of the circumcision for the truth of God, to confirm the promises made to the fathers."[7]

But why was circumcision performed on the eighth day? Many reasons can be cited. The first is based on a historical or literal understanding of the term *eighth day*. Rabbi Moses,[8] an eminent philosopher and theologian though a Jew, explains this. The flesh of a boy child only seven days old was still as tender as

---

[5] 1 Cor. 15:50. [6] Rom. 2:28–29. [7] Rom. 15:8.

[8] Moses ben Maimon, better known as Maimonides (1135–1204), known in his own time and since not only as an eminent philosopher and theologian but as a physician and author of medical books.

it had been in the mother's womb, but by the eighth day it became stronger and more solid. Therefore God did not want babies to be circumcised before the eighth day because the softness of their flesh might lead to serious injury. He also did not want postponement beyond the eighth day for three reasons, which are stated by the same philosopher. The first was to avoid danger, since the infant might die if there was a longer delay. Secondly, to mitigate the child's suffering: circumcision is very painful, so the Lord commanded that it be done while babies still have little imagination and would not feel the pain so much. Thirdly, to be considerate of the parents' grief, because a great many infants die as a result of being circumcised, and if boys were not circumcised until they were grown up and then died as a result, the parents would grieve more than if the children had died when they were only eight days old.

The second reason for holding to the eighth day is based on an anagogical or mystical understanding. The rite was performed on the eighth day to help us understand that within the octave of resurrection we will be circumcised of all punishment and all misery. By this reasoning the eight days are eight ages—from Adam to Noe, from Noe to Abraham, from Abraham to Moses, from Moses to David, from David to Christ, from Christ to the end of the world, then the age of the dying, and finally the age of the resurrection. Or by the eight days we are to understand eight goods that will be ours in eternal life. These are enumerated by Augustine, who says: "What does 'I will be their God' mean, if not 'I will be for them the gratification of their every honorable desire? I will be to them life, health, food, plenty, glory, honor, peace, and every good.'" Or by seven days we are to understand man himself, who consists of body and soul. Four of the days are the four elements of which the body is composed, and three are the three potencies of the soul, the concupiscible, the irascible, and the rational. Therefore man, who now has seven days, will, when conjoined to the unity of eternal immutability, have eight days, and on that eighth day will be circumcised of every penalty and fault.

The third way to understand the eighth day is in the tropological or moral sense, and in this sense the eight days can yield various meanings. The first day can be the knowledge of our sins: "For I know my iniquity, and my sin is always before me."[9] The second can be the decision to shun evil and do good, which we see in the prodigal son, who said: "I will arise and will go to my father."[10] The third day, shame for sin; so the apostle: "What fruit therefore had you then in those things of which you are now ashamed?"[11] The fourth, fear of the judgment to come: "For I have always feared God as waves swelling over me";[12] and Jerome: "Whether I eat or drink or whatever else I do, it seems to me that that voice is always sounding in my ears, 'Rise, O dead, and come to judgment.'" The fifth day will be contrition: "Make mourning as for an only son, a bitter

---

[9] Ps. 50:3.   [10] Luke 15:8.   [11] Rom. 6:21.
[12] Job 31:23 (Douay).

lamentation."[13] The sixth, confession: "I have acknowledged my sin to thee."[14] The seventh, hope of pardon; for although Judas confessed his sin, he did not hope for pardon and therefore did not obtain mercy. The eighth will be the day of satisfaction, and on that day man will be spiritually circumcised not only of his faults but of all punishment. Or the first two days are for sorrow for sin committed and the desire of amendment; the next two for confession of the wrongs we have done or the good we have failed to do; the other four are for prayer, shedding of tears, mortification of the flesh, and generous almsgiving. Or the eight days can be eight things which, diligently considered, will circumcise us of all will to sin, so much so that serious thought devoted to any one of them will make a great prescription for living a good life. Bernard enumerates seven of these, saying: "Seven things are of the essence of man, and if he pondered them, he would not sin forever: they are his vile matter, shameful conduct, lamentable outcome, unstable condition, pitiable death, miserable dissolution, and abominable damnation." The eighth day can be the consideration of ineffable glory.

A fourth way of understanding the eight days and the eighth day is the allegorical or spiritual interpretation. According to this, five days will be the five books of Moses, two will be the Prophets and the Psalms, and the eighth the Gospel doctrine. In the first seven days circumcision was not perfectly done, but on the eighth there is perfect circumcision of all faults and punishment, now hoped for, at last possessed. The reasons for circumcision can therefore be summed up as six: cautery, sign, merit, remedy, figure, and example.

What about the flesh removed by the Lord's circumcision? It is said that an angel carried it to Charlemagne, and that he enshrined it at Aix-la-Chapelle in the church of the Blessed Mary and later transferred it to Charroux, but we are told that it is now in Rome in the church called Sancta Sanctorum, where there is the following inscription:

Circumcisa caro Christi sandalia clara
atque umbilici viget hic praecisio cara,

which means, "Here are the circumcised flesh of Christ and his bright sandals, here too is preserved a precious cutting of his umbilicus." For that reason a station takes place at this church on this day. But if all this is true, it is certainly to be wondered at. Since the flesh belongs to the true human nature, we believe that when Christ rose, the flesh went back to its glorified place. There are some who say that this is true according to the opinion of those who hold that only what was handed on from Adam belongs to the true human nature, and that alone rose from the dead.

It is worthy of note that in ancient times the pagans and Gentiles observed many superstitious rites on the first day of January, and that the saints were at

[13] Jer. 6:26.   [14] Ps. 50:5.

great pains to uproot these superstitious practices even among the Christian folk. Augustine talks about this in one of his sermons. He says they believed that their leader Janus was some kind of god, to whom they paid much veneration on this day, and that they made his image with two faces, one looking forward and the other backward, because it was the end of one year and the beginning of the next. Also on this day some of them put on monstrous masks, others wore the skins of animals, still others the heads of beasts, thus showing that they not only dressed like beasts but had bestial feelings. There were even some who clothed themselves in women's dress, shamelessly tricking out their soldierly muscles in feminine finery. Others followed the auguries so closely that if someone asked for fire from their hearth or some other favor, they would refuse it. The giving and receiving of devilish gifts was also practiced. Others laid out sumptuous tables in the night and left them there all night long, believing that they would enjoy such abundant feasting throughout the year. And Augustine adds: "Anyone who participates in these pagan customs may well fear that the name of Christian will do him no good. Whoever takes a friendly part in the games of the ungodly may be sure that he also shares in their sins. Therefore, brothers, it is not enough for you to shun this evil. Wherever you see it, denounce it, rebuke it, put it down." So says Augustine.

14. The Epiphany of the Lord

On the feast day of the Lord's epiphany four miracles are commemorated, and therefore the day has four different names. On this day the Magi adored Christ, John baptized him, he changed water into wine, and he fed five thousand men with five loaves.

When Jesus was thirteen days old, the Magi, led by the star, came to him: therefore the day is called Epiphany, from *epi*, which means above, and *phanos*, meaning an appearing, because then the star appeared from above, or the star, appearing from above, showed the Magi that Christ was the true God. On the same day, twenty-nine years later, he had entered his thirtieth year (he was then twenty-nine years and thirteen days old) and, as Luke says, was beginning his thirtieth year; or, as Bede has it and the Roman church affirms, he was already thirty years old. Then, I say, he was baptized in the Jordan, and therefore the day is called Theophany, from *theos*, meaning God, and *phanos*, apparition. The whole Trinity appeared on that day, the Father by voice, the Son in the flesh, the Spirit as a dove.

On the same day one year later, when he was thirty or thirty-one years plus thirteen days old, he changed water into wine; so the day is called Bethany, from *beth*, house, because by working the miracle in a house he appeared as true God. Still another year thereafter, when he was thirty-one or thirty-two, he fed the five thousand men with five loaves, as Bede says and as we hear in the hymn that is sung in many churches and begins *Illuminans altissimus*. So the day is called Phagiphany, from *phagos*, which means a mouthful or to eat. There is some doubt, however, whether this fourth miracle occurred on this particular date. Bede does not say this explicitly in his original, and in John 6 we read: "The Pasch was near at hand."

Four appearances, then, happened on this day, the first through the star, in the manger; the second through the Father's voice, in the Jordan; the third in the changing of water into wine at the wedding feast; the fourth in the multiplication of the loaves in the desert. But the first appearance is the principal one celebrated on this date, and so we will go on with that story.

When the Lord was born, three Magi came to Jerusalem. In Greek their names were Apellius, Amerius, and Damascus; in Hebrew, Galgalat, Malgalat, and Sarachin; in Latin, Caspar, Balthasar, and Melchior. Concerning what sort of magi they were there are three opinions based on the threefold meaning of the word *magus*. Magus means deceiver, sorcerer, or wise man. Some say that these kings were called magi, deceivers, because of what they did, namely, that they deceived Herod by not returning to him. Hence the Scripture: "Herod, perceiving that he was deluded by the wise men, etc." Or magus may mean sorcerer, as Pharaoh's sorcerers were called magi. Chrysostom says that the three kings were called magi because they had been sorcerers but were later converted, and that the Lord chose to reveal his birth to them and to lead them to himself, thereby extending to all sinners the hope of pardon. Or again, magus is the equivalent of wise man; in Hebrew the magus is called a scribe, in Greek a philosopher; the Latin is *sapiens*, wise man, and the Magi were so called because they were men of great wisdom.

These three, wise men and kings, came with a numerous company to Jerusalem. But, it may be asked, why to Jerusalem, since the Lord was not born there? Remy assigns four reasons for this. His first is that the Magi knew the time of Christ's birth but not the place. Because Jerusalem was the royal city and the high priest had his seat there, they supposed that so great a child would be born nowhere else. His second reason is that the city where the scribes and those learned in the Law resided would be the place to learn where the child was born. The third, that the Jews would be left without an excuse, since otherwise they might have said: "We knew the place of his birth but not the time, and therefore we do not believe." Thus the Magi showed the Jews the time, and the Jews showed the Magi the place. The fourth reason would be that the Jews' indifference was condemned by the Magi's zealous search. The Magi believed one prophet, the Jews refused to believe a number of them; the former searched for a foreign king, the latter did not bother to look for their own; the Magi came a great distance, the Jews lived close by. These kings were Balaam's descendants, and they came having seen the star in accordance with their father's prophecy: "A star shall rise out of Jacob, and a man shall spring up from Israel."

Still another reason for their coming is adduced by Chrysostom in his commentary on Matthew. He asserts, referring to what some others said, that certain men who probed hidden secrets chose twelve from among their number, and if one of them died, his son or a close relative took his place. Year after year the chosen twelve went up once a month to the top of the mountain of victory, stayed three days, bathed, and prayed God to show them the star that Balaam had foretold. On the day of Christ's birth, while they were there, a star came to them above the mountain: it had the shape of a most beautiful child over whose head a cross gleamed. The child addressed the wise men, saying: "Go to the land of Judah as fast as you can, and you will find there the newborn king whom you seek"; and they set out immediately. But we must speak about how in so short a time, namely, in thirteen days, they were able to travel so great a distance, from the East to Jerusalem, which is said to be at the center of the world. According to Remy, this was possible because the Child toward whom they hastened had power to lead them to him in that brief space of time. Or it may be said, following Jeremiah, that they were mounted on dromedaries, very swift animals that run as far in one day as a horse can in three. The word dromedary, by the way, comes from *dromos*, running, and *ares*, strength.

When the Magi reached Jerusalem, they inquired, saying: "Where is he that is born king of the Jews?" They did not ask *whether* he was born because they already believed that, but *where* he was born; and as if someone had asked them how they knew that this king had been born, they added: "We have seen his star in the East, and are come to adore him"—in other words, "We, being in the East, have seen the star which showed that he was born." We have seen it, I say, placed over Judea. Or, "We, being in our own region, saw his star in the east" (meaning "to the east of us"). By these words, as Remy says in his *Original*, they professed their faith in the One who is true man, true king, and true God: true man, since they said, "Where is he who is born?"—true king, since they said, "king of the Jews"—true God, because they added, "We have come to adore him." The commandment was that none should be adored save God alone.

Herod, hearing this, was troubled, and all Jerusalem with him. The king was troubled for three reasons. First, the Jews might accept the newborn king as their own, and expel Herod as a foreigner. Hence Chrysostom: "As even a light breeze sways a branch high up on the tree, so a whisper of rumor can disturb men in high station, burdened as they are with the weight of their honors." Second, he was afraid the Romans would blame him if someone whom Augustus had not appointed were called king of Jerusalem, because the Romans had decreed that no god should be worshiped nor any man called king without the emperor's permission and approval. Third, this king, supreme in his land, was troubled because, as Gregory says, with the birth of the King of heaven the height of heaven is opened, and earthly heights are brought low.

All Jerusalem also was troubled, and this for three reasons. First, the impious cannot be gladdened by the coming of the just One. Second, they thought to flatter their troubled king by showing him that they too were disturbed. Third, as conflicting winds whip up the waves of the sea, so kings who are set against each other stir up the populace, and the Jews feared that contention between the present and the coming king could breed sedition among their own people. This last reason is Chrysostom's.

Herod then assembled all the priests and scribes and inquired of them where the Christ would be born. When they told him that this would be in Bethlehem of Judah, he secretly summoned the wise men and diligently questioned them about the time of the star, so that he might know what to do in case the Magi did not return to him; and he told them to bring him word once they had found the child, pretending that he himself wanted to adore him, whereas he intended to kill him.

Note that when the Magi entered Jerusalem, the star no longer guided them, and this for three reasons. The first was to make them look for Christ's birthplace, so that they would be assured of his birth both by the appearance of the star and by the predictions of the prophets; and so it happened. The second was that when they sought human help, they deserved to lose the help from above. The third was that, as the apostle says, signs are given to infidels but prophecy to the faithful: therefore the sign that was given to the Magi while they were still infidels would not appear to them while they were still among the believing Jews. These three reasons are touched upon in the *Gloss*.

When the Magi departed from Jerusalem, the star went before them until it came and stood above where the child was. There are three opinions—Remy gives them in his *Original*—about what sort of star this was. Some say it was the Holy Spirit, who appeared to the Magi as a star as he later descended as a dove upon Christ at his baptism. Others, including Chrysostom, say that the star was an angel, the same angel who appeared to the shepherds; but since the shepherds were Jews and used reason, the angel appeared to them as a rational being, whereas, since the Magi were pagans and did not have the use of reason, the angel appeared to them as a star. Still others hold what is thought to be the truer explanation, namely, that the star was newly created and returned to the underlying matter after its mission was accomplished.

This star, according to Fulgentius, differed from others in three ways: in its location, since it was not fixed in the firmament but was suspended at a level of the air close to earth; in its brilliance, because it was brighter than other stars, so bright indeed that sunlight could not dim it and even at midday it appeared brightest of all; and in its motion, because it went before the Magi like a traveler, not going round in circles but straight ahead. Three other differences are treated in the *Gloss* on Matthew 2, the first words of which are: "This star of the Lord's birth. . . ." Here the first difference is in the star's origin, because the other stars were created at the beginning of the world, this one at a moment in time. It was different, secondly, in its purpose, because the other stars, as Genesis tells us, were set in the heavens to be for signs and seasons, but this one to show the Magi their way. The third difference was in duration: the other stars are perpetual, but this one, once its purpose was fulfilled, returned to the underlying matter.

Seeing the star, they rejoiced with exceeding great joy. Note that the star the Magi saw was a fivefold star—a material, a spiritual, an intellectual, a rational, and a supersubstantial star. The first, the material star, they saw in the East. The spiritual star, which is faith, they saw in their hearts, for if this star of faith had not shone in their hearts, they never would have come to the vision of that first star. They had faith in Christ's humanity (for they said: "Where is he who is born . . ."), in his royal dignity (for they said: ". . . king of the Jews . . ."), and in his divinity (". . . we have come to adore him"). The third, the intellectual star, is the angel they saw in sleep, when they were warned by an angel not to go back to Herod: but according to some other *Gloss* it was not an angel but the Lord himself who warned them. The fourth, the rational star, was the Blessed Virgin, whom they saw with the Child. The supersubstantial star, which was Christ himself, they saw in the manger; and of these two last stars we read: "Entering into the house they found the Child with Mary his mother." Each of these five is called "the star." Thus the first, Ps. 8:4: "the moon and the stars which thou hast founded"; the second, Ecclus. 43:10: "the glory of the stars (i.e., of the virtues) is the beauty of heaven (i.e., of the celestial man)"; the third, Bar. 3:34: "The stars have given light in their watches and rejoiced"; the fourth in the hymn *Ave maris stella*; the fifth, Apoc. 22:16: "I am the root and stock of David, the bright and morning star."

At the sight of the first and second of these stars the Magi rejoiced. Seeing the third, they rejoiced with joy. The sight of the fourth made them rejoice with great joy, and of the fifth, with exceeding great joy. Or, as the *Gloss* says: "He who rejoices with great joy rejoices about God, who is the true joy," and adds, "with great joy" because nothing is greater than God, and "with exceeding great joy" because great joy may be more or less great. Or the evangelist intended to show, by the mounting emphasis in these words, that men rejoice more over things lost and found again than over what they had always possessed.

The Magi entered the little house and found the Child with his mother. They fell to their knees and offered their gifts of gold, frankincense, and myrrh. Here Augustine exclaims: "O infancy, to whom the stars are subject! O Infant, great and glorious, over whose swaddling clothes the angels keep watch, to whom the stars do obeisance, before whom kings tremble and seekers of wisdom kneel! O blessed house! O seat of God second only to heaven, lighted not by a lamp but by a star! O heavenly palace wherein dwells not a bejeweled king but a God clothed in flesh, who lies not on soft cushions but in a hard crib, sheltered not by a golden ceiling but by a roof of thatch blackened by soot yet studded with stars! I am amazed when I see the cloths and perceive the heavens, I am shaken when in the crib I look upon a beggar Child whose glory rises above the planets!" In the same vein Bernard writes: "What are you doing, O Magi, what are you doing? You worship a baby at the breast, wrapped in poor cloths, in a shabby hut! Is this a God? What are you doing? Offering him gold? Then he is a king! But where is his royal hall, where is his throne, where his throng of courtiers? Is this stable his palace, this manger his throne, his courtiers Joseph and Mary? Here the wise men give up their wisdom in order to become wise." Hilary also speaks about this in the second book of his treatise *On the Trinity*: "A virgin gives birth, but the birth is of God. The baby whimpers and the angels sing their praises, the cloths are soiled and God is adored. So the dignity of power is not lost as the humbleness of the flesh is made manifest. Behold in the infant Christ not only lowliness and weakness but the sublimity and excellence of divinity." And Jerome, in his commentary on the Epistle to the Hebrews, says: "Look upon the cradle of Christ and see heaven! You behold the infant crying in his crib, listen at the same time to the angels' songs of praise. Herod pursues, but the Magi adore, the One whom the Pharisees know not but the star points out. He is baptized by a menial but the voice of a thundering God is heard; he is immersed in the waters but the dove descends, indeed the Holy Spirit as a dove."

Why did the Magi offer these three gifts? There are several reasons. The first, it was traditional among the ancients, as Remy says, that no one presented himself empty-handed before a god or a king, and the Persians and Chaldeans were used to offering gifts such as these. The Magi, as we read in the *Scholastic History*, came from the borderland of Persia and Chaldea where the Saba river flows (so the region is called Sabaea). Another reason is given by Bernard: they offered gold to the holy Virgin to relieve her poverty, frankincense to dispel the bad odor of the stable, and myrrh to strengthen the child's limbs and drive out harmful worms. A third reason is that the gold was offered for tribute, the incense for sacrifice, and the myrrh for burial of the dead. So these three gifts corresponded to Christ's royal power, divine majesty, and human mortality. A fourth is that gold symbolizes love, incense prayer, and myrrh the mortification of the flesh; and these three we ought to offer to Christ. Lastly, the gifts signify three attributes of Christ, namely, his most precious divinity, his most devout soul, and his intact and uncorrupted flesh.

These three attributes were also symbolized by the three articles that were in the Ark of the Covenant. Aaron's rod, which blossomed, betokened the flesh of Christ, which rose from the dead; Ps. 27:7: "And my flesh hath flourished again." The tables of stone on which the commandments were written stood for his soul, in which were all the treasures of the knowledge and wisdom of the hidden God. The manna signified his divinity, which has all savor and all sweetness. The gold, therefore, being the most precious of metals, we understand to be the precious divinity of Christ, the incense his prayerful soul because incense signifies devotion and prayer; Ps. 141:2: "Let my prayer be directed as incense in thy sight." The myrrh, which preserves from corruption, prefigured his uncorrupted flesh.

The Magi, having been warned in sleep not to return to Herod, went back to their country by another route. See now the stages of their progress! A star led them and they followed it; men—nay, prophets—taught them; an angel showed them the way home; and they rested in Christ.

The bodies of the Magi used to be at Milan, in the church of the Friars Preachers, but are now in Cologne. Helena, the mother of Constantine, first brought them to Constantinople, and later they were transferred to Milan by Saint Eustorgius, the bishop of that city. After the emperor Henry took possession of Milan, he moved the bodies to Cologne on the Rhine river, and there they are honored by the people with great veneration and devotion.

15. Saint Paul, Hermit

This Paul was the first hermit, as Jerome, who wrote his life, testifies. To escape the persecution of Decius he took refuge in a boundless desert, and there, unknown to men, he lived for sixty years in a cave.

The emperor Decius had two names and was also known as Gallienus. His reign began in the year 256. Paul, seeing the tortures that Decius was inflicting on Christians, fled to the desert. At that time two young Christian men were apprehended. One of them had his whole body coated with honey and was exposed under a blazing sun to be stung to death by flies, hornets, and wasps. The other was laid upon a downy bed in a pleasant place cooled by soft breezes, filled with the sound of murmuring streams and the songs of birds, redolent with the sweet odor of flowers: he was bound down with ropes entwined with flowers, so that he could not move hand or foot. Then a very beautiful but totally depraved young woman was sent to defile the body of the youth, whose only love was for God. As soon as he felt the disturbance of the flesh, having no weapon with which to defend himself, he bit out his tongue and spat it in the face of the lewd woman. Thus he drove out temptation by the pain of his wound and won the crown of martyrdom. It was the sight of such tortures as these that caused Paul, terrified, to seek safety in the desert.

Meanwhile Saint Anthony thought that he was the first monk to live the eremitic life, but it was made known to him in a dream that there was another such hermit, holier than he. Anthony set out through the forest to find this hermit. First he met a hippocentaur, a creature half man and half horse, who directed him to go to the right. Next he encountered an animal carrying some dates, the upper part of whose body was that of a man, the lower parts those of a goat. Anthony required him in the name of God to say what he was, and he answered that he was a satyr (a creature the pagans erroneously believed was a god of the forest). Finally a wolf came to meet him and led him to Saint Paul's cell. Paul, however, knowing that Anthony was approaching, had closed and locked his door. Anthony begged him to let him in, declaring that he would rather die where he was than go away. After a time Paul yielded and opened the door, and they fell into a warm embrace.

When it was time for food, a crow flew down, carrying a loaf formed of two halves. Anthony wondered at this, but Paul told him that God provided him daily with food: this day the quantity was doubled to take care of the guest. There followed a pious argument: which of them was worthy to divide the loaf? Paul deferred to Anthony as his guest, Anthony to Paul as his senior. In the end both took hold of the loaf and broke it into two equal parts.

As Anthony was on his way back to his own cell, he saw angels bearing the soul of Saint Paul heavenwards. Hurriedly retracing his steps, he found Paul's body kneeling upright in the attitude of prayer. He thought the saint was still alive, but finding that he was indeed dead he exclaimed: "O blessed spirit, what you practiced in life you now exemplify in death!" He had no means of burying the body, but two lions came up, dug a grave, and, when the saint was buried, went back to the forest. Anthony took Paul's mantle, which was woven of palm leaves, and wore it on solemn occasions. Paul died about the year 287.

16. Saint Remy

The name Remigius (Remy) comes from *remi*, to feed, and *geos*, earth, one who feeds earthlings with sound doctrine. Or the name comes from *remi*, shepherd, and *gyon*, wrestling, one who tends his flock and wrestles. Remy fed his flock with the word of his preaching, the good example of his life, and the support of his prayer. Moreover, there are three kinds of arms—for defense, such as the shield, for attack, like the sword, and for protection, like the breastplate and the helmet. Remy struggled against the devil with the shield of faith, the sword of the word of God, and the helmet of hope. His life was written by Hincmar, archbishop of Rheims.

Remy was a glorious confessor of the Lord, noted for his learning. His birth was foreseen by a hermit in the following manner. When the Vandal persecution had devastated the whole of France, a certain recluse, a holy man who had lost the sight of his eyes, prayed the Lord for the peace of the Church in France. An angel appeared to him and said: "Know that the woman named Cilina will give birth to a son, Remy by name, who will free his people from the attacks of their wicked enemies." When the hermit awoke, he went immediately to the home of Cilina and told her all he had seen in a vision. She did not believe him because she was already old, but he went on: "Know this, that when you are nursing your child, you are to anoint my eyes with your milk and so restore my sight."

All these things happened as foretold, and in due time Remy fled from the world and became a hermit. His fame spread, and when he was twenty-two years old, the entire population of Rheims elected him their archbishop. He was so gentle that the birds came to his table and ate crumbs of food from his hands. And once when he was a guest in the house of a certain matron and her supply of wine was running short, Remy went to the cellar and made the sign of the cross over the wine cask; and after he had prayed, the wine overflowed the cask and half-filled the cellar.

Clovis, king of France, was at that time a pagan, and his wife, a very devout Christian, could not win him to the faith. But when he saw a huge army of the Alemanni coming against him, he made a vow to the Lord God whom his wife worshiped that if he was granted victory over the Alemanni, he would accept the faith of Christ. His wish was fulfilled, and Clovis went to the blessed Remy and asked to be baptized. When he arrived at the baptismal font, the sacred chrism was missing, but a dove flew down with a phial of chrism in its beak, and the bishop anointed the king with it. This phial is preserved in the church at Rheims, and to this day the kings of France are anointed with this chrism.

A long time passed, and a certain Genebald, a prudent, worthy man, took in marriage one of Remy's nieces; but for religious motives they separated, and Remy ordained Genebald as bishop of Laon. Genebald, however, allowed his wife to visit him often for instruction, and as a result of their frequent meetings his passions were aroused and the two lapsed into sin. The woman conceived and bore a son, and sent word to the bishop. He was dismayed and sent back the following message: "Because the child was acquired by robbery, I want him called Latro (robber)." However, to avoid arousing suspicion, Genebald allowed his wife to visit him as before, and, despite his tears over the first sin, they sinned again. This time she gave birth to a daughter, and when the bishop was informed of this, he answered; "Name this child Vulpecula (little fox)."

Finally Genebald came to his senses and presented himself to Saint Remy, prostrated himself at the prelate's feet, and wanted to take off the stole he wore as a bishop. The saint forbade him and, when he heard what had happened, gently consoled the penitent bishop and shut him up in a cramped cell for seven years, meanwhile governing the church of Laon himself. On Holy Thursday of the seventh year, while Genebald was absorbed in prayer, an angel of the Lord stood before him, told him that his sin was forgiven, and ordered him to leave his cell. He answered: "That I cannot do, because my lord Remy locked the door and put his seal upon it." The angel said: "So that you may know that heaven is opened to you, the door of this room will be opened without damage to the seal," and the door opened at once. But Genebald threw himself in the entrance with his arms extended in the form of a cross and said: "Even if my Lord Jesus Christ were to come to me here, I shall not go out unless my lord Remy, who shut me in, comes here himself." Then Saint Remy, admonished by the angel, went to Laon and reestablished the bishop in his see. Genebald persevered in holy works for the rest of his life, and his son Latro succeeded him as bishop, and he also was a saint.

Remy, renowned for his many virtues, went to his rest in peace about the year of the Lord 500. On this same day the birthday of Saint Hilary of Poitiers is celebrated.

* * *

17. Saint Hilary

Hilary, or Hilarius, looks much like *hilaris*, hilarious, cheerful, because the saint was always cheerful in the service of God. Or the name is like *alarius*, which comes from *altus*, high, and *ares*, virtue, because he was high in knowledge and virtuous in his life. Or the name is from *hyle*, the primordial matter, which is obscure, and Hilary's words, both spoken and written, were obscure and profound.

Hilary, a native of the region of Aquitania, who eventually became bishop of the city of Poitiers, rose like the bright morning star among the other stars. At first he was married and had one daughter, but while still a layman led the life of a monk. His way of life and the depth of his learning caused him to be elected bishop of Poitiers, and he defended the true faith against the heretics, not only in his own city but throughout France. At the urging of two bishops who had fallen into heresy, he, together with Saint Eusebius of Vercelli, was exiled by the emperor, who favored the heretics.

The Arian heresy was spreading in all directions, and the emperor gave permission to the bishops to convene and to debate the truths of the Christian faith. Hilary came to the meeting, but the same two bishops, who could not withstand his eloquence, had him sent back to Poitiers. He went to the island called Gallinaria, which was overrun by snakes, but the snakes fled from him. He raised a stake in the middle of the island as a boundary mark which he forbade the reptiles to pass, so that for them half the island was like the sea, not the land. And when he returned to Poitiers, he restored to life an infant who had died without baptism: the saint lay in the dust for a long time and prayed, and the two rose together, the old man from his prayer and the infant from death.

Hilary's daughter Apia wanted to marry, but the bishop persuaded her to choose holy virginity instead. Then, seeing her firm in her resolve but fearing that she might weaken, he prayed the Lord not to let her live any longer but to take her to himself. His prayer was heard: a few days later the maiden migrated to the Lord, and her father buried her with his own hands. The mother of the blessed Apia, weighing in her mind what had happened, begged the bishop to obtain the same grace for her that he had for their daughter. He did this, and by his prayers sent his wife ahead to the heavenly kingdom.

At that time Pope Leo, led astray by the perfidy of the heretics, convoked a council of all the bishops, and Hilary went to it though he was not invited. The pope, hearing that he had arrived, gave orders that no one should rise to greet him or offer him a seat. Hilary came in and Leo said to him: "Are you Hilary the cock?"[1] "I am not a cock," the saint responded, "but I was born in Gaul and I am a bishop from Gaul." Leo: "So you are Hilary from Gaul, and I am Leo, apostolic bishop and judge of the see of Rome!" Hilary: "You may be Leo, but not the Lion of Judah, and if you sit in judgment, it is not in the seat of majesty." The pope rose angrily, saying: "Wait a little while until I come back, and I'll deal with you as you deserve." Hilary: "If you don't come back, who will answer me in your place?" Leo: "I won't be long, and when I get back, I'll take your pride down a peg!"

The pope went out to take care of a need of nature, but was seized with dysentery and perished miserably. Meanwhile Hilary, seeing that no one gave him a seat, sat down on the ground, quoting the Ps. 23:1: "The earth is the Lord's." On the instant, by the will of God, the ground on which he sat rose up and put him on the same level with the other bishops. Then, when the pope's wretched end was made known, Hilary rose, confirmed all the bishops in the Catholic faith, and sent them home so confirmed.

There is, however, some doubt about this miraculous death of a Pope Leo, not only because there is nothing about it in the *Scholastic History* or the *Tripartite History*, but also because the *Chronicle* has no record of a pope by that name at that time. Furthermore, Jerome says: "The holy Roman church has always kept itself spotless and will so continue for all time, unstained by any heresy." It

---

[1] A play on words. *Gallus* means either "a Gaul" or "cock."

might, however, be thought that at that time someone named Leo was pope, not by canonical election but by tyrannical usurpation; or perhaps Pope Liberius, who was on the side of the heretical emperor Constantine, was also called Leo.[2]

At length, after performing many miracles, and being old and infirm, Hilary, knowing that his end was near, called for the priest Leontius, for whom he had deep affection. It was night, and he asked Leontius to go outside, and to report to him anything he heard. Doing as he was told to, Leontius came back and said he had heard nothing but the noise of the city crowds. The priest watched at the bedside of the dying bishop and again, around midnight, was ordered to go out and to report what he heard. This time he came back to say that he had heard nothing. Then a great light, so bright that the priest could not bear it, shone about the bishop, and as the light slowly faded, the saint departed to the Lord. He flourished about the year 340, in the reign of Constantine.[3] His feast day is on the octave of Epiphany.

Two merchants owned a block of wax, and one of them offered the wax at the altar of Saint Hilary though the other refused to do so. Promptly the wax split into two parts, one remaining with the saint, the other returning to the merchant who had refused to offer it.

✳

18. Saint Macarius

Macarius is derived from *macha*, skillfulness, and *ares*, virtue, or from *macha*, beating, and *rio*, master. Saint Macarius was skillful in outwitting the deceits of the demons and virtuous in his life; he beat his body to tame it and was masterly in ruling his brother monks.

Macarius the abbot, making his way one day across a vast desert, paused to sleep in a tomb where the bodies of pagans were buried, and pulled out one of the bodies to use as a pillow. The demons tried to frighten him, and one of them called to him in a woman's voice: "Get up and come bathe with us!" Another

---

[2] Indeed there was no Pope Leo before Pope Leo I the Great, 440–461. Pope Liberius was exiled by Constantius II (not "Constantine") for refusing to approve Arian errors. Later he subscribed to a compromise formula drawn up by Arian bishops, and still later repudiated his own subscription. Cf. references in n. 1 to chapter 103 on Saint Felix, Pope, below.

[3] According to *Butler's Lives of the Saints* (New York: P. J. Kenedy & Sons, 1963), 1:79, Hilary became bishop of Poitiers about the year 350 and died about the year 368.

demon entered the body and, as if he were the dead man, answered: "I cannot come because some pilgrim is lying on top of me!" But the saint, not terrified at all, answered the body, saying: "Get up and go, if you can!" Hearing this the demons fled, crying out in a loud voice: "Sir, you have defeated us!"

Another day, when abbot Macarius was passing through a swamp on his way to his cell, he met the devil, who carried a scythe with which he tried to cut down the saint but could not strike him. The devil addressed him: "I suffer much violence from you, Macarius, because I cannot prevail against you. How is this? Whatever you do, I do. You fast, I eat hardly anything. You deprive yourself of sleep, I am always awake. There is only one thing by which you outdo me!" "And what is that?" asked the abbot. "Your humility," the demon replied, "and that is why I cannot prevail against you."

Being sorely tried by temptations of the flesh, Macarius filled a large sack with sand and walked in the desert for several days carrying the sack over his shoulders. Theosebius met him and asked why he was carrying so heavy a load. His answer: "I am tormenting my tormentor!"

Another time the saint saw Satan passing by dressed like a man, and wearing a linen cloak with a number of flasks protruding from its pockets. "Where are you going?" Macarius asked him. "I am taking drink to the monks," was the answer. "But why so many bottles?" "I want to satisfy their tastes," said the devil. "If one flask doesn't please one of them, I offer a second and a third, until he finds one that he likes." Macarius met him again on his way back and asked: "How did you do?" Satan responded: "They are all so holy that no one consented to drink, except one whose name is Theotistus." Macarius hurried off in search of this monk and by his exhortations converted him. Another day he met the devil equipped as before and asked him where he was going. "To the brethren." On the way back the two met again and the old abbot asked: "How did things go today?" "Badly!" "How so?" "Because now they are all holy, and, worst of all, I have lost the one I had, and he has become the holiest of the lot!" At this the saint offered thanks to God.

One day Saint Macarius found the skull of a dead man and, having prayed, asked the skull whose head it had been. The answer was that he had been a pagan. Macarius put the question: "Where is your soul?" "In hell!" The next question was whether he was very deep in hell. "As deep as the distance between heaven and earth." "Are there any deeper down than you?" "Yes, the Jews!" "And still deeper than the Jews?" "The farthest down of all are false Christians, who, having been redeemed by the blood of Christ, think little of so great a price."

At times when Macarius walked farther and farther into the desert in search of solitude, he thrust a reed into the ground every so often, so as to be able to find his way back. But once, when he had gone ahead for nine days and stopped somewhere to rest, the devil collected all the reeds and laid them beside the saint's head. This made his return journey very difficult.

One of his monks was deeply troubled by the thought that as long as he stayed in his cell, he was useless, whereas if he lived among other people, he might be of service to many. The monk told Macarius about these disturbing thoughts, and the abbot said: "My son, this is the way to answer them: 'This at least I do for Christ. I stay here within the walls of my cell.'"

Once a flea bit Macarius and he killed it with his hand, and a great deal of blood came out of it. As a punishment for having so avenged the injury done him he lived naked in the desert for six months and came out with bites and scabs all over his body. After that he fell asleep in the Lord, renowned for his many virtues.

✳

19. Saint Felix

This saint is called Felix *in Pincis*, either from the place where he was buried, or because he is reputed to have been killed with styluses: *pinca* is the word for stylus. The story is that Felix was a schoolmaster and was exceedingly strict with his pupils. He was also a Christian, and as he professed his faith openly, the pagans seized him and turned him over to the boys he taught; and they stabbed him to death with their styluses. The Church, however, seems to hold that he was a confessor, not a martyr.

Whenever Felix was led before an idol to force him to sacrifice to it, he blew on it and it fell to pieces. Another account tells us that Maximus, bishop of Nola, was fleeing from his persecutors and fell to the ground exhausted from hunger and cold. An angel sent Felix to assist him, and Felix, who had no food with him, saw a cluster of grapes hanging from a thornbush and squeezed the juice into the bishop's mouth. Then he took the old man on his shoulders and carried him home. When the bishop died, Felix was elected to succeed him.

One day when he was preaching and his persecutors were looking for him, he slipped through a narrow opening in the wall of a ruined house and hid there. In a trice, by God's command, spiders spun a web across the space. The pursuers, seeing the web, thought that no one could have gone through the opening, and went on their way. Then Felix took refuge in another place and a widow brought him food for three months, but she never saw his face. Finally peace was restored and he returned to his church, where he went to his final rest in the Lord. He was buried outside the city, in a place called Pincis.

Felix had a brother who was also called Felix. When the persecutors tried to make him worship the idols, he said to them: "You are the enemies of your gods, because if you take me to them, I will blow upon them as my brother did, and they will be shattered."

Saint Felix is said to have kept a garden. It happened that some men came one night to steal his vegetables, but something forced them instead to spend the night cultivating the garden. Coming upon them in the morning Saint Felix greeted them, and they confessed the wrong they had intended to do. Then they went away, forgiven.

Some pagans came to seize Felix but were stricken with intolerable pain in their hands. They howled with the pain, and Felix said to them: "Say 'Christ is God' and the pain will leave you." They said the words and were cured. A priest of the false gods came to him and said: "Sir, my god saw you coming and took flight. I asked him why he fled, and he answered: 'I cannot bear this Felix's holiness!' Therefore, if my god fears you so much, how much more should I fear you!" Felix then instructed him and he was baptized. To some who were worshiping Apollo Felix said: "If Apollo is truly God, let him tell me what I am holding in my hand." What he held was a paper on which the Lord's Prayer was written. Apollo made no answer and the pagans were converted.

When the time came for him to die, Saint Felix celebrated mass, gave the *Pax* to his people, stretched himself on the floor of the church in prayer, and departed to the Lord.[1]

20. Saint Marcellus

Marcellus comes from *arcens malum*, keeping evil away, or from *maria percellens*, striking the seas, i.e., striking and beating back the adversities of life in the world. The world is likened to the sea, because as Chrysostom says in his *Commentary on Matthew*, in the sea there is confusion of sound, constant fear, the image of death, tireless clashing of the waves, and never-ending change.

---

[1] Some elements in this brief legend appear in the life of Saint Felix of Nola as written by Saint Paulinus of Nola. *Butler's Lives of the Saints* (New York: P. J. Kenedy & Sons, 1963), 1:81, notes ". . . the invention of a 'St. Felix in Pincis.' This confusion was probably due to the existence of a church on the Pincio at Rome dedicated to St. Felix of Nola." Saint Felix of Nola was commemorated in the pre–Vatican II Roman Calendar as "Priest and Martyr" but is not included in the current liturgical calendar.

Marcellus was supreme pontiff in Rome and reproached the emperor Maximian for his relentless cruelty to Christians. He celebrated the mass in the house of a Roman lady, which was consecrated as a church. The emperor in his wrath turned the house into a stable for cattle and confined Marcellus there to care for the animals. After many years of this servitude he fell asleep in the Lord about the year 287.

---

21. Saint Anthony

Anthony (Antonius) comes from *ana*, above, and *tenens*, holding, meaning one who holds on to higher things and despises worldly things. Saint Anthony despised the world because it is unclean, restless, transitory, deceptive, bitter. So Augustine says: "O sordid world, why are you so clamorous? Why do you mislead us? You want to hold us though you pass away: what would you do if you stayed? Whom would you not deceive with sweetness, you who, being bitter, lure with sweet foods?"

Saint Anthony's life was written by Saint Athanasius.

When Anthony was twenty years old, he heard the following words read in church: "If thou wilt be perfect, go sell what thou hast and give to the poor." He sold all he had, gave the proceeds to the poor, and from then on lived the life of a hermit. He bore countless trials inflicted by the demons. Once when he had overcome the spirit of fornication by the virtue of faith, the devil appeared to him in the form of a black child, prostrated himself, and admitted that he was conquered. Anthony had prayed to God to let him see this demon of impurity that plagued young people; and, seeing the demon in the form just described, he said: "Now that I have seen you in all your ugliness, I will fear you no longer."

Another time, when he was living hidden away in a tomb, a crowd of demons tore at him so savagely that his servant thought he was dead and carried him out on his shoulders. Then all who had come together mourned him as dead, but he suddenly regained consciousness and had his servant carry him back to the aforementioned tomb. There, lying prostrated by the pain of his wounds, in the strength of his spirit he challenged the demons to renew the combat. They appeared in the forms of various wild beasts and tore at his flesh cruelly with their teeth, horns, and claws. Then of a sudden a wonderful light shone in the place and drove all the demons away, and Anthony's hurts were cured. Realizing that Christ was there, he said: "Where were you, O good Jesus, where were you? Why did you not come sooner to help me and heal my wounds?" The Lord answered: "Anthony, I was here, but I waited to see how you would fight. Now, because you fought manfully, I shall make your name known all over the earth." Indeed, so great was the saint's fervor that when the emperor Maximian was putting Christians to death, Anthony followed the martyrs, hoping to merit martyrdom, and was exceedingly sad when that grace was not granted him.

Another time he had gone into a cave and found there a silver dish. He said to himself: "How did this silver dish get here, since there is no trace of man's presence? It is so big that if it had fallen from some traveler's pack, it could not have been missed. O devil, this is your doing, but you will never be able to change my will!" No sooner were the words uttered than the dish vanished in a puff of smoke. Later he found a huge mass of real gold, but the gold went up in flames.

Now the saint sought refuge in the mountains, where he lived for twenty years and became known for his innumerable miracles. Once when he was rapt in ecstasy, he saw the whole world covered with snares connected one to the other, and exclaimed: "Oh, how can anyone escape these traps?" And he heard a voice say: "Humility!" Again he was carried aloft by angels, but demons were there to bar his way, proclaiming the sins he had committed from childhood on. To them the angels said: "You should not tell these things, because by the mercy of Christ they are wiped away. If you know how he became a monk, tell that!" The demons had nothing more to say. Anthony was borne upward in freedom and freely set down on earth.

Anthony tells us this about himself: "I once saw a very tall devil who dared to claim for himself the power and knowledge of God, and he asked me: 'What do you want me to give you, Anthony?' But I spat in his face and set upon him armed with the name of Christ, and he vanished at once." Again the devil appeared to him in a shape so high that his head seemed to touch the sky. When Anthony asked him who he was, he said he was Satan, and added: "Why do the monks attack me and the Christians curse me?" Anthony answered: "What they do is just, because you harass them at all times with your insidious schemes." Satan: "I never harass them, but they harass each other! And I am reduced to nothing because Christ reigns everywhere!"

An archer once saw Saint Anthony taking his ease with his brethren and was displeased at the sight. Anthony said to him: "Put an arrow to your bow and shoot!" The archer did so, but when he was ordered to do the same thing a second and third time, he said: "If I go on doing this, my bow will break!" Anthony: "So it is with us as we do God's work. If we stretch ourselves unduly, we are quickly broken, so it is good for us to relax from our rigors from time to time." Hearing this, the man was edified and went his way.

Someone asked Anthony what he should do to please God. The saint replied: "Wherever you go, have God always before your eyes; follow the testimony of

Holy Scripture in all you do; and whenever you settle down someplace, don't be too quick to go somewhere else. Observe these three rules and you will be saved." An abbot asked him: "What should I do?" Anthony: "Don't trust in your own righteousness; practice moderation in food and talk; and don't worry about things done in the past." Again, Anthony said: "Just as fish too long out of water die, so monks who tarry outside their cells and keep company with lay people weaken in their resolve to live a quiet life." And again: "Anyone who lives in solitude and quiet is saved from three kinds of warfare—against hearing, talking, and seeing. All he still has to fight against is his heart."

Several monks came with an old man to visit Abbot Anthony, and the saint said to them: "You are in good company with this old man." Then he asked the man: "Good father, have you found these brothers good?" "They are good enough, but their house has no door on it. Anyone who wants to walks into the stable and unties the donkey." What he meant was that whatever came into their heads came out through their mouths. Abbot Anthony also said: "It is well to know that there are three movements of the body; one is from nature, one from too much food, and one from the devil."

A monk had renounced the world but not totally, because he kept some of his belongings. Anthony told him to go and buy meat, and he did so; and on the way back he was attacked and bitten by dogs. Anthony told him: "Those who renounce the world and still want to have money will likewise be assailed by demons and torn apart."

The saint was finding life in the desert tedious and prayed: "Lord, I want to work out my salvation, but I cannot control my thoughts." He arose and walked out, and saw someone sitting at work and then rising to pray; and this was an angel of the Lord, and the angel said to him: "Do as I am doing, and you will be saved."

Some of the monks asked Anthony about the state of their souls, and the following night a voice called him and said: "Get up, go out, and see what you see." What he saw was a huge, terrifying being whose head towered to the clouds, and also figures with wings trying to fly upwards but being held back by the monster's outstretched hands; yet there were others freely flying upwards, and these he could not stop. Anthony heard sounds of great joy mixed with sounds of grief, and understood that it was the devil, holding back some guilty souls and groaning because he could not halt the heavenward flight of the holy ones.

One day when Anthony was at work with his brethren, he looked up to heaven and beheld a sad vision. He knelt and begged God to avert the coming mischief; and, when the monks questioned him, with tears and sobs he said that a crime unheard-of throughout the ages was imminent. "I saw," he said, "the altar of God surrounded by a pack of horses that tore and trampled everything around them with their hooves; for the Catholic faith is about to be torn asunder by a violent storm, and men will trample like horses upon Christ's sacraments."

Then the voice of the Lord sounded, saying: "My altar will be dishonored." In fact, two years thereafter the Arians rose up and split the unity of the Church, defiled the baptistry and the churches, and slaughtered Christians on the altars as if they were lambs of sacrifice.

A certain highly placed Egyptian named Ballachius, an Arian, attacked the Church of God, turned virgins and monks out into the streets naked, and had them whipped in public. Anthony wrote him: "I see the wrath of God coming upon you. Stop persecuting Christians unless you want to incur God's anger, because he is threatening you with death soon to come." The unhappy man read the letter, laughed at it, spat on it, threw it to the ground, had its bearers whipped, and sent them back to Anthony with the following message: "You, who discipline your monks with such care. Soon the rigor of our discipline will be visited upon you!" Five days later, as he was about to mount his gentle horse, the animal bit him, knocked him to the ground, and trampled and crushed his legs. In three days he was dead.

Some of the monks asked Anthony to tell them the word of salvation, and he said: "You have heard the Lord saying, 'If someone strikes you on the right cheek, turn to him also the other.'" They replied: "That we cannot fulfill." He said: "Then at least bear the one blow patiently." "We cannot do that either." Anthony: "Well, at least do not strike rather than be struck." "Even that is too much!" So Anthony said to his disciple: "Prepare a fortifying drink for these brothers, because they are so frail!" But, to the brothers: "All I can say to you is, 'Pray!'" All this we read in *Lives of the Fathers*.

At last, in the 105th year of his life, the blessed Anthony embraced his brethren and expired in peace during the reign of Constantine, which began about the year 340.[1]

22. Saint Fabian

Fabian (Fabianus) is like *fabricans*, building, and Fabian built heavenly bliss for himself, gaining it by a triple right—by adoption, by purchase, and by a fight well fought.

---

[1] Constantine II, who reigned 337–340.

Fabian was a citizen of the city of Rome. When the pope died and the people gathered to elect a successor, Fabian went along to see what the outcome would be. Lo and behold, a white dove came down upon his head, and the people, filled with wonder, elected him as supreme pontiff.

Pope Damasus tells us that Pope Fabian sent seven deacons to all areas of the Church and assigned seven subdeacons to them to write down the Acts of the martyrs. Haymon wrote that when the emperor Philip wished to be present at the vigil of Easter and to share in the mysteries, Fabian forbade him to do so until he had confessed his sins and taken his place with the penitents.

In the thirteenth year of his pontificate Fabian was beheaded by order of the emperor Decius and so won the crown of martyrdom. He suffered about the year of the Lord 253.

---

23. Saint Sebastian

Sebastian comes from *sequens*, following, *beatitudo*, beatitude, *astim*, city, and *ana*, above; therefore one who pursues the beatitude of the city on high, the city of supernal glory—in other words, one who acquires and possesses that city. Augustine says that this possession costs five payments: poverty pays for the kingdom, pain for joy, toil for rest, dishonor for glory, and death for life. Or Sebastian is derived from *bastum*, saddle; for Christ is the horseman, the Church the horse, Sebastian the saddle on which Christ rode to do battle in the Church and obtain the victory of many martyrs. Or the name means surrounded, or going about; for the saint was surrounded by arrows as a porcupine is with quills, and he went about among the martyrs and strengthened them all.

Sebastian was a most Christian man. A native of Narbonne and a citizen of Milan, he was so well thought of by the emperors Diocletian and Maximian that they made him commander of the First Cohort and attached him to their personal retinue. Sebastian sought military rank for the sole purpose of being able to visit Christians under torture, to encourage them when he saw that their spirit was weakening.

Two twin brothers of the high nobility, named Marcellian and Marcus, were about to be beheaded for the faith of Christ, and their parents came to try to get them to change their minds. Their mother came first, her hair disheveled, garments torn, and breasts bare, and she cried: "O my dearest sons, misery unheard-of and grief unbearable surround me! Woe is me, I am losing my sons who go willingly to death! Yet if the enemy were taking them away, I would follow their captors through the thick of battle! If they were condemned to prison, I would break in if it cost me my life! What new way of dying is this, that the headsman is exhorted to strike, life's only wish is to be ended, death is invited to take over? New is this mourning, new this misery, when the youth of one's offspring is lost of their own accord, and in their pitiful old age the parents are forced to live on!"

Now the father arrived, supported by his slaves, his head sprinkled with dust, and he cried out to heaven: "I come to bid farewell to my sons on their way to death! Unhappy me, that the funeral rites I had prepared for myself I will carry out for my children! O my sons, staff of my old age and twin fruit of my loins, why do you love death so much? Come hither, young men, and mourn my sons with me! Come, old men, and weep with me for my sons! Gather here, you fathers, and see to it that you do not suffer woes like mine! Let my eyes fail with weeping, that I may not see my sons fall beneath the sword!"

Then came the wives of the two, setting their children in front of them and saying with loud cries: "To whom are you leaving us? Who will guide the lives of these infants? Who will divide your great possessions? Alas, what iron hearts are yours, that you disdain your parents, spurn your friends, cast away your wives, abandon your children, and of your own will hand yourselves over to the executioners!"

All this began to soften the hearts of the two men. Then Saint Sebastian, who was present, broke into the midst of the gathering and said: "O you strong soldiers of Christ, do not let these tearful blandishments cause you to forsake the everlasting crown!" And to the parents he said: "Do not fear, they will not be separated from you but will go to heaven and prepare starry dwellings for you. Since the world began, life has betrayed those who placed their hopes in it, has deceived their expectations, has fooled those who took its goods for granted, and so it has left nothing certain and proves itself false to all. Life induces the thief to steal, the angry to rage, the liar to deceive. It commands crimes, orders wickedness, counsels injustice. But this persecution, which we suffer here on earth, flames up today and tomorrow blows away, today burns hot and cools tomorrow: it comes on in an hour and in another is gone. But the pain of eternity is ever renewed to stab more deeply, is increased to burn more fiercely, is fanned to prolong the punishment. Therefore let us stir up our desire, our love for martyrdom! The devil thinks he conquers by making martyrs, but while he catches he is caught, while he binds he is bound, while he wins he loses, while he tortures he is tortured, while he strangles he is killed, while he mocks he is laughed at!" As Saint Sebastian was saying all this, suddenly a radiance shone from heaven and shed light upon him for almost an hour, wrapping him in its splendor like a shining cloak, and seven radiant angels surrounded him. A youth also appeared at his side and gave him the kiss of peace, saying: "You will always be with me!"

Now Zoe, the wife of Nicostratus in whose house the two holy young men were kept under guard, fell at the saint's feet and begged forgiveness, nodding and gesturing because she had lost the power of speech. Sebastian said: "If I am Christ's servant, and if all that this woman has heard from my mouth and has believed is true, may he who opened the mouth of Zechariah his prophet let her speak!" Immediately the woman's speech returned and she said: "Blessed be the words of your mouth, and blessed be all who believe what you have said! For I have seen an angel holding a book before you in which everything you said was written."

Hearing this, her husband also knelt at Saint Sebastian's feet and prayed for forgiveness. Then he loosed the martyrs' bonds and told them to go free. They answered that they would not give up the victory they were about to win. The Lord had endowed the saint's words with such grace and power that not only did he confirm Marcellian and Marcus in their acceptance of martyrdom but also converted their father, whose name was Tranquillinus, their mother, and many others of their household to the faith, and the priest Polycarp baptized all of them.

Tranquillinus suffered from a painful disease, but as soon as he was baptized, his illness was cured. The prefect of the city of Rome was afflicted with the same disease and asked Tranquillinus to bring to him the person who had cured him. So Sebastian and the priest Polycarp went to the prefect, who asked them to restore his health, and Sebastian told him that he would first have to renounce the worship of false gods and empower him to demolish his idols: then only would he regain his health. The prefect said that his slaves, not Sebastian, should destroy the idols, but Sebastian answered: "They are afraid to strike their gods, and if they did it and the devil harmed them, the infidels would say that this was because they had laid hands on their gods." So Polycarp and Sebastian girded themselves and reduced more than two hundred idols to fragments.

Then they said to Chromatius, the prefect: "We have shattered the idols and you are not cured. This must be because you have not yet renounced your false beliefs, or else you are holding back some idols." The prefect admitted that he had a room in which the whole order of the stars was represented. His father, he said, had spent two hundred pounds of gold on the work, and by it he could foretell future events. Sebastian insisted: "As long as you keep that room intact, you yourself will not be made whole." The prefect then gave his consent, but his son Tiburtius, a forthright young man, spoke up: "I will not suffer so great a work to be dismantled; but rather than seem to stand in the way of my father's recovery, I will have two ovens fired, and if my father is not cured once the room is destroyed, these two will be roasted alive!" Sebastian replied: "Do as you say!" While the room in question was being taken apart, an angel appeared to the prefect and told him that the Lord Jesus had cured him of his malady. The prefect realized that he was indeed cured, and ran after the angel to kiss his feet, but the angel would not allow this because the man had not yet received baptism. So he and his son Tiburtius and fourteen hundred persons among his family and retainers were baptized.

Meanwhile Zoe was seized by the pagans, subjected to long torture, and died a martyr. Learning of this, Tranquillinus burst out: "The women are winning the crown ahead of us! Why do we go on living?" And he was stoned to death a few days later. Saint Tiburtius was ordered to burn incense to the gods or to walk barefoot over burning coals. He made the sign of the cross and walked unshod over the coals, saying: "I feel as if I am treading on rose leaves in the name of our Lord Jesus Christ." Fabian, the prefect, retorted: "Everyone knows that Christ has taught you the arts of magic!" Tiburtius: "Be still, unhappy man! You are not worthy to pronounce that sweet holy name!" The prefect, indignant, had him beheaded. Marcellian and Marcus were tied to a stake and chanted the words of the Psalm: "Behold how good and how pleasant it is for brothers to dwell together in unity!" The prefect shouted at them: "Wretches, put aside your madness and save yourselves!" "Never have we feasted so well!" they responded. "Please leave us just as we are for as long as we are clothed in our bodies!" The prefect ordered soldiers to run them through with lances, and thus they consummated their martyrdom.

After all this, the prefect denounced Sebastian to the emperor Diocletian, who summoned the saint and said to him: "I have always had you among the first in my palace, and all this time you have been acting secretly against my welfare and offending the gods." Sebastian: "I have always worshiped God who is in heaven, and prayed to Christ for your salvation and the good estate of the Roman Empire." But Diocletian gave the command to tie him to a post in the center of the camp, and ordered the soldiers to shoot him full of arrows. They shot so many arrows into his body that he looked like a porcupine, and left him for dead. Miraculously set free, he stood on the steps of the imperial palace a few days later and, as the emperors came out, firmly reproached them for their cruel treatment of Christians. "Isn't this the Sebastian whom we ordered shot to death?" the emperors exclaimed. Sebastian answered: "The Lord deigned to revive me so that I could meet you and rebuke you for the evils you inflict on the servants of Christ!" The emperors then ordered him to be beaten with cudgels until he died, and had his body thrown into the sewer to prevent the Christians from honoring him as a martyr. The following night Saint Sebastian appeared to Saint Lucina, revealed to her where his body was, and asked that it be buried near the remains of the apostles, which was done. Sebastian suffered under the emperors Diocletian and Maximian, whose reign began about the year of the Lord 287.

In the first book of his *Dialogues* Pope Gregory reports that a woman in Tuscany, recently married, was invited by friends to attend the dedication of a church to Saint Sebastian; but the night before she was to go there, she was aroused by carnal desire and could not refrain from lying with her husband. Morning came, and, fearing to be shamed in the sight of men more than before God, she went to the church. No sooner had she set foot into the place where the saint's relics were kept than the devil seized her and began to torment her as all looked on. A priest of the church snatched the altar cloth from the altar and threw it around her, whereupon the devil laid hold of the priest. The woman's friends took her to sorcerers who might, by their incantations, drive the devil from her, but as the magic formulas were pronounced, by the judgment of God a legion of demons, 6,666 in number, infested the woman and tormented her more and more severely. Then a certain man eminent for his holiness, whose name was Fortunatus, prayed for her and she was saved.

In the *Annals of the Lombards* we read that during the reign of King Gumbert all Italy was stricken by a plague so virulent that there was hardly anyone left to bury the dead, and this plague raged most of all in Rome and Pavia. At this time there appeared to some a good angel followed by a bad angel carrying a spear. When the good angel gave the command, the bad one struck and killed, and when he struck a house, all the people in it were carried out dead. Then it was divinely revealed that the plague would never cease until an altar was raised in Pavia in honor of Saint Sebastian. An altar was built in the church of Saint Peter in Chains, and at once the pestilence ceased. Relics of Saint Sebastian were brought to Pavia.

Ambrose, in his Preface for Saint Sebastian, says: "Lord, the shedding of the blood of the blessed martyr Sebastian for the confession of your name shows your wonderful works: you confer strength in weakness and success to our efforts, and at his prayer give help to the infirm."

24. Saint Agnes, Virgin

The name Agnes comes from *agna*, a lamb, because Agnes was as meek and humble as a lamb. Or her name comes from the Greek word *agnos*, pious, because she was pious and compassionate; or from *agnoscendo*, knowing, because she knew the way of truth. Truth, according to Augustine, is opposed to vanity and falseness and doubting, all of which she avoided by the virtue of truth that was hers.

Agnes was a virgin most sensible and wise, as Ambrose, who wrote the story of her martyrdom, attests. When she was thirteen years old, she lost death and found life. Childhood is computed in years, but in her immense wisdom she was old; she was a child in body but already aged in spirit. Her face was beautiful, her faith more beautiful.

One day she was on her way home from school when the prefect's son saw her and fell in love. He promised her jewels and great wealth if she consented to be his wife. Agnes answered: "Go away, you spark that lights the fire of sin, you fuel of wickedness, you food of death! I am already pledged to another lover!" She began to commend this lover and spouse for five things that the betrothed look for in the men they are to wed, namely, nobility of lineage, beauty of person, abundance of wealth, courage and the power to achieve, and love transcendent. She went on: "The one I love is far nobler than you, of more eminent descent. His mother is a virgin, his father knows no woman, he is served by angels; the sun and the moon wonder at his beauty; his wealth never lacks or lessens; his perfume brings the dead to life, his touch strengthens the feeble, his love is chastity itself, his touch holiness, union with him, virginity."

In support of these five claims, she said: "Is there anyone whose ancestry is more exalted, whose powers are more invincible, whose aspect is more beautiful, whose love more delightful, who is richer in every grace?" Then she enumerated five benefits that her spouse had conferred on her and confers on all his other spouses: he gives them a ring as an earnest of his fidelity, he clothes and adorns them with a multitude of virtues, he signs them with the blood of his passion and death, he binds them to himself with the bond of his love, and endows them with the treasures of eternal glory. "He has placed a wedding ring on my right hand," she said, "and a necklace of precious stones around my neck, gowned me with a robe woven with gold and jewels, placed a mark on my forehead to keep me from taking any lover but himself, and his blood has tinted my cheeks. Already his chaste embraces hold me close, he has united his body to mine, and he has shown me incomparable treasures, and promised to give them to me if I remain true to him."

When the young man heard all this, he was beside himself and threw himself on his bed, and his deep sighs made it clear to his physicians that lovesickness was his trouble. His father sought out the maiden and told her of his son's condition, but she assured him that she could not violate her covenant with her betrothed. The prefect pressed her to say who this betrothed was, whose power over her she talked about. Someone else told him that it was Christ whom she called her spouse, and the prefect tried to win her over with soft words at first, and then with dire threats. Agnes met this mixture of cajolery and menace with derision, and said: "Do whatever you like, but you will not obtain what you want from me." The prefect: "You have just two choices. Either you will sacrifice to the goddess Vesta with her virgins, since your virginity means so much to you, or you will be thrown in with harlots and handled as they are handled."

Because she was of the nobility, the prefect could not bring force to bear upon her, so he raised the charge of her Christianity. Agnes said: "I will not sacrifice to your gods, and no one can sully my virtue because I have with me a guardian of my body, an angel of the Lord." Then the prefect had her stripped and taken nude to a brothel, but God made her hair grow so long that it covered her better than any clothing. When she entered the house of shame, she found an angel waiting for her. His radiance filled the place with light and formed a shining mantle about her. Thus the brothel became a place of prayer, and anyone who honored the light came out cleaner than he had gone in.

The prefect's son now came with other young men, and invited them to go in and take their pleasure with her, but they were terrified by the miraculous light and hurried back to him. He scorned them as cowards and in a fury rushed in to force himself upon Agnes, but the same light engulfed him, and, since he had not honored God, the devil throttled him and he expired. When the prefect heard of this, he went to Agnes, weeping bitterly, and questioned her closely about the cause of his son's death. "The one whose will he wanted to carry out," she said, "thus got power over him and killed him, whereas his companions, frightened by the miracle they saw, retreated unharmed." The prefect persisted: "You can prove that you did not do this by some magical art, if you are able to bring him back to life by your prayer." So Agnes prayed, and the youth came to life and began to preach Christ publicly. At this the priests of the temples stirred up a tumult in the populace, shouting: "Away with the witch, away with the sorceress who turns people's heads and befuddles their wits!" On the other hand the prefect, impressed by the miracle, wished to set her free but, fearing that he would be outlawed, put a deputy in charge and went away sadly.

The deputy, Aspasius by name, had Agnes thrown into a roaring fire, but the flames divided and burned up the hostile crowd on either side, leaving the maiden unscathed. Aspasius finally had a soldier thrust a dagger into her throat, and thus her heavenly spouse consecrated her his bride and martyr. It is believed that she suffered in the reign of Constantine the Great, which began in A.D. 309. Her kinsmen and other Christians buried her joyfully and barely escaped the pagans who tried to stone them.

Saint Agnes had a foster sister named Emerentiana, a holy virgin who had not yet received baptism. She stood by the grave and continued to berate the pagans, who proceeded to stone her to death. At once God sent an earthquake with lightning and thunder, and a large number of pagans perished; and from that time on they did not harm those who came to the virgin's tomb. The saint's parents and relatives, watching beside her grave on the eighth day, saw a chorus of angels clothed in shining gold garments, and in their midst Agnes, similarly clad and with a lamb whiter than snow standing at her right hand. Agnes consoled them: "Do not mourn my death but rejoice and be glad with me, because I now have a throne of light amidst all these holy ones." In memory of this, the octave of the feast of Saint Agnes is observed.

Constance, Constantine's daughter and a virgin, was stricken with leprosy, and when she heard of the vision just described, she went to the saint's grave. While praying there she fell asleep and saw Saint Agnes, who said to her: "Be constant, Constance! If you believe in Christ, you will be freed of your disease." Awakening at the sound of the voice she found herself completely cured. She received baptism and had a basilica erected over the saint's grave. There she continued to live a virginal life and by her example gathered many virgins around her.

Paulinus, a priest serving the church of Saint Agnes, was tormented by a violent temptation of the flesh and, not wishing to offend God, sought permission of the supreme pontiff to contract marriage. The pope, knowing the priest's goodness and simplicity, gave him a ring set with an emerald and ordered him to go before a beautiful statue of Saint Agnes that stood in her church, and to command her, in the pope's name, to allow herself to become his betrothed. When the priest delivered this order, the statue immediately extended the ring finger, accepted the ring, and withdrew the hand, and the priest was delivered of his temptation. It is said that this ring can still be seen on the finger of the statue. Elsewhere, however, we read that the pope told a priest that he wanted him to commit himself to a certain spouse, to take care of her and nourish her, and that this spouse was the church of Saint Agnes, which was falling into ruins. The pope gave him a ring that would mark his espousal to the aforesaid statue, and the statue extended its finger and withdrew it. Thus the priest espoused the statue.

In his book *On Virgins*, Ambrose says of Saint Agnes: "The old, the young, the children sing of her! No one is more worthy of praise than the one who is praised by all! All men are her heralds, who by speaking of her proclaim her martyrdom. Marvel, all of you, that she stood forth as God's witness although at her age she could not yet decide about herself! So it came about that what she said regarding God was believed, although what she said about man was not yet believed, because what is beyond nature is from the author of nature. This is a new kind of martyrdom! One hardly capable of suffering is already ripe for victory, one unready to fight is yet able to win the crown, one masters virtue before reaching the age of judgment! Bride hastens not to the bridal chamber as the virgin marched to the place of torture, joyous her approach, swift her stride!" And, from Ambrose's Preface: "Saint Agnes, disdaining the advantages of noble birth, merited heavenly honors; caring nothing for what human society desires, she won the society of the eternal king; accepting a precious death for professing Christ, she at the same time was conformed to his likeness."

25. Saint Vincent

The name Vincent may be interpreted as burning up vice, or as conquering fires, or as holding on to victory. Saint Vincent did indeed burn up vices, getting rid of them by mortification of the flesh; he conquered the fires of torture by dauntless endurance of pain and held on to victory over the world by despising it. He conquered three things that were in the world, namely, false errors, impure loves, and worldly fears, which he overcame by wisdom, purity, and constancy. In this regard Augustine says: "The martyrdoms of the saints have taught and do teach us how to conquer the world, with all its fallacies, fervors, and fears."

It is said that Augustine compiled an account of Vincent's passion. Prudentius celebrated it in verse.

Vincent, noble by birth and nobler by his faith and religious devotion, was deacon to Valerius the bishop.[1] Since he was readier of speech than the bishop, Valerius entrusted his office of preaching to the deacon and devoted himself to prayer and contemplation. The two were brought to Valencia by order of Dacian the governor and held in harsh confinement. Then, when he supposed that they were almost dead from hunger, he ordered them brought into his presence. When he found them in good health and spirits, he was angry and burst out: "What do you say for yourself, Valerius, you who act contrary to the rulers' decrees in the name of religion?" Valerius was hesitant in answering, and Vincent said to him: "Venerable father, don't mutter to yourself as if you were feebleminded, but speak out loud and clearly! Or, holy father, if you so command, I will undertake to reply to this judge." "My dear son," said the bishop, "I had long since commissioned you to speak for me; and now I leave it to you to answer for the faith in which we stand." Vincent then turned to Dacian and said: "What you have said comes down to our denying our faith; but know that for right-thinking Christians it is wicked and blasphemous to repudiate the worship of God!"

Wrathful, Dacian ordered the bishop to be sent into exile. On the other hand Vincent, that contumacious and presumptuous youth, had to be made an example that would put fear into others, so by the governor's command he was stretched on the rack and torn limb from limb. When he had been thus mutilated, Dacian said to him: "Tell me, Vincent, how does your miserable body look to you now?" But the saint, smiling, replied: "Indeed, this is what I have

[1] Of Saragossa.

always longed for!" Angrier than ever, the governor began to threaten him with every sort of torture unless he yielded to his commands, but Vincent exclaimed: "O happy me! The harder you try to frighten me, the more you begin to do me favors! Up, then, wretch, and indulge your malicious will to the full! You will see that by God's power I am stronger in being tortured than you are in torturing me!"

At this the governor began to shout and whip his brutal servants on with words and blows, whereupon Vincent taunted him: "The way you talk, Dacian! What you're saying proves me right and my torturers wrong!" At this the governor, beside himself with rage, called out to the ruffians: "Miserable wretches, you're getting nowhere! Get on with it! You've been able to torture parricides and adulterers into admitting anything and everything, yet this Vincent all alone has withstood everything you tried!" Challenged, the torturers drove iron hooks into the saint's sides so that the blood spurted from his whole body and the entrails hung out between the dislocated ribs.

Now Dacian spoke: "Have pity on yourself, Vincent! Recover your splendid youth and be spared further torments!" "You venomous tongue of the devil," Vincent retorted, "I have no fear of your torments! The only thing I do fear is that you pretend to want to have mercy on me. Indeed the more wrathful I see you, the greater and fuller is my rejoicing! Don't forgo a single jot or tittle of your tortures . . . then you will have to admit yourself defeated in all of them!"

So he was taken down from the rack and carried to a gridiron with a fire under it. The saint reproached the torturers for being too slow and hastened ahead of them toward the suffering that awaited him. Willingly mounting the grill he was seared, singed, and roasted, and iron hooks and red-hot spikes were driven into his body. Wound was piled upon wound, and, as the flames spread, salt was thrown on the fire so that the hissing flames could make the wounds more painful. The weapons of torture tore past his joints and into his belly, so that the intestines spilled out from his body. Yet with all this he remained unmovable and, turning his eyes toward heaven, prayed to the Lord.

When his men reported this to Dacian, he said: "Too bad! You're beaten so far, but now let us keep him alive and make him suffer longer! Shut him up in the darkest of dungeons, cover the floor with sharp fragments for him to lie on, shackle him to a post, leave him without any sort of human consolation, and when he is dead, let me know." The heartless knaves carry out the wishes of their still more heartless master. But behold! The King for whom the soldier suffers commutes his suffering to glory. The darkness of the dungeon is dispelled by dazzling light, the sharpness of the potsherds is changed into the softness of flowers, the shackles fall from his feet, the saint enjoys the solace of angels; and when he walks on the flowers and joins in the angels' chant, the lovely melody and the wonderful perfume of the flowers spread abroad. The guards are terrified by what they witness through the cracks in the dungeon walls, and are converted to the faith.

Hearing what had happened, Dacian, in a fury, said: "Now what more can we do to him? See, he has bested us! Let him be transferred to a couch and laid on soft pillows. We must not make him ever more glorious by having him die in torment, but after he is refreshed, let him be punished and tortured again!" So Vincent was carried to a soft couch, but after he had rested there for a short while, suddenly he breathed his last. This was about the year A.D. 287, in the reign of Diocletian and Maximian.

When this news came to him, Dacian, seeing himself thus defeated, was thunderstruck. "I was not able to break him while he was alive," he mused, "but I can still punish him now that he is dead, and so ease the pain I feel and claim the victory after all!" He gave orders to expose the saint's body in an open field to be devoured by bird and beast, but it was quickly surrounded by a guardian band of angels and no animal could reach it. Then a crow, voracious by nature, attacked birds bigger than himself and drove them away with the beating of his wings; and when a wolf came up, the crow chased him by biting him and cawing loudly. Then the bird lighted and turned his head toward the body, staring at it fixedly as if marveling at the guard of angels.

Learning of the latest events, Dacian said: "I can see that I can't take his measure even now that he's dead!" But he ordered the corpse to be weighted down with a huge millstone and cast into the sea, so that what could not be consumed by earthbound beasts might at least be devoured by marine monsters. Sailors therefore transported the body far out to sea and threw it overboard, but the corpse returned to the shore faster than the sailors could get there. Then Vincent revealed its whereabouts to a certain lady, who, with some others, found it and gave it honorable burial.

Of this martyr Augustine says: "Blessed Vincent was victorious in words, victorious in pain, victorious in confessing his faith, victorious in tribulation, victorious burned, victorious submerged, victorious ashore, victorious in death." Augustine also says: "He was stretched and twisted to make him suppler, scourged to make him learn better, pummeled to make him more robust, burned to make him cleaner." Ambrose in his Preface says of him: "Vincent is racked, beaten, scourged and burned but still unconquered: his courageous stance for the holy Name is unshaken, the fire of zeal heats him more than the hot iron, he is more bound by the fear of God than by fear of the world, he is determined to please God rather than the judge, he longs to die to the world rather than to God." And Augustine again: "We are confronted with a wondrous play—an iniquitous judge, a bloodthirsty torturer, a martyr unconquered, a contest between cruelty and piety."

Prudentius, who shone during the reign of Theodosius the Elder which began in A.D. 387, says that Vincent replied to Dacian: "Torments, dungeons, iron claws, fiery spikes, and death, the ultimate pain—all this is play to Christians." Then Dacian said: "Bind him, bend him, twist his arms, pull him apart until the joints of his limbs snap and break and through the wounds the palpitation of his liver can be seen." This soldier of God laughed, mocking the bloody hands that could not force the iron claws still deeper into his limbs. When he lay in the dungeon, an angel said to him: "Get up, glorious martyr, stand up fearless and be counted our comrade in the angelic troop. O soldier most unconquerable, stronger than the strongest, the cruel, bitter tormentors themselves fear you, their conqueror!" Prudentius exclaims: "O renowned above all, you have won the palm of a double victory, you have gained two laurel crowns together!"

---

26. Saint Basil, Bishop

Basil was a venerable bishop and an eminent doctor of the Church. His life was written by Amphilochius, bishop of Iconium.

Basil's great holiness was made manifest in a vision granted to a hermit named Ephrem, who, being rapt in ecstasy, saw a column of fire the tip of which touched heaven, and heard a voice from above saying: "Basil is as great as the immense column you see before you." Ephrem therefore went into the city on the feast of the Epiphany because he wanted to look upon this great man. When he saw the bishop clothed in shining white vestments, moving solemnly in procession with his clergy, he said to himself: "I know now that I have gone to all this trouble for nothing! This man, who enjoys such honor, certainly cannot be the great saint I expected to see! We who have borne the burden of the day and the heats are not so rewarded, whereas this man, with all his honors and his throng of attendants, is a column of fire. . . . I wonder!"

Basil knew in spirit what was going through Ephrem's mind and had the hermit brought before him; and when he came into the bishop's presence, he saw a tongue of flame coming out of his mouth as he spoke. "Truly Basil is great," Ephrem exclaimed, "truly Basil is a column of fire, truly the Holy Spirit speaks through his mouth!" And to the bishop Ephrem said: "I beg of you, my lord, to obtain for me the ability to speak Greek." "You have asked for something very difficult," Basil replied. Nevertheless he prayed for the hermit, who at once began to speak in Greek.

There was another hermit who, seeing Basil somewhere in procession in his pontifical robes, looked down on him, thinking in his heart that the bishop took much pleasure in such pomp. And a voice spoke to him, saying: "You there, you have more delight in stroking your cat's tail than Basil takes in his accoutrements!"

Emperor Valens, who was partial to the Arians, confiscated a church that belonged to the Catholics and gave it to the heretics. Basil went to the emperor and said: "Your majesty, it is written that the honor of the king loves judgment and the judgment of the king loves justice. Why then has your heart ordered that the Catholics be excluded from their church and it be given to Arians?" "So here you are, Basil," the emperor retorted, "shaming me again! This is unworthy of you!" Basil replied: "What is worthy of me is to die, if I must, for justice!"

Then Demosthenes, who was in charge of the emperor's table and was also a partisan of the Arians, spoke in defense of the heretics and treated the bishop insolently. "Your business is to see that the king's meals are well prepared," Basil answered, "and not to cook up divine dogmas!" The steward, in confusion, had no more to say.

Valens now addressed the bishop: "Basil, go and give judgment in this case, but do not be swayed by immoderate love of the people." So Basil went before the Catholics and Arians and proposed that the doors of the church be closed and sealed with the seal of each party, and that the church would belong to the party at whose prayer the doors opened. This satisfied everybody. The Arians then prayed for three days and three nights, but when they came to the church the next morning, the doors were not opened. Then Basil led a procession to the church, prayed, gave the doors a light blow with his pastoral crook, and said: "Lift up your heads, O ancient doors, that the king of glory may come in!"[1] The doors flew open at once, all the people went in, thanking God, and the church was returned to the Catholics.

As we read in the *Tripartite History*, Valens promised great rewards to Basil if the latter would come around to his way of thinking, but the bishop said: "That sort of promise might beguile children, but those who are nourished with the words of God do not allow one syllable of the divine dogmas to be altered." The emperor was indignant, the same history tells us, and prepared to write a decree sentencing the bishop to exile; but first one pen, then a second, then a third broke in his hand, and the hand began to tremble violently. The emperor gave up and destroyed the decree.

A highly respected man named Heradius had an only daughter whom he intended to consecrate to the Lord, but the devil, foe of the human race, got wind of this and inflamed one of Heradius's slaves with love for the girl. The man, knowing that as a slave he could not possibly win the embraces of so noble a lady, turned to a sorcerer and promised him a lot of money if he could advance his suit. The sorcerer told him: "I can't do that, but, if you wish, I'll send you to the devil my master, and if you do as he tells you, you will get what you desire." The young man said: "I'll do it!" Therefore the soothsayer wrote a letter

[1] Ps. 24:9 (RSV).

to the devil and sent it by the hand of the slave. The letter read: "Since it behooves me, my lord, with care and dispatch to draw people away from the Christian religion and attract them to your service so that you may grow day by day, I am sending you this youth who is burning with desire for a certain young woman. I ask that he may have his wish, so that in this individual I may gain glory and may be able to win over others to you."

When he gave the letter to the slave, he said: "Go and stand on the tomb of a heathen at midnight and cry out to the demons. Hold this letter up in the air, and they will come right away!" So the youth went and summoned the demons, throwing the letter into the air. In an instant the prince of darkness, surrounded by a swarm of demons, was at hand; and when he had read the letter, he asked: "Do you believe in me, that I can bring about what you want?" "I believe, my lord!" he answered. The devil: "And do you renounce your Christ?" The slave: "I renounce him!" "You Christians are a perfidious lot," the devil retorted. "Sometimes when you need me, you come to me. Then, when your wish is gratified, you deny me and turn to your Christ; and he, out of the abundance of his clemency, takes you back! But if you want me to fulfill your desire, write me a script in your own hand, in which you profess to renounce Christ, your baptism, and the Christian faith; to be my servant; and to be condemned with me at the Last Judgment."

The slave wrote as directed, repudiating Christ and indenturing himself to the service of the devil. At once his new master called up the spirits who were in charge of fornication, and commanded them to go to the aforesaid maiden and set her heart afire with love for the slave. They carried out his orders so thoroughly that the girl threw herself sobbing on the ground and cried out to her father: "Have pity on me, father, have pity on me! I am sorely tormented by my love for one of our slaves! Show me your fatherly love, and wed me to this man whom I love and for love of whom I suffer torture! Otherwise you will shortly see me dead and will have to account for me on the Day of Judgment!"

Her father wailed aloud and said: "Oh, wretched me! What has happened to my poor child? Who has stolen my treasure? Who has put out the soft light of my eyes? I had hoped to join you to your heavenly spouse, and counted on winning my salvation through you, and here you are, maddened by a lascivious love! O my daughter, let me join you to the Lord as I had planned! Do not drive my old age to the netherworld with grief!" The girl, however, continued to cry out: "Either grant my wish quickly, father, or you will see me dead very soon!" She was weeping bitterly and almost raving; and finally her father, in the depths of desolation and being badly advised by his friends, gave in to her wish, had her married to the slave, and handed over all he owned to her, saying: "Be on your way, my poor, poor daughter!"

Now, while the couple had made their home together, the young man did not go to church or make the sign of the cross, nor did he commend himself to God in any way. Some of their acquaintances noticed this and said to his wife:

"Do you know that your husband, whom you chose for yourself, is not a Christian and never enters a church?" When she heard this, she was filled with dread, threw herself to the ground, tore her flesh with her fingernails, beat her breast, and said: "O wretched me! Why was I born, and when I was born, why did not death take me at once?" She told her husband what she had heard, and he declared that there was not a word of truth in it; what she had been told was entirely false. "If you want me to believe you," she said, "you and I will go to church together tomorrow!"

Seeing that he could no longer hide the truth, the former slave then told his wife the whole story from the beginning, and the young woman groaned aloud. Then she hurried to blessed Basil and told him all that had happened to her husband and to herself. Basil summoned the husband, heard the story from him, and asked: "My son, do you want to turn back to God?" "I want to, my lord," he answered, "but I can't! "I made my profession to the devil, renounced Christ, put my renunciation in writing, and gave it to the devil."

"Don't worry, my son!" said Basil. "The Lord is kind and will accept you as a penitent." He laid his hands on the youth and made the sign of the cross on his forehead. Then he shut him in a cell for three days, after which he visited him and asked him how things were with him. "I can't stand it, my lord," he said. "They shout at me and terrorize me and attack me! They hold up my script as an excuse for their treatment, saying: 'You came to us, not we to you!'" "Don't be afraid!" Basil said. "Just believe!" He gave him a little food, again made the sign of the cross on his forehead, closed his cell, and prayed for him. A few days later he visited him and said: "How are things now, my son?" "I still hear their shouting and their threats, father," the man answered, "but I no longer see them." Basil again gave him food and blessed him, closed the door, and continued to pray for him. After a number of days he went back and asked: "How now?" The young man replied: "I'm doing well, O saint of God! Today I saw you in a vision, fighting for me and beating the devil!"

The bishop then led him out of his cell, summoned all the clergy and religious and the whole populace, and urged all to pray for the man. Then he took him by the hand and led him to the church. There the devil came on with a horde of demons and, though invisible, took hold of the slave and tried to tear him away from the bishop's grasp. The young man called out: "Saint of God, help me!" But the evil one assaulted him with such force that in dragging the one he wanted he was also pulling the saint along. Basil said to him: "Most wicked spirit, is your own damnation not enough for you, that you try to bring down God's handiwork with you?" "You wrong me, Basil!" said the devil. "I did not go after him, it was he who came to me! He denied his Christ and made his profession to me, and I have it in his own handwriting!" Basil answered: "We will not stop praying until you give up the script." And as Basil prayed and held up his hands to heaven, the script, carried down by the breeze, came and settled in Basil's hands as all looked on. He caught it and asked the youth: "Do you recognize this writing, brother?" "Yes, it is my own hand," he replied. Whereupon Basil destroyed the script, led him into the church, made him worthy to receive the sacrament, instructed him and gave him rules for right living, and restored him to his wife.

There was a woman who had many sins on her conscience and had written them down on paper; at the end of the list she added one sin more serious than the others. Then she gave the list to blessed Basil, asking him to pray for her and by his prayers to wipe out the sins. So he prayed and, when he opened the paper, found that all the sins were deleted except the most serious one. The woman said to Basil: "Take pity on me, servant of God, and beg forgiveness of that sin as you obtained it for the rest."

The bishop said to her: "Leave me, woman, because I am a sinful man and need forgiveness as much as you do!" When she insisted, however, he told her: "Go to that holy man Ephrem, and he will be able to obtain what you are asking for." So she went to the holy man Ephrem, and when she told him why she had come, he said: "Leave me, woman, because I am a sinful man, and go back to Basil, my daughter, and he, the one who obtained pardon for the rest of your sins, will be able to do the same for this one. But hurry, if you are to find him still alive!"

The woman came to the city only to find Saint Basil being carried to his tomb. She followed, however, and began to call out: "Let God look upon us and judge between you and me, because you, though you could have won God's mercy for me, sent me off to someone else!" Then she threw her paper on the bier. A moment later it fluttered down to her, and when she unfolded it, she saw that that sin had been completely deleted. So she, and all who were present, gave heartfelt thanks to God.

Before the man of God departed from his body but while he was seriously ill with the malady of which he was to die, he called for a Jew named Joseph, a man highly skilled in the art of medicine, as though he needed the physician's services. Basil loved this man dearly because he foresaw that he was to convert the Jew to the Christian faith. However, as soon as Joseph took the bishop's pulse, he knew that he was at death's door and said to those in attendance: "Get ready whatever is necessary for his burial, because his death is imminent."

Basil heard this and said to Joseph: "You don't know what you're saying!" Joseph answered him: "Believe me, my lord, as surely as the sun will set this afternoon, so surely will your light go out today!" Basil: "And if I do not die today, what will you say?" Joseph: "But that is not possible, my lord!" Basil: "And if I survive till tomorrow at the sixth hour, what will you do?" Joseph: "If you are still alive at that hour, I will be the one to die." Basil: "Yes, may you die to sin, but live to Christ!" Joseph: "I know what you mean. If you survive till that hour, I will do what you are exhorting me to do."

Then blessed Basil, although by the law of nature he should have died within minutes, besought the Lord to grant him a delay, and he lived to the ninth hour the next day. Joseph was amazed when he saw this and believed in Christ; and

Basil, overcoming the weakness of the body by the power of his spirit, rose from his bed, went to the church, and baptized the Jew with his own hands. Then he went back to his bed and joyfully yielded up his soul to God. He flourished about A.D. 370.

---

27. Saint John the Almsgiver

John the Almsgiver held the office of patriarch of Alexandria. One night while he was at prayer, he saw in a vision a very beautiful maiden standing by him, wearing a crown of olive leaves. Seeing her he was astonished and asked her who she was. "I am Pity," she said, "and it is I that brought the Son of God down from heaven. Take me for your spouse and all will be well with you." John saw that the olive crown represented pity and compassion, and from that day on he became so compassionate that he was called *Eleymon*, the compassionate, the almsgiver. He always called the poor his masters, as the Hospitalers to this day call the poor their masters. He therefore met with his serving people and said to them: "Go through the city and make me a list of my masters, down to the last one." They did not understand what he meant, so he said: "Those whom you call the poor, the beggars, they are the ones I declare are our masters and helpers, for they are able to help us to get to heaven."

To encourage people to give alms he used to tell them that once some poor men were warming themselves in the sun, and they began to talk about those who gave alms, praising the good and reviling the bad. There was a certain Peter, a tax-collector, very rich and powerful but utterly pitiless toward the poor. When they came to his door, he drove them away angrily, and not one of them could be found who had ever had an alms from him. Then one of these men said: "What will you give me if I get something from him today?" They made a wager, and he went to Peter's house and begged for an alms. Peter came home at that moment and saw the poor man standing at his door. Just then his slave was carrying some wheaten loaves into the house, and Peter, finding no stone to throw, snatched up a loaf and hurled it angrily at the beggar. The man caught it and hurried back to his companions, showing them the alms that he had received from the tax-collector's hand.

Two days later the rich man lay mortally ill and saw himself in a vision standing before the Judge. Some black men were heaping up his evil deeds on one side of the scale, while opposite stood some white-clothed persons who looked sad because they could find nothing to put on their side. Then one of them said: "True, we have nothing but one wheaten loaf, which he gave, reluctantly, to Christ two days ago." He put the loaf on the scale, and it seemed to balance all the bad deeds on the other side. The white-robed angels said to him: "Add something to this loaf, or the demons will have you!"

The tax-collector woke up and found that he was cured of his illness, and said: "If the one loaf that I threw at that man in anger could do me so much good, how much more would it do for me if I gave all I have to the needy!" Then, one day when he was walking along dressed in his finest garments, a man who had lost all he had in a shipwreck asked him for something to wear. At once he took off his expensive cloak and gave it to the man, who took it and sold it as soon as he could. When the tax-collector went home and saw his cloak hanging in its place in the house, he was so sad that he could not eat, and said: "I was not worthy to have a needy man keep something to remember me by." But then while he was asleep he saw a personage more brilliant than the sun, with a cross on his head and wearing the cloak that he, Peter, had given to the man in need. "Why are you weeping, Peter?" the apparition asked. When Peter explained the cause of his sadness, the other asked: "Do you recognize this cloak?" "Yes, Lord," he answered. "I have been wearing it," the Lord told him, "since you gave it to me, and I thank you for your kindness, because I was freezing from the cold and you covered me."

Peter came to himself, began to bless the poor, and said: "As God lives, I will not die until I have become one of them!" He therefore gave all he had to those in need, then called in his notary and said to him: "I'm going to tell you a secret, and if you breathe a word of it or if you don't heed what I say, I'll sell you to the barbarians!" Then he gave him ten pounds of gold and said: "Go to the holy city and buy goods for yourself, and sell me to some Christian stranger and give the proceeds to the poor!" The notary refused, but Peter told him: "If you don't listen to me, I'll sell you to the heathens!" So the notary took him as one of his slaves, clothed in rags, to a silversmith, sold him for thirty pieces of silver, took the money, and distributed it to the poor.

Peter, now a slave, did the most menial work, and was treated with contempt and pushed and struck by the other slaves, who even called him a fool. The Lord, however, appeared to him frequently and consoled him, showing him the clothing and other gifts given to the poor. Meanwhile the emperor and everyone else bemoaned the loss of so valuable a man. Then some of his former neighbors came from Constantinople to visit the holy places and at one point were invited by Peter's master to be his guests. While they were at dinner, they whispered to each other: "That servant looks like our friend Peter, doesn't he?" And as they stared at him curiously, one said: "It certainly is Peter, and I'll get up and hold him!" But Peter sensed what was going on and got away. The doorman was a deaf-mute who opened the door only at a signal, but Peter ordered him to open, not by signs but speaking. The man heard at once and received the power of speech, answered Peter, opened the door, and let him out. Then, going into the house, he said, to the surprise of all who heard him speak: "That slave who worked in the kitchen has gone out and run away, but wait! He must be a servant of God, because when he said to me, 'I tell you, open!' a flame came out of his mouth and touched my tongue and ears, and right away I could hear and speak!" They all jumped up and ran after Peter, but could not find him. Then everyone who belonged to that house did penance for the vile way they had treated so good a man.

A monk named Vitalis wanted to test Saint John to see whether he would listen to rumors and be easily scandalized, so he went into the city and got a list of all the prostitutes. He went to them one by one and said to each one: "Give me this night, and don't do any other business." Then he went to the woman's house, knelt in a corner, and stayed there praying for the woman. In the morning he left, forbidding everyone to reveal what he was doing. One of the women, however, did make his way of life known, and at once, in answer to the old man's prayer, she began to be tormented by a demon. All the others said to her: "You're getting what you deserve from God because you told a lie! That scoundrel went in to you to commit fornication and for nothing else!"

That evening Vitalis said to all who were listening: "I've got to go, because there's a certain lady who's expecting me!" To many who blamed him for doing wrong he replied: "Have I not a body like everyone else? Or is God angry only with monks? Monks are men just like the rest!" But some said to him: "Go ahead and take one wife, father, but stop wearing that habit and giving scandal to others!" Vitalis, pretending to be angry, said: "I won't listen to you, leave me alone! Anyone who wants to be scandalized, let him be scandalized and let him beat his head against the wall! Did God appoint you to judge me? Go and mind your own business! You won't have to account for me!" He said these things at the top of his voice, and complaints reached blessed John, but God hardened John's heart so that he did not credit what he heard. Vitalis pleaded with God to reveal to someone after his death what he had been doing, so that it should not be imputed as sin to those who were scandalized by his actions. And in fact, Vitalis brought many of those women to conversion and found places in a monastery for a number of them.

One morning, however, as he was leaving the house of one of the prostitutes, a man on his way in to commit sin met him and slapped his face, saying: "Isn't it time, you wretch, for you to mend your ways and quit your filthy conduct?" Vitalis answered: "Believe me, you'll get from me such a slap that all Alexandria will come running!" And so it happened . . . Some time later the devil in the guise of a Moor gave the man a blow, saying: "This is the slap that Father Vitalis sends you!" And at once a demon began to torment him, so that all came running at the sound of his cries; but he repented, and was set free by the prayer of Vitalis. And when the man of God felt his death approaching, he left a written admonition: "Judge not before the time!" The women confessed what he had done, and all glorified God, blessed John first of all, who said: "Would that I had received the slap that he received!"

A poor man in pilgrim's dress came to John and begged an alms. John called his steward and said: "Give him six gold pieces!" The man took the money, went away and changed his clothes, came back, and again begged alms of the patriarch, who called his steward and said: "Give him six gold pieces!" After the beggar had left, the steward told the patriarch: "That's the second time today. All he did was change his clothes, but because you asked, I gave." Blessed John pretended not to know this. The mendicant, however, changed clothes again and begged alms of John a third time. The steward touched the patriarch's arm and nodded that this was the same man. Blessed John responded: "Go and give him twelve gold pieces! It may be my Lord Jesus Christ, testing me to see whether this man can go on asking more than I can go on giving!"

One time a certain high official wanted to invest some of the church's money in trade, but the patriarch firmly refused to give his consent because he intended to dispense the money to the poor. The two argued the point acrimoniously and parted in anger. But as the day waned, the patriarch sent word by his archpriest to the gentleman, saying: "My lord, the sun is setting." Hearing this, the official burst into tears and came to John, begging his pardon.

A nephew of John had been grossly insulted by a shopkeeper. He complained tearfully to the patriarch and refused to be comforted, and the patriarch responded: "How could anyone dare to contradict you or say a word against you? Trust my insignificant self, my child! This very day I will do something to that man that will make all Alexandria wonder!" The boy took comfort at what he heard, thinking that his relative would have the shopkeeper soundly whipped. The patriarch, seeing that the youngster was calmer, clasped him to his bosom, kissed him, and said: "My son, if you are really the nephew of my humble self, prepare to be insulted and beaten by everybody! True kinship is not determined by flesh and blood but by strength of mind." Quickly therefore he sent for the shopkeeper and dispensed him from all rents and payments. All who heard about this marveled at it and understood what John had meant when he said he would do something to the man that would make all Alexandria wonder.

The blessed John learned of the custom that as soon as an emperor was crowned, tomb-builders should take four or five small samples of marble of different colors, call upon the emperor, and say: "Out of what marble or metal does your majesty desire that your tomb be built?" John followed the custom and gave orders for the construction of his sepulcher, but prescribed that the monument was to remain unfinished until his death, and further ordered that at any celebration or festivity, some of those present with him and his clergy should come and say to him: "My lord, your tomb is unfinished. Give the orders for its completion, because you know not at what hour the thief may come."

A certain rich man saw that blessed John's couch was covered with cheap, thin bedclothes because he gave away better ones to the poor, so he bought a very costly quilt and gave it to the patriarch. John, finding it over him, could not sleep all night, thinking that three hundred of his masters could be covered for the price of this one bedcover; and he lamented all night long, saying: "How many lay down tonight without supper, how many lie in the public square soaked with rain, how many are there whose teeth chatter with the cold? And here you are, fed with fine fat fish and resting in your big bed with all your sins on top of you, warming yourself with a bedcover worth thirty pieces of silver! Humble John will not be so covered another time!" So the next morning he had the article sold and the price distributed to the poor. His wealthy friend learned of this, bought the quilt back, and gave it to blessed John, asking him not to sell it this time but to cover himself with it. John accepted it but ordered it to be sold and the proceeds to be passed on to his masters. The rich man again went and bought back the coverlet, took it to John, and said to him with a laugh: "Let's see who will give up first, you with your selling or I with my buying back!" In this way the saint gently plucked the rich man, so to speak, and told him that one might thus rob the rich with the intention of benefiting the poor without committing a sin, because each party gained thereby—the one because he was saving souls, the others because they received so great a reward.

In his effort to motivate people to give alms generously, blessed John often told the story of Saint Serapion. Serapion had just given away his coat to a poor man when he met another one who was suffering from the cold. To him he gave his shirt and sat nearly naked with his gospel book in his hand. A passerby asked him: "Father, who robbed you?" Serapion showed him the gospel book and said: "This did." But later, seeing another poor man, he sold the book and gave him the price. Somebody asked him where his gospel book was, and he replied: "The Gospel commands us, 'Sell all you have and give to the poor,' and I had the Gospel here and sold it as it commanded."

Another time when someone asked blessed John for an alms and he ordered five pence to be given to him, the man was indignant that more had not been given, and burst out with obscenities and cursed the patriarch to his face. His attendants wanted to rush at the beggar and give him a thrashing, but John would have none of it and said: "Let him be, brothers, let him curse me. Here I am, sixty years old, insulting Christ with my misdeeds, and shall I not bear with one curse from this man?" And he had his purse placed open in front of the fellow so that he could take from it as much as he wanted.

People were going out of the church after the reading of the Gospel and standing around at the doors, exchanging idle talk. Once, after the reading, the patriarch went out with them and sat down in their midst. They all seemed surprised at this, but he said to them: "My children, where the sheep are, there should the shepherd be! Therefore either you go in and I will go in with you, or you stay out here and I will do the same." He did this just once and so taught the people to stay in church.

A young man had run off with a nun, and the clergy denounced him to Saint John, saying that he ought to be excommunicated on the ground that he had lost two souls, his and the nun's. John restrained them, saying: "Not so, my sons, not so! I will show you that you yourselves are committing two sins. The first is that you go against the Lord's commandment, which says, 'Judge not, that you may not be judged.' The second, because you do not know for certain that they are still living in sin today and have not repented."

It frequently happened that when blessed John was at prayer and was rapt in ecstasy of spirit, he was heard arguing with God in words like these: "So, good Jesus, let us see which of us outdoes the other—I in giving your gifts away, or you in providing them."

The time came when he was stricken with a high fever and realized that his end was near, and he said: "I thank you, O God, because you have listened to my indigence begging your bounty that when I die I should be found to possess no more than a single penny; and I now order that that penny be given to the poor." His venerable body was laid in a tomb in which the bodies of two other bishops had been buried, and in a wonderful way those bodies made room for Saint John and left him a place between them.

Shortly before he died, a woman had committed a sin so heinous that she dared not confess it to anyone ever, but John told her at least to write the sin down (since she knew how to write), seal the paper, and bring it to him, and he would pray for her. She agreed to this, wrote out the sin, carefully put her seal on the paper, and handed it over to the saint, but a few days later he sickened and fell asleep in the Lord. When the woman heard that he was dead, she feared that she would now be shamed and disgraced, thinking that he would have entrusted her paper to someone and that it would fall into the hands of some stranger. She approached Saint John's tomb and there, with floods of tears, cried out, saying: "Alas, I thought I would avoid dishonor, and now I am disgraced in the eyes of all!" She wept bitterly and asked Saint John to show her where he had put her writing; and behold, Saint John came forth from the tomb in full pontifical regalia and borne up on either side by the two bishops who lay at rest with him. He said to the woman: "Why do you come and disturb us? Why do you not leave me and these saints who are with me . . . why do you not leave us in peace? Look! Our stoles are wet with your tears!" Then he held out her writing, sealed as it had been before, and said: "There is your seal! Open the paper and read it!" She opened the paper and saw that her sin had been completely erased, and that in its place was written, "Because of John, my servant, your sin is wiped out." So the woman poured out her thanks to God, and blessed John returned to the tomb with the other bishops. He flourished about the year of the Lord 605, in the reign of Emperor Phocas.

28. The Conversion of Saint Paul, Apostle

Saint Paul's conversion took place in the same year during which Christ suffered and Stephen was stoned, counting the year not in the normal way from January to December, but simply as a space of twelve months; for Christ suffered on the 25th day of March and Stephen was stoned in the same year on the 3d day of August, while Paul was converted on the 25th day of January.

Why is Paul's conversion celebrated, while that of other saints is not? Three reasons are usually given for this. The first is the example that Paul set: no sinner, no matter how grievous his sin, can despair of pardon when he sees that Paul, whose fault was so great, afterwards became so much greater in grace. The second is the joy of the Church, which had been greatly saddened through his persecution and received so much greater happiness through his conversion. The third is the miracle by which the Lord turned this cruel persecutor into so faithful a preacher.

Paul's conversion was miraculous by reason of the one who brought it about, by reason of the means used to dispose Paul for conversion, and by reason of the subject, Paul himself. Miraculous, first, because the one who converted him was Christ, who showed his marvelous power in what he said: "It is hard for you to kick against the goad,"[1] and in changing Paul so suddenly that, once changed, he replied: "Lord, what do you want me to do?"[2] Augustine comments: "The Lamb that was slain by wolves turns a wolf into a lamb: he who previously spent his fury in persecuting is now ready to obey." Christ also showed his wondrous wisdom, in that he cured Paul of the tumor of pride, offering him the depths of humility, not the heights of majesty. "I who speak to you," he said, "am Jesus of Nazareth, whom you are persecuting." The *Gloss* adds: "He does not call himself God or the Son of God, but says, 'Take upon yourself the depths of my humility and rid your eyes of the scales of pride.'" Moreover, he showed his wondrous forbearance, since he converted Paul at the very moment when Paul, in act and in intention, was persecuting the Christians. Paul's mind was set on evil, since he breathed forth threats and the will to slaughter Christians; what he attempted was perverse, since he went to the high priest, forcing himself, as it were, upon him; and his action was malicious since he was on his way to Damascus to put the Christians in chains and take them bound to Jerusalem. Therefore his journey was utterly wrongful, yet the divine mercy converted him.

[1] Acts 9:5. [2] Acts 9:6.

Second, the conversion was miraculous because of the means used to dispose the one to be converted, namely, the light that made Paul ready for conversion. That light is said to have been sudden, immense, and heaven-sent: "And suddenly a light from heaven shone around him."[3] Paul had three vices, the first being wanton boldness, which he demonstrated by going to the high priests: "He was not summoned," says the *Gloss*, "but went on an impulse, driven by his zeal." His second vice was insolent pride, because he is said to have breathed out threats of violence against the disciples of the Lord. The third was that he understood the Law according to the flesh; so the *Gloss*, commenting on the words "I am Jesus whom you are persecuting," says: "It is I, God of heaven, speaking, whom you, with your Jewish way of judging things, think of as being dead." Therefore the divine light was sudden, in order to frighten the bold one, and immense, to bring the haughty, overbearing one down to lowly humility, and heavenly, to change his fleshly understanding and make it heavenly. Or it could be said that the disposing means was triple—the voice that called out, the shining light, and the display of divine power.

Finally, Paul's conversion was miraculous by reason of the subject in whom it was effected—Paul himself. Three things happened to Paul, outwardly and miraculously: he fell to the ground, he was blinded, and he had neither food nor drink for three days. He was thrown to the ground in order to be straightened up in his perverse intentions. Augustine: "Paul was prostrated in order to be blinded, blinded in order to be changed, changed in order to be sent, and sent in order that he might suffer for the truth." Augustine again: "He was enraged and was crushed in order to become a believer; the wolf was crushed and became a lamb; the persecutor was crushed and became the preacher; the son of perdition was crushed to be brought erect as the vessel of election." He was blinded to be enlightened in his darkened intelligence. Hence it is said that in the three days during which he remained blind, he was taught the Gospel, for he himself testifies that he did not receive it from man nor through a man, but through a revelation of Jesus Christ. Augustine: "I say that Paul was Christ's true fighter, taught by him, anointed by him, crucified with him, and glorious in him. He mortified his body so that the flesh would be ready for the doing of good. His body was thenceforth well disposed to every good work. He knew how to be full and to be hungry, to thirst and to abound; he was at home everywhere and could cope with every situation." Chrysostom: "Tyrants and peoples breathing fury he regarded as so many gnats, death and crucifixions and a thousand tortures were to him child's play and he embraced them willingly. He felt more adorned when bound with chains than if he were crowned with a royal diadem, and he accepted wounds more gladly than others would receive rich gifts." And three things are said to have been in him in contrast to three that

---

[3] Acts 9:3. The whole story of Paul's conversion, and much of the language used here, is found in this chapter.

were in our first parent. Adam stood up against God and Paul prostrated himself on the earth; Adam's eyes were opened and Paul's were blinded; Adam ate forbidden food and Paul abstained from permitted food.

29. Saint Paula

Paula belonged to the high Roman nobility. Saint Jerome wrote her life as follows.[1]

If all the members of my body were turned into tongues and all the skills of the human voice were applied to the task, I still could say nothing worthy of the virtues of the holy and venerable Paula. She was noble by birth but far more noble by her sanctity, powerful earlier by reason of her wealth but later more renowned for her poverty; and I call to witness Jesus and the holy angels, and particularly her own angel, the companion and guardian of this admirable woman, that I say nothing by way of flattery or blandishment, and that what I am about to say in testimony to her virtue falls far short of her deserts. Does my reader want to know Paula's virtues in brief? She left poor all those who belonged to her, she being poorer than any of them. As a jewel of inestimable price shines out among many gems, and as the radiance of the sun dims and darkens the tiny fires of the stars, so she surpassed all others by her humility and made herself least among all in order to be greater than all. The more she lowered herself, the higher she was lifted up by Christ. She hid but was not hidden: by fleeing vain glory she merited the glory that follows virtue like a shadow and evades those who seek it while seeking those who despise it.

Paula was the mother of five children—Blaesilla, over whose death I consoled her in Rome; Paulina, who made Pammachius, her saintly and admirable husband, heir to all her property and projects, for whom I wrote a small book about her death; Eustochium, the daughter who still lives in the Holy Land and is a precious adornment of the Church; Rufina, whose early demise sorely distressed

[1] This chapter is excerpted from Jerome's letter on the life of Saint Paula (cf. Migne, PL 22:878–906). All but a dozen or so words are taken from Jerome: Jacobus extracted paragraphs and snippets sufficient to establish Paula's sanctity by dwelling on the usual virtues—humility, charity, poverty, contemptus mundi, chastity. The "snippets" are often taken out of context, which at times obscures the train of thought. Jerome's "letter" is five or six times as long as Jacobus's chapter, and its rhetorical, eulogistic style is totally foreign to our author.

her mother's loving spirit; and a son, Toxocius. After Toxocius she bore no more children; from this you might understand that she did not wish to engage in conjugal union any longer. After her husband's death she mourned him so much that she almost died of grief, but then turned so ardently to the service of God that she might seem to have desired her spouse's death. And what is there to say about her giving to the poor all the abundant riches and treasures of her grand, noble house?

Paulinus, bishop of Antioch, and another bishop, Epiphanius, came to Rome, and Paula was so impressed by their virtues that she thought of leaving home and country. What more shall I say? She went down to the port, and her brother and close relatives and friends, and, more important than these, her children, followed her and tried to dissuade their most loving mother. Rufina, who was about to be married, held back her tears and begged her mother to wait for her wedding. While the sails were hoisted and the ship, propelled by the rowers, was heading toward the deep, little Toxocius stood on the shore with outstretched, pleading hands. Yet Paula, dry-eyed, looked toward heaven, putting her love of God above her love for her children. She knew not herself as mother in order to prove herself Christ's handmaid. As she fought her grief, her entrails were twisted in pain as if being torn from her body. Her full faith made her able to bear this suffering: more than that, her heart clung to it joyfully, and for love of God she put aside love of sons and daughters. Her only comfort was in Eustochium, who shared her plans and accompanied her on the voyage. The ship put to sea, and while all her fellow passengers were looking back to the shore, Paula looked away so as not to see what she could not see without pain.

The vessel reached port in the Holy Land, and the proconsul of Palestine, who knew her family very well, sent servants ahead to prepare rooms for her in his palace, but she chose a humble cell instead. She visited all the sites where Christ had left traces, with such ardor and zeal that she could hardly leave the first places she saw except that she wanted to hurry on to the others. She prostrated herself in adoration before the cross as if she could see the Lord hanging on it. On her way into the cave of the Resurrection she kissed the stone that the angel had removed from the entrance and, as if thirsting for the yearned-for waters of faith, licked with her tongue the place where the Lord's body had lain. What floods of tears, what storms of sighs, what torrents of grief she poured out there all Jerusalem, indeed the Lord himself whom she besought, can testify.

Next she went to Bethlehem and, entering the Savior's cave, saw the Virgin's sacred refuge; and in my hearing she swore that with the eyes of faith she saw the Infant wrapped in swaddling clothes, whimpering in the manger, the Magi adoring the Lord, the star shining overhead, the virgin mother, the watchful guardian, the shepherds coming in the night to see the word that had come to pass, as though to affirm again the words of John the Evangelist: "In the beginning was the Word, and the Word was with God, and the Word was made flesh." She saw the innocent children slain, Herod raging, Joseph and Mary fleeing to Egypt. Then she spoke with joy mixed with tears: "Hail, Bethlehem, house of bread, where that bread was born which came down from heaven! Hail, Ephrata, most fertile land whose fertility is God! David spoke confidently, saying, 'We will go into his tabernacle; we will adore in the place where his feet stood.' And I, a miserable sinner, am deemed worthy to kiss the crib in which the infant Lord cried, to pray in the cave where the virgin mother brought forth God. Here is my place of rest, because it is my Lord's native place. Here I shall dwell, because my Savior chose it."

Paula abased herself with such humility that someone who wanted to see her because of the renown of her name, seeing her, could not believe this was the woman he sought, but must be the lowest of the maidservants. She was surrounded by crowding choirs of virgins, yet in the way she dressed or spoke or walked, she seemed the least of all. Never, from the time her husband died until the day of her own passing, did she sit at table with any man, though she knew the man was saintly or was in high pontifical station. She did not use the baths unless illness demanded it. Except when beset with high fevers she had no bed craped with soft quilts but took her rest on the hard ground covered with sackcloth—if indeed one can speak of rest when her days and nights were joined together by almost continuous prayer. She wept so bitterly for slight faults that one would have thought her guilty of the grossest crimes; and when we admonished her, as we[2] frequently did, to spare her eyes and save them for reading the gospels, she said: "This face, which against God's command I used to paint with rouges and whiteners and mascaras, deserves to be made ugly! The body that enjoyed so many pleasures ought to be made to suffer! Long laughter must be atoned for by steady weeping, soft linens and costly silks call for the rough feel of the hair shirt as reparation. In the past I did everything to please my husband and our world. Now I want to please Christ."

If, among so many and such great virtues, I should wish to emphasize her chastity, such praise would seem superfluous. While she was still living a worldly life, she set an example for all the matrons of Rome and so conducted herself that even the meanest gossip would not dare to spread a false rumor about her. I admit the error I committed when I rebuked her for her prodigal almsgiving, quoting the words of the apostle: generosity yes, but "I do not mean that others should be eased and you burdened, but that as a matter of equality your abundance at the present time should supply their want, so that their abundance may supply your want."[3] I urged her to use foresight or she might not have anything left to give away, and other similar arguments. Her response was modest, brief, and wisely put: she called the Lord to witness that everything she did was done for his name, and her one wish and vow was that she might die a beggar, unable to leave as much as a penny to her daughter, and that for her burial she might be wrapped in a shroud that was not her own. In conclusion she said: "If I beg I

---

[2] Jerome.   [3] 2 Cor. 8:13–14.

shall find many who will give to me; but if one poor beggar should die because he does not receive from me what I can give him even if I have to use what belongs to someone else, who will be held accountable for his life?"

Paula was unwilling to pour out money for stones that will pass away with the earth and the world, but chose rather to spend it on the living stones that roll around on the earth, out of which, as John says in the Apocalypse, the city of God is built. Except on feast days she used little or no oil in her food, and that gives an idea of her attitude toward drink and fish and milk and honey and eggs and everything else that appeals to the sense of taste—things that some think they are very abstemious in using, and are sure of their virtuousness even while they gorge themselves. I know one scandalmonger (that vilest breed of man) who, as if he were doing a kindness, told Paula that she seemed to some people to be carried away by the ardor of her virtues, and to be out of her mind, and that she should take better care of her brain. To this she replied: "We have become a spectacle to the world, to angels, and to men; we are fools for Christ's sake, but the foolishness of God is wiser than men."[4]

She had founded a monastery for men and handed it over to be ruled by men. She had also gathered together a large number of young women coming from various regions and from the noble, middle, and lowest strata of society. For these women she established three groups and three monasteries, so that they worked and had their meals separately, coming together only for chanting the Psalms and praying. If disputes arose among them, she brought agreement about by the gentleness of her way of speaking. She curbed the fleshly urges of the very young ones by imposing frequent double fasts, preferring to have them suffer in body rather than in spirit. She said that cleanliness of body and dress was uncleanness of the soul, and that the same fault which men of the world regarded as light or of no consequence was, in the monasteries, a very serious matter. When others were ailing, she gave them whatever they wanted, even allowing them to eat meat, whereas if she was ill, she granted herself no such indulgence. In this her treatment was obviously unequal, since she compensated for her clemency to others by her hardness to herself.

What I am about to tell you I saw for myself. One year in the month of July Paula fell into a violent fever. After we had despaired of her life, she began, by God's mercy, to breathe more easily. The physicians determined that to recover her strength she should take a little thin wine, and should not drink water for fear of bringing on dropsy. I secretly asked the holy bishop Epiphanius to admonish or even compel her to drink wine. But she, quick and insightful as she was, saw through the ruse at once and smiled, knowing that what the bishop said came from me. What more is there to tell? When the holy pontiff, after delivering many exhortations, came outside, I asked him how he had fared, and he answered: "I succeeded so well that she almost persuaded me, an old man, not to drink wine!"

[4] 1 Cor. 4:9–10; 1:25.

She bore grief patiently but was stricken by the deaths of those dear to her, particularly of her children; the loss of her spouse and her daughters brought her close to death. She made the sign of the cross on her lips and her breast, hoping by that sign to ease the sorrow she felt as wife and mother, but she was overcome by her emotion, and the mother's inner pain disturbed her believing soul. Conquering by strength of spirit, she was conquered by the fragility of the body.

She had the Holy Scriptures by heart, and while she loved the story they told and called it the foundation of truth, she preferred the spiritual interpretation and made of it the summit of her soul's edification. And I shall say something else, though it may seem unbelievable to the envious. I studied the Hebrew language from adolescence with much toil and sweat, got to know it fairly well, and have kept at it constantly so as not to lose it. Paula wanted to learn Hebrew and did learn it so well that she sang the Psalms in Hebrew and spoke the language without any Latin peculiarities. Even today we see her sainted daughter Eustochium doing the same thing.

Thus far we have sailed with favorable winds, and our lithe ship has glided through the curling waves of the sea, but now rocks and shoals lie ahead for my story. Who indeed could speak without weeping about Paula's last days on earth? She was prostrated by a very serious illness—or better, she was finding what she most longed for, which was to leave us and be united more fully to the Lord. Why do I delay and by delaying make others endure my grief any longer? This most prudent of women felt the approach of death. Parts of her body and limbs were cold, and only the warmth of her soul kept life in her sacred, holy breast. Yet, as though she was on her way to her own and cared no longer about strangers, she kept whispering these verses: "I have loved, O Lord, the beauty of thy house and the place where thy glory dwells," and "How lovely are thy tabernacles, O Lord of hosts! I have chosen to be abject in the house of my God."[5] And when I asked her why she would not speak and did not answer when asked whether she had pain, she replied in Greek that she felt no trouble and saw everything as quiet and tranquil. After that she fell silent and lay with her eyes closed as if to shut out human things. Until she breathed forth her soul, she repeated the same verses, in so low a voice that even bending over to listen we could hardly hear what she was saying.

A great crowd of people from the cities of Palestine came to her funeral. No monk of those living hidden in the desert could bear to stay in his hovel, no virgin could be detained in the secrecy of her cell: all thought it would be a sacrilege not to pay their final duty to so wonderful a woman until she was laid to rest under the church and next to the cave where the Lord was born. Her venerable daughter the virgin Eustochium, like a child being weaned, could hardly be lifted from her mother's body, whose eyes she kissed, to whose cheeks she clung, whose whole body she embraced, with whom she herself wished to be buried. Jesus is witness that to her daughter the mother left not a penny but

[5] Ps. 25(26):8; 83(84):1, 11.

only the care of the poor, the immense multitude of brothers and sisters whom it is hard simply to feed, and impious to turn away.

Farewell, O Paula, and assist with your prayers your worshiper in his extreme old age!

---

30. Saint Julian

Julian, Julianus, begins like *jubilus*, jubilant, and *ana* means upward; so Julian is close to *Jubilans*, one who strives upward toward heaven with jubilation. Or the name comes from *Julius*, one who begins, and *anus*, old man, because in God's service Julian was old in his long-suffering, but one who began by knowing himself.

Julian was bishop of Le Mans. It is said that he was Simon the Leper, whom Christ cured of leprosy and who invited the Lord to a festal meal. After Christ's ascension the apostles ordained Julian as bishop of Le Mans. He was renowned for his many virtues. He raised three dead persons to life and in time went to his rest in peace. He is also said to be the Julian who is invoked by travelers in search of good lodging, for the reason that he welcomed Christ as a guest in his house. But it seems more likely that this was another Julian, namely, the one who killed both his parents unwittingly. The story of this Julian will be told further on.

There was another Julian, this one from Auvergne, noble by birth but more noble by his faith, who out of his desire for martyrdom went so far as to offer himself to the persecutors. Finally the consular official Crispinus sent one of his men to put Julian to death. When Julian got word of it, he jumped up at once, ran out, fearlessly set himself in front of the man who was looking for him, and welcomed the blow that beheaded him. The attackers picked up the sacred head and carried it to Saint Ferreolus, a friend of Julian, threatening him with the same death unless he sacrificed to the gods. He refused. They put him to death and buried Julian's head in one tomb with the body of Ferreolus. Many years later Saint Mamertus, bishop of Vienne, found Saint Julian's head held in Ferreolus's hands: the head was undamaged and free of wounds, as if it had been buried that very day.

Among this saint's many miracles, here is one that is often told. A certain deacon was about to make off with some sheep belonging to Saint Julian's church, and the shepherds tried to stop him in the name of the saint. "Julian doesn't eat sheep!" he retorted. Not long thereafter he was seized with a violent, debilitating fever and admitted that it was the martyr who was burning him. Then he had water splashed over him to cool the heat, but instantly a cloud of smoke and a horrible stench arose from his body. All those who were present fled, and the deacon died shortly afterwards.

Gregory of Tours tells us that there was a peasant who started out to plow his field on a Sunday, but at once the fingers of his right hand stiffened and stuck fast to the handle of the hatchet he used to clean the plowshare. Two years later, however, he prayed in Saint Julian's church and was cured.

There was still another Julian, the brother of Saint Julius. These two brothers went to the most Christian emperor Theodosius, asking his permission to tear down the temples of the idols wherever they found them, and to build churches of Christ. The emperor was pleased to grant their request and wrote a command that everyone should obey them and give them help, under pain of death. So the saintly brothers Julian and Julius were building a church at a place called Gaudianum, and, in obedience to the emperor's command, all who passed that way helped in the work.

It happened that some men were going by with a wagon, and they said to each other: "What excuse can we give these people so as to be able to go on freely and not have to give some work here?" And they concluded: "Let's put one of us into the wagon flat on his back and cover him up with sheets. We'll tell them we have a dead man in the cart, and they'll let us be on our way." So they picked one of their number and put him in the wagon, telling him: "Keep quiet and close your eyes and lie there like a dead man until we are in the clear!" So they covered him over and came to Julian and Julius, servants of God, who said to them: "Good fellows, stop for a bit and give us a hand here!" The men answered: "We can't stop here because we have a dead man in the wagon." Blessed Julian said to them: "What good does it do to tell us such lies?" "We are not lying, sir," they said, "and it's just as we told you!" Saint Julian replied: "So be it! Let things be as you have said."

The men goaded their oxen and moved on, and when they had gone far enough, they stood by the wagon and began to call their companion by name, saying: "Up with you now and drive the oxen, and we'll move along faster!" Getting no answer they nudged him and said: "Stop playing games! Come out and do your job!" When there still was no answer, they pulled off the covers and found him dead. Thereupon such fear penetrated one and all that no one dared to lie to the servant of God from then on.

There was another Julian, who unwittingly killed both his parents. When this Julian, noble by birth, was young, he went out one day to hunt and began to chase a stag whose trail he had picked up. Suddenly, by the will of God, the stag turned to face him and said: "Are you tracking me to kill me, you who are going to kill your father and mother?" Filled with dread at hearing this, and fearing that what he had heard from the stag might indeed happen to him, he left everything and went away secretly. Having reached a very remote region he took service with a prince, and carried on so manfully in wartime and peacetime that the prince dubbed him a knight and gave him a widow, a noblewoman, in marriage, with a castle as dowry.

Meanwhile Julian's parents, deeply saddened by the loss of their son, wandered everywhere in search of him and in time reached the castle where Julian made his home. As it happened, Julian was away, but his wife met them and asked who they were. They told her all about their son, and she realized that they were her husband's father and mother—I think because she had often heard the same story from her spouse. She therefore welcomed them cordially and, for love of them, left her husband's bed to them and slept in another room. In the morning she went to church. Julian, arriving home, went to his bedroom to awaken his wife. Finding a couple asleep in his bed and supposing that they were his wife and her lover, he silently drew his sword and killed them both. Then he went out of the castle and saw his wife on her way home from church. Surprised, he asked her who the couple were whom he had found in his bed, and she said: "They are your parents, they have been looking for you for the longest time, and I settled them in your bed."

At this news Julian almost fainted and, weeping bitterly, said: "Woe is me, wretch that I am, what shall I do now? I have slain my dear, dear parents! See . . . I have tried so hard to escape the stag's prediction, and now I have fulfilled it in this horrible way! But now, sweet sister, farewell! I shall not rest until I know that God will accept my penance!" But his wife responded: "Far be it from me, dearest brother, to desert you and let you go away without me! I have shared your joy, now I shall be with you to share your sorrow!"

They set out together and came to a broad river where many people were in danger of their lives. There they established a very large hospice in which they might work out their penance. They never failed to give transport to any who wished to cross the river, and received all poor folk kindly in their hospice. A long time passed, and one freezing night, when Julian, tired out, was getting some rest, he heard a plaintive voice calling his name and begging in the most doleful tones for transport. Quickly rising and going out, he found the man almost perishing from the cold, carried him into the house, lit a fire, and tried to warm him. But the stranger did not respond, and Julian, fearing that he might die, put him in his own bed and carefully covered him up. In a short while the stranger, who had looked so infirm and almost leprous, rose splendid in midair and said to his host: "Julian, the Lord sent me to tell you that he has accepted your penance, and that both of you will, in a little time, find rest in the Lord." The messenger disappeared, and not long thereafter Julian and his wife, full of good works and almsgiving, went to their eternal rest.

Finally there was another Julian, no saint but a most wicked wrongdoer, namely, Julian the Apostate. This Julian had been a monk and made a great show of religion and piety. A certain woman (as Master John Beleth tells us in his *Summa de officio ecclesiae*), had three jars filled with gold, but she filled the tops of the jars with ashes so as to conceal the gold. Then she entrusted the jars for safekeeping to Julian, whom she regarded as a very holy man, in the presence of several monks, without indicating in any way that there was gold in them. Julian accepted the jars and, finding this large supply of gold in them, stole the treasure and filled the jars with ashes. After a while, when the woman came to reclaim her deposit, he returned to her the jars filled with ashes: but when she looked for the gold, she could not convict him of stealing it, because there was no witness to say that there had been gold; the monks who had been present at the original transfer had seen nothing but ashes. So Julian got the gold, fled to Rome with it, and, by means of it, in time procured the consulship and eventually became emperor.

From childhood Julian had been instructed in the arts of magic, which delighted him, and he had many masters to teach him. We learn from the *Tripartite History* that one day, when he was still a child and his teacher had left him alone, he began to read the incantations of the demons, and a whole horde of demons appeared before him looking like black Ethiopians. Julian, seeing this, made the sign of the cross at once, and the whole crowd of demons vanished. When the master returned and Julian told him what had happened, his teacher explained that the evil spirits particularly hate and fear that sign.

When he acceded to the empire, he remembered this, and, since he intended to use magic to attain his ends, he renounced the Christian faith, destroyed crosses wherever he found them, and persecuted Christians to the full extent of his power, thinking that otherwise the demons would be less likely to obey him. We read in *Lives of the Fathers* that when Julian invaded Persia, he sent a demon to the West to bring back news from there. The demon arrived at a certain place but was immobilized there for ten days because a monk was praying day and night at that same spot. The demon went back having achieved nothing, and Julian asked him: "What took you so long?" The evil spirit answered: "For ten days I was held up by a monk praying out in the open, and, since I could not get past him, I came back empty-handed." This angered the emperor, who declared that when he reached that place, he would have his revenge on the monk. Since the demons had promised Julian a victory over Persia, his soothsayer asked some Christian: "What do you think the son of the carpenter is doing today?" The Christian answered: "Making a coffin for Julian!"

When the emperor had advanced as far as Caesarea of Cappadocia (as we read in a history of Saint Basil and as Fulbert, bishop of Chartres, confirms), Saint Basil met him and sent him four barley loaves as a gift. Julian was offended, disdained to accept the loaves, and in return sent Basil a bundle of hay, with the message: "You have offered us the fodder of irrational animals. Take back what you sent." Basil replied: "We indeed sent you what we ourselves eat, but you have given us what you feed your beasts with." To this, Julian responded angrily: "When I have subjugated Persia, I will raze this city and plow up the land, and it will be called not 'man-bearing' but 'grain-bearing.'"

The following night Basil had a vision in the church of Saint Mary in which he saw a multitude of angels, and in their midst a woman seated on a throne. The woman said to her attendants: "Quickly summon Mercury to me! He shall put to death the apostate Julian, who in his insolent pride blasphemes me and my Son!" This Mercury was a soldier who had been killed by Julian himself for the faith of Christ and was buried in this church. Instantly Saint Mercury, whose arms were preserved nearby, stood at attention and received her orders to prepare to fight. Basil woke up, went to the place where Saint Mercury lay at peace near his arms, opened the tomb, and found neither the body nor the weapons. He questioned the watchman as to whether he had removed anything from the tomb, and the man swore that he had seen the arms the evening before in the place where they had always been kept. Basil then went back to his house, but in the morning came again, and in the usual place found the saint's body and his weapons, including the lance, which was now covered with blood.

Then someone came from Julian's army and reported as follows: "While Emperor Julian was still with the army, an unknown soldier came up with his arms and his lance, put spurs to his horse and rushed with impetuous bravery upon Julian, drove his lance through his body, vanished, and was not seen again." Julian, while he was still breathing, filled his hand with his blood (as we are told in the *Tripartite History*) and tossed it into the air, saying: "Galilean, you have conquered!" With these words he expired miserably. His men left him unburied, and the Persians stripped off his skin and with it covered a cushion for the king's throne.

*About the feasts that occur within
the time of deviation*

Having spoken about the feasts that occur within the time that falls partly in the time of reconciliation and partly in the time of pilgrimage, which time the Church represents from the Birth of Christ to Septuagesima, we shall now take up the feasts that occur within the time of deviation, which the Church represents from Septuagesima to Easter.

31. Septuagesima

Septuagesima designates the time of deviation or turning away from God, Sexagesima the time of widowhood, Quinquagesima the time of pardon, Quadragesima, or Lent, the time for spiritual penance. Septuagesima begins on the Sunday on which the introit *Circumdederunt me gemitus mortis*[1] is sung, and ends on the Saturday after Easter.

Septuagesima was established for three reasons, as we learn from Master John Beleth's *Summa de officiis*. The first reason was to make compensation. The holy fathers had decreed that in order to pay due reverence to the day of the Lord's ascension, on which day our human nature rose to heaven and was lifted above the choirs of angels, Thursday should always be treated as a solemn holy day, and no fast should be observed on that day. Indeed, in the primitive Church, Thursday was celebrated equally with Sunday, and a solemn procession was held to represent the procession of the disciples or of the angels themselves. There was a popular proverb which said that "Thursday is Sunday's cousin," because in times past it was just as dedicated a day. But then the feasts of the saints intervened and it was burdensome to celebrate so many feasts, so the solemnizing of Thursday fell into disuse. By way of compensation the holy fathers added a week of abstinence before Lent and called it Septuagesima.

The second reason for the institution of Septuagesima is that this season signifies the time of deviation, of the fall away from God, of exile and tribulation for the whole human race from Adam to the end of the world. Now this exile extends through the period of seventy days and is included in the passage of seven thousand years: we understand seventy days as representing seventy hundreds of years. We count six thousand years from the world's beginning to the Lord's ascension, and we understand the remaining time to the end of the world as the seventh millennium: only God knows when it will end.

It was in the sixth age of the world that Christ snatched us, by baptism, out of this exile, restoring to us the robe of innocence and the hope of eternal reward, but it is when our time of exile is over that we shall be perfectly graced with both robes. That is why in this time of deviation and exile we put aside the chants of joy. In the office of the eve of Easter, however, we sing one Alleluia, expressing our thanks for the hope of an eternal homeland and the recovery, through Christ, of the robe of innocence in the sixth age of the world. This Alleluia is followed by a tract,[2] signifying the labor by which we still have to fulfill God's

---

[1] The sorrows of death surrounded me.

[2] The tract consisted of verses from the Psalms chanted or recited in the mass, replacing the Alleluia, on certain penitential days in the liturgical year.

commands. On the Saturday after Easter, which, as has been said, brings an end to Septuagesima, we sing two Alleluias, because when this world's term is completed, we will obtain the double robe of glory.

A third reason for the observance of Septuagesima is that it represents the seventy years the children of Israel spent in captivity in Babylon, when they hung up their lyres and said: "How shall we sing the Lord's song in a foreign land?" So we also, in Septuagesima, put aside our songs of praise. But then, when in the sixtieth year Cyrus gave them leave to return home, they began to rejoice, and we too, on Holy Saturday, as it were in the sixtieth year, sing Alleluia to recall their joy. They, however, had to work hard getting ready for the return journey and putting their baggage together, and we add to the Alleluia the tract which recalls that labor. Then on Easter Saturday, the last day of Septuagesima, we sing two Alleluias, symbolizing the fullness of joy with which they arrived in their own land.

The time of captivity and exile of the children of Israel also represents the time of our own pilgrimage, because as they were set free in the sixtieth year, we are liberated in the sixth age of the world. And as they worked hard to get their bundles ready, so we also, freed as we are, must labor to fulfill the commandments. But when we shall have come into our true homeland, all labor will cease, our glory will be complete, and we shall sing a double Alleluia in body and soul.

In this time of exile, therefore, the Church, weighed down with many troubles and almost driven to despair, with deep sighs cries out in her liturgy, saying: "The sorrows of death have surrounded me." Thus the Church describes the manifold tribulations she bears on account of the misery she has brought upon herself, the double punishment inflicted upon her, and the wrong done by some. Yet to save her from despair a triple healing remedy and a triple reward are offered both in the Gospel and in the Epistle.[3] The remedy, if she wishes to be completely delivered from her tribulations, is this: she must labor in the vineyard of the soul, pruning away vices and sins; in the race of the present life she must run by doing the works of penance; and then she must fight staunchly in the struggle against all the devil's trials. If she follows this prescription, she will receive a threefold reward, because to the laborer the day's wages will be given, to the runner the prize, and to the fighter the crown.

Then again, since Septuagesima signifies the time of our own captivity, we are offered a remedy by which we can be freed from captivity: by running, to escape from it, by fighting, to win over it, and with the day's wages, to buy our freedom.

[3] Readings in the mass of Septuagesima Sunday in the pre–Vatican II missal (1 Cor. 9:24–27 and 10:1–5; Matt. 20:1–16).

32. Sexagesima

Sexagesima begins on the Sunday when the introit *Exsurge, quare obdormis Domine*[1] is sung, and ends on the Wednesday after Easter. It was instituted as a compensation, a sign, and a representation.

First, as a compensation: Pope Melchiades and Saint Silvester decreed that two meals should be eaten every Saturday, for fear that due to abstinence from food on Friday, which is a fast day throughout the year, man's constitution would be weakened. To compensate for the Saturdays of this season, therefore, the popes added a week before Lent and called it Sexagesima.

Second, as a sign: Sexagesima (sixtieth day) signifies the time of the Church's widowhood and her grief at the absence of her Spouse, because a sixtieth part of the crop is owed to widows.[2] To console the widowed Church for the absence of her Spouse, who has been carried off to heaven, two wings are given to her, namely, the practice of the six works of mercy and the fulfillment of the Ten Commandments. Now *sexagesima* means 60—6 times 10—the 6 standing for the six works of mercy and the 10 for the Decalogue.

Third, as a representation: Sexagesima signifies not only the time of widowhood, but also the mystery of our redemption. The number 10 stands for man, who is the tenth drachma,[3] because man was created to make up for the ruin of the nine angelic orders. Or 10 means man because his body is composed of four humors and in his soul he has three powers—memory, intellect, and will—which were made to serve the most blessed Trinity, enabling us to believe in the three Persons faithfully, to love them fervently, and to keep them always in memory. The number 6 represents the six mysteries through which man, 10, is redeemed: they are Christ's incarnation, birth, passion, descent into hell, resurrection, and ascension into heaven.

Sexagesima is prolonged to the Wednesday after Easter, that day's introit being *Venite benedicti Patris mei*,[4] because those who have practiced the works of mercy will hear these words (as Christ himself testifies) when the door is opened to the Church-bride and she enjoys the embrace of her Spouse.

---

[1] Arise, why sleepest thou, O Lord?

[2] Commentators on Matt. 13:23, the parable of the sower, attribute the hundredfold yield to virgins, the sixtyfold to widows, and the thirtyfold to wives, according to their different degrees of merit.

[3] In chapter 37, "The Purification of the Blessed Virgin Mary," Jacobus notes that tithing (here called decimation) identified the redeemed," because the tenth drachma signified man."

[4] Come, ye blessed of my Father.

In the epistle of the mass for Sexagesima Sunday the Church is admonished to imitate Paul's example by bearing patiently the tribulation that is hers due to the absence of her Spouse. In the gospel she is encouraged to persevere in sowing the seed of good works. The Church, which almost in despair had cried out: "The sorrows of death have surrounded me," now, in control of herself again, prays for help in tribulation and to be freed of her troubles, saying: "Arise, why sleepest thou, O Lord? Arise, and cast us not off to the end. Why turnest thou thy face away and forgettest thou our want and our trouble? For our soul is humbled down to the dust: our belly cleaveth to the earth. Arise, O Lord: help us and redeem us for thy name's sake!" In this introit she repeats her "Arise" three times. There are those in the Church who are oppressed by adversity but not discouraged; others are oppressed and discouraged; still others are neither oppressed nor discouraged, but are in danger because they have no adversity to put up with and so may be broken by prosperity. Therefore the Church calls upon the Lord to arise from sleep, and to strengthen the first group, since by not rescuing them from their adversity he seems to be sleeping; to convert the second group, because he seems to have turned his face from them and somehow to have cast them off; to help the third group and set them free.

33. Quinquagesima

Quinquagesima lasts from the Sunday on which the introit *Esto mihi in Deum protectorem*[1] is sung until Easter Sunday. It was instituted as a completion, a sign, and a representation.

As a completion: we ought to fast for forty days as Christ did, but in Lent there are only thirty-six fast days because there is no fasting on Sundays. Sundays are exempted both to mark our joy and reverence for the Lord's resurrection, and to follow the example of Christ, who on the day of his rising from the dead took food twice—once when he came in to the disciples, the doors being closed, and they offered him a piece of a broiled fish and a honeycomb, and again, as some say, with the two disciples going to Emmaus. Therefore, to supply for the Sundays, four days of fast were added before Lent. Then the clergy, seeing that as they were ahead of the people by their ordination, they should also

---

[1] Be unto me a protecting God.

be ahead of them by their holiness, began to fast and abstain for two more days in addition to the added four. Thus a whole week was added before Lent and was called Quinquagesima, and Pope Telesphorus confirmed this, as Ambrose tells us.

Secondly, Quinquagesima signifies the time of remission, i.e., a season of penance in which everything is forgiven. Every fiftieth year was a jubilee year, a year of remission, because all debts were remitted, slaves were freed, and every man recovered his own property. This signified that by penance the debts of sins were wiped out, and everyone was freed from slavery to the devil and returned to the possession of heavenly dwellings.

Thirdly, as representation: Quinquagesima represents not only the time of remission, but the state of beatitude. In the fiftieth year slaves were set free; on the fiftieth day after the lamb was sacrificed, the Law was given; the fiftieth day after Easter the Holy Spirit was sent. Therefore the number 50 represents beatitude—the receiving of freedom, knowledge of the truth, and perfection of charity.

In the epistle and gospel of Quinquagesima Sunday three things necessary to make works of penance perfect are brought to our attention, namely, charity, which is proposed in the epistle, the reminder of the Passion, and faith, which is understood in the restoration of sight to the blind man. These are set forth in the Gospel: faith itself makes the works acceptable and appeasing to God, because without faith it is impossible to please God; and the memory of the passion of our Lord makes penance easy. Hence Gregory says: "If Christ's passion is kept in memory, there is nothing that will not be borne in tranquillity of spirit." Charity prompts continous works of penance, because, as Gregory says, the love of God cannot be idle: if there is love, it produces great works, and if no works are forthcoming, there is no love.

So, as at the beginning the Church, almost in despair, had cried out: "The sorrows of death have surrounded me," and later recovered herself and begged to be helped, now, her confidence renewed and her hope of pardon revived through penance, she prays, saying: "Be unto me a God, a protector, and a house of refuge, to save me. For thou art my strength and my refuge; and for thy name's sake thou wilt lead me and nourish me." Here she asks for four favors—protection, strength, refuge, and guidance. All her children are in the state of grace or the state of sin, in adversity or in prosperity. The Church prays for strength for those in grace, that they may be confirmed in grace; for those in sin she prays God to be their refuge; for those in adversity she asks protection in their troubles; and for the prosperous she prays that God may lead them to make innocent use of their goods.

Quinquagesima, as we have said, ends on Easter Sunday, because penance makes us rise to newness of life. During Quinquagesima the Fiftieth Psalm, the *Miserere*, is very frequently recited.

34. Quadragesima

For Quadragesima, the first Sunday of Lent, the introit *Invocavit me*[1] is sung. The Church, weighed down with so many tribulations, had cried out: "The sorrows of death surrounded me," and afterwards, having caught her breath, had called for help, saying: "Arise, O Lord" and "Be unto me a God, a protector." Now she shows that she has been heard, saying: "He has cried to me and I have heard him." Note, however, that Lent has 42 days, including the Sundays, but when six Sundays are taken out, only 36 days of fast are left. This number of days amounts to one-tenth of the year, because the year has 365 days, of which 36 days are one tenth. But four days are added preceding the first Sunday in order to fill out the sacred number of 40 days, which number the Savior consecrated by his fast in the desert.

Three reasons can be assigned to explain why we observe the fast for this number of days. The first, given by Augustine, is that Matthew has forty generations leading to the coming of Christ: "To this purpose the Lord came down to us through forty generations, that we should ascend to him through forty days of fasting." Augustine adds another explanation: "In order that we may reach the fiftieth, a tenth must be added to the fortieth, because in order to attain our blessed rest we must labor throughout the whole time of this present life. Hence the Lord stayed with his disciples for 40 days, and the tenth day thereafter sent the Holy Spirit, the Paraclete."

Master Praepositivus, in his *Summa de officiis*, gives a third reason, saying: "The world is divided into four parts and the year into four seasons; man is constituted of four elements and four complexions; and we have transgressed the New Law, which comprises the four gospels, and the Old Law in its Ten Commandments. It is proper, then, that the 4 be multiplied by the 10, making 40, and that we fulfill the commandments of the Old and New Laws throughout the time of this life. Our body, as we have said, consists of four elements, and these have, as it were, four 'seats' in us: fire is predominantly in the eyes, air on the tongue and in the ears, water in the genitals, and earth in the hands and the other members. So curiosity lodges in the eyes, scurrility in the tongue and ears, sensual pleasure in the sexual organs, cruelty in the hands and other members. The publican in the gospel confesses all four of these: he stood afar off to confess his sensuality, which smells bad, as if to say: 'I dare not come nearer, Lord, lest my

---

[1] He has cried to me.

stench reach your nostrils.' He did not lift his eyes to heaven, thus confessing his curiosity. He beat his breast with his hand, confessing cruelty. When he said: 'God, be merciful to me, a sinner,' he accused himself of scurrilous conduct, because sinners are often called buffoons, scurrilous fellows, or better, lechers." Thus far Praepositivus.

Gregory also, in one of his homilies, proposes three reasons: "Why is the number 40 retained for the fast, unless it is that the power of the Decalogue reaches its fullness through the four books of the holy Gospel? Moreover, we subsist by the four elements in this mortal body, and we contravene the Lord's commandments by indulging the body. Therefore, since we have violated the precepts of the Decalogue in yielding to the desires of the flesh, it is right that we should castigate the flesh 4 × 10 times over. Again, from Quadragesima Sunday to Easter day there are six weeks or 42 days, from which the six Sundays are subtracted from the fast, leaving 36 days of fasting. Now there are 365 days in the year, so we are, so to speak, giving a tenth of our year to God." This from Gregory.

Why is it that we do not observe our fast at the same time when Christ fasted? He began his fast immediately after he was baptized, but we connect ours rather with Easter. Master John Beleth, in his *Summa de officiis*, assigns four reasons for this. The first is that Christ suffered for us, and if we wish to rise with him, we ought to suffer with him. The second is that we imitate the children of Israel. Once when they made their exodus from Egypt, and again, from Babylonia, they celebrated the Pasch, thus proving that we are imitating them. And so, following their example, we fast at this time, in order to merit our escape from Egypt and Babylonia, i.e., from this world, and our passage into the land of our eternal heritage. A third reason is that the fires of lust usually burn more hotly in the spring, and to calm the body's cravings we have our longest fast in this season. And fourthly, immediately after the end of our fast we are to receive the Body of the Lord. As the Israelites, before they ate the paschal lamb, chastised themselves by eating wild bitter lettuces, so we ought to chastise ourselves by doing penance, in order to be worthy to eat the Lamb of life.

35. The Ember Day Fasts

The ember day, or four-season, fasts were instituted by Pope Callistus and are observed four times a year, following the four seasons of the year.

There are many reasons for this practice. The first is that spring is warm and humid, summer hot and dry, autumn cool and dry, winter cold and wet. Therefore we fast in the spring to control the harmful fluid of voluptuousness in us; in summer, to allay the noxious heat of avarice; in autumn, to temper the aridity of pride; in winter, to overcome the coldness of malice and lack of faith.

The second reason for these four periods of fast is that the first one falls in March, i.e., in the first week of Lent, so that the vices that are in us may wither—they cannot be completely extinguished—and the seeds of the virtues may sprout. The second fast falls in summer, in Pentecost week, because the Holy Spirit comes at that time and we ought to be fervent in the Spirit. In September we fast before Saint Michael's feast, because then the fruits of the earth are harvested and we should offer to God the fruits of good works. The fourth fast comes in December because then the grasses die, and we should die to the world.

The third reason is that we fast in order to imitate the Jews. They fasted four times a year—before Passover, before their Pentecost, before the feast of Tabernacles in September, and before the feast of Dedication in December.

The fourth reason is that man consists of the four elements, as regards the body and three powers, the rational, the concupiscible, and the irascible, as regards the soul. In order to control these elements and powers in us, we fast for three days four times a year, the number 4 referring to the body, the number 3 to the soul. These reasons are proffered by Master John Beleth.

The fifth reason, as stated by John of Damascus, is that in the spring there occurs an increase of blood, in the summer, of choler, in the autumn, of melancholia, and in winter, of phlegm. Therefore we fast in spring to weaken the blood of concupiscence and senseless gaiety in us; the sanguine person being libidinous and volatile. In summer we fast to weaken the bile of wrathfulness and falsity, because the choleric person is naturally inclined to bad temper and deception. In the autumn we fast to counteract the melancholia of cupidity and despondency, because the melancholic is naturally greedy and gloomy. In the winter our fasting reduces the phlegm of sluggishness and laziness, the phlegmatic being by nature dull and slothful.

The sixth reason is that spring is compared to air, summer to fire, autumn to earth, and winter to water. So in spring we fast to tame our high spirits and our

139

pride, in summer to damp the fire of greed and covetousness, in autumn to overcome the earth of spiritual frigidity and murky ignorance, in winter to harness the water of our lightheadedness and inconstancy.

A seventh reason is that spring is related to childhood, summer to adolescence, autumn to adulthood or the prime of life, and winter to old age. Therefore we fast in spring in order to preserve the innocence of the child, in summer to develop strength by living chaste lives, in autumn to grow young by constancy and mature by righteousness. In winter we strive by fasting to grow in prudence and virtuous living like the old, or rather, to make satisfaction for any offense we have given to God in earlier years.

William of Auxerre has given us an eighth reason: we fast four times in the year to atone for our failures in the same four seasons. Furthermore, we fast for three days in order to atone in a day for the faults committed in each month; we fast on Wednesday because Judas betrayed the Lord on that day, on Friday because that is the day Christ was crucified, on Saturday because that day he lay in the tomb and the apostles grieved over the violent death of their Master.

---

36. Saint Ignatius

The name Ignatius comes from *ignem patiens*, which means being afire with love of God.

Ignatius was a disciple of Saint John and bishop of Antioch. We read that he wrote a letter to the Blessed Virgin in these terms: "To Mary the Christ-bearer, her Ignatius. You ought to strengthen and console me, a neophyte and disciple of your John, from whom I have learned many things about your Jesus, things wondrous to tell, and I am dumbfounded at hearing them. My heart's desire is to be assured about these things that I have heard, by you who were always so intimately close to Jesus and shared his secrets. Fare you well, and let the neophytes who are with me be strengthened in the faith, by you, through you, and in you." The Blessed Virgin Mary, mother of God, answered him as follows: "To my beloved fellow disciple Ignatius, this humble handmaid of Christ Jesus. The things you have heard and learned from John are true. Believe them, hold on to them, be steadfast in carrying out your Christian commitment and shape your life and conduct on it. I will come to you with John to visit you and those who are with you. Stand firm and do manfully in the faith. Do not let the hardships of persecution shake you, and may your spirit be strong and joyful in God your salvation. Amen."

So respected was blessed Ignatius's authority that even Dionysius, the apostle Paul's disciple who was eminent in philosophy and supreme in divine knowledge, adduced Ignatius's work as authoritative in confirmation of what he himself taught. In his book *On the Divine Names*, Dionysius states that there are some who reject the use of the name *amor* in relation to the things of God, saying that in these things *dilectio* (*agape*, love) is more divine than *amor* (*eros*, love). Dionysius, wishing to show that the noun and name *amor* can be used in everything relating to God, says: "The divine Ignatius writes, 'My Love *(amor meus)* has been crucified.'"[1]

We read in the *Tripartite History* that Ignatius heard angels standing on a mountain and singing the antiphons. He thereupon made it a rule that the antiphons were to be sung in the Church, and the Psalms to be intoned in accordance with the antiphons.

Blessed Ignatius had for a long time prayed for the peace of the Church, fearing the danger of persecution not for himself but for weak Christians. Therefore when the emperor Trajan, who came to power in the year of the Lord 100, was returning from a victorious campaign in the East and was threatening all Christians with death, Ignatius went out to meet him and declared openly that he was a Christian. Trajan responded by having him loaded with chains and turning him over to ten soldiers with orders to take him to Rome; he also warned Ignatius that in Rome he would be given to the wild beasts and eaten alive. On the journey to Rome Ignatius wrote letters to all the churches, strengthening them in the faith of Christ. We read in the *Ecclesiastical History* that in one of these letters, addressed to Rome, he asked the faithful there not to interfere with his martyrdom. In this letter he says: "From Syria to Rome, by land and by sea, already I fight day and night with the beasts, being linked and chained to ten soldiers as savage as leopards, whose assignment is to guard me and get me to Rome. Kind treatment simply makes them more ferocious, but I learn more and more from their wickedness. . . . O salutary beasts that are being readied for me! When will they come? When will they be turned loose? When will they be allowed to feast on my flesh? I shall invite them to devour me! I shall beg them to begin, lest they be afraid to touch my body as they have been with some others. I shall use force, I shall throw myself upon them! Pardon me, Romans, I beg of you! I know what is best for me—fire, crosses, wild beasts, my bones scattered about, limb being torn from limb and flesh from bone, all the devil's tortures piled upon me, if only I may gain Christ!"

---

[1] The Greek distinction between *agape* and *eros*, and the Latin between *dilectio* or *caritas* and *amor*, does not come out in English, which translates all these terms as "love." In the passage referred to (*DN* 4.12, 708 B-C) Dionysius notes that the sacred writers used *diligo-dilectio* and *amo-amor* with the same meaning (cf. Pseudo-Dionysius, *The Complete Works* [New York: Paulist Press, 1987], p. 81).

When he arrived in Rome and was brought before Trajan, the emperor asked him: "Ignatius, why do you stir up rebellion in Antioch? Why do you try to convert my people to Christianity?" Ignatius answered: "Would I might convert you, too, so that you might possess the highest principate of all!" Trajan: "Offer sacrifice to my gods and you will be the chief of all the priests!" Ignatius: "Neither will I sacrifice to your gods nor do I aspire to your high rank. Whatever you wish to do to me, do it! You will not change me at all!" Trajan then issued orders: "Beat him about the shoulders with leaded scourges! Tear at his sides with nails and rub his wounds with sharp stones!" When all these things had been done to him and he remained unmoved, Trajan said: "Bring live coals and make him walk barefoot over them!" Ignatius: "Neither fiery flames nor boiling water can quench the love of Christ Jesus in me!" Trajan's answer: "It's the devil's magic at work, that you can suffer so much and still not give in!" Ignatius: "We Christians have nothing to do with sorcery, and our law condemns sorcerers to death, but you who worship idols, you are the sorcerers!" Trajan said: "Tear his back open with hooks and pour salt in his wounds!" Ignatius: "The sufferings of this time are not worthy to be compared with the glory to come!" Trajan ordered: "Now take him away chained as he is, and bind him to a stake! Keep him in the bottom of the dungeon, let him go without food or drink for three days, and then throw him to the beasts to be devoured!"

Three days later the emperor, the Senate, and the whole city gathered to see the bishop of Antioch in combat with the wild beasts, and Trajan said: "Since Ignatius is so haughty and hardheaded, bind him and loose two lions at him, so that there won't be any relics left of him!" Then Ignatius spoke to the people crowded around and said: "Men of Rome, know that my labors will not go unrewarded, and that it is not for loose morals that I suffer these pains but for loyalty to my duty." Then, as we read in the *Ecclesiastical History*, he continued: "I am the wheat of Christ! May I be ground fine by the teeth of the beasts, that I may be made a clean bread!" When the emperor heard these words, he said: "Great is the patience of the Christians! Where is the Greek who would bear so much for his God?" But Ignatius responded: "It is not by my own strength that I endure all this, but by the help of Christ!" Then he began to provoke the lions, egging them on to attack him and eat him. Two savage lions therefore leapt upon him, but they only smothered him, not breaching his flesh in any way. Seeing this, Trajan's wonder knew no bounds, and he left the scene with orders that anyone who wanted to remove the body should be allowed to do so. Christians then came and took the saint's body and gave it honorable burial.

When Trajan received letters in which Pliny the Younger expressed high esteem for the Christians whom the emperor had ordered put to death, he regretted his treatment of Ignatius and gave orders that Christians were no longer to be sought out, but that if a Christian fell into the hands of the law he should be punished. We also read that in the midst of all sorts of tortures blessed Ignatius never ceased calling upon the name of Jesus Christ. When the executioners asked him why he repeated this name so often, he replied: "I have this name written on my heart and therefore cannot stop invoking it!" After his death those who had heard him say this were driven by curiosity to find out if it was true, so they took the heart out of his body, split it down the middle, and found there the name *Jesus Christ* inscribed in gold letters. This brought many of them to accept the faith.

In his commentary on the Psalm *Qui habitat*,[2] Saint Bernard wrote of our saint: "That great Ignatius, who had listened to the disciple whom Jesus loved and was himself a martyr, whose precious relics enrich our poverty, in letters that he wrote to Mary saluted her as 'Christ-bearer'—a title of the highest dignity and a mark of immeasurable honor."

37. The Purification of the Blessed Virgin Mary

The purification of the Virgin Mary took place forty days after the birth of Jesus. This feast has traditionally been known by three names—Purification, Hypopanti, and Candlemas.

The feast is called Purification because on the fortieth day after her Son's birth the blessed Virgin came to the Temple in order to be purified according to the custom prescribed by the Law, although she was not bound by that Law. The twelfth chapter of Leviticus prescribed that a woman who had received seed and borne a male child would be unclean for seven days and must abstain from association with men and from entering the Temple. When the seven days were complete, she was clean as regards association with men, but as regards entering the Temple she was unclean for thirty-three days more. Thus, forty days having passed, on the fortieth day she should go to the Temple and offer her son with gifts. If, however, she had borne a daughter, the number of days was doubled as regards both association with men and entrance into the Temple.

To explain why God commanded that a male child should be offered in the Temple on the fortieth day, three reasons may be adduced. One is that the child is brought into the Temple building on the fortieth day, just as the soul most frequently enters the body, as into its temple, on the fortieth day: this we learn

[2] Psalm 90 (91).

from the *Scholastic History*. (The physicians, however, say that the male body is completely formed in forty-six days.) A second reason is that since the soul is stained by its infusion into the body on the fortieth day, it is fully cleansed of the stain on the fortieth day after birth when the child is brought into the Temple and gifts are offered for him. The third reason: we are given to understand that those who resolve by faith to observe the Ten Commandments proclaimed by the four evangelists will merit entrance into the temple of heaven.

In the case of a woman who gives birth to a female child the number of days is doubled as regards entering the Temple, just as the formation of the female body takes twice as many days. The organization of the male body takes forty days and the soul is infused most often in forty days, but the formation of the female body and the infusion of the soul take twice as long. There are three reasons (omitting the natural ones) for this doubling of the time. First, since Christ was to take flesh in the male sex, he willed to honor this sex and to endow it with more grace, so that the child would be formed and the mother cleansed sooner. Secondly, since the woman sinned more than the man, so her troubles are doubled above those of the man in the outer world and should be doubled inside the womb. Thirdly, this makes it clear that the woman has somehow wearied God more than man has, since she has sinned more. God is wearied somehow by our wicked doings, as he himself says (Isa. 43:24): "You have burdened me with your sins, you have wearied me with your iniquities"; and in Jeremiah he says (Jer. 6:11): "I am full of the wrath of the Lord, I am weary of holding it in."

The Blessed Virgin was not bound by this law of purification, because it was not by receiving seed that she conceived, but by a mystical inbreathing. That is why Moses added, "having received seed." He did not need to add this with regard to other women, all of whom conceive in the normal way; and Bernard notes that the words were added by Moses for fear that blasphemy might be visited upon the mother of the Lord.

Mary, however, wished to submit to this law for four reasons. Her first was that she might give an example of humility, wherefore Bernard says: "O blessed Virgin! You have neither cause nor need for purification, but did your Son need circumcision? Be among women as one of them, for so your Son is among boys." This humility was not only on the mother's side but on the Son's. He likewise willed to submit to the Law in this matter: by his birth he held himself as a poor man, by his circumcision as a poor and sinful man, but on this day as a poor and sinful man and a slave; as poor, in that he chose the offering of the poor, as sinner in that along with his mother he willed to be purified, as slave in that he willed to be redeemed. At a later time he willed also to be baptized, not that there was guilt to be purged, but that he might show the depth of his humility. Thus Christ chose to accept for himself all the remedies established against original sin, not because he had any need of them, but to manifest his humility and to show that these remedies were effective in their time.

Five remedies against original sin were instituted in the course of time. According to what Hugh of Saint Victor says, three of these, namely, offerings, tithing, and the killing of a sacrificial victim (which most fully expressed the work of our redemption), were established by the Old Law. The method of accomplishing redemption was expressed by the offering; the price of redemption by a sacrifice in which blood was shed, and the identity of the redeemed by tithing, because the tenth drachma signified man.

The first remedy, therefore, was offering: thus Cain offered gifts out of the fruits of the earth, and Abel out of his flocks. The second remedy, tithing: thus Abraham offered tenths to the priest Melchizedek, because, as Augustine says, tithes are given out of what the giver really cares about. In the case of the third remedy, the killing of a victim, the sacrifices themselves, according to Gregory, were directed against original sin because of the requirement that at least one of the parents be a believer, and sometimes both parents could be unbelievers. So a fourth remedy, circumcision, was instituted, because this was valid whether or not the parents were believers. But this remedy was effective and could open the gate of paradise only for males, so baptism, which was common to both sexes and opens paradise to all, succeeded circumcision.

We see that Christ took all five remedies upon himself in one way or another. As to the first, the Lord was offered by his parents in the Temple. As to the second, he fasted for forty days and nights, because, having no goods out of which to pay a tithe, he at least offered four times ten days to God. He made the third remedy his own both when his mother offered two turtledoves or young pigeons so that they could be sacrificed for him, and when he offered himself as a sacrifice on the cross. He accepted the fourth remedy when he allowed himself to be circumcised, and the fifth when he was baptized by John.

Christ's second reason for submitting to the Law was that he might fulfill the Law. The Lord had not come to abolish the Law but to fulfill it. If he had not abided by the Law, the Jews could have excused themselves and said: "We do not accept your teaching because you are not like our fathers and you do not observe the traditions of the Law." On this day, indeed, Christ and his mother submitted to a threefold law: first to the law of purification, as an example of virtue, so that we, after we have done all things well, may say that we are unworthy servants; second to the law of redemption, as an example of humility; third to the law of offering, as an example of poverty.

The Lord's third reason was that the law of purification was to be terminated; for as the coming of daylight dispels the darkness and at the sun's rising the night shadows vanish, so the coming of true purification put an end to symbolic purification. For then came our true purification, i.e., Christ, who is called purification in the active sense, since he purifies us through faith, as it is said: "cleansing their hearts by faith" (Acts 15:9). That is why fathers are no longer held to payment, nor mothers to going into the Temple and being purified, nor sons to being bought back.

The fourth reason was to teach us how we should be purified. There are five ways by which, beginning in infancy, we are to purify ourselves. They are the vow, which signifies renunciation of sin; water, which signifies washing by baptism; fire, which indicates infusion of spiritual grace; witnesses, signifying a multitude of good works; and war, which signifies temptation. So the blessed Virgin came to the Temple, offered her Son, and redeemed him with five shekels. Note that some firstborn were redeemed, like the firstborn of the twelve tribes, who were redeemed with five shekels: some were not redeemed, like the firstborn of the Levites, who were never redeemed but, when they grew to adulthood, always served the Lord in the Temple. There were also the firstborn of clean animals, which again were not redeemed but were offered to the Lord. Some firstborn animals were substituted for, as a lamb was offered in place of the firstborn of an ass, and some were killed, like the firstborn of dogs. So, since Christ was of the tribe of Judah, one of the twelve tribes, he should be redeemed, and they offered for him to God a pair of turtledoves or two young pigeons, these being the offering of poor people: rich people offered a lamb. Scripture does not say "young turtledoves" but "young pigeons," because young pigeons are always available while young turtledoves are scarce, though the mature doves can always be found. Nor are two pigeons called for, but two turtledoves, because the pigeon is a lascivious bird and therefore God did not want it offered to him in sacrifice: the dove, on the other hand, is a virtuous bird.

But have we not seen that the Blessed Virgin Mary had received a large amount of gold from the Magi only a short while earlier? It would seem, therefore, that she could have afforded to buy one lamb. It must be said, as Bernard asserts, that the Magi did indeed bestow a great weight of gold, because it is unlikely that such great kings would have offered a trifling amount to such a child. Yet there are those who think that the Blessed Virgin did not keep the gold but immediately disbursed it to the poor, or perhaps had the foresight to save for the impending seven-year sojourn in Egypt. Or it may be that they did not offer so large a quantity of gold, since the gift had a mystical significance. A commentator has it that three offerings were made for Christ: thus the first came *from* him by his parents, the second, namely, the birds, was made *for* him, and the third *by* him on the cross for all men. The first offering showed his humility, because he submitted to the Law, the second his poverty, because he chose the offering of the poor, the third his love, because he gave himself up for sinners. The characteristics of the turtledove are set down in the following verses:

> Alta petit turtur, cantando gemit, veniens ver
> Nuntiat et caste vivit solusque moratur,
> Pullos nocte fovet morticinumque fugit.[1]

---

[1] It soars to the heights, its song has a mournful note, / it announces the coming of spring, lives chastely and stays alone, / warms its young in the night, and shuns carrion flesh.

The pigeon's characteristics are likewise noted in verse:

> Grana legit, volitat sociata, cadavera vitat,
> Felle caret, plangit sociam, per oscula tangit,
> Petra dat huic nidum, fugit hostem in flumine visum,
> Rostro non laedit, geminos pullos bene nutrit.[2]

The second name for today's feast is *Hypopanti*, which is equivalent to Representation, because Christ was presented in the Temple. Or *hypopanti* signifies a meeting, because Symeon and Anna met the Lord when he was offered in the Temple. The word comes from *hypa*, which means to go, and *anti*, which means against, toward. So then, Symeon took the Child in his arms. Note that here Christ was overshadowed or made little of in three ways. Firstly, his truth was set at naught, for he, who is the truth and through himself as truth leads every man, and is the way that leads to himself as the life, on this day allowed himself to be led by others, when they carried the Child Jesus to Jerusalem, as the gospel tells us. Secondly, his goodness was hidden, since he, who alone is holy and good, chose to be purified with his mother as though he were unclean. Thirdly, his majesty was made little of, in that he, who upholds all things by the word of his power, on this day allowed himself to be held and carried in an old man's arms, although he upheld the one who carried him, as it is said: "The old man carried the child, the child governed the old man."

Then Symeon blessed him, saying:

> Now thou dost dismiss thy servant, O Lord, according to thy word,
>   in peace;
> Because my eyes have seen thy salvation,
> Which thou hast prepared in the face of all peoples,
> A light to the revelation of the Gentiles and the glory of thy people Israel.[3]

Symeon calls him by three names—salvation, light, and glory of thy people Israel. The meaning of this triple naming can be taken four ways. First, as related to our being made righteous, "salvation" means the remission of guilt, and the name Jesus is interpreted "savior" because he will save his people from their sins. "Light" indicates the giving of grace, "glory of the people" the giving of glory. Second, as related to our regeneration: the first name, salvation, is implied because the child is exorcised and baptized, and so, as it were, cleansed of sin; recalling the second name, light, a lighted candle is given to him; as to the third name, he is offered at the altar. Third, as related to the day's procession: candles are blessed and exorcised, then lighted and given into the hands of the faithful,

---

[2] It collects grains, flies in groups, avoids cadavers, / has no spleen, mourns a companion, touches with kisses; / nests in the rocks; it flies from the enemy seen in the river, / inflicts no wound with its beak, and carefully feeds its two young.

[3] Luke 2:29–32.

and the people go into the church singing hymns. Fourth, as related to the threefold naming of this feast: it is called Purification in relation to the cleansing from sin, and so is called "salvation." It is called Candlemas in relation to illumination by grace, whence the name "light." It is called Hypopanti in relation to the granting of glory, indicated by the words "the glory of thy people Israel"—for then we shall meet Christ in the air (1 Thess. 4:16). Again, it might be said that in this canticle Christ is praised as peace, salvation, light, and glory; peace, as our mediator; salvation, as our redeemer; light, as our teacher; glory, as our rewarder.

The third name for today's feast is Candlemas, because on this day candles are carried in the hand. The Church established this usage for four reasons. The first is to do away with an erroneous custom. On the calends of February the Romans honored Februa, mother of Mars the god of war, by lighting the city with candles and torches throughout the night of that day. This they did every fifth year (that span of years being called a *lustrum*) in order to obtain victory over their enemies from the son whose mother they so solemnly celebrated. Also in February the Romans sacrificed to Februus, i.e., to Pluto and the other gods of the underworld, that the gods might be propitious to the souls of their ancestors: they made solemn offerings to them and sang their praises throughout the night by the light of candles and torches. Pope Innocent says that the Roman wives observed a feast of lights that had its origin in some poets' fables, according to which Proserpina was so beautiful that the god Pluto, smitten with desire, abducted her and made her a goddess. Her kinsmen sought her for a long time through the forests and woodlands with torches and lanterns, and the Roman wives imitated this, going about with torches and candles. Since it is hard to relinquish such customs and the Christians, converted from paganism, had difficulty giving them up, Pope Sergius transmuted them, decreeing that the faithful should honor the holy mother of the Lord on this day by lighting up the whole world with lamps and candles. Thus the Roman celebration survived but with an altered meaning.

Another reason for solemnizing the feast of Candlemas was to show the purity of the Virgin Mary. Some people, hearing that she had accepted purification, might think that she had needed to be purified. Therefore, to show that she was totally pure and radiant, the Church ordered that we should carry luminous candles, as if the Church were in effect saying: "O blessed Virgin, you need no purification! You are wholly shining, wholly resplendent!" Mary needed no purification. She had not conceived by receiving seed and had been made perfectly clean and holy in her mother's womb. Indeed she was made so completely glorious and holy in the maternal womb, and in the coming of the Holy Spirit upon her, that no slightest inclination to sin remained in her. Moreover, the power of her holiness reached out to others and was poured into them, so that in them, too, every movement of concupiscence was extinguished. That is why the Jews say that despite Mary's exceeding beauty no man could ever desire her, for the reason that the power of her chastity penetrated all who looked upon her, and all lustful desires were quenched in them. So Mary is compared to the cedar tree, because as the cedar kills snakes with its odor, so her holiness shed its rays upon others and killed the snaky movements of the flesh in them. She is also compared to myrrh, because as myrrh kills worms, so her sanctity kills lust. Moreover, this prerogative was hers alone and was not granted to others who were sanctified in the womb nor to virgins: their holiness and chastity were not transfused into others and did not extinguish their fleshly desires, whereas the power of the Virgin's chastity penetrated the hearts of the libidinous so deeply that it immediately rendered them chaste.

The third reason for celebrating the feast of Candlemas is to recall the procession that occurred on this day, when Mary and Joseph and Symeon and Anna formed a solemn procession and presented the child Jesus in the Temple. On the feast day we too make a procession, carrying in our hands a lighted candle, which signifies Jesus, and bearing it into the churches. In the candle there are three things—the wick, the wax, and the fire. These three signify three things about Christ: the wax is a sign of his body, which was born of the Virgin Mary without corruption of the flesh, as bees make honey without mingling with each other; the wick signifies his most pure soul, hidden in his body; the fire or the light stands for his divinity, because our God is a consuming fire. So someone has written:

> Hanc in honore pio
> Candelam porto Mariae.
> Accipe per ceram
> Carnem de Virgine veram,
> Per lumen numen
> Majestatis que cacumen.
> Lychnus est anima
> Carne latens praeopima.[4]

The fourth reason for celebrating this feast is to instruct us. We learn that if we wish to be purified and clean before God, we must have three things in us, namely, true faith, good works, and a right intention. The lighted candle in the hand is faith with good works; for as a candle without a light is said to be dead, and as a light does not illumine without a candle and seems to be dead, so works without faith and faith without good works can be called dead. The wick hidden within the wax is the right intention, and Gregory says: "Let the work be visible to the public in such a way that the intention remains in hiding."

---

[4] This candle I carry in honor of holy Mary. / Take the wax for the true body born of the Virgin. / Take the light for God and his supreme majesty. / Take the wick for the soul concealed in the fat flesh.

37. THE PURIFICATION OF THE VIRGIN

A certain noble lady was deeply devoted to the Blessed Virgin. She had a chapel built next to her house and employed her own chaplain, and her wish was to hear mass in honor of Blessed Mary every day. As the feast of the Purification approached, the priest went off on some business of his own and the lady could not have mass on that day. Or, as we read elsewhere, for love of the Virgin she had given away everything she owned, even to her clothes; and so, having nothing to wear, she could not go to church and would be without mass on the feast day. She was grieved at this and went into her own chapel or her room and prostrated herself before the Blessed Virgin's altar. Then suddenly she was rapt in spirit, and it seemed to her that she was in a beautiful church. She looked and saw a large number of virgins coming into the church, led by a most radiant virgin who was crowned with a sparkling diadem. When they were all seated in the proper order, another group, this time of young men, came in and were seated in order. Then came a man carrying a large bundle of candles. He gave a candle to the virgin who had led the procession, then distributed them to the other virgins and the young men, and finally came to the lady and offered her a candle, which she gratefully accepted. Then she looked toward the choir of the church and saw two candle-bearers, a subdeacon, a deacon, and a priest wearing the sacred vestments, moving in procession to the altar to celebrate a solemn mass. The matron sensed that the two acolytes were Saint Vincent and Saint Laurence, the deacon and subdeacon were angels, and the priest was Christ himself.

After the recitation of the *Confiteor* two handsome young men went to the middle of the choir and with high, clear voices and fervent devotion began the office of the mass; and all those in the choir took up the chant. When it was time for the offertory, the Queen of the virgins and the other virgins, together with all those in the choir, genuflected and offered their candles to the priest, as is customary. The priest waited for the lady to offer her candle to him but she would not come forward, and the Queen of the virgins sent a messenger to tell her that it was rude of her to keep the priest waiting. She, however, answered that the celebrant should go on with the mass because she was not going to offer her candle. The Queen then sent another messenger, to whom the lady made the same response, namely, that she would give to no one the candle that had been given to her, but would keep it out of devotion. This time the Queen gave the following order to the messenger: "Go and ask her again to give up her candle, and if she refuses, take it away from her by force!" When the messenger went and heard the lady repeat her refusal, he said that his orders were to wrench the candle away from her. Then he tried with all his strength to take the candle away, but she clung to it even more strongly. A long struggle ensued, each of them pulling on the candle with might and main, until suddenly it broke, and one half remained in the messenger's hands, the other in the lady's. At that very moment she came to herself and found that she was still prostrated before her altar with the broken candle in her hand. Wondering at this, she offered devout

150

thanks to the Virgin Mary for not letting her go without mass on the feast day and providing a way for her to participate in the ceremony. She put the candle carefully away and kept it among her most precious relics; and it is said that all who touched it were freed at once from whatever infirmity befell them.

There was another matron who was pregnant and one night, in a dream, saw herself holding a banner tinted the color of blood. Awakening, she was promptly bereft of her senses, and the devil deluded her, so that she thought she was holding the faith of Christ, to which she had always adhered, between her breasts, but that it was escaping from her grasp. She found no cure for this delusion until she passed the whole night of this day's feast in a church of the Virgin Mary, and there was fully restored to health.

---

38. Saint Blaise

Blaise (Blasius) is like *blandus*, bland, or is formed from *bela*, meaning habit or disposition, and *syor*, small; for the saint was bland through the sweetness of his discourse, virtuous by habit, and small by the humility of his way of life.

Blaise set a powerful example of gentleness and holiness, and the Christians in Sebaste, a city in Cappadocia, elected him to be their bishop; but because Diocletian's persecution was raging, Blaise, though now a bishop, retired to a cave and there led the life of a hermit. Birds brought him food, and wild animals flocked to him and would not leave until he had laid hands on them in blessing. Moreover, if any of them were ailing, they came straight to him and went away cured.

The prefect of that region once sent his soldiers out to hunt, and they, after sighting no game elsewhere, came by chance upon Saint Blaise's cave, where they discovered a great herd of wild beasts standing in front of it. The hunters could not possibly take them all and, astonished at what they saw, reported it to their commander. The prefect at once dispatched more soldiers with orders to bring in the bishop and any Christians they found.

That same night Christ appeared three times to Blaise, saying: "Rise and offer sacrifice to me!" Then the soldiers arrived and said: "Come out, the prefect summons you!" Saint Blaise answered them: "You are welcome, my sons! Now I see that God has not forgotten me!" As he went along with them, he never stopped preaching and worked many wonders before their eyes. For instance, a woman, whose son was dying because a fish bone had stuck in his throat, laid the boy at the bishop's feet and tearfully begged him to cure her child. Saint Blaise laid his hands on him and prayed that this child, and anyone else who sought help from God in his name, should obtain the benefit of health. The boy was cured instantly. Another poor woman, a widow, possessed nothing but a single pig, and a wolf had violently made off with the pig. The woman implored Saint Blaise to get the pig back, and the saint smiled and said: "Good woman, don't be sad, your pig will be returned to you." Within minutes the wolf came up and gave the pig back to the widow.

Blaise now entered the city and, by the prefect's order, was locked up in jail. The next day, however, the prefect had him brought before him and, when he saw him, welcomed him with cozening words, such as: "Greetings, Blaise, friend of the gods!" "Greetings likewise to Your Excellency!" Blaise responded, "But do not call them gods but demons, because they are given over to eternal fire along with all who honor them!" This made the prefect angry, and he ordered Blaise to be beaten with cudgels and put back in jail. Blaise said to him: "Foolish man, do you hope that your punishments will take my love of God away from me, when I have my God in me to give me strength?"

The poor widow who had recovered her pig heard what had happened, killed the pig, and delivered its head, with the feet, a candle, and a loaf, to Saint Blaise. He thanked her, ate, and told her: "Every year offer a candle in the church named for me, and all will be well with you and with all who do the same." The widow year after year did as he told her and enjoyed great prosperity.

The prefect now had the bishop brought out of prison but could not induce him to bow to the gods, so he ordered the torturers to hang him from a rafter and tear his flesh with iron spikes, then to put him back in jail. Seven women, however, followed and collected the drops of his blood, so they were arrested and ordered to sacrifice to the gods. They said: "If you want us to adore your gods, place them reverently at the edge of the lake, so that we can wash their faces and worship them more cleanly!" This made the prefect happy, and what they had asked was quickly done. But the women snatched up the idols and threw them into the middle of the lake, saying: "Now we shall see if they are really gods!" When the prefect heard of this, he was beside himself with rage, beat himself with his fists, and shouted at his men: "Why didn't you hold on to our gods and keep them from being plunged into the bottom of the lake?" "The women fooled you with their talk," the men retorted, "And so the gods got immersed!" The women also had their say: "The true God can't be fooled, and if these idols were gods, they would have known ahead of time what we intended to do!"

Furious, the prefect called for the preparation of molten lead, iron combs, and seven breastplates fired red-hot and arranged to one side, seven linen shirts to the other. Then he ordered the women to choose which of these they wanted to put on. One of the women, who had two small children with her, boldly ran forward, picked up the linen shirts, and threw them into the fire. The children said to their mother: "Dearest mother, don't leave us behind! You have filled us with the sweetness of your milk, so fill us with the sweetness of the kingdom of heaven!" The prefect ordered the women to be hung up and their flesh to be slashed with iron rakes; and their flesh was seen to be white as driven snow, and from their torn bodies milk flowed instead of blood. They bore these tortures without flinching, and an angel of the Lord came to them and encouraged them stoutly, saying: "Have no fear! The good workman, who has started his work well and brings it to a good end, merits a blessing from the one for whom he works and receives a wage for his work; and joy is the wage he possesses!"

Then the prefect had them taken down and thrown into the furnace, but the fire was extinguished by God's power and the women emerged unharmed. The prefect admonished them: "Have done with your magical arts and adore our gods!" They answered: "Finish what you've started! We are called now to the heavenly kingdom!" So he sentenced them to be beheaded. They knelt in readiness for the blow of the sword and worshiped God, saying: "O God, you have brought us out of darkness and into your marvelous light, you have made us your sacrifice! Now receive our souls and let us enter into eternal life!" Their heads fell and they migrated to the Lord.

The prefect had Blaise brought before him and said to him: "Either adore the gods or don't!" "Impious man," Blaise retorted, "I do not fear your threats! Do as you will! I turn my body over to you completely!" The prefect ordered him to be thrown into the lake, but he made the sign of the cross over the water and instantly it became like dry, firm land under him. "If your gods are true gods," he said to the bystanders, "show their power by walking on the water!" Sixty-five men walked in and promptly drowned. Then an angel of the Lord descended and said to him: "Come out, Blaise, and receive the crown God has prepared for you!" He came out, and the prefect said: "Well, have you absolutely decided not to worship the gods?" Blaise answered: "Know, wretch, that I am a servant of Christ and do not adore demons!" The order was given to behead him, and he prayed to the Lord that anyone who besought his intercession when suffering from throat trouble or any other illness should be heard and healed immediately. And behold, a voice came to him from heaven, saying that what he prayed for would be done. And so the saint was beheaded with the aforementioned two children, about the year of the Lord 283.

39. Saint Agatha, Virgin

Agatha comes from *agios*, which means holy, and *theos*, God—hence saint of God. According to Chrysostom, there are three requirements for sainthood, and Agatha was perfect in all three—namely, cleanness of heart, the presence of the Holy Spirit, and abundance of good works. Or the name comes from *a*, which means without, *geos*, earth, and *theos*, God—therefore a goddess, as it were, without earth, i.e., without love of earthly things. Or it comes from *aga*, speaking, and *thau*, completion, and Agatha spoke completely and perfectly, as is clear from her answers. Or again from *agath*, servitude, and *thaas*, higher, because one of her answers was: "To be a slave of Christ is proof of the highest nobility." Or from *aga*, solemn, and *thau*, consummation, because she was solemnly consummated, i.e., buried, which refers to the angels who buried her.

The virgin Agatha was highborn and a great beauty, living in the city of Catania, where she worshiped God at all times and in all holiness. Quintianus, the consular official in Sicily, who was baseborn, libidinous, greedy, and a worshiper of idols, was determined to get her in his grasp. Being of low degree he would gain respect by lording it over a noble, her beauty would satisfy his libido, he would steal her riches to feed his avarice, and, being a pagan, he would force her to sacrifice to the gods.

So he had her brought before him and quickly perceived the firmness of her resolution. He therefore turned her over to a procuress whose name was Aphrodisia and her nine daughters who were as lascivious as their mother. He gave them thirty days to overcome her resistance. They tried to change her mind, at times by promising her pleasure, at others by threatening her with pain. They hoped to win her over from her good resolve, but blessed Agatha said to them: "My determination is built on rock and founded in Christ! Your promises are raindrops, your threats are rivers, and however hard they beat upon the foundation of my house, it cannot fall." Having said this, she prayed and wept day after day, thirsting to attain the palm of martyrdom. Aphrodisia saw that her will could not be shaken, and told Quintianus: "It would be easier to split rocks or reduce iron to the softness of lead than to move or recall that girl's mind from its Christian intention."

Then Quintianus summoned her again. "What is your social standing?" he asked. She answered: "I am freeborn and of illustrious lineage, as my ancestry attests." Quintianus: "If you are so highborn, why does the way you live make you seem to be of servile status?" Her answer: "I am the slave of Christ, there-

154

fore I show myself as a person in service." Quintianus: "If you are of noble birth, why do you call yourself a slave?" Agatha: "Because to be a slave of Christ is proof of the highest nobility." "Make your choice!" Quintianus said. "Either sacrifice to the gods or submit to torture!" Agatha retorted: "May your wife be like your goddess Venus, and may you be like your god Jupiter!" Quintianus ordered her to be slapped in the face, and said: "Don't let your loose tongue insult your judge!" Agatha answered: "I marvel that a sensible man like you can fall into such stupidity as to call gods those whose lives neither you nor your wife would want to imitate! Indeed you consider it an insult if you are said to follow their example. If your gods are good, I've made a good wish for you: if you repudiate any association with them, then you agree with me!" "What's the use of all this idle talk?" Quintianus exclaimed; "sacrifice to the gods or prepare to suffer!" Agatha: "If you promise me the wild beasts, the sound of Christ's name will gentle them! If you try fire, angels will serve me with a healing dew from heaven! If you resort to wounds and torments, I have the Holy Spirit, through whom I make naught of all that!" Then, because what she said was making him look foolish in the public eye, Quintianus had her put in jail; and to jail she went happy and triumphant, as if invited to a banquet, and commended her trial to the Lord.

The next day Quintianus said to her: "Forswear Christ and adore the gods!" When she refused, he ordered her stretched on the rack and tortured, and Agatha said: "These pains are my delight! It's as if I were hearing some good news, or seeing someone I had long wished to see, or had found a great treasure. The wheat cannot be stored in the barn unless it has been thoroughly threshed and separated from the chaff: so my soul cannot enter paradise unless you make the headsmen give my body harsh treatment." This made Quintianus so angry that he ordered the executioners to twist her breast for a long time and then cut it off. Said Agatha: "Impious, cruel, brutal tyrant, are you not ashamed to cut off from a woman that which your mother suckled you with? In my soul I have breasts untouched and unharmed, with which I nourish all my senses, having consecrated them to the Lord from infancy."

The tyrant ordered her back to prison, and forbade the jailers to allow any physician to care for her or anyone to bring her food or water. But toward the middle of the night an aged man, preceded by a boy carrying a light, came to her. He brought various medicaments and said to Agatha: "Though this mad consul has inflicted torments on you, the way you have answered him has tormented him even more, and though he has caused your breasts to be injured, his exuberance will turn to bitterness. I was there when all this was done to you, and I saw that your breast could be healed." Agatha: "I have never applied any material remedy to my body, and it would be shameful to lose now what I have preserved for so long." The aged man said to her: "I am a Christian, so you need not be ashamed." Agatha: "How could I be ashamed, since you are so old and a grandfather, and I am so cruelly mangled that no one could possibly desire me?

But I thank you, kind sir and father, for deigning to have such solicitude in my regard." "But why," the old man asked, "why do you not allow me to heal you?" "Because I have my Lord Jesus Christ," Agatha replied, "and he by a single word can cure everything and by his word restores all things. If he so wills, he can cure me instantly." The aged man smiled. "I am his apostle," he said, "and he sent me to you. Know that in his name you are healed." And Peter the apostle vanished. Agatha knelt in thanksgiving, and found that all her hurts were healed and her breast restored to her bosom. The jailers, terrified by the dazzling light, had fled and left the jail open, but some who were left asked her to go away. "Far be it from me," she said, "to run away and lose the crown of patience, and also to expose my guards to trouble!"

After four days passed, Quintianus again told her to worship the gods, or still worse punishments would be hers. Agatha answered: "Your words are silly and useless, they are wicked and pollute the air! You mindless wretch, how can you want me to adore stones and abandon the God of heaven who has healed me?" "Who healed you?" Quintianus asked. Agatha: "Christ the Son of God!" Quintianus: " You dare to pronounce the name of Christ again, when I do not want to hear it?" Agatha: "As long as I live I shall invoke Christ with heart and lips!" Quintianus: "Now we'll see if Christ will cure you!" He ordered Agatha to be rolled naked over potsherds and live coals strewn on the ground. While this was going on, a tremendous earthquake shook the city and caused the palace to collapse, crushing two of Quintianus's counselors. At this the whole populace came running and shouting that such things were being visited on them because of the unjust treatment meted out to Agatha. So Quintianus, caught between the earthquake and the popular uprising, ordered Agatha back to prison. There she prayed, saying: "Lord Jesus Christ, you created me, you have watched over me from infancy, kept my body from defilement, preserved me from love of the world, made me able to withstand torture, and granted me the virtue of patience in the midst of torments. Now receive my spirit and command me to come to your mercy." And, having finished her prayer, she called out in a loud voice and gave up her spirit, about the year of the Lord 253, in the reign of the emperor Dacian.[1]

Faithful Christians came, anointed her body with spices, and laid it in a sarcophagus. Then a young man clothed in silken garments and accompanied by over a hundred handsome youths wearing rich white vestments, none of whom had ever been seen in that region, approached the saint's body and placed at the head a marble tablet, after which he and his companions vanished from the sight of all. On the tablet was inscribed: MENTEM SANCTAM, SPONTANEAM, HONOREM DEO ET PATRIAE LIBERATIONEM, which may be understood as meaning: "She had a holy and generous soul, gave honor to God, and accomplished the liberation of her country." When this miracle was noised abroad, even pagans and Jews began to venerate the tomb in great numbers.

---

[1] Graesse notes that "recent editions add 'otherwise called Decius.'"

As for Quintianus, he was on his way to look for and make off with Agatha's riches when his two horses began to gnash their teeth and kick out with their hooves, and one of them bit him and the other kicked him into the river, and his body was never found.

One year from the day of Agatha's birth into the new life of heaven, the mountain that looms over Catania erupted and spewed a river of fire and molten rock down toward the city. Then crowds of pagans fled from the mountain to the saint's tomb, snatched up the pall that covered it, and hung it up in the path of the fire; and, on the very day of the virgin's birth, the stream of lava halted and did not advance a foot farther.

About this virgin saint, Ambrose says in his Preface: "O holy and glorious virgin, who faithfully shed her blood as a martyr in praise of the Lord! O illustrious, renowned virgin, upon whom shone a twofold glory: since amidst harsh torments she wrought all sorts of miracles and, strengthened by support from above, merited to be cured by the apostle's visitation! So the airs bore his bride heavenward to Christ, and glorious obsequies shine about her mortal frame as the angel choir acclaims the holiness of her soul and the liberation of her native land."

40. Saint Vaast

Vedastus, the Latin form of Vaast, comes from *vere*, truly, *dans*, giving, and *aestus*, heat, and the saint truly gave himself the heat of affliction and penance. Or the name may come from *veh*, woe, and *distans*, distant, because eternal woe was distant from him. The damned will say "woe!" continually—woe! because I have offended God, woe! because I did the devil's will, woe! that I was born, woe! that I cannot die, woe! because I am so sorely tormented, woe! because I shall never be set free.

Vaast was ordained bishop of Arras by Saint Remy. When he came to the city gate, he found two beggars there, the one blind, the other lame. They asked for an alms and he said to them: "I have neither silver nor gold, but what I have I give you"; whereupon he prayed, and both of them were made whole. Then there was an abandoned church, covered with thorns and brambles, in which a wolf had made his lair. Saint Vaast ordered the wolf to go away and not to dare come back, and the wolf obeyed.

After he had labored as bishop for forty years and by word and work had converted many to the faith, he saw a column of fire descending from heaven upon his house. He realized that his end was at hand, and a short while later he fell asleep in the Lord, about A.D. 550.

As the corpse was being transferred for burial, Audomatus, an old man who was blind, lamented that he could not see the bishop's body, and instantly his sight was restored. Later, however, at his prayer, he became blind again.

41. Saint Amand

The name Amand means lovable, and the name fitted the man, for he had three qualities that make a person lovable. First, he was friendly toward others; Prov. 18:24: "A man amiable in society will be more friendly than a brother." Second, he was honorable in his conduct, as it is said of Esther (Esther 2:15): "She was agreeable and amiable in the sight of all." Third, he was upright and virtuous; 2 Sam. 1:23: "Saul and Jonathan were lovely, and comely in their life."

Amand, the son of noble parents, entered a monastery. While he was walking in the monastery garden, he came upon a huge serpent and, by praying and making the sign of the cross, made it go back to its pit never to come out again. Then he went to the tomb of Saint Martin, where he stayed for fifteen years, wearing a hair shirt and living on barley bread and water.

Then he went to Rome and was spending the night in prayer in the church of Saint Peter, when the watchman irreverently put him out of the building. Saint Peter appeared to him as he slept at the church door, and directed him to go to Gaul and to rebuke King Dagobert for his crimes. The king resented this and ordered Amand out of his kingdom. Later the king, who had no son, prayed the Lord to grant him a son, and his prayer was answered. He began to think about whom he should have to baptize his son, and it came to him that Amand might be the one to ask. Amand was sought for and brought to the king, who knelt at his feet and begged the saint to forgive him and to baptize the son whom the Lord had granted him. Amand graciously consented to the first request but, fearing to become involved in worldly affairs, declined the second and left the court. In the end, however, he yielded to the king's prayer; and at the baptism, while all were silent, the infant pronounced the response: "Amen."

Dagobert then had Amand installed as bishop in the see of Maastricht, but the people there disdained his preaching, and he withdrew to Gascony.[1] There a jester who ridiculed him with scornful words was seized by a demon, and, tearing at his own flesh with his teeth, he confessed that he had wronged the man of God, and died a miserable death. Then there was a time when Amand was washing his hands and another bishop saved the water, with which he afterwards cured a blind man.

On another occasion Amand, at the king's bidding, wished to establish a monastery in a certain location, but the bishop of a nearby city took offense at this and sent his men either to kill Amand or force him to leave the place. They went to him and tried to deceive him: he was to come with them, they said, and they would show him a very good site for his monastery. Amand had foreknowledge of their evil intentions but, because he longed for martyrdom, went with them to the peak of the mountain where they planned to murder him. But suddenly the mountain was enveloped in rainstorms so dense that the murderers could not even see each other. Thinking that they were about to die, they fell to their knees and implored his pardon, also begging him to let them get away alive. He prayed fervently and the weather turned serene. The repentant fellows went home, and Amand, having escaped their plot, performed many other miracles and eventually died in peace. He flourished about A.D. 653, in the time of the emperor Heraclius.

42. Saint Valentine

The name Valentine, in Latin *Valentinus*, is made up of *valorem*, value, and *tenens*, holding; and Saint Valentine held on to—persevered in—holiness. Or the name is like *valens tiro*, valiant soldier of Christ. A valiant soldier is one who has never fallen, who strikes hard, defends himself bravely, and conquers decisively. Thus Valentine never failed by shunning martyrdom, he struck hard by putting down idolatry, he defended his faith by confessing it, he conquered by suffering.

---

[1] *Vasconia* in the text. Historically, Amand's activity as a missionary bishop was carried on in the area that is now Belgium. There is no evidence that he was ever in southern France. Cf. *Butler's Lives of the Saints* (New York: P. J. Kenedy & Sons, 1963), 1:263.

Valentine was a venerable priest, whom the emperor Claudius summoned before him. "What is this, Valentine?" he asked. "Why do you not win our friendship by adoring our gods and abandoning your vain superstitions?" Valentine answered: "If you but knew the grace of God, you would not say such things! You would turn your mind away from your idols and adore the God who is in heaven." One of the people standing by Claudius said: "Valentine, what have you to say about the holiness of our gods?" "All I have to say about them," Valentine replied, "is that they were wretched human beings full of every uncleanness!" Claudius spoke: "If Christ is true God, why do you not tell me the truth?" Valentine: "Truly Christ alone is God! If you believe in him, your soul will be saved, the empire will prosper, and you will be granted victory over all your enemies!" Claudius responded, saying to those around him: "Men of Rome, heed how wisely and rightly this man speaks!" Then the prefect said: "The emperor is being led astray! How shall we give up what we have believed from infancy?"

At this the heart of Claudius was hardened, and he turned Valentine over to the prefect to be held in custody. When Valentine came into this man's house, he said: "Lord Jesus Christ, true light, enlighten this house and let all here know you as true God!" The prefect said: "I wonder at hearing you say that Christ is light. Indeed, if he gives light to my daughter who has been blind for a long time, I will do whatever you tell me to do!" Valentine prayed over the daughter, her sight was restored, and the whole household was converted to the faith. Then the emperor ordered Valentine to be beheaded, about A.D. 280.

43. Saint Juliana

Juliana was betrothed to Eulogius, the prefect of Nicomedia, but refused to become his wife unless he accepted the faith of Christ. Her father therefore commanded that she be stripped and soundly beaten, then handed her over to the prefect. Eulogius said to her: "My dear Juliana, why have you played false with me, rejecting me this way?" She answered: "If you will adore my God, I will consent, otherwise I will never be yours!" "I can't do that, dear lady," the prefect replied, "because the emperor would have me beheaded." Juliana: "If you are so afraid of a mortal emperor, how can you expect me not to fear an immortal one? Do whatever you please, because you will not be able to win me over!"

So the prefect had her severely beaten, and ordered her hung up by the hair of her head for half a day, and molten lead to be poured on her head. None of this, however, did her the slightest harm, so he had her bound in chains and shut up in prison. There the devil came to her in the guise of an angel and said: "Juliana, I am an angel of the Lord, who has sent me to you to warn you to sacrifice to the gods, if you do not want to be subjected to long torture and die a dreadful death!"

Juliana wept and prayed, saying: "O Lord my God, do not let me perish, but show me who this is that's giving me such advice!" Then a voice spoke to her, telling her to lay hold of her visitor and force him to admit who he was. She grasped him firmly and questioned him, and he told her that he was a demon and that his father had sent him to deceive her. "And who is your father?" she asked. He answered: "Beelzebul, who sends us out to do all sorts of mischief and has us whipped unmercifully whenever we are outdone by Christians. So I know it will go hard with me because I have not been able to get the better of you!" He admitted, among other things, that he was kept farthest away from Christians when they were celebrating the mystery of the Lord's Body and when they were engaged in prayer and preaching. Juliana tied his hands behind his back, threw him to the ground, and gave him a thorough thrashing with the chain that had bound her, while the devil cried aloud, pleading with her and saying: "My lady Juliana, have pity on me!"

Now the prefect gave orders to bring Juliana out of jail, and she came out dragging the demon, still in bonds, after her. The demon continued to plead with her, saying: "Lady Juliana, stop making a fool of me or I'll never again be able to mislead anyone! Christians are supposed to be merciful, but you haven't shown me any mercy at all!" But she dragged him from one end of the market-place to the other and finally tossed him into a sewer.

When news of this reached the prefect, he had Juliana stretched on a wheel until all her bones were broken and the marrow spurted out, but an angel of the Lord shattered the wheel and healed her instantly. Seeing this happen, the people around believed, and 500 men and 130 women were beheaded forthwith. Then Juliana was put into a tub filled with molten lead, but the lead became like a cool bath. At this the prefect cursed his gods, who were unable to punish a mere girl for heaping such insults upon them. Then he ordered her beheaded, and while she was being led to the place of execution, the demon whom she had whipped appeared in the guise of a young man, shouting and saying: "Don't spare her! She slandered your gods and gave me a terrible beating last night! Give her what she deserves!" When Juliana opened her eyes a little and saw who was shouting, the demon ran away exclaiming: "Woe is me! I think she still wants to catch me and tie me up!"

When blessed Juliana had been beheaded, the prefect went to sea with thirty-four men, and a storm came up and they were all drowned; and when the sea cast the bodies on the shore, they were devoured by the birds and the beasts.

44. The Chair of Saint Peter

There are three kinds of "chair"—the royal chair, or throne, 2 Sam. 23:8: "David sitting in the chair, etc."; the priestly chair, 1 Kings 1:9: "Now Eli the priest was sitting on a stool before the door of the temple of the Lord"; and the magisterial or professorial chair, Matt. 23:1: "The scribes and the Pharisees have sat on the chair of Moses." Peter sat on the royal chair because he was first among all kings; on the priestly chair because he was the shepherd of all clerics; and on the magisterial chair because he was the teacher of all Christians.[1]

The Church commemorates the Chair of Saint Peter with a feast day because blessed Peter is said to have been raised on this day to the seat of honor in Antioch. There appear to be four reasons for the institution of this solemnity. The first is that when blessed Peter was preaching in Antioch, Theophilus, governor of the city, said to him: "Peter, why are you corrupting my people?" Peter then preached the faith of Christ to Theophilus, who immediately had him imprisoned and deprived of food and drink. The apostle was almost exhausted but regained some strength, turned his eyes to heaven, and said: "Christ Jesus, helper of the helpless, come to my aid! These trials have almost destroyed me!" The Lord answered him: "Peter, did you think I had deserted you? You impugn my kindness when you are not afraid to say such things against me! The one who will relieve your misery is at hand!"

Meanwhile Saint Paul heard of Peter's imprisonment. He presented himself to Theophilus, asserted that he was highly skilled in many arts and crafts, and said that he knew how to sculpt in wood and stone and could do many other kinds of work as well. Theophilus pressed him to stay on as a member of his household. A few days later Paul went secretly to Peter in his cell and found him very weak and almost dead. Paul wept bitterly and took Peter in his arms, weeping profusely, and burst out: "O my brother Peter, my glory, my joy, the half of my soul, now that I am here you must recover your strength!" Peter opened his eyes, recognized Paul, and began to cry but could not speak. Paul quickly opened the other's mouth, forced food into him, and thus got some warmth into his body. The food strengthened Peter, who threw himself into Paul's embrace and both of them shed a flood of tears.

---

[1] The term "chair" is derived from the Greek/Latin word *cathedra*, seat, and, as used here, usually indicates a seat of special dignity, a throne. In Church language the *cathedral* is the church in which the bishop's chair, *cathedra*, is located—the center, so to speak, of his "see," a word derived from the Latin *sedes*, which also means "seat."

Paul left the jail cautiously and went back to Theophilus, to whom he said: "O good Theophilus, great is your fame, and your courtliness is the friend of honor. But a small evil counteracts great good! Think about what you have done to that worshiper of God who is called Peter, as if he were someone of importance! He is in rags, misshapen, reduced to skin and bones, a nobody, notable only for what he says. Do you think it is right to put such a man in jail? If he were enjoying the freedom to which he is accustomed, he might be able to do you some useful service. For instance, some say that he restores the sick to health and the dead to life!" Theophilus: "Idle tales, Paul, idle tales! If he could raise the dead, he would free himself from prison!" Paul: "Just as his Christ rose from the dead (or so they say) yet would not come down from the cross, so Peter, following Christ's example (it is said), does not set himself free and is not afraid to suffer for Christ!" Theophilus: "Tell him, then, to bring my son, who has been dead for fourteen years, back to life, and I will release him unharmed and free!" Paul therefore went to Peter's cell and told him he had solemnly promised Theophilus that his son would be brought back to life. "That's a hard promise to keep, Paul," said Peter, "but God's power will make it easy!" Peter was taken out of prison and led to the tomb. He prayed, and the governor's son came to life immediately.

There are some things here, however, that sound improbable, for instance, that Paul would pretend that he had the natural skills needed to do and make a variety of things, or that the son's sentence of death was suspended for fourteen years. But however that may be, Theophilus and the whole population of Antioch, together with a great many other people, believed in Christ. They built a magnificent church and erected an elevated throne in the center, to which they lifted Peter up so that he could be seen and heard by everybody. He occupied that chair for seven years, but afterwards went to Rome and ruled the see of Rome for twenty-five years. The Church, however, celebrates this first honor because it was the beginning of the custom by which bishops are distinguished by place, power, and name. Thus what we read in Ps. 106:32 is fulfilled: "Let them exalt him in the church of the people, and praise him in the chair of the ancients."

Note that the church in which blessed Peter was exalted is threefold, namely, the church of the militant, the church of the malignant, and the church of the triumphant. He was exalted in this threefold church by the three feasts that are celebrated in his honor. In the church of the militant he was exalted by presiding over it and ruling it laudably in spirit, in faith, and in his virtuous life; and this refers to today's feast, which is named for the pontifical Chair, because Peter then assumed the pontificate in the church of Antioch and ruled it in a praiseworthy manner for seven years. Secondly, Peter is exalted in the church of the malignant, in that he dispersed it and converted it to the true faith; and this refers to the second feast honoring him, which is named after his chains, because he dispersed this church and brought many back to the faith. Thirdly, he is exalted in the church of the triumphant; and this refers to the third solemnization, which is that of his passion, because by his passion he entered the church triumphant.

Furthermore, the Church during the year celebrates three feasts in Peter's honor for many other reasons besides the above, among them his office, his benefits, our debt to him, and the example he set for us.

First, he is honored because he was privileged. Blessed Peter enjoyed three privileges that raised him above the other apostles, and because of these three privileges the Church honors him three times in the year. He enjoyed a higher dignity than the others by his authority, since he stood forth as prince of the apostles and received the keys of the kingdom of heaven. He was more fervent than the others in his love, for he loved Christ with greater fervor, as is manifest from many passages in the gospels. His power was more efficacious, since, as we read in the Acts of the Apostles, the infirm were cured when his shadow passed over them.

Second, he is honored because of his office in the Church. He was supreme pontiff over the universal Church, and, since he was prince and prelate of the whole Church that is spread over the three parts of the world, namely, Asia, Africa, and Europe, the Church celebrates his feast three times in the year. Third, he is honored for the benefits he provides. Having received the power of binding and loosing, he frees us from three kinds of sins, namely, sins of thought, of word, and of action, or our sins against God, our neighbors, and ourselves. And there is still another triple benefit that the sinner obtains through the power of the keys, namely, absolution from guilt, commutation of punishment from perpetual to temporal, and remission of part of the temporal punishment. And on account of this threefold benefit, Saint Peter is triply honored. Fourth, he is honored on account of our debt to him. Since he has fed and feeds us in three ways, namely, by word, by example, and by temporal aid or the suffrage of his prayers, we are triply indebted to him and therefore honor him with three feasts. A fifth reason is the example he gives us, because no sinner should despair even if he, like Peter, has denied God three times, provided that, like Peter, he confesses God in his heart, by his speech, and through his actions.

A second reason for the institution of today's feast is one that is taken from the *Itinerarium* of Saint Clement. There we read that Peter was going about, preaching the Gospel, and when he approached Antioch, all the people of that city came barefoot, clothed in sackcloth, and sprinkling ashes on their heads, to meet him. They did this by way of penance, because they had taken sides against him with Simon the Magician. Seeing their repentance, Peter thanked God. Then they brought to him all the people who were sickly or were possessed by demons. Peter had them laid out in front of him and called down God's blessing upon them, and an immense light appeared and all were cured, whereupon they ran after Peter and kissed his footprints. Within a week over ten thousand men were baptized. Theophilus, governor of the city, had his house consecrated as a basilica, in which he erected an elevated chair for Peter so that he might be seen and heard by all. Nor does this account contradict what has been said above. It is quite possible that after Peter, due to Paul's intervention, was magnificently welcomed by Theophilus and the townspeople, he may have left the city. Then Simon Magus may have perverted the people and stirred them up against the apostle, but later they would have done penance and again given Peter an honorable reception.

The feast of the Chair of Saint Peter used to be called the feast of Saint Peter's Banquet, and this brings us to the third reason for its institution. It was an ancient custom of the pagans (as Master John Beleth tells us) to offer a banquet on the tombs of their ancestors every year on a certain day in the month of February. Then, during the night, demons consumed the food, but the pagans thought it was the souls of the dead, which they called shades, that wandered among the tombs and did away with the viands. According to the same author the ancients said that when the souls are in the human body, they are called souls, when they are in the underworld, they are *manes*, ghosts, when they ascend to heaven, they are called spirits, and, when they are recently buried or wander around the tombs, shades. The holy fathers of the Church wanted to eradicate this custom of the banquets but saw that it would be difficult to do so, and in its stead instituted the feast of the Chair or Enthronement of Saint Peter. This combined the Roman and the Antiochene feasts on the same day when the old banquets were held, and so there are some even now who call this feast the Feast of Saint Peter's Banquet.[2]

The fourth reason for the institution of today's feast is reverence for the clerical tonsure. It is noteworthy that, according to a tradition held by some, the clerical tonsure had its origin here. When Peter began to preach the Gospel at Antioch, the pagans shaved the top of his head as a sign of contempt for the name of Christian; and in time the tonsure, which had been imposed on the prince of the apostles as a badge of shame, was passed on to all clerics as a mark of honor. There are three things worthy of note regarding this clerical "crown," namely, the shaving of the head, the cutting off of hair, and the circular shape of the tonsure. The top of the head is shaved for three reasons, of which two are given by Dionysius in the *Ecclesiastical Hierarchy*.[3] He says that the shaving of the head signifies a clean, plain, artless way of life; for three things follow upon the cutting off of hair or the shaving of the head, namely, preservation of cleanness, lack of ornament, and denudation. Preservation of cleanness follows, because hair collects dirt; lack of ornament, because hair is worn as an ornament. Thus the tonsure signifies a clean, unpretentious life. This means that clerics should have interior cleanness of mind and a lack of concern for external fashion. The

---

[2] The traditional date of this feast in the Roman calendar is 22 February, which almost exactly coincided with the final day of the Roman feasts of the dead, the 21st.

[3] Graesse mistakenly has *in Coelesti Hierarchia*. The correct reference is *The Ecclesiastical Hierarchy*, chap. 6, sec. 2, in Pseudo-Dionysius, *The Complete Works* (New York: Paulist Press, 1987), 246–247.

denuding of the scalp signifies that there should be nothing between the cleric and God: clerics should be immediately united to God and should behold the glory of the Lord with face unveiled. The cutting off of hair gives us to understand that clerics should cut away all superfluous thoughts from their minds and should have their hearing prepared and ready for the word of God, thus completely removing from themselves everything temporal except the strictly necessary.

There are many reasons for the circular shape of the tonsure. First, the circle has neither end nor beginning, and by this it is understood that clerics are ministers of God, who has neither beginning nor end. Second, the round shape has no angles, and this means that clerics should have no soiled areas in their lives, since (as Bernard says) where there are angles there are dirty spots. They should also have truth in their teaching, because truth (as Jerome says) does not like angles. Third, the circle is of all shapes the most beautiful; hence God made his heavenly creatures in this shape. This means that clerics should have beauty inwardly in their thoughts and outwardly in their conduct. Fourth, the circle is the simplest of all shapes, for no figure (as Augustine says) consists of only one line; the circle is the only one that is closed by a single line. This signifies that clerics should have the simplicity of doves, according to the word of the Lord: "Be simple as doves."

45. Saint Matthias, Apostle

The Hebrew name Matthias means given by God, or gift of God, or it can mean humble or small. Saint Matthias was given by God when God chose him out of the world and gave him a place among the seventy-two disciples. He was a gift of God when, being elected by lot, he won the name of apostle. He was small in that he always preserved true humility. Humility (as Ambrose says) is threefold. There is first the humility that is imposed from without on a person, who is then said to be humiliated; second, the humility of reflection, which comes out of one's self-knowledge; third, the humility of devotion, which proceeds from knowledge of the Creator. Matthias had the first humility by suffering martyrdom, the second by having a low estimate of himself, and the third by bowing before the majesty of God. Or his name may come from *manus*, which means good, and *thesis*, which means position. Matthias, the good, was positioned in the place of the evil one, Judas.

Bede is believed to be the author of the life of Matthias which is read in the churches.

Matthias the apostle was given the place of Judas; but first let us briefly see something of Judas's birth and origins. We read in a certain admittedly apocryphal history that there was in Jerusalem a man, Ruben by name, who was also called Simon, of the tribe of Dan, or, as Jerome has it, of the tribe of Issachar, and who had a wife named Cyborea. One night, after they had paid each other the marital debt, Cyborea fell asleep and had a dream that she related, terrified, sobbing and groaning, to her husband. She said: "I dreamed that I was going to bear a son so wicked that he would bring ruin upon our whole people." Ruben answered: "That's a very bad thing you are saying, a thing that should not be repeated, and I think a divining spirit had hold of you!" "If I find that I have conceived and if I bear a son," she said, "there can be no doubt that it was not a divining spirit but a revelation of the truth."

In due time the son was born, and the parents, filled with fear, began to wonder what to do with him. They abhorred the thought of killing him but were unwilling to nurture the destroyer of their people, so they put the infant in a basket, which they set afloat in the sea, and the waves carried it to an island called Scariot. Judas therefore took the surname of Iscariot from the island. The queen of this island, who was childless, was walking on the beach. She saw the basket floating in the surf and had it brought ashore. In it she found this beautifully formed infant and sighed: "Oh, if only I might have such a child, how relieved I would be, because my kingdom would not be left without a successor by my death!" She therefore had the infant nursed secretly while she pretended to be pregnant. When the time came, she lied by announcing that she had borne a son, and the word spread throughout the kingdom. The king was overjoyed at having a son, and the whole nation shared his joy. The child, of course, was brought up in royal style.

Not long afterward, however, the queen conceived of the king and gave birth to a son. As the two boys grew up, they often played together, and Judas frequently maltreated the royal child and made him cry. The queen resented this and, knowing that Judas was not her son, often chastised him for his misdeeds, but Judas continued as bad as ever. Finally the truth came out and it was known that he was not the queen's child but a foundling. When Judas himself learned this, he was bitterly ashamed and secretly killed the king's son, who had been thought to be his own brother. Then, fearing that he would be put to death for this crime, he fled to Jerusalem with other youths who were part of a tribute payment, and took service (like finding like) in the household of Pilate, who was then governor of Judea. Pilate noticed that Judas was a man after his own heart and began to treat him as a favorite, finally putting him in charge of his whole domain; and Judas's word was law.

One day Pilate was looking out from his palace at a nearby orchard and was seized with such a desire for some of the fruit that he almost fainted. The orchard belonged to Ruben, Judas's father, but Judas did not recognize his father nor did Ruben know his son, because Ruben thought that his child had perished in the sea, and Judas had no idea who his father was or where he came from. Pilate called for Judas and told him: "I crave that fruit so much that if I don't get some of it, I'll die!" Thus prompted, Judas jumped over into the orchard and speedily picked some apples. At that moment Ruben came along and found Judas picking his apples, whereupon a violent argument started, words led to insults, and insults to blows and injuries on both sides. Finally Judas struck Ruben at the back of the neck with a stone and killed him. He then delivered the apples to Pilate and told him what had happened.

As daylight faded and night came on, Ruben's body was found and it was thought that he had been overtaken by sudden death. Pilate awarded all Ruben's belongings, including his wife Cyborea, to Judas. Then one day Judas, finding Cyborea heavyhearted and tearful, urged her to tell him what was troubling her. "Alas, I am the unhappiest of women," she answered. "I drowned my baby son in the sea, I found my husband stricken with sudden death, and to all my sorrows Pilate has added a new one, handing me over, saddened as I am and totally unwilling, to be your wife!" She went on to tell him all about her baby, and Judas told her all that had happened to him. So they discovered that he had taken his mother to wife and had killed his father. Cyborea then persuaded him to repent, and he turned to our Lord Jesus Christ and begged forgiveness for all his crimes. So far, however, what we have set down comes from the aforesaid apocryphal history, and whether it should be retold is left to the reader's judgment, though probably it is better left aside than repeated.

Be that as it may, the Lord made Judas his disciple and then chose him to be an apostle. Indeed he loved him so dearly that he made him the keeper of the purse and finally bore with him as his betrayer. So Judas carried the purse and stole the alms that were given to Christ. At the time of the Lord's passion he protested because the ointment that was worth three hundred pence had not been sold so he could steal that money too. Then he went out and betrayed his Lord for thirty pieces of silver, each coin being worth ten pence, and so he made up the three hundred pence lost over the ointment—or, as some say, he regularly stole one-tenth of all that was given to Christ, and therefore sold the Lord for the tenth part of the lost sale price of the ointment, i.e., three hundred pence. However, he was sorry for what he had done, threw back the money, and hanged himself with a halter, and, as the gospel tells us, "burst asunder in the middle and all his bowels gushed out." Thus his mouth was spared defilement since nothing came out through it, for it would have been incongruous that a mouth which had touched the glorious lips of Christ should be so foully soiled.

It also was fitting that the bowels which had conceived the betrayal should burst and spill out, and that the throat from which had emerged the voice of the traitor should be strangled by a rope. Moreover, Judas perished in the air, so that the one who had offended the angels in heaven and men on earth was kept out of the regions belonging to angels and to men, and was left in the air in the company of demons.

Between the Lord's ascension and Pentecost the apostles were together in the upper room, and Peter remarked that the number twelve—the number of apostles chosen by the Lord to preach the faith of the Trinity to the four quarters of the world—was diminished. Rising in the midst of his brothers, he said: "Men and brothers, it behooves us to replace Judas with someone who will testify with us to Christ's resurrection, because the Lord told us, 'You will be witnesses to me in Jerusalem and in all of Judea and Samaria and to the uttermost part of the earth.' Now a witness should testify only to things he has seen, so we should choose one from among the men who have been with us all the time, and have seen the Lord's miracles and heard his teaching." They therefore put forward two disciples, namely, Joseph, who was called the Just on account of his holiness and was the brother of James of Alpheus, and Matthias, of whom nothing more is said in praise because his being chosen as an apostle is praise enough. They prayed, saying: "O Lord, you know the hearts of all! Show us which of these two brothers you have elected to take the place in this ministry and apostleship that Judas lost!"[1] They cast lots and the choice fell on Matthias, who therefore was numbered with the eleven apostles.

Note that this one example does not, as Jerome says, mean that the use of lots is approved as common practice: privileges allowed to a few do not make general law. Or again, as Bede says, before the truth came it was licit to make use of figures. The true host was immolated in the passion but consummated at Pentecost, and therefore in the election of Matthias lots were used so as not to depart from the Law which prescribed that the high priest be selected by lot. After Pentecost, when the truth had been made public, the seven deacons were ordained not by lot but through election by the disciples, the prayer of the apostles, and the laying on of hands. Regarding the kind of lots the above were, we have two opinions from the holy fathers. Jerome and Bede agree that they were the same kind of lots as those whose use we find very frequently in the Old Testament. On the other hand Dionysius, who was a disciple of Paul, considers it irreligious to hold this opinion and declares that as he sees it, this lot was nothing other than a brilliant ray of light sent down from God upon Matthias to show that he was to be received as an apostle. So, in *The Celestial History*,[2]

---

[1] Acts 1:23–26.

[2] Cf. *The Ecclesiastical Hierarchy* (again, not *The Celestial*), chap. 5, sec. 3, in Pseudo-Dionysius, *The Complete Works* (New York: Paulist Press, 1987), p. 241. Note that in this English version the translator has rendered the words *sors divina* as "divine *choice*," whereas I have translated them "divine *lot*."

Dionysius says: "Of the divine lot that by God's will fell upon Matthias, others have said different things, which, in my opinion, are not in accord with religion. I shall now state my own understanding: the Scriptures used the term 'lot' to describe a certain divine gift which showed the apostolic group that Matthias was accepted by divine election."

Judea was assigned to Matthias the apostle by lot, and he preached there assiduously, wrought many miracles, and went to his eternal rest in peace. In some codices, however, we read that he was crucified and ascended into heaven with the martyr's crown. It is said that his body is buried under a porphyry slab in the church of Saint Mary Major in Rome, and that his head is shown to the people there.

In another legend, found in Trier, we read among other things that Matthias, of the tribe of Judah, was born in Bethlehem of illustrious parentage. At his studies he quickly acquired much knowledge of the law and the prophets, shunned everything lascivious, and overcame the temptations of adolescence by the maturity of his conduct. He schooled himself in virtue and was quick in understanding, ready in compassion, not puffed up by prosperity, steady and intrepid in adversity. He made every effort to carry out in action what he prescribed by command, and to demonstrate his oral teaching by putting it in practice. While he was preaching throughout Judea, he cleansed the lepers, drove out demons, made the lame walk, the blind see, and the deaf hear, and raised the dead to life. He was brought before the high priest and to many accusations responded: "I do not need to say much about the things you charge me with, things you call crimes, because to be a Christian is not a matter of crime but of glory!" The pontiff asked him: "If you were given time to reflect, would you recant?" Matthias: "Far be it from me to apostatize and repudiate the truth, having once found it!"

Matthias was very learned in the law, clean of heart, prudent in judgment, keen in solving problems concerning the sacred Scripture, cautious in counseling, and frank in his speech. During his preaching in Judea he converted many to the faith by signs and miracles. This made the Jews envious and they haled him before the council. Two false witnesses, who had brought charges against him, were the first to hurl stones at him, and he demanded that these stones be buried with him in testimony against the witnesses. While he was being stoned, he was beheaded with an ax in the Roman manner, raised his hands to heaven, and breathed his last. His body was translated from Judea to Rome and from there to Trier.

In another legend we read that Matthias went to Macedonia and preached there. He was given a poisoned potion that had blinded all who drank it, but he drank it in Christ's name and it did him no harm. More than 250 people had been blinded by the drink, and Matthias restored their sight by laying his hand on each of them. But the devil appeared to them in the likeness of a child and persuaded them to kill him, on the ground that he was undermining their religion. He was there in their midst, but they looked for him for three days and could not see him. On the third day, however, he made himself known to them and said: "Here I am!" They tied his hands behind his back and put a rope around his neck, tortured him cruelly, then shut him up in prison. There the demons gnashed their teeth at him but could not get near him. The Lord came in a great light, lifted him from the ground, loosed his bonds, comforted him gently, and opened the door of the prison for him. He went out and resumed his preaching of the word of God. There were some who still obstinately resisted his preaching, and to them he said: "I give you notice that you will go to hell alive!" and the earth opened and swallowed them. The rest, however, were converted to the faith.

46. Saint Gregory

The name Gregory (Gregorius) is formed from *grex*, flock, and *gore*, which means to preach or to say, and Saint Gregory was preacher to his flock. Or the name resembles *egregarius*, from *egregius*, outstanding, and *gore;* and Gregory was an outstanding preacher and doctor. Or Gregorius, in our language, suggests vigilance, watchfulness; and the saint watched over himself, over God, and over his flock—over himself by virtuous living, over God by inward contemplation, over the flock by assiduous preaching—and in these three ways he merited the vision of God. So Augustine says in his book *De Ordine:* "He who lives well, studies well, and prays well sees God."

Gregory's life was written by Paul, historian of the Lombards, and at a later time was more carefully compiled by John the Deacon.[1]

Gregory was born into a senatorial family. His father's name was Gordianus, and his mother's, Silvia. While still an adolescent he reached a high level of learning. He was also exceedingly wealthy, yet he considered leaving all behind him and committing himself to a religious way of life. For a long time, however, he put off this conversion. He thought that he might more safely put himself in the service of Christ by appearing to remain in the world as an urban magistrate; but the demands of secular affairs soon weighed on him so heavily that he was snared in them not only in appearance but in his mind.

---

[1] Tradition has awarded Pope Saint Gregory I (590–604) the title "the Great." Only one other pope, Saint Leo (440–461), is so called.

After his father died, Gregory built six monasteries in Sicily and established a seventh in his own house within the city walls, dedicating this one in honor of Saint Andrew the Apostle. He lived there, laying aside his silken robes with their adornment of gold and gems for the rough tunic of a monk. In a short time he attained such holiness that in the very beginning of his new life he could already be counted among the perfect. Indeed the measure of his perfection may be gauged from words he later wrote in the prologue to his *Dialogues*: "My unhappy spirit, stricken with the wounds of its present cares, recalls how different life was in the monastery—how the spirit let everything go by beneath it, and rose above the transitory to think upon nothing but the things of heaven. Even while still retained in the body it escaped the confinement of the flesh by contemplation and loved death itself (the thought of which is so painful to most people) because death is the entrance to life and the reward of labor." Furthermore he chastised his body so severely that his stomach was weakened and he barely stayed alive. He frequently suffered the kind of fainting spell called *syncope* by the Greeks, at which times he seemed close to death.

One day when he was busy writing in one of his monasteries, over which he presided as abbot, an angel of the Lord came to him in the guise of a shipwrecked seaman and pleaded for help, shedding floods of tears. Gregory had some silver coins given to him, but he came back the same day, complaining that he had lost much and had been given little, and again he received money. Yet a third time he came, making a nuisance of himself with his loud demands for help. The monk in charge of the monastery's property informed Gregory that there was nothing left to give the beggar but a silver dish in which Gregory's mother in times past had sent vegetables for his meal. The saint immediately said to give the dish to the mendicant, who accepted it joyfully and went his way. But the beggar was really an angel of God, as he afterwards made himself known.

Another day, when Gregory was walking through the marketplace in Rome, he noticed a group of young men, handsome in form and features, whose blond hair attracted admiring attention. They were slaves and were being sold. Gregory asked the trader where they came from, and he answered: "From Britain, where all the inhabitants have the same fair skin and blond hair as these do." Gregory asked if they were Christians, and the merchant replied: "No, they are benighted pagans." Gregory groaned sadly and said: "What a pity, that the prince of darkness should possess these radiant faces!" He then asked the name of that people and was told that they were called Angles. "And well named!" he said "The name sounds like Angels, and their faces are angelic." He asked what their province was called and was told that their provincial name was *Deiri*. "Again well named," said Gregory, "because they are to be rescued *de ira*, from wrath." He inquired about the name of their king, and the trader said that he was called Aelle. "Aelle is right," said Gregory, "because *Alleluia* must be sung in that land."

Shortly thereafter Gregory called upon the pope, and the pontiff, yielding to his insistent pleading, agreed to send him to convert the English. He was well on his way when the Romans, distressed at his absence, went to the pope and addressed him as follows: "You have offended Saint Peter and destroyed Rome by sending Gregory away!" This alarmed the pope, who hastened to send messengers after the saintly abbot, calling him back. Gregory had been on the road for three days and had stopped to give his traveling companions a chance to rest. He himself was reading when a locust lighted on his book, forcing him to desist from his reading and making him realize, by the very meaning of the insect's name, that he should stay in that same locus: it was the spirit of prophecy that enabled him to understand this. He therefore exhorted his companions to resume their journey as fast as possible, while he waited for the papal messengers and was compelled to turn back to Rome, sad though he was to do so. Then the pope took him out of his monastery and ordained him to be his cardinal deacon.

The Tiber once overflowed its banks so far that it came over the city walls and demolished a large number of houses. The river carried a great many serpents and a huge dragon down to the sea, but the waves smothered the beasts and tossed them onto the shore. The stench of their rotting bodies bred a deadly pestilence called the bubonic plague, and people seemed to see arrows coming from heaven and striking this one and that one. The first to be stricken was Pope Pelagius, who died within hours, and the plague swept through the population so fatally that many houses stood empty in the city.

The Church of God, however, could not be without a head, and the people unanimously elected Gregory to be their bishop, although he made every effort to dissuade them. He had to be consecrated bishop of Rome, but the plague was causing havoc in the city, so he preached to the people, organized a procession, and had litanies recited, exhorting everyone to pray zealously to the Lord. Even while the entire population pleaded with God, however, in any one hour ninety men died; but Gregory continued to urge all to pray until the divine mercy should banish the plague.

When the procession was finished, Gregory tried to flee from Rome but could not, because they watched for him day and night at the city gates. At length he changed his clothes and persuaded some tradesmen to hide him in a wine cask and get him out of the city in a wagon. When they reached a forest, he made for a hiding place in the caves and hid there for three days. A relentless search for him was under way, and a bright column of light beamed down from the heavens and appeared over the place where he had concealed himself: a certain hermit saw angels descending and ascending in this beam. Of course this led the pursuers to Gregory, and they carried him back to Rome and consecrated him as supreme pontiff.

That he accepted this highest honor against his will is clear to anyone who reads his writings. In a letter to the patrician Narsus he wrote: "When you describe the heights of contemplation, you renew my grief at my own ruin, because I hear what I had lost inwardly when I unworthily mounted outwardly to this summit of power. I want you to know that I am oppressed with such grief that I can hardly speak. Therefore do not call me Noemi, i.e., beautiful, but call me Mara, because I am filled with bitterness." And elsewhere he wrote: "If, knowing that I have been raised to the order of bishop, you love me, weep, because I myself ceaselessly shed tears; and I beg you to pray God for me." In the prologue to his *Dialogues* he says: "Due to my pastoral responsibilities, my spirit suffers from engagement in the affairs of men of the world, and after having enjoyed the beauty of spiritual quiet it is soiled with the dust of earthly business. I ponder therefore what I have to put up with, I ponder what I have lost. As I fix my attention on what I have lost, my present burden grows heavier. See, I am tossed about as if by the waves of the sea, the mighty storm winds beat upon the ship of my mind; and when I recall my former life, my eyes look back, I see the shore, and I sigh."

The plague was still ravaging Rome, and Gregory ordered the procession to continue to make the circuit of the city, the marchers chanting the litanies. An image of Blessed Mary ever Virgin was carried in the procession. It is said that this image is still in the church of Saint Mary Major in Rome, that it was painted by Saint Luke, who was not only a physician but a distinguished painter, and that it was a perfect likeness of the Virgin. And lo and behold! The poisonous uncleanness of the air yielded to the image as if fleeing from it and being unable to withstand its presence: the passage of the picture brought about a wonderful serenity and purity in the air. We are also told that the voices of angels were heard around the image, singing

> Regina coeli laetare, alleluia,
> Quia quem meruisti portare, alleluia,
> Resurrexit sicut dixit, alleluia!

to which Gregory promptly added:

> Ora pro nobis, Deum rogamus, alleluia![2]

Then the pope saw an angel of the Lord standing atop the castle of Crescentius, wiping a bloody sword and sheathing it. Gregory understood that that put an end to the plague, as, indeed, happened. Thereafter the castle was called the Castle of the Holy Angel.

In time, moreover, the pope sent Augustine, Mellitus, John, and some other missionaries to England, as he had long wished to do; and by his prayers and merits he brought about the conversion of the English to the faith.

Gregory was so humble that he would not allow anyone to praise him. To Stephen, a bishop who had written him laudatory letters, he wrote: "In your

---

[2] Queen of heaven, rejoice, alleluia, / Because he whom thou didst bear, alleluia, / Hath risen as he said, alleluia! / Pray for us, we beg God, alleluia!

letters you show me much favor (far more than I, unworthy as I am, ought to hear), although Scripture tells us, 'Praise not any man as long as he lives.' Nevertheless, although I was unworthy to hear such things, I beg you to pray that I may become worthy of them, in order that, if you said that these good things are in me because they are not, they may be in me because you said they are." Likewise in a letter to the patrician Narsus: "When in writing to me you match the name to the thing and put forth resounding statements and rhetorical touches in my regard, surely, dearest brother, you are calling the monkey a lion, which we are seen to do when we call mangy kittens leopards or tigers." And in a letter to Anastasius the patriarch of Antioch: "When you speak of me as the mouth of the Lord, when you call me a lamp, when you say that by my speaking I can benefit many and enlighten many, you cause me to question seriously my own self-estimate, for I consider who and what I am and discern no such good in myself, and I also consider who you are and am sure you are incapable of lying. Therefore when I wish to believe what you say, my infirmity contradicts me, and when I wish to argue against what you say in praise of me, your holiness contradicts me. But, Your Holiness, I ask that some good come of this our disagreement, so that if what you say of me be not so, it be so because you say it."

He wanted no pompous or high-sounding titles. To Eulogius, the patriarch of Alexandria, who had called him the universal pope, he wrote: "In the foreword of the epistle that you addressed to me you made a point of imposing a word of prideful significance by calling me the universal pope. I beg your most kind holiness not to do this again, because what is attributed to another beyond what reason calls for is taken away from yourself. I do not seek to move ahead by means of words but by good conduct, and I do not regard as an honor something that I know causes my brother to lose honor. Therefore let words that inflate vanity and wound charity be banished." Again, when John, bishop of Constantinople, usurped this vainglorious title for himself and by fraud obtained from the synod the privilege of being called the universal pope, Gregory wrote this, among other things, about him: "Who is this man, who, contrary to evangelical statutes and canonical decrees, presumes to usurp a new name for himself, so that without lessening [the status of other bishops] he may be number one and yearns to be universal?" Nor did Gregory allow his fellow bishops to speak of him as "commanding." For this reason he wrote to Eulogius, bishop of Alexandria: "Your Charity speaks to me, saying, 'as you have commanded.' Please do not let me hear that word again, because I know who I am and who you (others) are. In terms of place you are my brothers, in terms of virtue you are my fathers."

It was also due to his profound humility that Gregory did not want women to call themselves his handmaids. Thus he wrote to the patrician lady Rusticana: "One thing I did not like in your letter was something that, while it may be said once, was said there several times—namely, again and again, 'your maidservant.'

By my office as bishop I became the servant of all: why do you speak of yourself as my servant, since even before I assumed the episcopate I was your servant? Therefore I beg of you by almighty God that I may never again find this word applied to me in your letters."

Out of humility he did not want his books to be made public during his lifetime: in his judgment they were worthless in comparison with the works of other authors. To Innocent, governor of the province of Africa, he wrote: "That you have expressed the wish to have my tract on the book of Job sent to you makes me rejoice at your interest; but if you wish to fatten on delicious food for the mind, read the treatises of your compatriot the blessed Augustine, and do not compare our bran with his wheat flour. Moreover, I do not want anything I may happen to have said to become readily available to people while I am in this body." We also read in a book translated from Greek into Latin that when a holy father, Abba John, came to Rome to visit the threshold of the apostles, he saw blessed Gregory walking in the middle of the city. He wished to meet him and do him reverence, as was proper; but blessed Gregory, seeing that the other was about to prostrate himself on the ground, anticipated John by dropping to his knees in front of him and would not rise before the father did. Here again his great humility was confirmed.

He was so generous in almsgiving that he saw to the needs not only of people close by but of others far away; thus he provided for the monks on Mount Sinai. He kept a register of those in need and took care of them liberally. He established a monastery in Jerusalem and made provision for the servants of God who lived there, and he reserved eighty pounds of gold annually for the daily expenses of three thousand handmaids of God. He invited pilgrims to his table every day. One day he was about to humble himself by pouring water on the hands of one such pilgrim and turned around to pick up a jug of water, but, when he turned back, the one whose hands he meant to wash had disappeared. He wondered at this, and that very night the Lord appeared to him and said: "On other days you have waited on me in my members, but yesterday it was I myself whom you welcomed."

Another time he ordered his steward to invite twelve pilgrims to dine with him, and the steward carried out his orders. When all were seated, however, the pope looked around and counted thirteen. He summoned the steward and asked why he had presumed, against his orders, to invite thirteen guests. The steward counted, and, finding only twelve, said: "Believe me, father, there are only twelve here." Then Gregory noticed that the countenance of one pilgrim, who was seated close to him, changed again and again: now it was the face of a young man, then was like that of a venerable ancient. When the meal was finished, the pope brought this man into a side room and insisted that he be good enough to make himself and his name known. The pilgrim answered: "Why do you ask me my name, which is marvelous? Nevertheless know that I am that shipwrecked seaman to whom you gave the silver dish in which your mother had sent you vegetables. Know for certain also that from the very day on which you gave me the dish, the Lord destined you to become the head of his Church and the successor of Peter the apostle." Gregory asked him: "How did you know that the Lord had destined me to rule over his Church?" The answer was: "I knew it because I am his angel, and the Lord sent me back so that I might always protect you, and through me you might obtain from him whatever you ask." And in the twinkling of an eye he disappeared.

At that time there was a certain hermit, a man of great virtue, who had given up all for God and possessed nothing but a cat, which he petted and fondled in his lap almost as if it were a woman who lived with him. The hermit prayed to God to deign to show him with whom he, who for love of him possessed no earthly wealth, might hope to dwell in the future by way of remuneration. One night it was revealed to him that he might hope to share a dwelling with Gregory the Roman pontiff. But the hermit groaned with disappointment, thinking that his voluntary poverty was of little benefit to him if he was to receive his reward with one who enjoyed such an abundance of worldly goods. As he went on day after day grieving at the thought of his poverty and Gregory's wealth, there came another night when he heard the Lord saying to him: "It is not the possession of wealth but the love of it that makes a man rich. How dare you compare your poverty with Gregory's riches—you, who prove every day that you love that cat, your treasure, by the way you stroke it, while he does not love the wealth that surrounds him, but despises it and gives it away openhandedly to all who need it?" The solitary therefore gave thanks to God and began to pray that he, who had thought his merit was belittled by being compared with the pope's, might in time be found worthy of dwelling with Gregory.

Upon being falsely accused before Emperor Maurice and his sons of having had something to do with the death of a certain bishop, Gregory wrote a letter to the emperor's deputy, in which he said: "One thing you might mention to my lords is that if I, their servant, had wished to have a hand in causing death or harm to Lombards, today the Lombard nation would have no king, no dukes, no counts, and would be in chaos: but because I fear God, I would be afraid to become involved in the death of any man." You see how humble he was, calling himself the emperor's servant and the emperor his lord and master, although he was the supreme pontiff. See his humility, when he refused to agree to the death of his enemies. And when Emperor Maurice persecuted Gregory and the Church of God, Gregory wrote this, among other things, to him: "Because I am a sinner, I believe that the more you inflict distress upon me, who serve him so badly, the more you placate almighty God."

One day a figure dressed in a monkish habit stood fearlessly before the emperor, brandished a drawn sword at him, and predicted that Maurice would die by the sword. The emperor, terrified, put an end to his persecution of the pope and earnestly begged him to pray that God would deign to punish him in this life for his wrongdoing, rather than reserving his punishment to the final judgment.

Then Maurice had a vision. He saw himself standing outside the judge's tribunal, and the judge calling out: "Bring Maurice here!" Thereupon the attendants seized him and set him down before the judge. The judge asked him: "Where do you want me to pay you back for the wrongs you perpetrated in this world?" The emperor answered: "Pay me my just deserts here, Lord, rather than in the life to come!" At once the voice of God gave orders that Maurice, his wife, and his sons and daughters be turned over to the soldier Phocas and be killed by him. And that is what happened: not long afterwards Phocas, one of his soldiers, put him and his whole family to death by the sword and succeeded him in the empire.

One Easter Sunday, when Gregory was celebrating the mass in the church of Saint Mary Major and pronounced the *Pax Domini*, an angel responded in a loud voice: *Et cum spiritu tuo!* From then on the popes made that basilica a station, and in testimony to this miracle no response is made when the *Pax Domini* is sung there.

Once when the Roman emperor Trajan was hurrying off to war with all possible speed, a widow ran up to him in tears and said: "Be good enough, I beg you, to avenge the blood of my son, who was put to death though he was innocent!" Trajan answered that if he came back from the war safe and sound, he would take care of her case. "And if you die in battle," the widow objected, "who then will see that justice is done?" "Whoever rules after me," Trajan replied. "And what good will it do you," the widow argued, "if someone else rights my loss?" "None at all!" the emperor retorted. "Then wouldn't it be better for you," the woman persisted, "to do me justice yourself and receive the reward, than to pass it on to someone else?" Trajan, moved with compassion, got down from his horse and saw to it that the blood of the innocent was avenged.

We also read that one of Trajan's sons was galloping his horse recklessly through the city and ran down the son of a widow, killing him. When the grief-stricken mother related this incident to Trajan, he handed over his own son—the one who had done the deed—to the widow, to replace the son she had lost, and endowed her liberally besides.

One day many years after that emperor's death, as Gregory was crossing through Trajan's forum, the emperor's kindness came to his mind, and he went to Saint Peter's basilica and lamented the ruler's errors with bitter tears. The voice of God responded from above: "I have granted your petition and spared Trajan eternal punishment; but from now on be extremely careful not to pray for a damned soul!" Furthermore, John of Damascus, in one of his sermons, relates that as Gregory was pouring forth prayers for Trajan, he heard a divine voice coming to him, which said: "I have heard your voice and I grant pardon to Trajan." Of this (as John says in the same sermon) both East and West are witness.

On this subject some have said that Trajan was restored to life, and in this life obtained grace and merited pardon: thus he attained glory and was not finally committed to hell nor definitively sentenced to eternal punishment. There are others who have said that Trajan's soul was not simply freed from being sentenced to eternal punishment, but that his sentence was suspended for a time, namely, until the day of the Last Judgment. Others have held that Trajan's punishment was assessed to him *sub conditione* as to place and mode of torment, the condition being that sooner or later Gregory would pray that through the grace of Christ there would be some change of place or mode. Still others, among them John the Deacon who compiled this legend, say that Gregory did not pray, but wept, and often the Lord in his mercy grants what a man, however desirous he might be, would not presume to ask for, and that Trajan's soul was not delivered from hell and given a place in heaven, but was simply freed from the tortures of hell. A soul (he says) can be in hell and yet, through God's mercy, not feel its pains. Then there are those who explain that eternal punishment is twofold, consisting first in the pain of sense and second in the pain of loss, i.e., being deprived of the vision of God. Thus Trajan's punishment would have been remitted as to the first pain but retained as to the second.

We are told, moreover, that the angel also said: "Because you pleaded for a damned person you are given a dual option: either you will endure two days of torment in purgatory, or you will certainly be harassed your whole life long by infirmities and pains and aches." Gregory chose to be stricken throughout his life by pains rather than to endure two days in purgatory, and so he was constantly struggling with fevers or coping with gout or shaking with severe pains or racked with excruciating stomach cramps. Indeed, he wrote as follows in one of his letters: "I am beset with so much gout and so many kinds of pain that my life is to me a most grievous punishment; daily I grow weak with suffering and sigh expectantly for the remedy of death." In the same vein, in another letter: "The pain I bear is mild at times and very severe at others, but never so mild as to go away and never so severe as to kill me. So it happens that though I am dying daily, I am held at bay by death. I am so thoroughly penetrated by noxious humors that living is an ordeal and I look forward eagerly to death, which I think is the only remedy for my sufferings."

A certain woman used to bring altar breads to Gregory every Sunday morning, and one Sunday, when the time came for receiving communion and he held out the Body of the Lord to her, saying: "May the Body of our Lord Jesus Christ benefit you unto life everlasting," she laughed as if at a joke. He immediately drew back his hand from her mouth and laid the consecrated Host on the altar, and then, before the whole assembly, asked her why she had dared to laugh. Her answer: "Because you called this bread, which I made with my own hands, the Body of the Lord." Then Gregory, faced with the woman's lack of belief, prostrated himself in prayer, and when he rose, he found the particle of bread changed into flesh in the shape of a finger. Seeing this, the woman recovered her faith. Then he prayed again, saw the flesh return to the form of bread, and gave communion to the woman.

Certain princes asked Gregory for some precious relics, and he gave them a swatch from the dalmatic of Saint John the Evangelist, but they regarded this as worthless and unworthy of their rank, and indignantly returned it to him. Then Saint Gregory, having prayed over it, asked for a knife and slashed the patch of cloth. Blood gushed at once from the cut, thus miraculously demonstrating the preciousness of relics.

One of Rome's rich men left his wife and for that was denied communion by the pope. The man took this as a personal affront but, since he could not openly resist the authority of the supreme pontiff, sought help from sorcerers. They promised to use their incantations to send a demon into the pope's horse, to madden it and endanger both horse and rider. So, when Gregory happened to be riding by on his palfrey, the magicians sent in their demon and upset the horse so much that no one could hold it. Gregory, however, knew by the Spirit that a demon was at work, and by making the sign of the cross over the animal delivered it from the spell, which fell upon the sorcerers in the form of perpetual blindness. They then admitted their guilt and later attained the grace of baptism. The pope, however, would not have their eyesight restored, for fear they might take up their magical arts again; but he gave orders that their living was to be provided from church funds.

We also read, in a book which the Greeks call *Lymon*, that the abbot who presided over Saint Gregory's monastery informed the pope that one of his monks had laid away three pieces of money for himself. Gregory, to put the fear of punishment in the other monks, excommunicated the guilty brother. Some time later the offender died, Gregory being unaware of his death; and he, aggrieved that the monk had died without absolution, wrote a prayer as an epitaph, absolving the defunct from the bond of excommunication. He gave this script to a deacon with orders to read it over the dead monk's grave. The order was carried out, and the following night the deceased appeared to the abbot and told him that he had been held in custody, but had been set free the previous day.

Gregory remodeled the Church's offices and chant, and founded a school for the chanters, for which he built two houses, one next to Saint Peter's basilica, the other near the Lateran church. There the couch on which he reclined while he attended to the singing and the rod with which he used to threaten the choir boys, together with an antiphonary from his own hand, are preserved with due veneration. To the canon of the mass he added the words *diesque nostros in tua pace disponas atque ab aeterna damnatione nos eripi et in electorum tuorum jubeas grege numerari*.[3]

---

[3] And [we pray thee] order our days in thy peace, and command that we be saved from eternal damnation and numbered in the flock of thy chosen.

At length blessed Gregory, having reigned for thirteen years, six months, and ten days,[4] departed this life full of good works. On his tomb these verses are inscribed:

> Suscipe terra tuo de corpore sumptum,
> Reddere quod valeas vivificante Deo,
> Spiritus astra petit, leti nil vira nocebunt,
> Cui vitae alterius mors magis ipsa via est.
> Pontificis summi hoc clauduntur membra sepulchro,
> Qui innumeris semper vixit ubique bonis.[5]

His death occurred in the year 604 from the incarnation of the Lord, under the emperor Phocas.

After blessed Gregory's death a great famine scourged the whole region, and the poor people, for whom Gregory always provided food, went to his successor and said: "Holy father, may Your Holiness not allow us to die of hunger, since our father Gregory used to feed us." These words angered the new pope, who answered: "Gregory, to win fame and praise, may have taken it upon himself to provide for all peoples, but we ourselves can do nothing for you," and he always sent them away empty-handed. Saint Gregory appeared to him three times and chided him gently for being so frugal and for speaking unkindly of him, but the pope made no move to change his conduct. So Gregory, now stern and fearsome, appeared a fourth time and struck him a lethal blow on the head, which caused him great pain and brought him to an early death.

The famine persisted, and some of Gregory's envious associates began to defame him, declaring that he was a spendthrift who had squandered the Church's wealth. They wanted to avenge this alleged prodigality by inducing others to burn the saint's books. Some were indeed burned and his critics were of a mind to burn all of them, but Peter, Gregory's deacon, who had been very close to him and is his interlocutor in the four books of his *Dialogues*, put up a vigorous resistance. He pointed out that their action would in no way detract from the late pope's memory since copies of his books were already in circulation in various regions of the world, and added that it would be a monstrous sacrilege to destroy so many great works of so great a father, over whose head he himself had often seen the Holy Spirit in the likeness of a dove. In the end he got them to agree that if he, Peter, merited immediate death by confirming by oath the truth of what he had told them, they would desist from burning the books, but if he was not to die but survived after giving his sworn testimony, he himself would lend a hand to the book burners. In fact we read that Gregory had told

---

[4] September 590–12 March 604.

[5] Receive, O earth, what was taken from thy body, / which thou canst give back when God vivifies it. / The spirit soars to the stars; no ills can harm the happy one / for whom death itself is the way to that other life. / In this tomb are enclosed the remains of that supreme pontiff / who ever and everywhere lived in good works.

Peter that if he publicized the miracle of the vision of the dove, he would die on the spot. Therefore the venerable Peter, dressed in deacon's robes and carrying the book of the Gospels, gave witness to Gregory's holiness and, in the very act of pronouncing the words of this true confession, gave up the ghost without suffering the last agony.

There was a monk in Saint Gregory's monastery who had put aside a sum of money. Blessed Gregory appeared to another monk and told him to direct the first one to get rid of his money and do penance, because he was to die in three days. Hearing this the guilty monk was shaken with fear, did penance, and gave up his money; but he was soon stricken with such a fever that from dawn to the third hour of the third day the burning was so intense that his tongue stuck out of his mouth and he seemed to be breathing his last. His brother monks stood around him chanting the Psalms, but after some time they interrupted their psalmody and began to talk about his faults. He then revived enough to smile and blink his eyes at them, saying: "May the Lord forgive you, brothers, for wanting to bring up my failings. You put me in a difficult dilemma, because I was being accused both by you and by the devil at the same time, and did not know which accusation to answer first. But if ever you see someone at the point of death, don't denigrate him but treat him with compassion as one who, with his accuser at his side, is going to be judged by a very strict judge. I stood for judgment with the devil accusing me, but with Saint Gregory's help I gave good answers to all his charges except one only, about which I was ashamed. For that one. as you have seen, I have been sorely punished and have not yet been able to get free of it." The brothers pressed him to tell them what he had been accused of, but he replied: "I dare not say, because when blessed Gregory commanded me to come back to you, the devil protested vehemently, thinking that God himself was sending me back to do penance for that one thing. Therefore I gave blessed Gregory my warrant that I would not reveal to anyone the calumny in question." Then he shouted: "O Andrew, Andrew, may you perish this year, because by your wicked counsel you brought me to this peril!" And then and there, rolling his eyes frightfully, he expired.

Now there was in the city a man named Andrew. At the very moment when the dying monk cursed him, this Andrew was seized by a malady so lethal that he was wasting away with the flesh falling from his bones yet could not die. He called the monks of Saint Gregory's monastery together and confessed to them that with the help of the aforementioned monk he had stolen certain papers belonging to the monastery and had sold them to outsiders for money; and this man, who had been unable to die, breathed his last as he was making his confession.

In this period, as we read in the life of Saint Eugene, the Ambrosian office rather than the Gregorian was still observed by the churches, and the Roman pontiff, whose name was Hadrian, convened a council at which it was decreed that the Gregorian office was to be followed universally. Emperor Charlemagne, acting as executor of this decree, traveled round the various provinces and, by threats and penalties, compelled all clerics to obey it. He also burned the books of the Ambrosian office wherever found and imprisoned many rebellious clergy.[6]

The blessed bishop Eugene set out for the council but found that it had disbanded three days before his arrival. It was his prudent decision to persuade the pope to recall all the prelates who had taken part in the council, though they were already three days on the road. At the newly convoked council it was the unanimous decision of the fathers that the Ambrosian and Gregorian missals should be placed on the altar of Saint Peter, the doors of the church should be closed tight and carefully sealed with the seals of a large number of bishops, and the bishops themselves should spend the night praying the Lord to indicate by some sign which of the two offices he wanted observed by the churches. Everything was done as ordered. When they opened the church doors in the morning, they found both missals lying open on the altar; or, as others state, they discovered the Gregorian missal broken up and its pages scattered here and there, whereas the Ambrosian volume was simply opened and lay where it had been placed on the altar. The bishops saw this as a sign from God, indicating that the Gregorian office should be spread throughout the world, while the Ambrosian was to be observed only in the church of Saint Ambrose. The holy fathers so decreed, and their decree is followed to this day.

John the Deacon, who compiled the life of Saint Gregory, relates that while he was gathering material and writing the life, a man dressed in priestly garments appeared to him in a dream and stood beside him (as he saw it) while he was writing by the light of a lantern. The man's outer garment was white and so thin that the blackness of the robe underneath it could be seen. The man came closer and puffed out his cheeks with boisterous laughter. When John asked him how a holder of such dignified office could laugh so rudely, he answered: "Because you're writing about dead people whom you never saw alive." John: "Although I never saw this man face to face, what I write about him I learned from reading him." "I see," said the other, "that you have done as you wished, and I shall go on doing what I can!" With that he blew out John's lamp and terrified him to the point that he screamed as though he thought the other had slashed his throat. At that moment Gregory appeared, having with him Saint Nicholas at his right and Peter the Deacon at his left, and he said to John: "Why did you doubt, O you of little faith?" The adversary was then trying to hide behind the bed-curtain, and Gregory snatched a large torch from the hand of Peter the Deacon who was holding it. With the flaming torch he burned the adversary's mouth and face, blackening him until he looked like an Ethiopian. A small spark fell on

---

[6] Hadrian I (772–795) had important and generally amicable dealings with Charlemagne, sole ruler of the Frankish realm from 771 to 814. This whole episode as related here, while historically improbable at best, is indicative of Jacobus's interest in liturgical developments and of his zeal for Roman authority.

his white garment and set it afire, and he was seen to be totally black. "We have blackened him enough," Peter said to Saint Gregory, who replied: "*We* haven't blackened him. We showed that he really *is* black!" And so they departed, leaving much light behind them.

47. Saint Longinus

Longinus was the centurion who with other soldiers stood by the Lord's cross, and who by Pilate's order pierced Christ's side with a spear. Seeing the signs that accompanied his death, the darkness and the earthquake, Longinus believed in Christ. Yet according to some accounts, what did most to convince him was that, age and infirmity having left him almost blind, the blood that ran down the shaft of the spear touched his eyes and at once he saw clearly.

Longinus then quit the military career and received instruction from the apostles at Caesarea of Cappadocia. He devoted the next twenty-eight years to living the monastic life, and by word and example made many converts to the faith. When the governor ordered him to worship the idols and Longinus refused, the governor commanded that all his teeth be pulled out and his tongue be cut off, but Longinus did not lose the power of speech. Moreover, he took an ax and with it smashed all the idols, saying: "We shall see whether they are gods!" The demons came out of the idols and infested the bodies of the governor and his attendants, and all of them began to rage and rant and bark like dogs, then collapsed at the feet of Longinus. He asked the demons: "Why do you live in idols?" They answered: "We can live anyplace where Christ's name is not heard and the sign of his cross is absent!"

The governor was still in a rage and had lost his sight, and Longinus told him: "Know that you cannot be cured unless you have me put to death. As soon as I am dead, I will pray for you and ask God to restore you to health of body and soul." So the governor ordered the beheading of Longinus, after which he went to the martyr's body, prostrated himself, and with tears did penance, whereupon his sight and health came back and he spent the rest of his life in good works.

✻
---

48. Saint Sophia and Her Three
Daughters

This is the legend of the holy martyrs Sophia and her three daughters, Faith, Hope, and Charity.[1] Note that the principal temple in Constantinople is named after Saint Sophia, whose name means Wisdom.

Saint Sophia wisely brought up her three daughters in the fear of God. The first daughter was eleven years old, the second ten, and the third eight when she came to Rome, where every Sunday she visited the churches and won over many women to Christ. For this reason she and her daughters were charged before Emperor Hadrian. The beauty of the three girls so charmed him that he wanted to adopt them as his own daughters, but they scorned him as dirt.

Faith was punished, first, by being beaten by thirty-six soldiers, secondly, by having her breasts torn off, and all saw milk flowing from the wounds and blood from the severed breasts. The witnesses cried out against the emperor's injustice, but the young girl rejoiced and hurled insults at him. Thirdly, she was thrown on a red-hot gridiron but was unharmed, then, fourthly, was put in a frying pan full of oil and wax, and, fifthly, was beheaded.

Her sister, Hope, was then summoned but could not be persuaded to sacrifice to the idols. Therefore she was first put into a caldron full of pitch, wax, and resin, drops from which fell on some unbelievers and cremated them: finally she was killed with a sword.

Charity, the third daughter, young child though she was, was encouraged by her mother and would not yield to Hadrian's blandishments, so the impious emperor firstly ordered her to be stretched on the rack until her limbs broke and her joints parted; secondly, to be beaten with clubs; thirdly, she was scourged with lashes. Fourthly, she was thrown into a fiery furnace, out of which the flames leapt over sixty yards and killed six thousand idolaters while the child walked unscathed in the midst of the fire and shone like gold. Fifthly, she was stabbed with white-hot nails and thus, with a martyr's dancing step, passed gladly by the sword to the crown.

Now, with many persons looking on, this most virtuous mother buried the remains of her incomparable daughters and, lying down on the grave, said: "Dearest daughters, my desire is to be with you." So she breathed her last in

---

[1] Graesse notes that this legend is lacking in more recent editions.

peace, and those present buried Saint Sophia with her beloved children. She had borne the sufferings of each of them and therefore was more than a martyr.

As for Hadrian, his whole body rotted and he wasted away to death, admitting the while that he had unjustly done injury to the saints of God.

❋

49. Saint Benedict

Benedict, whose name means blessed, was so called because he blessed many, or because he had many blessings, or again because all spoke well (*bene dicere*) of him, or because he merited eternal blessings. His life was written by Saint Gregory.

Benedict was a native of the province of Nursia. He was sent to Rome as a child for his liberal studies, but while still young he abandoned schooling and decided to retire to the desert. His nurse, who loved him dearly, followed him to a place called Effide. Once she borrowed a sieve from a neighbor to sift some wheat but let it fall off a table, and it broke into two pieces. Seeing her weep over this mishap, Benedict took the pieces, prayed, and found the sieve repaired.

Later on he secretly took leave of his nurse and lived for three years in a place where he was unknown to anyone except a monk named Romanus, who solicitously saw to his needs. There was no path, however, from Romanus's monastery to Benedict's cave, so the monk tied a loaf of bread to a long rope and lowered it to the saint. A little bell was attached to the rope, and when it rang, the man of God knew that Romanus had sent him food and came out and took it. But the ancient Enemy, envying the charity of the one and begrudging the other his nourishment, threw a stone and broke the bell; but Romanus found other ways to supply the saint's needs.

Some time later the Lord appeared to a priest who was readying his Easter dinner and said to him: "Here you are preparing delicacies for yourself, while yonder my servant is racked with hunger." The priest set out promptly and with much difficulty found Benedict, to whom he said: "Arise and let us take food together, because today is the Lord's Pasch." "I know it must be the Pasch," Benedict replied, "because I have the joy of seeing you." Indeed he lived so far away from anyone else that he had not known that this was Easter Sunday. The priest said: "Truly today is the day of the Lord's resurrection, and you should not be fasting, and that is why I have been sent to you." And so, blessing God, they took their meal.

One day a small black bird came to annoy Benedict, fluttering so close to his face that the saint could have caught it with his hand, but instead he made the sign of the cross and the bird flew away. Soon the devil brought to the holy man's mind the image of a woman whom he had once seen, and he was so aroused by the memory of her that he was almost overcome with desire, and began to think of quitting his solitary way of life. But suddenly, touched by the grace of God, he came to himself, shed his garment, and rolled in the thorns and brambles which abounded thereabouts; and he emerged so scratched and torn over his whole body that the pain in his flesh cured the wound of his spirit. Thus he conquered sin by putting out the fire of lust, and from that time on he no longer felt the temptations of the flesh.

Benedict's fame increased and spread abroad, and when the abbot of a nearby monastery died, the monks came to him in a body and begged him to preside over them. He refused and put them off for a long time, foreseeing that he would not be able to agree with their mode of life; but eventually he gave in and yielded to their entreaties. When he insisted that they observe the rule more strictly, however, they blamed each other for having pressed him to become their abbot, since their waywardness ran counter to his norm of right living. So, when they saw that he would not allow them to go on doing what was forbidden, and found it too hard to relinquish their bad habits, they mixed poison into his wine and served it to him at table. Benedict made the sign of the cross over it, and the wineglass shattered as if struck by a stone. Thus made aware that since it could not withstand the sign of life, it had been a drink of death, he rose at once, faced them calmly, and said: "May almighty God have mercy on you, brothers! Did I not tell you that I would not be able to fit my ways to yours?"

The saint then returned to the place of solitude that he had left. The wonders he performed multiplied, and so many disciples were drawn to him that he built twelve monasteries. In one of them there was a monk who could not stay very long at his prayers, but went out while the rest prayed and busied himself with worldly, transitory things. When the abbot of that monastery told Saint Benedict about this, the latter went there and saw a small black boy tugging at the fringe of the delinquent monk's habit and pulling him outside. He asked the abbot and a monk named Maurus: "Don't you see who it is that is pulling him away?" They answered no, and he said: "Let us pray that you also may see." They prayed, and Maurus saw but the abbot could not. The next day, when prayers were finished, the man of God found the monk outside the church and struck him with his staff to punish him for his blindness. Thereafter the monk stayed motionless at prayer, and the ancient Enemy, as if he himself had received the blow, dared not disturb his meditations.

Three of the twelve monasteries were built at the top of a steep mountain. It was a hard task to draw water at the bottom of the cliff and carry it to the top, so the brothers often besought the man of God to relocate their monasteries. Then one night he climbed the mountain with a young lad and, after praying for a long time, arranged three stones at the summit as a marker. In the morning, when he had returned to his abode and the monks came with the same request as usual, he said: "Go to the top of the cliff and you will find three stones set there. Dig at the place marked, for God can make water flow there for you." They went and found the spot, with water already oozing from the rock. They dug a hole and soon saw it filled with water; and even now it flows abundantly enough to pour down the cliff from top to bottom.

Once a man was clearing out brambles around Benedict's monastery with a scythe, and the blade came loose and fell into a deep part of the lake. The man was sorely disturbed about this, but the saint thrust the shaft into the water, and the blade came up and fastened itself to the shaft.

Placidus, a very young monk, went to draw water and fell into the river, and the current caught him and pulled him the distance of an arrow-shot from the bank, submerging him. Saint Benedict, sitting in his cell, immediately knew this by an inner vision. He called Maurus, told him what had happened, and ordered him to go and rescue Placidus. After receiving the abbot's blessing Maurus hurried on his errand, strode over the water thinking he was still on solid earth, reached the youth, and pulled him out by the hair. Maurus then went and described the incident to the man of God, but Benedict attributed the rescue not to his own merits but to Maurus's obedience.

There was a priest named Florentius whose ill will toward Benedict stirred such malice in him that he sent the saint a poisoned loaf as if it were blessed. Benedict accepted it with thanks, tossed it to a crow that regularly received bread from his hands, and said: "In the name of Jesus Christ take this bread away and drop it someplace where no one can find and eat it." The crow opened its beak, spread its wings, and began to fly around the loaf, cawing as if to say that it wanted to obey but could not do what was ordered. The saint nonetheless repeated his command over and over, saying: "Pick it up, pick it up, it won't hurt you, and get rid of it as I said to." Finally the bird carried the loaf away and came back three days later to receive the accustomed ration from the saint's hand.

Florentius, seeing that he could not kill the body of the master, burned with the desire to bring death to the souls of his disciples. To this end he ranged seven young women in the monastery garden to dance and sing in order to arouse the monks' passions. The holy man watched this from his cell and feared that his disciples might fall into sin, so he surrendered to his adversary's hostility and set out to find another place to live, taking several monks with him. Florentius, standing on a balcony, saw him depart and began to gloat; but suddenly the balcony collapsed and put an end to Florentius. Then Maurus ran after the man of God and said: "Come back, come back! The one who caused you such grief is no more!" But Benedict groaned with regret, both because his enemy had died and because his disciple was delighted over the enemy's death, and he imposed a penance on Maurus for presuming to rejoice over the death of a foe.

By going off to another area, however, he changed his location but not his real enemy. He came to Monte Cassino, where there had been a temple of Apollo. There he built an oratory in honor of Saint John the Baptist and converted the surrounding populace from idolatry to the true faith. The ancient Enemy, resenting what he had done, appeared to his bodily eyes in a horrible vision, raging at him visibly with flames shooting out of his eyes and mouth, and said: "Benedict, Benedict!" The saint did not answer, and the devil cried: "Maledict, Maledict, not Benedict, accursed, not blessed! Why do you persecute me?"

One day the brothers were trying to lift a stone that was lying on the ground to put it in the wall they were building, but they were unable to raise it: a great number of men were there but could not hoist the stone. Then the man of God came and gave a blessing, and the block was raised in no time at all. When they thought about this, they realized that the devil had been sitting on the stone and holding it down. Then, when the monks were building the wall a little higher, the evil spirit appeared to the saint and let him know that he was going after the brothers at work. Benedict immediately sent a message to them: "Brothers, be on your guard! The devil is coming after you!" The messenger had barely finished speaking when the devil overturned the wall and a young monk was crushed under the fallen stone. But the man of God had the dead body, mangled and lacerated as it was, brought to him in a sack, and by his prayer restored the youth to life and sent him back to his work.

A layman known for his virtuous life used to come once a year to visit the saint, fasting on the way. Once, while he was making this journey, another traveler, who carried provisions for the road, joined him and after some time said to him: "Come, brother, let us take some food to keep up our strength. We still have a long way to go." The pious man replied that he always fasted while making this journey, and the other said no more for a while, then renewed his invitation, meeting the same refusal. When another hour had passed and the long road had wearied them, they came to a meadow where there was a spring and whatever else might give refreshment and pleasure to the body. The fellow traveler pointed this out and urged the pilgrim to eat a little and take some rest. The proposal charmed his ears and the scene his eyes, and he consented. When he came to Saint Benedict, the saint said to him: "So, brother, the evil Enemy could not entice you the first time nor the second, but the third time he had the best of you." Thereupon the visitor threw himself at the saint's feet and bemoaned his fault.

Totila, king of the Goths, wanted to find out whether the man of God really had the spirit of prophecy, so he dressed his swordbearer in kingly garments and dispatched him to the monastery with all regal pomp. When Benedict saw him coming, he called to him: "Put off those clothes, they are not yours!" The man fell to the ground and expired, because he had dared to deceive so great a man.

A clerk who was possessed by the devil was brought to the man of God to be cured, and the saint drove the evil spirit out of him and said to him: "Go home, and from now on eat no meat, and do not take sacred orders: the day you do so you will be sold back into the power of the devil." The clerk obeyed this warning for some time, but then, seeing men younger than he being put above him by being ordained, he went against the saint's words as if he had long forgotten them, and had himself ordained to the priesthood. The devil who had left him soon took hold of him and did not stop tormenting him until he breathed his last.

A certain man sent a boy to the saint with two flasks of wine, but the boy hid one of them by the wayside and delivered the other. Benedict accepted it politely and, as the boy was leaving, warned him, saying: "Be careful not to drink from the flask you hid, but tip it cautiously and see what's inside." Abashed, the lad left him and on his way back decided to put what he had heard to the test; and when he tipped the flask, a snake wriggled out of it. And once, when the saint was at his supper, a monk, the son of a high official, was serving him and holding a light for him. This monk, stung by pride, began to think to himself: "Who is this man, whom I wait on while he has his supper, for whom I hold a light, to whom I pay service? And who am I, that I should be his servant? " Quickly the man of God said to him: "Cross your heart, brother, cross your heart! What are you saying to yourself?" Then he called the monks, had them take the lamp from the bearer's hands, and ordered him to go back to his cell and stay there quietly.

In the days of Totila a Goth named Galla, an Arian heretic, resorted to the most monstrous cruelties against the Catholic church's religious men. No cleric or monk who came face to face with him could escape death at his hands. One day, afire with the heat of greed and looking eagerly for plunder, he was inflicting various kinds of torture on a certain peasant, and the victim, unable to endure the pain, blurted out that he had put himself and his property under the protection of Benedict the servant of God. His tormentor believed this and allowed the suffering man a spell of relief, but, while desisting from his savage treatment of the peasant, had his arms bound with stout thongs and marched him ahead of his horse to find this Benedict who had taken over the man's goods. The peasant, his arms tied behind him, led his oppressor to the holy man's monastery and found him sitting at the door of his cell reading a book. The rustic said to Galla, who was following him fuming with rage: "This is Father Benedict, the one I spoke about."

Galla looked at the saint and, carried away by his perverse wrath, thought he would terrorize this monk as he was used to terrorizing others. He shouted at him: "Get up, get up, and return this fellow's property to him!" Hearing this voice, the man of God looked up from his book and stared at Galla and the man who was held in bonds. When the saint glanced at the peasant's arms, the thongs that held them miraculously fell off, more quickly than any man could have untied them. Galla, seeing the man who had been bound now standing free, was shaken at the sight of such power. He dismounted, fell to the ground, and bent his cruel, stiff neck at Benedict's feet, commending himself to the holy man's prayers. The saint hardly interrupted his reading, but called the monks and ordered them to take Galla inside, where he would receive a blessing and some food. When the Goth was brought back to him, Benedict admonished him to give up his insane cruelty. Galla took his leave and no longer dared to demand anything of the peasant whose bonds the saint had loosed, not with his hands but by a glance from his eyes.

There was a time when famine struck the region of Campania, and all the people suffered from a grievous lack of food. In Benedict's monastery the supply of wheat was already exhausted and almost all the bread had been consumed, until at mealtime the monks could find no more than five loaves. The venerable father, seeing them all in such distress, took care to correct their faintheartedness with a mild reprimand and to lift their spirits with a promise, saying: "Why are you so troubled by a shortage of bread? Today's dearth will be followed by tomorrow's plenty." The next day sacks containing two hundred measures of flour were found at the door of the saint's cell: almighty God had sent them, but by whose hands is not known to this day. When the brothers saw this, they gave thanks to God and learned not to doubt, whether in abundance or in need.

We also read that there was a man whose son was so badly afflicted with elephantiasis that his hair was falling out, his scalp was swollen, and the pus exuding from it could not be concealed. The father sent the boy to the man of God, who speedily restored him to health, for which favor they offered boundless thanks to God. Thereafter the boy persevered in good works until he fell asleep happily in the Lord.

On one occasion Benedict sent several monks to a certain place where they were to build a monastery, and set a day on which he would come and tell them how it was to be built. The night before the promised day dawned, however, he appeared in dream to the monk he had appointed as abbot and to his assistant, and designated in detail the places where the various buildings were to be constructed. But they put no faith in the vision and continued to await his arrival, until finally they went back to him and said: "Father, we waited for you to come as you had promised, but you did not come." "Why do you say this, brothers?" he answered. "Did I not appear to you and give you the ground plan? Go now and carry out the design as you saw it in the vision."

Not far from Benedict's monastery there were two nuns of noble birth who could not hold their tongues and often angered their superior with their indiscreet talk. The superior reported this to the man of God, who sent them the following order: "Curb your tongues or I will excommunicate you," not imposing the sentence of excommunication but threatening it. The nuns did not change their ways in the least, and in a few days they died and were buried in the church. When masses were celebrated there and the deacon pronounced the usual formula: "Let anyone who is not in communion go outside," the woman who had been their nurse and always made an offering on their behalf saw them come out of their tombs and leave the church. When she related this to Saint Benedict, he gave her an offering with his own hand and said: "Go and make this offering for them and they will no longer be excommunicated." This was done, and from then on, when the deacon made the customary announcement, the nuns were not seen leaving the church.

A monk who had left the monastery to visit his parents without obtaining the abbot's blessing died the very day he reached his home. He was buried, but once and again the earth threw him up. The parents came to Benedict and begged him to impart his blessing to the dead man. The saint gave them a consecrated Host and said: "Go and place this on his breast and return him to the grave." They did so, and the earth retained the corpse and did not reject it again.

Another monk, who was unhappy in the monastery and wanted to leave, importuned the man of God so much that finally, having had enough of this, he gave the needed permission. Hardly had the monk got outside the gate when he met with a dragon, which opened its maw and wanted to devour him. The monk cried out to some of the brothers who were nearby: "Hurry, hurry, this dragon wants to eat me!" They ran up but saw no dragon, and led the trembling, terrified brother back to the monastery, where he was quick to promise that he would never leave again.

A severe famine struck the whole province another time, and Saint Benedict gave away all he could find to the needy, so that there was nothing left in the monastery except a small quantity of oil in a glass jar. The saint ordered the cellarer to give this oil to someone who was asking for it. The cellarer heard the order but did not obey it, since no oil would be left for the brothers. When the man of God found out about this, he threw the jar of oil out the window, not wanting anything to be left in the monastery owing to disobedience. The glass jar landed on a huge rock, but it did not break nor was the oil spilled, and the abbot commanded that it be given to the one who had asked for it. Having sharply reprimanded the monk for his disobedience and lack of faith, the saint gave himself to prayer, and immediately a large cask that stood close by was so full of oil that it was seen to flow out over the stone floor.

Once the saint went down from the monastery to meet with his sister who had come to visit him, and while they sat at table in the evening, she asked him to stay on with her that night. He absolutely refused to do so. She then lowered her head in her hands to pray to the Lord, and when she raised her head, there came such flashes of lightning, such crashes of thunder, such torrents of rain, that no one could take as much as a step outside the house, although minutes before the sky had been marvelously clear. Her floods of tears had altered the serenity of the air and drawn down the rain. The man of God was aggrieved at this and said: "May God forgive you, sister! What have you done?" "I begged you," she answered, "and you would not listen to me. So I prayed to the Lord and he listened. Now go on your way if you can!" So it came about that they passed the whole night in holy conversation and mutual edification. And behold! Three days after he returned to his monastery, raising his eyes he saw his sister's soul in the form of a dove, penetrating the secret spaces of heaven. He then had her body brought to the monastery and laid to rest in the tomb he had prepared for himself.

One night when Saint Benedict was watching at his window and praying to the Lord, he saw spreading over the sky a light so bright that it dispelled all the darkness of the night, and the whole world was gathered as though beneath a single ray of the sun and brought before his eyes. There he saw the soul of Germanus, bishop of Capua, being carried up to heaven; and he learned later that at that same hour the bishop's soul had gone forth from his body.

During the year in which the saint was to leave this life, he predicted the day of his death to his monks. Six days before his departure he ordered his tomb to be opened. He suffered attacks of fever that grew worse day by day. On the sixth day he had himself carried to the church, and there received the Lord's Body and Blood in preparation for his end. Then, still standing and supported by his brother monks, he raised his hands to heaven and breathed his last in the midst of a prayer.

The day Saint Benedict departed this life and went to Christ, the same revelation came to two monks, one of whom was in his cell, the other some distance away. They saw a shining road strewn with rugs and lighted by countless lamps, rising toward the East from the blessed Benedict's cell to heaven. A man of venerable mien and shining aspect was standing above this road, and he asked them if they knew what the road was that they saw before them. They answered that they did not know, and he said: "This is the road by which Benedict, the beloved of God, is ascending to heaven."

The saint was buried in the oratory of Saint John the Baptist, which he had built over the ruined altar of Apollo. He flourished about the year of the Lord 518, in the time of Justin the Elder.

50. Saint Patrick

Patrick lived about A.D. 280. Once he was preaching to the king of the Scots about Christ's passion, standing before him and leaning on the staff that he held in his hand. By accident he put the sharp point of the staff on the king's foot and so pierced the foot. The king thought that the holy bishop had done this deliberately and that he himself could not receive the faith of Christ otherwise than by suffering like this for Christ, so he bore the pain patiently. Marveling at this, the saint prayed and healed the king's foot. He also obtained from God that no poisonous reptile could live in the whole province; and it is said that in answer to his prayer even the woods and bark from the trees in that region effectively counteract poison.

Then there was a man who stole a sheep from his neighbor and ate the sheep. Saint Patrick called upon the thief, whoever he might be, to make restitution for the theft, but no one came forward; so one day, when all the people were gathered together, he commanded in the name of Christ that the sheep should bleat in the belly of the one who had eaten it. The sheep bleated, the guilty man did penance, and from then on all were careful to avoid the sin of theft.

It was Patrick's custom devoutly to venerate every cross that he saw, but once he passed by a large, beautiful one without seeing it. Those who were with him wanted to know why he had not seen the cross and bowed before it. When Patrick prayed and asked the Lord whose cross this one was, he heard a voice coming out of the earth and saying: "Did you not see that I, who am a pagan, am buried there, and am unworthy of the sign of the cross?" So Patrick had the cross removed.

He preached throughout Ireland but with very meager results, so he besought the Lord to show some sign that would terrify the people and move them to repentance. He then did as the Lord commanded him, and in a certain place drew a large circle with a stick; and behold, the earth opened within the circle and a very deep, wide pit appeared. Then it was revealed to blessed Patrick that this was the place of Purgatory; that anyone who wished to go down into it would have no other penance to do and would endure no other purgatory for his sins; but that most would not come back from there, and that those who did come back would have had to stay below from one morning to the next. There were indeed many who went down into the pit and did not come out.

Long after Patrick died, a man named Nicholas, who had committed many sins, repented of his crimes and wanted to undergo the purgatory of Saint Patrick. He mortified himself by fasting for two weeks, as everyone did, then opened the gate with the key, which was kept in an abbey. He went down into the pit and discovered a door to one side, by which he went in, and saw a chapel there. Some monks in white habits were going into the chapel and reciting the office, and they told Nicholas to have courage, because he would have to endure many trials from the devil. When he asked them what help he might have against these trials, they said: "When you feel pain being inflicted upon you, cry out at once and say, 'Jesus Christ, Son of the living God, have mercy on me, a sinner!'"

The aforesaid monks then withdrew and demons appeared, urging Nicholas to change his mind and obey them. They started with bland promises, saying that they would take care of him and see that he returned unharmed to his own.

But when he refused to obey them, promptly he heard the roaring of wild beasts and a rumbling that sounded as if all the elements were in tumult. He shook with horrible fear at this and cried out: "Jesus Christ, Son of the living God, have mercy on me, a sinner!" And immediately the pandemonium was stilled.

Then Nicholas was led to another place where there was a crowd of demons who said to him: "Do you think you can escape from our hands? Never! Now, on the contrary, you will learn what it is to be mangled and tortured!" A towering, frightful fire appeared, and the demons said: "Unless you yield to us, we will throw you into the fire to be burned to ashes!" When he spurned them, they seized him and cast him into the terrible fire, and when he felt its pain, he cried out the prayer to Jesus, and the fire was extinguished.

He was led to still another place, where he saw some men being burned alive and having hot iron blades thrust deep into their bodies by the demons. Others lay prone on the ground and gnawed the earth for pain, screaming: "Spare us! Spare us!" while the devils set upon them still more grievously. He saw others being bitten by serpents, while demons dragged out their entrails with incandescent iron hooks. When Nicholas continued to resist them, they threw him into the same fire and made him feel the same blades, the same pains. But again he called upon Jesus Christ and was freed of the pain forthwith. Then he was taken to a place where men were being fried in great frying pans, and where there was a very large wheel full of flaming iron hooks upon which men were hanging by various parts of their bodies; and the wheel spun so rapidly that it threw off a globe of fire.

Next he saw a large building where there were trenches filled with molten metal, into which some men had one foot, some had two, and others were in up to the knees, others to the waist, to the chest, to the neck, to the eyes; but Nicholas called upon Christ and passed safely through all this. He proceeded farther and came in sight of a very wide hole out of which rose a horrible smoke and an intolerable stench, and men glowing like sparkling hot iron were trying to get out but were pushed back by the demons. These told Nicholas: "The place you are looking at is hell, in which our master Beelzebul dwells. We will throw you in there if you still refuse to do our will, and once you are thrown in there, you will never get help or be able to escape!" Nicholas disdained to listen to them, so they snatched him and cast him into the pit, and he was enveloped in such pain that he almost forgot to invoke the name of the Lord; but then he gathered his wits and cried out in his heart (he was unable to speak a word): "Jesus Christ, Son of the living God, have mercy on me, a sinner!" He emerged from the pit unhurt, and the horde of demons, acknowledging defeat, disappeared.

Now he was led to a place where he saw a bridge that it behooved him to cross. The bridge, however, was very narrow and as smooth and slippery as ice, and beneath it flowed a broad, deep river of sulfur and fire. He had no hope of being able to cross the bridge but remembered the words that had saved him so many times, so he confidently went toward the bridge and put one foot on it, reciting the prayer to Jesus Christ. A clamor of shouts broke out from below and frightened him so much that he barely kept his footing, but he went on with his prayer and came to no harm. Then he placed the other foot and repeated the same words, and continued to do so step by step until he was safely across.

When he reached the other side, he was in a pleasant meadow redolent of the perfume of all sorts of flowers. Now two handsome youths appeared to him and guided him toward a splendid city that gleamed marvelously with gold and precious stones. From the city gate a wonderful aroma drifted around him and refreshed him so much that he no longer seemed to sense any pain or bad odor. His guides told him that the city was Paradise. He wanted to go in, but they said that he must first return to his own, going back exactly the way he had come without any interference from the demons, who would take flight at the sight of him. After thirty days, they said, he would die a peaceful death and would come into the city as a perpetual citizen.

Nicholas went up out of the pit and found himself back in the place from which he had started. He told everyone about all the things that had happened to him, and after thirty days fell happily asleep in the Lord.

51. The Annunciation of the Lord

The feast is so named because on this day the coming of the Son of God was announced by an angel. It was fitting that the Annunciation should precede the Incarnation, and this for three reasons. The first is that the order of reparation should correspond to the order of transgression or deviation. Therefore since the devil tempted the woman to lead her to doubt, through doubt to consent, and through consent to sinning, so the angel brought the message to the Virgin by the announcement to prompt her to believing, through believing to consent, and through consent to the conceiving of the Son of God. The second reason has to do with the angel's ministry. The angel is God's minister and servant, and the Blessed Virgin was chosen to be God's mother; and as it is right for the minister to be at the service of his mistress, so it was fitting that the Annunciation be made to the Blessed Virgin by an angel. The third reason is that reparation was to be made for the fall of the angels. The Incarnation made reparation not only for human sin but for the ruin of the fallen angels. Therefore the angels were not to be excluded; and as womankind was not excluded from knowledge of the mysteries of the Incarnation and the Resurrection, neither was the angelic messenger excluded. God made both of these mysteries known through angels, the Incarnation to the Virgin Mary and the Resurrection to Mary Magdalene.

The Virgin Mary lived in the Temple from her third to her fourteenth year and made a vow to live in chastity unless God otherwise disposed. Then she was espoused to Joseph, God revealing his will by the flowering of Joseph's staff, as is more fully set forth in our account of the birth of Blessed Mary. Joseph went to Bethlehem, the city of his origins, to make the necessary preparation for the nuptials, while Mary returned to her parents' home in Nazareth. Nazareth means "flower"; hence Bernard says that the Flower willed to be born of a flower, in "Flower," in the season of flowers.

At Nazareth, then, the angel appeared to Mary and greeted her, saying: *Hail, full of grace, the Lord is with thee! Blessed art thou among women*. Bernard says: "We are invited to salute Mary by Gabriel's example, by John's joyous leaping in his mother's womb, and by the reward of being greeted in return."

Now we must first see why the Lord wanted his mother to be married. On this point Bernard gives three reasons, saying: "It was necessary that Mary be espoused to Joseph, because thereby the mystery was hidden from the demons; Mary's virginity was confirmed by her spouse; and her modesty and good name were protected." A fourth reason was that Mary's espousal took away dishonor from every rank and condition of womankind, namely, the married, virgins, and widows, since she herself was married, virginal, and widowed. A fifth: she was served and cared for by her spouse; a sixth, the genealogical line was established through the husband.

The angel said: *Hail, full of grace!* Bernard: "In her womb was the grace of the presence of God, in her heart the grace of charity, on her lips the grace of benignity, in her hands the grace of mercy and generosity." Bernard also says: "Truly *full of grace*, because from her fullness all captives receive redemption, the sick receive healing, the sorrowful consolation, sinners forgiveness, the righteous grace, the angels joy, and finally the whole Trinity receives glory and the Son of man the substance of human flesh."

The Lord is with thee. Bernard: "With you are the Lord God the Father, of whom the One you are conceiving is begotten, the Lord the Holy Spirit, of whom you conceive, and the Lord the Son, whom you clothe with your flesh." *Blessed art thou among women*. Bernard goes on: "You are blessed among women, blessed indeed above all women, because you will be a virgin mother and the mother of God."

Women had come under a threefold curse, namely, the curse of reproach when they were unable to conceive, wherefore Rachel, when she conceived and bore a son, said: "God has taken away my reproach";[1] the curse of sin when

---

[1] Gen. 30:23.

they conceived, whence the Psalm says: "Behold I was conceived in iniquities, and in sins did my mother conceive me";[2] and the curse of pain when they gave birth; so Genesis: "In pain you shall bring forth children."[3] The Virgin Mary alone was blessed among women, because to her virginity was added fruitfulness, to her fruitfulness in conceiving, holiness, and to her holiness in giving birth, happiness.

Mary is called *full of grace*, as Bernard says, because four kinds of grace shone in her spirit: the devotion of her humility, the reverence of her modesty, the greatness of her faith, and the martyrdom of her heart. She is told, *The Lord is with thee*, because four things, as the same Bernard says, shone upon her from heaven, these being Mary's sanctification, the angel's salutation, the overshadowing of the Holy Spirit, and the incarnation of the Son of God. Moreover she is told, *Blessed art thou among women*, because, according to the same author, four things also shone in her body: she was the Virgin of virgins, fruitful without corruption, pregnant without heaviness, and delivered without pain.

When Mary heard the angel's words, she was troubled and thought to herself what this greeting might mean. Here we see that the Virgin was worthy of praise in her hearing the words and her reception of them, and in her pausing to think about them. She was praiseworthy for her modesty when she heard the words and remained silent, for her hesitancy at receiving the words, and for her prudence in her thoughtfulness, because she thought about the sense of the greeting. Note that she was troubled by the angel's words, not at the sight of him: she had often seen angels but had never heard one speak as this one did. Peter of Ravenna says: "The angel had come kindly in manner but fearsome in his words," so that while the sight of him gave her joy, hearing what he said distressed her. Hence Bernard comments: "She was troubled, as befitted her virginal modesty, but not overly distressed, due to her fortitude; she was silent and thoughtful, evidence of her prudence and discretion."

To reassure her, the angel said: *Fear not, Mary, for thou hast found grace with God*;[4] and Bernard exclaims: "What grace indeed! Peace between God and men, death destroyed, life made whole!" *Behold, thou shalt conceive and bear a son and shalt call his name Jesus, which means savior, because he will save his people from their sins. He will be great and will be called the Son of the Most High*. Bernard: "This means that he, who is great God, will be great—a great man, a great teacher, a great prophet."

Mary asked the angel: *How shall this be done, because I know not man?*—i.e., I have no intention of knowing man. So she was virginal in her mind, in her body, and in her intentions. Here we see Mary questioning, and whoever questions, doubts. Why then was Zachary alone punished by being struck dumb? To this point Peter of Ravenna assigns four reasons, saying: "The One who knows

[2] Ps. 50:7.   [3] Gen. 3:16.   [4] Luke 1:28ff.

sinners attended not to their words but to their hearts, and judged not what they said but what they meant. Their reasons for questioning were not the same, their hopes were different. She believed, contrary to nature; he doubted, in defense of nature. She simply asked how such a thing could happen; he decided that what God wanted could not be done. He, though pressed by examples, failed to rise to faith; she, with no example to go by, hurried to faith. She wondered how a virgin could give birth; he was dubious about a conjugal conception. It was not the fact that she questioned, but how it could come about, the process of it, because there are three ways of conceiving—the natural, the spiritual, and the miraculous—and she was asking which of these would be the mode of her conception."

The angel answered: *The Holy Spirit will come upon thee, and it is he who will cause thee to conceive.* Hence the child to be born of her is said to be conceived of the Holy Spirit, and this for four reasons. The first is the manifestation of boundless love, in other words, to show that the Word of God took flesh out of God's ineffable love; John 3:16: "God so loved the world that he gave his only Son." That reason is given by the Master of the Sentences. The second was to make it clear that the conception proceeded from grace alone, not from merit: the angel's words showed that since the conception was of the Holy Spirit, it came about by grace alone, being preceded by no merit of any man. This reason is Augustine's. The third is the operative power of the Holy Spirit: the conception came about by the power and working of the Spirit: this from Ambrose. Hugh of Saint Victor adds a fourth reason, namely, the motive involved. He says that the motive leading to natural conception is the love of a man for a woman and the woman's love for the man. So, he says, because in the Virgin's heart there burned so great a love of the Holy Spirit, in her body the same love worked miracles.

And the power of the Most High will overshadow thee. This, according to the *Gloss*, is explained as follows: "A shadow ordinarily is formed by light falling on a solid body, and neither the Virgin nor any pure human being could contain the fullness of the deity: but '*the power of the Most High will overshadow thee,*' and in her the incorporeal light of the godhead took on the body of mankind, in order that she might bear God." Bernard seems to come close to this explanation when he says: "Because God is a spirit and we are the shadow of his body, he lowered himself to us so that through the solidity of his life-giving flesh we might see the Word in the flesh, the sun in the cloud, the light in the lamp, the candle in the lantern." Bernard also says that the angel's words can be read as if he said: "Christ, the power of God, will conceal in the shadow of his most secret counsel the mode by which you will conceive of the Holy Spirit, so that it will be known only to him and to you. And if the angel says, 'Why do you ask me? when you will soon experience what I am telling you!' You will know in yourself, you will know, you will happily know, but the One who works in you will be your teacher. I have been sent to announce the virginal conception, not to create it." Or, "*will overshadow thee*" means that she would be kept cool and shaded from all heat of vice.

And behold, thy kinswoman Elizabeth hath also conceived a son. According to Bernard, Elizabeth's conceiving was announced to Mary for four reasons: that she might be filled with joy, perfected in knowledge, perfected also in doctrine, and moved to a work of mercy. Jerome, indeed, says: "That her kinswoman, who was barren, had conceived was announced to Mary in order that as miracle was added to miracle, so more joy might be heaped upon her joy. Or the Virgin received the word immediately through an angel so that she might know it before it became common knowledge and not just hear it from someone else, and this lest it appear that the mother of God was kept apart from the counsels of her Son and unaware of what was happening close by on earth; or rather, so that by being fully informed of the coming, now of the forerunner and afterward of the Savior, and thus knowing the time and sequence of these events, she might later make the truth known to writers and preachers. Moreover, hearing of the older woman's pregnancy, the younger woman would think of going to her side, and thus the unborn prophet would be given the opportunity to do homage to his Lord, and the one miracle might furnish occasion for a more wondrous one."

Now Bernard: "Quick, Virgin, give your answer! O Lady, say the word and accept the Word, offer yours and accept God's, pronounce the transitory and embrace the everlasting, rise up, run, open yourself! Arise by faith, run by devotion, open by giving your consent!" Then Mary, raising her hands and her eyes to heaven, said: *Behold the handmaid of the Lord, be it done unto me according to thy word.* Bernard: "It is said that some have received the word of God in the mouth, others in the ear, still others in the hand. Mary received that word in her ear by the angel's greeting, in her heart by faith, in her mouth by her confessing it, in her hand when she touched it, in her womb when it took flesh in her, in her bosom when she nursed it, in her arms when she offered it."

Be it done unto me according to thy word. Bernard interprets this: "I will not have it *done unto me* as preached by some demagogue, or signified in a figure of speech, or imagined in a dream, but as silently breathed into me, in person incarnate, bodily living in my body." And in an instant the Son of God was conceived in her womb, perfect God and perfect man, and from the very first day of his conception he had as much wisdom and as much power as he had in his thirtieth year.

Then Mary arose and went into the hill country to Elizabeth, and John leapt in his mother's womb as a way of greeting the Virgin. The *Gloss* notes: "Because he could not give greeting with his tongue, he leapt for joy of spirit and so began to fulfill his office as Christ's forerunner." Mary attended Elizabeth for three months until John was born, and lifted him from the earth with her own hands, as we read in the *Book of the Just*. It is said that God wrought many works on this day as it came round in the course of the years, and a poet tells them in memorable verses:

> Salve justa dies quae vulnera nostra coerces!
> Angelus est missus, est passus in cruce Christus,
> Est Adam factus et eodem tempore lapsus,
> Ob meritum decimae cadit Abel fratris ab ense,
> Offert Melchisedech, Ysaac supponitur aris,
> Est decollatus Christi baptista beatus,
> Est Petrus ereptus, Jacobus sub Herode peremptus.
> Corpora sanctorum cum Christo multa resurgunt,
> Latro dulce tamen per Christum suscipit Amen.[5]

A rich and noble knight renounced the world and entered the Cistercian order. He was unlettered, and the monks, not wishing to number so noble a person among the lay brothers, gave him a teacher to see if he might acquire enough learning to be received as a choir monk. He spent a long time with his teacher but could learn no more than the two words *Ave Maria*, which he cherished and repeated incessantly wherever he went and whatever he was doing. At length he died and was buried among the brothers, and behold! a beautiful lily grew up above his grave, and one leaf had the words *Ave Maria* inscribed on it in letters of gold. Running to see this great spectacle, the monks dug down into the grave and discovered that the root of the lily sprang from the dead man's mouth. They then understood the depth of devotion with which he, whom God glorified with so prodigious an honor, had recited these two words.

A knight had a stronghold beside the road, and pitilessly robbed every passing traveler. Every day, however, he greeted the Virgin mother of God with the *Ave Maria*, never letting anything prevent him from so doing. It happened that a holy monk was making his way along the road and the aforesaid knight gave orders to waylay him, but the holy man begged the robbers to take him to their chief because he had a secret message to deliver to him. When he came before the knight, he asked him to summon his household and all the people in the castle, because he wished to preach the word of God to them. When they had come together, he said: "You are not all here! Someone is missing!" They told him that all were present, but he said: "Look around carefully and you will find that someone is absent!" Then one of them exclaimed that indeed the chamberlain had not come. "That's the one who's missing," said the monk. Quickly they went after him and brought him out in front of everybody; but when he saw the man of God, he rolled his eyes in fright, shook his head like a madman, and

---

[5] The verse begins, "Hail, good day that heals our wounds," and commemorates the sending of the angel, Christ's suffering and death, Adam's creation and fall, Abel's murder, Melchizedek's offering, the sacrifice of Isaac, the beheading of the Baptist, Peter's deliverance from prison, James's martyrdom under Herod, the rising of many bodies of the saints with Christ, and the happy end granted by Christ to the good thief.

dared come no closer. The holy man said to him: "I adjure you in the name of Jesus Christ our Lord to tell us who you are and to say openly why you are here!" The answer was: "Woe is me, the adjuration forces me against my will to admit that I am not a man but a demon who took human form and have stayed with the knight these fourteen years. Our prince sent me here to watch diligently for the day this knight would fail to recite his *Ave Maria*, thus falling into my power. I was to throttle him at once, and he, ending his life while engaged in wrongdoing, would be ours. Any day he recited his prayer I had no power over him; but, watch as I might, he never let a single day pass without praying to the Virgin."

When the knight heard this, his astonishment knew no bounds. He prostrated himself at the feet of the man of God, begged forgiveness for his sins, and thereafter mended his ways. The holy man then said to the evil spirit: "I command you, demon, in the name of our Lord Jesus Christ, to leave here and infest some place where you may not presume to harm anyone who invokes the glorious mother of God!" The demon vanished, and the knight reverently and gratefully allowed the holy man to resume his journey.

---

52. Saint Timothy

The feast of Saint Timothy is celebrated at Rome, to which city Timothy came from Antioch in the pontificate of Pope Melchiades and was appointed by the priest Silvester, who later became the bishop of the city, to perform functions which at that time the popes themselves were afraid to carry out. Silvester not only welcomed him to his house but, putting fear aside, praised his way of life and his teaching. Timothy preached the truth of Christ for a year and three months and made many converts, and then, being worthy of martyrdom, was captured by the pagan populace and turned over to Tarquin, the urban prefect. Weakened by torture and cast into prison for refusing to sacrifice to the idols, as a good athlete of God he was struck down on the third day and beheaded with several murderers.

Saint Silvester took the body to his house by night and invited Pope Saint Melchiades, who with all the priests and deacons spent the night praising and confirming his martyrdom. A most devoted woman named Theone asked the pope to allow her to raise a monument in her garden, at her own expense, in which Saint Timothy's body might be laid to rest near the tomb of Saint Paul. This was done, and the Christians were pleased because a martyr by the name of Timothy lay close to Paul the apostle, who had had a disciple of that name.[1]

※

53. The Passion of the Lord

The passion of Christ was bitter in its pains, scornful in the mockery it laid upon him, and fruitful in its manifold benefits.

The pain of the passion was of five kinds. The first was its shamefulness. It was shameful because it happened in a place of shame, namely, on Calvary, where malefactors were punished. The mode was shameful, because he was condemned to a most ignominious death, the cross being the instrument of punishment for thieves. Yet, shameful as it then was, the cross is now a sign of unbounded glory, as Augustine says: "The cross, which was the shame and torture of criminals, now adorns the forehead of emperors. If God has conferred such great honor on an instrument of punishment, how greatly will he honor his servant?"

The Lord's passion was shameful because of the company in which he suffered. He was reckoned with thieves and robbers who were criminals to begin with; but later one of them, Dismas, who was crucified at Christ's right side, was converted, as we read in the *Gospel of Nicodemus*, and the other, Gesmas, on the left side, was condemned. Thus to one the kingdom was given, to the other, torment. Ambrose says: "The author of mercy, hanging on the cross, divided the gifts and obligations of mercy among different recipients. He left persecution to the apostles, peace to the disciples, his body to the Jews, his garments to those who crucified him, his spirit to his Father, a guardian to his mother the blessed Virgin, paradise to the good thief, hell to sinners, the cross to penitent Christians. That is the testament which Christ made as he hung on the cross."

The passion was painful, secondly, because it was unjust. Christ had done no wrong, and there was no deceit in his mouth. Therefore what was done to him was done unjustly and caused him grievous pain. The principal charges unjustly brought against him were three: that he forbade the payment of tribute,

---

[1] Graesse notes that this legend is lacking "in recent (or more recent) books," and that it differs markedly from the legend with the same title, numbered 121 both here and in Graesse's edition.

that he called himself a king, and that he claimed to be the Son of God. In answer to these three acccusations we, speaking for the Savior, make three responses on Good Friday when we sing: "O my people, what have I done to you, etc.?" in which verse Christ brings up three benefits he conferred on them—delivering them from Egypt, guiding them in the desert, planting them as his fairest vine in a very good land—as if to say: "You accuse me regarding the payment of tribute; rather you ought to thank me for freeing you of tribute. You accuse me because I called myself a king; you ought to thank me for the royal fare I provided for you in the desert. You accuse me of calling myself God's Son; you should rather thank me for choosing you as my vine and planting you in a very good place."

Thirdly, Christ's passion was painful because it was his friends who brought it upon him. The pain would have been more bearable if it had been caused by people who had some reason to be his enemies, or by strangers or foreigners, or by people to whom he had been in some way troublesome. On the contrary he suffered at the hands of friends—i.e., of men who should have been his friends—and of his kinsmen—i.e., people of the same stock from which he was born. Of both of these Psalm 37:12 says: "My friends and companions stand aloof from my plague, and my kinsmen stand afar off," and Job says (19:13): "My acquaintances like strangers have departed from me, my kinsmen have forsaken me." Then there were those upon whom he had conferred many good things, as we read in John 10:32: "Many good works I have showed you from my Father. For which of these works do you stone me?" Bernard: "O good Jesus, how kindly you have dealt with men, what great and superabundant gifts you have lavished upon them, what keen, bitter sufferings you have borne for them—harsh words, harsher blows, most harsh torments!"

The fourth pain resulted from the tenderness of his body, as David says (2 Kings 23:23) in a figure of speech: "He was like the most tender little worm of the wood." Bernard: "O Jews, you are stones! You strike a softer stone, out of which the chime of mercy resounds and the oil of love gushes." Similarly Jerome: "Jesus was handed over to the soldiers to be scourged, and the scourges tore that most sacred body and the breast in which God dwelt."

The fifth pain sprang from the overall effect: it penetrated every part of his body, it smote all his senses. This pain was first of all in his eyes, because he wept, as Heb. 5:7 says, "with a strong cry and tears." Bernard: "He was lifted on high so that he might be heard over a greater distance, he spoke more loudly so that no one could have an excuse for not hearing, to his outcry he joined tears to stir men's compassion." He also wept at other times and places—at the resurrection of Lazarus and over Jerusalem. In the first instance he shed tears of love, so that some who saw him weeping said: "See how he loved him!" (John 11:35–36). In the second instance they were tears of compassion, but the third time they were tears of pain.

He suffered in his hearing, when insults and blasphemies were leveled at him. These were aimed at four particular prerogatives of Christ. He possessed preeminent nobility because in his divine nature he was the Son of the eternal King, and in his human nature he was of royal descent, so that as a man he was King of kings and Lord of lords. He possessed ineffable truth, because he is the way, the truth, and the life, and he also said of himself: "Your word is truth" (John 17:17), the Son being the Father's speech or word. He had insuperable power, because all things were made by him and without him nothing was made. And his was a unique goodness, because no one is good but God alone.

Christ heard insults and blasphemies aimed at each of these prerogatives. Against his nobility they asked: "Is not this the carpenter's son? Is not his mother called Mary?" (Matt. 13:55). His power was derided: "It is only by Beelzebul, the prince of demons, that this man casts out demons" (Matt. 12:24); and: "He saved others, he cannot save himself" (Matt. 27:42). They said he was powerless though he showed power enough to strike down his persecutors solely by the sound of his voice. When he asked: "Whom do you seek?" and they said: "Jesus of Nazareth," Jesus answered: "I told you that I am he," and they fell to the ground at once. Augustine: "He struck at this hate-ridden, fearfully armed mob with no weapon but a word; he repulsed them, laid them low by the power of his hidden divinity. What will he, who did this when about to be judged, do when he comes to judge? What will he who was about to die be able to do when he assumes his reign?"

His truth was denied: "You are bearing witness to yourself; your testimony is not true" (John 8:13). So they called him a liar, whereas he was the way, the truth, and the life. Pilate did not deserve to know or hear this truth, because he was not judging Christ according to the truth. He did begin his judging on the basis of truth, but he did not abide by the truth; therefore he was worthy to raise the question about truth, but not to hear the solution. Augustine gives another reason to explain why Pilate heard no solution to his question: it suddenly came to him that by Jewish custom one prisoner was released at the Passover, so he went out abruptly, not waiting for a solution. And Chrysostom offers a third reason, namely, that Pilate knew his question was so difficult that much time and discussion would be called for, whereas he was in haste to set Christ free and so hurried out. We read in the *Gospel of Nicodemus*, however, that when Pilate asked Jesus: "What is truth?" (John 18:38) Jesus answered: "Truth is from heaven." "Is there no truth on earth?" Pilate retorted. "How could there be truth on earth," Jesus replied, "when truth is judged by those who hold power on earth?"

As regards Christ's goodness, his accusers said that he was a sinner at heart: "We know that this man is a sinner" (John 9:24); also that he led people astray with his words: "He stirs up the people, teaching throughout all Judea, from Galilee even to this place" (Luke 23:5); and more, he violated the Law by his actions: "This man is not from God, for he does not keep the Sabbath" (John 9:16).

He suffered throughout his body, thirdly, in the sense of smell. A strong smell of decay pervaded the place of Calvary, where dead bodies were left to rot. The *Scholastic History* says that *calvaries* properly means the bare human skull: hence, because criminals were beheaded there and many skulls were strewn about, it was called the place of skulls or Calvary. Fourthly, he suffered in the sense of taste. When he cried out: "I thirst!" they gave him vinegar mixed with myrrh and gall, so that the vinegar would make him die more quickly and the guards would sooner be relieved of their watch; for it is said that the crucified died more quickly if they drank vinegar. The myrrh would also offend his sense of smell, and the gall his sense of taste. So Augustine says: "Purity is given vinegar to drink instead of wine, sweetness is drenched with gall, innocence stands in for the guilty, life dies for the dead."

Fifthly, he suffered pain through the sense of touch. In every part of his body, from the soles of his feet to the top of his head there was no soundness. Bernard says that he suffered in all his senses: "The head that angels trembled to look upon is stabbed with clustered thorns; the face, more beautiful than the faces of the children of men, is befouled by the spittle of the Jews; the eyes that outshine the sun are clouded over in death; the ears that hear the angels sing hear the taunts of sinners; the mouth that teaches angels is given gall and vinegar to drink; the feet whose footstool is adored because it is holy are fixed to the cross with a nail; the hands that shaped the heavens are spread open and nailed to the cross; the body is scourged, the side is pierced with a lance, and what more is there? Nothing is left in him except the tongue, so that he could pray for sinners and commend his mother to a disciple."

Christ's passion was painful, but it was also scornful in the mockery it visited upon him. He was mocked four times. The first was in the house of Annas, where he was blindfolded, slapped, and spat upon. Bernard: "Your lovely face, O good Jesus, that face the angels desire to look upon, they defiled with spittle, struck with their hands, covered with a veil in derision, nor did they spare it bitter wounds." The second time was in the palace of Herod, who deemed Jesus a simpleton and of unsound mind because he refused to answer him, and draped him in a white robe to make a fool of him. Bernard: "You, O man, are man and you are crowned with flowers, and I, who am God, have a crown of thorns. You have gloves on your hands and my hands have nails driven through them. You dance in white garments, and I, for your sake, was mocked when Herod clothed me in a white garment. You dance with your feet, and I have endured pain in my feet. You, in the dance, extend your arms like a cross in a gesture of joy, and I have had my arms stretched on the cross as a mark of opprobrium. I have borne pain on the cross and you take pleasure in shaping a cross with your arms. You uncover your chest and side as a sign of vainglory, and my side was pierced for you. But return to me and I will welcome you!"

But why did the Lord, in the course of his passion, remain silent before Herod, Pilate, and the Jews? We see three reasons for this. First, they were not worthy of hearing an answer; second, Eve had sinned by saying too much and Christ willed to make satisfaction by saying nothing; and third, no matter what he said, they would have distorted and perverted it.

Christ was mocked a third time in the house of Pilate, where the soldiers wrapped a scarlet cloak around him, put a reed in his hands and a crown of thorns on his head, and bending the knee, said: "Hail, king of the Jews!" We are told that the crown of thorns was plaited of furze, the thorns of which are very hard and penetrate deeply, whence it is thought that this crown drew blood from his head. About this Bernard says: "That divine head had clusters of thorns driven into the brain." There are three opinions about the principal seat of the soul in the body. It may be in the heart, since, according to Matthew (15:19): "From the heart come forth evil thoughts," or in the blood, according to Lev. 17:11 "The life of all flesh is in the blood," or in the head, since, according to John (19:30): "He bowed his head and gave up his spirit." It would seem that these three opinions were known to the Jews, at least to judge by what they did. In order to tear his soul from his body they sought it in his head by driving thorns all the way into the brain, looked for it in his blood by opening the veins in his hands and feet, and tried to reach it in his heart by piercing his side. In response to these scornful actions, on Good Friday we kneel three times before unveiling the cross, singing: "*Hagios ho theos*, Holy God, etc.," thrice honoring him who thrice was mocked for our sake.

On the cross Christ was mocked a fourth time, as we read in Matthew (27:41): "The chief priests, with the scribes and elders, mocked him, saying, 'If he is the king of Israel, let him come down now from the cross, and we will believe in him.'" On this Bernard says: "At this time he exhibits patience more than ever, commends humility, fulfills obedience, shows perfect love. These are the four jewels with which the four parts of the cross are adorned—charity at the top, obedience on the right, patience on the left, and humility, the root of all the virtues, below."

Bernard briefly sums up all that Christ suffered: "As long as I live, I will remember the labors he put forth in his preaching, his fatigues in explaining, his vigils in prayer, his temptations while he fasted, his compassionate weeping, the snares set for him in arguments with his opponents, and, lastly, in the insults, the spittings, the slappings, the derisive gestures, the nails, the reproaches."

Now we come to the manifold fruits of the Lord's passion, which can be described as threefold, namely, the remission of sins, the granting of grace, and the manifestation of glory. These three are indicated in the title placed over him on the cross: "Jesus" referring to the first, "of Nazareth" to the second, "king of the Jews" to the third, because in heavenly glory we will all be kings. Augustine says of the fruits of the passion: "Christ blotted out all guilt, present, past, and future—past sins by remitting them, present sins by holding us back from them, future sins by giving us grace to avoid them." On the same subject Augustine also says: "Let us wonder and rejoice, love and praise and adore, because through our redeemer's death we have been called from darkness to light, from death to life, from corruption to incorruption, from exile to the fatherland, from grief to joy."

How beneficial to us the mode of our redemption was is clear for four reasons: it was most acceptable to God as a peace offering, most suitable for curing humanity's illness, most efficacious to attract humankind, and best adapted to accomplish the defeat of man's Enemy.

First, the mode of our redemption was most acceptable to God as a way of placating him and reconciling us to him, for, as Anselm puts it in his book titled *Why God Became Man*, "There is nothing more painful or difficult that a man can do for God's honor than to suffer death voluntarily and not for debt but of his own free will, and no man can give himself more fully than by surrendering himself to death for God's honor." So we read in Eph. 5:2: "Christ delivered himself, an oblation and a sacrifice to God for an odor of sweetness." Augustine, in his book *On the Trinity*, tells us how this sacrifice placated God and reconciled us with God: "What could be so readily accepted as the flesh of our sacrifice being made the body of our Priest?" Thus, since four things are to be considered in every sacrifice—to whom it is offered, what is offered, for whom it is offered, and who offers it—in this sacrifice he who himself is the one mediator between the parties, reconciling us with God by the sacrifice of peace, could remain with him to whom he made the offering, could make those for whom he made the offering one in himself, and could himself be the one who made the offering and the offering he made.

Speaking about how we were reconciled through Christ, the same Augustine says that Christ is the priest through whom we are reconciled, the sacrifice by which we are reconciled, God, with whom we are reconciled, and the temple in which we are reconciled. Therefore, speaking in the person of Christ, he reproaches some who belittle this reconciliation: "When you were an enemy to my Father, he reconciled you through me; when you were far from him, I came to redeem you; when you were astray in the mountains and the forests, I came in search of you, found you amidst the rocks and the woods, and gathered you up lest you be torn to pieces by the swift teeth of wolves and savage beasts. I carried you on my shoulders, gave you back to my Father, labored, sweated, pressed thorns upon my head, exposed my hands to the nails, opened my side with a spear, was torn—I will not say by insults but by so many torments. I shed my blood, I gave my soul to unite you closely to myself . . . and you separate yourself from me."

Second, the mode of our redemption was most apt for curing humanity's sickness—apt from the point of view of the time, the place, and the way the cure was effected. It was fitting from the point of view of the time, because Adam was created and fell into sin in the month of March, on Friday the sixth day of the week and at the sixth hour of the day, and Christ chose to suffer on the day in March on which his coming was announced and on which he was put to death—the sixth day, Friday, at the sixth hour.

The place was also appropriate, whether it be considered as common, particular, or unique. The common place was the land of promise, the particular, Calvary, and the unique, the cross. In the common place the first man was formed, because it is said that he was formed in the region around Damascus, on that city's territory. Adam was buried in the particular place, or at least it is said that he was buried where Christ suffered. This, however, is not authentic, since according to Jerome Adam was buried on Mount Hebron, as is expressly stated in Josh. 14:15. Adam was deceived at the unique place—not that he was deceived on that wood on which Christ suffered, but in the sense that as Adam was deceived in the wood of the tree, so Christ suffered on the wood of the cross. A Greek history says, however, that it was the same wood.[1]

Third, the way the cure was effected was apt, because it operated through similarities and through opposites. Through similarities: thus Augustine, in his book *On Christian Doctrine*, says that as man was deceived by a woman, so men were liberated by a man born of a woman, mortals by a mortal, the dead by his death. Ambrose: "Adam was formed from the virgin earth, Christ was born of a virgin. Adam was made to God's image, Christ is the image of God. Folly came through a woman, through a woman wisdom. Adam was naked, Christ was naked. Death came by a tree, life by the cross. Adam was in the desert, Christ was in the desert."

The cure also came by way of opposites. According to Gregory, the first man had sinned by pride, disobedience, and gluttony: he wanted to be like God in the sublimity of his knowledge, to overstep the limit set by God, and to taste the sweetness of the apple. And since cures have to be worked by opposites, the way satisfaction was made for us was most fitting, because it was through humiliation, the fulfilling of God's will, and physical pain. These three are reflected in Phil. 2:8: [Christ Jesus] "humbled himself," referring to the first, "became obedient," to the second, "unto death," to the third.

Third, the mode of our redemption was the most efficacious way to attract humankind. In no other way could men have been more strongly drawn to love God and trust in him, without impairment of their freedom of choice. Bernard speaks about how we are drawn to love: "More than anything else, O good Jesus, the cup that you drank—the work of our redemption—makes you lovable. That work fully justifies your claim to our total devotion: it sweetly entices, justly demands, swiftly clasps, and strongly constrains our love. For when you emptied yourself and put off your natural splendor, then your compassion shone more brightly, your love gleamed more brilliantly, your grace cast its rays more

---

[1] For more of this kind of information about the wood of the cross, see the chapters on the Finding of the Cross (68) and on the Resurrection (54), below.

widely." And regarding our trust in God, Romans 8: "He who did not spare his own Son but gave him up for us all, has he not also given us all things with him?" On this point Bernard says: "Who is there who would not be caught up by the hope of obtaining confidence when we attend to the way his body is disposed—the head bowed to kiss, the arms outstretched to embrace, the hands pierced to pour out gifts, the side opened for love, the feet held fast to keep him with us, his body stretched to give himself wholly to us?"

Fourth, our redemption was best adapted to accomplish the defeat of man's Enemy; Job 26:12: "His wisdom has struck the proud one," and, further on, Job 40:20 (Douay): "Can you draw out Leviathan with a hook?" Christ had hidden the hook of his godhead under the bait of his humanity, and the devil, wanting to swallow the bait of his flesh, was caught by the hook of his divinity. About this artful trap Augustine says: "The redeemer came and the deceiver was vanquished; and what did the redeemer do to the one who had caught us? He held out a mousetrap, his cross, and baited it with his blood." He willed to shed his own blood, not the blood of a debtor, for which reason he withdrew from debtors. This sort of debt the apostle calls a chirograph, a handwritten bill, which Christ took and nailed to the cross. Augustine says of this bill: "Eve borrowed sin from the devil and wrote a bill and provided a surety, and the interest on the debt was heaped upon posterity. She borrowed sin from the devil when, going against God's command, she consented to his wicked order or suggestion. She wrote the bill when she reached out her hand to the forbidden apple. She gave a surety when she made Adam consent to the sin. And so the interest on the debt of sin became posterity's burden."

Bernard, speaking for Christ, reproaches those who belittle this redemption, by which he led us out from the power of the Enemy: "My people, says the Lord, what could I have done for you that I have not done? What reason is there for you to prefer to serve the Enemy rather than me? He did not create you or feed you. If this seems trivial to you, ingrates that you are, not he, but I redeemed you. What was the price? Not, indeed, corruptible gold or silver, not the sun or the moon, not one of the angels: I redeemed you with my own blood. For the rest, if such a manifold right does not elicit from you a sense of obligation to become my servants, at least, putting all else aside, agree with me for a penny a day."

Now because Christ was betrayed and brought to his death by Judas due to greed, by the Jews due to envy, and by Pilate due to fear, we might consider the punishments that God inflicted on them for this sin. But you will find an account of Judas's origin and punishment in the legend of Saint Matthias,[2] and the story of the Jews' punishment and downfall in that of Saint James the Less.[3]

---

[2] Chapter 45, above.
[3] Chapter 67, below.

What follows is what we read in a history, admittedly apocryphal, concerning the origin and punishment of Pilate.

There was a king, Tyrus by name, who seduced a girl named Pyla, daughter of a miller called Atus, and had of her a son. When her son was born, Pyla gave him a name composed of her own and her father's, and called him Pylatus, or Pilate. When Pilate was three years old, his mother sent him to the king, his father. The king already had a son born of the queen his wife, and this son was almost the same age as Pilate. As they grew older the two often competed with each other at wrestling, boxing, and shooting with a sling, but the king's legitimate son, just as he was of nobler birth, showed himself more vigorous and skillful in every sort of contest, and Pilate, consumed with jealousy and suffering from liver trouble, killed his brother in secret. When King Tyrus learned what had happened, he was grief-stricken and called his council together to decide what should be done with this criminal, murderous son of his. All were agreed that he was worthy of death; but the king, upon reflection, was unwilling to pile one wrong upon another and sent Pilate to Rome as a hostage for the tribute that he owed annually to the Romans. He hoped by this means to purge himself of the murder of his son and to be freed of the Roman tribute.

At that time there was in Rome a son of the king of France, who likewise had been sent there in lieu of tribute. He and Pilate became comrades, but Pilate, seeing himself surpassed by the other both in character and in action, and goaded by the stings of envy, took his companion's life. Now the Romans, wondering what to do with him, said: "If this fellow, who slew his brother and strangled a hostage, is allowed to live, he can be mighty useful to the Republic; and, being a brute himself, he will know how to handle our brutish enemies." They therefore decided: "He must be judged worthy of death, but let him be posted as a judge to the island of Pontus, where the people have never tolerated a judge. If his wickedness can tame their perversity, all the better; if not, let him get what he deserves." So Pilate was sent to Pontus and its hardheaded people. He knew that they were destroyers of judges and that his life hung in the balance, so he quietly worked out ways to save his skin, and by threats and promises, torture and bribery, completely subjugated this rebellious crowd. His victory won for him the title of Pilate of Pontus, or Pontius Pilate.

Herod heard about this man's way of doing things and, being a crafty schemer himself, was delighted with the other's stratagems and sent envoys with gifts and an invitation to visit. Then he made Pilate his deputy and gave him power over Judea and Jerusalem. Pilate proceeded to amass great wealth and went to Rome without informing Herod. In Rome he offered the emperor Tiberius a huge sum of money and pressed the ruler to vest him outright with the powers he held from Herod. This gave rise to enmity between the two until the time of the Lord's passion, when Pilate, to conciliate Herod, sent Christ to him. The *Scholastic History* tells us that there was another reason for their hostility. There was an individual who claimed to be the son of God and beguiled a great many people in Galilee. He led his followers to Garizim, where he said he was going to ascend into heaven. Pilate came upon them and killed them all, because he feared that the people of Judea might likewise be misled. This caused enmity between him and Herod, because Galilee was in Herod's jurisdiction. Both of these reasons may well be true.

When Pilate had handed Jesus over to the Jews to be crucified, he was afraid that his condemnation of innocent blood might offend Tiberius Caesar, and dispatched one of his familiars to make a case for him to the emperor. Meanwhile, it was announced to Tiberius, who was seriously ill, that in Jerusalem there was a physician who cured all diseases by his word alone. Therefore the emperor, not knowing that Pilate and the Jews had put this physician to death, said to one of his intimates, whose name was Volusian: "Cross the sea as fast as you can, and tell Pilate to send this healer to me so that he may restore me to health." Volusian came to Pilate and delivered the emperor's command, but Pilate, terror-stricken, asked for a fortnight's grace.

During this time Volusian made the acquaintance of a woman named Veronica, who had been in Jesus' company, and asked her where he might find Jesus Christ. She answered: "Alas, he was my Lord and my God, and Pilate, to whom he was handed over through envy, condemned him and commanded that he be crucified." Volusian was grieved at this and said: "I am deeply sorry that I cannot carry out the orders my master gave me." Veronica answered: "When the Teacher was going about preaching and I, to my regret, could not be with him, I wanted to have his picture painted so that when I was deprived of his presence, I could at least have the solace of his image. So one day I was carrying a piece of linen to the painter when I met Jesus, and he asked me where I was going. I told him what my errand was. He asked for the cloth I had in my hand, pressed it to his venerable face, and left his image on it. If your master looks devoutly upon this image, he will at once be rewarded by being cured." "Can this image be bought for gold or silver?" Volusian asked. "No," Veronica replied, "only true piety can make it effective. Therefore I will go with you and let Caesar look upon the image, after which I will return home." So Volusian came to Rome with Veronica and told Tiberius: "The Jesus you have long desired to see was unjustly given over to death by Pilate and the Jews, and, by reason of their envy, nailed to the gibbet of the cross. However, a lady came to me with a picture of Jesus, and if you look at it devoutly, you will obtain the benefit of your health." Caesar therefore had the road carpeted with silk cloths and ordered the image brought to him, and the moment he looked at it, he won back his pristine health.

Pontius Pilate was then taken prisoner at Caesar's command and shipped to Rome; and when the emperor heard that he had arrived, he was filled with fury and had him brought into his presence. Pilate, however, had taken with him the

Lord's seamless tunic and came before the emperor wearing it. As soon as Tiberius saw him clothed in the tunic, his anger vanished. He rose to meet Pilate and could not address a harsh word to him. So the emperor, who, when Pilate was absent, seemed so terrible and furious, now, in his presence, was somehow calmed. As soon as he had given him leave to go, on the other hand, he was again afire with rage and called himself a wretch for not having showed the culprit the anger that was in his heart. Swearing and protesting that Pilate was a son of death and that it was not right to let him live on the earth, he at once had him called back. But when he saw him, the emperor greeted him and his wrath subsided. All wondered, and he himself wondered, that he could be so wrought up against Pilate absent and could not so much as speak to him harshly when he was present. At length, at a sign from God, or perhaps a hint from some Christian, he had the man stripped of that tunic, and instantly his previous rage was rekindled. The emperor's astonishment mounted until he was told that the tunic had belonged to the Lord Jesus. He had Pilate remanded to prison until he could consult with a council of wise men about what should be done with the criminal. Pilate was forthwith sentenced to a shameful death, but when he heard of this, he killed himself with his own knife and so ended his life. When Caesar was informed of this, he said: "Truly he died a most shameful death, and his own hand did not spare him."

The corpse was weighted with a huge stone and thrown into the Tiber, but wicked, foul spirits made sport of the wicked, foul body, plunging it into the water and snatching it up into the air. This caused awesome floods in the water and lightning, tempests, and hailstorms in the air, and a widespread panic broke out among the people. The Romans therefore pulled the body out of the Tiber and, as a gesture of contempt, carried it off to Vienne and dumped it into the Rhone. The name of the city comes from *Via Gehennae*, the road to hell, because at that time it was a place of malediction. Or, more likely, the city was called Vienne or Bienna because it was said to have been built in a biennium. But there again the wicked spirits rallied and stirred up the same disturbances, and the people, refusing to put up with so great a plague of demons, removed that vessel of malediction from their midst and consigned it to burial in the territory of the city of Lausanne. There the populace, harried to excess by the aforesaid upheavals, took the body away and sank it in a pit surrounded by mountains, where, according to some accounts, diabolical machinations still make themselves felt. . . . Thus far we have quoted the aforementioned apocryphal history: let the reader judge whether the story is worth the telling.

It should be noted, however, that the *Scholastic History* tells us that the Jews accused Pilate to Tiberius of the savage massacre of the Innocents, of placing pagan images in the Temple despite the protests of the Jews, and of appropriating money taken from the corbona, or poor-chest, for his own uses such as building a water conduit into his house. For all these misdeeds he was deported into exile at Lyons, his city of origin, and there he died, despised by his own people. It could be, if there is any truth to this story, that Tiberius had decreed his exile and had had him deported to Lyons before Volusian came back to Rome from Jerusalem and reported to the emperor, but then, learning how he had put Christ to death, had the miscreant brought out of exile and returned to Rome. Neither Eusebius nor Bede says in his chronicle that Pilate was exiled, but only that he suffered many calamities and died by his own hand.

About the feasts that occur within the time
of reconciliation

We have considered the feast days that occur in the time of deviation, which began with Adam and ended with Moses, and which
the Church represents from Septuagesima to Easter. We now take
up the feasts that occur within the time of reconciliation, which the
Church represents from Easter to the octave of Pentecost.

54. The Resurrection of the Lord

Christ's resurrection took place on the third day after his passion. Concerning the resurrection there are seven questions that must be considered. First, how is it true to say that the Lord lay in the tomb for three days and three nights and rose on the third day? Second, why did he not come to life immediately after dying instead of waiting until the third day? Third, how he rose. Fourth, why he hurried his rising rather than wait for the general resurrection. Fifth, why he rose. Sixth, how many times he appeared after the resurrection. Seventh, how he brought out the holy fathers who were in limbo and what he did there.

Regarding the first question, note that according to Augustine, to say that Christ was in the tomb for three days and three nights is a figure of speech, synecdoche, the last part of the first day being taken for the whole, the second day being counted in its entirety, and of the third day the first part standing for the whole. Thus there were three days and each day had its night preceding it. According to Bede this reversed the usual order of day and night, because previously day came first and night followed, but after Christ's passion this order was changed so that the nights came first and the days followed. This agreed with the order of the mystery, since first man fell from the daylight of grace into the night of sin and then, through Christ's passion and resurrection, came back from the night of sin to the daylight of grace.

As to the second question, let it be known that it was right that Christ should not rise immediately after dying but should wait until the third day, and this for five reasons. The first is what this delay signified, namely, that the light of his death cured our double death: therefore he lay in the tomb for one whole day and two nights, so that the day could be understood as signifying the light of his death and the two nights as our twofold death. The *Gloss* gives this reason to explain Christ's words in Luke 24:46: "It is written that the Christ should suffer and on the third day rise from the dead." The second reason was to prove that he had really died, because just as in the mouth of two or three witnesses every word may stand, so after three days one realizes what has happened to him, and therefore Christ, in order to give proof of his death and to show that he had experienced death, chose to lie buried for three days.

The third reason was to show his power, because if he had risen immediately it might not be clear that he had the power to lay down his life and to rise again from death. This reason seems to be suggested in 1 Cor. 15:3: ". . . that Christ died . . . and that he was buried . . . and that he rose again on the third day." His death is mentioned first so that as the death is shown to be a fact, so also the truth of the resurrection is demonstrated. The fourth reason is that all that was to be restored was prefigured. Peter of Ravenna proposes this reason, saying: "He willed to be buried for three days to show that he was to restore what was in heaven, to repair what was on earth, and to redeem what was in the underworld." The fifth reason was to represent the three states of the just. Gregory gives this reason in his commentary on Ezechiel: "Christ suffered on Friday, rested in the tomb on Saturday, and rose from death on Sunday. For us the present life is Friday, the time when we suffer distress and pain, but on Saturday we are, as it were, at rest in the grave because after death we find rest for our soul, and on Sunday, the eighth day, we rise from that condition with the body and rejoice in the glory of soul and body. So pain is ours on the sixth day, rest on the seventh, and glory on the eighth."[1] Thus Gregory.

Regarding the third question, namely, how Christ rose, note first that he rose powerfully, i.e., by his own power; John 10:18: "I have power to lay down [my life] and I have power to take it up again"; and John 2:19: "Destroy this temple, and in three days I will raise it up." Second, he rose happily, all misery left behind; Matt. 26:32: "After I am raised up, I will go before you to Galilee." "Galilee" is interpreted "transmigration," and Christ, when he rose, went ahead into Galilee because he crossed over from suffering to glory, from corruption to incorruption. Pope Leo: "After Christ's passion the chains of death were broken; weakness passed into strength, mortality into eternity, shame into glory." Third, he rose usefully, because he seized prey; Jer. 4:7: "The lion is come up out of his den and the robber of nations has roused himself"; John 12:32: "And I, if I be lifted up from the earth, will draw all things to myself," i.e., when I am taken up from the earth, raising my soul out of limbo and my body from the tomb, I will draw all things, etc. Fourth, he rose miraculously, because the tomb remained closed. Just as he came forth at birth though his mother's womb remained closed, and as he came in to his disciples though the doors were shut, so also he was able to come out of the closed tomb. Hence we read in the *Scholastic History* that in the year 1111 from the Lord's incarnation a monk of Saint-Lawrence-outside-the-Walls marveled to see the cord that he wore as a cincture inexplicably thrown down in front of him, still knotted, while a voice sounded in the air: "Thus was Christ able to come out of the tomb." Fifth, he rose truly, i.e., with his own true body. Indeed, he gave six proofs that he had truly risen from the dead. First, the angel, who does not lie, said so, and second, by his frequent apparitions: in these two ways he showed that he had truly risen. Third, by eating he proved that he was not using any magical arts. Fourth, he let himself be touched, so it had to be his real body. Fifth, by showing his wounds, he proved that this was the same body in which he had died. Sixth, by coming in

---

[1] The "eighth day" is the day "after time," i.e., eternity.

through the closed doors of the house, he showed that he rose glorified.. Therefore it is evident that on all these points the disciples had had doubts about his resurrection.

Seventh, he rose immortally, since he was never to die again; Rom. 6:9: "Christ, rising again from the dead, dies now no more." Yet Dionysius, in his letter to Demophilus, said that Christ, after his ascension, told a man named Carpus: "I am ready to suffer again for man's salvation." Thus it is clear that if such a thing were possible, he was prepared to die again for mankind. The aforementioned Carpus, a man of admirable holiness, told the blessed Dionysius, as we learn from the same letter, that when a certain infidel had led one of the faithful astray, he, Carpus, took this so badly that he fell ill. Furthermore, though his sanctity was so great that he always experienced a heavenly vision before he celebrated the sacred mysteries, now, when he should have been praying for the conversion of the two men, on the contrary, he prayed daily that God would have no mercy and would put an end to their lives by burning them up. And once, when he awoke at midnight and began to say this prayer, the house he was in suddenly split in two and a huge furnace appeared in the middle. Then he looked upward and saw heaven open and Jesus there, surrounded by a multitude of angels. Next he saw the aforesaid two men standing terror-stricken near the furnace. Serpents came out of it and coiled themselves around the men, bit them, and tried strenuously to drag them into the furnace, while some other men pushed them toward it. Carpus took such pleasure at the sight of the suffering of the two that, paying no heed to the vision above, he fixed his attention on their trials and was sorry they did not fall into the furnace right away. In time, however, he looked up reluctantly and saw the heavenly vision as before; and now Jesus, taking pity on those men, rose from his supercelestial throne, came down with a company of angels, reached out, and lifted the two out of danger. Then Jesus said to Carpus, whose hand was raised: "If you wish to strike, strike me! I am ready to suffer for men's salvation. That is my pleasure, and not that other men sin."—It is to preserve these words of Christ that we have set down this account of the vision as Dionysius related it.[2]

As to the fourth question, namely, why the Lord did not wait to rise again with the rest at the general resurrection, there are three reasons for this choice. First, there is the dignity of his body. This body was of the highest dignity because it was deified, i.e., united to his divinity. Therefore, it would have been unseemly were the body to lie so long beneath the dust. Hence Ps. 15(16):10: "Nor wilt thou give thy holy one [i.e., the sanctified, deified body] to see corruption"; and Ps. 131(132):8: "Arise, O Lord, into thy resting place, thou and the ark, which thou hast sanctified." The body that contained divinity is here called the ark. A second reason would be the strengthening of faith, because if Christ had not risen at that time, faith would have perished and no one would

---

[2] Cf. Pseudo-Dionysius, *The Complete Works*, 278–280.

have believed that he was true God. This is obvious from the fact that all except the Blessed Virgin lost their faith at the crucifixion but recovered it once the resurrection was known; thus 1 Cor. 15:17: "If Christ be not risen again, then is our preaching vain, and your faith is also vain." A third reason is that Christ's resurrection was the exemplar of our own. Rarely would anyone be found who would hope for resurrection in the future unless it could be seen to have happened in the past. For this reason the apostle says that if Christ arose from the dead, we too shall rise, because his rising is the exemplary cause of our resurrection. Gregory: "The Lord showed by this example what he promised as a reward, so that as all the faithful knew that he had risen, so they would hope for the reward of resurrection at the end of the world." And Gregory also says: "He wanted his death to last no longer than three days, lest, if resurrection were delayed in him, in us it might be utterly despaired of. Therefore, knowing about the glory of our Head, we have hope of our own resurrection."

The fifth question asked for what purpose Christ rose. Let it be known that his resurrection procured four great benefits for us: it effected justification for sinners, taught a new way of life, stirred up hope for rewards to be received, and caused the resurrection of all. The first, justification: Rom. 4:25: "He was delivered up for our sins and rose again for our justification." The second, new way of living: Rom. 6:4: "As Christ is risen from the dead by the glory of the Father, so we also may walk in newness of life." The third, hope: 1 Pet. 1:3: "By his great mercy we have been born anew to a living hope through the resurrection of Jesus Christ from the dead." The fourth, resurrection for all: 1 Cor. 15:20: "Christ the Lord has been raised from the dead, the firstfruits of those who have fallen asleep. For as by a man came death, by a man has come also the resurrection of the dead."

Note also that, as is clear from what has been said, Christ's resurrection had four distinguishing marks. The first is that while our resurrection is deferred to the end, his was celebrated on the third day. The second is that we rise through him, whereas he rose through himself, through his own power, whence Ambrose says: "How could he, who brought others to life, look for help in restoring life to his own body?" Thirdly, we shall return to dust, but Christ's body could not be reduced to dust. Fourthly, his resurrection is the efficient, exemplary, and sacramental cause of our resurrection. Regarding the first of these causes, the *Gloss* on the verse of Ps. 29(30):6 ("In the evening weeping shall have place, and in the morning, gladness") says: "Christ's resurrection is the efficient cause of the soul's resurrection in present time and of the body's in the future." Regarding the exemplary cause, 1 Cor. 15:20: "Christ is risen from the dead, the first fruits of them that sleep." Regarding the sacramental cause, Rom. 6:4: "As Christ is risen from the dead, so we also may walk in newness of life."

We come to the sixth question: how many times did the risen Christ appear? Let it be known that he appeared five times on the day of his resurrection, and five more times on subsequent days. The first of his apparitions was to Mary

Magdalene, as in John 20:1–18 and in Mark 16:9: "[Jesus] rising early the first day of the week, appeared first to Mary Magdalene, etc." Here Mary represents all repentant sinners. Indeed, he willed to appear first to her for five reasons. The first, that she loved him more ardently; Luke 7:47: "Many sins are forgiven her because she loved much." The second, in order to show that he had died for sinners; Matt. 9:13: "I came not to call the just but sinners." The third, because harlots go ahead of the wise in the kingdom of heaven; Matt. 21:31: "The harlots will go into the kingdom of God before you." The fourth, that as a woman had been the messenger of death, so a woman should be the one to announce life: this according to the *Gloss*. The fifth, that where sin abounded, grace would superabound, as we read in Rom. 5:20.

The Lord's second apparition on Easter Day was to the women as they came back from the tomb, when he said to them: "All hail!" and they approached and took hold of his feet, as we read in the last chapter of Matthew. The women here stand for the humble, to whom the Lord shows himself because of their sex and because of their affection, for they held his feet.

His third apparition was to Simon Peter, but where and when we do not know, unless perhaps it was when Peter was returning from the sepulcher with John. It might be that Peter at some point took a different way from John's, and that then the Lord appeared to him (Luke, last chapter). Or it may have happened when Peter went into the sepulcher alone, as the *Scholastic History* says, or in a cave or underground cavern. The same history says that after he denied Christ, he fled to a cavern which is now called Gallicantus,[3] where, it is said, he wept for three days for having denied Christ, and that there Christ appeared to him and comforted him. The name "Peter" is interpreted as meaning "obedient," and Peter here represents the obedient, to whom the Lord appears.

His fourth apparition was to the disciples at Emmaus. The name is interpreted "desire for counsel" and signifies Christ's poor, who wish to fulfill this counsel: "Go, sell what you have and give to the poor." The fifth was to the disciples gathered together (John 20:19), where they represent the religious, the doors of whose senses are closed.

These five apparitions occurred on Easter Day, and the priest represents them in the mass when he turns to the people five times—the third time in silence because this turning stands for the apparition to Peter, the place and time of which are not known.

The sixth time Jesus appeared was on the octave day of the resurrection, when the disciples were together and Thomas, who had said he would not believe unless he saw and touched, was present. Here he represents those who hesitate in believing, John 20:26–29. The seventh apparition was to the disciples when they were fishing, John 21:4; they represent preachers, who are fishers of men. The eighth time was to the disciples on Mount Tabor, as in the last chapter

[3] *galli cantus*, i.e., cockcrow.

of Matthew: here the contemplatives are signified, because Christ was transfigured on that mountain. The ninth was when the eleven disciples were at table and Jesus upbraided them for their incredulity and hardness of heart, as we read in Mark 16:14; here we understand sinners placed in the number of transgression, which is eleven,[4] whom the Lord sometimes visits mercifully. The tenth and last apparition was to the disciples as they stood on Mount Olivet, as in the last chapter of Luke. From there he ascended into heaven, because "godliness is of value in every way, as it holds promise for the present life and also for the life to come," 1 Tim. 4:8.

Three other apparitions are referred to as having happened on the day of the resurrection, but the text has nothing about them. There is the one to James the Just, otherwise James of Alpheus, an account of which we shall find in the legend of James the Less.[5] It is said that Jesus was also seen on the same day by Joseph, as we read in the *Gospel of Nicodemus*. When the Jews heard that Joseph had asked Pilate for the body and had placed it in his own tomb, they were indignant, and took him and shut him up in a small room that they carefully locked and sealed. They intended to kill him after the Sabbath, but the very night of the resurrection the house was lifted up by the four corners and Jesus came in to him, dried his tears, embraced him, and, leaving the seals intact, led him out and brought him to his house in Arimathea.

The third apparition was to the Virgin Mary and is believed to have taken place before all the others, although the evangelists say nothing about it. The church at Rome seems to approve this belief, since it celebrates a station[6] at the church of Saint Mary on Easter Sunday. Indeed, if this is not to be believed, on the ground that no evangelist testifies to it, we would have to conclude that Jesus never appeared to Mary after his resurrection because no gospel tells us where or when this happened. But perish the thought that such a son would fail to honor such a mother by being so negligent! Still it may be that in this case the evangelists kept silence because their charge was only to present witnesses to the resurrection, and it would not be proper to have a mother testifying for her son. If indeed the words of the other women had been taken for ravings, how much more surely would a mother be thought to be making up stories for love of her son! So the evangelists judged it better not to write about this apparition, and left it to be taken for granted. Christ must first of all have made his mother happy over his resurrection, since she certainly grieved over his death more than the others. He would not have neglected his mother while he hastened to console others. Ambrose also testifies to this in the third book of his *De Virginibus*, say-

---

[4] Augustine, in Sermo 51, explains that since the number of commandments is 10, the number of sin is 11, because sin "transgresses"—oversteps—the number 10 (Augustinus, *Opera*, 5, col. 430 B–C; cf. Sermo 83, ibid., col. 645 A).

[5] Chapter 67, below.

[6] A "station" brought the people of the city together in one of the principal churches (in this instance, Saint Mary Major), where the pope led the solemn celebration of a major feast.

ing: "His mother saw the risen Lord, and saw him first and believed first." Mary Magdalene saw him although up to that moment she had hesitated to believe. And Sedulius,[7] treating of Christ's apparition, says:

> Semper virgo manet, hujus se visibus astans
> Luce palam Dominus prius obtulit, ut bona mater,
> Grandia divulgans miracula, quae fuit olim
> Advenientis iter, haec sit redeuntis et index.[8]

Regarding the seventh and last question, namely, how Christ led out the holy fathers who were in Limbo and what he did there, the Gospel tells us nothing openly. Yet Augustine, in one of his sermons, and Nicodemus in his *Gospel*, give us some information. Saint Augustine writes as follows: "As soon as Christ yielded up his spirit, his soul, united to his deity, went down to the depths of hell. When he came to the edge of darkness like some splendid, terrible raider, the impious infernal legions, terrified as they gazed on him, began to ask: 'Whence is he, so strong, so terrible, so splendid, so noble? That world which was subject to us never sent us a dead man like this, never destined such gifts to hell! Who then is this, who comes to our gates so boldly, and not only has no fear of our torments but also frees others from our chains? See how these, who used to moan under our blows, now, with salvation in sight, not only fear nothing but even threaten us! Never have the dead here below been so confident, nor was there a time when they could be so joyous in captivity! O our prince, wherefore have you willed to bring this one here? Your gladness has perished, your joys turned to lamentation! While you hang Christ upon the tree, you know not what losses you sustain in hell!'

"After these cries of the cruel infernal spirits, at the Lord's command all the iron bars were shattered and innumerable peoples of the saints, throwing themselves at his feet, called out with tearful voice: 'You have come, Redeemer of the world, you have come, you whom we longed for and waited for day by day! You have come down to hell for us! Leave us not when you ascend again to the upper world! Go up, Lord Jesus, leave hell stripped of its prey and the author of death bound again in his chains! Restore joy to the world, help us, put an end now to our fierce pains and in mercy set the captives free! While you are here, absolve the guilty! While you ascend, defend your own!'" Thus far Augustine.

In the *Gospel of Nicodemus* we read that Carinus and Leucius, sons of the aged Simeon, were raised to life with Christ and appeared to Annas and Caiaphas and Nicodemus and Joseph and Gamaliel, and at their urging told what Christ had done in hell. This is their story:

---

[7] Caelius Sedulius, a Christian poet of the second half of the fifth century.

[8] She remains ever virgin, to whose sight the Lord first offered himself at dawn, so that she, good mother, who in the past was the path for his coming, might, by making known the grand miracles, become also the signpost for his returning.

"While we were in thick darkness with all our fathers the patriarchs, a gold and royal purple sunlight suddenly burst upon us. At once Adam, father of the human race, rejoiced, saying, 'This is the Light of the Author of the everlasting light, who promised to send us his coeternal Light. And Isaiah exclaimed, This is the Light of the Father, the Son of God, as I, when I was alive on earth, predicted, saying, The people that walked in darkness have seen a great light.'

"Then our father Simeon came up and, rejoicing, said, 'Glorify the Lord, because I held the newborn infant Christ in my arms in the Temple and, moved by the Holy Spirit, proclaimed, Now my eyes have seen thy salvation, which thou hast prepared before the face of all peoples; a light to the revelation of the Gentiles and the glory of thy people Israel (Luke 2:25–32).' Next came one who dwelt in the desert and, when we asked who he was, said, 'I am John, who baptized the Christ and went before him to prepare his way, and I pointed him out with my finger, saying, Behold the Lamb of God! And I have come down to announce to you that Christ will soon visit us.'

"Then Seth said, 'I had gone to the gates of paradise and prayed the Lord to send his angel to give me some of the oil of mercy; I wanted to anoint the body of my father Adam who was infirm. The angel Michael appeared and told me, Do not weary yourself weeping as you pray for oil from the tree of mercy. That you cannot possibly receive until five thousand five hundred years have passed.'

"Hearing all this, the patriarchs and prophets rejoiced with great joy. Then Satan, prince and captain of death, said to Hell, 'Get ready to receive Jesus, who boasts that he is the Son of God, but is a mere man who fears death and says, My soul is sorrowful even unto death. Yet he has cured many whom I had made deaf, and has made those I lamed able to walk straight.' Hell answered, 'If you are so mighty, what sort of man is this Jesus, who fears death and yet defies your power? He says he is afraid of death because he wants to fool you, and woe to you forever and ever!' Satan answered: 'I have tempted him and stirred up the populace against him. I sharpened the spear, I mixed the gall and vinegar, I readied the wood of the cross. His death is at hand and I will bring him to you!' Hell: 'Is he the one who restored Lazarus, who was mine, to life?' Satan: 'The very one!' Hell: 'I adjure you by your power and mine, don't bring him to me! When I heard the command of his word, I shuddered with fear and couldn't even hold on to Lazarus, who shook free of his bonds and took off like an eagle, springing up with unbounded agility and getting away from us!'

"Now a voice like thunder was heard, saying, 'Lift up your gates, O princes, and be lifted up, eternal gates, and the King of glory will come in!' At the sound of the voice the demons ran and shut the bronze gates and put up the iron bars. Then David said, 'Did I not prophesy and say, Let them thank the Lord for his steadfast love, for he shatters the doors of bronze and cuts in two the bars of iron?'[9] Then again the voice rang out loudly, 'Lift up your gates, etc.' Hell,

[9] Ps. 106(107):15–16.

seeing that the voice had called out twice and feigning ignorance, asked, 'Who is this king of glory?' David replied, 'The Lord who is strong and mighty, the Lord mighty in battle, he is the King of glory!'[10]

"Then the King of glory came and poured light into the eternal darkness; and the Lord reached out and took Adam's right hand, saying, 'Peace be to you and all your sons, my just ones!' Whereupon the Lord ascended out of hell and all the saints followed him. The Lord, holding Adam's hand, entrusted him to the archangel Michael, who led him into paradise. Two men of great age came forward and the saints asked them, 'Who are you? You were not yet dead with us in hell and here you are in the body in paradise!' One of the two answered, 'I am Enoch, I was taken up here; and this is Elijah, who was carried up here in a fiery chariot. We have not yet tasted death but are being kept until the coming of the Antichrist. We will fight with him and be killed by him, and after three and one-half days will be assumed into the clouds.'

"As he spoke, another man came forward carrying the sign of the cross on his shoulders. Being asked who he was, he said, 'I was a robber and was crucified with Jesus. I believed that he was the Creator and I prayed to him and said, Lord, remember me when you come into your kingdom. Then he said to me, Truly, I say to you, today you will be with me in paradise;[11] and he gave me this sign of the cross, saying, Carry this, walk into paradise. If the angel on guard doesn't let you go in, show him this sign of the cross and say to him, Christ, who is now dying on the cross, sent me over. And when I did this and told the angel, he opened at once and led me in, placing me on the right side of paradise.'"

When Carinus and Leucius had said all this, suddenly they were transfigured and were seen no more.

Gregory of Nyssa, or, according to some books, Augustine, says about the above: "All at once, when Christ came down, the eternal night of hell was filled with light, and the dark gatekeepers, beset with fear, broke the shadowy silences between them and whispered: 'Who indeed is this terrible one who gleams with such splendor? Our hell never received such a one, never did the world disgorge the like into our cavern! He is an invader, not a debtor, a demolisher and destroyer, no sinner but a predator. We see a judge, not a suppliant, one who comes to fight, not to succumb, not to stay but to take from us what is ours.'"

---

[10] Ps. 23(24):7-10.
[11] Luke 23:42-43.

55. Saint Secundus

Secundus resembles *se condens*, which means establishing oneself, i.e., composing oneself by integrity of morals. Or the name is like *secundans*, i.e., *obsecundans*, complying with; so, complying with the commands of the Lord. Or the name is formed from *secum dux*, commander of oneself. Saint Secundus was his own commander, because he controlled sensuality by reason and directed his senses to the performance of all good works. Or *secundus*, the second, refers to *primus*, the first, for there are two roads that lead to eternal life, the first by lamenting in penance, the second by martyrdom. The precious martyr Secundus took not only the first road but also the second.

Secundus was a valiant soldier, a stout fighter for Christ, and a glorious martyr for the Lord. He won the martyr's crown in the city of Asti, and Asti is honored by his glorious presence and rejoices in having him as its special patron saint. He was instructed in the Christian faith by blessed Calocerus, who was held in prison in Asti by Sapritius the prefect. Blessed Marcianus was also imprisoned, in the city of Tortona, and Sapritius wanted to go there in order to compel him to offer sacrifice. Secundus went with him, his pretext being to have a holiday, his real purpose being to see Marcianus.

As they were riding along outside Asti, a dove came down and lighted on Secundus's head. Sapritius said to him: "You see, Secundus, our gods love you so much that they send birds from heaven to visit you!" When they came to the river Tanaro, Secundus saw an angel of the Lord walking over the water and saying to him: "Secundus, have faith, and you will walk like this over the worshipers of idols." Sapritius said: "Brother Secundus, I hear the gods talking to you!" Secundus replied: "Let us walk toward the fulfillment of our heart's desire!" When they came to the river Bormida, an angel appeared to him as before and asked: "Secundus, do you firmly believe in God, or do you perhaps have doubts?" Secundus answered: "I believe in the truth of his passion!" Sapritius exclaimed: "What *is* that that I'm hearing?" When they arrived in Tortona, Marcianus, following the angel's directions, came out of the jail and appeared before Secundus, saying: "Secundus, enter upon the way of truth and continue until you receive the palm of faith!" Sapritius said: "Who is that, speaking to us like someone in a dream?" Secundus: "A dream to you, to me an admonition and an encouragement!"

After that, Secundus went to Milan, and an angel led Faustinus and Jovita, who were being held in prison, to meet him outside the city; and he was baptized by them, a cloud providing the water. Then suddenly a dove came from heaven carrying the Body and Blood of the Lord, which it entrusted to Faustinus and Jovita. Faustinus in turn gave the sacred species to Secundus to be brought to Marcianus. By that time it was night, and when Secundus reached the bank of the river Po, the angel took hold of the horse's bridle and led him across the river and to Tortona, to Marcianus's prison. Secundus entered the prison and gave Faustinus's precious gift to Marcianus, who took it and said: "May the Lord's Body and Blood be with me unto eternal life!" Then, at the angel's command, Secundus left the prison and went to his lodging.

Soon Marcianus was condemned to die and was beheaded, and Secundus retrieved his body and buried it. Sapritius heard of this and summoned Secundus. "So far as I can see," he said, "you profess to be a Christian." Secundus: "Indeed I do profess to be a Christian!" Sapritius: "You desire a bad death!" Secundus: "Rather, that is what's coming to you!" Secundus refused to sacrifice to the gods and Sapritius ordered him to be stripped naked, but immediately an angel of the Lord was at his side and prepared covering for him. Then Sapritius had Secundus bound on a rack and stretched until his arms were drawn out of their sockets, but when an angel repaired the injury, the prefect remanded him to prison. There the angel came to him and said: "Stand up, Secundus, follow me and I shall lead you to your Creator!" Then the angel conducted him into the city of Asti and left him in the prison where Calocerus was, and the Savior with him. Seeing the Savior, Secundus prostrated himself at his feet. The Savior said to him: "Fear not, Secundus, for I am the Lord your God, and I will rescue you from all evils!" And he blessed them and ascended to heaven.

Morning came, and Sapritius sent men to the prison, but, though the doors were locked and sealed, they did not find Secundus. Sapritius therefore came from Tortona to Asti to punish Calocerus at least. He ordered Calocerus to be brought before him, and they came back and told him that Secundus was with Calocerus. So he had the two of them brought to him and said to them: "Since our gods know that you have no respect for them, they want you to die together." They refused to sacrifice, so he had pitch heated with resin and poured over their heads and into their throats. They swallowed the potion with relish, as if it were the sweetest of waters, and said loudly and clearly: "How sweet to my mouth are your words, O Lord!" Sapritius then sentenced Secundus to be beheaded in Asti, and Calocerus to be sent to Albenga and put to death there. When blessed Secundus had been decapitated, angels of the Lord took his body and with praises and chants gave it burial. He suffered on the thirtieth day of March.

56. Saint Mary of Egypt

Mary the Egyptian, who is called the Sinner, led a most austere life in the desert for forty-seven years, beginning about the year of the Lord 270 in the time of Claudius. A priest named Zozimus crossed the Jordan and began to wander through the broad forest, hoping to find some holy father there, and saw a figure walking about naked, the body blackened and burned by the fiery sun. It was Mary the Egyptian. She immediately took flight, and Zozimus ran after her as fast as he could. She said to him: "Father Zozimus, why are you pursuing me? Forgive me, I cannot face you because I am a woman and naked, but lend me your mantle so that I may see you without being ashamed." Astonished at being called by name, he gave her his mantle and prostrated himself on the ground, asking her to bless him. "It behooves you, father," she said, "to give the blessing, since you are adorned with the dignity of priesthood." When he heard that she knew both his name and his office, he marveled still more and urgently besought her to bless him. Then she said: "Blessed be God, the redeemer of our souls!" She extended her hands in prayer, and he saw her lifted some feet above the earth. The old man began to suspect that this might be a spirit pretending to pray. "May God forgive you," she said, "for thinking that I, a sinful woman, might be an unclean spirit."

Now Zozimus adjured her in God's name to tell him about herself. Her answer was: "Excuse me, father, because if I tell you who and what I am, you will flee as if frightened by a serpent, your ears will be contaminated by my words, the air will be polluted with filth."

The old man forcefully insisted nonetheless, so she began: "I was born in Egypt, brother, and went to Alexandria when I was twelve years old. There, for seventeen years, I plied my trade as a public woman and never refused my body to anyone. But there came a time when some people of that region were going up to Jerusalem to pay homage to the holy cross, and I asked the sailors to allow me to go with them. When they asked me for my fare, I said: 'Brothers, I have no other fare, but take my body in payment for the passage.' So they took me aboard and I paid my fare with my body.

"I arrived at Jerusalem and went to the church with the others to worship the holy cross, but suddenly, by an invisible force, I was pushed back from the door and not allowed to enter. Again and again I got to the threshold of the entrance and suffered the pain of being repulsed, while the others went in freely and encountered no obstacle. Then I came to myself and realized that this was happening to me because of my dreadful crimes. I began to beat my breast, I shed bitter tears and sighed from the bottom of my heart. Then, looking up, I saw there an image of the Blessed Virgin Mary. I began to pray tearfully to her, asking her to obtain pardon for my sins and to let me go in and worship the holy cross, promising that I would renounce the world and thenceforth live chastely. Having offered this prayer and putting my trust in the name of the Blessed Virgin, I went again to the door of the church and entered without difficulty.

"When I had worshiped the cross with the utmost devotion, someone gave me three coins with which I bought three loaves of bread, and I heard a voice saying to me: 'If you go across the Jordan, you will be saved.' I therefore crossed the Jordan and came into this desert, where I have stayed for forty-seven years without seeing a single human being. The loaves I had brought with me turned hard as stone, but they have sufficed me for food all these years. My clothes fell to pieces in time. For seventeen years I was troubled by temptations of the flesh, but now by the grace of God I have conquered them all. There now, I have told you my whole story, and I beseech you to pray God for me."

The priest knelt and blessed the Lord in his handmaid. She said: "I beg you to come back to the Jordan on the day of the Lord's Supper and to bring with you the Body of the Lord, and I will meet you there and receive the sacred Body from your hand, because since the day I came here I have not received the communion of the Lord." The old man returned to his monastery, and the following year, when Holy Thursday was drawing near, he took the sacred Host and went to the bank of the Jordan. He saw the woman standing on the other bank, and she made the sign of the cross over the river and walked across the water. Marveling at this, the priest prostrated himself at her feet. She said: "Do not do that! You have the sacrament of the Lord on your person and you shine with the dignity of priesthood. But I pray you, father, that you may deign to come again to me next year." Then, once again making the sign of the cross over Jordan waters, she went over and returned to the solitude of the desert.

The father went back to his monastery and a year later sought the place where he had first spoken to the woman. He came to the place and found her lying there dead. He began to weep and did not dare to touch her, saying to himself: "I wish I could bury the saint's body, but I fear this might displease her." As he was thinking about this, he noticed something written in the sand beside her head, and read: "Zozimus, bury Mary's little body, return her dust to the earth, and pray for me to the Lord, at whose command I left this world on the second day of April." Thus the old man knew for certain that she had reached the end of her days immediately after receiving the Lord's sacrament and returning to the desert, and that she had crossed this expanse of desert in one hour and migrated to God, whereas it took him thirty days to cover the same distance.

Zozimus tried to dig a grave but could not. Then he saw a lion meekly coming toward him and said to the lion: "This holy woman commanded me to bury her body here, but I am old and cannot dig, and anyway I have no shovel. Therefore you do the digging and we will be able to bury this holy body." The lion began to dig and prepared a suitable grave, and when that was finished went away like a gentle lamb, while the old man made his way back to his monastery, glorifying God.

57. Saint Ambrose

The name Ambrose comes from *ambra*, amber, which is a fragrant, precious substance. Ambrose was precious to the Church and spread a pleasing fragrance both in his speech and in his actions. Or Ambrose is derived from *ambra* and *syos*, which means God, he being, as it were, the amber of God, because through him God diffused fragrance everywhere, as amber does; for Ambrose was and is the good odor of Christ in every place. Or the name comes from *ambor*, which means father of light, and *sior*, small, because he was a father in begetting many spiritual children; he was luminous in his expounding of Holy Scripture; and he was small in the humble way he dealt with others. Moreover, in the *Glossary* we find *ambrosia*, the food of angels, and *ambrosium*, the heavenly honeycomb; for Ambrose was a heavenly perfume by the fragrance of his renown, a supernal flavor due to his contemplative prayer, a celestial honeycomb by the sweetness of his exposition of the Scriptures, a food for angels in his glorious fruitfulness.

Paulinus, bishop of Nola, wrote the saint's life and gave it to Saint Augustine.

Ambrose, son of Ambrose the prefect of Rome, lay asleep in his cradle in the atrium of the palace when all of a sudden a swarm of bees flew in and covered his face and mouth so completely that the bees seemed to be moving in and out of their hive. Then they soared upward to such a height that the human eye could barely follow them. Witnessing this, the infant's father was astonished, and said: "If this child lives, something great will come of him." Later on, when Ambrose, now an adolescent, saw his mother and his sister, a professed virgin, kissing the hands of priests, he playfully offered his right hand to his sister, saying that she might well do the same for him.[1] She regarded this as coming from one too young to know what he was talking about, and refused.

Ambrose made his studies in Rome and pleaded cases in the courts with such eloquence that the emperor Valentinian appointed him to govern the province

---

[1] Jacobus omits Paulinus's explanatory clause, ". . . if she kept in mind that he was to be a bishop."

of Liguria-Emilia. After his arrival in Milan, the capital of the province, the bishop of the city died and the populace gathered in the cathedral to choose a new bishop. A noisy disturbance broke out, however, between the Arians and the Catholics over the election, and Ambrose went to the church to quell the commotion. As he entered, a child's voice was heard, crying "Ambrose for bishop!" All present took up the cry and unanimously acclaimed Ambrose as their bishop.

Ambrose thereupon tried to frighten the people into changing their minds. He left the church, went straight to his tribunal, and there, contrary to his usual moderate practice, sentenced several persons to be tortured. The populace, un-deterred, shouted: "Your sin be upon us!" Deeply troubled, Ambrose went home and tried to pose as a mere teacher of philosophy, but the public would have none of it and called him out again. Then he publicly had women of the street brought to his house, hoping that the people, seeing this, would revoke their decision; but this, too, failed, and the crowds continued to take his sin upon themselves. Then he determined to flee the city by night, but in the morn-ing, when he thought he had reached Pavia, he found himself at the gate of Milan called the Porta Romana. There the people found him and would not let him out of their hands.

All this was reported to the most clement emperor Valentinian, who was delighted that judges appointed by him should be considered for the priesthood, and the worthy ruler was particularly pleased that his word to Ambrose had been fulfilled. When he had dispatched him to Milan with his new commission, he had said to him: "Go, and act not like a judge but like a bishop." Meanwhile, in the interval before the answer to the report came back, Ambrose managed to hide again, but the people found him. Then it was realized that he was only a catechumen. He was baptized immediately and within a week was elevated to the episcopal throne. Four years later, when he was visiting Rome, his sister the consecrated virgin kissed his right hand. He smiled and said: "See, I told you back then that you would kiss this bishop's hand!"

On one occasion he went to another city to ordain the newly designated bishop, to whose election the empress Justina and other heretics objected, hop-ing that someone from their own party would be appointed instead. One of the young Arian women, more impudent than the rest, went up to the pulpit and grasped Saint Ambrose by the sleeve of his vestment, attempting to drag him over to the women's area, where they might beat him and drive him contumeli-ously out of the church. Ambrose said to her: "I may be unworthy of this high priestly rank, but you have no right to lay hands on any priest, and you should have feared God's judgment and the punishment that might befall you." The sequel confirmed what he had said: the very next day he conducted her body to the grave, thus repaying insult with blessing. This put the fear of God in everyone.

After his return to Milan, Ambrose had to contend with all sorts of plots instigated by the empress Justina, who offered bribes and honors to people to win them to her cause; so there were many who tried to force him into exile. One such, more unlucky than others, was stirred to such fury that he rented a house next to the cathedral and kept a fully equipped wagon with a team of four horses there. Thus he was ready to carry the bishop into exile the moment he succeeded, with Justina's connivance, in laying hold of Ambrose. But God's judgment dictated otherwise. The very day the abduction was planned for, the plotter was taken from his house and carried into exile in his own quadriga. Ambrose, however, returning good for evil, saw to it that the man's needs were provided for.

The saint made the rules for the chant and the liturgy to be followed in the church of Milan.

In his time there were in Milan many who were possessed by demons, who cried out that they were being tortured by Ambrose. Justina, and many Arians who were in her entourage, declared that the bishop paid people to say, falsely, that they were troubled by unclean spirits and that Ambrose was tormenting them. Then, all of a sudden, one of the heretics present was seized by a demon and leapt into the midst of the crowd, shouting: "May those who do not believe Ambrose be tortured as I am tortured!" The heretics, thrown into confusion, plunged the man into a pool and drowned him.

Another heretic, particularly sharp in debate, hardheaded and totally resistant to conversion, one day heard Ambrose preach and saw an angel whispering in his ear the words the bishop was speaking to his people. Having seen this, the erstwhile heretic began to defend the faith he had previously persecuted.

There was a soothsayer who summoned demons and sent them to wreak harm on Ambrose, but they came back and told him that they not only could not reach the bishop but were unable to come near the doors of his house, because an unquenchable fire protected the whole building and scorched them even though they stood far off. And when this same soothsayer was delivered by the judge to the torturers to be punished for his evil deeds, he cried out that Ambrose tortured him even more sorely than they did.

When a certain possessed man entered Milan, the demon left him but came back into him when he quit the city. Asked about this, the demon explained that he was afraid of Ambrose.

Another man, aided and abetted by Justina, made his way into the bishop's bedroom by night in order to kill him with a sword, but when he lifted the sword to strike, his arm withered instantly.

The citizens of Thessalonica had aroused the emperor's wrath, but at Ambrose's request he had pardoned them. Later the ruler, secretly influenced by some malicious courtiers, ordered the execution of a huge number of those he had pardoned. Ambrose knew nothing of this at the time, but when he learned what had happened, he refused to allow the emperor to enter the church. Theodosius pointed out that David had committed adultery and homicide, and Ambrose responded: "You followed David in wrongdoing, follow him in repentance." The most clement emperor accepted the order gratefully and did not refuse to do public penance.[2]

A man possessed of the devil began to shout that he was being tortured by Ambrose. Ambrose ordered him to be quiet and said: "O devil, it is not Ambrose that tortures you, but your envy, because you see those who are going up to the place from which you fell so ignominiously. Ambrose knows no pride!" Instantly the possessed man was quiet. And once when the bishop was walking in the city, it happened that a man accidentally fell and lay prostrate on the ground. Seeing this, a passerby began to laugh at him. To this man Ambrose said: "You're standing now, but be careful that you don't fall!" The words were hardly spoken when down the man went and lamented his own fall as he had laughed at the other's.

Another time Ambrose went to the palace of Macedonius, master of the offices, to intercede for someone in trouble, but he found the doors closed and could not gain entrance, so he said: "Very well! One of these days you yourself will come to the church and won't be able to get in—not that the doors will be closed, because they will be wide open." Some time later Macedonius, fearful of his enemies and seeking refuge, fled to the church but could not find a way in although all the doors stood open.

The saint's abstinence was so strict that he fasted every day but Saturdays, Sundays, and major feast days. His generosity was such that he gave away everything he had to the churches and the poor, keeping nothing for himself. He was so compassionate that when someone confessed his sin to him, he wept so bitterly that the sinner himself was compelled to weep. He was humble and hardworking, and wrote out his books with his own hand except when bodily weakness forbade it. So loving and kindhearted was he that when the death of a holy priest or bishop was announced to him, he wept so copiously that he could hardly be consoled. When he was asked why he grieved so bitterly for holy men who had gone to glory, he said: "Don't think I'm weeping because they are gone, but because they have gone ahead of me, and it will be hard to find anyone worthy to replace them." His constancy and courage were so great that far from indulging the vices of emperor or prince, he was loud and persistent in reproving them.

When a certain man had perpetrated a heinous crime and was brought before him, Ambrose said: "He must be handed over to Satan to die in the flesh, lest he dare to commit any more such crimes." And no sooner had these words been

[2] Graesse (252n) remarks that the "little story" (*historiola*) told in this paragraph "is lacking in the editio princeps." The story is repeated below in greater detail.

pronounced than the unclean spirit, as is his wont, began to tear at the guilty man.[3]

The story is told that once when blessed Ambrose was on his way to Rome, he found hospitality in a Tuscan villa, the home of an exceedingly wealthy man. Ambrose asked him solicitously how things were with him, and he answered: "Everything has always gone well, even famously, with me. As you see, I have riches galore. I have more slaves and servants than I need. I have always had everything to my liking, nothing untoward has ever happened to me, nor anything to be sad about." Ambrose, taken aback at hearing this, said to his traveling companions: "On your feet and away from here as fast as we can go, because the Lord is not in this place. Quick, my sons, hurry! We must lose no time getting away, or the divine vengeance may catch us here and involve us also in the sins of these people." So he and his company fled, and when they had gone some distance, the earth suddenly opened behind them and swallowed that man and all that belonged to him so completely that not a trace remained. Observing this, Ambrose said: "See, brothers, how mercifully God spares those to whom he sends adversity, and how severe his anger can be against those who always enjoy prosperity." It is said that in that same place there is a very deep ravine, which stands as a reminder of what happened there.

Ambrose was aware that greed, the root of all evil, was increasing more and more among men, especially among those who wielded power and would sell anything for a price, and among those in high church office. He was deeply grieved at this and prayed God instantly to deliver him from the ills of this world. When he knew that his wish was about to be granted, he rejoiced and revealed to his brethren that he would be with them only until Easter. Then, a few days before he had to take to his bed, he was dictating a commentary on the Forty-third Psalm to his secretary, who suddenly saw a small fire in the shape of a shield covering the saint's head and then going slowly into his mouth, like a householder entering his house. His face turned white as snow but afterwards resumed its normal look. That day put an end to his writing and dictating. He was not able to complete his explanation of the Psalm, and some days later his bodily condition worsened. Then the count of Italy, who was in Milan, convoked the ranking men of the province. He told them that the death of so great a man could be a threat to the welfare of Italy, and asked them to wait upon the man of God and beg him to obtain from God the space of one more year of life. When Ambrose heard their plea, he answered: "I have not lived among you in such a way that I should be ashamed to live on, nor am I afraid to die, since we all have the good Lord."

---

[3] Graesse notes (253n) that the Ed. Pr. omits this anecdote. "Ed. Pr." might mean "first edition," or "principal edition." Neither designation could have a precise meaning.

At that time four of the bishop's deacons met and talked about who might be the right man to succeed him. They were meeting at a distance from the place where Ambrose the man of God was dying; but when they had silently nominated Simplicianus and hardly had time to pronounce his name, the saint, far from them as he was, three times exclaimed: "Old he is, but he is the right man!" When the deacons heard this, they scattered in fear and after Ambrose's death chose none but Simplicianus.

In the place where the saint lay on his deathbed, he saw Jesus coming toward him smiling joyfully. And Honorius, the bishop of Vercelli, who was expecting Ambrose's death, was asleep when he heard a voice call out three times: "Get up, because the time of his passing is near." He rose and hurried to Milan, arriving in time to give the dying bishop the sacrament of the Lord's Body. Moments later Ambrose extended his arms in the form of a cross and breathed his last with a prayer on his lips. He flourished about the year of the Lord 379. When his body was transported to the cathedral on the night of Easter, a number of baptized children saw the saint. Some of them saw him seated on the episcopal throne, some pointed him out to their parents as he went up to it; still others told how they had seen a star above his body.

A certain priest was at dinner with several others and began to speak ill of Saint Ambrose. At once he was stricken with a mortal illness, was carried to his bed, and died. In the city of Carthage three bishops were dining convivially, and one of them spoke disparagingly of Ambrose. He was told what had happened to that priest, but scoffed at the story. Immediately he received a lethal wound and ended his days then and there.

Saint Ambrose set an example by his many virtues. Firstly, he was remarkably generous: all he possessed belonged to the poor. In this regard he tells about himself that when the emperor demanded that he surrender his basilica, he responded (as recorded in the decree *Convenior*, XXIII, qu. 8): "If he had asked me for what was mine—my property, my money, and the like—I would not have opposed him, since all that is mine belongs to the poor." Secondly, he was spotlessly pure; indeed, he was a virgin. Hence Jerome tells us that Ambrose said: "We not only praise virginity, we practice it." Thirdly, he was firm in his faith. When the emperor demanded the basilica, Ambrose said (as this is recorded in the chapter quoted above): "He will take away my life before he gets my see from me." Fourthly, he invited martyrdom eagerly. In his letter *De basilica non tradenda* we read that the deputy of the emperor Valentinian sent his orders to Ambrose, saying: "Fail to respect Valentinian and I will have your head." Ambrose's answer: "May God allow you to carry out your threat, and may God turn her enemies away from the Church! Let them aim all their spears at me and slake their thirst in my blood."

Fifthly, he is a model of perseverance in prayer. Thus we read in the eleventh book of the *Ecclesiastical History* that Ambrose defended himself against the queen's fury not with his hand but with fasting and continuous vigils; with his prayers at the foot of the altar he gained God as defender for himself and for the Church. Sixthly, there was the abundance of his tears. He had three kinds of tears—tears of compassion for the sins of others, as Paulinus tells us in his *vita* that when someone confessed his sin, Ambrose wept so abundantly that he compelled the sinner to weep likewise; tears of devout yearning for the joys of eternity, as Paulinus, already quoted, says that when the saint was asked why he wept so much for holy men when they died, he answered: "Because they have gone ahead of me to glory"; tears shed for wrongs done by others, as he said of himself and we read in the decree cited above: "Against the Gothic troops my weapons are my tears, for they are enough defense for a priest. I ought not and cannot offer any other resistance."

Seventhly, consider his unyielding courage, which manifested itself through three of his guiding principles. The first of these was the defense of Catholic truth. We read in the eleventh book of the *Ecclesiastical History* that Justina, mother of the emperor Valentinian, who supported the Arian heresy, began to disturb the good order of the Church, and threatened bishops with expulsion and exile unless they revoked the decrees of the Council of Rimini. With warfare like this she beat upon that wall and tower of the Church, the most valiant Ambrose. In the preface of the mass of his feast the following is sung of him: "Thou didst strengthen Ambrose with such virtue and adorn him with so great a gift of constancy that by him demons were driven out and tortured, the Arian apostasy was crushed and withered away, and the necks of secular princes were bent to thy yoke and made humble."

The second principle that shaped his actions was the protection of the Church's freedom. Thus when the emperor wanted to take possession of a certain basilica, Ambrose opposed the monarch, as he himself attests and as it is set down in Decree XXIII, qu. 6: "I myself met with the counts, who delivered the emperor's command to yield the basilica forthwith, saying that it was his right to demand it. I responded: 'If he wants my patrimony, let him take it; if he wants my body, I am ready, and if in fetters, put them on. Do you want me dead, your will is mine. I will not use the crowd as my shield, I will not cling to the altar begging for my life but will gladly be immolated for the altars. You bring me the emperor's order to give up the basilica: we are under pressure from the royal commands: but our resolve is strengthened by the words of Scripture. Emperor, you talk like one of the foolish virgins. Do not burden yourself with the thought that you have any right to the things that are God's. Palaces belong to the emperor, churches to the priests. Saint Naboth defended his vineyard with his own blood. He did not surrender his vineyard: shall we hand over the church of Christ? Tribute is due to Caesar, let it not be denied him. The church belongs to God, let it not be donated to Caesar. If something is demanded of me or taken forcibly—my property or my house or my gold or my silver, whatever belongs to me by right—I will offer it willingly, but from the temple I can give away nothing, not one chip, since I have received it in trust, not to be picked apart.'"

His third principle was the denunciation of vice and all iniquity. Thus we read in the *Tripartite History* and in another chronicle that at one time rioting had broken out in the city of Thessalonica and the rioters had stoned several judges. Theodosius, enraged, ordered all to be put to death, making no effort to separate the innocent from the guilty, with the result that almost five thousand men were killed. So, when the emperor came to Milan and was about to enter the church, Ambrose met him at the door and forbade him entrance, saying: "Why, O emperor, do you not recognize the enormity of your presumption after doing such wrong in anger? Or can it be that imperial power precludes the admission of sin? It behooves you to let reason control power. O emperor, you are the prince, but your subjects are servants of God just as you are. With what eyes do you look upon the temple of our common Lord? How dare you set foot upon this holy pavement? How can you stretch out the hands that are still dripping with blood unjustly spilled? How could you presume to take into your mouth a taste of the Blood of the Lord, when by the fury of your words so much blood has been shed unjustly? Stand back! Go away! Do not try to add a second sin to your already great guilt! Accept the bond with which the Lord has now bound you, for it is the best medicine, the surest way to health."

In obedience to these words the emperor, groaning and weeping, withdrew to his palace. When he continued to mourn for a long while, Rufinus, commander of the army, asked him what caused such sadness. "You cannot know how sad I feel," he answered. "The churches are open to slaves and beggars, but I cannot enter them." And his speech was broken by sobs. "If you wish," said Rufinus, "I'll go straight to Ambrose and have him loose the bond he has put upon you." "You can't change Ambrose's mind," said the emperor, "because no fear of the imperial power will make him deviate from divine law." But when Rufinus assured him that he would bring the bishop around, the emperor told him to go, and he himself followed closely after him. However, the minute Ambrose saw Rufinus, he said: "You act like an impudent dog, Rufinus! You, the perpetrator of such a slaughter, you don't wipe the shame from your face, you don't blush while you bark at the divine majesty!" Rufinus nevertheless continued to plead for the emperor and said that the latter was coming after him. Afire with heavenly zeal, Ambrose said: "I declare to you that I forbid him to cross the sacred threshold, and if he goes from power to tyranny I willingly accept being put to death."

When Rufinus reported this to Theodosius, the emperor replied: "I will go to him and let him shame me to my face as I deserve!" So he went to Ambrose and implored him to remove his bonds, but Ambrose met him and refused to let him come into the church, asking: "What penance have you done for such crimes?" He answered: "It is for you to impose, for me to obey." And when the emperor pointed out that David had committed adultery and homicide, Ambrose replied: "You have followed him in sin, follow him in repentance." Willingly agreeing to this, Theodosius did not refuse to do public penance; and being thus reconciled, he went into the church and stood inside the gates of the chancel. Ambrose asked him why he was waiting there. He said that he was waiting to take part in the sacred mysteries, to which Ambrose replied: "O emperor, the space inside the chancel is reserved for priests. Go outside therefore, and participate with the rest of the people. The purple makes emperors, not priests." The emperor promptly obeyed.

Upon his return to Constantinople, Theodosius took his place outside the chancel when he went to church, but the bishop sent word to him to come inside. "It was hard for me to learn the distinction between emperor and priest," the emperor said, "and it took time to find someone to teach me the truth. Now Ambrose is the only one I would call a bishop."

Eighthly, Ambrose was outstanding for the purity of his doctrine, which had many qualities. It was profound, as Jerome says in his book *De XII Doctoribus*: "Ambrose was lifted above the depths and, a bird of the air though he went into the deep, he is seen to have gathered his fruit from on high." His doctrine was firm and solid, as Jerome says in the same book: "All his sentences are firm pillars of the faith, of the Church, and of every virtue." His work had beauty and elegance, as Augustine says in his book *On Marriage and Contracts*: "Pelagius the heresiarch praises Ambrose, saying, 'The blessed bishop Ambrose, in whose books the Roman faith shines, emerges like a flower among Latin writers.'" And Augustine adds: "No enemy has dared to question his faith nor his very correct understanding of the Scriptures." His doctrine had great authority, because the ancient authors, Augustine among them, considered his words authoritative. Hence Augustine writes to Januarius that when his mother Monica wondered that there was no fasting on Saturday in Milan, and Augustine asked Ambrose about it, Ambrose answered: "When I go to Rome I fast on the Sabbath. So you also, observe the usage of any church you happen to visit, and you will not scandalize anyone nor have anyone scandalize you." Augustine adds: "I have thought about this sentence many times, and have always held it to be and have accepted it as an oracle from heaven."

The life and martyrdom of Tiburtius and Valerian is contained in the passion of Saint Cecilia.[4]

---

[4] See chapter 169, below.

58. Saint George

The name George is derived from *geos*, meaning earth, and *orge*, meaning to work; hence one who works the earth, namely, his own flesh. Now Augustine writes in his book *On the Holy Trinity* that good earth is found high on the mountains, in the temperate climate of the hills, and in level ground: the first bears good grass, the second, grapes, and the third, the fruits of the fields. Thus blessed George was on the heights because he disdained base things and so had the fresh green of purity; he was temperate by his prudence and so shared the wine of heavenly joy; he was lowly in his humility and therefore bore the fruits of good works. Or George is derived from *gerar*, holy, and *gyon*, sand, therefore, holy sand; for he was like sand, heavy with the weight of his virtues, small by humility, and dry of the lusts of the flesh. Or again, the name comes from *gerar*, holy, and *gyon*, struggle; so a holy fighter, because he fought against the dragon and the executioner. Or George comes from *gero*, pilgrim, *gir*, cut off, and *ys*, counselor, for he was a pilgrim in his contempt for the world, cut off by gaining the crown of martyrdom, and a counselor in his preaching of the Kingdom. At the council of Nicaea his legend was included among the apocryphal writings because there is no sure record of his martyrdom. In Bede's *Calendar* we read that he was martyred in the Persian city of Dyaspolis, which formerly was called Lidda and is near Joppe. Elsewhere we read that he suffered under the emperors Diocletian and Maximian, or under the Persian emperor Dacian in the presence of seventy kings of his empire. Or we are told that he was put to death by the prefect Dacian during the reign of Diocletian and Maximian.

George, a native of Cappadocia, held the military rank of tribune. It happened that he once traveled to the city of Silena in the province of Lybia. Near this town there was a pond as large as a lake where a plague-bearing dragon lurked; and many times the dragon had put the populace to flight when they came out armed against him, for he used to come up to the city walls and poison everyone who came within reach of his breath. To appease the fury of this monster the townspeople fed him two sheep every day; otherwise he would invade their city and a great many would perish. But in time they were running out of sheep and could not get any more, so, having held a council, they paid him tribute of one sheep and one man or woman. The name of a youth or a maiden was drawn by lot, and no one was exempt from the draft; but soon almost all the young people had been eaten up. Then one day the lot fell upon the only daughter of the king, and she was seized and set aside for the dragon. The king, beside himself with grief, said: "Take my gold and my silver and the half of my kingdom, but release my daughter and spare her such a death." But the people were furious and shouted: "You yourself issued this decree, O king, and now that all our children are dead, you want to save your own daughter! Carry out for your daughter what you ordained for the rest, or we will burn you alive with your whole household!" Hearing this, the king began to weep and said to his daughter: "My dearest child, what have I done to you? Or what shall I say? Am I never to see your wedding?" And turning to the people he said: "I pray you, leave me my daughter for one week, so that we may weep together." This was granted, but at the end of the week back they came in a rage, crying: "Why are you letting your people perish to save your daughter? Don't you see that we are all dying from the breath of the dragon?" So the king, seeing that he could not set his daughter free, arrayed her in regal garments, embraced her tearfully, and said: "Woe is me, my darling child, I thought I would see sons nursing at your royal breast, and now you must be devoured by the dragon! Alas, my sweetest child, I hoped to invite princes to your wedding, to adorn the palace with pearls, to hear the music of timbrel and harp, and now you must go and be swallowed up by the beast." He kissed her and sent her off, saying: "O, my daughter, would that I had died before you, rather than lose you this way!" Then she threw herself at his feet and begged his blessing; and when, weeping, he had blessed her, she started toward the lake.

At this moment blessed George happened to be passing by and, seeing the maiden in tears, asked her why she wept. She answered: "Good youth, mount your horse quickly and flee, or you will die as I am to die." George responded: "Lady, fear not; but tell me, what are all these people waiting to see?" The damsel: "I see, good youth, that you have a great heart, but do you want to die with me? Get away speedily!" George: "I will not leave here until you tell me the reason for this." When she had told him all, he said: "Don't be afraid, child! I am going to help you in the name of Christ!" She spoke: "Brave knight, make haste to save yourself; if not, you will die with me. It is enough that I die alone, for you cannot set me free and you would perish with me."

While they were talking, the dragon reared his head out of the lake. Trembling, the maiden cried: "Away, sweet lord, away with all speed!" But George, mounting his horse and arming himself with the sign of the cross, set bravely upon the approaching dragon and, commending himself to God, brandished his lance, dealt the beast a grievous wound, and forced him to the ground. Then he called to the maiden: "Have no fear, child! Throw your girdle around the dragon's neck! Don't hesitate!" When she had done this, the dragon rose and followed her like a little dog on a leash. She led him toward the city; but the people, seeing this, ran for the mountains and the hills, crying out: "Now we will all be eaten alive!" But blessed George waved them back and said to them: "You have nothing to fear! The Lord has sent me to deliver you from the trouble this dragon has caused you. Believe in Christ and be baptized, every one of you, and I shall slay the dragon!" Then the king and all the people were baptized, and George, drawing his sword, put an end to the beast and ordered him to be moved out of the city, whereupon four yoke of oxen hauled him away into a broad field outside the walls. On that day twenty thousand were baptized, not counting the women and children. The king built a magnificent church there in honor of Blessed Mary and Saint George, and from the altar flowed a spring whose waters cure all diseases. He also offered a huge sum of money to blessed George, who refused to accept it and ordered it to be distributed to the poor. Then he gave the king four brief instructions: to have good care for the church of God, to honor the priests, to assist with devotion at the divine office, and to have the poor always in mind. Finally, he embraced the king and took his leave. Some books, however, tell us that at the very moment when the dragon was about to swallow the girl alive, George, making the sign of the cross, rode upon him and killed him.

At this time, in the reign of Diocletian and Maximian, the prefect Dacian launched against the Christians a persecution so violent that in one month seventeen thousand won the crown of martyrdom, while many others, being threatened with torture, gave in and offered sacrifice to the idols. Seeing this, Saint George, overcome with grief, gave away all his possessions, laid aside his military trappings, and put on the garb of the Christians. He then pushed into the middle of the crowd and cried out: "All your gods are demons, and our God alone is the Creator of the heavens!" This angered the prefect, who retorted: "By what rashness do you dare to call our gods demons? Where do you come from and what is your name?" George answered him: "My name is George, I come of noble forebears in Cappadocia. With the help of Christ I have conquered Palestine; but now I have left all that to serve the God of heaven more freely." The prefect, seeing that he could not win him over, commanded that he be stretched on the rack and had him torn limb from limb with hooks. His body was burned with flaming torches, and salt was rubbed into his gaping wounds. That very night the Lord appeared to him in the midst of a great light and so sweetly comforted him with his presence and his words that the saint thought nothing of his torments.

Dacian, now convinced that the infliction of pain was of no avail, summoned a certain magician and said to him: "It must be by their magical arts that the Christians make light of our tortures, and they hold sacrifice to our gods to be worthless." The magician replied: "If I cannot overcome his spells, let my head be forfeit." Thereupon, relying on his magic and invoking the names of his gods, he mixed poison into some wine and gave it to blessed George to drink; but the saint made the sign of the cross over the wine, drank it, and suffered no harm. The magician then put a stronger dose of poison into the wine, but the saint, again making the sign of the cross over the cup, drank with no ill effect. At this the magician prostrated himself at George's feet, begged his pardon with loud lamentation, and asked that he be made a Christian: for this he was beheaded in due time. The following day the prefect ordered George to be bound upon a wheel that was fitted with sharp knives, but the wheel fell apart at once and the saint remained unharmed. Dacian then had him plunged into a caldron of molten lead, but George made the sign of the cross and, by God's power, settled down as though he were in a refreshing bath.

Now, realizing that he was getting nowhere with threats and torments, Dacian thought he might bring the saint around with soft speech. "George, my son," he said, "you see how long-suffering our gods are; they put up with your blasphemies so patiently yet are ready to forgive you if you consent to be converted. Follow my advice, then, dearest son. Give up your superstition, sacrifice to our gods, and win great honors from them and from ourselves." George smiled and replied: "Why did you not say kind things to me before, instead of trying to overcome me by torture? So be it: I am ready to do as you say." Dacian, deluded, was glad to hear this and ordered the herald to call the whole populace together to see George, who had resisted so long, finally yield and worship the gods. The city was strung with garlands and filled with rejoicing, and all stood by as George came into the temple to offer sacrifice. He fell to his knees and prayed the Lord to destroy the temple with its idols so completely that, for the glory of God and the conversion of the people, nothing would be left of it. Immediately fire came down from heaven and consumed the temple, the idols, and the priests, and the earth opened and swallowed up anything that was left. Saint Ambrose says in his Preface for Saint George: "While Christianity was professed only under cover of silence, George, most loyal soldier of Christ, alone and intrepid among Christians openly professed his faith in the Son of God; and the grace of God, in return, gave him such fortitude that he could scorn the commands of tyrants and face the pain of innumerable torments. O blessed and noble fighter for the Lord! Not only was he not won over by the flattering promise of earthly power, but he fooled his persecutor and cast the images of his false gods into the abyss." Thus Ambrose.

When Dacian heard what had happened, he had George brought before him and said: "How evil can you be, you wickedest of men, that you could commit so great a crime!" George retorted: "You do me wrong, O king! Come along with me and watch me offer sacrifice again!" "You trickster!" Dacian exclaimed. "What you want to do is to get me swallowed up as you made the earth swallow the temple and my gods." "Miserable man!" George answered, "how can your gods, who could not help themselves, help you?" Enraged, the king said to Alexandria, his wife: "I shall faint, I shall die, because I see that this man has got the best of me." Her response was: "Cruel, bloodthirsty tyrant! Did I not tell you not to go on mistreating the Christians, because their God would fight for them? And now let me tell you that I want to become a Christian." Stupefied, the king cried: "Oh, worse and worse! So you too have been led astray!" Thereupon he had her hung up by the hair of her head and beaten with scourges. While she was being beaten, she said to George: "O George, light of truth, what do you think will become of me since I have not been reborn in the waters of baptism?" "You have nothing to fear, lady!" he answered. "The shedding of your blood will be both your baptism and your crown." With that she prayed to the Lord and breathed her last. Ambrose testifies to this, saying in his Preface: "For this reason the queen of the pagan Persians, though she had not yet been baptized, was shown mercy and received the palm of martyrdom when her cruel spouse had condemned her to death. Hence we may not doubt that she, crimson with the dew of her blood, gained entrance through the celestial portal and merited the kingdom of heaven." Thus Ambrose.

The following day George was sentenced to be dragged through the whole city and then beheaded. He prayed the Lord that all who implored his help might have their requests granted, and a heavenly voice came to him saying that it would be so. His prayer finished, his head was cut off and his martyrdom accomplished in the reign of the emperors Diocletian and Maximian, which began about the year of our Lord 287. As for Dacian, while he was on his way back to his palace from the place of execution, fire fell from above and consumed him and his attendants.

Gregory of Tours relates that some men were carrying away relics of Saint George and were given hospitality at a certain chapel overnight; and in the morning they were absolutely unable to move the casket containing the relics until they had shared them with the oratory. And in the *History of Antioch* we read that during the Crusades, when the Christians were on their way to besiege Jerusalem, a very beautiful young man appeared to a certain priest. He told the priest that he was Saint George, the captain of the Christian host, and that if the Crusaders carried his relics to Jerusalem, he would be with them. Then, when they had laid siege to the city, they did not dare mount the scaling ladders in the face of the Saracens' resistance; but Saint George appeared to them wearing white armor marked with the red cross, and made them understand that they could follow him up the walls in safety and the city would be theirs. Thus reassured, the army took the city and slaughtered the Saracens.

59. Saint Mark, Evangelist

Marcus, the Latin form of Mark, is interpreted: sublime by mandate, or certain, or bent over, or bitter. Mark the evangelist was sublime by mandate by reason of the perfection of his life: he observed not only the common commands but the sublime ones, such as the counsels. He was certain because he was sure about the doctrine of his gospel: he handed down the doctrine of his gospel as certain doctrine inasmuch as he had learned it from Saint Peter, his master. He was bent over in his profound humility, for it was due to his humility that he cut off his thumb, as we are told, in order to be judged unfit for the priesthood. He was bitter by the bitterness of the punishment he suffered, being dragged through the streets of the city and dying in the midst of these torments. Or Marcus may simply be *marcus*, a heavy hammer that breaks down the iron, rings out a musical note, and strengthens the anvil. Thus Mark, by the sole doctrine of his gospel, strikes down the perfidy of the heretics, rings out the praise of God, and strengthens the Church.

Mark the evangelist belonged by birth to the priestly tribe of Levi. He was a son of the apostle Peter by his baptism, and his disciple in the word of God. Mark went to Rome with Peter, and when the apostle preached the Gospel there, the faithful in Rome asked blessed Mark to put it in writing, so that it could be remembered in perpetuity. He did indeed write down the Gospel just as he had heard it from the lips of his master blessed Peter; and Peter, after examining the written text and finding it fully correct, approved it for acceptance by all Christians.

Peter saw Mark's constancy in the faith and sent him to Aquileia, where he preached the word of God and converted an innumerable multitude of pagans to the faith of Christ. He is said to have written a copy of his gospel there, and to this day the manuscript is shown in the church at Aquileia and is preserved with due devotion. Mark converted a citizen of Aquileia whose name was Hermagoras, and brought him to Peter in Rome to be consecrated as bishop of Aquileia. Hermagoras assumed the office of bishop and ruled the church in Aquileia perfectly until he was taken by the infidels and crowned with martyrdom.

Peter then sent Mark to Alexandria, and he was the first to preach the word of God there. Philo, that most learned of Jews, tells us that from the time of Mark's arrival in Alexandria a great multitude was brought together in faith and devotion and the practice of continence. Papias, the bishop of Hierapolis, also expounds his praises in exquisite language. Peter Damian has this to say about him: "[God] granted him so much grace in Alexandria that all those who flocked together to receive the rudiments of faith, quickly, by continence and perseverance in a totally holy way of living, winged their way upwards to a peak of perfection that was really monastic. To this Mark urged them on not only by performing prodigious miracles nor by the eloquence of his preaching, but also by his illustrious example." Further on, Peter Damian continues: "It also came about that after he died, he was returned to Italy, so that the land where it had been given him to write his gospel won the privilege of possessing his sacred remains. Blessed are you, O Alexandria, purpled by that triumphal blood! Happy are you, O Italy, enriched by the treasure of that body!"

It is said that Mark was so humble that he amputated his thumb so that he could not by any human judgment be promoted to the order of priesthood. Nevertheless, Saint Peter's decision and authority prevailed, and he made Mark bishop of Alexandria. Just as he arrived in that city, his shoe fell apart, and in this Mark saw a spiritual meaning: "Truly God has cleared the road for me and has not allowed Satan to put obstacles in my way, since my dead works were already forgiven by the Lord." Mark saw a cobbler mending some old boots and gave him his shoe to be repaired, but in the course of the work the man wounded his left hand gravely and he exclaimed aloud: "One is God!" The bishop heard this and said: "Truly the Lord has prospered my journey!" He made clay with his spittle and spread it on the cobbler's hand, which was healed in an instant. Seeing this display of power, the man took Mark into his house and questioned him closely about who he was and where he came from. Mark told him forthrightly that he was a servant of the Lord Jesus. The man said: "I would like to see him!" Mark replied: "I will show him to you!" He began to instruct him about Christ, and the man was baptized with his whole household.

Now the men of that city heard that some Galilean had come there and was denouncing the cult of the gods, and they began to plot against him. Mark knew this, so he ordained the man he had healed, whose name was Anianus, to be bishop of Alexandria, and he himself went to Pentapolis. After preaching there for two years he returned to Alexandria and built a church on the rocks near the sea, at a place called Bucculi, where he found that the number of the faithful had grown substantially. The priests of the temple tried to lay hold of him, and while blessed Mark was celebrating mass on Easter Sunday, they all met there, put a rope around his neck, and dragged him through the city, shouting: "Let's haul the wild ox to the slaughterhouse!" Scraps of his flesh were strewn on the road and the stones were drenched with his blood. Then he was shut up in a jail, where he was comforted by an angel, and the Lord Jesus Christ came to give him courage, saying: "Mark, evangelist mine, fear not! I am with you to deliver you!"

When morning came, they again put a rope around his neck and dragged him hither and yon, calling out: "Haul the wild ox to the shambles!" As Mark was dragged along, he gave thanks, saying: "Into your hands, O Lord, I commend my spirit," and with these words he expired, in the reign of Nero, which began about the year of the Lord 57. The pagans wanted to burn the martyr's body, but suddenly the air was turbulent, hail drummed down, lightning flashed, and everyone's thought was to find shelter, so they left the holy body untouched, and Christians took it away and buried it with all reverence in the church.

Saint Mark was a well-built man of middle age, with a long nose, fine eyes, and a heavy beard, balding and graying at the temples. He was reserved in his relations and full of the grace of God. Saint Ambrose says of him: "Blessed Mark shone as a worker of countless miracles. It happened that a cobbler who was repairing a shoe for him wounded his left hand badly and cried out: 'One is God!' The servant of God rejoiced at hearing this. He made clay with his spittle, spread the clay on the man's hand, and cured the wound, and the cobbler was able to finish his work. Thus the saint imitated a miracle wrought by him whose Gospel he preached, who opened the eyes of the man born blind." Thus Ambrose.

In the year 468 after the incarnation of the Lord, in the reign of Emperor Leo, Venetians transferred the body of Saint Mark from Alexandria to Venice and built a wondrously beautiful church in his honor. The way this happened was that some Venetian merchants, who had business in Alexandria, by presents and promises induced the two priests who had charge of Saint Mark's body to let them secretly remove it and transport it to Venice. When the body was lifted from the tomb, an odor spread over the whole city of Alexandria—an odor so sweet that all the people wondered where it came from. As the sea journey progressed, the sailors let the crews of other ships know that they had the saint's body aboard. One of those informed said: "Maybe they gave you the corpse of some Egyptian, and you think it's the body of a saint!" Right away the ship that carried the saint's body turned itself around with astonishing speed, rammed the doubter's vessel, and could not be pulled loose until all aboard made it clear that they believed it was really Saint Mark's body.

Then one night when the ships were scudding before a high wind and the seamen, shaken by the violence of the storm and bewildered by the darkness, had no idea where they were headed, Saint Mark appeared to a monk who was guarding his body, and said: "Tell them to lower the sails quickly, because they are not far from land!" The sails came down, and at dawn all saw that they were lying close to an island. Wherever they went ashore, keeping the holy treasure hidden from everyone, the natives nonetheless came and called out: "Oh, how lucky you are to be carrying the body of Saint Mark! Do let us worship and pray to him!" Moreover, there was one incredulous seaman who was grabbed by a demon and sorely harassed until he was brought to the holy relic and declared that he believed. Being freed of the demon, he gave glory to God and thereafter held Saint Mark in high devotion.

The saint's body had been enclosed within a column formed of marble stones, and the location of the column in the church was known to very few persons, for reasons of security. What happened was that once these persons had departed this life, there was no one who knew where the sacred treasure was or could give any clue as to its whereabouts. This caused much lamentation in the church. A feeling of desolation spread among the faithful, and a cloud of grief hung over all; the devout folk, indeed, feared that their renowned patron had been taken away by stealth. Therefore a solemn fast was decreed; and lo and behold, in full sight and to the wonderment of all, the stones bounced out of the column and the casket that hid the saint's body was visible. Prayers of praise went up to the

Creator, who had deigned to show their patron to the people, and the day that had been glorified by such a prodigious event was observed as a feast in later years.

A young man whose chest was being eaten away by cancer began to implore Saint Mark's help with heartfelt devotion. Then, while he slept, someone in the garb of a pilgrim, who seemed to be hurrying to reach some destination, appeared to him. The young man asked the pilgrim who he was and where he was going in such haste. He answered that he was Saint Mark, and that he was hurrying to reach a ship in danger, whose crew was calling upon him for help. Mark extended his hand and touched the sick man, who woke up in the morning to find himself cured. In a short time that ship came to a Venetian port, and the seamen reported the danger they had been in and how Saint Mark had saved them.

In Alexandria some Venetian merchants had taken passage in a Saracen ship and, when they were at sea, saw that the ship was in imminent danger. They therefore got into the skiff that was towed by the vessel and cut the rope, whereupon the ship sank and a voracious wave swept all the Saracens under. One of them, however, invoked Saint Mark as he was able to do, and bound himself by a vow to be baptized if the saint came to his rescue, and to visit his church. Instantly a shining man appeared to him, plucked him out of the sea, and deposited him in the skiff with the Venetians. This man finally got back to Alexandria and, showing no thankfulness for his rescue, neither made a visit to Saint Mark's church nor received the sacraments of our faith. Mark appeared to him again and reproached him for his ingratitude. So, realizing the wrong he had done, he went to Venice, was reborn at the sacred font of baptism, took the name of Mark, professed faith in Christ, and lived out his life in good works.

A man was working at the top of the bell tower of Saint Mark's in Venice, and suddenly and unexpectedly fell from the tower, injured in every limb; but even as he fell, he was not forgetful of Saint Mark. He besought the saint's aid and landed on an unhoped-for plank that jutted out from the structure. A rope was passed to him, and, with all his hurts mended, he devoutly went up to finish the work he had started.

A man who was temporarily in service to a certain provincial noble had made a vow to visit the body of Saint Mark but could not obtain his master's permission to do so. In time, however, he put the fear of the Lord ahead of the fear of his master in the flesh and, without a word of farewell, devoutly went off to visit the saint. The master felt resentment at this and, when the servant came back, ordered his eyes put out. The ruffians who waited on him, more cruel than their master and ever ready to do his bidding, threw the servant of God to the ground as he invoked Saint Mark, and set about poking his eyes out with sharp-pointed sticks; but try as they might, they got nowhere with the sticks, which simply went to pieces. Their master then ordered them to break the man's legs and cut off his feet with hatchets, but the hard iron of the tools melted into lead. "Well, then, smash in his mouth and knock out his teeth with iron hammers!" But the iron forgot its strength and by God's power was blunted. The master, seeing all this, was taken aback, begged God's pardon, and with his servant visited the tomb of Saint Mark with earnest devotion.

A knight in battle had his arm so grievously wounded that the hand hung loose from the wrist. The doctors and his friends advised him to have the hand amputated, but the knight, thinking of the embarrassment of being maimed, instead had the hand tied in place with bandages and medicaments. He then invoked Saint Mark's aid, and the injury was immediately righted. All that was left of the wound was the scar, as evidence of the miracle and a monument to the great blessing granted to the knight.

A man in the city of Mantua was falsely accused by slanderers and put in prison. After forty days he could not stand confinement any longer. He disciplined himself by fasting for three days, then prayed to Saint Mark for help. The saint appeared to him and ordered him to leave the prison without hindrance. Half asleep with boredom, he thought he was suffering illusions and did not obey the saint's order, but Mark repeated the visit and the order a second and third time. Now the prisoner paid attention, and, seeing the door wide open, broke his shackles as if they were flaxen thread and walked out at midday unmolested, passing by the jailers and everyone else, seeing them all but invisible to them. He went to Saint Mark's tomb and devoutly paid his debt of thanks.

There was a time when the earth lay sterile throughout Apulia, and no rain fell to bless it with fertility. Then by a revelation it was known that this plague had befallen the land because the feast of Saint Mark was not observed there. The people therefore invoked the saint and promised that they would celebrate his feast, so Mark banished the sterility and, by sending salubrious air and the needed rain, provided the people with plenty.

About the year of the Lord 1212, in the city of Pavia and the convent of the Order of Friars Preachers, there was a friar named Julian, a native of Faenza who was known for his religious and holy life. He was young in body but aged in wisdom, and he lay mortally ill. Julian talked with the prior of the house and asked about his condition, and the prior told him that he was close to death. At once his face shone with happiness. He applauded with his hands and his whole body, and loudly exclaimed: "Make room, brothers, because for the great abundance of its gladness my soul is about to leap out of my body, and I have already heard happy rumors about it!" He raised his hands to heaven and said: "Bring my soul out of prison, that I may praise thy name! Unhappy man that I am, who shall deliver me from the body of this death?"

With this he fell into a deep sleep and saw Saint Mark coming to him and lying down beside him. Then he heard a voice saying: "What are you doing here, Mark?" Mark answered: "I have come close to this dying friar because his ministry is accepted by God!" Again the voice: "Why have you come especially to this man among so many other saints?" And Mark: "Because he had special

247

devotion for me and with constant piety visited the place where my body rests. Therefore I came to visit him in the hour of his extremity." Then others, clad in white garments, filled the whole house. "Why have you come?" Mark asked them. "To bring the soul of this friar into the presence of the Lord," they answered.

The friar awakened and immediately sent for the prior of the house (from whom I myself heard all this), told him all that he had seen, and with much joy fell happily asleep in the Lord.

60. Saint Marcellinus, Pope

Marcellinus ruled the Church of Rome for nine years and four months. By order of Emperors Diocletian and Maximian he was taken prisoner and brought forward to offer sacrifice. At first he refused and was threatened with various kinds of torture, and for fear of the threatened suffering he put down two grains of incense in sacrifice to the gods. This gave great joy to the infidels but caused the faithful immense sadness. However, under a weak head strong members rise up and make little of the threats of princes; so the faithful came to the pope and reproached him severely. He realized the gravity of his error and offered himself to be judged by a council of bishops. The bishops responded: "It is not possible for the supreme pontiff to be judged by anyone; but you yourself weigh your case in your own mind and pronounce your own judgment." The pope, repentant, lamented his fault and deposed himself, but the whole gathering immediately reelected him. When the emperors heard of this, they had him arrested again. He absolutely refused to offer sacrifice, so they sentenced him to beheading. Then the persecution was renewed with such fury that in one month seventeen thousand Christians were put to death.

When Marcellinus was about to be beheaded, he declared himself unworthy of Christian burial and excommunicated all who might presume to bury him. Thus his body lay above ground for thirty-five days. At the end of that time the apostle Peter appeared to Marcellus, who had succeeded as pope, and said: "Brother Marcellus, why do you not bury me?" Marcellus replied: "Have you not yet been buried, my lord?" Peter: "I consider myself unburied as long as I see Marcellinus unburied!" "But don't you know, my lord," Marcellus asked, "that he laid a curse on anyone who buried him?" Peter: "Is it not written that he who humbles himself shall be exalted? You should have kept this in mind! Now go and bury him at my feet!" Marcellus went straightaway and carried out the orders laudably.

※

---

61. Saint Vitalis

Vitalis could be from *vivens talis*, living such or living the same as, because Saint Vitalis lived outwardly in his works such as he was inwardly in his heart. Or the name comes from *vita*, life, or the word is formed from *vivens alis*, i.e., shielding oneself with the wings of the virtues. The saint was like one of the animals of God that Ezechiel saw, having four wings—the wing of hope, by which he flew to heaven, the wing of love, by which he flew to God, the wing of fear, by which he flew to hell, and the wing of knowledge, by which he flew into himself.

The account of his martyrdom is thought to have been found in the book of Saints Gervasius and Protasius.

Vitalis, a consular knight, fathered Gervasius and Protasius by his wife, Valeria. He once went to Ravenna with Paulinus, a judge, and there observed the trial of a physician named Ursicinus. Having undergone many tortures and been condemned to be beheaded, Ursicinus was shaking with fear, and Vitalis called out to him: "O doctor and brother Ursicinus, you have made a practice of curing others, do not now kill yourself with an eternal death! You have come to the palm by caring for the sufferings of many. Do not lose the crown prepared for you by God!" Ursicinus was strengthened by these words, repented of his fears, and freely accepted martyrdom; and Saint Vitalis saw to it that he received honorable burial.

After this experience Vitalis could not bring himself to rejoin his superior, Paulinus. The judge took this very badly, not simply because Vitalis would not come back to him, but also because he had dissuaded a willing Ursicinus from sacrificing to the idols, and because he had publicly declared himself a Christian. He therefore ordered him to be stretched on the rack. "Stupid man," Vitalis said, "do you think you can fool me, when I have been so zealous about liberating others?" "Take him to the palm tree," Paulinus ordered, "and if he will not sacrifice, dig a ditch there so deep that you reach water, and bury him alive and lying on his back!" His men did as ordered and buried Vitalis alive, in the reign of Nero, which began about A.D. 52.

The pagan priest who had recommended this form of punishment was seized at once by a demon, and raged and raved for seven days at the site of the burial, crying out: "You are setting me on fire, Vitalis!" On the seventh day he was pitched into the river by the demon and perished miserably.

Valeria, the wife of Saint Vitalis, was on her way to Milan when she saw some men sacrificing to the idols. They urged her to join them and to eat some of the immolated foods, but she responded: "I am a Christian, and it is not licit for me to eat food from your sacrifices!" Hearing this, they beat her so brutally that the men who accompanied her brought her half dead into Milan, and three days later she migrated happily to the Lord.

※

---

62. A Virgin of Antioch

There was a certain virgin in Antioch whose story Ambrose set forth in the second book of his *De Virginibus*, as follows.

In recent times there was a virgin in Antioch who shrank from being seen in public. But the more she avoided the eyes of the lustful, the more she enkindled their desire. Beauty that is heard about but not seen is the more desired, due to two stimuli, erotic love and knowledge, since nothing displeasing meets the eye, and beauty known about is imagined as all the more pleasing. The eye is not exploring in order to judge, but the lustful heart craves.

This holy virgin was determined to safeguard her virtue and shut herself off from the eyes of the libidinous so as to discourage their hopes; but she did this so thoroughly that they stopped longing for her and sought to betray her. Hence persecution. The girl had no means of fleeing and, being young, feared that she might fall into traps set by the impure, so she prepared herself to be strong. She was so religious that she did not fear death, so chaste that she looked forward to it. The day of her crowning was at hand, and great was the expectation of all: a young girl is brought forward who professes herself ready to wage a twofold war, for her virginity and her religion. But when they recognized the constancy of her profession and her fear for her virtue, when they saw her blushing when looked at but prepared to suffer torture, they began to consider how to take away her religion and leave her the hope of saving her chastity, so that when she had been deprived of what mattered the most, they might then snatch away what was left. So the order is given: either the virgin sacrifices to the gods or she is prostituted in a brothel.

How can they think they are worshiping their gods when they vindicate them by such means? How do they live, those who judge this way? This girl has no doubts about her religion but fears for her purity and says to herself: "What do we do today—martyrdom or virginity? Either crown is denied us. But the very name of virgin is unknown to whoever denies the author of virginity. How can you be a virgin and worship a harlot? How can you be a virgin and love an adulterer? How can you be a virgin if you seek carnal love? It is more meritorious to keep the mind virginal than the flesh. Both are good if possible, but if not possible, let us at least be chaste in God's sight if not in men's. Rahab was a harlot, but after she believed in the Lord, she found salvation. Judith decked herself in silks and jewels in order to charm an adulterer, but, because she did this for religion's sake and not for love, no one thought of her as an adulteress. The example is well found, because if Judith, who committed herself to religion, saved both her chastity and her country, perhaps we too, by keeping our religion, will preserve our chastity. But if Judith had thought more of her chastity than of her religion, having lost her country she would likewise have lost her purity."

Strengthened by the thought of these examples, the virgin silently pondered in her mind the words of the Lord: "He that shall lose his life for me shall find it."[1] She wept, saying no words lest an adulterer should even hear her speak; nor did she choose injury to her chastity but recoiled from doing injury to Christ. Judge whether she, who would not commit adultery even by the sound of her voice, could commit it with her body.

This long time what I have been saying has made me feel shame, and now I shudder to bring up a series of ignominious deeds and dwell upon them. Virgins of God, shut your ears! The maiden of God is led to the bawdy house. But open your ears, virgins of God! A virgin may be exposed to prostitution, she cannot be made an adulteress. Wherever a virgin of God is, there is Christ's temple. Brothels do not defile chastity, but chastity abolishes the shame even of such places.

Now comes a rush of the wanton to the house of ill fame. Holy virgins, learn here the miracles of the young martyr, learn the language of these places! The dove is caught within, the birds of prey clamor without, all fight to see who will be the first to pounce on the prey. But she raises her hands to heaven as if she had come to a house of prayer and not to an abode of lust, and says: "O Christ, for a virgin you made wild lions tame, you can also tame the fierce hearts of men. Fire rained down on the Chaldeans. By your mercy and not by its nature the sea divided to make way for the Jews. Susanna went to her knees on the way to

[1] Matt. 10:39.

execution and triumphed over the lecherous old men. The right hand that was desecrating the gifts of your temple shriveled. Now vile hands are reaching for the body that is your temple. Do not allow this incestuous sacrilege, you who would not allow the thief to steal. And blessed be your name, because I came here to be ravished of my virginity, I will leave here still a virgin."

Hardly had she finished her prayer when a knight, formidable of aspect, broke through the crowd around her. How must the maiden have trembled, when the people made way for fear of him! But she did not forget what she had read. "Daniel," she said to herself, "had come merely to see judgment done on Susanna, but he, single-handed, won freedom for her whom the crowd condemned. It may be that a sheep is hiding here under wolf's clothing. Christ too has his soldiers, indeed his legions. Or it may be the headsman who has come, but fear not, my soul! Headsmen make martyrs!"

O virgin, your faith has saved you! The knight says to her: "Do not be afraid, my sister! I came here to save your soul, not to lose it. Save me, so that I may save you! I came in like an adulterer, but if you will it, I shall go out a martyr. Let us exchange our clothing. Mine will suit you and yours me, and both will suit Christ. Your garb will make me a true soldier and mine will keep you a virgin. You will be well clothed, and I will be better off unclothed, so that the executioner may recognize me. Take my clothing, which will hide the fact that you are a woman, and give me yours, which will consecrate me for martyrdom. Wrap this cloak around you to conceal your maidenly form and protect your chastity. Put on this bonnet, to cover your hair and hide your face: those who have been in a brothel usually hide their blushes. Be careful not to look back when you go out of here. Remember Lot's wife, who lost her natural life because she looked at unchaste men, even though with chaste eyes. Have no fear, nothing will be missing in the sacrifice. In your place I will make myself an offering to my God, and in my place you will be a soldier of Christ, fighting the good fight of chastity, waged for eternal wages—the breastplate of righteousness to clothe the body with spiritual protection, the shield of faith to ward off wounds, and the helmet of salvation. Where Christ is, there is the stronghold of our salvation. As the husband is the head of the wife, so Christ is the head of virgins."

As he said these words he took off the cloak that made him seem both a persecutor and an adulterer. The virgin offered her head to the executioner, the knight his mantle to the virgin. What a spectacle! What grace, when in a house of sin the actors, a knight and a virgin, vie with each other for martyrdom! By nature they are unlike, yet are similar by God's mercy; and the oracle "The wolf and the lamb shall feed together"[2] is fulfilled. Indeed they do not merely feed together, they are immolated together.

What more can I tell you? The cloak is exchanged, the girl flies out of the trap, yet not on her own wings, since she is borne up on spiritual wings; and—

[2] Isa. 65:25.

what had never before been seen down through the ages—a virgin of Christ walks out of a brothel. But those who saw with their eyes and did not see with their heart—wolves they were!—roared at their prey like wolves in pursuit of a lamb. One of them, more shameless than the rest, went in, but when his eyes took in the situation, he exclaimed: "What's this? A girl came in here, but I see a man! This is no fabulous doe in place of a maiden. This is real! A maiden is changed into a knight! I had heard and had not believed that Christ had changed water into wine, but here is a change of sex. Let us get out of here while we still are what we were! Could it be that I myself am changed—I who think I see one thing and see something different? I came to the brothel: what I see is a switch of persons. The change is made. I will leave, I will go out pure, I who came in an adulterer!" So the knight is judged guilty and the crown belongs to this great winner. He is condemned in place of the virgin because he was apprehended in place of the virgin. So not only virgins but martyrs came out of that house.

The story goes on that the girl ran to the place of torture, and that the two contended for the right to die. The knight said: "I'm the one who's condemned to death. That sentence sets you free. I'm the one they arrested!" The maiden cried out: "I didn't choose you to stand in for me! I wanted you as a protector of my virtue. If they're after my chastity, I'm still a woman, but if blood is what they want, I don't want anyone to bail me out. I have what I need to pay what I owe, and I'm the one for whom the sentence was intended. Certainly if I had given you as surety for a sum I owed, and when I stayed away and the judge made you pay my debt to the lender, you could get a court order compelling me to reimburse you out of my inheritance. If I refused, who would not deem me worthy of death? And how much more so when a capital sentence is involved! I will die innocent so as not to die guilty! There is no middle ground now; either I will be guilty of your blood or I will shed my own as a martyr! I came here in such haste: who will dare to shut me out? If I had stayed away, who would dare to absolve me? I would owe more to the laws as guilty not only of being a fugitive but of causing the death of another. My body is strong enough to bear death, but I could not bear to do such an injustice. There is room in this virgin for wounds, but none for dishonor. I have shrunk from shame, not from martyrdom. I changed my clothing, I have not changed what I professed to be. If you snatch my death away from me, you will not have redeemed me: you will have cheated me! So please don't argue with me, don't dare to contradict me. Don't take away the good you have done me. When you deny this latest sentence against me, you revive the earlier one. The earlier sentence voids the later one; if the second does not hold me, the first one does. We can satisfy both sentences if you allow me to suffer first. They can inflict other punishments on you, but in a virgin the price will be her chastity; so you will win greater glory if you make a martyr out of a virgin than if you turn a martyr into an adulteress."

What outcome do you expect? the two compete and the two win: the crown is not divided, a second crown is added. So the two holy martyrs did well for each other—she by giving him the opportunity for martyrdom, he by allowing her to profit by it.

The schools of the philosophers make much of two Pythagoreans named Damon and Pythias, one of whom, having been sentenced to death, asked for some time to settle his private affairs. The wily tyrant who had condemned him, figuring that he would be unable to find a bondsman, demanded that he designate someone who would suffer in his place if he failed to appear. Which of the two was the more renowned I do not know: both were famous. The one found a surety for his death, the other offered himself. So when the condemned man did not appear at the appointed time, the guarantor, unperturbed, did not refuse to die in his place. As he was being led to the place of execution, the guilty man came back, pushed his friend aside, and put his head on the block. The tyrant, admiring the conduct of the philosophers who held friendship dearer than life, begged the two whom he had condemned to admit him to their friendship: such was the grace of virtue that it won the tyrant over. . . . Praiseworthy, yes, but less so than our pair. For one thing, the others were both men, whereas one of ours was a young woman who had first to overcome the weakness of her sex; the other two were friends while our two were unknown to each other; the friends offered themselves to one tyrant, but ours to several even crueler ones; and the one tyrant granted pardon while the cruel ones dealt death. Of the two men one was bound by a compelling need, in our two there was complete freedom of choice on both sides. The two men were more calculating, having more at stake, namely, their friendship: for the virgin and the knight the goal was martyrdom. The friends contended for men, the martyrs for God. Thus Ambrose.

63. Saint Peter Martyr

The name Petrus, Peter, is interpreted as knowing or recognizing, or as taking off one's shoes; or Peter comes from *petros*, firm. Hence three privileges possessed by Saint Peter are indicated. He was an outstanding preacher and therefore is called knowing, because he had perfect knowledge of the Scriptures and, in preaching, recognized what met the needs of each hearer. He was a most pure virgin and so is called one who takes off his shoes, because he removed and put off all earthly love from the feet of his affections and inclinations: in that way he was virgin not only in his body but in his mind. Third, he was a glorious martyr of the Lord and so was firm, because he bore martyrdom with constancy in defense of the faith.

Peter the New, called Peter Martyr, of the Order of Preachers,[1] a renowned fighter for the faith, was a native of the city of Verona. He emerged like a radiant light in a cloud of smoke, or a white lily among briars, or a red rose among thorns. This brilliant preacher was the son of parents who were blinded by error; his virginal honor rose from among people corrupt in body and soul; this celebrated martyr stood out from among thorns, meaning those destined for eternal fire.

Peter did indeed have unbelieving, heretical parents, but he kept himself unsullied by their error. Once when he was seven years old and was home from school, his uncle, who reeked of heresy, asked him what he was learning. He answered that he had learned: "I believe in God the Father almighty, creator of heaven and earth." His uncle retorted: "Don't say 'creator of heaven and earth,' because God was not the creator of visible things. The devil created all that is visible."[2] The boy answered that he would rather say what he had learned and read, and would rather believe what Scripture says. Then the uncle tried to change the boy's mind by quoting his authorities, but Peter, being filled with the Holy Spirit, turned them against the uncle and slew the man with his own sword, so to speak, leaving him disarmed and unable to parry. The uncle was indignant at being outdone by a mere child and reported the whole incident to the father, using every argument he could think of to induce the father to take little Peter out of school. "I am afraid," he said, "that when young Peter has finished his studies, he will rally to the harlot church of Rome and thus confuse and destroy our faith." He did not know how truly he spoke when, like Caiaphas, he prophesied that Peter would destroy the false doctrines of the heretics. But because God was in control, the father did not agree with his brother, hoping that as Peter progressed in the grammatical arts, some master heretic would draw him into their sect.

The holy youngster saw that it was not safe to dwell with scorpions, so he left the world and his family behind and joined the Order of Friars Preachers. Pope Innocent in his letter stresses the praiseworthy life that Peter lived in that Order. "Peter in his adolescent years," he wrote, "prudently turned away from the world's deceits and entered the Order of Friars Preachers. For thirty years, upheld by a troop of virtues with faith in the lead, hope standing by, and charity accompanying, he prevailed and progressed in the defense of the faith, for which he burned with zeal. Against its fierce enemies he waged continuous warfare with intrepidity of mind and fervor of spirit, and happily brought his long struggle to a close with the victory of martyrdom. Thus Peter, firm upon the rock of

[1] The Order of Saint Dominic, or Dominicans.

[2] The Catharist heresy, like the Albigensian, against which Peter of Verona fought as an inquisitor, condemned all matter as evil.

faith and hurled against the rock of suffering, rose, worthy of the martyr's crown, to the rock of Christ."

Peter always guarded his virginity of mind and body, and never felt the touch of mortal sin, as is proved by the faithful testimony of his confessors. Because a slave too delicately nourished may turn against his master, Peter subdued his body by the sparse use of food and drink. For fear that through idleness and sloth he might fall victim to the wiles of the enemy, he constantly subjected himself to the just ordinances of the Lord. Since he was totally occupied with what was commanded, there was no room in his life for what was forbidden, and he was safe from spiritual failings. During the silent hours of night that are given to man for his repose, Peter, after a brief sleep, applied himself to the study of the readings[3] and spent the time for sleep in prayerful watching. It would soon be day with its tasks—the needs of souls to be cared for, sermons to be prepared and preached, confessions to be heard, and the heretics' pestiferous doctrine to be refuted with valid reasonings, for which he was blessed with a gift of special grace. Pleasing to God in his devoutness, mild in his humility, calm in obedience, tender in kindness, compassionate in his feeling for others, constant in patience, preeminent in charity, and well founded in the maturity of his conduct in all circumstances, he attracted people by the spreading aroma of his virtues. He was also a fervent lover of the true faith and zealous in practicing it, and he fought strenuously in its defense. The faith was so deeply imprinted upon his spirit, and he bound himself so totally to its service, that every one of his words and works reflected the virtue of faith. He also longed to suffer death for the faith and is known to have begged the Lord, with frequent, earnest appeals, not to let him leave this life until he had drunk for him from the chalice of his passion. Nor was he disappointed of his hopes.

Blessed Peter was renowned for the many miracles he performed in his lifetime. For instance, in Milan he was examining a heretical bishop whom the faithful had taken prisoner, and many bishops and religious and the greater part of the city population had gathered to witness the trial. Moreover, with his preaching and his questioning of the bishop the hours were getting longer and the extreme summer heat was bothering all those present, when the heresiarch said for all to hear: "O wrongheaded Peter, if you are as holy as these stupid people say you are, why are you letting them die of the heat? Why don't you ask the Lord to put a cloud in front of the sun to keep the people from death by overheating?" To this Peter responded: "If you are willing to promise to renounce your heresy and return to the Catholic faith, I will ask the Lord and he will do as you said." The backers of the heretics called out to the heresiarch, saying: "Promise! Promise!" They thought, of course, that what Peter had pledged himself to do before all the people could not be done, especially since

---

[3] No doubt the lessons from Scripture, the martyrology, and elsewhere, which were read in the liturgical hours and at other assemblies.

there was not so much as a wisp of cloud in the sky. On the other hand, the Catholics began to worry about Peter's promise, fearing that by it the Catholic faith might be discredited.

The heretical bishop refused to commit himself, but blessed Peter, with sure confidence, said: "To the end that the true God be shown to be the creator of all that is visible and invisible, and for the reassurance of the faithful and the confusion of heretics, I ask God to make some small bit of cloud form and place itself between the sun and the people." He made the sign of the cross, and for a whole hour a cloud spread across the sky like a tent, protecting the people from the sun.

A man named Asserbus, who had been paralyzed for five years and had to be pulled from place to place on a kind of sled, was brought to blessed Peter in Milan. When Peter made the sign of the cross over him, he was cured forthwith and stood up.

Pope Innocent, in the letter already referred to, relates some more miracles that God wrought through Peter in the saint's lifetime. He says: "The son of a certain nobleman had such a large growth in his throat that it was very hard for him to speak or even to breathe. Blessed Peter raised his hands over him and put his mantle around him, and the sick man was cured instantly. The same nobleman was stricken later on with violent convulsions. Thinking and fearing that he was in imminent danger of death, he had the saint's mantle, which he had kept, brought to him. He placed it on his chest and quickly vomited a worm that had two heads and was covered with thick hairs. This achieved his complete cure. The saint put his finger into the mouth of a mute young man, broke the string that tied his tongue, and obtained for him the blessing of speech. God deigned to do these and many other miracles through Peter during his lifetime." Thus far Innocent.

The plague of heresy was spreading in Lombardy and already infecting many cities with its pestiferous contagion. To wipe out this diabolical pestilence, the supreme pontiff dispatched a number of inquisitors, all members of the Order of Friars Preachers, to various areas of the province. In Milan the heretics were very numerous, occupied places of secular power, and made effective use of their fraudulent eloquence and devilish knowledge. The pope knew that blessed Peter was a man of great courage and was not to be intimidated by great numbers of enemies. He also was aware of the unshakable virtue that would keep Peter from making the slightest concession to his adversaries' power. Furthermore he knew that Peter's eloquence could easily lay bare the heretics' deceptions and that he was deeply learned in divine wisdom and could by reasoning refute the frivolous arguments of the heretics. Therefore the pope appointed this stout fighter for the faith to the city and county of Milan, and made him his chief inquisitor with plenary authority.

Peter applied himself diligently to his work as inquisitor and sought out the heretics wherever they were, giving them neither rest nor quarter. He ably confounded and powerfully repulsed them, wisely and subtly arguing with them so that they could not resist the wisdom and the Spirit that spoke through him. The heretics saw this and were pained by it, so they began to take counsel with their henchmen about killing him. They thought they would be able to live in peace if this mighty persecutor was removed from their midst. So, one day when the intrepid preacher, soon to be a martyr, was traveling from Como to Milan to search for heretics, he won the palm of martyrdom on the way.

Innocent describes the event as follows: "He was on the road from the city of Como, where he was prior of the house of the friars of his Order, to Milan, to carry on the inquisition against the heretics that had been entrusted to him by the Holy See. Then, as he had predicted in his public preaching, one of the heretics' men, won over by their pleas and payments, fell upon him furiously as he pursued his salutary purpose. It was the wolf against the lamb, the savage against the meek, the impious against the pious, the enraged against the gentle, the furious against the calm, the profane against the saint. He undertakes the assault, carries out his attempt with murderous intent, cruelly strikes the sacred head, and inflicts frightful wounds until his sword is glutted with the blood of the just. Meanwhile the venerable victim does not turn away from his assailant but presents himself as a willing sacrifice, patiently submitting to his attacker's savage blows. So he sent his spirit soaring heavenward at the very spot where he suffered, while the sacrilegious murderer still rained blows upon the minister of Christ. He uttered no word of complaint, no groan or moan, but suffered all patiently and commended his soul to the Lord, saying: 'Into thy hands, O Lord, I commend my spirit.' He also began to recite the Creed, of which even at the moment of death he was still the herald. This was reported by the assassin himself, who was captured by the faithful, and by a Dominican friar who had accompanied Peter, and was mortally wounded by the same assailant and died a few days later. But even while the Lord's martyr was breathing his last, the cruel killer snatched up a dagger and drove it into his side."

Thus, on the day of his martyrdom, Saint Peter somehow merited to be confessor, martyr, prophet, and doctor. He was confessor in that amidst torments he, with utmost constancy, confessed the faith of Christ, and on that same day, having made his confession in the usual way, he offered the sacrifice of praise to God. He was martyr in that he shed his blood in defense of the faith, prophet in that on the morning of that day he made a prediction. He had come down with the quartan fever, and his companions told him that they would not be able to reach Milan from Como. He answered: "If we cannot get as far as the friars' house, we can lodge for the night at Saint Simplicianus." And that is what happened. The brothers carried the sacred body to Milan, but the crowds were so dense that they could not get to the priory. So they deposited the holy remains for the night in the church of Saint Simplicianus. He was doctor in that even as he suffered he taught the true faith, reciting the Creed in a loud, clear voice.

Peter's venerable passion is seen to be similar in many ways to the passion of Christ. Christ suffered for the truth that he preached, Peter for the truth of the faith that he defended; Christ was made to suffer by the unbelieving Jewish people, Peter by the unbelieving crowd of the heretics; Christ was crucified at the time of Passover, Peter suffered martyrdom in the same season; when Christ suffered he said: "Into thy hands, O Lord, I commend my spirit"; Peter loudly pronounced the same prayer in his last moments. Christ, moreover, was betrayed and crucified for thirty pieces of silver, Peter was betrayed and murdered for forty pounds Pavian. By his passion Christ brought many to the faith, Peter by his martyrdom converted many heretics; for although this eminent doctor and fighter for the faith had done much in his lifetime to eradicate the pestiferous dogma of the heretics, after his death, due to his merits and sparkling miracles, the heresy was uprooted so far that great numbers relinquished their error and hurried back to the bosom of holy Church. The city and county of Milan, where many clusters of heretics had existed, were so thoroughly purged of heresy that, with many heretics exiled and many more converted to the faith, none dared to show themselves there any longer. Moreover, many of the greatest and most famous preachers of the time entered the Order, and until now[4] they are pursuing heretics and their partisans with admirable zeal. So our Samson has killed more Philistines by dying than he killed while alive. Thus the grain of wheat, falling into the ground and caught and killed by the hands of unbelievers, brings forth abundant fruit; thus the bunch of grapes, crushed in the winepress, gives out juice in plenty; thus spices, ground in the mortar, pour forth a richer perfume; thus mustard seed is all the stronger once it is pulverized.

After the holy man's glorious triumph the Lord honored him with many miracles, some of which the supreme pontiff has related, saying: "After Peter's death the lamps that hang around his tomb have several times lighted up by divine action, without any human assistance; it was indeed appropriate that for one who had shone brilliantly with the fire and light of faith, so singular a miracle of fire and light should occur. A man who, while he was at table with some others, spoke disparagingly of Peter's holiness, to prove his point took a morsel of food, saying that if what he said about Peter was unfair, he would be unable to swallow the morsel. Quickly he felt the food stick in his throat so that he could neither swallow it nor cough it up, and, as his face changed color, he realized that he could choke to death. He repented of his malicious talk and inwardly made a vow that he would never again say such things, and at once he was able to bring up the morsel and his life was saved. A woman who suffered

---

[4] Peter was martyred in 1252, and Jacobus compiled the *Legenda* in the late 1250s. "Until now" (*usque nunc*) suggests a period of time later than the composition of the *Legenda*. Graesse, 284 n. 2 and 288 n. 1, notes that most of the anecdotes in the second half of this chapter, beginning with the one that opens "In Florence a young man, a heretic . . . ," are not in the Ed. Pr. and therefore are later additions.

from dropsy came, with the help of her husband, to the place where Saint Peter had been killed. There she prayed to him and quickly recovered her health.

"The martyr himself helped women possessed by demons, forcing the evil spirits to come out of the women's bodies with much vomiting of blood; and he cured fevers and many other and diverse afflictions. A man had a skin disease that punctured a finger on his left hand in many places. Peter cured him and gave him wonderful comfort. A child had suffered a fall and was so badly injured that he had neither feeling nor movement and was mourned as dead, but some of the earth that had been spattered by the martyr's sacred blood was placed on the boy's chest and he stood up unhurt. Another woman whose flesh was being eaten away by a cancer had some of this same earth applied to her wound and was cured. And there were others who had various diseases and were brought to the saint's tomb in wagons or other vehicles. There their ills were fully cured and they were able to go home without further help."

When Pope Innocent iv inscribed blessed Peter's name in the catalog of the saints, the friars met in chapter at Milan and resolved to transfer the martyr's body to a higher place, since it had lain below ground for over a year. They found the body sound and uncorrupted, without the slightest odor of decay, as if it had been buried that very day. The friars with great reverence placed the body on a large catafalque beside the road where he had been murdered, and then displayed it whole and entire for all the people to see and venerate.

Besides the miracles above described as related in the pope's letter, a great many more are remembered. Many religious men and women and numbers of other people have seen lights descending from heaven over the site of the martyrdom, and have testified that they saw two friars in Dominican habits surrounded by these lights.

A young man named Geoffrey or Godfrey, who lived in the city of Como, had a piece of cloth that was cut from Saint Peter's mantle. A certain heretic laughed at him and said that he would believe Peter was a saint if the youth threw the cloth into the fire and the cloth did not burn. This would prove beyond any doubt that Peter was a saint, and the heretic would adhere to his faith. So the young man threw the cloth on burning coals, but the cloth bounced high out of the fire, and then on its own power jumped back upon the coals and extinguished them completely. The unbeliever said: "So! My own cloak would do the same thing!" They lighted another fire and a piece of the heretic's cloak was laid on one side, and the cloth from Saint Peter's on the other. The minute the heretic's cloth felt the heat of the fire, it went up in flames, whereas Peter's patch prevailed over the fire and put it out, and not a thread of the cloth was as much as scorched. The heretic observed this, returned to the way of faith, and told everyone about the miracle.

In Florence a young man, a heretic and a profligate, was in the friars' church with some companions, looking at a painting that depicted the martyrdom of Saint Peter; and, seeing the assassin striking him with his unsheathed sword, the young man exclaimed: "If I had been there, I'd have hit him harder!" No sooner had he uttered these words than he was stricken dumb. When his companions asked him what was the matter with him, he could not answer, so they took him home. But on the way he saw the church of Saint Michael, slipped away from his friends, and went into the church. He knelt and prayed from the heart to Saint Peter, asking the saint to spare him, binding himself by a vow to confess his sins and renounce all heresy if he was cured. Suddenly he recovered the power of speech, went to the friars' house, abjured his heresy, and confessed his sins, giving his confessor permission to preach about this to the people. Then, in the middle of the sermon, the young man stood up and, in the presence of a great multitude, told the whole story himself.

A ship was in distress far out at sea, enveloped in the blackness of night and almost swamped by the fury of the waves. The people aboard called for help from various saints but, seeing no sign of rescue, were overcome with fear of imminent doom. Then one of them, a Genoese, called for silence and addressed them as follows: "Men and brothers, have you not heard how a friar of the Order of Preachers, Friar Peter by name, was recently killed by heretics because of his defense of the faith, and how God has marked him out by many signs? Now therefore let us devoutly implore his protection, because I have good hope that we shall not have prayed in vain!" All agreed and invoked blessed Peter, asking for his help with devout prayers. As they prayed, the yardarm from which the sail hung was seen to be studded with lighted candles. The darkness was dissipated by the marvelous gleam of the candles, and in no time the blackness of the night was changed into the brightness of daylight. Looking up they saw a man, who wore the habit of the Friars Preachers, standing atop the sail, and no one doubted that it was Saint Peter. When the crew, unharmed, reached Genoa, they went to the house of the Friars Preachers, gave thanks to God and blessed Peter, and told the friars the whole story of the miracle.

A woman in Flanders had had three miscarriages, which made her husband hate her. She asked Saint Peter to come to her aid. In time she give birth to a fourth child, this one dead like the others. The mother took the child with her and committed herself totally to praying to Saint Peter, begging him devoutly to make her son live. The child came to life, and when he was to be baptized, it was decided that he would be called John; but the priest did not know what name he was to be given, and called him Peter, which name the new Christian made his own out of devotion to Saint Peter.

At Utrecht in the Teutonic province, some women sat at streetside, spinning and watching a great concourse of people going to the church of the Friars Preachers to honor Saint Peter Martyr. "You see?" they said to people standing around, "Those friars know all about raising money! Now they want to pile up a lot of money to build big palaces, so they've invented a new martyr!" While they were saying things like this, suddenly all the thread they were spinning was soaked in blood and their fingers were covered with blood. They were astonished at the sight of this and wiped their hands carefully to see if perhaps they had cut themselves. But when they found that their fingers showed no cuts, and that it was the thread itself that was running with blood, trembling and repentant they said: "Truly it's because we said bad things about the blood of the precious martyr that this stupendous miracle of blood has happened to us." They ran therefore to the house of the friars and told the story to the prior, presenting the bloody thread to him. After much urging the prior convoked a solemn preaching service, at which he related what had happened to the women, and showed all present the bloodstained thread.

Now a very opinionated master of arts heard this and began to make fun of the whole story, saying to those around him: "Just look at the way these friars beguile the hearts of simple people! Here they've got together some nice little neighbor women and had them dip thread into some blood and then pretend that a miracle had happened!" While he was still speaking, the wrath of God was visited upon him. As many looked on, he was stricken with a fever so intense that his friends had to hold him by the hand, take him away from the service, and lead him home. But the fever continued to affect him so violently that he feared he was dying, so he sent for the prior and confessed his sin to God, and made a vow to Saint Peter in the presence of the said prior, promising that if by the saint's merits he recovered his health, he would always have special devotion to him and would never again say such scandalous things. Wonder of wonders! No sooner had he pronounced his vow than he was well again.

The subprior of the aforesaid priory was bringing some very large and beautiful stones for the construction of the church already mentioned, and the boat that was carrying the stone unexpectedly ran aground and was so firmly locked in the sand that it could not be budged. The crew got down from the vessel and tried to push it free, but to no avail. They thought they had lost their ship until the subprior, ordering the others to stand aside, put his hand on the hull and, pressing lightly, said: "In the name of Saint Peter Martyr, in whose honor we are carrying these stones, back off!" Immediately the vessel was afloat, undamaged, and the seamen, climbing aboard safe and sound, sailed joyfully home.

At Sens in the province of France, a girl fell into a swift-flowing stream and was in the water for a long time, finally being pulled out dead. Her death was proven by four facts: the length of time in the water and the rigidity, coldness, and blackness of the corpse. Still, some people carried her to the church of the friars, and when they had commended her to Saint Peter, she was restored to life and health.

In Bologna, Friar John of Poland was ill with the quartan fever but was due to preach to the community on the feast of Saint Peter Martyr. In the natural course of the fever he expected an attack the night before the sermon and was afraid he might be unable to preach. He turned to Saint Peter's altar and prayed that by the saint's merits he might preach his glory, and so it happened: that very night the fever left him and he never suffered it again.

A woman by the name of Girolda, the wife of James of Vallesana, who for thirteen years was possessed by unclean spirits, went to a certain priest and told him: "I am possessed, and the evil spirit harasses me!" The priest was frightened and repaired to the sacristy, where he found a book containing the formulas for exorcism. He put on a stole under his cape and, with some other people, returned to the woman. As soon as she saw him, she said: "Where did you go, you wicked thief? And what are you wearing hidden under your cape?" The priest got nowhere with his exorcisms and could effect no cure. Then the woman went to blessed Peter while he was still alive and besought his help. Speaking like a prophet he answered her: "Have confidence, my daughter, do not despair! If I cannot at present do what you ask, the time will come when you will obtain in full whatever you ask of me." This came true: after his passion the aforesaid woman went to his tomb and was completely delivered of vexation by demons.

A woman named Euphemia, from a place called Corriongo in the diocese of Milan, was tormented by demons for seven years. When she was brought to Saint Peter's tomb, the demons began to disturb her more than usual and through her mouth to cry out: "Mary, Mary! Peter, Peter!" Then the spirits went out of her, leaving her for dead, but in a short time she arose completely cured. She declared that the demons harassed her most on Sundays and feast days, especially when the mass was being celebrated.

A woman of Beregno, Verbona by name, was plagued by demons for six years, and when she was brought to Saint Peter's tomb, a dozen men could not hold her. One of these men was a certain Conrad of Ladriano, a heretic who had come there to mock Saint Peter's miracles. He was restraining the woman with the others when the demons, speaking through the woman, said to him: "You belong to us! Why are you holding us? Did we not carry you to a certain place and did you not commit a murder? Haven't we conducted you to such and such places and haven't you committed such and such crimes?" And when they had told his many sins, which no one but he alone knew about, he was frightened beyond words. The demons tore the skin from the woman's neck and breast and went out of her leaving her half dead, but after a while she arose hale and hearty. Conrad, the aforesaid heretic, saw all this and was converted to the Catholic faith.

Once during the saint's lifetime, when a particularly acute and singularly eloquent heretic was debating with Peter, he expounded his errors with such subtlety and force that Peter, try as he might to respond effectively, did not have much success. He asked for time to think, went into a nearby chapel, wept and prayed God to defend the cause of his faith, and either to bring this prideful speaker back to the true faith or to punish him by silencing his tongue. Then he confronted the heretic and openly, before the whole audience, called upon him to state his arguments again. The man, however, was stricken mute and could not proffer so much as a word. This confounded the heretics, who took their departure, while the Catholics gave thanks to God.

A man named Opiso, a convinced heretic, had come to the friars' church to meet a female relative of his, also a heretic, and, passing by Saint Peter's tomb, saw two coins lying on it. "Fine!" he said. "We'll drink these!" Then of a sudden he began to shake all over and could not move an inch from where he stood. Frightened, he put back the coins and so was able to leave. This experience showed him Saint Peter's power, and he abandoned his heresy and converted to the Catholic faith.

In Germany, at the monastery of the Order of Saint Sixtus at Ottenbach in the diocese of Constance, there was a nun who for a year or more had suffered from painful gout in her knee, and no remedy had been found to cure it. She was unable to visit Saint Peter's tomb bodily both because she lived under a religious rule and because her serious physical condition forbade such a journey; so she thought of traveling to the tomb in her mind at least, and to visit it with sincere devotion. She learned that it would take thirteen days to go from Ottenbach to Milan, so for each of the next thirteen days she recited one hundred Our Fathers in honor of Saint Peter. Wonderful to relate, as she continued this journey in her mind, day by day and little by little she felt better, and when the last day was done and her mental stride carried her to the tomb, she knelt as if she were there in the body and with wholehearted devotion read the entire Psalter. When she had finished that, she felt freed of her infirmity to the degree that only a little pain was left. She then made the return trip just as she had made the outward one, and before she had completed thirteen days, she was entirely cured.

A man named Rufinus, from Canapicio of the Villa Mazzati, fell seriously ill. A vein had ruptured in the lower part of his body and blood flowed out continually; and no doctor was able to find a remedy. When this had gone on for six days and nights, Rufinus devoutly invoked the aid of Saint Peter and was cured so suddenly that between the offering of the prayer and the cessation of the hemorrhage there was no interval of time. When Rufinus fell asleep, he saw a friar dressed in the Dominican habit, stout and dark complexioned, whom he took to be a companion of Saint Peter Martyr, as indeed there had been one who looked like that. The friar held out his hands full of blood and sweet-smelling ointment to Rufinus, saying: "This blood is still fresh; come then to the fresh blood of Saint Peter." When he woke up, he decided to visit Saint Peter's tomb.

Several noblewomen of the castle of Masino in the diocese of Ivrea had special devotion to Saint Peter, fasted on his vigil, and went to his church to hear vespers. One of them, to honor Saint Peter Martyr, lighted a candle and placed it in front of the altar of Saint Peter the apostle. After the ladies went home, a greedy priest blew out the candle, but a flame quickly appeared and relighted it. He tried two or three times to extinguish the candle, but each time the light came back. He got tired of doing this and went to the choir, where he saw another candle before the high altar. A cleric who also fasted for the saint's vigil had lighted it in honor of Saint Peter. The priest tried twice to put this candle out and failed. The clerk watched this and called out angrily: "You devil, don't you see that this is a miracle? Don't you see that Saint Peter doesn't want you to extinguish his candle?" Both of them were astonished and terrified, and priest and clerk went up to the castle and told everybody about the miracle.

A man of Meda whose name was Roba had lost everything he owned, except the clothes he wore, at the gaming table. He went home late in the night, lighted a lamp, and went to his bed; but when he saw the tattered sheets and thought about his losses, he felt so despondent that he began to invoke the demons and to commend himself to them with impious words. At once three demons came and threw the lamp on the terrace, then seized Roba by the neck and throttled him until he could not speak a word. They made so much noise that the people in the lower part of the house came up and said: "What are you doing, Roba?" The demons answered them: "Go in peace and get back to bed!" They thought they were hearing Roba's voice and went their way. When they were gone, the demons tormented him more and more viciously. The people below realized what was happening and called in a priest, who adjured the demons in Saint Peter's name to be gone. Two of them departed. The next day Roba was taken to Saint Peter's tomb. Friar William of Vercelli came to him and began to rebuke the demon, who called him by name though he had never seen him. "Brother William," the demon said, "I will not go out of this man for you, because he is ours and does our works!" When William asked the spirit his name, he said: "I am called Balcephas." However, when he was ordered in Saint Peter's name to leave the man, he threw his victim to the ground and went out of him. Roba was well again and accepted a salutary penance.

One Palm Sunday when Saint Peter preached in Milan and a very large number of men and women had come to hear him, he said publicly and clearly: "I know for certain that the heretics are dealing for my death and that for this purpose money has already changed hands. But let them do whatever they can, I will persecute them more when I am dead than I have in this life!" It is obvious that what he said came true.

In a monastery in Florence a sister was at prayer the day blessed Peter was done to death, and in a vision saw the Blessed Virgin enthroned in glory on a high throne, and two friars of the Order of Preachers ascending to heaven and taking their places at either side of her. The nun asked who these were, and heard a voice telling her: "This is Friar Peter, who in the sight of the Lord ascends glorious like the smoke of incense." It has been corroborated that Peter's death occurred the day this religious had the vision. She suffered a long and serious illness, but devoted herself wholly to prayer to Saint Peter and soon was restored completely to health.

A schoolboy on his way from Maguelone to Montpellier jumped and fell, suffering a rupture in the groin so painful that he could not take a step. The lad had heard a preacher tell about a woman who had been cured by placing earth on which Saint Peter's blood had fallen on the cancer that was consuming her flesh. Picking up a handful of dirt, he said: "Lord God, I don't have any of that earth, but you gave that earth so much power by the merits of Saint Peter, you can give the same power to this earth!" He made the sign of the cross over it, invoked the martyr, spread the earth on the injured part, and was healed at once.

In the year of the Lord 1259, in the city of Apostella, there was a man named Benedict whose legs were swollen like wineskins, whose belly bulged like a pregnant woman's, whose face was hideous with sores, and whose whole body was so bloated that he seemed a monster. Barely holding himself erect with a staff, he begged an alms of a woman, who answered: "You are in need of a grave more than of anything else, but follow my advice! Go to the house of the Friars Preachers, confess your sins, and invoke the aid of Saint Peter!" Early the next morning he went to the house of the friars, but the door of the church was locked and he set himself down outside the door and went to sleep. And lo! a venerable man in the habit of the Preachers appeared to him, covered him with his own cloak, and led him into the church. Benedict awoke and found himself inside the church, completely cured. Many people were moved to admiration and surprise at the sight of the man who had been as good as dead and now, suddenly, was freed of his grave infirmity.

64. Saint Fabian

Saint Fabian ruled the Church of Rome for many years and finally suffered martyrdom in the reign of Decius. At his election as bishop of the city of Rome the Spirit, appearing in the form of a dove, was seen by many. Fabian ordered accounts of the passions of the martyrs, which are not carefully preserved by notaries, to be collected, and put in writing. He also had many basilicas built at the martyrs' tombs, and dedicated them himself. He established the practice of burning the old chrism and consecrating fresh chrism every year on Holy Thursday. Look for more about him at the feast of blessed Fabian and Sebastian, martyrs.[1]

---

[1] This chapter obviously duplicates the legend of Saint Fabian, pope and martyr, the subject of chapter 22. There is no reference to a Pope Fabian in the legend of Saint Sebastian. Graesse notes (291 n. 1) that the present chapter does not appear "in more recent editions."

65. Saint Philip, Apostle

Philippus, the Latin form of Philip, can be interpreted as *os lampadis*, mouth of a lamp, or as *os manuum*, mouth of hands; or it is composed of *philos*, which means love, and *yper*, above. The apostle is called mouth of a lamp because of his luminous preaching, mouth of hands because of his tireless work, and lover of the things above because of his heavenly contemplation.

After Philip the apostle had preached throughout Scythia for twenty years, the pagans laid hold of him and thrust him before a statue of Mars to make him sacrifice. Then suddenly a huge dragon emerged from the base of the statue, killed the pagan priest's son, who was tending the fire for the sacrifice, slew two tribunes whose men were holding Philip in chains, and infected the rest with the stench of its breath so that all were made ill. Philip then said: "Believe what I tell you! Smash that statue and in its place worship the cross of the Lord, and your sick will be cured and your dead restored to life." But those who were suffering called out: "Just let us be cured and we will quickly smash this Mars!" Philip commanded the dragon to hie himself to a desert place where he could do no harm to anyone, and the beast went away and was seen no more. Then he cured the sick and obtained the gift of life for the three who had died. All the people accepted the faith, and he preached to them for a whole year and ordained priests and deacons for them. The apostle went to the city of Hierapolis in Asia and there put down the heresy of the Ebionites, who taught that the body assumed by Christ was only a phantom. There with him were his two daughters, dedicated virgins both of them, through whom the Lord converted many to the faith.

Seven days before his death Philip convoked the bishops and priests and said to them: "The Lord has granted me these seven days so that I might give you good counsel." He was then eighty-seven years old. The infidels seized him, and, like his Master whom he had preached, he was nailed to a cross, and so migrated to the Lord and happily finished his life.

Isidore, in his book *On the Life, Birth, and Death of the Saints*, writes of Philip as follows: "Philip the Galilean preached Christ and led the barbarian peoples, who lived in darkness on the shores of the wild Ocean, to the light of knowledge and the haven of the faith. At the end he was crucified and stoned at Hierapolis, a town in the province of Phrygia. He died and reposes there together with his daughters." This from Isidore.

Jerome, in his *Martyrology*, says of the Philip who was one of the seven deacons, that he died at Caesarea on the sixth day of July, distinguished for the signs and wonders he worked. Three of his daughters were buried with him there; the fourth was laid to rest at Ephesus. The above Philip is not the same as this Philip, because the former was an apostle and the latter a deacon; the former reposes at Hierapolis, the latter at Caesarea; the former had two daughters who had the gift of prophecy, the latter had four daughters. The *Ecclesiastical History*, however, seems to say that Philip the apostle had four daughters who were prophetesses; but in this instance Jerome is more credible.

※

---

66. Saint Apollonia

During the reign of the emperor Decius a savage persecution broke out in Alexandria against the servants of God; but a man named Divinus, a wretch of the demons, anticipated the ruler's edict and stirred up the superstitious rabble against the servants of the same Christ, and the mob, thoroughly aroused, thirsted for nothing less than the blood of the pious. Their first captives were dedicated religious, both men and women. Some of them they tore limb from limb, hacking them to pieces. They mutilated the faces of others and put their eyes out with pointed sticks, and threw them out of the city. Still others they led to the idols, pressing them to worship, and when these refused and cursed the idols, they had their feet chained together and were dragged through the city streets, until this brutal, horrid torture reduced their bodies to shreds and tatters.

At this time there lived in Alexandria an admirable virgin, well along in years, named Apollonia. She was wreathed with the flowers of chastity, sobriety, and purity, and stood like a sturdy column strengthened by the Spirit of the Lord, perceived by the Lord for the merit and virtue of her faith, admired by the angels, and offering a spectacle and example to men. When the furious mob was surging through the houses of the servants of God, breaking up everything with hostile cruelty, blessed Apollonia was carried off to the tribunal of the impious, innocent in her simplicity, dauntless in her virtue, bringing with her nothing more than the constancy of her intrepid spirit and the purity of her untroubled conscience. Thus she offered her devout soul to God and handed over her most chaste body to the persecutors to be tortured. The executioners, cruelly wreaking their wrath upon her, first beat out all her teeth. Then they piled up wood and built a huge pyre, telling her they would burn her alive unless she took part in their impieties. But she, seeing the pyre already burning and after a brief moment of recollection, suddenly broke free from the hands of the wicked and of her own will threw herself into the fire with which they had threatened her. Her merciless tormentors were shocked beyond measure at finding a woman even more eager to undergo death than they to inflict it. This fearless martyr, already tried by so many kinds of torture, would not be conquered by the torments visited upon her nor by the heat of the flames, because her spirit was on fire with the far more ardent rays of truth. So it was that the material fire, ignited by the hands of mortals, could not overcome the heat infused by God in that indefatigable breast.

Oh, great and wondrous struggle of this virgin, who, by the grace of a compassionate God, went to the fire so as not to be burned and was burned so as not to be consumed, as if neither fire nor torture could touch her! There would have been safety in freedom, but no glory for one who avoided the fight. Apollonia, the stalwart virgin martyr of Christ, contemns the world's pleasures, tramples on worldly prosperity by her contemptuous appraisal, yearns only to please her spouse Jesus Christ. By a happy perseverance in her resolution to stay a virgin she remains unshaken in the midst of excruciating torments. The merit of this virgin, so gloriously and blessedly triumphant, excels and shines out among martyrs. Indeed this woman's virile spirit did not give way under the great weight of her struggle. By her love of heaven she expelled every earthly fear and grasped the trophy of the cross of Christ. Armed against fleshly lusts and all tortures by her faith rather than by the sword, she fought and she won. And this may he deign to grant us, who lives and reigns with the Father and the Holy Spirit forever and ever.[1]

67. Saint James, Apostle

Jacobus, the Latin form of James, is interpreted as one who causes to fall, or trips someone who is in a hurry, or as one who prepares. Or Jacobus comes from *Ja*, a name of God, and *cobar*, which means burden or weight. Or again, as if the name were Jacopus, it might come from *jaculum*, lance, and *cope*, a cutting, so

---

[1] Graesse (293 n. 1), notes that this chapter is absent from "more recent editions."

one cut down with lances. James therefore was one who brought the world to a fall by his contempt for it, he tripped up the devil who is always in a hurry, and he prepared his body for every good work. Evil passions are in us due to three causes, as Gregory of Nyssa says—namely, bad bringing up or bad associations, bad bodily condition, and the vice of ignorance. And he says that those bad passions are cured by good habits, good exercise, and the study of good doctrine. Blessed James took good care of himself and so had his body prepared for every good work. He is also called a divine weight due to the gravity of his conduct, and he was cut down with lances in his martyrdom.

This apostle James is called James of Alpheus, meaning the son of Alpheus; the brother of the Lord; James the Less; and James the Just. He is called James son of Alpheus not only according to the flesh but according to the meaning of that name. Alpheus is interpreted as learned, or document, or fugitive, or thousandth, because James was learned through inspired knowledge, a document by instructing others, a fugitive from the world because he despised it, and thousandth because of his reputation for humility.

He is called the brother of the Lord because he is said to have borne a very strong resemblance to Jesus, so that very often they were mistaken one for the other. Hence when the Jews set out to capture Christ, they had to avoid taking James because he looked like Christ; so they engaged Judas, who could distinguish the Lord from James due to long familiarity with them, to point Christ out by giving him a kiss. Ignatius confirms this likeness in his letter to John the Evangelist when he says: "If I have your permission, I want to come up to Jerusalem to see the venerable James, surnamed the Just, who they say resembled Jesus Christ so closely in his features, his life, and his way with others that he might have been born his twin brother; so that, as they say, if I see James I see Christ Jesus so far as all bodily features are concerned."

Again, James is called the brother of the Lord since Christ and James, being descended from two sisters, were thought of as being descended from two brothers, Joseph and Cleophas. He is not called the brother of the Lord on the ground that he was the son of Joseph, the spouse of Mary, by another wife, as some would have it, but because he was the son of Mary the daughter of Cleophas, and this Cleophas was the brother of Joseph, Mary's spouse—although Master John Beleth says that Alpheus, James's father, was brother to Joseph, Mary's spouse. But this is not thought to be true: the Jews called "brothers" those who were related on both sides. It may also be that James was called the brother of the Lord on account of the excellence of his sanctity, which gave him right of preference, so that of all the apostles he was the one ordained to be bishop of Jerusalem.

He is called James the Less to distinguish him from James, the son of Zebedee, for James of Zebedee was born earlier than James of Alpheus, and James of Alpheus was called to be an apostle later. In many religious communities it is customary that the one who enters earlier (*prior*) is called the greater (*major*), and the one who comes later (*posterior*) is called the less (*minor*), though "the less" may be either older in years or more worthy in holiness.

James is called the Just because of the merit of his most excellent holiness. According to Jerome his holiness was so revered by the people that they strove eagerly to touch the hem of his garment. Hegesippus, who lived close to the time of the apostles, wrote as follows about James's sanctity, as we read in the *Ecclesiastical History*: "James, the brother of the Lord, assumed the rule of the Church. He has universally been called the Just from the time of the Lord down to our own. From his mother's womb he was holy. He drank no wine or strong drink, never ate meat, no razor ever came near his head, no oil anointed him, he never bathed. His clothing consisted of a linen garment. He knelt so often in prayer that his knees were calloused like the soles of his feet. For this ceaseless and surpassing righteousness he was called the Just and Abba, which is interpreted to mean the stronghold of the people and righteousness. Because of his eminent sanctity he alone of the apostles was allowed to enter the Holy of Holies." So far Hegesippus.

It is also said that he was first among the apostles to celebrate the mass. In recognition of his superior holiness the apostles awarded him the honor of being the first among them to offer mass in Jerusalem after the Lord's ascension. This was before he was ordained bishop, since we read in the Acts of the Apostles that even before his ordination the disciples were persevering in the doctrine of the apostles and in the communication of the breaking of bread, which is understood to be the celebration of mass. Or perhaps he is said to have been the first to celebrate because we are told that he was the first to say mass in pontifical vestments, just as Peter later on did in Antioch and Mark in Alexandria. James was a virgin all his life, as Jerome attests in his book *Contra Jovinianum*.

Josephus, and Jerome in the book *De viris illustribus*, tell us that after the Lord died on the day before the Sabbath, James made a vow that he would not eat until he saw Christ risen from the dead. On the day of the resurrection, when James had not tasted food until then, the Lord appeared to him and said to those who were with him: "Lay the table and prepare the bread!" Then he took the bread, blessed it, and gave it to James the Just, saying: "Rise, my brother, and eat, because the Son of man has risen!"

In the seventh year of his episcopate, when on Easter Sunday the apostles had gathered in Jerusalem, James asked each of them how much the Lord had done among the people through them, and they gave their accounts. Then for seven days James and the other apostles preached in the Temple before Caiaphas and a number of Jews, and the time was at hand when they would have wished to be baptized. Suddenly a man came into the Temple and shouted: "O men of Israel, what are you doing? Why do you let these sorcerers delude us?" He stirred up the people so much that they wanted to stone the apostles. The man climbed up to the platform from which James was preaching and threw him to the floor below, and as a result James limped badly for the rest of his life. This happened to him in the seventh year after the Lord's ascension.

In the thirtieth year of his episcopate, the Jews, seeing that they could not kill Paul, who had appealed to Caesar and been sent to Rome, turned their tyrannical persecution on James. Hegesippus reports, as we find in the *Ecclesiastical History*, that the Jews came together to him and said: "We pray you, call the people back, because they are wrong about Jesus, thinking that he is the Christ! We beg you therefore to speak to all these people who are coming for the day of the Pasch, and to disabuse them about Jesus. We all will comply with what you say, and we, together with the people, will testify that you are a righteous man and that you are no respecter of persons." They stood him therefore on the pinnacle of the Temple and shouted: "Most righteous of men, to whom we all owe deference, the people are wrong in following Jesus who was crucified! Tell us plainly what you think about him!" James responded: "Why do you question me about the Son of man? Behold, he is seated in the heavens at the right of the sovereign Power, and he will come to judge the living and the dead!"

The Christians rejoiced at hearing this and listened to him gladly. The Pharisees and the Scribes said to each other: "We made a mistake in allowing him to give such testimony to Jesus! Now let us go up and throw him down! That will frighten this crowd and they won't dare believe what he said!" Then all together, and as loudly as they could, they shouted: "Oh! Oh! The just man has erred!"

Then they went up and threw him down, and came down again and began to stone him, saying: "Let us stone James the Just!" But James, though beaten to the ground, not only could not die but even turned over, raised himself to his knees, and said: "I pray you, Lord, forgive them, for they know not what they do!" At this, one of the priests, of the sons of Rahab, exclaimed: "Stop! What are you doing? This just man whom you're stoning is praying for you!" But one of the others snatched up a fuller's club, aimed a heavy blow at James's head, and split his skull. That is how Hegesippus describes the martyrdom. James migrated to the Lord under Nero, who began to reign in the year of the Lord 57. He was buried there beside the Temple. The people were determined to avenge his death and capture and punish the malefactors, but these quickly got away.

Josephus says that the destruction of Jerusalem and the dispersion of the Jews were a punishment for the sin of killing James the Just. Jerusalem, however, was destroyed not only on account of James's death but especially on account of the death of the Lord, according to what Christ himself said: "They will not leave one stone upon another in you, because you did not know the time of your visitation."

But because the Lord does not wish the death of a sinner, and so that the Jews would have no excuse for their sin, he gave them forty years to do penance, and called upon them to do so through the apostles and especially through James the brother of the Lord, who continuously preached repentance among them.

When no amount of admonition availed, God willed to terrify them with wonders. During the forty years he had granted them for penance, many prodigies and portents occurred, as Josephus tells us. An extraordinarily brilliant star, similar in shape to a sword, hung over the city for a whole year, shooting out deadly flames. On a certain feast of Unleavened Bread, at the ninth hour of the night a light shone around the altar of the Temple, so brilliant that all thought a marvelously bright day had dawned. On the same feast day a heifer that was already in the hands of the ministers to be sacrificed brought forth a lamb. Some days later, at the hour of sunset, cars and chariots were seen racing across every quarter of the sky, and battalions of armed men clashing in the clouds and surrounding the city with unlooked-for troops. On another feast day, which is called Pentecost, the priests went at night to the Temple to conduct the usual ministries, and heard movements and crashing noises and voices saying: "Let us get away from this place!" And four years before the war, at the feast of Tabernacles, a man by the name of Jesus, son of Ananias, suddenly began to shout: "A voice from the East, a voice from the West, a voice from the four winds, a voice over Jerusalem and over the Temple, a voice over husbands and wives, a voice over the whole people!" The man was caught, beaten, whipped, but could say nothing else, and the more he was whipped, the louder he shouted. He was brought before the judge, tortured, mangled until his bones showed through the torn flesh, but he neither begged nor wept, only howling at each blow and repeating the same words, adding: "Woe, woe to Jerusalem!" All this from Josephus.

The Jews were neither converted by admonitions nor frightened by marvels, so after forty years the Lord brought Vespasian and Titus to Jerusalem, and they razed the city to its foundations. The reason for their coming to Jerusalem is explained in a certain admittedly apocryphal history. There we read that Pilate, realizing that in Jesus he had condemned an innocent man and fearing the displeasure of Tiberius Caesar, sent an envoy named Albanus to present his excuses to the emperor. Pilate's envoy was driven ashore in Galatia by contrary winds and taken to Vespasian, who at that time held the governorship of Galatia from Tiberius. The prevailing custom in that country was that anyone who had been shipwrecked had to give his goods and his service to the ruler. So Vespasian asked Albanus who he was, where he came from, and where he was going. Albanus answered: "I live in Jerusalem, that is where I came from, and I was on my way to Rome." Vespasian: "You come from the land of the wise men, you know the art of medicine, you are a physician! You must cure me!" In fact since childhood he had had some kind of worms in his nose, whence his name Vespasian. Albanus: "My lord, I know nothing of medicine and therefore am unable to cure you." Vespasian: "Cure me or die!" Albanus: "He who gave sight to the blind, drove out demons, and raised the dead, he knows that I have no knowledge of the art of healing." Vespasian: "Who is this that you say such great things about?" Albanus: "Jesus of Nazareth, whom the Jews, in their envy, put to death! If you believe in him you will obtain the grace of health." Vespasian:

"I believe, because he who raised the dead will be able to free me of this ailment."

As he said this, the worms fell out of his nose and he received his health then and there. Filled with joy, he said: "I am sure that he who was able to cure me is the Son of God. I will seek permission of the emperor and go with an armed band to Jerusalem, and I will overthrow all those who betrayed and killed this man!" And Vespasian said to Albanus, Pilate's envoy: "Your life and goods are safe and unharmed, and you have my permission to return home."

Vespasian then went to Rome and obtained Tiberius Caesar's permission to destroy Jerusalem and Judea. For years during the reign of Nero, when the Jews were rebelling against the empire, he built up several armies: hence (according to the chronicles) he was acting not out of zeal for Christ but because the Jews were renouncing Roman rule. Vespasian then marched upon Jerusalem with a huge force, and on the day of the Pasch laid siege to the city and trapped the innumerable multitude gathered there for the festal day. Some time before Vespasian's arrival the Christian faithful who were in Jerusalem had been warned by the Holy Spirit to leave the city and to take refuge in a town called Pella, across the Jordan. Thus, with all her holy men withdrawn, Jerusalem became the place where the vengeance of heaven fell, upon the sacrilegious city and its criminal people.

The Romans' first assault, however, was against a town of Judea called Jonapata, in which Josephus was both leader and ruler, and he and his people put up a brave resistance; but at length Josephus, seeing that the city's fall was inevitable, took eleven Jews with him and sought safety in an underground room. After four days without food his associates, though Josephus disagreed, preferred to die there rather than submit to servitude under Vespasian. They wanted to kill each other and offer their blood in sacrifice to God; and, since Josephus held first rank among them, they thought he should be the first to die, so that by the shedding of his blood God would be the sooner placated. Or (as another chronicle has it) they wanted to kill each other so as not to fall into the hands of the Romans.

Now Josephus, being a prudent man and not wanting to die, appointed himself arbiter of death and sacrifice, and ordered the others to cast lots, two by two, to determine which of each pair would put the other to death. The lots were cast and one man after the other was consigned to death, until the last one was left to draw lots with Josephus. Then Josephus, who was a strong, agile men, took the other man's sword away from him, asked him which he preferred, life or death, and ordered him not to waste time choosing. The man, afraid, answered promptly: "I do not refuse to live, if by your favor I am able to save my life."

Josephus now had a talk in hiding with an intimate of Vespasian with whom he himself was on friendly terms: he requested that his life be spared by Vespasian, and what he requested he obtained. He was taken before Vespasian, who said to him: "You would have deserved death, if this man's petition had not secured your freedom!" Josephus: "If anything wrong has been done, it can be set right!" Vespasian: "What can a conquered man do?" Josephus: "I will be able to do something, if what I say wins me a favorable hearing." Vespasian: "It is granted that you may say what you have to say, and if there is any good in it, it will be listened to quietly." Josephus: "The Roman emperor has died, and the Senate has made you emperor!" Vespasian: "If you are a prophet, why did you not prophesy to this city that it was about to fall under my sway?" Josephus: "I foretold it publicly for forty days!"

Shortly thereafter legates arrived from Rome, affirmed that Vespasian had indeed been elevated to the imperial throne, and took him off to Rome. Eusebius, too, states in his chronicle that Josephus prophesied to Vespasian both about the emperor's death and about his own elevation.

Vespasian left his son Titus in charge of the siege of Jerusalem. We read in the same apocryphal history that Titus, hearing of his father's accession to the empire, was so filled with joy and exultation that he caught a chill and suffered a contraction of nerves and muscles that left him painfully paralyzed in one leg. Josephus heard that Titus was paralyzed, and diligently sought information regarding the cause of the disease and the time it had struck. The cause was unknown, the nature of the illness also unknown, but the time was known: it happened to Titus when he learned of his father's election. Josephus, quick and foresighted as he was, put two and two together, and, knowing the time, surmised both the nature of the ailment and its cure. He knew that Titus had been debilitated by an excess of joy and gladness, and, keeping in mind that opposites are cured by opposites, knowing also that what is brought on by love is often dispelled by dislike, he began to ask whether there was anyone who was particularly obnoxious to the prince. There was indeed a slave who annoyed Titus so much that the very sight of him, and even the sound of his name, upset him completely. So Josephus said to Titus: "If you want to be cured, guarantee the safety of any who come in my company." Titus: "Whoever comes in your company will be kept secure and safe!"

Josephus quickly arranged a festive dinner, set his own table facing that of Titus, and seated the slave at his right side. When Titus saw the fellow, he growled with displeasure; and as he had been chilled by joy, he now was heated by his fit of fury: his sinews were loosened, and he was cured. Thereafter Titus granted his favor to the slave and took Josephus into his friendship. Whether this story is worth telling is left to the reader's judgment.

Titus maintained the blockade of Jerusalem for two years. Among the other ills that weighed heavily on the people in the besieged city, there was a famine so severe that parents snatched food from their children and children from parents, husbands from wives and wives from husbands—snatched it not only from their hands but out of their mouths. Young people, though stronger by their age, wandered about the streets like phantoms and fell down exhausted by hunger. Those who were burying the dead often fell dead on top of those they were burying. The stench from the cadavers was so unbearable that they were being buried out of public funds, and when the funds ran out, the unburied corpses were so numerous that they were thrown over the city walls. Titus, making a tour around the walls and seeing the moats filled with cadavers and the whole area infected with the smell of death, raised his hands to heaven, wept, and said: "God, you see that not I am doing this!"

The hunger was so acute that people chewed their shoes and their shoelaces. The *Ecclesiastical History* tells the story of a woman noble by birth and by riches, whose house was broken into by robbers who stole all she had, including the last bit of food. She held her suckling infant in her hands and said: "Unhappy son of an unhappier mother, for whom should I keep you alive amid war and famine and pillaging? Come now therefore, my firstborn, be food to your mother, a scandal to the robbers, a testament to the ages!" She strangled her child, cooked the body, ate half, and hid the other half. The robbers, smelling cooked meat, rushed back into the house and threatened the woman with death unless she gave up the food. She uncovered what was left of the infant. "Look here," she said, "you see I saved you the best part!" But they were filled with such horror that they could not even speak. "This is my son," she said. "The sin is mine! Don't be afraid to eat, because I who begot him ate first. Don't be either more religious than the mother or more softhearted than women! But if piety overcomes you and you dread to eat, I will eat the rest, since I've already eaten half!" Trembling and terrified, the robbers slunk away.

Finally, in the second year of Vespasian's reign, Titus took Jerusalem, reduced the city to ruins, and leveled the Temple; and as the Jews had bought Jesus Christ for thirty pieces of silver, Titus had Jews sold at the rate of thirty for one silver coin. Josephus tells us that 97,000 were sold and 110,000 perished of hunger or by the sword. We also read that when Titus entered the city, he noticed one particularly thick wall and gave orders to break into it. Inside the wall they found an old man, venerable in age and appearance. When asked who he was, he replied that he was Joseph, from Arimathea, a city of Judea, and that the Jews had had him shut in and immured because he had buried Christ. He added that from that time to the present he had been fed with food from heaven and comforted by divine light. In the *Gospel of Nicodemus*, however, it is said that though the Jews had walled him in, the risen Christ broke him out and brought him to Arimathea. It could be said that once released he would not desist from preaching Christ and therefore was walled in a second time.

Vespasian died and his son Titus succeeded him as emperor. He was a clement and generous man. His goodness was so great that, as Eusebius of Caesarea in his chronicle and Jerome both affirm, when one evening he remembered that on that day he had done nothing good nor given anything to anyone, he said: "Oh, my friends, I have lost the day!"

Long afterwards some Jews set out to rebuild Jerusalem, and when they went out the first morning, they found crosses of dew on the ground. Frightened, they fled. The second morning they came back, and, as Miletus says in his chronicle, each of them found a bloody cross sketched on his clothing. Again they fled in terror. When they returned on the third day, a fiery vapor came out of the ground and consumed them utterly.

✳

68. The Finding of the Holy Cross

This feast is named for the finding of the holy cross because, it is said, the cross was found on this day. It had been found earlier by Adam's son Seth in the earthly paradise, as we shall see below, by Solomon in Lebanon, by the queen of Sheba in Solomon's temple, by the Jews in the water of the pond; and on this day it was found by Helena on Mount Calvary.

The finding of the holy cross occurred more than 200 years after the Lord's resurrection. We read in the *Gospel of Nicodemus* that when Adam became infirm, his son Seth went to the gates of paradise and begged for some oil from the tree of mercy, with which he might anoint his father's body and restore his health. The archangel Michael appeared to him and said: "Waste no toil or tears trying to obtain oil from the wood of mercy, because there is no way you can acquire it before 5,500 years have gone by!" . . . this although it is believed that only 5,199 years elapsed from Adam's day to Christ's passion. Elsewhere we read that the angel offered Seth a shoot from the tree and ordered him to plant it on the mount of Lebanon. In a certain admittedly apocryphal history of the Greeks we read that the angel gave him a branch from the tree under which Adam committed his sin, informing him that when that branch bore fruit, his father would be made whole. When Seth went back and found his father dead, he planted the branch over Adam's grave, where it grew to be a great tree and was still standing in Solomon's time. Whether any of this is true we leave to the reader's judgment, because none of it is found in any authentic chronicle or history.

Solomon admired the beauty of this tree and had it cut down and used in the building of his forest house.[1] John Beleth says, however, that it was not possible to find a place where the trunk of the tree could be fitted in: it was always too

---

[1] I owe to the Abbé Roze (*La légende dorée* [Paris: Ed. Rouveyre, 1902], 2:53–54) a note to the effect that this house is referred to in 1 Kings 7. It was called "forest house" because so many cedar trees had been used in its construction.

long or too short. If it did not fit into a place too narrow for it and it was carefully shortened, it was immediately seen to be so short as to be completely useless. Therefore the workmen would have nothing more to do with it, and it was thrown over a certain pond to serve as a bridge for those wishing to cross.

When the queen of Sheba came to hear Solomon's words of wisdom and was about to cross this bridge, she saw in spirit that the Savior of the world would one day hang upon this very same wood. She therefore would not walk on it but immediately knelt and worshiped it. In the *Scholastic History*, however, we read that the queen of Sheba saw the wood in Solomon's forest house, and when she returned home, she sent word to Solomon that a certain man was to hang upon that wood, and that by this man's death the kingdom of the Jews would be destroyed. Solomon therefore had the wood taken out and buried in the deepest bowels of the earth. Later on the pond called Probatica[2] welled up at that spot, and the Nathineans[3] bathed the sacrificial animals there. So it was not only the occasional descent of an angel of the Lord, but also the power of the wood, that caused the motion of the water and the healing of the sick.

When Christ's time to suffer was drawing near, the aforesaid wood floated up to the surface of the pond, and the Jews, seeing it, used it in making the Lord's cross. It is said that the cross was made out of four kinds of wood, namely, palmwood, cedar, cypress, and olivewood. Hence the verse:

Ligna crucis palma, cedrus, cypressus, oliva.

There were four wooden parts to the cross—the upright shaft, the crossbeam, the tablet above, and the block into which the cross was fixed, or, as Gregory of Tours says, the crosspiece that supported Christ's feet. Hence each of these parts might be made of any of the kinds of wood enumerated above. The apostle seems to have this variety of woods in mind when he says: "You may be able to comprehend, with all the saints, what is the breadth and length and height and depth." The eminent doctor,[4] at the place referred to, explains these words as follows: "The breadth of the Lord's cross is the crossbeam upon which his hands were extended; the length means the shaft from the ground to the crossbeam, where the whole body hung from the hands; the height means from the crossbeam to the top, where the head touched; the depth is the part hidden by the earth in which the cross stood. By this sign of the cross all human and Christian action is described: to do good works in Christ and to cling to him perseveringly, to hope for heaven, and to avoid profaning the sacraments."

This precious wood of the cross lay hidden underground for over two hundred years and was rediscovered by Helena, mother of Constantine. At that time

---

[2] John 5:2.

[3] *Natmei* (in Graesse) is no doubt a scribe's error (or Graesse's) for the *Nathinaei* of 1 Chron. 9:2, which the New English Bible translates "temple-servitors."

[4] Most likely Augustine, whom Jacobus, elsewhere in the *Legenda aurea*, calls *doctor egregius*, the term he uses here.

an innumerable horde of barbarians gathered on the bank of the Danube: their aim was to cross the river and to subjugate all the lands as far as the western limit. When Emperor Constantine learned of this, he moved his camp and took his stand with his army along the opposite bank of the Danube; but more and more barbarians were arriving and were beginning to cross the river, and Constantine, seeing that they were bent on drawing him into battle the next day, was stricken with terror. That night an angel awakened him and urged him to look upwards. The emperor looked toward heaven and saw the sign of the cross formed in flaming light, with the legend *In hoc signo vinces* written in golden letters. Heartened by the celestial vision he had a facsimile of the cross made, and ordered it to be carried at the head of the army. Then his troops rushed upon the enemy and put them to flight, killing a great many of them. Soon thereafter Constantine called the heads of all the temples and questioned them closely, seeking to find out what god had the cross as his sign. They said they did not know, but then some Christians came along and told him about the mystery of the cross and the faith in the Trinity. Constantine believed perfectly in Christ and received the sacrament of baptism from Pope Eusebius, or, as some books have it, from the bishop of Caesarea. Many of the things stated in this account, however, are contradicted by the *Tripartite History* and the *Ecclesiastical History*, as well as by the life of Saint Silvester[5] and the *Acts* of the Roman pontiffs. There are those who hold that it was not Constantine the great emperor who was converted and baptized by Pope Saint Eusebius, as some historians seem to imply, but Constantine's father, also named Constantine, as we find in some other histories; for this latter Constantine came to the faith a different way, as we read in the legend of Saint Silvester, and he was baptized not by Eusebius but by Silvester.

When the elder Constantine died, the younger, remembering the victory his father had won by virtue of the holy cross, sent his mother Helena to Jerusalem to find the cross, as is related below. The *Ecclesiastical History* gives a different account of this victory: it says that when Maxentius invaded the Roman empire, Emperor Constantine arrived at the Albine[6] bridge to do battle with him. Constantine was exceedingly anxious about this battle and often raised his eyes to heaven in search of help from above. Then in a dream he saw, in the eastern part of the sky, the sign of the cross blazing with fiery brilliance, and angels standing by and saying to him: "Constantine, in this sign you will conquer." And, as we read in the *Tripartite History*, while Constantine puzzled about the meaning of this, the following night Christ appeared to him with the sign he had seen in the sky, and ordered him to have a standard made with this sign on it, because this would be of help to him in combat. So Constantine, again happy and confident of victory, drew on his forehead the sign of the cross that he had seen in the sky, had the military standards changed to the shape of the cross, and carried a gold

---

[5] See above, chapter 12.

[6] Why the text has this term for what is commonly called the Milvian bridge is not clear.

cross in his right hand. After that he prayed the Lord not to allow his right hand, which he had armed with the salutary sign of the cross, to be bloodied or stained by spilled Roman blood, but to grant him victory over the tyrant without bloodshed.

Maxentius meanwhile gave orders to arrange his boats as a trap, stringing floats across the river to look like a level bridge. Now, when Constantine drew up to the river, Maxentius rushed upon him with a small band of troops, commanding the rest to come after him; but he forgot his own stratagem and started across the false bridge, thus being caught by the ruse with which he had hoped to deceive Constantine, and was drowned in the depths of the stream. Thereupon Constantine was unanimously acclaimed emperor by all present.

We read in a fairly reliable chronicle that at that time Constantine's faith was not yet perfect and that he had not yet been baptized, but that after an interval he had a vision of Saints Peter and Paul[7] and was reborn by holy baptism at Pope Silvester's hands. Then, cured of his leprosy, he believed perfectly in Christ and so sent his mother Helena to Jerusalem to search for the Lord's cross. Ambrose, however, in his letter about the death of Theodosius, and the *Tripartite History* both say that he received baptism only in his last hours, having put it off in order that he might be able to be baptized in the river Jordan. Jerome says that he became a Christian under Pope Silvester. There is doubt about whether or not he delayed baptism, so that Saint Silvester's legend is likewise questionable on more than one point. This account of the finding of the cross, which we read in the *Ecclesiastical History*, seems more authentic than the story usually read in the churches. In the latter many things are stated which clearly are not in accord with the truth, unless perhaps one would choose to say, as was said above, that not Constantine but his father, also called Constantine, was the one concerned; but this does not seem very likely, although that is what we read in certain histories from overseas.[8]

When Helena arrived in Jerusalem, she gave orders that all the Jewish wise men located throughout the entire area should come together in her presence. This Helena had previously been an innkeeper or inn-servant,[9] but because of her beauty Constantine [the elder] had attached her to himself. Ambrose has this to say about her: "They assert that this woman had been an innkeeper or servant, but was joined to Constantine the elder, who later became emperor. She was a good innkeeper, who diligently sought a crib for the Lord, a good hostess who knew about the innkeeper who healed the wounds of the man who fell among

---

[7] See the legend of Saint Silvester, chapter 12 above.

[8] The confusion about Constantine's part in the finding of the cross (or his father's, whose name was not Constantine but Constantius) no doubt goes back to the manuscript sources available to Jacobus, including not only Eusebius and the *Tripartite History* but the more or less "authentic," or frankly apocryphal, documents to which Jacobus refers. The uncertainty about the time of his baptism persists among present-day scholars.

[9] The word *stabularia* can mean either innkeeper or servant in an inn.

robbers, a good servant, who preferred to spurn all things as dung in order to gain Christ: therefore Christ lifted her up from the dunghill to the throne." Thus Ambrose. Others, however, assert, and we read in a reasonably authentic chronicle, that this Helena was the only daughter of Clohel, king of the Britons. When Constantine came to Britain, he took Helena to wife, and so the island devolved to him after Clohel's death. Even British sources attest this; yet elsewhere we read that Helena was a native of Trier.

Be that as it may, the Jewish scholars, somewhat alarmed, asked each other: "Why do you think the queen has summoned us?" One of their number, Judas by name, said: "I know why! She wants to learn from us the whereabouts of the wood of the cross on which Christ was crucified. Be cautious, therefore, and let no one of us presume to tell her! Otherwise you can be absolutely sure that our Law will be annulled and the traditions of the fathers completely wiped out. My grandfather Zacheus foretold this to my father Simon, and on his deathbed my father said to me: 'Look, my son! When they come searching for Christ's cross, show them where it is or you will be tortured; for from then on the Jewish nation will never reign, but those who adore the Crucified will rule, because Christ was indeed the Son of God.' I asked him: 'Father mine, if our forefathers truly knew that Jesus Christ was the Son of God, why did they nail him to the gibbet of the cross?' 'God knows,' he replied, 'that I was never in their counsels and often spoke against them. But because Christ denounced the vices of the Pharisees, they had him put to death on the cross. He rose again on the third day and ascended to heaven as his disciples looked on. My brother Stephen believed in him and the Jews in their madness stoned him to death. Be careful therefore, my son, and do not rashly blaspheme him or his disciples.'" It does not seem very probable, however, that this Jew's father could have lived at the time of Christ's passion, because from that time to Helena's, when this Judas is supposed to have told his story, more than 270 years had elapsed—unless, perhaps, it could be said that men lived longer then than they do now.

However that may be, the Jewish scholars now said to Judas: "We have never heard anything like that; but if the queen questions you, see to it that you tell her nothing!" When they all stood before her, she asked them about the place where the Lord had been crucified. They refused absolutely to say where it was, and she condemned them all to die by fire. This frightened them and they handed Judas over to her, saying: "This man is the son of a just man and a prophet. He is learned in the Law and will give you the answers to all your questions." So she dismissed them all except Judas, to whom she said: "You have the choice of death or life: choose which one you prefer! Show me the place called Golgotha, where the Lord was crucified, so that I may find his cross." "How could I know the place?" he responded; "More than two hundred years have gone by since then!" "I swear by the Crucified," the queen said, "that I will starve you to death unless you tell me the truth!" She therefore had him thrown into a dry well and left him to suffer the pangs of hunger. After he had been without food for six days, he asked to be pulled out of the well on the seventh, and promised to show where the cross was. He was lifted out, and when he came to the place and prayed there, the earth suddenly quaked and a mist of sweet-smelling perfumes greeted their senses. Judas, filled with wonder, clapped his hands and said: "In truth, O Christ, you are the Savior of the world!"

The *Ecclesiastical History* tells us that at that place there was a temple of Venus, which Hadrian had built so that any Christians who came to pray there would seem to be adoring Venus. For this reason few came and the place was almost consigned to oblivion; but Helena had the temple razed and the site plowed up. After that, Judas girded himself and started manfully to dig, and when he had dug down twenty yards, he found three crosses buried and took them forthwith to the queen. Since they had no way of distinguishing Christ's cross from those of the thieves, they placed them in the center of the city and waited for the Lord to manifest his glory; and behold! At about the ninth hour the body of a young man was being carried past, and Judas halted the cortege. He held the first cross and the second over the body, but nothing happened. Then he extended the third cross, and the dead man immediately came back to life. In the histories of the Church we also read that when one of the leading women in the city lay close to death, Macarius, the bishop of Jerusalem, brought in first one and then another of the crosses, to no effect; but when he placed the third beside the lady, she opened her eyes at once and rose up cured.

Ambrose says that Judas determined which was the Lord's cross by finding and reading the title that Pilate had placed on the cross. At that moment the devil was up in the air screaming and shouting: "O Judas, why have you done this? My Judas did just the opposite: I pressed him and he betrayed his master, but you, despite my interdict, have found the cross of Jesus! Through the other Judas I gained the souls of many; through you I seem to be losing those I gained. Through him I reigned among the people, through you I will be expelled from my realm. But I will pay you back in turn: I will raise up another king against you, a king who will abandon the faith of the Crucified and by torture will make you deny the Crucified!" It would seem that he said this referring to Julian the Apostate, who, when Judas had become bishop of Jerusalem, inflicted many torments on him and made him a martyr of Christ. Judas heard the devil shouting and screaming but was not frightened in the least. Unshaken, he cursed the evil spirit, saying: "May Christ damn you to eternal fire!"

Judas was later baptized and given the name Quiriacus. When the bishop of Jerusalem died, Quiriacus was ordained bishop. Now the blessed Helena did not have the nails from Christ's cross and asked the new bishop to go to the place and try to find them. He went there and prayed profusely, and at once the nails appeared on the surface, gleaming like gold, and he collected them and delivered them to the queen, who fell to her knees and bowed her head, worshiping them with much reverence. Helena brought a piece of the cross to her son and left other pieces, encased in silver, in the place where the cross had been found.

She also brought to Constantine the nails that had held the Lord's body on the cross. Eusebius of Caesarea reports that the emperor had one of them fashioned into a bit for his war bridle, and had the others welded into his helmet. Some assert, however, as does Gregory of Tours, that four nails had pierced Christ's flesh, and that Helena put two of them in the emperor's bridle, fixed the third into the statue of Constantine that dominates the city of Rome, and cast the fourth into the Adriatic sea, which until then had been a whirlpool perilous to mariners. She also commanded that this feast be solemnly celebrated annually in honor of the finding of the holy cross.

Ambrose has more to say on this subject: "Helena sought the Lord's nails and found them, and had one of them made into a bit and the other worked into the royal crown: it was right that the nail be on the head, the crown at the top, the bridle in the hand, so that the mind should be preeminent, the faith should shine forth, and the royal power should rule."

At a later time Julian the Apostate put Bishop Saint Quiriacus to death because he had found the holy cross while the emperor was trying to destroy the sign of the cross everywhere. When Julian was on his way to attack the Persians, he invited Quiriacus to sacrifice to the idols, and when the bishop refused, Julian ordered his right hand to be cut off, saying: "With that hand you wrote many letters recalling many people from the cult of the gods." Quiriacus answered him: "You are doing me a favor, you rabid dog, because before I believed in Christ, I often wrote letters to the Jewish synagogues to dissuade everyone from believing in Christ, and now you have cut this scandal from my body." Then Julian had lead melted and poured into the saint's mouth, and an iron bed prepared on which Quiriacus was laid while hot coals and fat were sprinkled over him. When the saint lay there motionless, Julian said to him: "If you will not sacrifice to the gods, at least say that you are not a Christian!" Quiriacus cursed him and refused, so he ordered a deep trench to be dug and venomous snakes to be put in it, and Quiriacus to be thrown in on top of them; but the snakes died instantly. The emperor commanded that the bishop be thrown into a caldron full of boiling oil, and the saint, making the sign of the cross, was about to step into it of his own volition, and prayed the Lord to baptize him again with the bath of martyrdom. This angered Julian, who ordered the soldiers to plunge a sword into Quiriacus's chest, and so the saint merited to finish his life in the Lord.

The great power of the cross is evident in the experience of a young notary, a Christian. A sorcerer had deluded him and promised him great wealth, then led him to a place to which the sorcerer had summoned the demons. There the notary saw a huge Ethiopian[10] seated on a high throne, around which stood other Ethiopians armed with spears and cudgels. The large Ethiopian asked the

---

[10] *Aethiops*, in Jacobus's time, meant a black man, the color black standing for evil as white for virtue. This followed patristic exegesis of passages in the Old and New Testaments. There was no racial implication, because black people were rarely if ever known in Jacobus's time and place.

sorcerer: "Who is this boy?" The sorcerer: "My lord, he is our slave." The demon to the notary: "If you will adore me and be my servant, and deny your Christ, I will have you seated at my right hand." The notary quickly made the sign of the cross and declared that he was in all freedom the servant of Christ his Savior; and the minute he made the sign of the cross, the horde of demons vanished. There came a time when this notary went into the church of Saint Sophia with his master, and they both stood before an image of Christ the Savior. The master noticed that the image had its eyes fixed on the notary, looking at him attentively. The master wondered at this and directed the young man to move to the right, and he saw that the image's eyes turned and were again fixed on the notary. He had the youth go to the left, with the same result. The master begged him to say how he had merited of God that the sacred image should so keep its eyes on him. The young man answered that he was not aware of having done anything meritorious, unless it was that he had refused, before the devil, to deny his Lord.

69. Saint John before the Latin Gate

While John the apostle and evangelist was preaching at Ephesus, he was taken prisoner by the proconsul and invited to sacrifice to the gods. He refused and was remanded to prison, and a letter was sent to Emperor Domitian that described John as guilty of great sacrileges, namely, of despising the gods and of worshiping a crucified man. By Domitian's order he was brought to Rome, and all his hair was cut off in mockery. Then at the city portal called the Latin Gate he was plunged into a caldron of hot oil over a blazing fire, but felt no pain and came out unscathed. (Therefore the Christians built a church at the spot and solemnized that day as the day of the apostle's martyrdom.) When even the caldron did not deter John from preaching Christ, by order of Domitian he was relegated to the island of Patmos.

The reason the Roman emperors persecuted the apostles was not that they preached Christ, since the emperors themselves did not exclude any god, but that without the authorization of the Senate they had declared Christ divine—something the Senate forbade anyone to do. Indeed we read in the *Ecclesiastical History* that Pilate once wrote to Tiberius concerning Christ, and on the strength of that letter Tiberius would have allowed the Christian faith to be preached to the Romans, but the Senate rejected the idea on the ground that Christ could not be called a god by authority of the emperor.

Another reason given in a chronicle for the persecutions was that Christ had not appeared to the Romans first. Still another was that he banned the cult of all the gods, which the Romans practiced. Another was that he preached contempt of worldly goods, and the Romans were avaricious and ambitious. Moreover, Christ himself did not want the Senate to confirm his divinity, lest that be attributed to human power. According to Master John Beleth, another reason the emperors and the Senate persecuted the apostles was that he seemed to them too proud and grudging a god, in that he did not condescend to have any other god sharing his divinity. Orosius assigns another reason, namely, that the Senate was offended because Pilate had addressed letters about Christ's miracles to Tiberius and not to themselves, wherefore the Senate would not allow Christ to be consecrated among the gods. This stung Tiberius, and he proceeded to have many of the senators put to death and condemned others to exile.

When John's mother learned that he was a prisoner in Rome, she was moved by maternal compassion and went to Rome to visit him. Upon arrival there she found that he had been sent into exile, so she set out on the homeward journey and got as far as the city of Nerulana in Campania, where she died. Her body lay for a long time in a cave, until the location was revealed by her son to Saint James. The body, giving off a pervading perfume, was transferred with much honor to the aforementioned city and occasioned many miracles.

70. The Greater and Lesser Litanies

The litanies occur twice in the year. The first time is on the feast of Saint Mark, and this is called the Greater Litany. The second, or Lesser Litany, falls on the three days before the feast of the Lord's ascension into heaven. The word "litany" means prayer, supplication, rogation.

The first litany has three names: Greater Litany, Septiform Procession, and Black Crosses. It is called the Greater Litany for three reasons: the first, the one who instituted it, namely, Pope Gregory the Great; the second, the place where it was instituted, namely, Rome, mistress and head of the world due to the presence there of the body of the chief of the apostles and of the apostolic see; the third, the occasion for its institution, which was a widespread and deadly pestilence. The Romans, having lived a continent and abstemious life throughout Lent and having received the Body of the Lord at Easter, afterwards threw off all restraints in feasting, in games, and in voluptuous living. Therefore God, offended by these excesses, sent a devastating plague upon them—a malady called *inguinaria* because it caused a swelling or abscess in the groin. The plague was so virulent that people died suddenly while walking in the street or at table or at play or just talking to each other. It frequently happened that someone sneezed, as they say, and expired in the very act of sneezing; so, if one heard a person sneeze, one quickly said, "God bless you!" This is said to be the origin of the custom that still prevails, of saying "God bless you" when we hear anyone sneeze. Moreover, it is said, when anyone yawned, it was often that person's last breath; so if one felt a yawn coming on, one quickly made the sign of the cross—another custom still common among us. A full account of this plague is included in the life of Saint Gregory.

Secondly, the Greater Litany is called the Septiform Procession because Saint Gregory arranged the processions associated with the litany according to seven orders or classes: first, the clergy; second, all the monks and religious men; third, the women religious; fourth, all the children; fifth, all the laymen; sixth, all widows and unmarried women; and seventh, married women.[1] In our day we cannot count on that many people, so we supply by providing seven litanies to be recited before the insignia are lowered.

Thirdly, the Greater Litany is called the Black Crosses because, as a sign of their grief over the death toll of the plague, people put on black clothing, and, probably for the same reason, crosses and altars were shrouded in sackcloth. In these days of penance likewise, penitential clothing should be worn.

The other litany, which occurs on the three days before Ascension Thursday, was instituted by Saint Mamertus, bishop of Vienne, in the time of the emperor Leo, who began to reign in 458. It began earlier, therefore, than the institution of the Greater Litany and has three names: Lesser Litany, Rogations, and Procession. It is called Lesser to differentiate it from the Greater, because it was inaugurated by a lesser bishop, in a less distinguished place, and on account of a less grave situation than the above-described plague.

The reason for the institution of this litany was the following. At that time Vienne suffered frequent earthquakes, so violent that they leveled many houses and churches, and rumblings and crashes were often heard at night. Then something more terrible happened: on Easter Sunday fire fell from heaven and reduced the king's palace to ashes. And, yet more dreadful: as in the past God had allowed demons to enter into swine, now, the Lord permitting because of the

---

[1] Graesse has the seventh category as *omnes conjugati*, presumably therefore married men and women. He notes that the Ed. Pr. has *conjugatae*, married women—"falsely," he says. But it would seem from the preceding enumeration that there was no class left *except* married women.

sins of men, evil spirits entered wolves and other wild beasts, and these, fearing no man, came running openly over the roads and into the city itself, and at times devoured children and old men and women. The bishop, faced daily with such woeful calamities, proclaimed a three-day fast and instituted litanies, and so brought these tribulations to an end. At a later time the Church established and confirmed this litany for universal observance.

The Lesser Litany is called Rogations because in these three days we implore the help of the saints. This practice should certainly be maintained, and the prayers to the saints and the fasts insisted upon, for several reasons. First, we ask God to end the wars that so often erupt in springtime. Second, we ask him to preserve and multiply the still-tender young fruits of the earth. Third, we seek his help so that everyone may be able to control the impulses of the flesh, which at this season are stronger than usual; for in the spring the blood is hotter and temptations to wrongdoing abound. Fourth, we pray for help in preparing to receive the Holy Spirit: fasting is an excellent preparation and our supplications increase our worthiness.

Master William of Auxerre offers two further reasons for observing the Rogations. The first is that as Christ, ascending, says: "Ask and you shall receive," the Church may petition him more confidently. The second is that the Church fasts and prays in order to have less flesh by mortification, and by prayer to acquire wings, because prayer is the soul's wing by which it flies to heaven. So the soul will be able freely to follow Christ in his ascent: he ascended, opening the road before us, and he flew on the wings of the winds. For a bird that has much flesh and little plumage cannot fly very well: consider, for instance, the ostrich.

The Lesser Litany is called the Procession, because on this occasion the Church holds a great procession at which the cross is borne aloft, the bells are rung, the standard is carried. In some churches men carry a dragon with a huge tail. All the saints are besought one by one for their protection. In this procession we carry the cross and ring the bells to make the devils flee in terror; for just as a king in the midst of his army has the royal insignias, namely, trumpets and standards or banners, so Christ the eternal King in the midst of his Church militant has bells for trumpets and crosses for standards. Any tyrant would be terrified if he heard in his land the trumpets and saw the banners of some powerful king, his enemy; and so the demons who are in that murky air are sore afraid when they hear Christ's trumpets—the bells—and catch sight of his standards—the crosses. It is said that this was the reason for ringing the church bells when storms were brewing, namely, that the demons who stir up the storms should hear the trumpets of the eternal King and flee aghast, letting the storms die down. Of course, there was another reason, which was that the bells would warn the faithful and incite them to pray hard in view of the impending danger.

The cross itself is the banner of the eternal King, as a hymn for Passiontide has it:

Vexilla Regis prodeunt;
Fulget crucis mysterium;
Qua vita mortem pertulit
Et morte vitam protulit.[2]

The demons are afraid of this standard, according to what Chrysostom says: "Wherever the demons see the Lord's sign, they take flight, fearing the rod that scourged them." Moreover, this is why, in certain churches, when storms come up, the cross is brought out of the church and held up against the tempest, precisely so that the evil spirits may see the standard of the King and flee in terror. There, to sum up, is why the cross is held aloft in the procession and the bells are rung—that the demons who are in the air may flee in fright and desist from harassing us.

Another reason for carrying the standard in the procession is to represent the victory of Christ's resurrection and the victory of his ascension. He ascended to heaven with much booty: thus the banner advancing through the air is Christ ascending to heaven, and as a multitude of the faithful follows the standard carried in the procession, so a great assemblage of saints accompanies Christ ascending.

The chants sung in the procession stand for the chants and praises of the angels who met the ascending Christ and led him with his company into the heavens with choruses of praise. In some churches and especially in France, the custom obtains of carrying a dragon with a long tail stuffed with straw or some such material: the first two days it is carried in front of the cross, and the third day, with the tail empty, behind the cross. The significance of this is that on the first day, before the Law, and on the second, under the Law, the devil reigned in this world, but on the third, the day of grace, he was expelled from his realm by the passion of Christ.

Again, in that procession we ask for the protection of all the saints. Several reasons for this have already been noted, but there are other general reasons for which God has commanded us to pray to the saints: our neediness, the saints' glory, and the reverence due to God. The saints can know about the prayers of their supplicants, because in that eternal mirror they perceive whatever pertains to their joy or to our aid. Therefore, the first reason is our neediness, which may be due to a lack of merit, in which case, our merits not sufficing, we pray that others may supply for us. Or we may be deficient in contemplation, and since we cannot look upon the supreme light in itself, we pray to be able at least to see it in the saints. Or our shortcomings may be in our loving, because it is not uncommon for imperfect man to feel himself more drawn to one particular saint than even to God. The second reason is the glory of the saints, for God wills that we invoke the saints in order that, obtaining what we ask for through their

---

[2] The standards of the King advance; / The mystery of the cross shines out; / the cross on which life suffered death / and by death brought forth life.

intercession, we may enhance their greatness and by glorifying them join in praising them. The third reason is the reverence due to God, in that we sinners, because we offend God, do not dare, so to speak, to approach him in his own person, but can implore the support of his friends.

In these litanies the angelic canticle *Sancte Deus, sancte fortis, sancte et immortalis, miserere nobis*[3] would frequently be sung. John of Damascus tells us in Book III that on one occasion, when, on account of some public tribulation, the litanies were being celebrated, a boy was caught up from the midst of the people and carried to heaven. There he learned this canticle, then returned to the congregation and, in full view of the people, sang the canticle and the tribulation was ended. At the Council of Chalcedon the canticle was approved. Damascenus concludes as follows: "We say also that through this canticle the demons go away." The praiseworthiness and authority of the canticle are assured in four ways: first, from the fact that an angel taught it; second, because when it was sung publicly the said tribulation ceased; third, that the Council of Chalcedon approved it; fourth, that the demons fear it.

---

71. Saint Boniface, Martyr

Saint Boniface[1] suffered martyrdom under Emperors Diocletian and Maximian in the city of Tarsus but was buried at Rome on the road called the Via Latina.

Boniface was the chief steward in charge of the properties of a noble lady named Aglaë. The two lived in illicit union, but in time, touched by divine grace, they took counsel and decided that Boniface should go in search of the bodies of some martyrs. Their hope was that if they served and paid honor to the holy martyrs by venerating their relics, they might obtain salvation through the prayers of these saints.

After traveling for some days Boniface arrived at the city of Tarsus and said to those who were with him: "Men, go and find lodging for us! I am going to look for those I want so much to see, the martyrs in their trials!" He hurried to a place where he saw the blessed martyrs—one hanging by his feet with a fire burning below him, another stretched on a rack and tormented as he had been for a long

---

[3] O holy God, holy and strong, holy and immortal, have mercy on us.
[1] Graesse notes (316) that this legend is missing in more recent books.

time, another being torn with hooks, another with his hands cut off, another raised from the ground by a stake driven through his neck. Looking from a distance at these various kinds of torture and martyrdom devised by an impious executioner, and himself aflame with love of Christ, he began to call upon the great God of the holy martyrs, and ran up and sat at their feet, kissing their chains and saying: "O struggling martyrs of Christ, trample on the devil! Persevere for a short while! The labor is slight, and much rest and ineffable satiety will follow! The torments you are suffering for the love of God are temporary and will be over in a moment, and after the briefest interval of time you will pass over to the joys of perpetual happiness! Then, clothed in the glory of immortality and enjoying the vision of your King, you will render him praises of heavenly song amidst the choirs of angels and will see these wicked men, who are torturing you now, themselves being tortured in the abyss of eternal calamity!"

Simplicius the judge saw all this and had Boniface brought before his tribunal. "Who are you?" he asked him. Saint Boniface replied: "I am a Christian and am called Boniface!" The judge angrily ordered him to be hung up and his body to be slashed with hooks until the bones showed; then splinters of wood were driven under his fingernails. The martyr of God looked up to heaven and eagerly bore his pains, and the impious judge, seeing this, ordered molten lead to be poured into his mouth. The holy martyr said: "I give you thanks, Lord Jesus Christ, Son of the living God!" Then the judge ordered a tub to be brought and filled with boiling pitch, into which the holy martyr was plunged head first, but again he remained unharmed, so at the judge's command his head was cut off with a sword. The moment this was done, a tremendous earthquake shook the ground, and many of the infidels, perceiving the power of Christ in and through the martyr, became believers.

Meanwhile the fellow servants of Boniface the martyr looked for him all night everywhere in the city and, not finding him, said to each other: "He's with some whore, or else he's dead drunk in some tavern!" As they talked, it happened that they met one of the town's prison-keepers and asked him: "Have you seen a stranger anywhere, a Roman?" He answered: "Yesterday a foreigner was beheaded in the stadium!" They asked again: "What did he look like? Our man is a sturdy fellow, heavy build, thick head of hair, and was wearing a red cloak." The jailer said: "The man you're looking for died a martyr here yesterday!" They objected: "The man we're looking for is a woman-chaser and a drunkard!" The other said: "Come and see him!" When he showed them the holy martyr's corpse and precious head, they said to him: "He's the man! Please, give him to us!" "I can't give you his body without payment," said the jailer. They gave him five hundred sols and received the holy martyr's body, anointed it with sweet spices, and wrapped it in fine linen. Then they placed it in a litter and so carried it back to Rome, rejoicing and glorifying God.

An angel of the Lord now appeared to the lady for whom Boniface had worked, and informed her about what had happened to the blessed martyr. She hurried to meet the holy body with all veneration, built a monument worthy of it about a half-mile outside the city of Rome, and laid it to rest there.

Boniface was martyred on the fourteenth day of May in Tarsus, the metropolis of Cilicia, and was buried near Rome on the ninth day of June. Blessed Aglaë renounced the world and its pomps and distributed everything she owned to the poor and to monasteries, also freeing her slaves. She devoted her life to constant prayer and fasting, and merited such great graces from the Lord Jesus Christ that she became illustrious by the miracles she wrought in his name. She lived in the habit of a religious for twelve years, died worn out by her pious works, and was buried close to the holy martyr.

※

72. *The Ascension of the Lord*

The Lord's ascension occurred forty days after his resurrection. Concerning this event seven questions are to be considered—where he ascended from; why he did not ascend immediately after the resurrection but waited forty days; in what manner he ascended; with whom he ascended; by what merit he ascended; where he ascended to; and why he ascended.

On the first point, note that he rose to heaven from the Mount of Olives, out toward Bethany. This mountain, following another translation, was also called the Mount of Three Lights, because from the west the light from the Temple fell upon it by night, for a fire burned continually on the altar; in the morning it caught the sun's rays from the east before they reached the city; and the hill's olive trees produced a plentiful supply of oil, which feeds light.

Christ appeared twice to his disciples on the day of his ascension and ordered them to go to this mountain. The first time, he appeared to the eleven apostles as they were eating in the cenacle. (All the apostles and other disciples, as well as the women, were living in the section of Jerusalem called Mello, or else on Mount Sion where David had built his palace. There was a large furnished upper room where the Lord had ordered the two disciples to prepare the paschal meal for him, and the eleven apostles were staying in this room while the rest of the disciples and the women were lodged nearby.) They were at table in the cenacle when the Lord appeared to them and rebuked them for their lack of faith; and after he had eaten with them, he ordered them to go to the Mount of Olives, on the road to Bethany, as aforesaid. There he appeared to them again and responded to their untimely questioning, then raised his hands and blessed them. After that, as they looked on, he ascended into heaven.

Regarding the place from which Christ ascended, Sulpicius, bishop of Jerusalem, says, and the *Gloss* also says, that when a church was built there later on, the spot where Christ had stood could never be covered with pavement; and more than that, the marble slabs placed there burst upwards into the faces of those who were laying them. He also says that footmarks in the dust there prove that the Lord had stood on that spot: the footprints are discernible and the ground still retains the depressions his feet had left.

On the second point, namely, why Christ waited forty days to ascend to heaven, let it be known that he did this for three reasons. The first was to provide sure evidence of his resurrection from the dead. It was harder to prove the fact of the resurrection than that of the passion, because from the first day to the third the passion could be proved, but more days were required to establish the truth of the resurrection; therefore a longer time was necessary between the resurrection and the ascension than between the passion and the resurrection. Pope Leo, in his sermon on the Lord's ascension, says: "Today the period of forty days is rounded out, a period fixed by the most sacred planning and lengthened to serve our instruction, so that while the Lord extended his bodily sojourn among us over these days, faith in the resurrection might be supported by necessary evidence. We are grateful for the divine ordering and for the holy fathers' need of delay. They doubted in order that we might not doubt." The second reason was the consolation of the apostles, because the divine consolations are more abundant than our trials, and the time of the Lord's passion was a time of tribulation for the apostles, so the days of consolation had to outnumber the days of tribulation. Thirdly, there was a mystical meaning involved: we were given to understand that the divine consolations are to be compared with our tribulations as a year is compared with a day, a day with an hour, an hour with a moment. The comparison of year to day we find in Isa. 61:2: "To proclaim the acceptable year of the Lord and the day of vengeance of our God." Thus one day of trial yields a year of consolation. The ratio of day to hour is manifest from the fact that the Lord lay dead for forty hours, a time of tribulation, and, rising from the dead, appeared to the disciples over forty days for their consolation. Hence the *Gloss* says: "He had been dead for forty hours, so for forty days he demonstrated that he was alive." The ratio of hour to moment is suggested in Isa. 54:8: "In a moment of indignation have I hid my face a little while from thee, but with everlasting kindness have I had mercy on thee."

The third question concerned the manner of his ascension. First of all, he ascended powerfully, because he did so by his own power, as we read in Isa. 63:1: "Who is this that cometh from Edom . . . walking in the greatness of his strength?" and John 3:13: "No one has ascended into heaven but he who descended from heaven." Admittedly he ascended in a globe of cloud, but he did not do this because he needed the help of a cloud, but to show that every creature was ready to serve its creator. He rose by the power of his godhead, and this indicates a difference, according to the *Scholastic History*: whereas Enoch was translated into paradise and Elijah went up by a whirlwind into heaven, Jesus ascended by his own power. Enoch, according to Gregory, was engendered by coitus and in turn engendered, Elijah was engendered but did not engender, and Jesus was not engendered nor did he engender.

Secondly, he ascended openly, because the disciples were there to observe it, according to Acts 1:9: "While they looked on, he was raised up." John 16:5: "Now I am going to him who sent me, yet no one of you asks me, 'Where are you going?'" The *Gloss*: "Therefore openly, so that no one needs to ask about what he sees happening with the eyes of his body." He willed to have them see him ascending so that they would be on hand as witnesses of his ascension, would rejoice that a human being was carried up into heaven, and would desire to follow him there.

Thirdly, he went up joyfully, because the angels were jubilant, whence Ps. 46:6 (47:5) says: "God ascended with jubilee." Augustine: "As Christ ascends, the whole heaven quakes, the stars marvel, the heavenly hosts applaud, trumpets sound and blend their dulcet harmonies with the joyous choirs."

Fourthly, he went up swiftly, as Ps. 18:6 b (Douai) says: "He has rejoiced as a giant to run the way." He must have ascended with great speed, since he traversed such a distance, as it were in a moment. Rabbi Moses,[1] the great philosopher, tells us that each orbit or heaven of any of the planets is 500 years across, i.e., the distance from one side to the other is as far as someone could travel on a level road in 500 years, and the distance between one heaven and the next is also, he says, a journey of 500 years. Therefore, since there are seven heavens, from the center of the earth to the vault of the heaven of Saturn, the seventh heaven, there will be, according to Rabbi Moses, a journey that would take 7,000 years, and to the dome of the empyrean, 7,700—i.e., as far as one would go on a level road in 7,700 years if he lived that long, each year comprising 365 days and a day's march 40 kilometers, each kilometer being 2,000 paces or cubits long. This is what Rabbi Moses says: whether it be true or not only God knows, for he, who made all things in number, weight, and measure, knows this measurement. So it was a great leap that Christ made from earth to heaven; and about this leap and some others that Christ made, Ambrose says as follows: "By a leap Christ came into this world: he was with the Father and came into the Virgin and leapt from the Virgin to the manger, went down into the Jordan, went up to the cross, went down into the tomb, rose out of the tomb, and is seated at the Father's right hand."

As to the fourth point, namely, with whom Christ ascended, let it be known that he ascended with a great catch of people and a great multitude of angels. That he took a catch of men with him is obvious from what Ps. 68:18 (RSV)

---

[1] Moses Maimonides, Jewish philosopher (1135–1204).

says: "Thou didst ascend the high mount, leading captives in thy train." That he ascended with a multitude of angels is clear from the question which the lesser angels, seeing Christ ascending, asked of the greater ones, as we read in Isa. 63:1: "Who is this that comes from Edom, in dyed garments from Bosra?" The *Gloss* explains that there were some angels who were not fully cognizant of the mystery of the Lord's incarnation, passion, and resurrection, and, seeing him ascending to heaven by his own power with a multitude of angels and holy men, they wondered at this mystery and said to the angels who accompanied the Lord: "Who is this king of glory?" Dionysius, in the seventh chapter of his book *On the Celestial Hierarchy*, seems to insinuate that, while Christ was ascending, three questions were asked by the angels. The superior angels exchanged the first question among themselves, the same superior angels posed the second to Christ as he ascended, and the inferior angels asked the third of the superior ones.

The superior angels, therefore, ask each other: "Who is this who comes from Edom in dyed garments from Bosra?" Edom is interpreted as meaning "bloody" and Bosra as "armed," as if they said: "Who is this who comes from a world bloodied by sin and armed with malice toward God?" or, "Who comes from a bloody world and a fortified hell?" The Lord responds (Isa. 63:1 b): "It is I, that speak justice, and am a defender, to save." Dionysius puts it this way: "For I," he says, "speak of justice and of the judgment of salvation." In the redemption of the human race there was justice, insofar as the Creator brought back his estranged creature from his master; and there was judgment, insofar as by his power he cast the devil, who had no right to invade men, out of the man he had possessed. But in this connection Dionysius raises the following question: "Since these superior angels are close to God and are enlightened immediately by God, why do they question each other as if desiring to learn from each other?" But, as he himself resolves the question and as the commentator expounds it, by the very fact that the angels ask, they show that they seek knowledge. In the fact that they first confer among themselves, they show that they dare not anticipate God's communication to them. They therefore think it best to ask questions among themselves first, lest by too hasty interrogation they forestall the illumination that comes to them from God.

The same superior angels directed the second question to Christ, saying: "Why then is thy apparel red, and thy garments like those of the one who treads in the winepress?" (Isa. 63:2). Here the Lord is said to have had a garment, namely, his body, that was red because it was running with blood, since even then, while he was ascending, he still bore open scars in his body. Here is what Bede says: "The Lord kept his wounds and will keep them until the Judgment, so that he may build up the faith in his resurrection, that he may present his wounds to his Father as he pleads for humankind, that the good may see how mercifully they were redeemed and the bad may recognize how justly they are damned, and that he may carry with him forever the trophies of his victory." Therefore the Lord answers this question as follows: "I have trodden the winepress alone, and not a man of the Gentiles was with me" (Isa. 63:3). The cross may be called a winepress, because on it he was crushed as in a press and his blood gushed forth. Or he may be calling the devil a winepress, because the evil spirit has so bound and entangled the human race with the cords of sin that whatever was spiritual in them is squeezed out and nothing but the sour pulp is left. But our warrior trampled the winepress, broke the sinners' bonds, and, ascending into heaven, opened the heavenly inn and poured the wine of the Spirit.

The third question is the one the minor angels directed to their superiors, saying: "Who is this king of glory?" (Ps. 24:8, 10). The superior angels answered them: "The Lord of hosts is the king of glory!" With regard to this question and this answer Augustine says: "The vastnesses of the air are sanctified by the divine retinue, and the whole crowd of demons flying about in the air flee away from Christ ascending. Angels, hurrying up, ask, Who is this king of glory? The others answer, There he is, the one who is shining white and rose-colored! He is the one who has neither form nor beauty, who was weak on the cross and strong in plunder, worthless in his poor body, armed in battle, foul in death, comely in resurrection, white from the Virgin, rosy from the cross, dark in shame, and bright in heaven!"

On the fifth point—by what merit Christ ascended—be it known that it was by a threefold merit, about which Jerome says this: "Because of truth, since you fulfilled what you had promised; because of meekness, since you are sacrificed like a sheep for the life of the people; because of justice, since you delivered man not by power but by justice; and your right hand, in other words, power and virtue, will lead you wondrously—i.e., up to heaven." (Cf. Ps. 44:5 Douai.)

The answer to the sixth question, namely, where Christ ascended to, is that he rose above all the heavens, according to what we read in Eph. 4:8–10: "He that descended is the same also that ascended above all the heavens that he might fulfill all things." The text says "above all the heavens" because there are several heavens—the material, the rational, the intellectual, and the supersubstantial—beyond which he ascended. The material heaven is multiple and includes the aerial, the ethereal, the Olympian, the fiery, the starry, the crystalline, and the empyrean heavens. The rational heaven is the just man, who is called a heaven by reason of the divine indwelling, because as heaven is God's seat and dwelling place according to Isa. 66:1—"Heaven is my throne"—so also the righteous soul is the seat of wisdom, according to the Book of Wisdom. He is called heaven also by reason of holy conversation, because by their conversation and desire the saints are always dwelling in heaven, as the apostle says: "Our conversation is in heaven." Or again, by reason of continuous operation, because just as heaven is moved continuously, so the saints are continuously in motion by their good works.

The intellectual heaven is the angel. Angels are called heaven because they are like heaven by reason of their dignity and excellence. Of this dignity and excellence Dionysius, in the fourth chapter of his book *On the Divine Names*, says: "The divine minds *are* above all other existent beings, they live above all other living beings, they understand above all sense and reason, and, more than all other existences, they desire the beautiful and the good and participate therein." Secondly, they are most beautiful by reason of their nature and glory. Of this beauty Dionysius in the same book says: "The angel is a manifestation of the hidden light, a mirror pure, brilliant, uncontaminated, undefiled, unspotted, receiving, if it be allowable so to speak, the beauty of the boniform deiformity of God." Thirdly, they are very strong by reason of their virtue and their power. Speaking about the strength of the angels John of Damascus, in Book II, chapter 3, says: "They are strong and ready to carry out God's will, and they are to be found promptly wherever the divine nod commands." For heaven has height, beauty, strength. Of the first two we read in Ecclus. 43:1: "The firmament on high is his beauty, the beauty of heaven"; and of the third, Job 37:18: "Thou [Job] perhaps hast made the heavens with him, which are most strong."

The supersubstantial heaven is equality with the divine excellence, from which Christ came and to which he later ascended. Of this Ps. 18:7 says: "His going out is from the end of heaven, and his circuit even to the end thereof." Therefore Christ went up above all these heavens to the supersubstantial heaven itself. That he ascended through all the material heavens is assured by what is said in Ps. 8:2: "Thy magnificence is elevated above the heavens." He went through all the material heavens to reach the empyrean heaven, but his ascension was not like that of Elijah, who went up in a fiery chariot to the sublunar region but did not go beyond it. Elijah was transferred into the terrestrial paradise, which is as high as the sublunar region but does not transcend it. Christ therefore resides in the empyrean heaven, and this is the special and proper dwelling for him and for the angels and other saints: the habitation befits the inhabitants. This heaven surpasses the other heavens in dignity, priority, location, and extent, and therefore is a fitting habitation for Christ, who transcends all the rational and intellectual heavens in dignity, eternity, immutability, and the range of his power. Likewise, it is a suitable dwelling for the saints, for that heaven is uniform and immobile and has perfect luminosity and limitless capacity, and so is suitable for the angels and the saints, who were uniform in their works, immobile in love, luminous in faith and in knowledge, and capacious in their reception of the Holy Spirit.

That Christ ascended above all the rational heavens, i.e., above all the saints, is clear from what we read in the Song of Sol. 2:8: "Behold, he comes, leaping upon the mountains, bounding over the hills." Here the mountains stand for angels and the hills for saintly men. That he ascended higher than all the intellectual heavens, i.e., the angels, is evident from what Ps. 103:2 says: "Who makest the clouds thy ascent, who walkest upon the wings of the winds," and from what we read in Ps. 17:11: "He ascended upon the cherubim, and he flew; he flew upon the wings of the winds."

Christ ascended all the way to the supersubstantial heaven, which means that he ascended to equality with God, and this is clear from the last chapter of Mark (16:19): "The Lord Jesus, after he had spoken to them, was taken up into heaven and sits at the right hand of God." The right hand of God is coequality with God. Bernard: "To my Lord, and to him alone, the Lord promised and gave a seat at the right hand of his own glory, as being equal in glory, consubstantial in essence, alike in generation, not unequal in majesty nor later in time because eternal." Or it can be said that Christ in his ascension was sublime in four distinct ways—in terms of place and of the reward received, and in his knowledge and his virtue. Of the first, Eph. 4:10: "He that descended is the same also that ascended above all the heavens"; of the second, Phil. 2:8–9: "He humbled himself, becoming obedient unto death, etc." To this, Augustine says: "Humility merits glory, glory is the reward of humility." Of the third, Ps. 17:11 (Douai) says: "He sits enthroned upon the cherubim," i.e., above all the fullness of knowledge. The fourth sublimity is evident because he also ascended above the seraphim; Eph. 3:19: "To know also the charity of Christ, which surpasses all knowledge."

Regarding the seventh question, namely, why Christ ascended, it is to be noted that his ascension was fruitful or beneficial in nine ways. The first is that it brought down the love of God upon us; John 16:7: "If I go not, the Paraclete will not come to you; but if I go, I will send him to you." The second fruit is our greater knowledge of God; John 14:28: "If you loved me, you would indeed be glad because I go to the Father, for the Father is greater than I." To this Augustine says: "Therefore I take away this servile form, in which the Father is greater than I, so that you may be able the better to see God otherwise, as spirit." The third benefit is the merit of faith. Of this Pope Leo says in his sermon on the Lord's ascension: "Then a more instructed faith began to advance, with the stride of the mind, toward the Son as equal to the Father, contact with the corporeal substance in Christ, by which he is less than the Father, no longer being needed. For this is the strength of great minds—to believe without hesitating things that the eye of the body cannot see, and to fix desire on what you cannot reach by sight." Augustine, in the *Confessions*: "He has rejoiced as a giant to run the way: he did not tarry but ran, crying out by words, by deeds, by death, by life, by descent and ascension, crying out to us to return to him, and he departed from our sight that we might come back into our hearts and find him there."

The fourth fruit is our security. Christ ascended in order to be our advocate with the Father. We can be secure indeed when we realize that we have such an advocate to plead our cause; 1 John 2:1: "We have an advocate with the Father, Jesus Christ the just; and he is the propitiation for our sins." About this security

Bernard says: "O man, you have sure access to God, when the mother stands before the Son and the Son stands before the Father, the mother shows her Son her bosom and her breasts, the Son shows his Father his side and his wounds. Surely then, where there are so many marks of love, there can be no refusal."

The fifth benefit is our dignity. Very great indeed is our dignity, when our nature is exalted to the right hand of God! The angels, having in mind this dignity of mankind, forbade men to worship them, as we read in Apoc. 19:10: "I fell down at his feet to adore him. And he said to me, You must not do that. I am a fellow servant with you and your brethren." To this the *Gloss* adds: "[The angel] allowed himself to be adored, but after the Lord's ascension, seeing a man exalted above himself, he was afraid to receive adoration." Pope Leo, in a sermon on the Lord's ascension, says: "On this day the nature of our humanity was raised up beyond the height of every power to be seated with God the Father, in order that God's grace should become more wondrous, since what men had thought to have a just claim to their veneration had been removed from their sight, yet faith did not falter nor hope waver nor charity grow cool."

The sixth fruit of the Lord's ascension is the strengthening of our hope; Heb. 4:14: "Having therefore a great high priest who has passed into the heavens, Jesus the Son of God, let us hold fast the confession of our hope"; and Heb. 6:18–19 (RSV): "That we who fled for refuge might have strong encouragement to seize the hope set before us. We have this as a sure and steadfast anchor of the soul, a hope that enters into the inner shrine behind the curtain, where Jesus has gone as a forerunner in our behalf." On this, Leo again: "Christ's ascension is our elevation, and where the glory of the head has gone before, there the hope of the body tends also."

The seventh benefit is that the way is marked out for us; Mic. 2:13: "He shall go up that shall open the way before them." Augustine: "The Savior himself has become your way: arise and walk, you have the way, don't be sluggish!" The eighth fruit is the opening of the gate of heaven; for as the first Adam opened the gates of hell, so the second the gates of paradise. So the Church sings: "You overcame the pain of death and opened the kingdom of heaven to those who believe." The ninth is the preparation of the place; John 14:2: "I go to prepare a place for you." Augustine: "O Lord, do prepare what you are preparing: for you are preparing us for yourself and you are preparing yourself for us when you prepare a place both for yourself in us and for us in yourself."

73. The Holy Spirit

On this day of Pentecost, as sacred history testifies in the Acts of the Apostles, the Holy Spirit was sent upon the apostles in tongues of fire. About this sending or coming eight points are to be considered: first, by whom the Spirit was sent; second, in how many ways he is or was sent; third, the time at which he was sent; fourth, how many times he was sent; fifth, how he was sent; sixth, upon whom he was sent; seventh, for what reasons he was sent; eighth, what led to his being sent.

On the first point, let it be noted that the Father sent the Spirit, the Son sent him, and the Holy Spirit gave and sent himself. The Father sent him; John 14:25: "The Counselor, whom the Father will send in my name. . . ." The Son sent him; John 16:7: "If I do go away, I will send him to you." In worldly affairs one can discern a triple comparison to illustrate the relationship of the sender to the person or thing sent. The sender gives being to what is sent, as the sun sends its rays; the sender gives power to what is sent, as the lancer sends the lance; the sender gives jurisdiction and authority, as the ruler sends the ambassador. This triple relationship can be seen in the sending of the Holy Spirit: he is sent by the Father and the Son as having from them being, power, and authority to act. Nevertheless, the Holy Spirit gave and sent himself, as seems to be indicated in John 16:13, where we read: "But when the Spirit of truth comes, he will guide you into all the truth." Pope Saint Leo says in a sermon for Pentecost: "The Blessed Trinity, the immutable Godhead, is one in substance, undivided in operation, unanimous in willing, equal in omnipotence, equal also in glory. The mercy of the Trinity apportioned the work of our redemption within Itself, so that the Father is propitiated, the Son propitiates, the Holy Spirit lights the fire of love."

The Holy Spirit is God, and therefore it is rightly said that he gives himself. Ambrose, in his book *On the Holy Spirit*, shows that the Spirit is God, saying: "Four things prove the manifest glory of his divinity. He is known to be God either because he is without sin, or because he forgives sins, or because he is not a creature but the Creator, or because he does not adore but is adored." And how the Blessed Trinity has given Itself to us totally is shown in this: the Father has offered us all he had, because, as Augustine says, he sent his Son as the price of our redemption and the Holy Spirit as the privilege of our adoption, and himself he holds in reserve as the inheritance due to us as adopted sons and daughters. Likewise the Son has offered himself to us totally, because, as Bernard says, he is himself shepherd, himself pasture, himself redemption, for he gave us his soul as ransom, his blood as drink, his flesh as food, and his divinity as reward. The Holy Spirit, too, offered and offers all his gifts totally to us, as we read in I Cor. 12:8–10: "To one indeed, by the Spirit, is given the word of wisdom; and to another the word of knowledge, according to the same Spirit; to another, faith by the same Spirit," and so on. Pope Leo says: "The Holy Spirit is the inspirer of faith, the teacher of knowledge, the font of love, the seal of chastity, and the cause of the whole of salvation."

On the second question, namely, the number of ways the Spirit is or was sent, note that he is sent in two ways, visibly and invisibly—invisibly when he penetrates into holy souls, visibly when his presence is shown by some visible sign. Of the invisible sending John 3:8 says: "The Spirit breathes where he wills, and you hear his voice but you do not know whence he comes or whither he goes." No wonder, because, as Bernard says regarding the invisible Word: "It does not come in through the eyes, because it has no color; nor through the nostrils, because it does not mingle with the air but with the mind, nor does it taint the air but makes it; nor through the jaws, because it cannot be chewed or gulped; nor through corporeal touch, because it is not palpable. So you ask: if the ways of the Word are so untraceable, how do you know he is present? The answer: I have known his presence when my heart was touched with fear; when I fled from vice, I knew the strength of his power; from what my eyes tell me and make me see, I marvel at the depth of the Word's wisdom; from the slightest amendment of my manner of life, I have come to experience his kindness and gentleness, and from the reformation and renewal of the spirit of my mind, I have somehow perceived the splendor of his beauty; and seeing all this at once, I stand in awe of the multiplicity of his greatness." Thus far Bernard.

The sending is visible when it is marked by some visible sign. It is to be noted that the sending of the Holy Spirit was shown by five kinds of visible signs. Firstly, he appeared in the form of a dove over Christ at his baptism; so Luke 3:22: "The Holy Spirit descended upon him in bodily form as a dove." Secondly, he came in a shining cloud around Christ transfigured; Matt. 17:5: "He was still speaking when lo, a bright cloud overshadowed them." As at the Lord's baptism so also at his glorification, the Holy Spirit manifested the mystery of the Blessed Trinity, in the former as a dove, in the latter as a bright cloud. Thirdly, he came as a breath; John 20:22: "He breathed upon them and said to them, 'Receive the Holy Spirit, etc.'" Fourthly, as fire, and fifthly, in the shape of a tongue; and in this double form he appeared on this day.

The Spirit showed himself in the forms of five different things to let it be known that he produces the properties of these things in the hearts in which he makes his dwelling. First, he was seen in the form of a dove. The dove's call is a moaning sound, it has no bile or bitterness, it nests in the clefts of the rock. So the Holy Spirit makes those whom he fills moan over their sins; Isa. 59:11: "We shall all roar like bears and shall lament as mournful doves"; Rom. 8:26: "The Spirit himself intercedes for us with sighs too deep for words"—i.e., he makes us plead and groan. The Spirit also frees us of the bile of bitterness; Wisd. 12:1: "O how good and sweet is thy Spirit, O Lord, in all of us"; and in the seventh chapter of the same book he is called gentle, loving, and beneficent because he makes us gentle in speech, loving in heart, and beneficent in action. He lives in "the clefts of the rock," by which we understand the wounds of Christ. In the Song of Sol. 2:10 we read: "Arise, make haste, my love, my bride, and come, my dove in the clefts of the rock," and the *Gloss* explains: "Keep my nestlings warm for me by the inpouring of the Holy Spirit"; and the *Gloss* on the clefts of the rock: "in Christ's wounds." In Lam. 4:20 Jeremiah says: "The breath (*spiritus*) of our mouth, Christ the Lord, is taken in our sins, to whom we said, Under thy shadow we shall live among the Gentiles"—as if he said: "The Holy Spirit (who is the breath of our mouth, since our mouth is Christ the Lord because he is our mouth and our flesh) makes us say to Christ, 'We shall live in your shadow, that is, in your passion (in which Christ was in darkness and despised), by remembering it continually.'"

The second visible sign was the cloud. A cloud is lifted above the earth, it cools the earth and generates rain. So the Spirit lifts those whom he fills by making them look down on the things of earth; Ezek. 8:3: "The spirit lifted me up between earth and heaven, etc."; also the same, 1:19–21: "When the living creatures rose from the earth, the wheels rose. Wherever the spirit would go, they went, and the wheels rose along with them; for the spirit of life was in the wheels." Similarly Gregory: "Once the spirit has been tasted, all flesh loses its savor."

The Spirit provides cooling against the incitements of vice; so Mary was told: "The Holy Spirit will come upon you and the power of the Most High will overshadow you"—i.e., will give you coolness from all heat of vices. Hence also the Holy Spirit is called water, which has regenerative power; John 7:38–39: "Scripture says, 'Out of his belly shall flow rivers of living water.' Now this he said of the Spirit which those who believed in him were to receive." Thirdly, the Spirit generates a rain of tears; Ps. 147:18: "His wind shall blow and the waters shall run"—i.e., the waters of tears.

Third, he was shown in the visible form of breath. Breath is mobile, hot, smooth, and necessary for breathing. So the Holy Spirit is mobile, i.e., quick at diffusing himself; indeed he is more mobile than all else that moves. On the text, "Suddenly a sound came from heaven like the rush of a mighty wind," the *Gloss* says: "No obstacles can slow the grace of the Holy Spirit." Second, he is hot in order to start a fire; Luke 12:49: "I came to cast fire upon the earth and would that it were already kindled." Hence the Spirit is compared to the hot south wind; Song of Sol. 4:16: "Awake, O north wind, and come, O south wind. Blow upon my garden, let its fragrance be wafted abroad." Third, the Spirit is smooth in order to smooth and soften. To convey this he is called by the name of ointment, as is clear from the first letter of John, 2:27: "His anointing teaches you about everything." Also by the name of dew, so the Church sings: "May he make you fruitful by the inward shower of dew." Or he is called a gentle breeze; 1 Kings 19:12: "And after the fire a whistling of a gentle air," and there was the Lord. Moreover, breath is necessary for breathing—so necessary, indeed, that if it was taken away even for a short time, a man would die very quickly. This is also to be understood of the Holy Spirit. So Ps. 104:30: "Thou shalt take away their breath and they shall fail and shall return to their dust; thou shalt send forth thy Spirit and they shall be created, and thou shalt renew the face of the earth." So also John 6:63: "It is the Spirit that gives life."

Fourth, the Holy Spirit was shown in the appearance of fire, and fifthly, in the shape of tongues, as we read: "There appeared to them parted tongues, as it were of fire: and it sat upon every one of them." Why the Spirit appeared on this day in the double form of fire and tongues will be explained further on.

About the third question, namely, at what time the sending of the Spirit occurred, note that he was sent on the fiftieth day after Easter. This day was chosen to make it clear that from the Holy Spirit come the perfection of the law, eternal reward, and remission of sins. The perfection of the law is his work, because, according to the *Gloss*, on the fiftieth day, after the preliminary immolation of the lamb, the law was given in fire, and in the New Testament, on the fiftieth day from Christ's Pasch the Spirit descended in fire; the law on Mount Sinai and the Spirit on Mount Sion, the law at the top of a high mountain and the Spirit in the upper room. By this it is implied that the Holy Spirit himself is the perfection of the whole law because the fullness of the law is love.

The fiftieth day signifies eternal reward. The *Gloss* says: "Just as the period of forty days after his resurrection, during which Christ was with his disciples, stands for the present Church, so the fiftieth day on which the Spirit is given signifies the wage of eternal reward." And the remission of sins is indicated, as the *Gloss* points out: "Therefore in the fiftieth year the jubilee indulgence was granted and sins were remitted by the Holy Spirit . . ." and the *Gloss* continues: "In the spiritual jubilee the guilty are absolved, debts are forgiven, exiles are called back to their homeland, the lost heritage is restored, slaves—i.e., men sold into sin—are freed from the yoke of servitude." Thus far the *Gloss*. Those under sentence of death are pardoned and set free, hence Rom. 8:2: "The law of the Spirit of life in Christ Jesus has set me free from the law of sin and death." The debts of sin are remitted, because love covers a multitude of sins. Exiles are called back to their homeland, so Ps. 142:10: "Thy good spirit shall lead me into the right land." The lost heritage is regained; Rom. 8:16–17: "It is the Spirit himself bearing witness with our spirit that we are children of God, and if children, then heirs." Slaves are liberated; 2 Cor. 3:17: "Where the Spirit of the Lord is, there is freedom."

Now for the fourth question, namely, how many times the Spirit was sent to the apostles. According to the *Gloss* he was given to them three times—before Christ's passion, after his resurrection, and after his ascension. The first time he came to empower them to perform miracles, the second time to forgive sins; the third time he gave them strength of heart.

First, then, because the Lord was sending the apostles to preach and drive out demons and cure sickness, he gave them the power to do miracles, and these miracles are the work of the Holy Spirit, as we read in Matt. 12:28: "If it is by the Spirit of God that I cast out demons, then the kingdom of God has come upon you." It does not follow, however, that everyone who has the Holy Spirit can perform miracles. Miracles, as Gregory says, do not make a man a saint; they show that he is a saint. Nor does it follow that everyone who does miracles has the Holy Spirit, because the wicked declare that they have performed them, saying: "Lord, Lord, have we not prophesied in thy name and cast out devils in thy name and done many miracles in thy name?" God does miracles by his own authority, angels because they are superior to matter, demons through natural forces inherent in things, magicians through secret contracts with demons, good Christians by justice publicly recognized, bad Christians by such justice simulated.

The second time Christ gave the Spirit to the apostles was when he breathed upon them and said: "Receive the Holy Spirit. Whose sins you shall forgive they are forgiven them, whose sins you shall retain they are retained." Yet no one can remit sin as to the stain which it produces in the soul, nor as to the guilt, i.e., the eternal punishment that it calls for, nor as to the offense to God: all these are remitted only by the infusion of grace and by virtue of contrition. The priest is said to absolve because he declares that the fault has been remitted, because he commutes the penalty of purgatory to a temporal one, and because he dispenses a part of the temporal punishment.

The third time the Spirit was given was on this day, when the disciples' hearts were so strengthened that they had no fear of torments; Ps. 32:6: ". . . all the power of them by the spirit of his mouth." Augustine says: "Such is the grace of the Holy Spirit that if he finds sadness he dispels it, if an evil desire he quells it, if fear he drives it out." Pope Leo says: "The apostles hoped for the Holy Spirit, not that he would then come to dwell in holy souls for the first time but that he would inflame hearts that were already sanctified with still greater fervor, and would inundate them more copiously, piling up his gifts, not starting them or working something new, but rather lavishing greater riches."

Our fifth point is the manner of the Spirit's sending, and we note that he was sent with sound and in fiery tongues, and that these tongues of fire appeared sitting upon the apostles. The sound was sudden, heavenly, vehement, and filling: sudden because no obstacle can slow the Spirit's action; heavenly because he produces heavenly effects; vehement because he induces filial fear, or because he repels eternal woe (*vehemens* = *veh adimens*, taking away woe) or because he moves the mind away from all carnal love (*vehens mentem*, moving the mind). The sound was filling because the Holy Spirit filled all the apostles, as we read:

"They were all filled with the Holy Spirit." There was in the apostles a threefold sign of this fullness. The first sign consists in not resounding, as a full wine cask does not resound, and as in Job 6:5: "Will the ox low when he stands before a full manger?"—as if to say that when the manger of the heart contains the fullness of grace, there should be no lowing of impatience. The apostles had this sign because in tribulation they uttered no complaint but rather went from the presence of the council rejoicing that they were accounted worthy to suffer reproach for the name of Jesus (Acts 5:41).

The second sign of fullness is that no more can be taken in—in other words, that's enough. When a vessel is filled with a fluid, it cannot take any more; similarly, when a man has eaten his fill, he has no more appetite. So the saints, who have the fullness of grace, can no longer receive another fluid, namely, that of earthly love; Isa. 1:11: "I am full, I desire not holocausts." In the same way those who have tasted the sweetness of heaven do not thirst for earthly pleasure. Augustine: "When anyone has drunk from the river of Paradise, one drop of which is greater than the ocean, in him the thirst for this world is quenched." This sign was in the apostles: they wanted to have nothing of their own and to share everything in common.

The third sign of fullness is overflow, as is seen in a river in flood; Ecclus. 24:23: "It overflows, like the Pishon, with wisdom." Literally, that river regularly overflows its banks and inundates the adjacent land. The apostles began to overflow, because they started to speak in various languages. The *Gloss* says: "Behold a sign of fullness; the full vase bursts, fire cannot be hidden in a man's bosom"; and so they began to irrigate what lay around them, Peter started to speak, and three thousand were converted.

The Spirit was sent in tongues of fire, and about this we shall see three things: why he came in tongues conjoined with fire, why in fire rather than in some other element, and why in tongues rather than in some other member.

First, note that there are three motives for his appearing in fiery tongues. The first was to enable the apostles to proclaim words of fire: the second, that they might preach a law of fire, namely, the law of love. Of these two Bernard says: "The Holy Spirit came in fiery tongues in order that they might speak words of fire in the languages of all the peoples, and that fiery tongues might preach a law of fire." The third reason is that they should know it was the Holy Spirit, who is fire, that spoke through them; they were not to have any doubt about this, nor to claim the conversion of others as their own doing. Thus all who heard their words heard them as the words of God.

On the second point, let it be known that there are several reasons for the sending of the Spirit in the form of fire. The first is related to his sevenfold grace, for the Spirit, like fire, lowers the lofty by the gift of fear, softens the hard by the gift of piety, enlightens the obscure through knowledge, restrains the unsure by the gift of counsel, reinforces the weak through fortitude, refines the metals by removing dross through the gift of understanding, and mounts upward by the gift of wisdom.

The Spirit came as fire also by reason of his dignity and excellence. Fire surpasses the other elements by its appearance, its rank, and its power: by its appearance because of the beauty of its light, in rank by the sublimity of its position, in power by its vigor in action. So too the Spirit excels in all these respects—in the first, because he is called the Holy Spirit without stain, in the second because he penetrates all intelligent spirits, in the third because he possesses all power, as we read in Wisd. 7:22–23.

The third reason for the Spirit's coming in fire is its manifold efficacy. This reason is explained by Rabanus as follows: "Fire has four natures; it burns, it purges, it heats, and it gives light. So likewise the Spirit burns away sins, purges hearts, dispels tepidity, enlightens ignorance." Thus Rabanus. The Spirit burns away sins; Zech. 13:9: "I will bring them through the fire and will refine them as silver is refined." The prophets prayed to be burned with this fire, saying (Ps. 25:2 Vulgate): "Prove me, O Lord; burn my reins and my heart." He purges hearts; Isa. 4:4: "When the Lord shall wash away the blood of Jerusalem from its midst by the spirit of judgment and by the spirit of burning." He dispels tepidity, and Rom. 12:11 describes those whom the Holy Spirit fills as "aglow with the Spirit." Gregory says: "The Holy Spirit appeared in fire, because he drives the torpor of coldness out of every heart he fills, and sets that heart afire with desire for his eternity." He enlightens ignorance; Wisd. 9:17: "Who shall know thy thought, except thou give wisdom, and send thy Holy Spirit from above?" And 1 Cor. 2:10 says: "God has revealed to us through the Spirit."

The fourth reason is the nature of love itself. Fire expresses the significance of love in three ways. First, fire is always in motion, and love keeps those whom the Holy Spirit fills always moving in good works. So Gregory says: "The love of God is never idle. If it is love, it accomplishes great things, and if it accomplishes nothing, it is not love." Second, of all the elements fire is the most formal: it has little matter and much form. In the same way the love of the Holy Spirit makes those whom he fills have little love for earthly things and much love for celestial and spiritual things, so that it is not carnal things loved carnally but rather spiritual things loved spiritually. Bernard distinguishes four ways of loving: to love the flesh for the flesh, the spirit for the flesh, the flesh for the spirit, and the spirit for itself. Third, fire has the power to bend high things downwards, to tend upwards, to bring fluids together and coagulate them; and by that we are to understand the triple force of love, as we learn from Dionysius's words in the book *On the Divine Names*: "Love has three kinds of force, namely, the inclinative, the elevative, and the coordinative: it inclines the higher toward the lower, elevates the lower toward the higher, and coordinates equals with equals." Thus Dionysius. The Holy Spirit produces this triple power of love in those whom he fills, because he lowers them by humility and contempt of self, elevates them toward desire for the things that are above, and coordinates them by uniformity of moral values.

Now why did the Spirit appear in the shape of a tongue rather than in that of another member? For three reasons. The tongue is the member ignited by the fire of Gehenna, is hard to control, and is useful when well controlled. Therefore, because the tongue was inflamed by hellfire, it needed the fire of the Holy Spirit; James 3:6: "Our tongue is a fire, a world of iniquity." Because it is hard to control the tongue, it needs the grace of the Spirit more than the other members do; James 3:7: "Every nature of beasts and of birds and of the rest is tamed by the nature of man, but the tongue no man can tame." Because the tongue is very useful if well controlled, it needed to have the Holy Spirit as its controller.

By appearing in the shape of a tongue, the Spirit also indicated how necessary he is to preachers. Preachers need him because he makes them speak fervently, without hesitation, and therefore he was sent in the appearance of fire. Bernard: "The Holy Spirit came upon the apostles in tongues of fire so that they might speak fiery words and that fiery tongues might preach a law of fire." They could speak confidently, not faintheartedly; Acts 2:4, 4:29: "They were all filled with the Holy Spirit and began to speak the word with all confidence." They could speak differently according to the different capacities of their hearers, and Acts says that they spoke in various tongues. They spoke usefully, for edification and benefit; Isa. 61:1: "The Spirit of the Lord is upon me, because the Lord has anointed me" . . . to bring good tidings to the afflicted.

The tongues of fire appeared sitting upon the apostles, to signify that he was needed by those who preside; and indeed the Spirit is needed by presiders and judges because he confers authority to remit sin; John 20:23: "Receive the Holy Spirit. Whose sins you shall forgive, etc." They need wisdom in order to judge; Isa. 42:1: "I have put my spirit upon him; he will bring forth justice to the nations." They need kind hearts in order to give support; Num. 11:17: "I will give them some of the spirit that is upon you; and they shall bear the burden of the people with you." The spirit of Moses was the spirit of kindness, as is clear from Num. 12:3: "now the man Moses was very meek." And they should be adorned with holiness so as to communicate holiness; Job 26:13: "His spirit has adorned the heavens."

Our sixth question concerns those upon whom the Spirit was sent, and we note that he was sent upon the disciples, who were clean receptacles, apt to receive the Holy Spirit due to seven qualities that were in them. First, they were quiet, restful people, as is indicated in the Scripture: "When the day of Pentecost had come . . . ," i.e., the day of rest. The feast of Pentecost was appointed for rest; Isa. 66:1c–2: "What is this place of my rest? . . . To whom shall I look, but to him that is humble and of a contrite spirit?" Second, they were united in love, as we read: "They were all together"—meaning of one heart and one soul. For just as a man's spirit does not give life to the members of his body unless they are united, neither does the Holy Spirit vivify spiritual members [unless they are united]. And as a fire is extinguished when the burning wood is scattered, so discord among men puts out the Holy Spirit, whence we sing about the apostles: "The God of gods found them united in charity and flooded them with his light." Third, they were in a secret place, as the text notes, "in one place," namely, in the cenacle; hence Hos. 2:14: "I will bring her into the wilderness and speak tenderly to her." Fourth, they were zealous in prayer, whence the text: "All these with one accord devoted themselves to prayer." So we sing

> Apostolis orantibus
> Repente de coelo sonus
> Deum venisse nuntiat.[1]

Prayer is necessary for the reception of the Holy Spirit, as we know from Wisd. 7:7: "I called upon God, and the spirit of wisdom came upon me." We also read in John 14:16: "I will pray the Father and he will give you another counselor."

Fifth, they were graced with humility, which is indicated when they are described as "sitting." So Ps. 104:10: "Thou makest springs to gush forth in the valleys," i.e., you give the grace of the Holy Spirit to the humble; and "What is this place of my rest? . . . him that is humble, etc." Sixth, they were joined together in peace, as we see from the fact that they were in Jerusalem, which name means "vision of peace." The Lord shows that peace is necessary for the receiving of the Holy Spirit; John 20:19f.: he first offered peace, saying "peace be with you," then breathed upon them and said: "Receive the Holy Spirit." Seventh, they were lifted up in contemplation, which is indicated by the fact that they received the Spirit in the upper room. To this the *Gloss* says: "Whoever desires the Holy Spirit rises above his fleshly dwelling and tramples it by spiritual contemplation."

The seventh point, for what reasons the Spirit was sent: note that he was sent for six reasons, which are noted in Christ's promises at the Last Supper: "The Paraclete, the Holy Spirit, etc."; John 14:26ff. Firstly, he is sent to console the sorrowful, because he is called the Paraclete, which also means consoler; Isa. 61:1–2: "The Spirit of the Lord is upon me . . . to bring good tidings to the afflicted . . . to those who mourn in Sion." Gregory: "The Spirit is called the Consoler because while he prepares the hope of pardon in those who grieve for having committed sin, he lifts their spirit out of the affliction of sadness." Secondly, he is sent to give life to the dead, and so is called Spirit, because it is the spirit that gives life; Ezek. 37:4: "O dry bones, hear the word of the Lord. Behold I will cause breath to enter you and you shall live." Thirdly, to sanctify the unclean, and so he is called *sanctus*, holy; for as he is called the Spirit, which gives life, so he is also called *sanctus*, because he sanctifies, makes holy and cleanses. Hence "holy" and "clean" are equivalent. Ps. 45(46):5: "The stream of the river makes the city of God joyful," i.e., the cleansing and overflowing grace

---

[1] While the apostles are at prayer / suddenly a sound from heaven / announces that God has come.

of the Holy Spirit gives joy to the city of God, meaning the Church of God, and by that river he has sanctified his most high tabernacle.

Fourthly, to establish love among those divided by discord and hatred: this is indicated by the title "Father." He is called Father because by his nature he loves us; John 16:27: "The Father himself loves you." Thus the Father, and we his children, and brothers toward each other and among brothers, persevere in perfect friendship. Fifthly, to save the just; this is shown by the words "in my name," the name Jesus meaning salvation. Therefore the Father sent the Spirit in the name of Jesus, in the name of salvation, to show that he came to save the nations. Sixthly, to teach the ignorant, so: "He will teach you all things."

On the eighth point, be it noted that the Spirit is given or was sent in the primitive Church, first in response to prayer: the apostles were praying, and (Luke 3:21) Jesus was praying and the Holy Spirit descended upon him. Second, through devout and attentive hearing of the word of God; Acts 10:44: "While Peter was still saying this, the Holy Spirit fell on all who heard the word." Third, through assiduous doing of works, as is indicated in the laying on of hands; Acts 8:17: "Then they laid their hands upon them, and they received the Holy Spirit." Or the laying on of hands signifies absolution, as is done in confession.

※

---

74. Saints Gordianus and Epimachus

Gordianus comes from *geos*, which means dogma or house, and *dyan*, which means bright; hence a bright house in which God dwelt. Thus Augustine says in the book *The City of God*: "A good house is one in which the parts fit well together, and which is spacious and full of light." So Saint Gordianus was well disposed by maintaining harmony, spacious through charity, and filled with the light of truth. Epimachus comes from *epi*, above, and *machin*, king, so a high king; or from *epi*, above, and *machos*, fight, so a fighter for the things above.

Gordianus was a commissioner of Emperor Julian. Once he was trying to compel a Christian named Januarius to sacrifice to the gods, but listened to his preaching and, with his wife Mariria and fifty-three others, was converted to the faith. When Julian learned of this, he sent Januarius into exile and condemned Gordianus to be beheaded if he refused to offer sacrifice. So blessed Gordianus was beheaded and his body thrown to the dogs, but when it lay untouched for a week, his retainers took it away and buried it with the body of Saint Epimachus, whom the aforesaid Julian had had put to death a short time earlier. They were buried about a mile from the city about A.D. 360.

---

75. Saints Nereus and Achilleus

Nereus is interpreted counsel of light, or it is derived from *nereth*, i.e., never guilty. Saint Nereus was a counsel of light by his preaching of virginity; he was a lamp in his virtuous everyday life; he was hasty in his fervor for heaven, and *ne reus*, i.e., never guilty, in the purity of his conscience. Achilleus comes from *achi*, which means my brother, and *lesa*, salvation, as the saint was the salvation of his brothers. The passions of these two saints were written by Euthices, Victorinus, and Macro, servants of Christ.

Nereus and Achilleus were the eunuchs in charge of the private chambers of Domitilla, the niece of the emperor Domitian. When this lady was about to be married to Aurelian, the son of a consul, and was arrayed in jewels and purple garments, Nereus and Achilleus preached the Christian faith to her and commended virginity to her for many reasons. They showed her that virginity was dear to God, related to the angels, and innate in human beings. On the other hand, a wife was subject to her husband and exposed to kicks and punches. She might give birth to one or more deformed children. Furthermore, they said, she found it hard to accept correction from her loving mother, but she would have to put up with her spouse's high-handed reprimands.

Domitilla said many things in reply, among them this: "I know my father was a jealous man and my mother had to take much abuse from him. Is my husband bound to be like that?" They answered: "As long as men are simply betrothed, they are all sweetness and light, but once they are married, they are cruel and domineering, and sometimes they prefer the chambermaid to her mistress! Moreover, every virtue, if lost, can be recovered by doing penance: virginity alone cannot be recalled to its pristine state. The guilt can be expunged by penance, but virginity cannot be regained." Having heard them out, Flavia Domitilla accepted the faith, made a vow of virginity, and took the veil from Pope Saint Clement.

When her husband-to-be was apprised of all this, he obtained the emperor's permission and sent the virgin with Saints Nereus and Achilleus into exile on the island of Pontus, hoping that this would change her decision. Some time later he himself went to the island and offered many gifts to the saints to induce them to persuade the virgin to change, but they wanted none of it and, to the contrary, strengthened her in her faith in the Lord. When they were under pressure to offer sacrifice, they said that they had been baptized by the apostle Saint Peter and that nothing would make them offer sacrifice to the idols, so they were beheaded about A.D. 80, and their bodies were buried near the tomb of Saint Petronilla.

There were others, namely Victorinus, Euthices, and Marco, to whom Domitilla was attached, and these men Aurelian compelled to work all day as slaves on his estates, giving them dog's food to eat at nightfall. In the end he had Euthices beaten until he expired, and had Victorinus suffocated in fetid waters. Marco he ordered to be crushed to death under an enormous rock. When this monstrous rock, which seventy men could hardly budge, was thrown on Marco, he caught it on his shoulders and carried it for two miles, as if it were as light as chaff. This brought many to embrace the faith, and the consul's son had Marco put to death.

After that, Aurelian took Domitilla back from exile and sent two young women named Euphrosina and Theodora, who were foster-sisters of hers, to induce her to change her mind, but instead, she converted them to the faith. Then Aurelian came to Domitilla with three minstrels and the pledged spouses of the two maidens, to proceed with the celebration of her wedding, after which he would take her to bed, by force if necessary. But Domitilla had already converted the two young men, so Aurelian brought Domitilla into the bedchamber and there ordered the minstrels to sing and the others to dance with him, intending to ravish the virgin thereafter. But the mimes fainted with exhaustion due to their singing, and the others likewise due to their dancing, except Aurelian himself, who danced without stopping for two days, until he collapsed and expired. His brother Luxurius, with the emperor's permission, had all the believers killed. He had a fire set in the room where the three virgins were lodged, and as they prayed together, they breathed their last. The next morning Saint Caesarius recovered their bodies, still unmarked, and buried them.

76. Saint Pancratius

Pancratius[1] comes from *pan*, meaning all or the whole, *gratus*, pleasing, and *citius*, faster, so the whole more quickly pleasing, because Saint Pancratius was pleasing to God quickly, in his childhood. Or, as the *Glossary* says, *pancras* means booty, a *pancranarius* is one who is beaten with scourges, *pancras* is a varicolored precious stone. So Saint Pancratius robbed a booty of captives, was subjected to the scourges of torture, and was varicolored by the variety of his virtues.

Pancratius was born of parents belonging to the high nobility. He was bereaved of father and mother while in Phrygia, and was left to the care of his uncle Dionysius. They went to Rome, where they had a large patrimony. In a village that was on their estates Pope Cornelius was in hiding with a number of the faithful, and Dionysius and Pancratius were converted to the faith of Christ by this Cornelius. In time Dionysius died a peaceful death, and Pancratius was taken prisoner and presented to the emperor Diocletian. He was then about fourteen years old.

Diocletian said to him: "My dear boy, take my advice and save yourself from a bad death! Because you are still a child, you are easily misled, and because you are certainly noble and the son of a man whom I esteemed very highly, I beg of you, give up this madness, and I will treat you as if you were my own son." Pancratius answered: "I may be a child in body but my mind is older, and, by the power of my Lord Jesus Christ in me, your terror means no more to me than that idol we are looking at. As for the gods you bid me worship, they were deceivers and corrupters of their own women, who did not spare even their kin. If you today knew that your slaves were like those gods, you would promptly have them put to death! I marvel that you can worship such gods without being ashamed!" The emperor, conscious of having been outdone by a child, ordered him beheaded on the Via Aureliana, about A.D. 287. Cocavilla, the wife of a senator, took care to have him buried.

Gregory of Tours says that anyone who dared to swear falsely near the tomb of Pancratius would either be driven mad by a demon or would fall on the flagstones and die before he reached the grille of the choir. There was the case of two men who were engaged in a serious legal controversy. The judge knew perfectly well which one was the guilty party, but his zeal for justice made him lead the two to the altar of Saint Peter. There he compelled the guilty man to

[1] Pancras in England.

swear to his pretended innocence, and prayed to the apostle to show the truth by some sign. The man swore, but nothing happened to him. The judge, aware of his guilt and still eager to see justice done, exclaimed: "Either old Saint Peter is too forgiving, or he is deferring to one younger than himself! Let us go to young Pancratius and put the question to him!" They went, and the guilty man dared to pronounce his false oath with his hand upon the saint's tomb; but then he could not pull his hand free and eventually died there. So it is that even now it is the custom to settle difficult cases by oath, over the relics of Saint Pancratius.

---

*About the feasts that occur within the
time of pilgrimage*

Having dealt with the feasts that occur within the time of reconciliation, which the Church represents from Easter to the octave of
Pentecost, we now turn to the feasts that fall within the time
of pilgrimage, which the Church represents from the octave of
Pentecost to Advent. This period does not always begin at this point
in the sequence of feast days, because it varies according to the
date of Easter.

---

77. Saint Urban

Urban comes from *urbanitas*, and Saint Urban was an urbane man. Or the name comes from *ur*, which means light or fire, and *banal*, which means response; and Urban was a light in his honorable conduct, a fire through his ardent love, and a response through his teaching. He was a beacon or a light because light is agreeable to look at, immaterial in its essence, heavenly in its source, and useful and helpful in its action. So this saint was agreeable in his relations with people, immaterial in his contempt for the world, heavenly in his contemplation, and useful and helpful in his preaching.

Urban succeeded Pope Callistus, during whose pontificate there was much persecution of Christians. Then Alexander, whose mother Ammaea had been converted to the Christian faith by Origen, assumed the throne of empire. His mother pleaded with him to put an end to the persecution, but the urban prefect Almachius, who had had blessed Cecilia beheaded, continued his cruel pursuit of the faithful. With the help of an adjutant named Carpasius he instituted a thorough search for Saint Urban. The pope was finally found hiding in a cave with three priests and three deacons, and was imprisoned. Then Almachius had Urban brought before him and accused him of misleading five thousand persons, among them the blasphemer Cecilia and two illustrious men, Tiburtius and Valerian. He also demanded the surrender of Cecilia's treasure. Urban answered him: "I see that greed, rather than piety toward the gods, is what motivates your cruel treatment of the saints. Cecilia's wealth had gone up to heaven by the hands of the poor!"

Saint Urban and his companions were then lashed with whips laden with lead. Urban invoked the Lord by his name Elyon, and the prefect, sneering, said: "The old man wants to look wise and therefore speaks an unknown language!" The captives could not be won over and so were remanded to prison, and Urban baptized three tribunes who came to him there with Anolinus, the jailer. When Almachius heard that Anolinus had become a Christian, he summoned him and, upon his refusal to sacrifice, had him beheaded. Saint Urban with his companions was led before an idol and ordered to sprinkle incense on the fire, but Urban prayed, and the idol fell from its pedestal and killed twenty-two priests, ministers of the fire. Again the prisoners were cruelly beaten and then led to the altar of sacrifice, but they spat on the idol, made the sign of the cross on their foreheads, gave one another the kiss of peace, and were beheaded under Alexander, whose reign began about A.D. 220.

Immediately Carpasius was seized by a demon, blasphemed his gods and praised the Christians despite himself, and was strangled by the demon. Having witnessed this, his wife and her daughter and her whole household were baptized by the priest Fortunatus, after which they buried the bodies of the saints with honor.

78. Saint Petronilla

Petronilla, whose life was written by Marcellus, was the daughter of Saint Peter the apostle. She was very beautiful, and therefore by her father's will she suffered continually from fever. The disciples were at table one day with Peter, and Titus said to him: "You have cured all sorts of illnesses, why do you leave Petronilla so sick?" "Because it's for her own good," Peter replied. "But lest it be thought that I said that because it was impossible for me to cure her," he turned and said to her, "Get up right away, Petronilla, and wait on us!" When all had been served, however, Peter said: "Now, Petronilla, back to bed!" She promptly returned to bed and the fever came back as before, but when she began to be perfect in the love of God, he cured her perfectly.

A count named Flaccus, much taken with Petronilla's beauty, came to ask her to be his wife. She responded: "If you want me for your wife, command maidens to come to me, and theirs it will be to accompany me to your house." While the count prepared the maidens for their task, Petronilla began a regimen of fasting, prayer, and the reception of the Body of the Lord, took to her bed, and after three days migrated to the Lord.

Flaccus, seeing that he had been deceived, turned to Felicula, one of Petronilla's companions, and ordered her either to marry him or to sacrifice to the idols. She refused to do either, and the prefect kept her in jail for seven days without food or drink and then tortured her on the rack, put her to death, and threw her body into the sewer. Saint Nicodemus recovered the body and buried it. For this, Flaccus had Nicodemus summoned before the judge, and when he refused to sacrifice, he was beaten with leaden rods and killed. His body was thrown into the Tiber, but was lifted out and honorably buried by a cleric named Justus.

---

79. Saint Peter the Exorcist

Peter the Exorcist was held in prison by the jailer Archemius. The daughter of Archemius was possessed of a demon and he often complained about this to Peter, who told him that if he believed in Christ, his daughter would be freed of the demon at once. Archemius said: "I wonder how it is that your Lord will be able to free my daughter but cannot free you from suffering for him as you are doing!" Peter answered: "My God has the power to set me free, but his will is that by way of a transitory passion we arrive at eternal glory." Archemius: "If I clamp double chains on you and your God frees you and cures my daughter, I will believe in Christ immediately!" All he had asked for happened, and Saint Peter appeared to him clad in white garments and holding a cross in his hand. Archemius prostrated himself at the saint's feet, and, since his daughter was cured, he and his whole house received baptism. He also permitted the other prisoners to go free, and any who wished to become Christians to do so; and many believed and were baptized by blessed Marcellinus, a priest.[1]

The prefect heard of this and ordered all the prisoners to be brought before him. Archemius called them together, kissed their hands, and said: "If any one of you desires to come to martyrdom, let him come fearlessly; but anyone who does not so desire may go from here unhurt." The judge learned that Marcellinus and Peter had baptized them, so he summoned them and jailed them separated from one another. Marcellinus was laid out naked on broken glass and deprived of light and water, and Peter was bound to a stake in a narrow cell high up in a tower, but an angel looked upon him, cut him loose, and put him and Marcellinus back in the house of Archemius, telling them to comfort those in the house for seven days and then to present themselves again to the judge.

When the said judge did not find his prisoners in prison, he called for Archemius, and when Archemius refused to offer sacrifice, the judge ordered him and his wife to be strangled in an underground crypt. Saints Marcellinus and Peter got wind of this and came to the place, and there, with Christians standing guard, Marcellinus celebrated the mass for seven days. The Christians said to the unbelievers: "See, we could have set Archemius free and then gone into hiding, but we would not do either the one thing or the other!" The pagans were angry at this, slew Archemius with the sword, and stoned the mother and the daughter. Marcellinus and Peter they beheaded at a black forest that is now called

---

[1] Graesse notes (343) that recent editions add "Marcellinus" to the title of this chapter.

"white" in memory of their martyrdom. This took place in the reign of Diocletian, which began in A.D. 287. An executioner named Dorotheus saw their souls, gowned in splendid, jeweled vesture, taken up to heaven by angels. This caused him to become a Christian, and eventually he died a happy death.

---

80. Saints Primus and Felicianus

Primus means highest and great. Felicianus is derived from *felix* and *anus*, meaning a happy old man. Saint Primus was called highest and great because of the dignity he gained by suffering martyrdom, of the power he displayed by performing miracles, of the holiness of his perfect life, and of the happiness he has in the glorious fulfillment of his life. Saint Felicianus was called an old man not only because he lived to a great age but on account of his venerable dignity, his mature wisdom, and the sobriety of his way of life.

Primus and Felicianus were denounced to Diocletian and Maximian by the priests of the temples, who told the emperors that if they did not make the two Christians offer sacrifice to the gods, they would not be able to obtain any benefits from the gods. By command of the emperors, therefore, the two were clapped into prison but were set free by an angel. Later they were again presented before the emperors, but clung firmly to their faith and were cruelly beaten. Then they were separated, and the prefect told Felicianus that he ought to have some regard for his age and therefore ought to sacrifice to the gods. Felicianus replied: "Look, I am eighty years old, and it is thirty years since I recognized the truth and chose to live for God, who can deliver me from your hands!" The prefect had him bound and nailed down by the hands and feet, and said to him: "You will stay there till you yield to us!" As the saint did not change the joyous expression on his face, the prefect gave orders that he was to be tortured, and nothing helpful was to be done for him.

Next the prefect had Saint Primus brought before him and said to him: "See here! Your brother has bowed to the emperors' decrees and therefore is respected as a great man in the palace! Now you do likewise!" Primus: "Though you are a son of the devil, what you said is true in part: my brother has bowed to the decree of the emperor of heaven!" This angered the prefect, and he ordered flaming torches to be held to the saint's sides and molten lead to be poured into his mouth, while Felicianus, whom they hoped to frighten, looked on; but Primus drank the lead with pleasure, as if it were cool water. This was too much for the prefect, who had two lions loosed upon the martyrs, but the beasts stretched themselves at their feet like gentle lambs. Then savage she-bears were let loose but became as gentle as the lions. Over twelve thousand men witnessed this spectacle, and five hundred of them believed in the Lord. The prefect, however, had the saints beheaded and their bodies thrown to the dogs and the birds, but the bodies remained untouched and were buried with honor by the Christians. They suffered about A.D. 287.

81. Saint Barnabas, Apostle

Barnabas is interpreted as son of one arriving, or son of consolation, or son of a prophet, or son who encloses. Saint Barnabas is called "son" four times because of his fourfold sonship: the Scriptures call him son by reason of his birth, his instruction, his imitation, and his adoption. He was reborn in Christ through baptism and instructed by the Gospel; he imitated Christ by his martyrdom and was by him adopted through being rewarded in heaven. This fourfold sonship applied to Barnabas himself. With regard to others he was one who arrived, consoled, prophesied, and enclosed. He arrived by going from place to place and preaching everywhere, which we know because he was companion to Saint Paul. He consoled the poor and the afflicted—the poor by bringing alms to them and the afflicted by addressing letters to them at the behest of the apostles. He prophesied because he was gifted with the spirit of prophecy. He enclosed and united a great multitude in the faith, as is clear from his being sent to Antioch. We find these four notes in the Acts of the Apostles (11:24): "For he was a good man and full of the Holy Spirit and of faith, and a great multitude was added to the Lord." As to the first, he was a man, i.e., manly, virile; as to the second, he was good; as to the third, he was full of the Holy Spirit, and as to the fourth, he was a man of faith. His passion was compiled by his cousin John, also called Mark, and covered especially the time from this John's vision almost to the end of the saint's life. It is believed that Bede translated this life from Greek into Latin.[1]

Barnabas, a Levite and a native of Cyprus, was one of the Lord's seventy-two disciples. He is extolled and praised on many grounds in the Acts of the Apostles, for he was very well disposed and in good order as regarded himself, his God, and his neighbor.

First, he maintained good order within himself in relation to the three powers—the rational, the concupiscible, and the irascible.[2] His rational power was illumined by the light of knowledge, whence we read in Acts (13:1): "There were in the church which was at Antioch prophets and doctors, among whom was Barnabas." He had his concupiscible power in good order in that it was cleansed of the dust of worldly affections; thus we read in Acts (4:36–37) that Joseph, who by the apostles was surnamed Barnabas, had a field, but sold it and brought the price and laid it at the feet of the apostles. The *Gloss* on this text says: "He proves that one should rid oneself of what one avoids touching, and teaches that the gold which he had laid at the apostles' feet should indeed be trodden under foot." His irascible power was strengthened by his indomitable uprightness, so that he manfully undertook arduous tasks, persevered in doing what called for strength, and showed constancy in adversity. That he undertook the arduous courageously is shown by the fact that he accepted the task of converting the great city of Antioch, and also by what we read in Acts (9:26f.), namely, that when Paul, after his conversion, went to Jerusalem and wanted to join the apostles, all of whom shunned him like lambs fleeing a wolf, Barnabas boldly took him and led him to meet them. He persevered in doing what called for strength, because he chastised his body and disciplined it by fasting, whence Acts (13:1–3) says of Barnabas and several others: "They were ministering to the Lord and fasting." He bore adversity with constancy, as the apostles gave testimony about him, saying: ". . . with our well-beloved Barnabas and Paul, men who have given their lives for the name of our Lord Jesus Christ. . . ."

Second, he was in good order in his relations with God, deferring to God's authority, majesty, and goodness. He deferred to God's authority, as we see from the fact that he did not simply take upon himself the office of preaching but wanted to receive it by God's authority. We read in Acts (13:2): "The Holy Spirit said to them, 'Set apart for me Barnabas and Paul for the work to which I have called them.'" He deferred to God's majesty. As Acts (14:10f.) has it, some men wished to attribute divine majesty to him and to offer sacrifice to him

---

[1] J.-B. M. Roze (*La légende dorée* [Paris: Ed. Rouveyre, 1903], 2:132) notes that no such translation is found among the Venerable Bede's works.

[2] The concupiscible appetite, according to Thomas Aquinas, has as its object good or evil as agreeable or repellent in itself. The irascible appetite has as its object the good perceived as subject to some condition of difficulty or danger.

as to a god, calling him Jove as being the older, and Paul Mercury as being a man of foresight and eloquence. But Barnabas and Paul, rending their clothes, shouted: "Men, what are you doing? We are mortals just like yourselves, preaching to you to be converted away from these useless gods and toward the living God!" And he deferred to God's goodness. We read in Acts (15:5) that some Jewish converts wanted to restrict and diminish the goodness of God's grace (by which we are saved freely and not by the Law), asserting that this was by no means sufficient without circumcision. Paul and Barnabas bravely resisted them and proved that the goodness of God's grace alone, without the Law, sufficed. Furthermore, they referred the question to the apostles and persuaded them to write a letter refuting the error of the dissidents.

Third, he maintained good order in his relations with his neighbor, because he nurtured his flock by word, by example, and by works of mercy. He fed them with the word because he preached the Gospel with care, whence it is said in Acts (15:35): "Paul and Barnabas continued at Antioch, teaching and preaching, with many others, the word of the Lord." We see his care also in the great multitude he converted in Antioch, where for the first time the disciples were called Christians. He nurtured his flock by example, because his life was to all a mirror of holiness and an example of true religion. In every work of his he was virile, religious, and strong, conspicuous in the goodness of his way of doing things, full of every grace of the Holy Spirit, outstanding in all virtue and faith. Of these four qualities we read in Acts (11:22f.): "They sent Barnabas to Antioch," and "he exhorted them all to remain faithful to the Lord with steadfast purpose, for he was a good man, full of the Holy Spirit and of faith." He nurtured the flock with works of mercy. There are two kinds of alms or works of mercy, namely, the temporal, which consists of providing for temporal needs, and the spiritual, which consists of forgiving offenses. Barnabas had the first kind when he brought alms to the brethren who were in Jerusalem. We read in Acts (11:27f.) that when there was a great famine during the reign of Claudius, as Agabus had prophesied, "the disciples determined, every one according to his ability, to send relief to the brethren who lived in Judea; and they did so, sending it to the elders by the hand of Barnabas and Paul." And he did the spiritual work when he forgave the offense committed by John whose surname was Mark; for when this disciple left Barnabas and Paul but then came back repentant, Barnabas forgave him and again received him as a disciple, whereas Paul refused to receive him again. This caused a division between Paul and Barnabas, each of them acting for a pious reason and intention. Barnabas took John back out of the kindness of mercy, Paul refused out of strict concern for uprightness. So the *Gloss* on Acts 15 says: "Because [John Mark] had confronted him to the face but showed himself too timid, Paul rightly turned him away, lest by the contagion of his example the strengths of others might be contaminated." This division therefore did not grow out of unworthy hard feelings: it was their response to the Holy Spirit's inspiration, namely, that they should separate so that they might preach to more people.

That is what happened. When Barnabas was in the city of Icona, his cousin, the aforementioned John, had a vision in which a man splendid to look upon appeared to him and said: "Be steadfast, John, because shortly you will be called not John but Elevated!" John related this to Barnabas, who counseled him: "Take care to tell no one about the vision you have had, because last night the Lord appeared to me in the same way and said: 'Be steadfast, Barnabas! You will gain an eternal reward because you left your own people and gave your life for my name!'" And, when Paul and Barnabas had preached for a long time in Antioch, an angel of the Lord appeared to Paul and said: "Make haste and go to Jerusalem, because there a certain brother awaits you!"

Barnabas wished to go to Cyprus to visit his parents, and Paul wanted to hasten to Jerusalem, so, the Holy Spirit guiding them, they decided to separate. When Paul told Barnabas what the angel had made known to him, Barnabas responded: "The will of the Lord be done! Now I am going to Cyprus and will end my days there, and I shall see you no more!" He wept and fell humbly at Paul's feet, and Paul said with compassion: "Do not weep, because that is the will of the Lord; for the Lord also appeared to me in the night and said, 'Do not stop Barnabas from going to Cyprus, because there he will give light to many and will die a martyr's death!'"

Barnabas then departed for Cyprus with John, taking with him the book of the gospel of Saint Matthew: he held the book over sick people and thus, by the power of God, cured many. As they were leaving Cyprus, they found Elymas, the sorcerer whom Paul had deprived of his sight for a time. Elymas opposed them and forbade them to go to Paphos. And one day Barnabas saw nude men and women running to celebrate their feast. Indignant at the sight he cursed their temple, and a section of it fell in and crushed many people. Finally he arrived at Salamina, and there the sorcerer stirred up a riot against him. The Jews laid hold of him and, after inflicting many injuries upon him, haled him before the judge of the city and demanded that he be punished. Then it was learned that Eusebius, a prominent and powerful man who was related to Nero, had arrived in Salamina, and the Jews were afraid he would take Barnabas away from them and let him go free; so they put a rope around his neck, dragged him out of the city, and burned him alive. Even then the impious Jews were not satisfied. They stowed his bones in a leaden urn, intending to cast it into the sea; but John, his disciple, rose in the night with two companions, got hold of the relics, and buried them secretly in a crypt. There they remained hidden, as Sigebert says, until the year of the Lord 500, in the time of Emperor Zeno and Pope Gelasius, when the place was revealed by Barnabas and the relics were recovered.

Blessed Dorotheus says: "Barnabas first preached in Rome and became bishop of Milan."

82. Saints Vitus and Modestus

The name Vitus comes from *vita*, life. Augustine distinguishes three kinds of life: the active; the leisurely, which pertains to spiritual leisure or quiet; and the contemplative, which combines the other two. These three kinds of life were in Saint Vitus. Again, Vitus is close to *virtus*, and Vitus was a virtuous man.

The name Modestus has the sense of standing in the middle, the middle being virtue, for virtue, as a middle, stands between two extremes, which are vices. The extremes of prudence are craftiness and foolishness; of temperance, overindulgence of carnal desires and excessive self-mortification; of fortitude, cowardice and rashness; of justice, vindictiveness and excessive leniency.

Vitus, a remarkable child and a Christian, suffered martyrdom in Sicily when he was only twelve years old. His father often whipped him because he despised the idols and refused to worship them. The prefect Valerian heard of this and summoned the boy, and, when he would not offer sacrifice, ordered him beaten with rods; but the arms of the men beating him and the hand of the prefect withered at once, and the prefect cried out: "Alas, alas! I've lost a hand!" Vitus said to him: "Call on your gods and let them heal you if they can!" Valerian to Vitus: "Can you do it?" Vitus: "In the name of my Lord, I can!" He prayed and obtained instant cure for the prefect, who then said to the father: "Take your boy in hand, or he'll come to a bad end!"

The father brought him home and tried to change the son's mind by surrounding him with music and sporting girls and other kinds of pleasure. Then he shut the boy up in his bedroom, and a wonderful fragrance came out of it, steeping the house and the people in it with its odor. The father looked in through the door and saw seven angels surrounding his son, and exclaimed: "The gods have come into my house," and immediately was stricken with blindness. His cries were so loud that the whole city of Lucania was disturbed, and Valerian came on the run and demanded to know what had happened to him. He answered: "I saw fiery gods and I could not bear to look at their faces!"

They conducted the father to the temple of Jove and promised a bull with gilded horns for the recovery of his sight, but to no avail. Then he begged his son to obtain his healing, and at the son's prayer the father saw the light again. When even then he did not believe, but rather thought to kill the child, an angel appeared to Vitus's tutor, Modestus, and commanded him to take the boy in a boat and go to another land. While they were at sea, an eagle brought them their food, and they wrought many wonders when they landed.

Meanwhile the son of the emperor Diocletian was seized by a demon, who declared that unless Vitus of Lucania came, he, the demon, would never come out of the son. Vitus was sought and found and brought to the emperor, who asked him: "Boy, can you heal my son?" Vitus answered: "Not I but the Lord can!" He placed his hand on the son and the demon fled instantly. Diocletian: "Boy, take thought to yourself and sacrifice to the gods, or die a dreadful death!" Vitus refused and was put in jail with Modestus, but the chains with which they were shackled softened and fell off, and the jail was flooded with brilliant light. When this was reported to the emperor, Vitus was put into a fiery furnace but came out unscathed. Then a fierce lion was brought in to devour him, but the beast was tamed by the power of his faith. Finally Vitus, Modestus, and Crescentia, his nurse who had followed him everywhere, were stretched on the rack; but suddenly the air became turbulent, the earth shook, thunder rolled, and the temples of the idols fell in and killed many worshipers.

The emperor was frightened and hurried away, beating his breast and saying: "Woe is me, I've been worsted by one mere child!" The martyrs were quickly freed by an angel and found themselves beside a river, where they paused and prayed and gave themselves up to the Lord. Eagles guarded their bodies, which were found and given honorable burial by an illustrious lady named Florentia, to whom Saint Vitus had revealed their whereabouts.[1] They suffered under Diocletian, whose reign began in A.D. 287.

83. Saint Quiricus and His Mother Saint Julitta

The name Quiricus comes from *quaerens arcum*, seeking a bow, or from *chisil*, which means fortitude, and *cus*, black; hence strong in virtue and black by humility. Or the name comes from *quiris*, javelin, or from *quiriles*, seat. Saint Quiricus[1] was a bow, i.e., curved in his humility and in the torments of his passion. He was black in his low estimate of himself, a javelin in his conquest of the

---

[1] Graesse notes (351n) that all the details regarding the finding and burial, except the name of the lady, are more recent additions. But the account as given here is certainly in the style of Jacobus.

[1] Perhaps better known as Cyr or Cyricus.

enemy, a seat because God dwelt in him. All this, which his age denied him, was supplied in him by the grace of God.

Julitta is like *juvans vita*, aiding by life, because the saint lived a spiritual life and thereby aided many.

Quiricus was the son of Julitta, a most illustrious lady of Iconium. Wishing to evade the persecution raging there, she went to Tarsus with her three-year-old son and two servingmaids. There she was brought before Alexander, the governor, carrying her child in her arms. The maids, seeing this, ran away leaving their mistress. The governor took the child in his arms, and when the mother refused to sacrifice to the gods, had her scourged with raw thongs. When the child saw his mother being scourged, he wept bitterly and uttered loud cries. The governor, holding him on his lap, tried to calm him with kisses and other endearments, but the child, looking back toward his mother, shrugged away from the ruler's embraces, turned his head indignantly, and scratched the man's face with his fingernails, crying out, in harmony with his mother's voice: "I too am a Christian!" He struggled for a long time and finally bit the governor on the shoulder, and Alexander, enraged and in pain from the wound, threw him from the height of the tribunal, his tender brains spilling down the steps. Julitta saw this happen and joyfully gave thanks to God that her son had gone before her to the kingdom of heaven. Then Alexander ordered her to be flayed alive, plunged into boiling pitch, and finally beheaded.

The governor had the bodies of mother and son cut up so that the Christians would not be able to bury them, but the pieces were collected by an angel and buried at night by Christians. In the time of Constantine the Great, when peace was restored to the Church, one of the two maids, who had survived, showed where the martyrs' bodies were, and the relics are held in great devotion by the whole populace. They suffered about the year of the Lord 230, under Emperor Alexander.

84. Saint Marina, Virgin

The virgin Marina was her father's only child. When he was widowed and entered a monastery, he changed his daughter's attire and dressed her as a male. He then asked the abbot and the monks to admit his only son, and, when they agreed, Marina was received as a monk and was called Brother Marinus by all.

"Marinus" then began to live the religious life and to observe strict obedience. When he was twenty-seven years old and the father felt the approach of death, he called his daughter, encouraged her to remain firm in her resolution, and ordered her never to reveal to anyone that she was a woman.

Marinus often went out with an oxcart to bring back wood to the monastery, and now and then stopped at the house of a man whose daughter conceived a child by a soldier. She was questioned and declared that the monk Marinus had ravished her. When Marinus was asked why he had committed such a shameful crime, he admitted that he had sinned and was banished from the monastery. He stayed outside the gate for three years, living on scraps of bread. When the woman's son was weaned, he was sent to the abbot and entrusted to Marinus to be brought up, and he stayed with Marinus for two years. Marinus accepted all this with the utmost patience and in all things rendered thanks to God. Finally the monks, moved by his humility and patience, took him back into the monastery and assigned some of the meanest labors to him. He accepted everything cheerfully and did his work with patience and devotion.

At length, having led a life filled with good works, he migrated to the Lord. When it came time to bathe the corpse before burying it in some grubby corner, the monks saw that it was the body of a woman. They were stupefied and frightened, and admitted that they had grossly maltreated this handmaid of God. They therefore gave her honorable burial in the church. As for the woman who had defamed the servant of God, she was seized by a demon, confessed her crime, came to the virgin's tomb, and was freed of the demon. People came from everywhere to visit the tomb, and many miracles took place there. Saint Marina died on the eighteenth day of June.[1]

---

[1] "*xiv kalendas Julii.*" The usual date is 20 July.

According to *Butler's Lives of the Saints* (New York: P. J. Kenedy & Sons, 1963), 1:314, "the story of this Marina is simply one of those popular romances of women masquerading as men." *The Golden Legend* includes, besides the Marina story, those of "Saints" Eugenia (mentioned several times in the legend of Saints Protus and Hyacinthus), Theodora (who used to be celebrated on 11 September), Margaret (also called Pelagia), and Pelagia (also called Margaret). The last two had the same feast day, 8 October.

85. Saints Gervasius and Protasius

Gervasius comes from *gerar*, sacred, and *vas*, vase; or from *gena*, a stranger, one not a dweller, and *syor*, small. So, Gervasius was sacred by his meritorious life, a vase as a receptacle of virtues, a stranger by contempt for the world, small by his humble estimate of himself.

Protasius comes from *protos*, first, and *syos*, God or godly, or from *procul*, at a distance, and *stasis*, position. This Protasius was first by his dignity, godly through his love, distant from any attachment to the world.

Ambrose found their passion written in a small book placed at their head.

Gervasius and Protasius were twin brothers, the sons of Saint Vitalis and the blessed Valeria. They had distributed all their goods to the poor and were living with Saint Nazarius, who was building an oratory near Embrun. A boy named Celsus was carrying stones for him. (But what is said about Nazarius having Celsus with him at that early date may be by way of anticipation, since we gather from the legend of Nazarius[1] that Celsus was entrusted to him at a much later time.) The three men were brought before the emperor Nero, and the boy Celsus followed them wailing and complaining. One of the soldiers slapped the lad and Nazarius rebuked him for doing so, whereupon the soldiers kicked and trampled the saint, jailed him with others, and later cast him into the sea. Gervasius and Protasius were taken to Milan, and Nazarius, miraculously saved from the sea, came to the same city.

At that time Count Astasius arrived in Milan on his way to make war on the Marcomanni. The worshipers of the gods came to meet him, asserting that the gods would not respond to them unless Gervasius and Protasius first offered sacrifice. The two were promptly apprehended and urged to sacrifice. But Gervasius said that all the idols were deaf and dumb, and that Astasius would have victory from the almighty God alone. The count, angered, had him beaten with leaded whips until he died. Then he summoned Protasius and said to him: "Wretch, take thought and live, and don't die a miserable death the way your brother did!" Protasius: "Who is the wretch—I, who do not fear you, or you, who are proving that you fear me?" Astasius: "How can you, miserable man, say that I fear you?" Protasius: "You prove that you are afraid of me and afraid I will do you harm if I do not sacrifice to your gods. If you were not afraid I would do you harm by not sacrificing, you would not force me to worship the idols!" The

---

[1] See below, chapter 102.

count then ordered him to be hung on the rack. Protasius: "I am not angry with you, Count, because I expect the eyes of your heart to be blind; but I pity you, because you do not know what you are doing! Finish what you have begun, then, so that the loving-kindness of our Savior may embrace me with my brother!" Then the count ordered him to be beheaded. Philip, a servant of Christ, and his son took away the saints' bodies and buried them secretly in their house in a stone coffin, and placed at their head a small book containing the martyrs' birth, life, and death. They suffered under Nero, whose reign began in A.D. 57.

The bodies of these two martyrs remained hidden for centuries but were found in Ambrose's time in the following way. Ambrose was at prayer in the church of Saints Nabor and Felix, and was neither wide awake nor sound asleep when two handsome youths, dressed in white tunics and mantles and shod with short boots, appeared to him and prayed with him. Ambrose prayed that if this apparition was an illusion it would not occur again, but if it was a true one it would be repeated. At cockcrow the two youths again appeared in the same way, praying with him; but on the third night, fully awake though his body was worn out with vigils, he was astonished when they appeared to him with a third person, who looked like Paul the apostle in a painting Ambrose had seen. The two young men were silent, but the apostle said to him: "Here are two who desired nothing the earth could give them, but followed my counsels. You will discover their bodies at the place where you are standing. At a depth of twelve feet you will find a coffin covered with earth, which contains their bodies and a small book telling their origin and their death."

Ambrose convoked the neighboring bishops, was the first to dig down into the earth, came to the coffin, and found all just as Paul had said. Although more than three hundred years had passed, the bodies were found to be in the same condition as if they had been laid to rest that very day. Moreover, a most sweet, noble odor rose from them. A blind man touched the coffin and received his sight. Many others were cured by the merits of these saints.

It was on their feast day that peace was concluded between the Lombards and the Roman Empire. In memory of that event Pope Gregory established the custom of chanting *Loquetur Dominus pacem in plebem suam*[2] at the introit of the mass of the feast. So it is that the office of that day refers partly to the saints and partly to events that occurred at the same date.

In the twentieth[3] book of his work *On the City of God*, Augustine relates that he himself was present, as were the emperor and a great throng, when, at the tomb of Saints Gervasius and Protasius in Milan, a blind man recovered his sight. (It is not known whether this was the same blind man as the one previously mentioned.) Augustine also relates in the same place that at a villa called Victori-

[2] The Lord will speak peace unto his people (Ps. 84:9 [85:8]).
[3] Correctly, bk. 22, chap. 8.

ana, some thirty miles from Hippo, a young man was bathing his horse in the river when suddenly a demon seized him, tormented him, and threw him into the river as if he were dead. In the evening vespers were sung in the nearby church of Saints Gervasius and Protasius, and the young man, as if struck by the voices, came into the church screaming and clung to the altar as though he were tied to it, and could not be moved away. The demon was conjured to go out of the man and threatened to tear him limb from limb if he went out. When the demon finally did go out, one of the young man's eyes hung down his cheek by a thin vein, but they put the eye back in its place as well as they could, and in a few days, by the merits of Saints Gervasius and Protasius, the youth was completely cured.

Ambrose, in his Preface for the saints, says: "These are the ones who, signed with the celestial banner, took up the victorious weapons of the apostle, were loosed from worldly bonds, broke through the lines of the wicked enemy's vices, and, free and unhampered, followed Christ the Lord! Oh, how happy the twins who, living by the word of God, could not be soiled by any earthly stain! Oh, how glorious the cause for which they fought and won the same crown just as they issued from the same maternal womb!"

※

86. The Birth of Saint John the Baptist

John the Baptist has many titles. He is called prophet, friend of the bridegroom, lamp, angel, voice, Elijah, baptizer of the Savior, herald of the judge, and forerunner of the King. Each of these titles denotes a particular prerogative of John: the title of prophet, his prerogative of foreknowledge; the title of friend of the bridegroom, his prerogative of loving and being loved; burning light, his prerogative of sanctity; angel, his prerogative of virginity; voice, his prerogative of humility; Elijah, his prerogative of fervor; baptizer, the wonderful honor of baptizing the Lord; herald, the prerogative of preaching; and forerunner, the prerogative of preparation.

The birth of John the Baptist was announced by the archangel in the following manner. The *Ecclesiastical History* tells us that in order to broaden divine worship, King David established twenty-four high priests, of whom one was superior and was called prince of priests. He designated fifteen men from the lineage of

Eleazar and eight from that of Ithamar, and gave each a week to serve by lot. The eighth week fell to Abijah, of whom Zechariah was a descendant. Zechariah and his wife Elizabeth were old and childless.

One day when Zechariah went into the Temple of the Lord to offer incense, and a multitude of people waited outside, the archangel Gabriel appeared to him. The vision startled him, but the angel said "Fear not, Zechariah, your prayer is heard!" It is the way of the good angels, according to the *Gloss*, to reassure by kindly words those who are alarmed at seeing them, whereas the bad angels transform themselves to look like angels of light, and, if they sense that anyone is terrified by the vision of them, they terrorize him still more.

Be that as it may, Gabriel announced to Zechariah that he was to have a son whose name would be John, who would drink no wine or strong drink and would go before the Lord in the spirit and power of Elijah. John is called Elijah by reason of place, because both lived in the desert; by reason of what they ate, because both ate little; by reason of their external appearance, because both cared little about what they wore; by reason of their office, since they were both forerunners, though Elijah was forerunner to the Judge and John to the Savior; and by reason of zeal, because their words burned like torches.

Zechariah, thinking about his old age and his wife's sterility, began to doubt and, as the Jews used to do, asked the angel for a sign. Because Zechariah had not believed the message, the angel gave him a sign by striking him dumb. Note, however, that at times one may doubt and be excused for doubting. This may be because so much is promised, as, for instance, in Abraham's case. When the Lord had promised him that his seed would possess the land of Canaan, Abraham said to him: "Lord God, how can I know that I am to possess it?" God, responding, said: "Bring me a heifer three years old, etc." (Gen. 15:9f.). Sometimes it may be in consideration of one's own frailty, as in the case of Gideon, who said: "I beseech thee, my Lord, how can I deliver Israel? Behold, my clan is the weakest in Manasseh, and I am the least in my father's house!" (Judg. 6:15). So he asked for a sign and received one. Sometimes what is promised seems naturally impossible, as in the case of Sara. The Lord had said: "I will return to you and Sara will have a son," and Sara laughed behind the door of the tent, saying: "After I have grown old and my husband is an old man, shall I give myself to pleasure?" (Gen. 18:12).

Why, then, is it that Zechariah is the only one punished for doubting? In his case there was the magnitude of the promise and the awareness of his own frailty, since he considered himself unworthy to have such a son, and there was the natural impossibility. It is thought that there are several reasons for this. The first, according to Bede, is that he voiced his disbelief, and was stricken dumb so that by keeping silent he might learn to believe. The second is that he was made mute so that the miracle of his son's birth might be more obvious, since the father's speech was restored at the son's birth and one miracle was piled on top of the other. Third, it was appropriate that he should lose his voice, when a voice was being born, and silence being imposed on the Law. Fourth, Zechariah had asked for a sign from God and muteness was the sign he received. When he went out to the people and they saw that he was unable to speak, they knew, as he nodded agreement, that he had seen a vision in the Temple.

He completed his week of service and went home, and Elizabeth conceived. She then hid herself for five months, because, as Ambrose says about this, she felt some shame at having a child at her age, fearing that she might seem to have indulged in lustful pleasure despite her years. Yet she also rejoiced at being rid of the reproach of sterility. It is a source of shame for women not to have the reward that belongs to marriage, since it is in view of that reward that marriage is a happy event and that carnal union is justified.

In Elizabeth's sixth month Mary, who had already conceived, came to her, the fruitful virgin to the woman relieved of sterility, feeling sympathy for her in her old age. When she greeted her cousin, blessed John, already filled with the Holy Spirit, sensed the Son of God coming to him and leapt for joy in his mother's womb, and danced, saluting by his movements the one he could not greet with his voice. He leapt as one wishing to greet his Lord and to stand up in his presence. The Blessed Virgin stayed with her cousin for three months, helping her, and when the child was born, as we read in the *Scholastic History*, she lifted it from the earth with her holy hands, kindly acting as a nursemaid would.

This holy forerunner of the Lord enjoyed nine special and singular privileges, namely:

the same angel who announced the coming of the Lord announced the coming of John;
he leapt in his mother's womb;
the mother of the Lord lifted him from the earth;
he unlocked his father's tongue;
he was the first to confer baptism;
he pointed out Christ with his finger;
he baptized Christ;
Christ praised him above all others;
he foretold Christ's coming to the souls in Limbo.

On account of these nine privileges, the Lord himself called John a prophet and more than a prophet. Chrysostom asks why Christ called him more than a prophet, and answers: "It befits a prophet to receive a gift from God, but does it belong to a prophet to give God the gift of baptism? It befits a prophet to prophesy about God, but is it for God to prophesy about the prophet? All the prophets prophesied about Christ, but no one prophesied about them. Yet not only did John prophesy about Christ, but other prophets also prophesied about John. All were bearers of the word, John was the voice itself; and by as much as the voice is closer to the word (yet is not the word), by so much was John closer to Christ yet was not Christ."

According to Ambrose, John's praiseworthiness derives from five causes, namely, his parentage, his moral conduct, his miracles, his office, and his preaching.

The praise based upon his parentage, again according to Ambrose, is manifested in five ways: "Perfect praise," he says, "is for him whose good lineage shows in his moral conduct, his conduct in fairness, his office in priesthood, his deeds in conformity to the law, his righteousness in righteous decisions."

John's praiseworthiness derives, secondly, from his miracles. Some of these took place before he was conceived in the womb, namely, the announcement of his birth by an angel, the imposition of his name, and his father's loss of voice. Some were related to his conception in the womb, namely, the supernatural conception itself, and his sanctification and the fulfillment of the gift of prophecy in the womb. Some were connected with his birth from the womb, namely, the attainment of the spirit of prophecy by each of his parents, because his mother knew what his name was to be and his father gave forth the canticle. The father recovered the power of speech and was filled with the Holy Spirit, whence we read: "Zechariah his father was filled with the Holy Spirit and he prophesied" (Luke 1:67). Ambrose says: "Look at John and see how much power there was in the sound of his name, which, being pronounced, gave his voice to a mute, a son to his father, piety and a priest to the people. Before, Zechariah was speechless of tongue, sterile of offspring, bereft of his office: John is born, suddenly his father becomes a prophet, recovers his speech, receives offspring from the Holy Spirit, and again assumes his function as a priest."

Thirdly, John is praised for his conduct, because his life was one of perfect holiness. Chrysostom speaks of this holiness: "John's way of life made everyone else's look blameworthy. For instance, if you see a white garment, you say, 'That is pure white,' but if you hold it against snow, it begins to look soiled even though it is not soiled. Thus everyone seemed unclean by comparison with John."

His holiness had three kinds of testimony. The first was the supercelestial, coming from the Trinity itself: from the Father, who called John an angel; Malachy (3:1): "Behold, I send my angel, and he shall prepare the way before my face." "Angel" is the name of an office or function, not of a nature, and therefore an angel is so called by reason of his office or function; and John is called an angel because he is seen to have fulfilled the offices of all the angels. He had the office of the Seraphim. That name is interpreted as meaning ardent, because the Seraphim make us ardent and in the love of God they are more ardent, more afire. Of John it is said in Ecclus. (48:1): "The prophet Elijah arose like a fire," and John came in the spirit and power of Elijah. Second, he had the office of the Cherubim. That name is interpreted as meaning the fullness of knowledge, and John is called *lucifer*, the light-bearer, the morning star,[1] because he was the end

---

[1] Cf. Job 38:32.

point of our ignorance and the starting point of the light of grace. Third, he had the office of the Thrones, whose function it is to judge, and of John it is said that he reproved Herod, saying: "It is not lawful for you to have your brother's wife." Fourth, he had the office of the Dominations, who teach us how to rule over subjects, and John was loved by those under him and was feared by kings. Fifth, the office of the Principalities, who teach us to have proper respect for those above us, and John said of himself: "He who is of the earth belongs to the earth and of the earth he speaks," but of Christ he says: "He who comes from heaven is above all."[2] He also says, speaking of Christ: ". . . the latchet of whose shoes I am not worthy to loose."[3] Sixth, the office of the Powers, by whom the harmful powers of the air are kept in check. They could not harm John because he was already sanctified, and he kept them away from us by disposing us to the baptism of penance. Seventh, the office of the Virtues, by whom miracles are performed, and blessed John showed many miracles in himself: it is a great miracle to live on wild honey and locusts, to wear camel's hair, and the like. Eighth, the office of the Archangels, when he made revelations of greater importance, such as those that pertain to our redemption, when he said: "Behold the lamb of God, behold him who takes away the sin of the world!" Ninth, the office of the Angels, when he announced lesser truths, such as those that pertain to morals, when he said: "Do penance," and: "Do violence to no man; neither calumniate any man."[4]

Second, John had the testimony of God the Son, as is clear from the eleventh chapter of Matthew, where Christ commends him wonderfully and in many ways, saying, among other things: "Among those born of women there has risen no one greater than John the Baptist." Peter Damian says: "From that word all praises of John derive, as by that word the earth was founded, the stars are moved, and the elements have their being." And third, John had the testimony of the Holy Spirit, who, speaking through Zechariah, said: "You, child, will be called the prophet of the Most High."

Secondly, he had the testimony of the angels and heavenly powers, as we see in the first chapter of Luke, where the angel commended him in many ways. He showed how great John's dignity was in relation to God when he said: "He shall be great before the Lord"; showed how holy he was in his treatment of himself, saying: "He shall drink no wine or strong drink, and shall be filled with the Holy Spirit even from his mother's womb"; and showed how usefully he served his neighbor, when he said: "And he shall convert many of the children of Israel to the Lord their God." And thirdly, he had the testimony of subcelestial beings, namely, men and women, his father and their neighbors, who said: "What then will this child be? For the hand of the Lord was with him."[5]

---

[2] John 3:31. [3] Luke 3:16.
[4] Luke 3:14. [5] Luke 1:66.

Fourthly, John's praiseworthiness is founded on the gifts God gave him in his office. He was gifted while he was still in the womb, when he emerged from the womb, in his life in the world, and in his departure from the world.

In his mother's womb he had the wondrous gift of a threefold grace. First came the grace by which he was made holy in the womb, so that he was sanctified before he was born; Jeremiah (1:4f.): "Before I formed you in the womb I knew you, and before you were born I sanctified you." Second was the grace by which he was made worthy to prophesy, as when by leaping in his mother's womb he recognized the presence of God. Chrysostom, in order to show in what ways John was more than a prophet, says: "It befits a prophet to receive the gift of prophecy for the merit of his way of life and his faith. Did it befit a prophet to be a prophet before he was a man?" Moreover, the custom was to anoint prophets, and when the Blessed Virgin greeted Elizabeth, Christ anointed John as prophet in the womb, according to what Chrysostom says: "Therefore Christ made Mary salute Elizabeth, so that the words, proceeding from the womb of his mother where Christ dwelt, would enter through Elizabeth's ears and go down to John in order to anoint him there as prophet."

Third was the grace that enabled him by his merits to pass on to his mother the spirit of prophecy. Chrysostom, continuing to show how John was more than a prophet, says: "Which of the prophets, by being a prophet, could make someone else a prophet? Elijah, indeed, anointed Elisha as a prophet but did not confer on him the grace of prophesying. John, on the other hand, while still in his mother's womb, bestowed knowledge of the coming of God into her house upon his mother, and opened her mouth to the word of confession of faith, so that she recognized the dignity of the one whom she did not see in person, saying, 'Why is this granted me, that the mother of my Lord should come to me?'"

At his emergence from the womb he had a threefold gift of grace, in that his birth was miraculous, holy, and joyful. Because it was miraculous, he was not born powerless; because it was holy, he was without guilt; because it was joyful, there was no lamenting, no sorrow. According to Master William of Auxerre, John's birth or nativity is celebrated for three reasons. The first is his sanctification in the womb. The second is the dignity of the office to which he was born, for he came as a bearer of light and was the first to announce eternal joy to us. The third is the joy surrounding his birth, for the angel had said: "Many will rejoice at his birth," and therefore it is right that we too should rejoice at his birth.

In his life in the world John had many gifts. The excellence of the divers gifts of grace that were his appears in this, that he had the perfection of all the saints. He was a prophet when he said: "There shall come one mightier than I." He was more than a prophet when he pointed his finger to identify Christ. He was an apostle, for an apostle is one who is sent, and he was "a man sent from God, whose name was John."[6] He was a martyr, because he endured death for justice's sake. He was a confessor, because he confessed and did not deny. He was a virgin, and because of his virginity he was called an angel, as we have read in Malachy: "Behold, I send my angel, etc."

In his departure from the world John had a triple gift. He was made an unconquered martyr, for he then acquired the palm of martyrdom. He was sent as a precious messenger, because he then brought to those in limbo the precious announcement of the coming there of Christ and of their redemption. And his glorious death is honored because, of all those who went down into limbo, his exodus therefrom is specially solemnized and gloriously celebrated by the Church.

Fifthly, John's praiseworthiness is based upon his preaching. The angel brought out four things about his preaching when he said: "He shall convert many of the children of Israel to the Lord their God. And he shall go before him in the spirit and power of Elijah; that he may turn the hearts of the fathers unto the children and the incredulous to the wisdom of the just, to prepare unto the Lord a perfect people." There four points are touched upon, namely, the fruit of the preaching, its order, its power, and its purpose, as is clear from the letter of the text.

Note also that John's preaching was commendable for three reasons: he preached fervently, efficaciously, and judiciously. He spoke with fervor when he said to the Pharisees: "You serpents, generation of vipers, how will you flee the judgment of hell?" Yet his fervor was inflamed with charity, because he was a burning light; whence he himself, speaking in the person of Isaiah, says: "[The Lord] made my mouth like a sharp sword." His fervor was informed by truth, because he was a shining light; John 5:53: "You sent to John and he gave testimony to the truth." It was directed by discernment or knowledge, so he interpreted the law to the people at large, or to tax-collectors and soldiers, according to the needs of each. It was firm in its constancy: he preached with such constancy that it cost him his life. His zeal had to have those four qualities, according to what Bernard says: "Let charity inflame your zeal, truth inform it, knowledge rule it, and constancy sustain it."

He also preached efficaciously, since so many were converted by his preaching. He preached by word through his assiduous teaching; by example through the holiness of his life; and, preaching by his meritorious life and his devout prayer, he converted many. And he preached judiciously. The prudent good judgment he brought to his preaching came out in three ways. First, he used threats to put fear in the perverse, saying: "Now the ax is laid to the root of the trees; every tree therefore that does not bear good fruit is cut down and thrown into the fire." Second, he used promises to entice the good, saying: "Repent, for the kingdom of heaven is at hand." Third, he used moderation, attracting the

---

[6] John 1:6.

mediocre toward perfection little by little, imposing light obligations on people in general, and on tax-gatherers and soldiers in particular, in order later to carry them forward to greater things—the people at large to do works of mercy, the publicans to abstain from hungering for what belonged to others, the soldiers not to rob anyone or accuse anyone falsely, and to be satisfied with their wages.

It is to be noted that Saint John the Evangelist went to heaven on the same day the birth of John the Baptist is celebrated. The Church, however, instituted the celebration of the Evangelist's feast on the third day following the nativity of Christ because his church was dedicated on that day, and the solemnization of the birthday of John the Baptist kept its date because the angel had certified it as the day for rejoicing over the birth of the Forerunner. There is no need to dogmatize about whether the Evangelist had to yield his day to the Baptist as the lesser to the greater. It is not appropriate to argue about which of them was the greater, as is clear from a heaven-sent example. We read that there were two doctors of theology, one of whom favored John the Baptist, the other John the Evangelist. They finally agreed on a formal disputation, and each one put great care into his search for authorities and convincing arguments with which to back his particular John. On the day of the disputation, however, each of the saints appeared to his champion and said to him: "We get along very well to-gether in heaven! Don't start disputes about us on earth!" They made the visions known to each other and to the public, and gave thanks to the Lord.

Paul, historian of the Lombards, was a deacon of the Roman church and a monk of Monte Cassino. One day he was to bless a candle, but his throat be-came hoarse though previously he had been in good voice. In order to obtain the restoration of his voice he composed the hymn *Ut queant laxis resonare fibris / Mira gestorum famuli tuorum*[7] for the feast of Saint John the Baptist. In the first verse he prays that his voice be restored . . . as Zechariah's was.

There are people who on this day burn the bones of dead animals, collected wherever they are found. There are two reasons for this, as John Beleth says. One is an observance that goes back to antiquity: there are animals called drag-ons, which fly in the air, swim in water, walk on land; and sometimes when they travel through the air they are lustfully aroused and drop their sperm into wells and flowing waters. This causes a year of plague. A preventive against this dan-ger was invented that consisted of making a bonfire of the bones of animals, the smoke from which drove the dragons away. Since this was usually done around the time of Saint John's feast day, some people continue to observe the custom. The other reason is to represent the burning of Saint John's bones by the infidels in the city of Sebaste.

---

[7] The third and fourth lines of the first verse are *Solve polluti labii reatum / Sancte Joannes*. Loosely, the English of it would be: In order that your servants may sing the wonders of your deeds with relaxed vocal cords, absolve the guilt of polluted lips, O Saint John! The whole charming hymn may be seen in *Hymni Ecclesiae* (London: Macmillan, 1865), 282.

Lighted torches are also carried around this bonfire, because John was a burning and a shining torch, and a wheel is spun because the sun then begins to be lower in its cycle. This signifies the decline of Saint John's fame, by which he was thought to be Christ, as he himself testified when he said: "I must decrease, but he must increase." According to Saint Augustine, this is also signified in their births and deaths. About the time of John's birth the days begin to be shorter, and about the time of Christ's birth they grow longer, as the maxim has it: *Solstitium decimo Christum praeit atque Joannem.*[8] So it was also in their deaths: Christ's body was heightened on the cross, John's was lessened by a head.

Paul the Deacon tells us in the *History of the Lombards* that Rothari, king of the Lombards, was buried, with a wealth of precious ornaments, beside the church of Saint John the Baptist. Then a man, seduced by greed, broke into the tomb and stole all the treasure. Saint John appeared to this man and said: "How dared you touch what was committed to my care? From now on you cannot enter my church!" And that is exactly how things went: whenever the man tried to enter this church, he was repelled by a mighty blow to the throat, and fell back at once.

87. Saints John and Paul

John and Paul were high officials in the household of Constantia, the daughter of Emperor Constantine. At the time the Scythians were invading Dacia and Thrace, and Gallicanus, commander of the Roman army, was about to lead his troops against them. Gallicanus demanded that Constantia be given to him in marriage in return for his leadership in the war, and the chief men of Rome urged the emperor to agree. The father, however, was saddened, because he knew that his daughter, after she was cured by Saint Agnes, had made a vow of virginity and would rather die than consent to marriage; but the virgin, trusting in God, advised her father to promise her to the general when and if he came back a victor. Moreover, he had two daughters of his now-deceased wife, and he would be asked to leave them with Constantia, so that she might learn their father's ways and wishes from them. In return for this Constantia offered him the services of John and Paul, hoping for greater security; and she prayed that God would convert both the father and the daughters. These arrangements pleased all parties.

---

[8] The solstice comes ten days before Christ and before John.

Gallicanus, with John and Paul and a large army, marched off to war, but the Scythians smashed the Roman force and besieged the remnants in a town in Thrace. At this point John and Paul went to the general and said to him: "Make a vow to the God of heaven, and you will win a victory greater than any you have won before!" Gallicanus made his vow, and a youth carrying a cross immediately appeared to him and said: "Gird on your sword and follow me!" He assented and followed the youth. They sped through the enemy's camp, reached their king and slew him, and by fear alone subjugated the army and made it tributary to the Romans. Two knights in armor appeared to him in the fight and supported him on either side.

Gallicanus, now a Christian, returned to Rome and was welcomed with much honor. He asked the emperor to pardon him that he no longer wished to wed his daughter, because he had made a vow of continence to Christ. Meanwhile Constantia had converted his two daughters, and Constantine was very pleased to grant his request regarding the marriage. The general now resigned his command, distributed his wealth to the poor, and served God in poverty with other servants of the Lord. He wrought many miracles, and at the mere sight of him the demons fled out of the bodies of the possessed. The fame of his holiness spread throughout the world, and people came from the east and the west to see this Roman patrician washing the feet of the poor, serving them at table, pouring water over their hands, ministering kindly to the sick, and engaging in other forms of holy servitude.

Emperor Constantine the Great died and was succeeded by his son Constantius, who was tainted with the Arian heresy. Another Constantine, this one the brother of Constantine the emperor, had left two sons, Gallus and Julian. Emperor Constantius appointed the said Gallus a caesar and sent him to put down rebellious Judea, but later put him to death. Julian, fearing that Constantius would do away with him as he had with his brother, entered a monastery and made so great a show of religiosity that he was ordained to the office of lector. He also consulted the devil through a sorcerer and received the answer that he would become emperor.

Some time later, due to the pressure of events in the empire, Constantius appointed Julian a caesar and sent him to Gaul, where he carried out his mission effectively. When Constantius died, Julian, by then an apostate, was raised to the empire as Constantius had ordered. Julian gave orders that Gallicanus should either sacrifice to the gods or go into exile: he did not dare kill so widely admired a man. Gallicanus went to Alexandria, where the infidels stabbed him to the heart and he won the crown of martyrdom.

Julian, consumed by sacrilegious greed, covered his avarice by quoting the Gospel. When he robbed Christians of their possessions, he said: "Your Christ says in the Gospel that unless you renounce all you possess, you cannot be his disciple." Then he heard that John and Paul were supplying the needs of poor Christians out of the riches the virgin Constantia had left, and he informed them that as they had served Constantine, it was their duty to be at his service. They said: "Emperors Constantine and Constantius were proud to be servants of Christ, and we gladly served them; but since you have abandoned the religion of all the virtues, we have absolutely renounced your service and would despise ourselves if we obeyed you!" Julian replied: "I was an ordained cleric in your church, and if I had wanted to, I could have been pope. But I thought it was a waste to do nothing and live in idleness. So I made my choice for the military life, offered sacrifice to the gods, and with their help rose to the empire. You therefore, since you were raised in the imperial court, should not leave my side. I should have you with me as the first men in my palace. But if you persist in despising me, I shall have to take action, because I must not be despised!" They answered: "Since we put God before you, we certainly do not fear your threats! If we did, we might incur the enmity of the eternal God!" "If within ten days you have not changed your attitude toward me," said Julian, "you will be forced to do what you do not care to do of your own volition!" "Act as if the ten days were past, and do what you have been threatening to do!" said the saints. The emperor replied: "You think the Christians will make martyrs of you, but I will punish you not as martyrs but as public enemies!"

John and Paul spent the next ten days distributing all their wealth to the poor. On the tenth day Terentianus was sent to them and he said: "Our master Julian has sent a small gold statue of Jove to you. You are to burn incense to it, otherwise you die, both of you!" The two responded: "If Julian is your master, keep peace with him! We have no master except our Lord Jesus Christ!" He then ordered them to be beheaded secretly, and their bodies to be buried in a grave inside the house; and he circulated the rumor that they had been sent into exile. Shortly thereafter, Terentianus's son was seized by a demon and began to cry out through the house that a demon was tormenting him. Seeing this, Terentianus confessed his crime, became a Christian, and wrote an account of the passion of the martyrs. They suffered about the year A.D. 460.

Pope Gregory, in a homily on the Gospel text "If any man will come after me, let him deny himself and take up his cross," tells the story of a lady who regularly visited the church of the martyrs. One day when she went in, she found two monks in pilgrim attire standing in the church. Thinking that they were pilgrims, she ordered her attendant to give them an alms. While the attendant went about doing so, the pilgrims stood close to the lady and said: "You visit us now. On the day of judgment we shall seek you out and do whatever we can for you!" And they vanished out of her sight.

Ambrose, in his Preface for these martyrs, says: "The blessed martyrs John and Paul truly fulfilled what the voice of David said, 'Behold how good and how pleasant it is for brothers to dwell together in unity' (Ps. 133:1). These were brothers by the law of their birth, bound together in their common faith, equal to each other in their martyrdom, and forever glorious in the one Lord!"

88. Saint Leo, Pope

We read in the book of the *Miracles of the Blessed Virgin* that one day when Pope Leo was offering mass in the church of Saint Mary Major and was distributing communion to the faithful, a woman kissed his hand, and he experienced a violent temptation of the flesh. The man of God, taking cruel vengeance on himself that same day, secretly cut off the hand that had scandalized him, and threw it away. In time the people began to murmur at the pope for not celebrating the divine mysteries as usual. Then Leo turned to the Blessed Virgin and committed himself totally to her care. She quickly appeared at his side and with her holy hands put back his hand and made it firm, ordering him to proceed as before and offer sacrifice to her Son. Leo therefore proclaimed to all the people what had happened to him, and showed the restored hand to everyone.

This pope called the Council of Chalcedon and decreed that from then on virgins alone could take the veil. This council also decreed that Mary should be called "Mother of God."

At that time Attila was devastating Italy. Saint Leo spent three days and nights in prayer in the church of the apostles and then said to his associates: "If any of you wish to follow me, come along!" He went out of the city and moved toward Attila and his band. The Hun, seeing the blessed Leo, dismounted, knelt at the pope's feet, and begged him to ask for anything he wanted. Leo asked him to withdraw from Italy and to set his prisoners free. Attila's people protested: was the conqueror of the world to be conquered by a priest? Attila answered them: "I acted for my own good and yours! I saw standing at his right side a mighty warrior with his sword drawn, who said to me, 'Unless you obey this man, you and your people will perish!'"

At another time Leo prayed and fasted for forty days at Saint Peter's tomb, asking the apostle to obtain for him the remission of his sins. Saint Peter appeared to him and said: "I have prayed the Lord for you and he has forgiven all your sins. You will be held responsible only for the laying on of hands; that is to say that you will be asked whether you ordained anyone whether he was worthy or not."

Saint Leo died about A.D. 460.

89. Saint Peter, Apostle

Peter had three names. First, he was called *Simon Bar-Jona. Simon* is interpreted as obedient, or as accepting sadness; *Bar-Jona* as son of the dove, since *Bar* means son in Syriac, and *Jona* means dove in Hebrew. Peter indeed was obedient when Christ called him: at a single word of command he obeyed the Lord. He accepted sadness when, having denied Christ, he went outside and wept bitterly. He was a son of the dove because his whole intention was to serve God in simplicity. Secondly, he was called *Cephas,* which is interpreted head, or rock, or speaking forcefully: head, because he was the chief among the Church's prelates; rock, because of his endurance in his passion; speaking forcefully, by reason of his constant preaching. Thirdly, he was called *Petrus,* Peter, which is interpreted as recognizing, or taking off one's shoes, or unbinding. Peter recognized Christ's divinity when he said: "You are the Christ, the Son of the living God." He stripped the feet of his attachments to any dead and earthly works when he said: "Behold we have left all things and have followed you." He unbound us by removing the bonds of sin, which he did with the keys he received from the Lord.

Peter also had three surnames. He was called Simon *Johanna,* which means beauty of the Lord; Simon *Johannis,* meaning to whom it is given; and Simon *Bar-Jona,* son of the dove. By these surnames we are given to understand that Peter had beauty of conduct, gifts of virtue, and abundance of tears, the last because the dove's song is mournful. As to the name Peter, first Jesus *promised* that that would be his name; John 1:42: "You shall be called Cephas, which means Peter." Second, Jesus *gave* him the name; Mark 3:16: "And to Simon he gave the name Peter." Third, he *confirmed* the name; Matt. 16:18: "And I tell you, you are Peter, and on this rock I will build my Church."

Marcellus, Pope Linus, Hegesippus, and Pope Leo wrote accounts of Peter's passion.

Peter the apostle stood out among and above the other apostles. He wanted to know who the Lord's betrayer was, because, as Augustine says, if he had known, he would have torn the individual apart with his teeth. Therefore Christ would not name the traitor, because, as Chrysostom says, Peter would have risen up and killed him immediately. He walked over the water to the Lord, who chose him to be present at his transfiguration and at the raising to life of the ruler's daughter, found the coin of the tribute in the fish's mouth, received the keys of the kingdom of heaven from the Lord, accepted the charge of feeding Christ's sheep, converted three thousand men by his preaching on the day of Pentecost, foretold the deaths of Ananias and Saphira, cured Aeneas the paralytic, baptized Cornelius, brought Tabitha back to life. The shadow of his body cured the sick, and he was jailed by Herod and set free by an angel.

What food he ate and what clothes he wore he himself, as quoted in Saint Clement's book, tells us: "All I eat is bread with olives and sometimes vegetables. What I wear is what you see—a tunic and a cloak. I don't need anything else." It is also said that inside his tunic he always carried a towel with which to wipe away his frequent tears, because, when the dear memory of the Lord's presence and speech came to his mind, the surge of love made him unable to contain his weeping. When he remembered how he had denied his Lord, his sense of guilt made him shed tears again. Indeed, weeping became so habitual with him that, as Clement says, his whole face seemed to be burned with tears. Clement also tells us that when Peter heard the cock crow at dawn, he rose to pray and as usual burst into tears. He tells us—and we find this also in the *Ecclesiastical History*—that when Peter's wife was led to her martyrdom, he was overjoyed and called to her by her name, saying: "Dear wife, remember the Lord!"

Once when Peter sent two of his disciples away to preach and they had been traveling for twenty days, one of them died, and the other returned to Peter and told him what had happened. It is said that the one who died was Martial, though some say it was Maternus. Elsewhere we read that the first disciple was blessed Fronto, and his companion, who died, was a priest named George. However that may be, Peter handed his staff to the surviving disciple and ordered him to go back to his dead friend and to lay the staff upon him. He did this, and the man who had been dead for forty days promptly stood up alive.

At the time there was in Jerusalem a conjurer named Simon, who claimed to be the source of all truth. He declared that he would make those who believed him immortal, and that nothing was impossible to him. We read also in Clement's book that Simon said: "I will be publicly worshiped as God, and I will be given divine honors. Whatever I may wish to do I will be able to do. When my mother Rachel told me to go out to the wheatfield and reap the grain, I saw a scythe lying on the ground and I commanded the scythe to do the reaping by itself, and it reaped ten times as much as the other reapers did." Jerome says that Simon added: "I am the word of God, I am the beautiful one, I am the Paraclete. All that God is, I am!" At his command bronze serpents moved, bronze and stone statues laughed, and dogs sang.

According to Pope Linus, this Simon wanted to debate with Peter and to prove that he was God. On the appointed day Peter came to the meeting place and said to those gathered there: "Peace be with you, brothers who love the truth!" Simon said to him: "We have no use for your peace! If there is peace and harmony, we will make no progress in our search for the truth. Thieves keep peace among themselves! Therefore do not invoke peace but war! When two fight, there will be peace when one or the other is defeated!" Peter: "Why are you afraid to hear of peace? Wars are born of sin, but where there is no sin, there is peace. Truth comes out in discussion, righteousness is found in deeds." Simon: "Idle talk! I will show you the power of my divinity so that you may adore me at once! I am the first power! I can fly through the air, make new trees, change stones into bread, stand in fire without injury. I can do anything I choose to do!" But Peter refuted him point by point and exposed all his magical hoaxes. Then Simon, seeing that he could not prevail over the apostle and for fear of being exposed as a sorcerer, threw all his books of magic into the sea and went to Rome, where he might be accepted as a god. But Peter learned of this and followed him, and this brought him to Rome.

It was in the fourth year of the reign of Emperor Claudius that Peter came to Rome. He held his see in Rome for twenty-five years and, as John Beleth says, ordained two bishops, Linus and Cletus, to assist him, one within the city of Rome and the other outside the walls. He preached assiduously and made many converts to the faith, and cured a great many sick people of their illnesses. In his preaching he always praised and stressed chastity. This so changed the lives of four of the prefect Agrippa's concubines that they refused to have anything more to do with him. This made him angry, and he watched for an opportunity to get the better of the apostle. Then the Lord appeared to Peter and said: "Simon and Nero are plotting against you, but have no fear, because I am with you and will shield you! I will also give you my servant Paul as a solace. He will arrive in Rome tomorrow!" Peter, knowing now, as Linus says, that the time to put off his mortal tent was at hand, presided over a meeting of his brethren at which he took Clement by the hand, ordained him a bishop, and installed him in his own prelatial chair. Then Paul arrived in Rome as the Lord had foretold, and with Peter began to preach Christ.

Meanwhile Simon Magus was in high favor with Nero, and people thought without a doubt that he was the guardian of the emperor's life and welfare and that of the whole city. One day, as Pope Leo tells it, Simon was standing in Nero's presence and his visage suddenly changed so that at one moment he looked older and the next moment younger. Nero saw this and was sure that Simon was the son of God. The sorcerer, as the same Leo reports, then said to Nero: "You know perfectly well, Emperor, that I am the son of God, so order me to be beheaded, and on the third day I will rise again!" Nero therefore ordered the executioner to cut off Simon's head. The executioner proceeded to cut the head off a ram but thought he had indeed beheaded a man, Simon having created this illusion by his magical arts. Thus Simon escaped. He gathered up the animal's remains and hid them, leaving the blood to congeal on the pavement, and remained in seclusion for three days. Then he made his appearance before Nero and said: "Have my blood, which I shed, wiped up, because, though I was beheaded, here I am, risen on the third day as I promised!" The emperor was dumbfounded and was more sure than ever that Simon was God's son. This from Leo. Another time, when Simon was inside with the emperor, a demon assumed his appearance and harangued the populace outside the palace. In the end the Romans held him in such veneration that they made a statue of him and inscribed this title on it: SIMONI DEO SANCTO.[1]

Pope Leo affirms that Peter and Paul went to Nero and exposed all the mischief Simon was doing; and Peter added that as there are two substances in Christ, the divine and the human, so there were two substances in this magician, the human and the diabolical. Then, as Saint Marcellus and Pope Leo aver, Simon said: "I will not tolerate this enemy any longer! I will command my angels and they will avenge me!" Peter said to him: "I am not afraid of your angels, but they are afraid of me!" "What!" said Nero, "Are you not afraid of Simon, who proves his divinity by his acts?" Peter: "If there is any divinity in him, let him tell me what I am thinking or what I am doing; but first I shall whisper in your ear what I am thinking, so that he won't dare to lie!" Nero: "Come close and tell me what you are thinking!" Peter came close to him and said: "Have a loaf of bread brought and given to me in such a way that he can't see what is happening!" The loaf was brought and Peter blessed it and hid it in his sleeve, and said: "Let Simon, who has made himself God, say what I have thought, said, and done!" Simon answered: "Rather let Peter say what I am thinking!" "I will show what Simon is thinking," Peter responded, "by doing what he's thinking!" Then Simon shouted angrily: "Let big dogs come in and devour him!" Suddenly huge dogs appeared and rushed upon Peter, but he brought out the blessed bread and the dogs turned and fled. Then Peter said to Nero: "See, I have shown, not by words but by action, that I knew what Simon had in mind. He had promised that he would bring his angels against me, but what he brought was dogs, showing that his angels are not godlike but canine!" Simon retorted: "Listen, Peter and Paul, if I cannot do anything to you here, we will go to a place where it suits me to judge you. For the time being I spare you!" This from Leo.

Then, as Hegesippus and Linus tell us, Simon, carried away by pride, dared to boast that he could raise the dead, and it happened that a young man had just died. So Peter and Simon were summoned, and all agreed with a proposal by Simon that the one who was unable to raise the dead man should be killed. Simon then began his incantations over the corpse, and those standing around saw the dead man move his head. The witnesses shouted and wanted to stone Peter, but the apostle, having barely succeeded in quieting them, said: "If the man is alive, let him rise, walk, and talk! Otherwise be aware that it was a demon that moved his head! Let Simon be moved away from the bier so that the devil's features may be fully unmasked!" Simon was moved away and the youth lay

[1] TO SIMON THE HOLY GOD.

motionless until Peter, standing at a distance, prayed and then said loudly: "Young man, in the name of Jesus Christ the Nazarene, arise and walk!" And the youth instantly arose and walked about.

Now the people wanted to stone Simon, but Peter said: "He is punished enough, since he has to admit that he and his witchcraft are defeated. Our master has taught us to return good for evil!" Then Simon spoke. "Peter and Paul, know that what you desire, namely, that I would deign to award you the crown of martyrdom, will not happen to you!" Peter: "May what we desire come for us, but may no good ever come to you, because every time you speak, you lie!"

Then, as Saint Marcellus says, Simon went to the house of Marcellus, a disciple of his, and tied an enormous dog at the door of the house, saying: "Now we'll see whether Peter, who usually comes to you, will be able to get in!" In a little while Peter arrived, made the sign of the cross over the dog, and turned it loose. The animal was gentle with all the others, but chased Simon, caught him and pulled him to the ground, leapt upon him and was about to take him by the throat; but Peter ran up and called to the dog not to hurt Simon. The dog therefore did not injure his body but tore his clothes to shreds and left him naked. Then the crowd, and especially the children and the dog, ran after him until they chased him out of the city as they would chase a wolf.

Unable to bear the shame of this episode, Simon kept out of sight for a whole year. Marcellus, however, witnessed these miracles and became a follower of Saint Peter. Later, Simon came out and was welcomed back into Nero's friendship. Furthermore, as Leo tells it, he called the people together and declared that he had been gravely offended by the Galileans and therefore had decided to leave the city, which he had protected until then. He also set a day upon which he was to ascend to heaven, because he did not deign to dwell on earth any longer. The day arrived and he climbed a high tower—or, according to Linus, he went up to the top of the Capitol—wearing a crown of laurel. He jumped off and began to fly. Paul said to Peter: "I'm the one to pray now; you're the one to command!" To Nero he said: "This man Peter is truthful, you and yours are seducers!" Peter said to Paul: "Paul, raise your head and look up!" When Paul looked up, he saw Simon flying and said to Peter: "Peter, what are you waiting for? Finish what you've started, because the Lord is already calling us!" Then Peter said: "I adjure you, angels of Satan, you who are holding Simon up in the air, I adjure you in the name of Jesus Christ our Lord! Stop holding him up and let him fall!" They released him at once and he crashed to the ground, his skull was fractured, and he expired. Nero grieved at the loss of such a man and said to the apostles: "You have aroused my suspicions, and therefore I shall lose you, too, and make you a horrible example!" This from Leo.

So the emperor gave Peter and Paul into the hands of Paulinus, a man of high station, and Paulinus turned them over to the custody of Mamertinus to be guarded by two soldiers, Processus and Martinianus; but Peter converted the soldiers, and they opened the prison doors and set the apostles free. (After the martyrdom of Peter and Paul, Paulinus had Processus and Martinianus brought before him for having done this, and, when he learned that they were Christians, had them beheaded by order of Nero.) The brethren urged Peter to leave the city. He was unwilling to do so, but finally, overcome by their insistence, he started out. When he got outside the city gates, as Leo and Linus have it, and reached the place that is now called Saint Mary at the Footprints, he saw Christ coming toward him and said: "Lord, where are you going?" Christ answered: "I am going to Rome to be crucified again!" Peter: "You will be crucified again?" Christ: "Yes!" And Peter said: "In that case, Lord, I'm going back to be crucified with you!" When these words had been spoken, the Lord ascended to heaven, while Peter watched and wept. And when he realized that what had been said concerned his own passion, he returned to the city and told the brethren what had happened.

Now he was taken prisoner by Nero's men and brought to the prefect Agrippa; and, as Linus says, his face shone like the sun. Agrippa said to him: "So you are the one who glories among the common people and the little women whom you wean from their husbands' beds!" But the apostle broke in to say that he gloried only in the cross of Jesus Christ. Then Peter, being an alien, was condemned to be crucified, while Paul, because he was a Roman citizen, was sentenced to beheading. Dionysius wrote about this judgment scene in his letter to Timothy on the death of Saint Paul: "O my brother Timothy, if you had seen the way they were treated in their last hours, you would have fainted with sadness and grief. Who would not weep in that hour when the sentence came down that Peter was to be crucified and Paul to be beheaded! Then you would have seen the mob of pagans and Jews striking them and spitting in their faces! And when came the awful moment of their consummation, they were separated from each other, and these pillars of the world were put in chains as the brethren groaned and wept. Then Paul said to Peter: 'Peace be with you, foundation stone of the churches and shepherd of the sheep and lambs of Christ!' Peter said to Paul: 'Go in peace, preacher of virtuous living, mediator and leader of the salvation of the righteous!' When the two were taken away in different directions because they were not put to death in the same place, I followed my master." So Dionysius.

Pope Leo and Marcellus assert that when Peter came to the cross, he said: "Because my Lord came down from heaven to earth, his cross was raised straight up; but he deigns to call me from earth to heaven, and my cross should have my head toward the earth and should point my feet toward heaven. Therefore, since I am not worthy to be on the cross the way my Lord was, turn my cross and crucify me head down!" So they turned the cross and nailed him to it with his feet upwards and his hands downwards. At the sight of this the people were enraged, and wanted to kill Nero and the prefect and free the apostle, but he pleaded with them not to hinder his martyrdom. Hegesippus and Linus say that the Lord opened the eyes of those who were weeping there, and they saw angels standing with crowns of roses and lilies, and Peter standing with them at the cross, receiving a book from Christ and reading from the book the words that he spoke. According to the same Hegesippus, Peter began to speak from the cross. "I chose to imitate you, Lord, but I had no right to be crucified upright. You are always upright, exalted, and high. We are children of the first man, who lowered his head to the earth, whose fall is signified by the manner of man's birth, for we are born in such a way that we seem to be dropped prone upon the earth. Conditions are changed, and the world thinks that right is left and left is right. You, Lord, are all things to me. All that you are, and nothing else but you alone, is all there is to me. I give you thanks with the whole spirit by which I live, understand, and call upon you!" (In these words two other reasons for his not wishing to be crucified in an upright position are touched upon.) Finally, Peter, knowing that the faithful had seen his glory, gave thanks, commended the faithful to God, and breathed forth his spirit. Marcellus and his brother Apuleius, Peter's disciples, took his body down from the cross and buried it embalmed with sweet spices.

Isidore, in his book *On the Birth and Death of the Saints*, says: "After Peter founded the church in Antioch, he went to Rome under Emperor Claudius to oppose Simon Magus, preached there, and for twenty-five years was bishop of that city. He was crucified head down, as he had wished, in the thirtieth year after the Lord's passion." Thus Isidore.

On the day of their death Peter and Paul appeared to Dionysius, according to what he says in the aforementioned letter: "My brother Timothy, hear the miracle, see the marvel, of the day of their martyrdom! For I was present at the moment when they were separated: after their death I saw them coming in hand in hand at the gate of the city, clothed in luminous garments and crowned with crowns of brilliance and light." Thus Dionysius.

Nero did not go unpunished for this crime and others he committed, for he put an end to his life with his own hand. Here we may add a brief notice of some of these crimes.

We read in a certain history, admittedly apocryphal, that when Seneca, Nero's tutor, was looking forward to a reward worthy of his labors, Nero ordered him to choose which branch of a given tree he would prefer to be hanged from, saying that this was the reward he was going to receive. When Seneca asked why he was being condemned to death, Nero brandished a sharp sword over his head, and Seneca bowed his head and backed away from the sword, stricken with fear at the threat of death. Nero asked him: "Master, why do you bow your head and dodge the sword?" Seneca answered: "Because I am a man and therefore I fear death and am unwilling to die." Nero: "And I fear you even now, as I feared you as a child! That is why I cannot live in peace and quiet as long as you are alive!" "If I must die," said Seneca, "at least allow me to choose the mode of death that I would prefer!" Nero: "Choose quickly! Don't delay your death!" Then Seneca lay in a bathtub filled with water and opened the veins in both arms; and as the blood flowed out, his life ended. So his very name, *Seneca*, was a presage. *Se necans* means killing oneself, and though he was forced to do so, he died by his own hand.

We also read that Seneca had two brothers. One was Julianus Gallio, the famous orator who committed suicide, and the other was Mela, father of the poet Lucan—the Lucan who, we read, died by opening his veins by order of Nero.

The same apocryphal history tells us that Nero, obsessed by an evil madness, ordered his mother killed and cut open so that he could see how it had been for him in her womb. The physicians, calling him to task over his mother's death, said: "Our laws prohibit it, and divine law forbids a son to kill his mother, who gave birth to him with such pain and nurtured him with so much toil and trouble." Nero said to them: "Make me pregnant with a child and then make me give birth, so that I may know how much pain it cost my mother!" He had conceived the notion of bearing a child because on his way through the city he had heard the cries of a woman in labor. They said to him: "That is not possible because it is contrary to nature, nor is it thinkable because it is contrary to reason." At this Nero said to them: "Make me pregnant and make me give birth, or I will have every one of you die a cruel death!"

So the doctors made up a potion in which they put a frog and gave it to the emperor to drink. Then they used their skills to make the frog grow in his belly, and his belly, rebelling against this unnatural invasion, swelled up so that Nero thought he was carrying a child. They also put him on a diet of foods they knew would be suitable for the frog, and told him that, having conceived, he had to follow the diet. At length, unable to stand the pain, he told the doctors: "Hasten the delivery, because I am so exhausted with this childbearing that I can hardly get my breath!" So they gave him a drink that made him vomit, and out came a frog horrible to see, full of vile humors and covered with blood. Nero, looking at what he had brought forth, shrank from it and wondered why it was such a monster, but the physicians told him that he had produced a deformed fetus because he had not been willing to wait the full term. He said: "Is this what I was like when I came out from my mother's womb?" "Yes!" they answered. So he commanded that the fetus be fed and kept in a domed chamber with stones in it. All this, however, is not contained in the chronicles and is apocryphal.

Then Nero began to wonder about the manner and extent of the burning of Troy, and made Rome burn for seven days and seven nights. He watched the fire from the highest available tower, being delighted with the beauty of the flames and reciting verses from the *Iliad* in a grandiose, bombastic style.

The chronicles tell us that Nero fished with gold nets, and that he worked hard at music and singing so as to surpass all harpists and actors. He took a man as his wife and was accepted as wife by a man, Orosius says. Finally the Romans could tolerate his insanity no longer, so they rose up against him and drove him out of the city. Seeing that no escape was possible, he sharpened a stick to a point with his teeth and drove it through his middle, thus putting an end to his life. Elsewhere we read that he was devoured by wolves.

When the Romans came back into the city, they found the frog hiding in its nest, hurried it out beyond the walls, and set it afire. Some say that the section of the city where the frog hid is called the Lateran for that reason.[2]

In the time of Pope Saint Cornelius some Greek Christians stole the bodies of the two apostles and were carrying them off, but demons living in the idols were forced by the power of God to cry out: "Men of Rome, help! Your gods are being carried away!" The faithful took this to mean the apostles, and the pagans to mean their gods, so believers and unbelievers came together and pursued the Greeks. These were fearful, and threw the apostles' bodies into a well near the catacombs, where the faithful recovered them at a later time. Gregory, however, says in his *Register* that a violent storm of thunder and lightning frightened and dispersed them so that they left the relics in or near the catacombs.

Then there was uncertainty about which bones were Saint Peter's and which Saint Paul's. The faithful prayed and fasted persistently and obtained a response from heaven: "The larger bones belong to the preacher, the smaller ones to the fisherman." So the bones were separated and each apostle's lot was placed in the church that had been raised in his honor. Others say that Pope Silvester, when he was about to consecrate the churches, put both the large and the small bones on a scale, weighed them with much reverence, and allocated equal halves to the two churches.

Gregory, in his *Dialogue*, tells of one Agontius, a man of great humility and sanctity, who lived in the church where Saint Peter's body reposes. There was also a girl living in the church, a paralytic who crawled on her hands and knees, dragging her body along the pavement because her lower limbs were crippled. For a long time she had been imploring Saint Peter to cure her, and finally he appeared to her and said: "Go to Agontius, who lives here, and he will restore you to health." So she began to drag herself here and there in the great church, looking in every nook and cranny and trying to find out who this Agontius was. Then suddenly the man she sought was in front of her, and she said to him: "Our shepherd and foster father Saint Peter has sent me to you to have you free me from my infirmities." "If you have been sent by him," Agontius answered, "stand up!" He gave her his hand and helped her to her feet, and she was completely cured, not a trace of her debility remaining.

In the same book Gregory tells us about Galla, a young girl of the highest Roman nobility, daughter of Symmachus, a consul and patrician. Galla was given in marriage, but in the space of one year her husband died and she was left a widow. Both her age and her fortune pointed to a second marriage, but she chose to be united to God in spiritual nuptials, which begin in grief but lead to eternal joys, rather than subject herself to marriage in the flesh, which always

---

[2] *Lateranus* from *latente rana*, hiding frog.

begins happily but tends toward a sad end. Galla, however, was a very hot-blooded woman, and her doctors told her that unless she gave herself again to the embraces of a husband, the excessive internal heat would cause her to grow a beard, unnatural as that would be. This actually happened, but she felt no concern about the external deformity because she loved inner beauty more, nor did she fear that if the beard made her ugly her heavenly spouse would not love her. She therefore put off her secular attire and entered the monastery attached to the church of Saint Peter, where she served God for many years in simplicity, prayer, and almsgiving. Then she was stricken with a cancer of the breast. Beside her bed there were always two candlesticks with lighted candles, because, being a lover of light, she hated not only spiritual but also material darkness. At a given moment she saw Saint Peter the apostle standing at the foot of her bed between the two candles. Thrilled with joy and drawing boldness from her love, she said: "What is it, my lord? Are all my sins forgiven me?" Peter, his face beaming with kindness, nodded and said: "All forgiven! Come!" She said: "I ask that Sister Benedicta may come with me." "No," said Saint Peter, "but that other sister may come with you." Galla told all this to the abbess, and three days later she died with the other sister.

In the same book Gregory says that there was a priest, known for his holiness, who, when he was dying, cried out joyously: "Welcome, my lords! Welcome, my lords, that you have deigned to come to me, poor little servant man that I am! I come, I come! Thank you! Thank you!" When those attending him asked him to whom he was talking, he was surprised and answered: "Don't you see the holy apostles Peter and Paul, who have come here together?" And when he had repeated those same words over and over, his holy soul was released from his body.

There are some who question whether Peter and Paul suffered martyrdom on the same day. Some say it was on the same day, but that one suffered a year later than the other. But Jerome and almost all the holy fathers who have dealt with this question agree that they suffered on the same day and in the same year. This is clear also from the letter of Dionysius; and Pope Leo (or Maximus, as some think) says in a sermon: "We have good reasons to think it happened that on one day and in one place they were sentenced to death by the one tyrant.. They suffered on one and the same day so that they could go to Christ at the same time; in one and the same place so that Rome might possess both of them; under one persecutor, that equal cruelty should befall them both. The day therefore was decreed to show their merit, the place to show their glory, and the persecutor to show their bravery." So Leo.

Granted, however, that they suffered on the same day and at the same hour, they did not suffer at the same spot but at different locations. When Leo says that they suffered in the same place, he means that they were both martyred in Rome. Someone put this in verse:

> Ense coronatur Paulus, cruce Petrus, eodem
> Sub duce, luce, loco, dux Nero, Roma locus.[3]

Another put it this way:

> Ense sacrat Paulum, par lux, dux, urbs, cruce Petrum.[4]

Although they died on the same day, however, Gregory decreed that on that day the offices should celebrate Peter more specially, and that commemoration of Paul be made the following day. This is because the church of Saint Peter was dedicated on that day, because Peter was higher in dignity and was converted earlier, and because he was the primate of Rome.

※
---

90. Saint Paul, Apostle

The name Paul, or Paulus, is interpreted to mean mouth of a trumpet, or their mouth, or wonderfully chosen, or miracle of election. Or Paulus comes from *pausa*, which in Hebrew means quiet or repose, and in Latin means a moderate man. These meanings denote six privileges that Paul possessed more than others do. The first is the privilege of fruitful speech, because he preached the Gospel from Illyria to Jerusalem and therefore is said to be the mouth of a trumpet. Secondly, his love of others was visceral and made him say: "Who is weak, and I am not weak? Who is scandalized, and I am not on fire?" Therefore he is called the mouth of them, i.e., the mouth of the heart, of which he himself says: "Our mouth is open to you, O Corinthians, our heart is wide." The third privilege is his miraculous conversion, and so he is called wonderfully chosen because he was chosen and converted miraculously. Fourthly, he had the hands of a workman, for which reason he is said to be a miracle of election, because it was a great wonder that he chose to earn his living with his own hands and to preach tirelessly. His fifth privilege was that of blissful contemplation. He was caught up to the third heaven and there became the quiet of the Lord, because contemplation

---

[3] Paul was martyred with a sword, Peter on a cross, the same / Ruler, day, place, the ruler Nero, the place Rome.

[4] Paul is sainted by the sword, same day, ruler, city, Peter by the cross.

requires quiet in the mind. Sixthly, he had the virtue of humility and so could be called moderate.

There are three opinions concerning Paul's name. Origen held that he always had two names and was called either Saul or Paul. Rabanus Maurus believed that originally he was called Saul after Saul the proud king but after his conversion was called Paul, which means small, because of his moderate and humble spirit. Thus he was interpreting his own name when he said: "I am the least of the apostles, not worthy to be called an apostle." Bede, however, thought that he took the name Paul from the proconsul Sergius Paulus, whom he converted to the faith. Pope Linus wrote Paul's passion.

After his conversion the apostle Paul suffered many forms of persecution, which Saint Hilary sums up as follows: "At Philippi Paul the apostle was beaten with rods and imprisoned, and had his feet bound to a log of wood; he was stoned in Lystra, pursued by evil men in Iconium and Thessalonica, thrown to the wild beasts in Ephesus. At Damascus he was let down over the city wall in a basket, in Jerusalem he was haled to court, whipped, bound, and conspired against, in Caesarea he was put in jail and charged with crimes, on the way to Italy by sea he was put in danger of shipwreck, and arriving in Rome he was tried and put to death under Nero." This from Hilary.

Paul was awarded the apostolate to the Gentiles. At Lystra he made a crippled man walk straight up, restored to life a youth who had fallen from a window, and performed many other miracles. At Mitylene a viper bit him on the hand but did him no harm; instead he shook off the beast into the fire. It is also said that those who are descended from the man whose guest Paul was are never harmed in any way by venomous snakes: for this reason, when a child is born to a man of that lineage, the father puts a serpent into the cradle, so as to be assured that the infant really is his child.

We find also that at different times Paul is portrayed as Peter's inferior, as greater than Peter, or as Peter's equal, but the fact is that he was inferior in dignity, greater in preaching, and equal in holiness. Haymon tells us that from cockcrow until late morning Paul plied a manual trade, then proceeded to preach, and that sometimes his sermons went on till nightfall. The remaining time sufficed for taking food and for rest and prayer.

When Paul arrived in Rome, Nero was not yet confirmed as emperor, and when he heard that Paul was engaged in arguing with the Jews about Jewish law and the Christian faith, he paid little attention. The apostle therefore was at liberty to go where he pleased and to preach freely. Jerome, in his book *On Illustrious Men*, says that in the twenty-fifth year from the Lord's passion, i.e., the second year of Nero's reign, Paul was sent to Rome in chains and was held in loose custody for two years during which he debated with the Jews, and then was set free by Nero and preached the Gospel in lands to the west. In Nero's fourteenth year, however, he was beheaded, in the same year and on the same day on which Peter was crucified. So Jerome.

Paul became widely known and was admired for his wisdom and the depth of his religious devotion. He became friendly with a number of people in Nero's immediate company and converted them to the faith of Christ. Some of his writings were read before the emperor and were applauded by all who heard them. Even the Senate thought highly of him. One day toward evening, however, he was preaching in a crowded upper room. A young man named Patroclus, who was Nero's cupbearer and dear to the emperor, climbed up and sat on a windowsill in order to hear him better, but after a while dozed off, fell to the ground, and was killed. Nero took the news of his favorite's death very hard and promptly appointed another to take his place. Paul knew about this by the Spirit and told some of the people present to bring him the body of Patroclus. He then restored the youth to life and sent him and his companions to the emperor.

So Nero, lamenting the death of his cupbearer, all of a sudden was told that Patroclus, very much alive, was at the door. Hearing that the youth, whom a moment ago he mourned as dead, was alive, he was frightened and refused to let him in, until finally his attendants persuaded him to admit the young man to his presence. Nero said to him: "Patroclus, you are alive?" The answer: "Caesar, I am alive." Nero: "Who brought you to life?" Patroclus: "Jesus Christ, the King of all the ages." Nero, angrily: "So he will reign forever and will do away with all the world's kingdoms?" Patroclus: "Yes, Caesar!" Nero slapped him, saying: "So now you are that king's soldier?" Patroclus: "Yes, I am his soldier because he brought me back from the dead." Then five of the emperor's ministers, who were always at his side, said to him: "Why, Emperor, do you strike this estimable youth, who is giving you truthful answers? For we too are soldiers of that unconquered king!"

At this, Nero shut them up in prison, intending to torture them as much as he had loved them previously. Then he gave orders to round up all Christians and punish and torture them without a hearing. Paul, along with the rest, was brought before him in chains. Nero said to him: "Well, sir, you serve a great king, but here you are, conquered by me! Why do you lure my soldiers away from me and attach them to yourself?" "I don't draw soldiers only from your corner of the earth," Paul answered, "but from the whole wide world, and our King will lavish upon them such gifts as will never be lacking and will exceed every need. If you consent to be a subject of this King, you will be saved. His power is so great that he will come to judge all men and will dissolve the figure of this world by fire."

Nero was enraged at what he heard; and because Paul had said that the figure of the world would be dissolved by fire, he ordered all the soldiers of Christ to be burned to death, and Paul to be beheaded for the crime of lese majesty. So massive was the ensuing slaughter of Christians that the Roman people besieged the palace and were stirring up a general sedition, shouting: "Caesar! Put a stop to this massacre, countermand your order! You are killing our fellow citizens, the guardians of the Roman Empire!"

This made Nero fearful, and he changed his edict to the effect that no Christians were to be touched until the emperor came to a considered judgment about them. So Paul was brought back and set before the emperor, and when he saw him, Nero shouted at the top of his voice: "Rid me of this malefactor! Off with this impostor's head! Away with this seducer of reason! Rid the earth of this perverter of minds!" "Nero," Paul replied, "I will suffer for a short time and will live forever unto the Lord Jesus Christ!" Nero called out: "Off with his head! Let him know that I am stronger than his king, that I have beaten him! Then we shall see whether he can live forever!" Paul: "So that you may know that I live eternally after the death of the body, when my head has been cut off, I will appear to you alive. Then you will be able to realize that Christ is the God of life, not of death."

When he had said this, Paul was led to the place of execution. On the way there the three soldiers who were guarding him asked: "Tell us, Paul, who is this king of yours whom you love so well that you would rather die for him than stay alive? What sort of reward do you expect for this?" Paul then preached to them about the kingdom of God and the pains of hell, so effectively that he converted them to the faith. They begged him to go away freely wherever he wanted to, but he said: "I am no deserter but an enrolled soldier of Christ, and I know that I shall pass out of this transitory life into eternal life. As soon as I have been decapitated, men of my faith will come and take away my body. You yourselves must note the spot and come back to it tomorrow morning. Beside my grave you will find two men praying. They will be Titus and Luke. You must tell them my reason for sending you to them. They will baptize you and make you fellow citizens and coheirs of the kingdom of heaven."

While Paul was speaking, Nero sent two soldiers to see whether he had been put to death. He wanted to convert them, but they said: "When you're dead and come back to life, then we'll believe what you say. Now come on and take what's coming to you!" When they arrived at the Ostia gate, near which he was to suffer, he came face to face with a lady who was a disciple of his. Her name was Plantilla, although according to Dionysius she was known by another name, Lemobia, perhaps because she had two names. She was weeping and began to commend herself to his prayers. "Don't be upset, Plantilla, daughter of eternal salvation," said Paul. "Lend me the veil you are wearing over your head. I will cover my eyes with it and return it to you afterwards." She handed him her veil, and the executioners laughed, saying: "Why do you let this impostor, this charlatan, have your costly veil? Now you've lost it!"

When Paul reached the place of execution, he faced the East, raised his hands to heaven, prayed for a long time in his mother tongue, and gave thanks to God. Then he bade his brethren farewell, tied Plantilla's veil over his eyes, knelt on the ground on both knees, bent his neck, and so was beheaded. As soon as his head bounded from his body, it intoned, in Hebrew and in a clear voice, "Jesus Christ," the name that had been so sweet to him in life, and that he had pronounced so often. It is said that in his letters he used the name Jesus or Christ, or both, five hundred times. From his wound a stream of milk spurted upon the soldiers' clothing, followed by a flow of blood. A vast light shone in the air, and a very sweet odor emanated from the saint's body.

Dionysius, in a letter[1] to Timothy about Paul's death, says: "In that grief-filled hour, my beloved brother, the executioner said to Paul, Bend your neck! Then the blessed apostle looked up to heaven, marked his forehead and breast with the sign of the cross, and said: My Lord Jesus Christ, into your hands I commend my spirit! Then, without hesitation or compulsion, he extended his neck and so received the martyr's crown as the executioner made his stroke and cut off Paul's head. As the blow fell, blessed Paul took off the veil, caught his own blood in it, rolled it up and folded it, and gave it to the woman.

"When the executioner returned, Lemobia asked him: 'Where have you laid my master Paul?' The soldier answered: 'He lies with his companion in the Valley of the Boxers outside the city, and his face is covered with your veil.' But she replied: 'Look! Peter and Paul have come here clothed in shining garments and wearing crowns gleaming with light on their heads.' Then she held out the veil dripping with blood and showed it to them, and because of this, many believed in the Lord and became Christians." So Dionysius.

Hearing how things had gone, Nero was frightened out of his wits, and called in friends and philosophers to discuss what had happened. While they were talking, Paul came in, though the doors were closed. He stood before the emperor and said: "Caesar, here I am, Paul the soldier of the eternal and unconquered king. Now believe, because I am not dead but alive, and you, poor wretch, will die the eternal death for having unjustly killed the saints of God." That said, he disappeared. By this time Nero was beside himself with fear and did not know what to do next, but his friends calmed him, and advised him to release Patroclus and Barnabas with the others and let them go wherever they wished.

The next morning the two soldiers, Longinus the commander and Accestus, went to Paul's grave and there saw two men, Titus and Luke, praying, and Paul standing between them. Titus and Luke were alarmed at the sight of the soldiers and started to run away, and Paul disappeared. The soldiers shouted after the two fugitives, saying: "We're not pursuing you as you think! We want you to baptize us, as Paul, whom we just saw praying with you, told us to do." The other two, hearing this, came back and baptized them joyfully.

Paul's head was thrown into a trench and could not be found because so many other people had been put to death and their heads and bodies piled into the same trench. However, we read in that same letter of Dionysius that at a later

---

[1] This "letter" is unknown.

time the trench was cleaned out, and Paul's head was tossed up along with other detritus. A shepherd stuck the head on his staff and stood the staff up in his sheepfold. Then for three consecutive nights the sheepherder and his master saw an ineffable light shining above the head. They made this known to the bishop and the faithful, who said: "That must be Paul's head!" So the bishop and a huge crowd of the faithful went out and took possession of the head, which they placed on a gold table. They wanted to put the head in its place with the body, but the patriarch responded: "We know that a great many Christians were killed and that their heads were scattered here and there, and I hesitate to put this head with Paul's body. Let us instead place the head at the feet of the body, and we will pray almighty God that if this be indeed the right head, the body may turn around and be joined to it." This suggestion appealed to everyone, and they placed the head at the feet of the saint's body. Then they prayed, and lo! to the wonderment of all, the body turned around and joined itself to the head where it belonged. So all blessed God and were sure that this was truly Paul's head. Thus Dionysius.

Gregory of Tours, who flourished in the reign of Justin II, tells us that a certain man who had lost all hope was preparing a noose to hang himself yet kept calling upon the name of Paul, saying: "Saint Paul, help me!" Then a sordid shade stood by him and urged him on, saying: "Go ahead, good fellow! Get it over with, don't waste time!" The man went on preparing his noose but continued to say: "Most blessed Paul, help me!" When the noose was ready, another shade appeared—this one in the form of a man—and said to the one that was coaxing the poor fellow: "Begone, wretch! Saint Paul has been called and is coming!" The foul shade vanished, and the man came to his senses, threw the noose away, and did suitable penance.

Gregory also says in his *Register*: "Numerous miracles come from Saint Paul's chains. Many people ask for some filings. A priest is at hand with a file, and for some of those who ask he strikes off a few filings easily and with no delay. For others who ask he files away long and hard at the chains, but nothing comes off."

In the letter we have already quoted, Dionysius piously deplores the death of his teacher Saint Paul, saying: "Who will give water to our eyes and a fountain of tears to our pupils, to enable us to mourn day and night the light of all the churches that is extinguished? Who will not weep and groan, who will not put on the weeds of mourning, will not be stunned in mind and overcome with grief? Behold! Peter, the foundation of the churches and glory of the holy apostles, has departed and left us orphans, and Paul, the friend of the Gentiles and consoler of the poor, has gone from us and is nowhere to be found! He was the father of fathers, the teacher of teachers, the shepherd of shepherds—Paul, I say, the abyss of wisdom, the high-sounding shepherd's pipe, the tireless preacher of the truth, the noblest of the apostles! This angel of earth and man of heaven, image and likeness of deity and deiform spirit, has left us—us, I say, the needy and unworthy—in this contemptible, evil world. He has gone to God, his lord and friend. Alas, my brother Timothy, beloved of my soul, where is your father, your master who loved you? Where now will he greet you from? See, you have been orphaned and left alone. No longer will he write to you with his most holy hand and say to you: Dearest son, come! My brother Timothy, what has befallen here of sadness and darkness and loss, that we have been made orphans? No longer do his letters come to you, letters that started: Paul, modest servant of Jesus Christ. No longer will he write to various cities on your behalf: Welcome my beloved son . . . Close the books of the prophets, brother, and seal them closed, because we have no one to interpret their parables and paradigms and speeches. The prophet David bewailed his son and said, Woe is me, my son, woe is me! And I say, Woe is me, my master, truly woe is me! No longer will your disciples flock to Rome and ask for us. No longer will anyone say: Let us go and see our teachers and ask them how we may best rule the churches entrusted to us, and they will interpret for us the sayings of our lord Jesus Christ and the sayings of the prophets. Yes, woe to these sons, my brother, because they are bereft of their spiritual fathers; the flock is bereft of them. And woe to us also, brother, who are bereft of our spiritual masters, who had gleaned understanding and knowledge of the Old and New Law and brought all this together in their letters. Where now is Paul's course, and the labor of his holy feet? Where now the eloquent mouth, the counseling tongue, the spirit ever pleasing to his God? Who may not wail and mourn, for those who merited glory and honor before God have been handed over to death like evildoers. Woe is me, the hour that I have looked upon that holy body, bloodied with innocent blood! Alas, my father, my master and teacher, for no guilt of yours did you die such a death! Now where shall I go to look for you, O glory of Christians and praise of the faithful! Who has silenced your voice, O high-noted reed pipe of the churches, precious pick to pluck the ten-stringed psaltery? Behold, you have gone in to the Lord your God, whom you desired, for whom you longed with your whole heart! Jerusalem and Rome, in a crooked friendship, have become equal in evil. Jerusalem crucified our Lord Jesus Christ and Rome did his apostles to death: Jerusalem now serves him whom she crucified, Rome glorifies those she slew by celebrating their memory. And now, my brother Timothy, those whom you loved and yearned for wholeheartedly, Saul I say and Jonathan, were not separated in life or in death, and I am not separated from my lord and master except insofar as base and wicked men have separated us. And this separation is only for a time, and his soul knows whom he loves, even without their speaking to him, they who are now at a distance from him. But on the day of resurrection it were a great loss to be separated from them." Thus Dionysius.

Chrysostom, in his *De laudibus Pauli*, commends this glorious apostle in many ways. He says: "He who called Paul's soul a preeminent meadow of virtues and a spiritual paradise was in no way at fault. What tongue could be found equal to praising him, since his soul possessed all the goods that are in all men, and held together not only all that is good in men but also—and this is much greater—all that is good in the angels? We will not be silent about this; indeed we really have to talk about it. For this is the highest kind of praise (the virtues and greatness of the one praised exceeding the powers of rhetoric), and so for us it is more glorious often to be bettered than always to be best. Where then can we more fittingly open the exordium of his praises than at this very point—namely, first, that we show him as possessing the good that is in all others. Abel offered sacrifice and is praised for so doing, but if we turn our attention to Paul's sacrifice, it will appear as far superior as heaven is to earth. He immolated himself day after day in and by a double sacrifice, offering the mortification both of his heart and of his body. It was not sheep or oxen that he offered, but himself doubly immolated. Nor was he satisfied even with this but strove to offer the whole world. He traveled by land and by sea, winging his way, as it were, over Greece and the lands of the heathen and every region under the sun, making angels of men—nay, more, turning these very men from demons into angels.

"What can possibly be found to equal this host, which Paul offered by the sword of the Holy Spirit on that altar which is located above the heavens? But Abel died at the hand of his envious brother, while Paul was killed by those whom he wished to rescue from innumerable evils. Do you want me to show you his countless deaths, deaths as numerous as the days of his life? We read that Noe saved only himself and his children in the ark. Paul, however, freed the whole world endangered by the waves of a far wilder flood, not by building an ark out of planks, but by writing epistles instead of shaping planks. This ark sails not just to one place but to the ends of the earth. It is not caulked with bitumen or pitch; its planks are held together by the Holy Spirit. This ark takes aboard men more witless than irrational animals and makes them imitators of the angels. Noe's ark took on a crow but sent it off again still a crow, and shipped a wolf but could not tame its savageness, but this ark did better, taking aboard hawks and vultures and making doves of them, subduing all savagery and inducing mildness of spirit.

"Abraham is admired by all because at God's command he left fatherland and kinsmen, but how could he be compared with Paul, who not only left home and kin but set no value on the whole world and indeed on heaven and the heaven of heavens, accepting Christ, clinging to this sole good, namely, the love of Christ, in place of all the rest? Neither things present, he says, nor things to come, nor might, nor height, nor depth, nor any other creature, shall be able to separate us from the love of God that is in Christ Jesus our Lord. Yes, Abraham put himself in danger when he rescued his brother's son from his enemies, but Paul snatched the whole world out of the grip of the devil, endured dangers without number, and by his own daily deaths won complete safety for others. Abraham was willing to sacrifice his son: Paul sacrificed himself a thousand times.

"There are those who admire Isaac for his patience when his enemies stopped up the wells he had dug; but Paul, seeing his wells, namely, his own body, stopped up with stones, not only accepted this, as Isaac had done, but strove to carry off to heaven those at whose hands he suffered. However much that font was stopped up, it burst forth all the more and, overflowing, fed many rivers that rose out of it. Scripture wonders at Jacob's patience and forbearance, but is there anywhere a soul staunch enough to imitate Paul's patience? It was not seven years but a lifetime of servitude that he bore for the spouse of Christ, enduring a thousand trials, burned by the sun's heat by day and chilled by the night cold, now cut by whips and bruised by stones and wrung by struggles, always jumping up to seize the captive sheep from the jaws of the devil. Then there was Joseph, who was adorned with the virtue of purity, but I am afraid it may seem ridiculous to praise Paul on this ground. He crucified himself, and not only the beauties of the human body, but also all that seems brilliant and comely in material things, looked to him as dust and ashes look to us. He was like a dead man motionless beside a corpse.

"Job, too, is admired, and he was a marvelous contender; but Paul held out not for months but for many years of struggle and emerged with honor, not scraping his ulcerous flesh with a fragment of a broken pot, but frequently plunging into the monstrous maw of the lion and fighting against innumerable trials, bearing them imperturbable as a stone. He sustained shameful treatment not from three or four friends but from all the infidels and even from his brethren, being spat upon and cursed by all. Job practiced openhanded hospitality and cared for the poor, but the care that Job gave to those weak in body Paul dispensed to sick souls. Job threw open his house to every comer; Paul's soul stood open to the whole world. Job possessed great herds of sheep and cattle and gave freely to the poor; Paul, owning nothing more than his body, ministered bodily to those in need, as he reminds us somewhere, saying: Such things as were needful for me and them that are with me, these hands have furnished (Acts 20:34). Worms and wounds inflicted sharp pains on holy Job; but if you consider the scourgings, the hunger, the chains, and the perils inflicted upon Paul by those of his own household, by strangers, and by the rest of the world, his solicitude for all the churches, his being burned by scandal given to anyone, you will see that his soul was harder than any rock, and surpassed iron and steel in strength. The pains that Job suffered in his body, Paul suffered in his spirit: a sadness more poignant than any sorrow consumed him when anyone fell into sin, so that torrents of tears flowed ceaselessly from his eyes not only by day but by night. He was afflicted more sorely than a woman in labor and said: My little children, of whom I am in labor again until Christ be formed in you.

"To save the Jews, Moses chose to be wiped out of the book of the living, and therefore offered himself to perish with the rest, but Paul offered himself *for* the rest. He wished to perish, not with those perishing; but in order that the others might be saved, he would give up eternal glory. And Moses resisted Pharaoh, but Paul resisted the devil daily. Moses resisted for the sake of one people, Paul fought for the whole world, not by sweat but by blood. John had locusts and wild honey for food, but Paul was caught up amidst the crash and clatter of the world, not settled, like John, in the quiet and peace of the desert; and for nourishment he had no locusts or honey, but satisfied his needs with much coarser food and with his zeal for preaching. John's attitude regarding Herodias was indeed very courageous, but Paul rebuked not one or two or three but many persons in similar positions of power, and tyrants far fiercer than any of them.

"It remains for us to compare Paul to the angels, and again we declare that he is magnificent, because he obeyed God with the utmost care, which is what David, admiring, said about the angels: O you his angels, you mighty ones who do his word, hearkening to the voice of his word! And what else does the prophet admire in the angels? He says: [Lord] who makest the winds thy messengers, fire and flame thy ministers! But we can find this in Paul, who purged the whole world as fire and wind do. But he had not yet won heaven, and this is above all to be wondered at, because he was busy on earth and was still encased in his mortal body. How worthy we are of condemnation, we who do not even try to imitate at least to a small degree this man who brings together in himself such a sheaf of virtues! No other nature was allotted to him than to us, he gained no soul different from ours, he lived in no other world but on the same earth and in the same area as we do. He grew up under the same laws and customs, yet in virtue of spirit he transcends all men who now are or ever were. Nor indeed is he to be admired only because in the abundance of his devotion he somehow did not feel the pains he accepted for the sake of virtue: he even thought of virtue as its own reward. We ourselves strive for virtue in view of the recompense held out to us, but he embraced and loved it even without any thought of reward. All the difficulties that seem to us to interfere with virtue he bore with perfect equanimity. He got up every day more ardent than the day before and faced the dangers that threatened him with ever-increasing bravery. When he saw that his death was imminent, he invited others to share his delight and his joy, saying: Rejoice and congratulate with me! Therefore he hurried toward the confusions and hurts that he sustained because of his zeal for preaching, rather than toward the enjoyment of the good things of life. He looked forward to dying rather than living, desired poverty rather than riches, sought toil much more than others seek rest after toil, chose grief more than others seek pleasure, prayed more earnestly and fruitfully for his enemies than others pray against theirs. To him there was one thing to be dreaded and feared, and that was to offend God, just as there was nothing desirable except to please the Lord always. I do not say just that he had no desire for present goods: he looked for nothing for the future. Do not talk to me about prizes and peoples, armies and wealth, provinces, powers: these he valued as little as if they were cobwebs. Talk to me about the goods that are promised us in heaven, and then you will see his burning love for Christ. There was nothing he craved in place of the love of Christ—not the high state of angels or archangels or anything of the kind. He enjoyed what was greater than all that, namely, Christ's love. Having that, he deemed himself blessed above all: without that love he wanted no association with lords and princes. With that love he would have preferred to be the last, the least, even one of the damned, rather than without it to live with the highest, most sublime honors. To be separated from Christ's love was to him the greatest, the only torment, to him it was hell, the only punishment, infinite, intolerable torture; but to enjoy that love was life, the world, the kingdom, it was the promise, it was blessings uncountable.

"So the things we are afraid of seemed no more important to Paul than withered grass. To him tyrants and enemies breathing wrath were so many gnats, death and torture and a thousand punishments mere child's play as long as he could suffer something for Christ. The chain he wore as a prisoner was to him more precious than the diadem with which he might be crowned. Confined in a dungeon he dwelt in heaven; he took lashes and wounds more gladly than others win laurels. He loved pains no less than prizes, and when pains came his way instead of prizes, he called them a favor, since the things that cause us sadness pleased him greatly. Moreover, he was burned with deep grief, as he said: Who is scandalized and I am not on fire?—although some say that there is a kind of pleasure in grief, for many who are wounded by the deaths of their children get some consolation out of their weeping, and grieve more when they are forbidden to grieve. Thus Paul, too, by night and by day found consolation in tears, and no one was more affected by his own ills than Paul by the ills of others. Indeed you may well judge how affected he was when he wept for the loss of sinners, since he yearned to be excluded from the glory of heaven if only they might be saved. He considered it a more painful thing that they were not to be saved than that he himself should perish.

"Therefore to whom or to what can anyone compare this man? To iron? To steel? One might well call that soul golden or steely, for it was stronger than any steel, more precious than gold or jewels, and surpassed the one metal in hardness and the other in price. And what is there to which this man's soul might be compared? To none of the things that exist . . . not one! But if the strength of steel were given to gold and the glitter of gold to steel, then perhaps such a comparison would fit Paul's soul. But suppose I suggest a likeness betweeen steel and gold and Paul, and you put the whole world on the other side of the scale: you will see that Paul obviously outweighs the world. Therefore we say that Paul is worth more or is more worthy than the world and all that is in it. Well, then, if the world is not worthier or worth more than Paul, how about heaven? But we find heaven, too, less worthy. And if he put not only heaven but whatever is in the heavens second to the love of God, how would the Lord, who is as much more generous than Paul as kindness is better than malice, not judge him more worthy than unnumbered heavens? Not only does God love us as much as he is loved by us, but so much more generously that no words can express it. God snatched Paul up into paradise and raised him to the third heaven, and not without good reason, since Paul, striding over the earth, conducted himself in all things as though he already enjoyed the company of angels. Still bound to a visible body he shared their perfection: still subject to so many bodily weaknesses he strove to appear as in no way inferior to their supernal virtues. As one having wings he flew over the whole earth by his teaching; being in the body he made little of labors and dangers; as though already possessing heaven he despised everything earthly, and he watched with unremitting concentration of his mind as though already living with the incorporeal powers.

"It has often happened that this or that people has been placed under the care of angels, but no angel ever had such authority over a nation that was committed to him as Paul has had over the whole world. Just as a long-suffering father is disposed toward a deranged son, whom he pities and weeps for the more the son abuses him, so Paul showed the greatest effusions of fatherly affection to those who plagued him the most. He often wept and grieved for those who had scourged him five times and thirsted for his blood, and prayed for them: Brethren, he said, my heart's desire and prayer to God for them [the Jews] is that they may be saved. Seeing them on the way to perdition he was sorely troubled and torn. As iron put in the fire quickly itself becomes fire, so Paul, suspended in love, became wholly love. As though he were the common father of the whole world, in love and actions he imitated the fathers of men, and went beyond not only fleshly but also spiritual fathers in solicitude and devotion. He wanted to hold up every last human being in God's sight as if he had begotten the whole world and yearned to lead all into the kingdom of God, and he spent himself soul and body for those he loved. This un-noble man, who went from place to place and made his living working on animal pelts, grew so powerful that in the space of barely thirty years he brought Romans and Persians, Parthians and Medes, Indians and Scythians, Ethiopians and Sarmatians and Saracens and every race of men under the yoke of truth; and, like a live coal thrown into a pile of hay, his fire burned up the works of the demons. His voice swept in more ardent than any fire, and everything—devil worship and tyrants' threats and traps set by false followers—gave way. More, just as before the rays of the rising sun darkness vanishes, adulterers and thieves hide in pits, bandits and murderers flee into caves, and everything is made shining and bright by the sunbeams, so, as Paul spread the Gospel abroad, error was driven out and truth came in, adultery and other abominations were chased and consumed like straw by the heat of that fire. At the same time the clear renown of truth rose like flame resplendent and mounted to the heights of heaven, raised up by those who rather seemed to be holding it down, and neither peril nor attack could stop it.

"The nature of error is such that if it meets no resistance, it goes out of fashion and fades away. On the other hand, it is of the nature of truth that under attack it comes to life and grows. God has so ennobled our race that we aspire to bear his image and likeness. We do not think that that is impossible: after all, Paul had the same body and the same soul as we have and ate the same food. God formed him as he formed you, and Paul's God is your God. Do you want to know God's gifts to Paul? Paul's very garments struck terror to the demons. More admirable than that, when Paul plunged into danger, he could not be accused of rashness, nor when dangers rose around him could he be called timid. He loved his present life because it allowed him the benefit of teaching, but at the same time disdained it because of the philosophical attitude to which contempt for the world had brought him. Finally, if you find Paul running away from danger, admire him no less than when he rejoices to confront danger; the latter is the part of courage as the former is the part of wisdom. Similarly if you find Paul boasting a little about himself, admire him as you would if you saw him despising himself, because this is the part of humility while the other is the part of greatness of soul. It was more meritorious of him to speak in praise of himself than to say nothing; indeed, if he said nothing, he would be more blameworthy than those who learned from this to praise themselves for no reason at all. If he had not been glorified, he would have caused loss to all those who had been entrusted to him, because while he humbled himself, he would have built up their pride. So Paul did better by boasting than another man would do by hiding the praises due him: the latter would gain less merit by concealing his merits than Paul gained by putting his on display. It is a serious fault to say something great and admirable about oneself, and to want to draw praise to oneself in the absence of some urgent necessity is sheer folly. It would not indicate that one was speaking according to God; rather, it is a sign of mindlessness. Such vainglory forfeits any reward that toil and sweat may have earned, for to talk boastfully about oneself is the act of a pompous, insolent person, whereas to say what is strictly necessary to the case at issue is the way of one who loves and has the good and welfare of many in mind. This was what Paul did. When he was slandered and lied about, he was forced to praise his accomplishments, particularly such as would show his worthiness, while he kept silent about other and still greater ones. I will come now, he says, to visions and revelations of the Lord . . . but I refrain (2 Cor. 12:1, 6). He had longer and more frequent converse with the Lord than any of the prophets and apostles, and was made the humbler thereby. He seems to have feared blows, but this was so that you might learn that by nature he was simply one of many: by his will he was not only above all men but was one of the angels. Not that fearing blows calls for reproach; what does deserve it is doing something unworthy of true piety out of fear of blows. The very fact that one who fears blows and wounds does not give up in a fight makes him more worthy of admiration than one who has no fear. So also, grieving is not blameworthy, but to say or do out of grief something that displeases God . . . that is blameworthy.

"What sort of man Paul was is shown by the fact that though he shared our human nature, he was somehow able to live above nature, so that even fearing death he did not refuse to die. There is nothing wrong about having a nature that is beset with weaknesses. What is wrong is to be a slave to those weaknesses. It is meritorious and admirable to overcome the weakness of nature by strength of will, as Paul did in dismissing John, also called Mark. He was perfectly right in doing this: it was called for by his commission to preach. Anyone who assumes that office must be not soft or lax but strong and firm in all circumstances. No one ought to aspire to the duties of that high office unless he is ready to expose his soul to a thousand deaths and dangers. If he is not of this stripe, he will doom many others by his example: it would be more helpful on his part to keep quiet and look out for himself. No one who yearns to govern, no one destined to fight the wild beasts or to perform as a gladiator in the arena, no one at all needs a soul and spirit so prepared to face danger and death as does the one who undertakes the office of preaching. Nowhere are the perils greater or the adversaries more cruel, nowhere are the stakes of the contest the like of those faced by the preacher: he is offered heaven as reward, hell as punishment.

"If, however, there is a display of anger among some preachers, do not regard this as evil. To be stirred to anger is not wrong, but to be angry unreasonably and with no just cause is sinful. Our provident Creator planted this emotion in us to spur somnolent and weakling souls out of their inertia and apathy. Just as the sword has an edge, so God has endowed our mind with an edge of ire for us to use if needed. Mildness of spirit is always good when it suits the moment, but when the circumstances do not call for it, even mildness is a vice. Thus Paul often put this emotion to use and was better angry than those who used impudent language.

"What was wonderful in Paul was that shackled, whipped, and wounded he was far more splendid than those adorned with jewels and purple robes, and that when he was taken in chains over the vast sea, he rejoiced as if he were on his way to a high throne of empire. He reached Rome but was not content to stay there and went running off to Spain, and there allowed no day to go by in idleness and rest, but, more ardent in preaching than fire itself, he feared no dangers and felt no shame when he was mocked. And what is still more worthy of admiration is this, that audacious as he was, always girded as for battle and breathing the fire of war, he could still show himself responsive and flexible. When the brethren ordered him, furious or rather fervent as he was, to go to Tarsus, he did not refuse. When they said he might best be lowered over the wall in a basket, he allowed it. And he did all this for the sake of one thing, namely, to have more time to preach, and so to go to Christ with many who believed through his preaching. He was fearful that he might leave this life poor, not having done enough for the salvation of many. And then . . . when those who are fighting under a commander and see the commander himself wounded and shedding his blood yet not yielding an inch to the enemy but standing firm, wielding his spear, laying his adversaries low with repeated blows, and sparing no pain, of course they follow so great a leader with all the more alacrity.

"So it was with Paul. They saw him chained and shackled in prison and preaching nonetheless. They saw him wounded yet capturing his tormentors themselves with his speech, and it built up their trust in him. This is what he meant when he said that most of the brethren had been made confident in the Lord because of his imprisonment and were much more bold to speak the word of God without fear. This in turn stimulated Paul's zeal, and he went after his opponents more relentlessly. As when fire, falling into a pile of material, spreads and burns all around it, so Paul's preaching drew in whoever heard him. His assailants became spiritual food for the fire, because through them the flame of the Gospel spread." Thus Chrysostom.

91. The Seven Brothers, Sons of Saint Felicity

Saint Felicity had seven sons, whose names were Januarius, Felix, Philip, Silvanus, Alexander, Vitalis, and Martial. By order of Emperor Antoninus, Publius the prefect summoned all of them, together with their mother, to appear before him, and tried to persuade the mother to spare herself and her sons. Her answer was: "I can neither be seduced by your blandishments nor frightened by your threats, for my security is from the Holy Spirit who is with me; and alive I will withstand you, and will vanquish you completely when you kill me!" Then, turning to her sons, she said: "My sons, look to heaven and fix your gaze above, because Christ awaits us there, so fight bravely for Christ and show yourselves faithful in the love of Christ!" Hearing this, the prefect commanded his men to slap her. Since mother and sons were obviously firm in the faith, all the sons were tortured and put to death while their mother looked on and encouraged them.

Gregory calls this blessed Felicity "more than martyr," because she suffered seven times in her seven sons and an eighth time in her own body. In his homilies Gregory says: "Saint Felicity, who by her believing stood out as a servant of Christ, by preaching became also a martyr of Christ. She feared to leave her sons after her, alive in the flesh, as other parents usually fear that their children may die before they themselves do. She brought forth her sons in the Spirit as she had borne them in the flesh, in order to give them to God by her preaching as she had given them to the world in the body. Knowing that they were the children she had borne in the flesh, she could not see them die without grieving for them, but the love that was in her was so strong that it overcame the grief she felt in her body. Rightly therefore I have said that this woman was more than martyr—this woman who died in each one of her sons and with as much desire as they had. While gaining this sevenfold martyrdom she also went beyond the palm of martyrdom, because her love of Christ was far from satisfied by her dying only once for him."

The martyrs suffered about the year of the Lord 110.

92. Saint Theodora

Theodora, a woman of noble rank, married to a wealthy, God-fearing man, lived in Alexandria in the time of Emperor Zeno. The devil, envious of Theodora's holiness, stirred up lust for her in another rich man, who sent her many messages and gifts in order to induce her to assent to him; but she rebuffed the messengers and spurned the gifts. He bothered her so much, however, that she had no peace of mind and her health began to suffer. Finally he sent a certain sorceress to her, who urged her forcefully to have pity on this man and to yield to his desire. Theodora answered that she would never commit so great a sin before the eyes of God who sees all, but the witch added: "Yes, God knows and sees everything that is done by day, but anything committed at dusk and sundown God does not see." The young woman asked the witch: "Is what you say true?" "It certainly is true!" the witch replied. The young woman was deceived and told the witch to have the man come to her as daylight waned, and she would do his will. When the man received this news, he was delighted, went to the lady at the appointed hour, lay with her, and left.

Theodora now came to her senses and wept bitterly, beating herself on the face and saying: "Alas, woe is me! I have lost my soul, I have destroyed the beauty of my virtue!" When her husband came home, he found her desolate and grieving, and, not knowing the reason, did his best to console her, but she would accept no comfort. The next morning she went to a monastery of nuns and asked the abbess whether God could know about a grave sin that she had committed at eventide. The abbess answered: "Nothing can be hidden from God, who knows all and sees all that is done, no matter the time it is done." Theodora wept profusely and said: "Give me the book of the gospels, that I may draw my own lot!" She opened the book and came upon the passage: "What I have written, I have written." She went home and, one day when her husband was away, cut her hair, put on men's clothing, and hurried to a monastery. She asked to be taken in with the monks and her request was granted. Asked what her name was, she said she was called Theodore. Then, as Brother Theodore, she humbly performed all the tasks assigned to her, and her service was welcomed by all.

Some years later the abbot called Brother Theodore and ordered him to yoke a team of oxen and haul a tun of oil out from the city. Her husband had wept much, fearing that she had gone off with another man; but now an angel of the Lord said to him: "Get up tomorrow and stand in the street called the Martyrdom of Peter the Apostle, and the first person you meet will be your wife." Theodora came along with her camels, saw her husband, recognized him, and said within herself: "Alas, my good husband, how hard I work to be delivered of the wrong I did you!" When she came near him, she greeted him, saying: "Joy to you, sir!" But he did not recognize her at all, and waited all day long and into the night before crying out that he had been deceived. In the morning a voice came to him, saying: "The one who greeted you yesterday was your wife."

Theodora's holiness was so great that she performed many miracles. Thus she took hold of a man who had been fatally mauled by a wild beast, and by her prayers brought him back to life, then tracked down the beast and cursed it, whereupon the animal dropped dead. And one time the devil, unable to bear her sanctity, appeared to her and said: "You whore of whores, you adulteress, you left your husband to come here and put me to shame! I shall use my fearsome powers to stir up a battle against you, and if I can't make you deny the Crucified, you can say that I don't exist!" But she made the sign of the cross and the demon vanished.

Another time, when she was on her way back with the camels and stopped someplace overnight, a girl came to her and said: "Sleep with me!" When Theodora spurned her, she went and lay with a man who was resting in the same place. When her belly grew big, she was asked who had got her pregnant, and she said: "That monk Theodore slept with me!" When the child was born, they turned it over to the abbot of the monastery. The abbot upbraided Theodore, who begged for forgiveness, and the abbot laid the baby on his shoulders and expelled him from the monastery.

Theodore—Theodora, after her expulsion, stayed outside the monastery for seven years, nourishing the child with milk from the herd. The devil, envious of such patience, transfigured himself, assuming the likeness of her husband, and said to her: "What are you doing here, my lady? Behold, I have pined for you all this time and have found no consolation. Come then, light of my life, because I forgive you even if you have lain with another man!" But Theodora, thinking that this was indeed her husband, told him: "I shall never again live with you, because the son of John the knight slept with me, and I wish to do penance for the sin I committed against you!" And when she prayed, he vanished and she knew it had been the devil.

At another time the devil, wishing to terrorize her, sent demons against her in the likeness of fierce beasts, and a man goaded them on and said: "Devour this whore!" But she prayed and they disappeared. Again a large troop of soldiers came, led by a prince to whom the others offered worship, and the soldiers said to Theodora: "Rise and adore our prince!" She answered: "I adore the Lord God!" When this response was reported to the prince, he ordered her to be brought and beaten until she was thought to be dead, after which the horde vanished. Still another time she saw before her a large quantity of gold, but she crossed herself and fled from the gold, recommending herself to God. Then one day she saw a man carrying a basket filled with all sorts of delicious foods, and the man said to her: "The prince who had you beaten says to accept this food and eat it, because he did that unknowingly." But she crossed herself and the man disappeared instantly.

When seven years had passed, the abbot, impressed by Theodora's patience, reconciled her and took her and her boy back into the monastery. After she had lived a praiseworthy life there for two years, she took the lad into her cell and closed the door. This was made known to the abbot, who sent some monks to listen attentively to what she might say to the boy. She embraced him and kissed him, and said: "My sweetest son, the term of my life is nearing its end. I leave you to God: you are to have him for father and helper. Sweetest son, persevere in fasting and prayer, and serve your brothers with devotion!" With these words she breathed her last and fell asleep happily in the Lord about A.D. 470, and the child, seeing her dead, wept floods of tears.

That very night a vision was shown to the abbot. He saw preparations being made for a great wedding, to which came the orders of angels and prophets and martyrs and all the saints; and behold, in their midst walked a woman alone, enveloped in ineffable glory. She came to the wedding site and sat on the bridal bed, and all stood around her and called upon her. Then a voice was heard saying: "This is Brother Theodore, who was falsely accused of fathering a child! Seven years have elapsed since then, and she has been punished for sullying her husband's bed." The abbot woke up, hurried with the monks to her cell, and found her already dead. They went in and uncovered her, and saw that she was a woman. The abbot sent for the father of the girl who had defamed her, and said to him: "Your daughter's husband has died!" The father put aside the clothing and saw that the husband was a woman. A great fear came upon all who heard this.

An angel of the Lord now spoke to the abbot, saying: "Get up quickly, mount your horse, and ride into the city. If anyone comes to meet you, take him up and bring him here!" As the abbot rode along, a man ran to meet him. The abbot asked him where he was going, and he answered: "My wife has died, and I am on my way to see her." The abbot took him up on his horse, and when they came to Theodora's body, they both wept abundantly. Then they buried her with many praises.

Her husband then occupied Theodora's cell and lived in it until he fell asleep in the Lord. Her son followed his foster-mother's example and lived her virtuous life, and when the abbot of the monastery died, the monks unanimously elected him to be their abbot.

✳

93. Saint Margaret

The name Margaret is also the name of a precious jewel called *margarita*, pearl, which is shining white, small, and powerful. So Saint Margaret was shining white by her virginity, small by humility, and powerful in the performance of miracles. The power of the pearl is said to work against effusion of blood and against the passions of the heart, and to effect the strengthening of the spirit. Thus blessed Margaret had power over the effusion of her blood by her constancy, since she was most constant in her martyrdom. She had power over the heart's passions, i.e., in conquering the demon's temptations, since she overcame the devil. She strengthened the spirit by her doctrine, since her doctrine strengthened the spirits of many and converted them to the faith of Christ.

Her legend was written by Theotimus, a learned man.

Margaret, a native of Antioch, was the daughter of Theodosius, a patriarch among the pagans. She was entrusted to the care of a nurse and, when she reached the age of reason, was baptized, for which reason her father hated her. One day, when she had grown to the age of fifteen and was guarding her nurse's sheep with other young girls, the prefect Olybrius was passing by and caught sight of this very beautiful girl. He burned with desire for her immediately and sent his men after her, saying: "Go and seize her! If she's freeborn, I'll make her my wife: if she's a slave, she'll be my concubine!"

Margaret was therefore presented for his inspection, and he questioned her about her parentage, her name, and her religion. She answered that she was noble by birth, that her name was Margaret, and that she was a Christian. Said the prefect: "The first two titles fit you perfectly, because you are known to be noble and you are as lovely as a pearl; but the third does not suit you at all! No beautiful and noble girl like you should have a crucified God!" "How do you know," Margaret asked, "that Christ was crucified?" "From the Christians' books," he replied. Margaret: "Since you read in them both of Christ's suffering and of his glory, you should be ashamed to believe the one and yet deny the other!" She went on to declare that Christ had of his own will been crucified for our redemption but now lived immortal in eternity. This angered the prefect, and he ordered her to jail.

The next day he had her haled before him and said: "Vain girl, pity your beauty and adore our gods, and all will go well for you!" Margaret: "I adore the God before whom the earth trembles, the sea storms, and all creatures are fearful!" The prefect: "Unless you yield to me, I'll have your body torn to shreds!" Margaret: "Christ gave himself up to death for me, and therefore I want to die for Christ!"

By the prefect's order she now was hung upon a rack and was beaten with rods and then lacerated with iron rakes, so cruelly that her bones were laid bare and the blood poured from her body as from a pure spring. The people standing by wept and said: "O Margaret, truly we grieve for you, because we see how cruelly your body is torn! Oh, what beauty you have lost by not believing in the gods! Now, then, believe, so as at least to remain alive!" Margaret: "O bad counselors, go away! Begone! This torture of the flesh is the salvation of the soul!" To the prefect she said: "Shameless dog! Ravenous lion! You have power over the flesh, but Christ keeps the soul to himself!" Meanwhile, the prefect, unable to bear the sight of such bloodletting, drew his hood over his eyes.

Margaret was taken down and put back in jail, where a marvelous light shone around her. There she prayed the Lord to let her see the enemy who was fighting her, and a hideous dragon appeared, but when the beast came at her to devour her, she made the sign of the cross and it vanished. Or, as we read elsewhere, the dragon opened its maw over her head, put out its tongue under her feet, and swallowed her in one gulp. But when it was trying to digest her, she shielded herself with the sign of the cross, and by the power of the cross the dragon burst open and the virgin emerged unscathed. What is said here, however, about the beast swallowing the maiden and bursting asunder is considered apocryphal and not to be taken seriously.

Again the devil, still trying to deceive Margaret, changed himself to look like a man. She saw him and resorted to prayer, and when she rose, the devil approached, took her hand, and said: "Let all you've done be enough for you, and just let me be!" But she grabbed him by the head, pushed him to the ground, planted her right foot on his head, and said: "Lie still at last, proud demon, under the foot of a woman!" The demon cried out: "O blessed Margaret, I'm beaten! If I'd been beaten by a young man I wouldn't mind, but by a tender girl . . . ! And I feel even worse because your father and mother were friends of mine!"

Margaret then forced him to tell her why he had come. He said it was to press her to obey the prefect's orders. She also made him say why he tempted Christians in so many ways. He answered that it was his nature to hate virtuous people, and that though he was often repulsed by them, he was plagued by desire to mislead them. He begrudged men the happiness that he had lost and could not retrieve for himself, so he strove to take it away from others. He added that Solomon had confined an infinite multitude of demons in a vase, and after his death the demons had caused fire to issue from the vase. This made men think that it contained a huge treasure. They therefore smashed the vase, and the demons escaped and filled the air. Then, after all this had been said, the virgin lifted her foot and said: "Begone, wretch!" and the demon promptly vanished.

Margaret therefore was reassured: she had defeated the chief, she would certainly outdo his hireling. The following day she was presented to the judge before a large gathering of people. Refusing again to sacrifice to the gods, she was stripped of her clothes and her body was burned with torches; and all wondered how so delicate a girl could withstand such torture. Then the judge had her bound and put in a tub full of water, in order to increase the suffering by varying the pain; but suddenly the earth shook and the virgin came out unharmed. At that five thousand men accepted the faith and were sentenced to death for the name of Christ. The prefect, fearing that still others would be converted, quickly gave orders to behead blessed Margaret. She asked for time to pray, and prayed devoutly for herself and her persecutors and for all who would honor her memory and invoke her, adding a prayer that any woman who invoked her aid when faced with a difficult labor would give birth to a healthy child. A voice from heaven announced that her petitions had been heard, and she rose from her prayer and said to the headsman: "Brother, take your sword and strike me!" He did so and took off her head with a single stroke, and so she received the crown of martyrdom. Margaret suffered on the twentieth day of July, or, as we read elsewhere, on the twelfth of that month.

A certain saint says of this holy virgin: "Blessed Margaret was filled with the fear of God, endowed with righteousness, clothed with religion, imbued with compunction, praiseworthy for her integrity, beyond compare in her patience. Nothing contrary to the Christian religion could be found in her. She was hated by her father and beloved of Jesus Christ."

94. *Saint Alexis*

The name Alexis is composed of *a*, which means much or very, and *lexis*, which means word. Alexis therefore was very powerful in the word of God.

Alexis was the son of Euphemianus, a member of the highest Roman nobility who was in the first rank at the emperor's court. Three thousand slaves wearing golden girdles and silk clothing waited on him. As a high officer in the city Euphemianus was temperate in the exercise of his authority. Moreover, every day he had three tables set up in his house for the poor and for orphans, widows, and strangers in need. He himself served at these tables and did not until late in the evening take food in the fear of the Lord with other religious men. His wife, Aglaë, shared both his religious fervor and his attitude toward others. They were childless until in answer to their prayers the Lord granted them a son, after whose birth they agreed to live in chastity.

Their son was instructed in the liberal disciplines and made rapid strides in all the philosophic arts. When he was still a youth, a girl of the imperial household was chosen for him and the wedding was celebrated. On their wedding night, as he and his bride met in the silence and secret of their chamber, the saintly youth began to instruct his spouse in the fear of God and urged her to remain in the pure state of virginity. Then he gave her his gold ring and the cincture he wore around his waist, and said: "Take this and keep it as long as God pleases, and may the Lord be always between us!" Then he took some of his wealth and went to the coast, where he secretly boarded a ship and sailed to Laodicea, going from there to Edessa, a city in Syria, where an image of our Lord Jesus Christ on a fine cloth, an image no human hand had made, was preserved. Once in Edessa he distributed everything he had brought with him to the poor, put on ragged clothes, and began to sit with the other mendicants in the porch of the church of Mary the mother of God. Of the alms he received he kept the bare minimum he needed to live on and gave the rest to the other poor people.

All this time his father, sorrowful and mourning over his son's departure, sent his slaves into every corner of the world to look for him. Some of them came to Edessa and were recognized by the son, but did not recognize him and gave alms to him as they did to the other beggars. He accepted the alms and gave thanks to God, saying: "I thank you, O Lord, that you have allowed me to receive an alms from my own slaves." The servants went home and reported to the father that they had not found his son anywhere. His mother, from the day of his departure, spread a sack on the floor of her bedchamber and lay awake at night, murmuring dolefully: "Here shall I stay always in sorrow until I recover my son." The young bride, too, said to her mother-in-law: "Until I hear from my sweet spouse, I shall stay with you, like a lonely turtledove."

When Alexis had spent seventeen years in God's service in the porch of the aforesaid church, the image of the Blessed Virgin that was in the church spoke to the watchman, saying: "Bring in the man of God, because he is worthy of the kingdom of heaven. The Spirit of God rests upon him, and his prayer rises like incense in the sight of God." But the watchman did not know who this man was, so the image spoke again: "The man who sits outside at the door, that's the one." The watchman hurried out and led Alexis into the church. When other people noticed this, they began to pay him reverence, so he left the place in order to escape human glory, went back to Laodicea, and took ship to go to Tarsus in Cilicia.

By God's dispensation the ship was driven by the wind into the port of Rome. When he became aware of this, Alexis said to himself: "I will go and stay unknown in my father's house and so will not be a burden to anyone else." Therefore he waited in the street as his father was on his way back from the palace surrounded by a number of suppliants, and called after him: "Servant of God, give orders that I, a pilgrim, be taken into your house, and that the crumbs from your table be given to me as food. And may the Lord deign to be merciful to you, too, who also are a pilgrim." When Euphemianus heard this, he thought lovingly of his son, gave orders that the stranger be welcomed, and designated a cubbyhole for him in the house. He also provided that the visistor should have food from the master's table, and appointed one slave to look after him. Alexis persevered in prayer and disciplined his body with fasting and vigils. The house servants made fun of him, spilled dirty water on his head, and plied him with insults, but he bore all this with unshaken patience.

For seventeen years Alexis lived unrecognized in his father's house. Then, knowing by the Spirit that the end of his days was near, he asked for paper and ink and wrote out a full account of his life. On a Sunday, after the celebration of mass, a voice rang out in the church: "Come to me all you who labor and are burdened, and I will refresh you." All present were frightened and fell to their knees while the voice came again, saying: "Seek out the man of God, that he may pray for Rome!" They looked around but found no one, and a third time the voice sounded: "Look in the house of Euphemianus!" Euphemianus was questioned but said he did not know what this was all about. Then the emperors Arcadius and Honorius, in company with Pope Innocent, came to the house. The slave who took care of Alexis came to his master and said: "Could our stranger be the man you are looking for? He is a man of good life and great patience."

Euphemianus ran to the stranger's cubbyhole and found him dead, his face shining like the face of an angel. He tried to take the paper from the dead man's hand but could not. He went out therefore and came back with the emperors and the pope. They went in to the dead man and the emperors said: "Sinners though we are, we two rule the state, and with us is the pontiff who has pastoral care of the whole world. Therefore give us the paper you are holding, and let us see what is written on it." The pope then went up and took the script, which was relinquished readily, and had it read before Euphemianus and a great crowd of people. The father, hearing what was read, was overwhelmed with grief; his strength deserted him and he fell down in a faint. When after a while he came to himself, he tore his garments and began to pull out his gray hair and beard, threw himself on his son's body, and cried out: "Woe is me, my son! Why have you saddened me this way? Why have you stricken me all these years with grief and lamentation? Woe, woe is me, I see you now, the staff of my old age, lying on a litter and not speaking to me! Alas, alas, what consolation will I ever find?"

The mother, hearing all this, came like a lioness breaking out of a net. Tearing her robes, her hair in wild disarray, she raised her eyes to heaven, then rushed to where her son lay; but such a crowd had gathered that she could not reach the holy body. She cried out: "Make way for me, you men, let me see my son, let me see my soul's consolation, the one who suckled at my breast!" And when she finally got to the body, she lay upon it and lamented: "Alas, my son, light of my eyes, why did you do this? Why have you treated us so cruelly? You saw your father and miserable me shedding tears, and did not make yourself known to us! Your servants hurt you and made sport of you, and you allowed it!" Again and again she prostrated herself upon the body, now spreading her arms over it, now feeling the angelic face with her hands and kissing it. "Weep with me, all of you here present," she cried, "because for seventeen years I had him here in my house and did not recognize him! Because he was my only son! Because even the slaves heaped contempt on him and dealt him blows! Woe is me! Who will give my eyes a fountain of tears, so that night and day I may pour out the sorrow that is in my soul?" The bereaved spouse also ran up weeping and saying: "Ah, woe, woe! Today I am left alone, have become a widow, have no one to gaze upon or lift my eyes to. Now my mirror is broken and my hope gone. Now begins the grieving that has no end!" And the people standing around heard all this and wept loud and long.

Now the pope and the emperors placed the body on a princely litter and went before it into the heart of the city. Announcement was made to the populace that the man of God whom the whole city had been seeking had been found. The people all ran to be near the saint. Any among them who were sick and touched the holy body were cured instantly, the blind received their sight, the possessed were delivered of the demons. Seeing these wonders, the emperors and the pope undertook to carry the bier themselves, in order that they too might be sanctified by the holy corpse. The crowds were so dense that the emperors gave orders to scatter gold and silver coins in the streets and squares, hoping that the common people would be drawn away by their love of money and would let the funeral procession get through to the church. The people, however, checked their greed and in ever greater numbers rushed to touch the saint's most sacred body; but the cortege finally succeeded in getting to the church of Saint Benedict Martyr. There they worked continuously for seven days, praising God as they raised a monument adorned with gold, gems, and precious stones, and reverently laid the holy body to rest in it. From this monument emanated a fragrance so powerful that everybody thought the tomb was filled with perfumes.

Alexis died the seventeenth day of July about the year A.D. 398.

95. Saint Praxedes

Praxedes was sister to blessed Pudentiana, and they were sisters of Saints Donatus and Timothy, who were instructed in the faith by the apostles. At a time when persecution was raging, they buried the bodies of many Christians. They also distributed all their goods to the poor. Finally they fell asleep in the Lord about the year of the Lord 165, in the reign of Emperors Marcus and Antoninus II.

96. Saint Mary Magdalene

The name Mary, or Maria, is interpreted as *amarum mare*, bitter sea, or as illuminator or illuminated. These three meanings are accepted as standing for three shares or parts, of which Mary made the best choices, namely, the part of penance, the part of inward contemplation, and the part of heavenly glory. This threefold share is what the Lord meant when he said: "Mary has chosen the best part, which shall not be taken away from her." The first part will not be taken away because of its end or purpose, which is the attainment of holiness. The second part will not be taken because of its continuity: contemplation during the earthly journey will continue in heavenly contemplation. And the third part will remain because it is eternal. Therefore, since Mary chose the best part, namely, penance, she is called bitter sea because in her penances she endured much bitterness. We see this from the fact that she shed enough tears to bathe the Lord's feet with them. Since she chose the best part of inward contemplation, she is called enlightener, because in contemplation she drew draughts of light so deep that in turn she poured out light in abundance: in contemplation she received the light with which she afterwards enlightened others. As she chose the best part of heavenly glory, she is called illuminated, because she now is enlightened by the light of perfect knowledge in her mind and will be illumined by the light of glory in her body.

Mary is called Magdalene, which is understood to mean "remaining guilty," or it means armed, or unconquered, or magnificent. These meanings point to the sort of woman she was before, at the time of, and after her conversion. Before her conversion she remained in guilt, burdened with the debt of eternal punishment. In her conversion she was armed and rendered unconquerable by the armor of penance: she armed herself the best possible way—with all the weapons of penance—because for every pleasure she had enjoyed she found a way of immolating herself. After her conversion she was magnificent in the superabundance of grace, because where trespass abounded, grace was superabundant.

Mary's cognomen "Magdalene" comes from Magdalum, the name of one of her ancestral properties. She was wellborn, descended of royal stock. Her father's name was Syrus, her mother was called Eucharia. With her brother Lazarus and her sister Martha she owned Magdalum, a walled town two miles from Genezareth, along with Bethany, not far from Jerusalem, and a considerable part of Jerusalem itself. They had, however, divided their holdings among themselves in such a way that Magdalum belonged to Mary (whence the name Magdalene), Lazarus kept the property in Jerusalem, and Bethany was Martha's. Magdalene gave herself totally to the pleasures of the flesh and Lazarus was devoted to the military, while prudent Martha kept close watch over her brother's and sister's estates and took care of the needs of her armed men, her servants, and the poor. After Christ's ascension, however, they all sold their possessions and laid the proceeds at the feet of the apostles.

Magdalene, then, was very rich, and sensuous pleasure keeps company with great wealth. Renowned as she was for her beauty and her riches, she was no less known for the way she gave her body to pleasure—so much so that her proper name was forgotten and she was commonly called "the sinner." Meanwhile, Christ was preaching here and there, and she, guided by the divine will, hastened to the house of Simon the leper, where, she had learned, he was at table. Being a sinner she did not dare mingle with the righteous, but stayed back and washed the Lord's feet with her tears, dried them with her hair, and anointed them with precious ointment. Because of the extreme heat of the sun the people of that region bathed and anointed themselves regularly.

Now Simon the Pharisee thought to himself that if this man were a prophet, he would never allow a sinful woman to touch him; but the Lord rebuked him for his proud righteousness and told the woman that all her sins were forgiven. This is the Magdalene[1] upon whom Jesus conferred such great graces and to whom he showed so many marks of love. He cast seven devils out of her, set her totally afire with love of him, counted her among his closest familiars, was her guest, had her do the housekeeping on his travels, and kindly took her side at all times. He defended her when the Pharisee said she was unclean, when her sister implied that she was lazy, when Judas called her wasteful. Seeing her weep he could not contain his tears. For love of her he raised her brother, four days dead, to life, for love of her he freed her sister Martha from the issue of blood she had suffered for seven years, and in view of her merits he gave Martilla, her sister's handmaid, the privilege of calling out those memorable words: "Blessed is the womb that bore you!" Indeed, according to Ambrose, Martha was the woman with the issue of blood, and the woman who called out was Martha's servant. "She [Mary] it was, I say, who washed the Lord's feet with her tears, dried them with her hair and anointed them with ointment, who in the time of grace did solemn penance, who chose the best part, who sat at the Lord's feet and listened to his word, who anointed his head, who stood beside the cross at his passion, who prepared the sweet spices with which to anoint his body, who, when the disciples left the tomb, did not go away, to whom the risen Christ first appeared, making her an apostle to the apostles."

Some fourteen years after the Lord's passion and ascension into heaven, when the Jews had long since killed Stephen and expelled the other disciples from the confines of Judea, the disciples went off into the lands of the various nations and there sowed the word of the Lord. With the apostles at the time was one of Christ's seventy-two disciples, blessed Maximin, to whose care blessed Peter had entrusted Mary Magdalene. In the dispersion Maximin, Mary Magdalene, her brother Lazarus, her sister Martha, Martha's maid Martilla, blessed Cedonius, who was born blind and had been cured by the Lord, and many other Christians, were herded by the unbelievers into a ship without pilot or rudder and sent out to sea so that they might all be drowned, but by God's will they eventually landed at Marseilles. There they found no one willing to give them shelter, so they took refuge under the portico of a shrine belonging to the people of that area. When blessed Mary Magdalene saw the people gathering at the shrine to offer sacrifice to the idols, she came forward, her manner calm and her face serene, and with well-chosen words called them away from the cult of idols and preached Christ fervidly to them. All who heard her were in admiration at

---

[1] The question of the identity of several Marys named in the gospels, including Mary Magdalene, will not be discussed here.

her beauty, her eloquence, and the sweetness of her message . . . and no wonder, that the mouth which had pressed such pious and beautiful kisses on the Savior's feet should breathe forth the perfume of the word of God more profusely than others could.

Then the governor of that province came with his wife to offer sacrifice and pray the gods for offspring. Magdalene preached Christ to him and dissuaded him from sacrificing. Some days later she appeared in a vision to the wife, saying: "Why, when you are so rich, do you allow the saints of God to die of hunger and cold?" She added the threat that if the lady did not persuade her husband to relieve the saints' needs, she might incur the wrath of God; but the woman was afraid to tell her spouse about the vision. The following night she saw the same vision and heard the same words, but again hesitated to tell her husband. The third time, in the silence of the dead of night, Mary Magdalene appeared to each of them, shaking with anger, her face afire as if the whole house were burning, and said: "So you sleep, tyrant, limb of your father Satan, with your viper of a wife who refused to tell you what I had said? You take your rest, you enemy of the cross of Christ, your gluttony sated with a bellyful of all sorts of food while you let the saints of God perish from hunger and thirst? You lie here wrapped in silken sheets, after seeing those others homeless and desolate, and passing them by? Wicked man, you will not escape! You will not go unpunished for your long delay in giving them some help!" And, having said her say, she disappeared.

The lady awoke gasping and trembling, and spoke to her husband, who was in like distress: "My lord, have you had the dream that I just had?" "I saw it," he answered, "and I can't stop wondering and shaking with fear! What are we to do?" His wife said: "It will be better for us to give in to her than to face the wrath of her God whom she preaches." They therefore provided shelter for the Christians and supplied their needs.

Then one day when Mary Magdalene was preaching, the aforesaid governor asked her: "Do you think you can defend the faith you preach?" "I am ready indeed to defend it," she replied, "because my faith is strengthened by the daily miracles and preaching of my teacher Peter, who presides in Rome!" The governor and his wife then said to her: "See here, we are prepared to do whatever you tell us to if you can obtain a son for us from the God whom you preach." "In this he will not fail you," said Magdalene. Then the blessed Mary prayed the Lord to deign to grant them a son. The Lord heard her prayers and the woman conceived.

Now the husband began to want to go to Peter and find out whether what Magdalene preached about Christ was the truth. "What's this?" snapped his wife. "Are you thinking of going without me? Not a bit of it! You leave, I leave. You come back, I come back. You stay here, I stay here!" The man replied: "My dear, it can't be that way! You're pregnant and the perils of the sea are infinite. It's too risky. You will stay home and take care of what we have here!"

But she insisted, doing as women do. She threw herself at his feet, weeping the while, and in the end won him over. Mary therefore put the sign of the cross on their shoulders as a protection against the ancient Enemy's interference on their journey. They stocked a ship with all the necessaries, leaving the rest of their possessions in the care of Mary Magdalene, and set sail.

A day and a night had not passed, however, when the wind rose and the sea became tumultuous. All aboard, and especially the expectant mother, were shaken and fearful as the waves battered the ship. Abruptly she went into labor, and, exhausted by her pangs and the buffeting of the storm, she expired as she brought forth her son. The newborn groped about seeking the comfort of his mother's breasts, and cried and whimpered piteously. Ah, what a pity! The infant is born, he lives, and has become his mother's killer! He may as well die, since there is no one to give him nourishment to keep him alive! What will the Pilgrim[2] do, seeing his wife dead and the child whining plaintively as he seeks the maternal breast? His lamentations knew no bounds, and he said to himself: "Alas, what will you do? You yearned for a son, and you have lost the mother and the son too!"

The seamen meanwhile were shouting: "Throw that corpse overboard before we all perish! As long as it is with us, this storm will not let up!" They seized the body and were about to cast it into the sea, but the Pilgrim intervened. "Hold on a little!" he cried. "Even if you don't want to spare me or the mother, at least pity the poor weeping little one! Wait just a bit! Maybe the woman has only fainted with pain and may begin to breathe again!"

Now suddenly they saw a hilly coast not far off the bow, and the Pilgrim thought it would be better to put the dead body and the infant ashore there than to throw them as food to the sea monsters. His pleas and his bribes barely persuaded the crew to drop anchor there. Then he found the ground so hard that he could not dig a grave, so he spread his cloak in a fold of the hill, laid his wife's body on it, and placed the child with its head between the mother's breasts. Then he wept and said: "O Mary Magdalene, you brought ruin upon me when you landed at Marseilles! Unhappy me, that on your advice I set out on this journey! Did you not pray to God that my wife might conceive? Conceive she did, and suffered death giving birth, and the child she conceived was born only to die because there is no one to nurse him. Behold, this is what your prayer obtained for me. I commended my all to you and do commend me to your God. If it be in your power, be mindful of the mother's soul, and by your prayer take pity on the child and spare its life." Then he enfolded the body and the child in his cloak and went back aboard the ship.

When the Pilgrim arrived in Rome, Peter came to meet him and, seeing the sign of the cross on his shoulder, asked him who he was and where he came

---

[2] The noun is capitalized in Graesse and presumably in the original, apparently to make it serve as a proper name.

from. He told Peter all that had happened to him, and Peter responded: "Peace be with you! You have done well to trust the good advice you received. Do not take it amiss that your wife sleeps and the infant rests with her. It is in the Lord's power to give gifts to whom he will, to take away what was given, to restore what was taken away, and to turn your grief into joy."

Peter then took him to Jerusalem and showed him all the places where Christ had preached and performed miracles, as well as the place where he had suffered and the other from which he had ascended into heaven. Peter then gave him thorough instruction in the faith, and after two years had gone by, he boarded ship, being eager to get back to his homeland. By God's will, in the course of the voyage they came close to the hilly coast where he had left the body of his wife and his son, and with pleas and money he induced the crew to put him ashore. The little boy, whom Mary Magdalene had preserved unharmed, used to come down to the beach and play with the stones and pebbles, as children love to do. As the Pilgrim's skiff drew near to the land, he saw the child playing on the beach. He was dumbstruck at seeing his son alive and leapt ashore from the skiff. The child, who had never seen a man, was terrified at the sight and ran to his mother's bosom, taking cover under the familiar cloak. The Pilgrim, anxious to see what was happening, followed, and found the handsome child feeding at his mother's breast. He lifted the boy and said: "O Mary Magdalene, how happy I would be, how well everything would have turned out for me, if my wife were alive and able to return home with me! Indeed I know, I know and believe beyond a doubt, that having given us this child and kept him alive for two years on this rock, you could now, by your prayers, restore his mother to life and health."

As these words were spoken, the woman breathed and, as if waking from sleep, said: "Great is your merit, O blessed Mary Magdalene, and you are glorious! As I struggled to give birth, you did me a midwife's service and waited upon my every need like a faithful handmaid." Hearing this, the Pilgrim said: "My dear wife, are you alive?" "Indeed I am," she answered, "and am just coming from the pilgrimage from which you yourself are returning. And as blessed Peter conducted you to Jerusalem and showed you all the places where Christ suffered, died, and was buried, and many other places, I, with blessed Mary Magdalene as my guide and companion, was with you and committed all you saw to memory." Whereupon she recited all the places where Christ had suffered, and fully explained the miracles and all she had seen, not missing a single thing.

Now the Pilgrim, having got back his wife and child, joyfully took ship and in a short time made port at Marseilles. Going into the city they found blessed Mary Magdalene with her disciples, preaching. Weeping with joy, they threw themselves at her feet and related all that had happened to them, then received holy baptism from blessed Maximin. Afterwards they destroyed the temples of all the idols in the city of Marseilles and built churches to Christ. They also elected blessed Lazarus as bishop of the city. Later by the will of God they went to the city of Aix, and, by many miracles, led the people there to accept the Christian faith. Blessed Maximin was ordained bishop of Aix.

At this time blessed Mary Magdalene, wishing to devote herself to heavenly contemplation, retired to an empty wilderness, and lived unknown for thirty years in a place made ready by the hands of angels. There were no streams of water there, nor the comfort of grass or trees: thus it was made clear that our Redeemer had determined to fill her not with earthly viands but only with the good things of heaven. Every day at the seven canonical hours she was carried aloft by angels and with her bodily ears heard the glorious chants of the celestial hosts. So it was that day by day she was gratified with these supernal delights and, being conveyed back to her own place by the same angels, needed no material nourishment.

There was a priest who wanted to live a solitary life and built himself a cell a few miles from the Magdalene's habitat. One day the Lord opened this priest's eyes, and with his own eyes he saw how the angels descended to the already-mentioned place where blessed Mary Magdalene dwelt, and how they lifted her into the upper air and an hour later brought her back to her place with divine praises. Wanting to learn the truth about this wondrous vision and commending himself prayerfully to his Creator, he hurried with daring and devotion toward the aforesaid place; but when he was a stone's throw from the spot, his knees began to wobble, and he was so frightened that he could hardly breathe. When he started to go away, his legs and feet responded, but every time he turned around and tried to reach the desired spot, his body went limp and his mind went blank, and he could not move forward.

So the man of God realized that there was a heavenly secret here to which human experience alone could have no access. He therefore invoked his Savior's name and called out: "I adjure you by the Lord, that if you are a human being or any rational creature living in that cave, you answer me and tell me the truth about yourself!" When he had repeated this three times, blessed Mary Magdalene answered him: "Come closer, and you can learn the truth about whatever your soul desires." Trembling, he had gone halfway across the intervening space when she said to him: "Do you remember what the Gospel says about Mary the notorious sinner, who washed the Savior's feet with her tears and dried them with her hair, and earned forgiveness for all her misdeeds?" "I do remember," the priest replied, "and more than thirty years have gone by since then. Holy Church also believes and confesses what you have said about her." "I am that woman," she said. "For the space of thirty years I have lived here unknown to everyone; and as you were allowed to see yesterday, every day I am borne aloft seven times by angelic hands, and have been found worthy to hear with the ears of my body the joyful jubilation of the heavenly hosts. Now, because it has been revealed to me by the Lord that I am soon to depart from this world, please go to blessed Maximin and take care to inform him that next year, on the day of the Lord's resurrection, at the time when he regularly rises for matins, he is to go alone to his church, and there he will find me present and waited upon by angels." To the priest the voice sounded like the voice of an angel, but he saw no one.

The good man hurried to blessed Maximin and carried out his errand. Saint Maximin, overjoyed, gave fulsome thanks to the Savior, and on the appointed day, at the appointed hour, went alone into the church and saw blessed Mary Magdalene amidst the choir of angels who had brought her there. She was raised up a distance of two cubits above the floor, standing among the angels and lifting her hands in prayer to God. When blessed Maximin hesitated about approaching her, she turned to him and said: "Come closer, father, and do not back away from your daughter." When he drew near to her, as we read in blessed Maximin's own books, the lady's countenance was so radiant, due to her continuous and daily vision of the angels, that one would more easily look straight into the sun than gaze upon her face.

All the clergy, including the priest already mentioned, were now called together, and blessed Mary Magdalene, shedding tears of joy, received the Lord's Body and Blood from the bishop. Then she lay down full length before the steps of the altar, and her most holy soul migrated to the Lord. After she expired, so powerful an odor of sweetness pervaded the church that for seven days all those who entered there noticed it. Blessed Maximin embalmed her holy body with aromatic lotions and gave it honorable burial, giving orders that after his death he was to be buried close to her.

Hegesippus (or, as some books have it, Josephus) agrees in the main with the story just told. He says in one of his treatises that after Christ's ascension Mary Magdalene, weary of the world and moved by her ardent love of the Lord, never wanted to see anyone. After she came to Aix, she went off into the desert, lived there unknown for thirty years, and every day at the seven canonical hours was carried up to heaven by an angel. He added, however, that the priest who went to her found her closed up in a cell. At her request he reached out a garment to her, and when she had put it on, she went with him to the church, received communion there, and, raising her hands in prayer beside the altar, died in peace.

In Charlemagne's time, namely, in the year of the Lord 769, Gerard, duke of Burgundy, being unable to have a son of his wife, openhandedly gave away his wealth to the poor and built many churches and monasteries. When he had built the monastery at Vézelay, he and the abbot sent a monk, with a suitable company, to the city of Aix in order to bring back the relics of Saint Mary Magdalene, if possible. When the monk arrived at the aforesaid city, however, he found that it had been razed to the ground by the pagans. Yet by chance he discovered a marble sarcophagus with an inscription which indicated that the body of blessed Mary Magdalene was contained inside, and her whole story was beautifully carved on the outside. The monk therefore broke into the sarcophagus by night, gathered the relics, and carried them to his inn. That same night blessed Mary appeared to him and told him not to be afraid but to go on with the work he had begun. On their way back to Vézelay the company, when they were half a league from their monastery, could not move the relics another step until the abbot and his monks came in solemn procession to receive them.

A certain knight, whose practice it was to visit the relics of Saint Mary Magdalene every year, was killed in battle. As he lay dead on his bier, his parents, mourning him, made pious complaint to the Magdalene because she had allowed her devotee to die without making confession and doing penance. Then suddenly, to the amazement of all present, the dead man rose up and called for a priest. He made his confession devoutly and received viaticum, then returned to rest in peace.

A ship crowded with men and women was sinking, and one woman, who was pregnant and saw herself in danger of drowning, called upon Magdalene as loudly as she could, and vowed that if by Mary's merits she escaped death and bore a son, she would give him up to the saint's monastery. At once a woman of venerable visage and bearing appeared to her, held her up by the chin, and, while the rest drowned, brought her unharmed to land. The woman in due time gave birth to a son and faithfully fulfilled her vow.

There are some who say that Mary Magdalene was espoused to John the Evangelist, who was about to take her as his wife when Christ called him away from his nuptials, whereupon she, indignant at having been deprived of her spouse, gave herself up to every sort of voluptuousness. But, since it would not do to have John's vocation the occasion of Mary's damnation, the Lord mercifully brought her around to conversion and penance; and, because she had had to forgo the heights of carnal enjoyment, he filled her more than others with the most intense spiritual delight, which consists in the love of God. And there are those who allege that Christ honored John with special evidences of his affection because he had taken him away from the aforesaid pleasures. These tales are to be considered false and frivolous. Brother Albert,[3] in his introduction to the gospel of John, says firmly that the lady from whose nuptials the same John was called away persevered in virginity, was seen later in the company of the Blessed Virgin Mary, mother of Christ, and came at last to a holy end.

A man who had lost his eyesight was on his way to the monastery at Vézelay to visit Mary Magdalene's body when his guide told him that he, the guide, could already see the church in the distance. The blind man exclaimed in a loud voice: "O holy Mary Magdalene, if only I could sometime be worthy to see your church!" At once his eyes were opened.

There was a man who wrote a list of his sins on a sheet of paper and put it under the rug on the Magdalene's altar, asking her to pray that he might be pardoned. Later he recovered the paper and found that his sins had been wiped out.

---

[3] No doubt Saint Albert the Great, O.P., an older contemporary of Jacobus.

A man who lay in chains for having committed the crime of extortion called upon Mary Magdalene to come to his aid, and one night a beautiful woman appeared to him, broke his fetters, and ordered him to be off. Seeing himself unshackled, he got away as fast as possible.

A clerk from Flanders, Stephen by name, had fallen into such a welter of sinfulness that, having committed every sort of evil, he could do no works of salvation nor even bear to hear of them. Yet he had deep devotion to blessed Mary Magdalene, observed her vigils by fasting, and celebrated her feast day. Once when he was on a visit to her tomb and was half asleep and half awake, Mary Magdalene appeared to him as a lovely, sad-eyed woman supported by two angels, one on either side, and she said to him: "Stephen, I ask you, why do you repay me with deeds unworthy of my deserts? Why are you not moved with compunction by what my own lips insistently say? From the time when you began to be devoted to me I have always prayed the Lord urgently for you. Get up, then! Repent! I will never leave you until you are reconciled with God!" The clerk soon felt so great an inpouring of grace in himself that he renounced the world, entered the religious life, and lived a very holy life thereafter. At his death Mary Magdalene was seen standing with angels beside the bier, and she carried his soul, like a pure-white dove, with songs of praise into heaven.

97. Saint Apollinaris

The saint's name is formed of the words *pollens*, which means powerful, and *ares*, meaning virtue; and Apollinaris was powerful in virtue. Or the name comes from *pollo*, admirable, and *naris*, by which discretion is understood; and it indicates a man of admirable discretion. Or the name is formed from *a*, meaning without, *polluo*, pollute, and *ares*, virtue, and Apollinaris was a man virtuous and unpolluted by vices.

Apollinaris was a disciple of the apostle Peter and by him was sent from Rome to Ravenna, where he cured the wife of a tribune and baptized her, along with her husband and the whole family. This was reported to the judge, who summoned Apollinaris first to appear before him. The saint was then led to the temple of Jupiter to offer sacrifice there, but he told the priests that the gold and silver which was hung around the idols would better be given to the poor than dangled before demons. He was made prisoner and beaten with rods until he was left half dead, but his disciples carried him away and brought him to the house of a widow, where he stayed for seven months and recovered his health.

He then went to the city of Classe to cure a nobleman who was mute. When he entered the house, a girl who was possessed of an unclean spirit shouted at him, saying: "Leave this place, servant of God, or I'll have you bound hand and foot and dragged out of the city!" Apollinaris rebuked the girl and drove the demon out of her. Then he invoked the name of the Lord over the mute and cured him instantly, whereupon more than five hundred men accepted the faith. The pagans, however, had him beaten with clubs and forbade him to pronounce the name of Jesus; but he, lying on the ground, cried out that Jesus was true God. They made him stand barefoot on live coals, and when he continued to preach Christ with undiminished zeal, they cast him out of the city.

At that same time, however, Rufus, a patrician of Ravenna, had a daughter who was in failing health. He called Apollinaris to come and cure her, but just as the saint entered the house, the daughter died. Rufus said to him: "Would that you had not come into my house, because the great gods are angry with me and have not willed to cure my daughter! But what can you do for her?" Apollinaris replied: "Have no fear! Only swear to me that if the girl is restored to life, you will not keep her from following God her creator!" Rufus gave his word. Apollinaris prayed and the girl arose and confessed the name of Christ, was baptized with her mother and many others, and from then on remained a virgin.

The emperor heard of this and wrote to the praetorian prefect, ordering him to make Apollinaris sacrifice to the gods, or, if he refused, to send him into exile. The prefect, failing to make him offer sacrifice, first had him scourged and then ordered him to be stretched on the rack. When the saint persisted in preaching Christ, the prefect had boiling water poured into his wounds, weighed him down with chains, and was about to send him into exile, but the Christians, witnessing such inhumanity, attacked the pagans and killed over two hundred of their men. The prefect saw what was happening and went into hiding, meanwhile shutting Apollinaris up in a narrow cell. Then he put him in chains aboard a ship, with three clerics who followed him into exile and two soldiers. With two of the clerics and the two soldiers the saint survived the perils of a storm at sea, and baptized the soldiers.

Apollinaris went back to Ravenna, and was captured by the pagans and taken to the temple of Apollo. He cursed the statue of the god and it crumbled to the ground. The priests of the temple saw this and presented Apollinaris to the judge, whose name was Taurus; but the man of God restored the sight of the judge's blind son, and Taurus was converted to the faith and kept the saint on his estate for four years. After that the pagan priests accused him before Vespasian, who issued a decree that anyone who insulted the gods must either sacrifice or be excluded from the city: for it is not right, he said, that we men should avenge the gods; they themselves, if they are angered, are able to punish their enemies.

Then the patrician Demosthenes handed Apollinaris, who still refused to sacrifice, over to a certain centurion, who already was a Christian. This man asked him to go and live in a settlement of lepers in order to escape the wrath of the pagans, but these latter pursued him and beat him until he was near death. He lived, however, for seven days, and then, after giving good counsel to his disciples, breathed his last and was given honorable burial by the Christians, under Vespasian, whose reign began about the year A.D. 70.

Ambrose, in his Preface, says of this martyr: "Apollinaris, that most worthy prelate, was sent by Peter, the prince of the apostles, to Ravenna, to preach the name of Jesus to the unbelievers. There he worked many miracles in Christ on behalf of those who believed in him. He was often beaten with rods, and his already aged body was mangled with horrible tortures by the impious. But, lest the faithful might be troubled at the sight of his sufferings, by the power of the Lord Jesus Christ he worked many signs, as the apostles had done. After he had been tortured, he restored a young girl to life, gave sight to the blind and speech to a mute, freed a woman possessed of the devil, cleansed a leper of his disease, strengthened the limbs of a victim of the plague, brought down an idolatrous image and the temple that sheltered it. O pontiff most worthy of admiration and commendation, pontiff who merited the power of the apostles along with the episcopal dignity! O bravest athlete of Christ, who still, even in advanced age and constantly in pain, preached Jesus Christ the redeemer of the world!"

98. Saint Christina

Saint Christina's name suggests *chrismate uncta*, anointed with chrism. She had the balm of good odor in her relationships with others, and the oil of devotion in her mind and benediction in her speech.[1]

Christina was born of parents of the highest rank, at Tyro in Italy. Her father shut her up with twelve waiting women in a tower, where she had silver and gold idols with her. She was very beautiful and many sought her in marriage, but her parents would give her to none of her suitors because they wanted her to remain in the service of the gods. She, however, was taught by the Holy Spirit

[1] The reader will sense how completely the following story disagrees with the "etymology" with which the chapter opens. According to *Butler's Lives of the Saints* ([New York: P. J. Kenedy & Sons, 1963], 3:173–174), this legend grew out of confusion between the story of an Eastern Saint Christina of Tyre, which contained the implausible "popular" episodes related above, and the memory of another Saint Christina, otherwise unknown, who was thought to have been martyred near Bolsena.

and shrank from sacrificing to the idols, hiding in a window the incense she was supposed to burn to them.

Her father came to see her and the servingwomen told him: "Your daughter, our lady mistress, abhors the worship of our gods and declares that she is a Christian!" The father spoke softly to her, seeking to win her to the cult of the gods, but she said: "Do not call me your daughter, but the child of him to whom the sacrifice of praise is due, for I offer sacrifice not to mortal gods but to the God of heaven!" "Daughter mine," the father responded, "don't offer sacrifice to one god only, or the others will be angry with you!" Christina: "Though you don't know it, you speak the truth, because I offer sacrifice to the Father, the Son, and the Holy Spirit!" The father: "If you adore three gods, why not adore the others too?" Christina: "The three I adore are one godhead!"

After this, Christina smashed her father's idols and distributed the gold and silver to the poor. The father came back to worship his gods and could not find them, but the women told him what Christina had done with them. He was angry and ordered her to be stripped and beaten by twelve men, and they beat her until they themselves dropped, exhausted. Then Christina said to her father: "O man without honor, shameless man, abominable before God, pray your gods to give the men who are worn out with beating me the strength to continue, if you can!" But he had her bound in chains and thrown into prison.

Her mother, hearing about all this, tore her garments, went to the jail, and prostrated herself at her daughter's feet, saying: "Christina, daughter mine, have pity on me!" She answered: "Why do you call me your daughter? Don't you know that I bear the name of my God?" The mother could not win her over, and went and told her husband how Christina had answered her. He then had her brought before his tribunal and said to her: "Sacrifice to the gods! Otherwise you will suffer all sorts of torments and will no longer be called my daughter!" Christina: "You do me a great favor by not calling me a daughter of the devil! What is born of the devil is a demon, and you are the father of Satan himself!"

The father then ordered her flesh to be torn off with hooks and her tender limbs to be broken; and Christina picked up pieces of her flesh and threw them in her father's face, saying: "Take that, tyrant, and eat the flesh that you begot!" Then the father stretched her on a wheel and lighted a fire with oil under her, but the flames leapt out and killed fifteen hundred men. The father attributed all this to magic and remanded her to prison. When it was night, he ordered his henchmen to tie a large stone around her neck and throw her into the sea. They did this, but immediately angels bore her up, whereupon Christ came down to her and baptized her in the sea, saying: "I baptize thee in God my Father, in myself, Jesus Christ his Son, and in the Holy Spirit." He then committed her to the care of the archangel Michael, who led her ashore. When the father learned of this, he beat his forehead and exclaimed: "By what witchcraft do you do this, that you work your magic in the sea?" Christina answered: "Foolish, unhappy man! I had this favor from Christ!" He sent her back to prison to be beheaded

in the morning, but he, her father, whose name was Urbanus, was found dead
that very night.

A wicked judge named Elius succeeded him. Elius had an iron cradle prepared and fired with oil, pitch, and resin. Christina was then thrown into this
cradle and four men were ordered to rock it back and forth so as to burn her to
death more quickly. Then Christina praised God, who willed that she, so recently reborn by baptism, should be rocked in a cradle like a newborn babe. The
judge, angrier than ever, had her head shaved and ordered her to be led naked
through the city to the temple of Apollo. There she directed a command to the
idol, which collapsed into a heap of dust. At this the judge was stricken with fear
and expired.

He was succeeded by another judge, named Julianus, who had a furnace
stoked and fired, and ordered Christina to be thrown into it. There for five days
she walked about, singing with angels, and was unharmed. Being informed of
this, Julianus ascribed it to magical arts, and had two asps, two vipers, and two
cobras put in with her; but the vipers licked her feet, the asps clung to her breasts
without hurting her, and the cobras wrapped themselves around her neck and
licked her sweat. Julian called to the court conjurer: "You're a magician too,
aren't you? Stir those beasts up!" The conjurer did as ordered, and the serpents
came at him and killed him in a trice. Then Christina commanded the reptiles
to hie themselves to a place in the desert, and brought the dead man back to life.

Next, Julianus had Christina's breasts cut off, and milk flowed from them
instead of blood. Lastly, he had her tongue cut out, but she, never losing the
power of speech, took the severed tongue and threw it in Julianus's face, hitting
him in the eye and blinding him. Goaded to wrath, Julianus shot two arrows
into her heart and one into her side, and she, pierced through and through,
breathed forth her spirit to God about the year 287, under Diocletian. Her body
rests near a fortified place called Bolsena, between Orvieto and Viterbo. The
tower[2] which once was near that town has been completely demolished.

[2] Graesse notes (421 n. 2) that the Ed. Pr., instead of *turris*, has *Tyrus*, which might be the Tyro
mentioned earlier.

INDEX

THE GOLDEN LEGEND

NIHIL OBSTAT: Otto L. Garcia, S.T.D.
                    Censor Librorum

IMPRIMATUR: +Thomas V. Daily, D.D.
                    Bishop of Brooklyn

Brooklyn, New York: August 25, 1992